BATTLE

A VISUAL JOURNEY THROUGH 5,000 YEARS OF COMBAT

R. G. GRANT

LONDON, NEW YORK, MELBOURNE,
MUNICH, AND DELHI

SENIOR EDITOR David John
EDITORS Philip Parker, Sam Atkinson,
Andrew Campbell, Andrew Szudek
EDITORIAL ASSISTANCE Miezan van Zyl
SENIOR ART EDITOR Mabel Chan
DESIGNERS Maxine Lea, Victoria Clark, Francis Wong,
Paul Drislane, Steve Woosnam-Savage, Colin Brown
DESIGN ASSISTANCE Clare Joyce,
Jane Tetzlaff, Vikram Pattwal
DTP DESIGNER John Goldsmid
PICTURE RESEARCH Anne-Marie Ehrlich
and Alison Walker at The Picture Desk
DK PICTURE LIBRARY Claire Bowers
SPECIAL PHOTOGRAPHY Gary Ombler
CARTOGRAPHY Advanced Illustration Ltd.
PRODUCTION Melanie Dowland
MANAGING ART EDITOR Philip Ormerod
ART DIRECTOR Bryn Walls
MANAGING EDITOR Debra Wolter
PUBLISHING MANAGER Liz Wheeler
PUBLISHER Jonathan Metcalf

ADDITIONAL TEXT CONTRIBUTIONS
Jake Field (pages 88–89; 120–121; 154–155)
Phillip Williams (pages 136–137; 242–243; 150–163)
Neil Grant (pages 184–195; 234–245; 260–263)
Rob Colson (pages 216–223; 246–253)
Simon Adams (pages 332–333; 338–339;
344–345; 350–353)
EDITORIAL CONSULTANTS
Dr. Hugh Bowden, Dr. Guy Halsall, Dr. David Parrott,
Professor Alan Forrest, Matthew Parker
PROOFREADER Alan Heal
US EDITOR Margaret Parrish
INDEXER John Noble

First American Edition, 2005
This revised edition published in 2009
Published in the United States by
DK Publishing
375 Hudson Street
New York, New York 10014

09 10 11 12 13   10 9 8 7 6 5 4 3 2 1

175207—September 2009

DK books are available at special discounts when
purchased in bulk for sales promotions, premiums, fund-
raising, or educational use. For details, contact: DK
Publishing Special Markets, 375 Hudson Street, New York,
New York 10014 or SpecialSales@dk.com.

Color reproduction by GRB, Italy
Printed and bound in Singapore by Star Standard

Discover more at
www.dk.com

CONTENTS

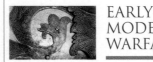

EMPIRES AND REVOLUTIONS
180

ERA OF WORLD WARS
264

— FOREWORD —

Like most of my generation of Europeans, born after World War II, I have no personal experience of armed conflict. Also like most of my generation, I had a father, grandfather, and uncles who had fought in wars—and who were mostly not inclined to talk about what they had seen and done. Growing up surrounded by adults who have lived through battle bred in me a fascination with warfare and an urge to understand the experience of violence that those reticent elders had undergone.

The most casual flick through the following pages would convince anyone that war is, and always has been, a major human activity. Military historian John Keegan goes so far as to say that "all civilizations owe their origins to the warrior." The fortunes of war have determined the growth of empires, the spread of ideologies and religious beliefs, and the building of nations. There has been a fashion in recent times to downplay the importance of battles. Doubt has been cast on the Greeks' victory over the Persians at Marathon, for example. Was that battle truly the salvation of western civilization, as many historians would have us believe? Yet the fortunes of war certainly do make a difference. Can it be doubted that a British victory in North America was certainly possible in 1776, and that if it had occurred the fledgling United States of America might not have survived? Is there not a real chance that Hitler might have confirmed his rule over mainland Europe had Stalingrad not been so desperately and, in the end, so skillfully defended in 1942?

This book is primarily about how, rather than why, wars were fought—a viewpoint reflecting that of the ordinary soldier through the ages, so often only dimly aware of any purpose beyond his own survival. It is partly a story of technological development, overall in the direction of greater distance. Through much of history, warfare was personal and face-to-face, conducted at the distance a bow could shoot an arrow or a catapult hurl a rock. Even when gunpowder weapons began their transformation of battle, for centuries it was still impossible to kill someone you could not see. Now conflict may be fought by men tracking icons on computer screens, potentially at intercontinental range. With the invention of nuclear weapons, the potential for destruction has increased beyond any military requirement—although it should not be forgotten that the Mongol conqueror

Timur destroyed the population of a city as effectively as any atom bomb, by the simple expedient of ordering every one of his tens of thousands of soldiers to bring him a severed head. The destructiveness of nuclear weapons once seemed likely to make armed conflict obsolete. But the stark choice presented by philosopher Bertrand Russell in 1954: "Shall we put an end to the human race? Or shall mankind renounce war?" has proved ill-founded. War has remained very much an option.

Another theme of the book is command, for inspired generalship has time and again triumphed against the odds. The styles of commander have varied from leaders-from-the-front, always at the head of the charge, to masters of maneuver like Napoleon or Lee, or those unflinching applicants of overwhelming force who are so often the victors in the attritional long haul. And then there are the fighting men themselves, the anonymous makers of history: the medieval knights who reveled in war as the pursuit of glory, the seasoned soldiers of 18-century Britain, stoical in their professionalism, or the conscripts of the two world wars—civilians in uniforms who nonetheless showed as much courage as any of their predecessors.

The phrase "the fog of war" has many times been used to convey the sheer chaos of the battlefield, defying tidy plans and clear-cut stratagems. The author faced with the task of describing battles meets this fog in the form of conflicting accounts and irreconcilable assertions of fact. Nowhere is this more evident than in war statistics. I have attempted, in collaboration with consultants, to produce figures for the numbers of troops and casualties in as many battles as possible. The reader should be aware, however, that all such figures are to be treated with caution. What they do convey is, in broad terms, the scale of warfare at any given time and the extraordinary loss of life it has entailed.

General William T. Sherman—a man who knew what he was talking about—said that "war is cruelty." But it is also many more positive things: courage, leadership, organization, comradeship, skill, and ingenuity. War has, quite rightly, acquired a bad reputation over the past century. But this disapproval should never extend to those who do the fighting. To them this book is dedicated.

R. G. Grant

R. G. Grant
SEPTEMBER 2005

WARFARE IN THE
ANCIENT WORLD

3000 BCE – 476 CE

THE ORIGINS OF WARFARE

WARFARE HAS BEEN CENTRAL TO the development of civilization. From earliest times, civilized states have flourished or fallen through their performance on the battlefield. The history of warfare begins with conflicts between different groups within limited areas of settled civilization—Persians against Greeks, for example, or Carthaginians against Romans—and between these settled civilizations and their "barbarian" neighbors, nomadic or otherwise.

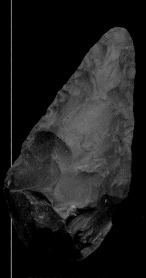

PALEOLITHIC AX
This 250,000-year-old hand ax could have been an early tool or weapon.

The nature and extent of primitive warfare—in other words, warfare in prestate societies—asks a fundamental question about human nature: were humans once peaceful, living in harmony with each other, or is warfare and all the horrors that accompany it "natural"? Those who take an optimistic view of uncorrupted human nature argue that, even when hunter–gatherers or simple agricultural societies entered into conflicts, these were fought in a ritualized manner designed to minimize casualties. Individuals engaged in ritual displays of aggression in the face of the enemy, after which there might be single combat between warriors or an exchange of missiles—arrows, spears, or stones—at a distance. Both sides would then go home with little harm done. More pessimistic historians and anthropologists, while accepting the existence of such ritualized encounters, paint a far darker picture. They point to evidence that "primitive" societies engaged in constant raiding against their neighbors—a state of permanent warfare. What is more, these raids could conclude

with the virtual extermination of the losing side, massacre or enslavement of the defeated being the rule rather than the exception. The Maori of New Zealand provide a historical example of primitive warfare. Living in fortified settlements, Maori groups fought one another every summer, often on a point of honor or to avenge an insult. Maori warfare included ritualized displays such as war dances and individual combat between warriors, but it also involved ambushes and raids that could lead to slaughter. The victors burned the villages and crops of the defeated and enslaved the survivors. They also feasted on their dead enemies and delighted in making fishhooks out of their bones.

"CIVILIZED" WARFARE

The history of "civilized" warfare, if such a term can be allowed, begins with the development of complex societies, made possible by the production of agricultural surpluses, mostly through irrigated farming. Such societies emerged over time in Mesopotamia, the Nile valley, the eastern

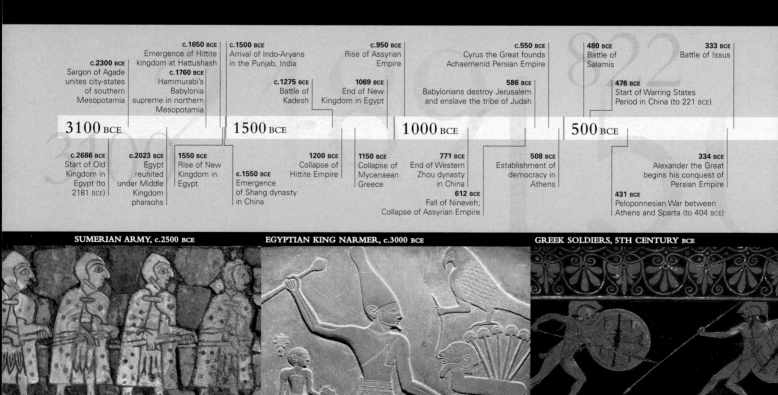

		c.1650 BCE Emergence of Hittite kingdom at Hattushash	**c.1500 BCE** Arrival of Indo-Aryans in the Punjab, India		**c.950 BCE** Rise of Assyrian Empire		**c.550 BCE** Cyrus the Great founds Achaemenid Persian Empire	**480 BCE** Battle of Salamis	**333 BCE** Battle of Issus
	c.2300 BCE Sargon of Agade unites city-states of southern Mesopotamia	**c.1760 BCE** Hammurabi's Babylonia supreme in northern Mesopotamia	**c.1275 BCE** Battle of Kadesh		**1069 BCE** End of New Kingdom in Egypt		**586 BCE** Babylonians destroy Jerusalem and enslave the tribe of Judah	**476 BCE** Start of Warring States Period in China (to 221 BCE)	

3100 BCE   **1500 BCE**   **1000 BCE**   **500 BCE**

c.2686 BCE Start of Old Kingdom in Egypt (to 2181 BCE)	**c.2023 BCE** Egypt reunited under Middle Kingdom pharaohs	**1550 BCE** Rise of New Kingdom in Egypt		**1200 BCE** Collapse of Hittite Empire	**1150 BCE** Collapse of Mycenaean Greece	**771 BCE** End of Western Zhou dynasty in China	**508 BCE** Establishment of democracy in Athens		**334 BCE** Alexander the Great begins his conquest of Persian Empire
			c.1550 BCE Emergence of Shang dynasty in China			**612 BCE** Fall of Nineveh; Collapse of Assyrian Empire		**431 BCE** Peloponnesian War between Athens and Sparta (to 404 BCE)	

SUMERIAN ARMY, c.2500 BCE   **EGYPTIAN KING NARMER, c.3000 BCE**   **GREEK SOLDIERS, 5TH CENTURY BCE**

Mediterranean, the Indus valley, China, and parts of the Americas. Because of the scale of their resources and their organizational ability, these states were capable of deploying large-scale armies that allowed kings or emperors to extend their dominion over subject peoples and to fight other empires in struggles for supremacy.

TECHNOLOGY OF WARFARE

Technology developed alongside the growth of armies. The introduction of bronze from the third millennium BCE, followed by iron from around 1200 BCE, created more effective weapons, replacing stone and bone in the production of spearheads, axheads, and arrowheads, as well as providing metal armor. To defend settlements and provide bases for military operations, armies began to build fortifications, as well as methods for attacking them in sieges. The most spectacular early battlefield technology, dating from around 1700 BCE, was the war chariot, made possible by the domestication of the horse. The riding of horses as cavalry—probably initiated by the nomadic peoples of the central-Asian steppes—did not become a major factor in armies until later, around the 8th century BCE, in Mesopotamia. Warfare also spread to the sea, with the development of oared warships. The first true warships came into existence around 1000 BCE, when the Greeks began to build galleys with wooden rams at the bow, capable of sinking enemy craft.

ORGANIZING ARMIES

By the 1st millennium BCE all the major elements of warfare as it would be practiced up to the gunpowder age were already in position. There were footsoldiers armed with weapons for slashing and stabbing, as well as missile weaponry such as bows, javelins, and slingshots. There were cavalry, who also used bows or lances. And there was a variety of siege machinery, including giant catapults, first used by Greeks in Sicily in the 4th century BCE. The great question was how to organize and motivate armies to use these technologies. The Assyrians were the first to create a force of regularly paid fighters supported by a properly organized system of supply. But this model of the professional army, replicated with impressive effect by the Roman Empire from the 1st century BCE, did not have a monopoly on success. In the 5th century BCE, for example, the Greek city-states showed that part-time citizen-soldiers could be formidable fighters, too. And nomadic horsemen such as the Huns, fighting as bands of mounted archers, frequently proved devastatingly effective against even the best armies of settled civilizations. The one constant factor revealed at this early stage in the history of warfare was that discipline and leadership could give the edge to any fighting force.

CAVALRY WARFARE
This 4th-century BCE marble relief depicts Alexander the Great in battle against the Persians. Alexander's cavalry was the driving force behind many of his victories.

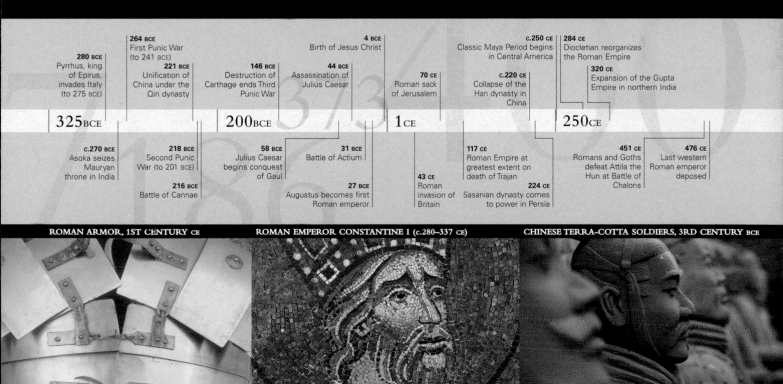

280 BCE
Pyrrhus, king of Epirus, invades Italy (to 275 BCE)

264 BCE
First Punic War (to 241 BCE)

221 BCE
Unification of China under the Qin dynasty

146 BCE
Destruction of Carthage ends Third Punic War

44 BCE
Assassination of Julius Caesar

4 BCE
Birth of Jesus Christ

70 CE
Roman sack of Jerusalem

c.250 CE
Classic Maya Period begins in Central America

c.220 CE
Collapse of the Han dynasty in China

284 CE
Diocletian reorganizes the Roman Empire

320 CE
Expansion of the Gupta Empire in northern India

325 BCE   **200 BCE**   **1 CE**   **250 CE**

c.270 BCE
Asoka seizes Mauryan throne in India

218 BCE
Second Punic War (to 201 BCE)

216 BCE
Battle of Cannae

58 BCE
Julius Caesar begins conquest of Gaul

31 BCE
Battle of Actium

27 BCE
Augustus becomes first Roman emperor

43 CE
Roman invasion of Britain

117 CE
Roman Empire at greatest extent on death of Trajan

224 CE
Sasanian dynasty comes to power in Persia

451 CE
Romans and Goths defeat Attila the Hun at Battle of Chalons

476 CE
Last western Roman emperor deposed

ROMAN ARMOR, 1ST CENTURY CE

ROMAN EMPEROR CONSTANTINE I (c.280–337 CE)

CHINESE TERRA-COTTA SOLDIERS, 3RD CENTURY BCE

BETWEEN HISTORY AND LEGEND

THE HISTORY OF WARFARE emerges from legend
sometime between 3000 and 1000 BCE in Mesopotamia
and the eastern Mediterranean. While archeology
reveals much about arms and conquests, legends such
as the Sumerian epic of Gilgamesh and the Greek *Iliad*
provide information about the earlier part of this period.

THE EARLIEST ARMIES

The first armies we know about existed from about 2500 BCE, in the
city-states of Sumeria in southern Mesopotamia. Most battles between
these cities involved infantry that wielded spears, axes, or daggers. There
were also battlewagons, or primitive chariots—vehicles with four solid-
wooden wheels, pulled by asses. Each vehicle had a crew of two:
a driver and an elite soldier, probably armed with a javelin. Among the
deadliest weapons in use by early armies was the composite bow. Made
of strips of wood, bone, and tendon, it was far more powerful than a
self bow, which was a simple bow made out of a single piece of wood.
Composite bows may have
been rare, however; there is
only one contemporary
Sumerian depiction of
them in battle. But the
limited technological
resources and small armies
of the early city-states
belied their potential:
dominant cities such as
Agade and Babylon
succeeded in carrying out
operations across
Mesopotamia, as well as
conquering other cities far
from their home bases.

EARLY WARRIORS
*This 3rd-millennium BCE
Sumerian inlaid box, the
Standard of Ur, shows ass-drawn
chariots and infantry with spears.*

KEY

▨ Sumer during Early Dynastic period c.3000–2360 BCE	▨ Babylonian Empire of Hammurabi c.1782–50 BCE
▨ Empire of Sargon I of Akkad c.2360–2230 BCE	➡ migration of Semites
	➡ campaigns of Sargon

0 km   125   250
0 miles   125   250

THE RISE OF THE CHARIOT

Horses were introduced into warfare sometime in the 2nd millennium
BCE and gave rise to a major technological innovation: the lightweight,
two-wheeled horse-drawn chariot. Used mostly as a platform for an
archer, horse-drawn chariots dominated warfare for
about a thousand years. The cost of breeding and
stabling the horses, building and maintaining the
chariots, and training the chariot crews was very
high, but the Egyptians, the Hittites, and the
Assyrians were able to field chariot forces in their
thousands. The Egyptian New Kingdom (1550–
1069 BCE) demonstrated how much power a state
could wield with the military resources of the
time, carrying out campaigns as far south as Nubia
(present-day Sudan) and as far north as Syria.

ROYAL ARCHER
*This Ancient Egyptian treasure
chest shows Pharaoh Tutankhamun
in a two-wheeled chariot,
slaughtering warriors from Nubia.*

THE BIRTH OF THE ARMY

THE FIRST RECORDED ACCOUNTS of warfare, between the city-states of Mesopotamia in the 3rd millennium BCE, depict warfare on a relatively small scale, fought by armies of a few thousand men. The only vehicles used in these conflicts were chariots drawn by asses. The growth of larger empires during the 2nd and 1st millennia BCE inevitably gave rise to bigger armies and costlier battles. By the second half of the 2nd millennium BCE, the Egyptians and the Hittites were vying for control of the countries of the eastern Mediterranean, with forces numbering anything up to 20,000 on either side. These powerful empires deployed thousands of two-wheeled horse-drawn war chariots, the most expensive military technology of its day.

SUMERIAN CITY-STATES

Lagash defeats Umma

DATE
c.2450 BCE

FORCES
Lagash's army: unknown; Umma's army: unknown

LOCATION
Sumeria, southern Mesopotamia

CASUALTIES
No reliable estimates

The best surviving information about warfare in early Sumeria comes from an inscribed pillar known as the Stele of Vultures, which the city-state of Lagash erected to commemorate the victory over its

WAR HELMET
This Sumerian battle helmet, made of a silver and gold alloy, was probably worn by a ruler.

LAGASH INFANTRY
The Stele of Vultures shows the army of Lagash advancing into battle against Umma. The footsoldiers carry spears and wear helmets of leather or copper.

neighbor Umma. After a border dispute arose between the states, Eanatum, the ruler of Lagash, inspired by Ningirsu, the god of his city, led an army to attack Umma. The Stele shows him advancing in a chariot, followed by his infantry. When the two sides meet, Eanatum dismounts to lead his men on foot. They lower their spears and press forward in a dense phalanx, treading on the bodies of their fallen enemies. Although struck in the eye by an arrow, Eanatum survived to enjoy his army's triumph—the Stele shows vultures picking his enemy's bones. Further records from Eanatum's time suggest that he led forces as far east as Elam (present-day western Iran).

SARGON'S CONQUESTS

Conquests of Sargon of Agade

DATE
c.2340–2284 BCE

FORCES
Sargon: a standing army of 5,400 men

LOCATION Mesopotamia (modern Iraq and eastern Syria)

CASUALTIES
No reliable estimates

Sargon of Agade was the first military adventurer to carve out an empire by conquest. According to legend, Sargon was of humble origins, discovered as a baby in a basket by a gardener. He founded his own city at Agade, the exact site of which remains unknown. From there he conquered the powerful city of Uruk and all the other Mesopotamian city-states, from Ur in Sumeria to Ebla in Syria, creating an empire covering roughly the area of modern-day Iraq. But Sargon's campaigns probably extended farther, perhaps to the Mediterranean and Anatolia. One inscription tells us that he won 34 battles; another suggests that he had a standing army, recording that "5,400 soldiers eat bread before him each day." Sargon's infantry probably used bronze weapons and composite bows,

VICTORY MONUMENT
A fragment from the Victory Stele of Sargon of Agade, erected to celebrate Sargon's military triumphs. His fame as a conqueror is reflected in the name given to the Assyrian king Sargon II (d.705 BCE).

and he would also have possessed four-wheeled chariots pulled by asses. This army could cope with siege warfare, since records tell of Sargon destroying the walls of the cities he captured. Sargon died about 2284 BCE and his empire survived for 125 more years. Later Mesopotamians regarded him as the founder of the region's tradition of expansion by military conquest, as exemplified by the Assyrians, Babylonians, and Persians.

RISE OF BABYLON

Campaigns of Hammurabi

DATE
c.1763–c.1758 BCE

FORCES
Hammurabi's army: unknown

LOCATION
Northern and southern Mesopotamia

CASUALTIES
No reliable estimates

Hammurabi came to the throne of the small city-state of Babylon early in the 18th century BCE. He was initially part of an alliance led by the relatively powerful kingdom of Assyria. Correspondence exists to show that Babylon and Assyria agreed to support each other with troops if needed. In about 1763 BCE,

HAMMURABI
This diorite sculpture of Hammurabi, the self-proclaimed "ruler of the four worlds," was found in Shush in southwestern Iran.

however, Hammurabi moved away from this alliance. He led a coalition of forces from Babylon and the allied cities of Eshnunna and Mari to defeat King Rim-Sin of Larsa, another of Hammurabi's former allies, who controlled the most important cities in southern Mesopotamia, including Uruk and Ur. Archeological evidence suggests that Hammurabi dammed up a main watercourse that supplied Larsa, achieving victory either by suddenly releasing the water and flooding the city or by withholding water from its desperate inhabitants. He then turned upon his newer allies, defeating Eshnunna in 1761 and conquering Mari in 1760. The latter revolted against its conqueror in 1758, but Hammurabi again defeated it and ordered the destruction of its walls. These victories gave Hammurabi control of an area that extended from the Syrian desert to the Persian Gulf. He built fortifications to defend this territory, but following his death the empire disintegrated.

NEW KINGDOM EGYPT

Megiddo

DATE	
c.1468 BCE	
FORCES	
Egyptians:	
10,000–20,000;	
Palestinians: unknown	
LOCATION	**CASUALTIES**
Near Haifa,	Palestinians: 83 killed;
northern Israel	340 captured

Pharaoh Thutmosis III (ruled 1479–1425 BCE) led an army out of Egypt to suppress an alliance of the princes of Megiddo and Kadesh in Palestine. The army took 10 days to march to Gaza, drinking from wells that had been dug along the desert roads. After halting to rest and scout out the ground ahead, Thutmosis took a huge gamble. Instead of proceeding around the mountains that lay to the north, he marched his men through the narrow Aruna Pass, thus exposing them to easy attack if caught. But the gamble paid off; the Egyptians' swift advance surprised the king of Kadesh, who had expected Thutmosis to take the longer route around the mountains. Thutmosis, leading his forces in a chariot of electrum (an alloy of gold and silver), overawed the forces of Kadesh, which fled toward the safety of the fortress of Megiddo. The town's gate was firmly closed, but those inside hauled the escaping soldiers over the walls with ropes made of clothing. The Egyptians collected plunder from the battlefield, and then began a siege of the fortress. Those inside surrendered after seven months.

COMBAT MEDALS
Gold medals in the shape of biting flies were awarded to Egyptian soldiers in return for "stinging" the enemy.

NEW KINGDOM EGYPT

Kadesh

DATE	
c.1275 BCE	
FORCES	
Egyptians: 20,000 men	
and 2,000 chariots;	
Hittites: 15,000 men	
and 3,500 chariots	
LOCATION	**CASUALTIES**
Along the Orontes	No reliable estimates
river, western Syria	

The battle at Kadesh is the most famous encounter from the era of chariot warfare, with thousands of the two-wheeled vehicles engaged on each side. Its origins lay in the contest between the Egyptians and the Hittites for control of Lebanon and Syria, which lay between their two empires. In the first year of the war, Pharaoh Ramesses II carried out a successful campaign up the eastern Mediterranean coast, apparently catching the Hittites off guard. But when he returned the following year, the Hittite king Muwatalli had assembled an army from all his domains to confront the Egyptians. Ramesses's forces consisted of four divisions, with chariots at the core of each. Drawn by two horses, the chariots were light and fast, traveling at speeds of up to 24mph (38kph), and capable of very sharp turns on their widely spaced wheels. Each vehicle had a crew of two, one to steer and one to fight, the charioteers' main weapon being the composite bow. The Hittites also depended on chariots, although theirs were heavier and slower, with a crew of three. The extra crew member may have acted as shield-bearer or may have jumped off the chariot and onto the battlefield to provide infantry support—a role played in the Egyptian force by specially trained soldiers who ran alongside the chariots. If the Egyptian charioteers had a shield, the driver probably held it as well as the reins. On the day of the battle, Ramesses's divisions advanced toward Kadesh, a city on the Orontes River. Ramesses and his lead division, believing the Hittites to be some distance away, set up camp near the city. Muwatalli had set a trap, however: his men were concealed on the other side of the Orontes, from where 2,500 Hittite chariots emerged to attack the Egyptian divisions still approaching Kadesh. The Hittites routed one of the divisions, then swung around to advance on the pharaoh's camp, at the same time that Muwatalli unleashed a thousand more chariots across the Orontes. According to the Egyptian version of events, Ramesses mounted his chariot and single-handedly cut down thousands of his enemies, forcing them to flee into the river. It certainly seems that an Egyptian counterattack,

> ## "His majesty [Ramesses II] drove his horse at a gallop and charged the forces of the Hittite foe…and found 2,500 chariots attacking him, all the fast army of the foe."
>
> Egyptian inscription at Thebes, 13th century BCE

RAMESSES' WAR CHARIOT
An Egyptian relief depicting Ramesses II at the battle of Kadesh. In reality, he would have had a driver in his chariot, too.

c.1304–c.1212 BCE

RAMESSES II

The most famous of Egypt's New Kingdom rulers, Ramesses II inherited the throne in 1279 BCE and held it for 67 years. He strove to project an image of himself as a successful war leader: in his many monuments and temples, he often had himself represented as a charioteer trampling upon his enemies or smiting captives with a mace. Besides the Hittites, Ramesses waged wars against the ancient kingdoms of Moab, Edom, and Negeb, as well as the Libyans.

STONE CARVING OF RAMESSES II, ABU SIMBEL, EGYPT.

demonstrating superior chariot speed and archery power, carried the day, but the battle was not the clear-cut victory the Egyptians proclaimed; Ramesses withdrew his forces after the engagement, and, when both sides agreed to what was effectively the world's first peace treaty, Kadesh remained a Hittite possession. The Hittites had thwarted the renewal of Egyptian power in Syria.

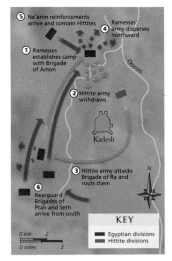

⑤ Ne'arim reinforcements arrive and contain Hittites
④ Ramesses' army disperses northward
① Ramesses establishes camp with Brigade of Amon
② Hittite army withdraws
③ Hittite army attacks Brigade of Ra and routs them
⑥ Rearguard Brigades of Ptah and Seth arrive from south

Orontes
Kadesh

KEY
0 km   2
0 miles   2

■ Egyptian divisions
■ Hittite divisions

EGYPTIAN WEAPONRY

One of the most effective weapons in the armies of Ancient Egypt was the composite bow. Consisting of a wooden core with horn glued on the front and sinew on the back, this was a powerful device that could shoot an arrow a distance of 575ft (175m). In Egypt's New Kingdom period (1550–1069 BCE), the arrowheads were mostly bronze, although iron or bone were also used. Soldiers also employed a range of axes, hatchets, and swords, most made of bronze. Distinctive epsilon-style axes (so called because they resembled the Greek letter) were much in use in the earlier Middle Kingdom period (2023–1720 BCE).

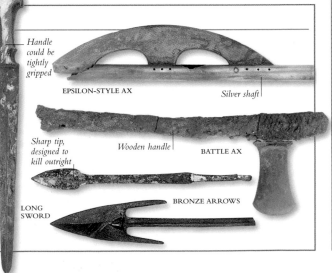

Handle could be tightly gripped

EPSILON-STYLE AX

Silver shaft

Sharp tip, designed to kill outright

Wooden handle

BATTLE AX

LONG SWORD

BRONZE ARROWS

Troy

DATE
c.1250 BCE

FORCES
Greeks: 102,000

CASUALTIES
No reliable estimates

LOCATION
Hisarlik,
northwest Turkey

The siege of Troy is narrated in the *Iliad*, attributed by the Ancient Greeks to the poet Homer. It tells of a conflict between Trojans and Greeks that starts when Paris, prince of Troy, abducts Helen, the wife of King

Menelaus of Sparta. Menelaus's brother Agamemnon, king of Mycenae, takes an army in "a thousand" ships to besiege Troy. The siege lasts 10 years, during which time many heroic combats are fought by heroes such as the Greek Achilles and the Trojan Hector. Eventually, the Greeks take the city by a trick. Pretending to abandon the siege, they leave behind a wooden horse with a force of men hidden inside. A further Greek left behind, Sinon, tells the Trojans that the horse is an offering to the goddess Athena, and persuades them to drag it into their city, enabling the men inside to emerge at night and open the city gates to the rest of the Greek force. The Greeks had no doubt that

this story represented a historical event. Alexander the Great (356–323 BCE) made a pilgrimage to the site traditionally identified as Troy—Hisarlik in modern Turkey—before embarking on his conquest of the Persian Empire. Archeologists have discovered Bronze Age settlements at this site, one of which seems to have been destroyed in the 13th century BCE. There is speculation that the *Iliad* represents a folk memory of a real event—a war between the Mycenaeans and an enemy tentatively identified as

TROJAN HORSE
Greek soldiers emerge from the horse that the Trojans unwisely dragged inside their city walls, on this 7th-century BCE amphora.

MYCENAEAN ARMOR
This bronze suit of armor, dating from around 1450 BCE, was probably more suited to a charioteer than a footsoldier.

the Hittites. Mycenae was certainly a flourishing, warlike power in Greece in the 13th century BCE. It was ruled by a king with the support of a warrior aristocracy, who rode chariots and used bronze weapons and armor. Mycenae exercised influence over a wide area and had trade contacts with the city we can, for convenience, call Troy. A plausible case has been made for the Mycenaeans raiding Troy, either for plunder or with the goal of establishing permanent control over a key point in its regional trading network. It is a large leap, however, from plausibility to fact. The Trojan War remains a legend, even if one with some historical basis.

Sea Peoples' Raids

DATE
1176 BCE

FORCES
Sea Peoples: unknown;
Egyptians: unknown

CASUALTIES
No reliable estimates

LOCATION
Nile delta,
northern Egypt

During the reign of Pharaoh Ramesses III (1184–1150 BCE), Egypt came under pressure from raiders known as the Sea Peoples. Little is known for certain about their origins, although they may have come from Anatolia. They fought on land as well as on sea, occupying parts of Syria and Palestine (one of the Sea Peoples were the Philistines), but it was the impact of their ships that made the greatest impression on the Egyptians. Their sea raids along Egypt's Mediterranean coast required Ramesses to assemble a fleet of his own and fight back. The result was history's first recorded sea battle. Since

the Egyptian vessels were designed for use on the Nile, not at sea, they confronted the raiders at the Nile delta at the mouth of the river. Both sides' ships had sails, but they almost certainly used oars for greater maneuverability when closing in for battle. The Egyptians aimed to draw close to their enemy and then unleash missile fire—arrows, javelins, and stones—from soldiers on the deck or up in the masts. As the Sea Peoples' fleet was drawn into the narrow waterways of the delta, Egyptian

bowmen also shot at them from the shore. In some cases Egyptians armed with swords and shields boarded enemy vessels, and may even have capsized some ships by hauling on grapnels hooked into the rigging. The Sea Peoples were heavily defeated. In the words of an Egyptian inscription, the enemy was "slain and made [into] heaps from stern to bow of their galleys."

SEA BATTLE
This Egyptian relief shows the battle against the Sea Peoples in the Nile delta. It was a fight not between ships, but between shipborne soldiers.

Mount Gilboa

DATE
c.1100 BCE

FORCES
Israelites: unknown;
Philistines: unknown

CASUALTIES
No reliable estimates

LOCATION
Plain of Esdraelon,
northern Israel

According to the Bible, Saul, the king of the Israelites, went to war against the Philistines, who were attacking his kingdom. Facing a more numerous and sophisticated enemy, Saul used guerrilla tactics, but was eventually forced to confront a Philistine army. Sure to be defeated on level ground, where the Philistines could use their chariots, the Israelites withdrew to the steep, rocky ridge of Mount Gilboa. Yet the Philistines were not deterred by the terrain: they stormed the ridge, taking a heavy toll from the Israelites. As his army fell around him, including his three sons, Saul took his own life rather than fall into enemy hands.

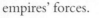

THE MIGHT OF MESOPOTAMIA

FOR MOST OF THE PERIOD from the 9th to the 5th century BCE, successive single states were dominant in the Near East—first Assyria, then Babylonia, and finally Persia. These powerful empires used large, well-organized armies to extend and enforce their rule. Weapons were now mostly of iron, while cavalry and siege engines joined the mix of the empires' forces.

RISE AND FALL
From the 10th century BCE the Assyrians developed a vast empire that remained unchecked until the 7th century.

Map labels

PHRYGIA
LYDIA
Sardis 547 BCE
Gordium
Anatolia
Halys
Taurus Mountains
CILICIA
Cyprus
Carchemish
605 BCE: Defeat of Assyrian and Egyptian armies by combined armies of Babylonia and Media bring Assyrian empire to an end
Scythians
Lake Van
Toprakkale
Tushpa
Harran 608 BCE: destroyed by Babylonians
KINGDOM OF URARTU
Khorsabad
Lake Urmia
MANNEA
Nineveh 612 BCE: Assyrian capital destroyed by Babylonians
ASSYRIA
Nimrud
Ashur 614 BCE: destroyed by Babylonians
MEDIA
Ecbatana
Mesopotamia
Diyala River 693 BCE
Tigris

Mediterranean Sea
Byblos
Sidon
Tyre
Damascus
SYRIA
Syrian Desert
Megiddo 605 BCE
ISRAEL
Gaza
Jerusalem 587 BCE: destroyed by Babylonians
Qarqar 853 BCE
Lachish 701 BCE
689 BCE: Babylon is destroyed by Assyrian king, Sennacherib. Rebuilt by his successor Esarhaddon and by Babylonian king Nebuchadnezzar II (605–562 BCE)
Babylon
BABYLONIA
Uruk
Ur
Persi
present-day coastline/ri

669 BCE: Egypt is conquered by Assyrian king Esarhaddon and ruled through native princes

EGYPT
Memphis 671 BCE: captured by Esarhaddon
Sinai
Nile
Arabian Peninsula
ELAM
648–47 BCE: Ashurbanipal destroys kingdom of Elam for its support of Babylonia; lands are sown with salt

0 km 100 200
0 miles 100 200

663 BCE: destroyed by Assyrian king, Ashurbanipal
Thebes
Red Sea

KEY
- under Ashur-dan II (934–912 BCE)
- added by death of Shalmaneser III (858–824 BCE)
- added by death of Sargon II (745–705 BCE)
- added by death of Ashurbanipal (668–626 BCE)
- New Babylonian Empire (625–539 BCE)

THE ASSYRIANS

Between the 9th and the mid-7th century BCE, Assyria carried the practice of warfare to a new level of efficiency. Its army was an instrument of terror, using torture, massacre, and mass deportation to wreak vengeance on any people that resisted Assyrian rule. At its peak under King Tiglath-pileser III (reigned 745–727 BCE), Assyria had a large army hierarchically organized into units led by professional generals. Tiglath-pileser's army was ethnically mixed, with foreign mercenaries and prisoners of war constituting major elements in the ranks. These soldiers were paid regularly and supplied with weapons and other materiel from centralized arms depots.

ASSYRIAN CHARIOT
An 8th-century BCE Assyrian relief depicting a two-horse chariot. Around this time three- and four-horse chariots also came into use.

PERSIAN KING
The conquests of Darius the Great (548–486 BCE) consolidated the frontiers of the Achaemenid Persian Empire.

THE PERSIANS

The Achaemenids, who took their name from the founding kings of the Persian Empire, also made cavalry a central element of their armies. Like the Assyrians, they assembled multiethnic forces, composed of conscripts and mercenaries from across their empire. Different peoples provided different specialties—Greek mercenaries served as infantry, Phoenicians as sailors, Medes and Scythians as horsemen. Strict training welded these forces into disciplined armies that, when needed, could move swiftly along Persia's excellent network of roads to defend or extend the empire.

HORSEMEN

The Assyrians still used chariots, introducing heavier, four-man vehicles, but by the end of the 8th century cavalry was overtaking chariots in importance. Steppe horsemen such as the Scythians had shown the effectiveness of lightly armored mounted archers, who could outrun enemies and subject them to arrow fire from powerful composite bows. By the late years of the Assyrian Empire, mounted archers were a vital component of its army, which also equipped its horsemen with spears. The advent of cavalry brought a new flexibility of maneuver to the battlefield.

SCYTHIAN GOLD
This 2,400-year-old gold Scythian comb shows a horseman in battle—a fitting object for a member of one of the first people to demonstrate the effectiveness of cavalry.

ASSYRIAN CONQUESTS

Qarqar

DATE 853 BCE

FORCES Assyrians: up to 100,000; Syrian-led alliance: c.70,000

CASUALTIES Assyria claimed it killed 14,000 of its opponents

LOCATION Northwest of Hamath, western Syria

By the 9th century BCE Assyria was the most powerful state in western Asia, using military might to dominate and extend its large empire. But in 853, 12 states in the eastern-Mediterranean region, led by Hadadezer of Damascus and including King Ahab of Israel, formed an alliance to resist further Assyrian conquest. The Assyrian king

Shalmaneser III led a huge force against this alliance that would result in a battle on a scale greater than any previously recorded. He advanced across the Tigris and Euphrates and into Syria, brushing aside resistance along the way. After sacking the city of Qarqar, he met the forces of the Syrian-led alliance near the Orontes River. The Assyrian army was a mix of chariots, cavalry, and footsoldiers. Assyrian reliefs suggest that horsemen fought in pairs, side by side, with one man holding the reins of both horses while the other fired his composite bow. The infantry, by

far the most numerous element, was mostly archers and spearmen. These men probably fought in pairs, too, the spearman defending the bowman with his weapon and shield. Like the Assyrians, the Syrian-led alliance had several thousand chariots, many of them provided by King Ahab, but considerably fewer horsemen. Oddly,

FLEXIBLE ARMOR
These small bronze plates, laced together with twine, were probably part of an Assyrian hauberk (armored tunic).

their forces included a contingent of camels, provided by the king of Arabia, although it is not known how they were used. Indeed, nothing is recorded about the course of the battle. Shalmaneser claimed a victory, boasting of inflicting 14,000 casualties and capturing countless chariots and horses. Yet none of his enemies lost their thrones—Hadadezer, for example, ruled Damascus for another 12 years, fighting the Assyrians on half a dozen more occasions. It was not until the reign of Tiglath-pileser III in the following century that Assyria conquered Syria and Palestine.

ASSYRIAN CONQUESTS

Siege of Lachish

DATE 701 BCE

FORCES Assyrians: unknown Judaeans: unknown

CASUALTIES No reliable estimates

LOCATION Present-day Tel Lakhish, southern Israel

In 701 BCE Assyria's King Sennacherib led an army into Palestine to punish subject peoples who—probably with the encouragement of Egypt—had revolted against Assyrian rule. One of these rebels was the Judaean people. Sennacherib's forces laid siege to the Judaean capital, Jerusalem, and to the walled city of Lachish. The siege of Lachish is especially well known

SIEGE WARFARE

The most formidable aspect of the Assyrian army was its ability at sieges. Instead of sitting out long blockades, the Assyrians preferred to take cities by assault. Engineers were skilled at undermining walls and building ramps, up which they pushed siege engines combining a ram with a tower manned by archers. When a besieged city fell, the Assyrians either killed or deported its inhabitants.

SOLDIERS ON THE WALLS OF A BESIEGED FORTRESS.

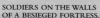

RAMMING ENGINE
This detail from the reliefs in Sennacherib's palace shows the Assyrians' siege engine mounting the ramp to hit the wall with its ram, while archers exchange fire.

because it was depicted on reliefs with which Sennacherib subsequently decorated his palace in Nineveh. Arriving in front of the city, the Assyrians called upon the inhabitants to surrender, offering them leniency if they opened their gates. The Judaeans, however, chose to resist and the siege began. The Assyrians encircled Lachish with troops, but, instead of waiting for a blockade to take effect, they prepared to assault the city. First they sent archers forward on foot, each accompanied by a shield-bearer. Protected from enemy arrows by large shields with curved-over tops, the archers shot at defenders on the ramparts, using their powerful composite bows. Their arrows provided cover for engineers to advance toward the walls. From the Nineveh reliefs it appears that engineers hacked at the base of the walls and tried mining under the foundations. But their main work was the construction of a ramp, made from dirt piled up in a steep slope to a point partway up the walls. When complete, the engineers paved it with stone slabs to smooth the surface. The Assyrians' idea was to propel a siege engine up this slope and attack the top of the wall. The siege engine was a wooden tower mounted on four wheels. Archers manned the top of the tower, while one or two battering rams protruded below. The whole structure was covered with dampened leather hides to protect it from flaming arrows—an incendiary weapon apparently used by both sides. Soldiers pushed the siege engine up the slope so that the ram

could batter the wall while the archers shot their arrows into the fortified town. At the same time, Assyrian infantry assaulted another section of the walls with scaling ladders, while being covered by shots from still more archers and stone-slingers. We do not know how long the assault on Lachish lasted or what the casualties were on either side, but the fighting was probably very fierce. Once the Assyrians had broken into the town, slaughter followed. The Nineveh reliefs show some Judaeans

> "I captured 46 towns …by consolidating ramps to bring up battering rams, by infantry attacks, mines, breaches, and siege engines."
>
> *Sennacherib* in the Old Testament (1 Kings, 18)

impaled on stakes and others pleading for their lives. Archeological evidence confirms that hundreds of men, women, and children were indeed massacred. In contrast to Lachish, the siege of Jerusalem was not a success for the Assyrians. They failed to take the city by assault and, after a lengthy blockade, raised the siege, probably because illness had broken out in their camp. By the end of Sennacherib's reign, however, the Assyrians returned and incorporated Judaea into their empire.

ASSYRIAN CONQUESTS

Diyala River

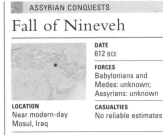

DATE
c.693 BCE

FORCES
Assyrians: unknown;
Elamites: unknown

CASUALTIES
No reliable estimates

LOCATION
Diyala River,
central Mesopotamia

In 694 BCE, to impose his rule on the troublesome Elamites at the southern edge of his empire, the Assyrian king Sennacherib invaded Elam and sacked its cities. The Elamites remained uncowed: the following year, with their allies from Chaldea in southern Babylonia, they mounted a counterinvasion. Both sides met at the Diyala River. In the words of Sennacherib's court chronicler, the king "cut [the Elamites'] throats like sheep … [filling] the plain with the corpses of their warriors like herbage." No Elamite account of the battle survives, but the Assyrian army may have suffered many fatalities itself since, unusually, it did not campaign the next year.

ASSYRIAN CONQUESTS

Fall of Nineveh

DATE
612 BCE

FORCES
Babylonians and
Medes: unknown;
Assyrians: unknown

CASUALTIES
No reliable estimates

LOCATION
Near modern-day
Mosul, Iraq

In 626 BCE Nabopolassar, whose background is unknown, took the throne of Babylon, then subject to the Assyrian Empire. By 616 he had evicted the Assyrian garrisons in the region, and then began probing attacks into Assyrian territory along the middle section of the Euphrates River, plundering and sacking cities. The Assyrians' ineffective response encouraged Nabopolassar to push

HORSE POWER
*A terra-cotta model of
an Assyrian warrior,
armed with a shield,
astride his horse.*

farther north, and in 615 his forces penetrated the Assyrian heartlands as far as the city of Ashur. There he suffered a serious defeat, however, and was forced to take refuge in the citadel of Tikrit. But the Assyrians, now under fire from another enemy, the Medes, were unable to follow up their success. Led by Cyaxares, the Medes formed an alliance with the Babylonians that sealed Assyria's fate. In 612 Cyaxares and Nabopolassar's armies joined up in Babylonia and marched north to the Assyrian capital, Nineveh, which fell

SPEAR, ARROW, AND CHARIOT
The spoked wheels on the chariot in this Assyrian relief were a development from earlier solid wheels, but during the 1st millennium BCE cavalry superceded chariots.

after a three-month siege. The Assyrian king Sin-shar-ishkun was probably killed, and the city was certainly looted and sacked. With Egyptian support, the Assyrians continued to fight, and moved their capital farther west to Harran, but in 608 Harran itself fell. The Assyrian Empire was crumbling.

BABYLONIAN–EGYPTIAN WARS

Fall of Jerusalem

DATE
586 BCE

FORCES
Babylonians:
unknown; Zedekiah's
army: unknown

LOCATION
Jerusalem
(present-day Israel)

CASUALTIES
No reliable estimates

The states of Palestine were caught in the middle of a confrontation between Babylon and Egypt in the early 6th century BCE. Zedekiah, the king of Judah, sided with Egypt, so in 597 Nebuchadnezzar, ruler of Babylon, besieged and captured Jerusalem, Judah's capital. Many of the city's inhabitants suffered the punishment of captivity in Babylon. The lesson was not learned, however. Ten years later, when the Egyptian pharaoh Hophra invaded Palestine, forcing out Babylonian garrisons, Zedekiah again allied himself with Egypt. Nebuchadnezzar responded by dispatching a powerful army to Palestine, forcing the Egyptians to withdraw and leaving Judah exposed to Babylonian revenge. Jerusalem was blockaded for 18 months until, in the words of the Bible, "there was no bread for the people of the land." It appears that Zedekiah and his army abandoned the city to its besiegers, but met the pursuing Babylonians on the plains of Jericho, where Zedekiah had to watch as his sons were killed in front of him. He was then blinded and carried off to Babylon, along with a large part of Judah's population.

A CHRISTIAN PERSPECTIVE
This early-modern tapestry of the Fall of Jerusalem portrays the combatants wearing the dress and carrying the weapons of Ottoman Turks.

Megiddo

DATE
605 BCE

FORCES Egyptians presumably far outnumbered the forces of Judah

LOCATION
Near Haifa, northern Israel

CASUALTIES
No reliable estimates

In 605 BCE the Egyptian pharaoh Necho II advanced through Palestine to aid the Assyrian forces still resisting Babylonian leader Nabopolassar in western Assyria (see the Fall of Ninevah). King Josiah of Judah, who sided with the Babylonians, led out an army to harass Necho on his way north. According to the Bible, Necho urged Josiah to let him pass, pointing out that he had no quarrel with Judah. Josiah, however, "did not turn away from him…but went to the valley of Megiddo to fight." No details of the battle are known, although there were presumably many chariots on both sides. An Egyptian victory was secured when Josiah died, falling to an arrow. Yet the triumph brought Necho no lasting advantage. He advanced into Syria, joining up with the remnants of the once-great Assyrian army, but was then attacked by forces led by Nabopolassar's son, Nebuchadnezzar, at Carchemish, on the west bank of the Euphrates River. The Egyptians and Assyrians got the worst of a hard-fought battle and Necho fled back to Egypt, his prestige ruined. The prophet Jeremiah commented sardonically, "Pharaoh king of Egypt is but a noise." The Assyrian cause was lost.

STRATEGIC SITE
The site of the ancient city of Megiddo, where battles were fought in 1468 BCE, 609 BCE, and 1918 CE.

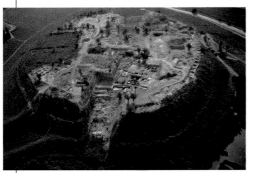

WAR CHARIOT

An Egyptian chariot was a lightweight vehicle designed for maximum speed and maneuverability. Its main function was as a mobile missile platform from which a warrior—who trained by using a rocking stool—shot arrows or threw javelins. It could also be used for shock effect in a high-speed charge, to move equipment around the battlefield, or to rescue the wounded.

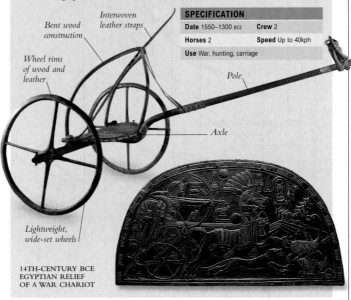

Intervowen leather straps
Bent wood construction
Wheel rims of wood and leather
Pole
Axle
Lightweight, wide-set wheels

SPECIFICATION	
Date 1550–1300 BCE	**Crew** 2
Horses 2	**Speed** Up to 40kph
Use War, hunting, carriage	

14TH-CENTURY BCE EGYPTIAN RELIEF OF A WAR CHARIOT

Sardis

DATE
546 BCE

FORCES
Persians: c.50,000; Lydian alliance: unknown (but greater)

LOCATION The plain of Thymbra, outside Sardis, Anatolia

CASUALTIES
No reliable estimates

In 550 BCE the Persian ruler Cyrus established a power base that would grow into an empire when he took control of the kingdom of Media in Ancient Iran. This takeover led to conflict with neighboring Lydia, a major power in western Anatolia. After an indecisive battle at Pteria in 547, Cyrus invaded Lydia and advanced on its capital, Sardis. The Lydian ruler, Croesus, confronted the Persian with a large army formed with the help of his Egyptian, Babylonian, and Spartan allies. Outnumbered, Cyrus formed his forces into a defensive square with his baggage camels in front and his archers in the middle. The smell of the camels disturbed the Lydian horses, disrupting their charge, while high-trajectory fire from the Persian bowmen inside the square caused the Lydians and their allies to flow around it in some disorder. A Persian counterattack swiftly turned into a rout, and Sardis fell soon afterward.

ROYAL WARRIOR
One of the "Immortals," an elite Persian guard. If one Immortal died he was immediately replaced—hence the name.

Fall of Babylon

DATE
539 BCE

FORCES
Persians: unknown; Babylonians: unknown

LOCATION Babylon, southern Mesopotamia (modern-day Iraq)

CASUALTIES
No reliable estimates

After his conquest of Lydia in 546 BCE, Cyrus went on to confront the Babylonian king Nabonidus. In 539 Cyrus invaded Babylonia with, as an ancient text tells us, "massive troops, whose number was immeasurable, like the water of a river." At the city of Opis, east of the Tigris, Cyrus defeated a Babylonian army, plundering the city's wealth and massacring its people afterward. But this is only one version of events, written down in a Babylonian chronicle. According to texts written in praise of Cyrus, the Persian ruler's progress was peaceful and unopposed. His army "marched with their arms at their sides," and entered Babylon "without battle [or] fighting." The truth appears to be that Cyrus sent his general Gobryas ahead to besiege Babylon. When the siege had succeeded, Gobryas having taken the city and made Nabonidus a prisoner, Cyrus led a peaceful, triumphal procession into Babylon, posing as a liberator of the city's inhabitants. There was some justification to this posture: the people of Babylon, including its priests, had been unhappy under Nabonidus's rule.

CYRUS THE GREAT

Cyrus, the founder of the Persian Achaemenid Empire, began his remarkable career of conquest by taking over the kingdom of the Medes from its ruler, Astyages. By 546 BCE, when he defeated Croesus of Lydia, Cyrus controlled western Iran, northern Mesopotamia, and most of Anatolia. His capture of Babylon and subsequent campaigns extended Persian rule over a vast area from the Mediterranean to the borders of India. Cyrus's military success resulted from an unmatched ability to organize and supply large-scale forces, drawn from all parts of his empire. In addition, he won the support of many of his conquered peoples with a policy of religious tolerance.

GREEK TRIUMPHS

THE CITY-STATES THAT FLOURISHED in Greece from around the 7th century BCE were small and apparently weak entities compared to the mighty empires of the Assyrians and the Persians. But their citizen armies, fighting shoulder to shoulder as spear-bearing infantry, proved more than a match for the subject soldiers of Persia. In the 4th century the Macedonian Greeks created an empire that stretched from the Mediterranean to India.

FORTIFIED HEIGHTS
The acropolis in Athens, like those in other Greek cities, was a walled fortress to be defended when an enemy laid siege to the city.

CITY-STATE WARFARE

The city-states of Ancient Greece based their armed forces upon the obligation of free citizens to fight when required, usually as hoplites (heavily-armed footsoldiers). Since the city-states were quarrelsome and fought one another repeatedly, citizens were frequently called upon to fulfill this military requirement. The citizen armies were not large and could not campaign for long—most hoplites were farmers who needed to be at home at key points in the year—but their battles were ruthless and bloody, fought at close quarters with spears.

GREEK ARMOR

The Greeks adopted bronze armor in the 8th century BCE. The full panoply consisted of a helmet, a cuirass for the upper body, and greaves for the knees and shins. Along with the spear, sword, and, above all, shield, this armor was considered the distinguishing equipment of the hoplite. Yet not all city-state soldiers wore it. The hoplite was expected to provide his own armor and many could afford only a helmet, or possibly a helmet and greaves. A full set of bronze armor was thus a status symbol and provided an opportunity for a conspicuous display of wealth.

Bronze helmet with cheek guards

Bronze cuirass made of two plates held together at the sides by leather straps

Molding idealizes warrior's muscles

BRONZE PANOPLY
The armor of a Greek hoplite was designed both to protect and to impress. Polished bright, it made a dazzling display.

SPARTA AND ATHENS

The two most powerful city-states were Sparta and Athens. Sparta created the most formidable army in Ancient Greece by training its citizen elite for war from the age of seven. The Spartans prized hardiness and fitness above all else, and group exercises were performed each day. In adulthood, male citizens were assigned to a mess where they were obliged to eat communally, and each belonged to a band of 40 soldiers who were sworn to obey their commanders. These bands were the basic units of the Spartan army, which alone among the city-state forces had a clear hierarchy of command. The army of Athens, on the other hand, was made up of citizens who had no particular training but shared the belief that a citizen's first duty was to fight. If Sparta excelled on land, the Athenian warships dominated at sea.

KEY

▭	annexed by Persians
▬	Persian campaigns against Greece 490-479 BCE
⚔	Greek victory
⚔	Persian victory
⚔	indecisive battle
▬	Persian Royal Road

GREECE VERSUS PERSIA
In the early 5th century BCE, faced with almost impossible odds, the Greek city-states united to repulse successive waves of Persian attack.

THE ADVENT OF MACEDONIAN POWER

The citizen army of hoplites fighting in phalanxes represented the Ancient Greek ideal of warfare. In reality, however, armies were a mixture of citizens, noncitizens, and mercenaries. Poorer men generally fought as skirmishers, harassing phalanxes with stones and arrows, while peltasts were specially trained javelin-throwers, who proved capable on occasion of inflicting defeat even on the hardy Spartan hoplites. The Greeks eventually lost their independence to their northern neighbors, the Macedonians (also Greek in culture), who had perfected their own form of warfare: a mixed force of professional infantry fighting in a phalanx, skirmishers on foot and on horseback, and an elite cavalry accompanying their chief.

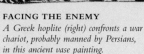

FACING THE ENEMY
A Greek hoplite (right) confronts a war chariot, probably manned by Persians, in this ancient vase painting.

MACEDONIAN CONQUEST

Under Philip of Macedon and Alexander the Great, the Greek phalanx was reinvented and cavalry armed with lances became a crucial force on the battlefield. Hoplites were organized in a tighter formation of greater depth than before, and each carried a two-handed 20–23ft- (6–7m-) long spear, the *sarissa*. Under Alexander's inspired generalship, the cavalry, infantry phalanx, and light skirmishers were combined to maximum effect, achieving conquest on an unprecedented scale by seizing the Persian Empire and Asia as far as northern India. The impact of this encounter with Asia was already visible before Alexander's death, with Persians taking important positions in the Macedonian forces. The Asian influence continued in the successor states to Alexander's empire—in Persia, Egypt, and Greece—which would in turn eventually prove vulnerable to the rising power of Rome.

PERSIAN CAVALRY
The Alexander Sarcophagus dramatically depicts a Persian horseman, riding without saddle or stirrups, battling the Macedonians.

PHALANX

Ancient Greek infantry fought in a phalanx, a close formation typically eight ranks deep. Each hoplite had a shield (the *hoplon*) on his left side and in his right hand a thrusting spear around 6½ft (2m) long. When opposing phalanxes confronted one another, they advanced until shield butted against shield and then they pushed with all their weight, while those in the front ranks, wielding spears overarm, stabbed at the enemy.

PHALANX CLASH
Hoplites armed with *hoplon* (shield), spear, and sword.

GREEK–PERSIAN WARS

AT THE BEGINNING OF THE 5th century BCE, Greeks in Anatolia revolted against the rule of the expanding Persian Empire. Despite support from two Greek cities, Athens and Eretria, the Persian emperor Darius the Great crushed the uprising. He then decided to punish the Greek cities that had aided the rebels. The first Persian invasion was repulsed at Marathon in 490, but 10 years later Darius's successor, Xerxes, made a more determined effort at conquest. The Greeks rose to the challenge once more, holding up the Persians at Thermopylae and defeating them at Salamis and Plataea. An Athenian-led alliance continued to fight the Persians in the Mediterranean until 448, but Greece was not invaded again.

GREEK–PERSIAN WARS

Marathon

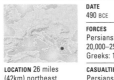

DATE
490 BCE

FORCES
Persians:
20,000–25,000;
Greeks: 10,000

LOCATION 26 miles (42km) northeast of Athens

CASUALTIES
Persians: 6,400 killed;
Greeks: 192 killed

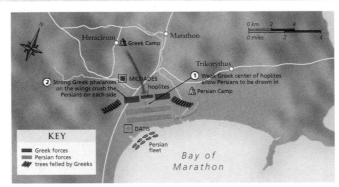

The invasion force sent to Greece by Darius in 490 BCE was commanded by a Median general, Datis. A fleet of 600 triremes (see p.31) carried the Persian army across the Aegean to land at Marathon, close to the main target, Athens. The Athenians, meanwhile, mustered their hoplites and marched north, joined only by a small force from Plataea. When they arrived at Marathon, the Athenian commanders hotly debated whether they should fight the Persians at once or wait for their allies, the Spartans. Miltiades, the most aggressive of the Athenians, won the argument, and the

TREASURY OF TRIUMPH

The Athenians' treasury at Delphi celebrated their triumph at Marathon. They filled it with the spoils of war as an offering to the god Apollo.

Greeks immediately advanced to confront the Persian host. The hoplites arranged themselves in a broad phalanx between two streams. In order to avoid being outflanked by the larger Persian army, Miltiades had to stretch his line, which was left thin at the center. One source also suggests that he protected his flanks with ramparts of felled trees. To the amazement of the Persians, the outnumbered Greek footsoldiers advanced aggressively, in close formation, straight at the enemy. On the flanks the Persian line collapsed under the charge, but in the center it was the Greek phalanx that broke under a hail of arrows and the axes of Persian auxiliaries.

The hoplites on the flanks responded by turning back from the hot pursuit of their opposite numbers and enveloping the Persian center from both sides. The battle disintegrated into a disorganized melée on the beach as the defeated Persians sought to reembark on their triremes. About two-thirds of their force escaped. According to Athenian legend, the runner Pheidippedes was sent to carry the news of the victory back to Athens—the original "marathon."

"The Persians…when they saw the Greeks coming on at speed made ready to receive them, although it seemed to them that the Athenians were bereft of their senses and bent upon their own destruction, for they saw a mere handful of men coming on at a run without…horsemen or archers."

WITNESS TO WAR

HERODOTUS

The Greek historian Herodotus (c.485–425 BCE) is our main source of information about the Greek-Persian Wars. Although he was born too late to have seen the events he describes, his accounts are full of vivid details that may have been told to him by eyewitnesses.

GREEK–PERSIAN WARS

Thermopylae

DATE
August 480 BCE

FORCES
Greeks: 7,000;
Persians: 200,000

LOCATION
Thessaly,
northern Greece

CASUALTIES
Greeks: 2,500;
Persians: 20,000

The Persian emperor Xerxes succeeded his father Darius in 486 BCE. Determined to expand his empire and avenge the defeat at Marathon, he set in motion meticulous preparations for the conquest of Greece. Faced with this new threat, most Greek cities chose to give in and accept Persian suzerainty. But Athens and the cities of the Peloponnese, including Sparta, remained defiant. In 480 Xerxes' preparations were complete and he led his army across the Hellespont (the straits between mainland Asia and Europe) and down through northern Greece, accompanied by his fleet, sailing down the coast.

BATTLE SITE
In 480 BCE Thermopylae was a narrow pass between the mountains and the sea, but silting has turned it into a broader coastal plain.

The Athenian leader Themistocles persuaded his Peloponnesian allies to confront the Persians by land and sea well to the north of Athens. A force of hoplites and skirmishers led by Spartan king Leonidas took up position at Thermopylae—a narrow defile between Mount Kallidromon and the sea—while a predominantly Athenian fleet of triremes was stationed off the island of Euboea. The Persian naval force was battered by storms on its way down the coast and, severely weakened, fought cautiously in an indecisive battle with the Greeks at Artemisium. On land, however, the Greeks faced the full might of the Persian army. For three days Leonidas's vastly outnumbered army held the pass, the narrowness of the battlefield preventing the Persians from taking advantage of their numbers. Man for man, the Greeks

CRESTED HERO
A statue of Leonidas, hero of Thermopylae, with a horsehair helmet crest and a shield emblazoned with a Gorgon's head.

proved a match even for the Immortals, Xerxes' elite imperial guard. In the end, however, the Greeks were undone by a traitor who revealed to Xerxes a mountain track that led around Thermopylae. When the Immortals appeared behind their position, the Greeks were doomed. Leonidas and his 300 Spartan hoplites, along with a thousand or more other Greek soldiers, fought courageously to their deaths.

GREEK–PERSIAN WARS

Salamis

DATE
September 480 BCE

FORCES
Greeks: 300–500 ships;
Persians: 500–700 ships

LOCATION
Off the Greek island of Salamis

CASUALTIES Greeks:
40 ships; Persians:
200–300 ships

After the battle of Thermopylae the Peloponnesian cities withdrew their forces south of the Isthmus of Corinth, leaving Athens indefensible. The Athenian leader Themistocles took as many as possible of the city's population on board the Greek fleet, which

had sailed south to Piraeus, and ferried them to the relative safety of the island of Salamis. The Persian army seized the acropolis in Athens after a short siege, plundering or burning everything inside. In the face of this disaster, Themistocles remained convinced that a victory at sea could turn the tables on the invaders. The Greek fleet was sheltered in the channel between Salamis and the mainland. Hoping to draw the Persian fleet into these

CORINTHIAN HELMET
This style of hoplite helmet, giving maximum facial protection, was common in the 5th century BCE.

narrow waters, Themistocles sent Xerxes a message saying that, if the Persian fleet attacked, his Athenians would change sides and the rest of the Greeks would flee. This message had credibility since many Greeks had already joined the Persian forces. The following day, Xerxes watched from a hilltop as most of his fleet rowed into the eastern end of the Salamis channel. As the channel narrowed, the triremes bunched together, creating confusion and limiting movement. At that point, the Greek fleet attacked, the ranks of oarsmen rowing with all their strength to ram into the enemy warships. Much of the battle was fought with arrows, spears, and axes as marine infantry and archers clashed, fighting on ships locked together. The conflict lasted seven hours, before the Persian fleet was decisively put to flight. With winter approaching and resupply by sea no longer possible, Xerxes withdrew his army to the north.

OARED WARFARE
At Salamis, as in all naval battles of this period, the goal was to sink the enemy by ramming or to get shipborne soldiers onto enemy vessels.

GREEK–PERSIAN WARS

Battle of Plataea

DATE
July 479 BCE

FORCES
Persians: 100,000;
Greeks: 80,000

LOCATION
South of Thebes,
Greek mainland

CASUALTIES
Persians: 50,000;
Greeks: 1,500

In 479 BCE the Persians, commanded by Mardonius, once more marched south into Greece. Sparta, Athens, and their allies assembled a substantial army and faced the Persians in front of Thebes. After an eight-day standoff, the Greeks decided on a night withdrawal to Plataea. This maneuver went chaotically wrong. By daybreak the center had successfully withdrawn, but the Spartans on the right and Athenians on the left were still close to the enemy. Sensing an opportunity to crush the Spartans, Mardonius launched his infantry against them. But the Spartans, unsurpassed in close combat, took out many of the Persian footsoldiers. By luck, the withdrawn Greek center returned just in time to intercept an encirclement of the Athenians by Persian cavalry. Mardonius was killed fighting the Spartans and the battle turned into a rout as Persian soldiers were hacked down while attempting to flee. A further Greek victory at Mycale the following month brought the Persian invasion to an end.

GREEK VERSUS GREEK

THE PELOPONNESIAN WAR, between 431 and 404 BCE, was started by Sparta in an attempt to reduce Athenian power. In search of a decisive result, Athens was forced to challenge Spartan superiority on land; in turn, Sparta had to contest Athenian control of the sea. When the Spartan navy achieved victory at Aegospotami, the Athenians lost the war. Yet Athens remained a player in the complex wars of the first half of the 4th century, in which the city-state of Thebes proved more than a match for the Spartan hoplites.

KEY

Athenian Empire c.431 BCE	
Athenian ally	
Sparta and allied states	
Neutral territory	
Athenian victory	
Spartan victory	
borders	

GREEK WARS

A system of alliances pulled much of Greece and the west coast of Anatolia into the Peloponnesian War of the late 5th century BCE.

PELOPONNESIAN WAR

Siege of Syracuse

DATE
415–413 BCE

FORCES
Athenians 30,000; Spartans: 3,000; Syracusans: unknown

LOCATION
Syracuse, east coast of Sicily

CASUALTIES
Entire Athenian force killed or captured

In 415 BCE the Athenians sent an expedition under the politician and general Nicias to capture the Greek city of Syracuse, a Sicilian ally of the Spartans. The force sailed in 100 triremes and, after landing, laid siege to the city. At this time, Greek armies had no siege engines with which to break down city fortifications, so the Athenians set about building a wall to enclose the city on its landward side. The goal was to starve the

defenders to death. In 414, however, the arrival of a 3,000-strong Spartan expedition, led by a commander Gylippus, interrupted this slow labor. Gylippus blocked the completion of the Athenian wall by building a counterwall across its path. The arrival of reinforcements from Athens led by Demosthenes only fed more men into an increasingly desperate situation. Disease broke out in the Athenian camp and the Syracusans blockaded the Athenian fleet in harbor. After a breakout attempt by the fleet failed, the trapped Athenians tried to escape overland. Caught in mountainous terrain under constant harassment from light forces with bows, javelins, and slingshots, the remaining 7,000 Athenians finally surrendered. Their generals were executed and the rest sent to die as slave workers in the stone quarries of Sicily.

SHIELD AND SPEAR

The hoplite's wooden shield, sometimes sheeted with bronze, weighed around 15lb (7kg). His spear typically had an iron head, balanced by a bronze spike at the other end.

PELOPONNESIAN WAR

Pylos

DATE
425 BCE

FORCES Athenians: 800 hoplites, 2,000 other troops; Spartans: 420 hoplites

LOCATION
West coast of the Peloponnese

CASUALTIES
Spartans: 128 killed, the rest captured

After war broke out between Athens and Sparta in 431 BCE, the Athenians could not prevent the Spartans from raiding up to the walls of Athens. They hit back by landing a garrison, led by Demosthenes, on the Peloponnesian coast at Pylos and using this base to launch raids into Sparta. In 425 the Spartans failed to retake Pylos with a combined land and sea operation. Even worse, hoplites they had placed on the nearby island of Sphacteria were cut off by the arrival of an Athenian fleet. Demosthenes himself then landed on the island with 800 hoplites and a large number of skirmishers. Driven back by the arrows of these troops, the Spartans were unable to engage in battle. Those that the Athenians did not kill they took prisoner.

PELOPONNESIAN WAR

Delium

DATE
November 424 BCE

FORCES Athenians: 7,000 hoplites; Boeotians: 7,000 hoplites, 1,000 cavalry, 10,000 light troops

LOCATION
Boeotia/Attica, east-central Greece

CASUALTIES Athenians: almost 1,000 hoplites

Led by the general Hippocrates, an Athenian army returning from a foray into Boeotia, northwest of Athens, was caught by an army from that region. The Boeotian general Pagondas drew up his phalanxes on ground hidden by a hill. When the phalanxes came over the hill to attack, the Athenians had to respond swiftly. They charged uphill to meet the enemy, and, in the words of historian Thucydides, the opposing phalanxes "crashed into one another on the run" and then "stood pushing against each other with their shields in a brutal battle." On the right the Theban phalanx was 25 ranks deep and pressed back the eight-deep Athenian ranks. But on the left the Athenians got the upper hand and butchered many of their enemies when the Boeotian phalanx collapsed. Pagondas ordered his cavalry to attack in support of his weakest wing. Luckily for him, when the horsemen appeared over a hill, the Athenians mistakenly believed a new army was joining the battle. As panic spread, the Athenian force turned and ran back toward the city of Delium, pursued by the Boeotians. Almost 1,000 Athenians were killed, including Hippocrates.

PELOPONNESIAN WAR

Aegospotami

DATE 405 BCE

FORCES
Athenians: 200 warships; Spartans: unknown

LOCATION
On the Hellespont, off the coast of Thrace

CASUALTIES
Athenians: more than 190 ships captured or destroyed

After its defeat at Syracuse, Athens was seriously weakened. The Spartans put the city under almost permanent siege by land; all that they needed for a complete victory was to overcome Athenian domination at sea. Athens survived by importing shiploads of grain from the Black Sea, recognizing that if the Spartans cut that lifeline it was doomed. Under the direction of admiral Lysander, the Spartans had their new fleet ready for battle in 406 BCE. Results were at first mixed. Lysander was victorious at Ephesus, only to be removed from his post because Spartan law limited an admiral's command to one year. The Athenians then crushingly defeated the Spartans under Callicratidas at Arginusae. In return for funding more shipbuilding in the wake of this defeat, the Persian prince Cyrus insisted on Lysander's return. In 405 the Athenian fleet established itself at Aegospotami on the Hellespont. Lysander, shadowing their movements but avoiding battle, positioned himself on the opposite shore. He observed that the Athenian sailors had fixed habits: they set sail each morning, paraded on the sea, then returned to shore for lunch. Lysander saw an opportunity not to be missed. A single scout vessel was sent to watch the Athenian base. When a signal flashed from the spy ship, informing Lysander that the

RAM ATTACK
The heavy ram on a Greek warship was designed to crash through an enemy vessel's hull.

Athenians were ashore, the Spartan fleet descended on the enemy, seizing empty triremes and landing marines to butcher the Athenians on the beach. Only eight Athenian warships escaped. The following year, facing starvation, Athens surrendered.

> "The Peloponnesians fell upon the rest of the ships, some of which they took entirely empty and others they disabled while their crews were still getting aboard. And the men, coming up unarmed and in straggling fashion, perished at their ships, or if they fled by land, their enemies, who had disembarked, slew them. Lysander took three thousand men prisoners…[and] sailed back…to the sound of pipes and hymns of victory."

WITNESS TO WAR
PLUTARCH
The Greek biographer Plutarch (46–c.119 CE) wrote about the battle of Aegospotami in his biography of the Spartan general Lysander. Plutarch was writing about five centuries after the Peloponnesian War, but he was a meticulous researcher—this description is based on contemporary sources.

> "The Athenians, panic-stricken at the unexpected move, held out for a short while and then gave way, and at once, some deserting the ships, others the camp, they took flight in whatever direction each man hoped to find safety."

Diodorus Siculus, Library of History, 1st century BCE

THEBAN WARS

Leuctra

DATE July 371 BCE

FORCES Spartans: 11,000; Thebans: 6,000

LOCATION Boeotia, central Greece

CASUALTIES Spartans: 2,000 killed; Thebans: negligible

In 379 BCE the Boeotian city-state of Thebes revolted against the Spartans, who had achieved dominance over Greece through their victory in the Peloponnesian War. In 371 the Spartans advanced into Boeotia. On the plain of Leuctra the Spartans spread their hoplites evenly across the battlefield with—as was traditional—their commander and best infantry on the right. Sparta's experienced, larger force had every expectation of crushing the Thebans. But the Theban leader Epaminondas adopted an unprecedented battle formation. He concentrated his hoplites in a column 48 ranks deep on the left of his line, where he also placed his elite infantry, the Sacred Band. This left only a thin line of hoplites in the center and on his right, screened by skirmishers on foot and horseback. The skirmishers held the Spartans off while Epaminondas's column crashed into the enemy's right, causing it to scatter. Epaminondas now attacked the Spartans' exposed flank and put the superior Spartan force to flight.

THEBAN WARS

Mantinea

DATE 362 BCE

FORCES 25,000 on each side

LOCATION The Peloponnese, north of Sparta

CASUALTIES Athenian–Spartan alliance: 1,000 killed, 2,000 captured; Thebans: similar losses

The victory at Leuctra initiated a period of Theban dominance in Greece, guaranteed by the military genius of Epaminondas. Sparta and Athens allied to challenge Thebes, but it was only in 362 BCE that enough other states joined the alliance to pose a serious threat. Epaminondas responded by seizing the strategic initiative, sending his army deep into the Peloponnese. When a direct advance on Sparta was blocked by the Spartan army, the Thebans turned to threaten the city of Mantinea, one of Sparta's allies. The arrival of an Athenian force held up the Theban maneuver and Athenians, Spartans, and Mantineans were able to join up to confront Epaminondas. As usual, Epaminondas placed his elite infantry on the left of his line, while Theban horsemen were deployed on both flanks, supported by *hamippoi* (runners trained to keep up with cavalry on foot). When battle was joined, Epaminondas led his hoplite elite in a crushing charge against the Mantineans, who held the right of the enemy line, while the Theban cavalry swept Athenian horsemen from the field. The Mantinean infantry broke into flight, but in the moment of victory Epaminondas himself was slain. The Thebans failed to follow through the pursuit and, without their leader, Thebes quickly fell from preeminence.

CONFLICT ZONE
Mantinea in the Peloponnese was the site of three battles. The first, between Sparta and Athens in 418 BCE, occurred during the Peloponnesian War. The second brought a victory for Thebes in 362. The third, and least, was a defeat for Sparta in 207.

c.490–429 BCE

PERICLES

The Athenian statesman Pericles led the city in its golden age. Identifying the interests of his city with the development of trade around the Mediterranean, he encouraged Athenians to sever their ties with Greece. He enclosed Athens and its seaport at Piraeus behind long walls, forcing the city to trade by sea. As a result the city's economy flourished, but Pericles's policies failed to prevent war with Sparta in 431 BCE. After falling from grace, he died during the plague of 429.

THE CONQUESTS OF ALEXANDER

THE TRIUMPH OF ALEXANDER of Macedon over the mighty Persians between 334 and 323 BCE was an exploit of unparalleled audacity, creating an empire stretching from Greece to India. He achieved this feat with the army he had inherited from his father, Philip, with its irresistible cavalry, hardened infantry, and light forces of auxiliaries. The make-up of this force reflected Alexander's proclaimed desire to wage war on behalf of all Greeks: it included Macedonians, Thessalians, and Thracians, as well as Cretans and Balkans. He himself was an indomitable leader, seizing the initiative on all occasions and pursuing the destruction of his enemies in battle.

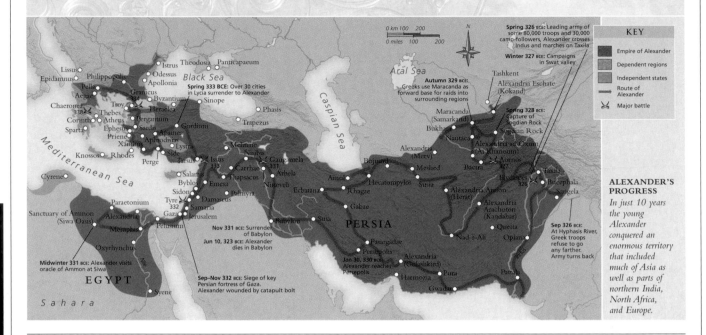

KEY

- Empire of Alexander
- Dependent regions
- Independent states
- Route of Alexander
- ⚔ Major battle

Spring 326 BCE: Leading army of some 80,000 troops and 30,000 camp-followers, Alexander crosses Indus and marches on Taxila

Winter 327 BCE: Campaigns in Swat valley

Autumn 329 BCE: Greeks use Maracanda as forward base for raids into surrounding regions

Spring 328 BCE: Capture of Sogdian Rock

Spring 333 BCE: Over 30 cities in Lycia surrender to Alexander

Sep 326 BCE: At Hyphasis River, Greek troops refuse to go any farther. Army turns back

Nov 331 BCE: Surrender of Babylon

Jun 10, 323 BCE: Alexander dies in Babylon

Midwinter 331 BCE: Alexander visits oracle of Ammon at Siwa

Jan 30, 330 BCE: Alexander reaches Persepolis

Sep–Nov 332 BCE: Siege of key Persian fortress of Gaza. Alexander wounded by catapult bolt

ALEXANDER'S PROGRESS

In just 10 years the young Alexander conquered an enormous territory that included much of Asia as well as parts of northern India, North Africa, and Europe.

WARS OF PHILIP OF MACEDON

Chaeronea

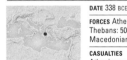

DATE 338 BCE

FORCES Athenians and Thebans: 50,000; Macedonians: 32,000

CASUALTIES Athenians and Thebans: 20,000; Macedonians: no reliable estimates

LOCATION 30 miles (50km) north of Thebes, Boeotia

In the spring of 338 BCE, an army fielded by Athens and Thebes confronted Philip's Macedonians outside the Boeotian town of Chaeronea. The Athenian–Theban force outnumbered their enemy, but they were far less diversified, consisting mainly of hoplites. In contrast, Philip, influenced by Epaminondas (see Theban Wars, p.25), had created an army in which the infantry phalanx was only one element. There were also 2,000 cavalry, missile troops, and the hypaspists (elite infantry who fought with more flexibility than the phalanx). There were two key moments in the battle. One was when Philip drew the Athenian hoplites out of formation with a feigned retreat and then turned to attack them. The other was a charge by the Macedonian cavalry, led by Alexander, which shattered the Theban forces. Thebes' elite infantry, the Sacred Band, fought on until only 46 of their 300 men were left alive.

382–336 BCE

PHILIP II OF MACEDON

When Philip secured the throne in 359 BCE, Macedonia was a backward state on the periphery of Greece. His energetic rule transformed Macedonia into a great power, through diplomacy and military innovations. Philip was a born warrior (he lost an eye in battle) who insisted on toughness and discipline in the large standing army he created. Victory at Chaeronea in 338 won him control of Greece, which he intended to use as a springboard for an ambitious campaign against the Persians, but his assassination in 336 meant that the task fell instead to his son, Alexander.

CONQUESTS OF ALEXANDER

Granicus

DATE May 334 BCE

FORCES Macedonians: 40,000; Persians: 35,000 (including up to 8,000 Greek mercenaries)

LOCATION Granicus River, western Anatolia

CASUALTIES Persians: more than 15,000

Succeeding his murdered father in 336 BCE, Alexander first consolidated his hold on Greece, brutally suppressing a rebellion by Thebes. By 334 he felt secure enough to embark on the campaign against Persia that his father had planned. Alexander's army sailed across the Hellespont into Anatolia, in itself a complex operation involving thousands of troops as well as siege equipment. It then marched east into Persian-ruled territory, Alexander intending to follow the coastline since his army would depend on resupply by sea. Mounted scouts rode in front of the main body, and it was they who reported the presence of Persian forces drawn up on the far bank of the Granicus River. The army assembled by local Persian commanders included a large number of Greek mercenaries. It was outnumbered by Alexander's forces but had taken up a strong defensive position. The river ran fast and its banks were steep: an opposed crossing would be a risky venture. Reaching the river in the late afternoon, Alexander led across a cavalry attack. Battle was joined on the far bank as the Persian cavalry attempted to push the Macedonians back into the river, horse pressing against horse. In the thick of the fighting, Alexander lost his spear and almost his life. But the Persian horsemen soon broke before the ferocious Macedonian onslaught and Alexander's infantry were able to wade across to join in. They quickly surrounded the Persian forces, massacring more than 15,000 of them. Those whom the Macedonians took prisoner they sent to work as slaves.

MEDIEVAL VIEW

Under a shower of javelins, Alexander's shock cavalry cross the Granicus River in this 15th-century CE French illustration.

CONQUESTS OF ALEXANDER

Gaugamela (Arbela)

DATE October 331 BCE

FORCES Macedonians: 40,000 infantry, 7,000 cavalry; Persians: 200,000

LOCATION West of Arbela (present-day Irbil in north Iraq)

CASUALTIES Macedonians: 500 killed, 3,000 wounded; Persians: 50,000 killed

After his victory at Issus (see pp.28–29), Alexander spent a year subduing the cities of Syria and Palestine and occupying Egypt, where he founded Alexandria. In the spring of 331 BCE, hearing that the Persian king Darius III was assembling a vast army in Mesopotamia, Alexander ordered his army to march east toward Persia itself. Darius, determined to defeat Alexander this time, waited for him on the Plain of Gaugamela. The Persian army was different from the one at Issus. Most Greek mercenaries were gone, leaving the infantry weaker, but other forces had been summoned from Darius's Asian empire, including elephants from India and hosts of Scythian and Afghan horsemen to augment the Persian cavalry. Darius also deployed 200 chariots with scythed wheels, flattening the ground in advance so that the vehicles could operate. Coming within sight of the Persian army in late September, Alexander pitched camp and considered how to take on forces outnumbering his own by four to one. He rejected a night attack and instead planned a variant on his usual tactics. Since it was impossible to avoid being outflanked on the open plain, he assigned cavalry and light infantry to defend the flanks and stationed a reserve force of infantry behind the front line. The Macedonians advanced toward the Persians with Alexander and the elite Companion cavalry leading on the right and the phalanx infantry and other cavalry wing in echelon behind. Darius's charioteers charged the Macedonian phalanx, but proved hopelessly vulnerable to its light skirmishers, who struck most of them down with javelins. On the left, Alexander's flank guards fought desperately to hold the enveloping Scythian horsemen, but on the right the Macedonian cavalry and hypaspists (elite infantry) broke through, driving a path toward Darius in the Persian center. Once again, the Persian emperor was obliged to flee the field. Alexander gave chase but gave up when he discovered that his army was getting the worst of fierce fighting behind him, where Persian infantry and cavalry had fought through to the rear of the Macedonian army. The arrival of Alexander's cavalry soon ended this melée around the baggage train. The Persians had once more been routed. In the aftermath of the battle, Darius was murdered by his own nobles and Alexander advanced to take the Persian capital, Babylon.

MACEDONIAN ARMOR

This metal breastplate was recovered from the tomb of Philip of Macedon in Vergina.

DELAYED REVENGE

Persepolis was the ceremonial center of the Persian Empire. In 330 BCE Alexander plundered it and burned the palace of Xerxes, probably as revenge for the burning of Athens in 480.

CONQUESTS OF ALEXANDER

Hydaspes

DATE May 326 BCE

FORCES Alexander: 6,000 infantry, 5,000 cavalry; King Porus: 30,000

LOCATION Hydaspes River, northwest India

CASUALTIES Alexander: 310 killed; King Porus: 23,000 killed (allegedly)

In 326 BCE, with the Persian Empire conquered, Alexander led a campaign into northern India. This brought him into confrontation with Parvataka (usually referred to as King Porus), the leading rajah of the Punjab. The two sides faced each other across the unfordable Hydaspes (now Jhelum) River. Alexander split his forces, leaving one part opposite Porus's position while marching the rest upstream, crossing the river in boats under cover of darkness. When Porus, to his surprise, discovered Alexander on his side of the river, he drew up his army, with its left wing by the water's edge. More than 100 war elephants were spaced out across the entire breadth of his line in front of his troops, with archers and javelin throwers on their backs, making a kind of movable fortification. Alexander ordered part of his cavalry to make a wide circuit around the right of Porus's line to attack from the rear. At the same time, javelin throwers were sent forward to harass the elephants, causing many of the beasts to panic and trample the troops behind them. As Porus's army wavered, Alexander led the Companion cavalry in a charge along the riverbank, while his infantry phalanx also moved inexorably forward with shields locked. The fighting was fierce, but, attacked from all sides, Porus's men finally took flight and Porus himself was captured. It was Alexander's last major battle.

ELEPHANTS AT WAR

By the time Alexander encountered war elephants at Gaugamela and Hydaspes, they had been in use in Indian armies for about 700 years. Aside from inspiring terror, elephants were fast on the charge and hard to stop, and could carry several archers or spearmen in a howdah, or canopied saddle, on their backs. On the downside, wounded elephants were liable to panic, trampling friend and foe alike. It was said that elephants were scared of pigs, and porcine countermeasures were allegedly used successfully against them on at least one occasion. Nonetheless, war elephants became a common feature of armies in the Mediterranean region in the centuries after Alexander.

CONQUESTS OF ALEXANDER

Issus

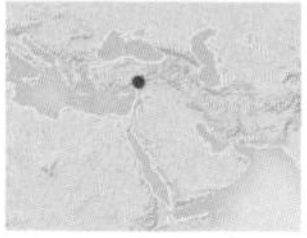

DATE
November 333 BCE

FORCES
Macedonians: 35,000;
Persians: 110,000

LOCATION Plain on the
Gulf of Iskenderun,
present-day Turkey

CASUALTIES
Macedonians: 450;
Persians: 50,000
(allegedly)

By the fall of 333 BCE, Alexander had conquered the Mediterranean coast of Anatolia. The Persian king Darius III set out with a large army to counter the Macedonian invasion of his territory, searching for Alexander's forces around northern Syria. In turn, Alexander, whose strategy was not to avoid battle but to seek it, was looking for the Persians. The Macedonians were advancing into Syria when they discovered that Darius's force was behind them, to the northeast. Alexander turned his army around and advanced to meet the Persians. Darius was forced to fight on a narrow plain between mountains and the sea, a location that limited the impact of his superior numbers. Although Alexander's forces were stretched thin, with the phalanx in the center far shallower than the traditional Macedonian 16 ranks,

he was able to extend his line from the foothills to the beach. As at Granicus, however, the Persians drew up behind a river, and reinforced their position with palisades placed where the river banks were lowest. These defenses only heartened Alexander and his Companion cavalry, who saw it as a sign that the Persians lacked the stomach for a fight. The battle began with Darius sending troops into the foothills in an attempt to outflank the Macedonians, but this maneuver was seen off by Alexander's archers. Alexander then seized the initiative, ordering a general advance. The infantry stepped

GOLD CHARIOT
This Persian model chariot can be compared to a cylinder-seal illustration of the Persian king Darius's vehicle.

356–323 BCE

ALEXANDER THE GREAT

The greatest general of antiquity, Alexander the Great was the son of Philip II of Macedon. Rumors that he had a hand in his father's assassination in 336 BCE are probably unfounded, but he certainly seized power with enthusiasm, despite having barely reached manhood. Alexander believed in his own image as a godlike hero, descended from Achilles and destined for great deeds. Utterly ruthless and impulsive, he led from the front. After the conquest of Persia in 330, he adopted some Persian customs and incorporated Persians into his army. This "orientalizing" of Greek culture alienated Alexander from many of his fellow Macedonians, one of whom he murdered at a drunken banquet in 328. One of Alexander's biggest mistakes followed his victory at Hydaspes in India in 326, when he opted to return to Persia across the desert, which turned into a death march for many of his men. Alexander died at Babylon in 323, possibly from poisoning, but more probably of a fever.

forward in tight phalanx formation, sarissas (long spears) lowered in the front ranks to spear the enemy and raised in the back ranks to ward off missiles. Alexander, who had positioned himself on the right of his line with the Companion cavalry, led the charge across the river into a combined force of heavily armored Persian cavalry and light infantry. On the beach on his left, Alexander's Thessalian horsemen and the Persian cavalry ran into one another at the charge. The Macedonian infantry was soon in trouble. Fording the river, they lost formation and gaps began to open in the bristling wall of sarissas, allowing Darius's Greek mercenary footsoldiers to get in among their opponents. But on the right, the shock effect of the Macedonian cavalry was irresistible. Carrying all before them, Alexander and the Companions were able to swing left, driving into the Persian flank. The Greek mercenaries, pressing forward in the center, faced encirclement. Darius himself came under threat and, as the Macedonian cavalry fought their way toward him, he fled the battlefield. When the defeat of the Persian army was complete, Alexander tried to hunt Darius down, but, although his wife, mother, and children were taken, the Persian king escaped to fight again.

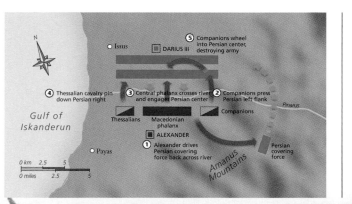

FLIGHT OF DARIUS

This Roman mosaic shows Darius fleeing in his chariot as Alexander (left) spears a Persian horseman. The long spears in the scene were a feature of the Macedonian phalanx; the artist has, rightly or wrongly, attributed them to Darius's Greek mercenary infantry.

3000 BCE – 476 CE

AFTER ALEXANDER

AFTER HIS DEATH in 323 BCE, Alexander's empire was divided between his generals. Ptolemy took Egypt, Seleucus gained Syria and Iran, and Antigonus controlled Anatolia. These powers fought numerous battles throughout the 3rd century, and while their armies were large, their style of warfare remained static—a repetition of Alexander's tactics without his genius. When they faced the growing might of Rome in the 2nd century, the Ptolemies, Seleucids, and Antigonids had no answer to its innovative strategies and ruthless aggression.

ANTIGONIDS VERSUS SELEUCIDS

Ipsus

DATE 301 BCE	
FORCES Antigonus: 70,000 infantry, 10,000 cavalry, 75 elephants; Seleucus: 64,000 infantry, 10,500 cavalry, 400 elephants	
LOCATION Phrygia, west-central Anatolia	**CASUALTIES** No reliable estimates

More than 20 years after Alexander's death, his former general Antigonus the One-Eyed still aspired to defeat Seleucus and Ptolemy and win control of the Hellenistic world. Antigonus, who was more than 80 years old, called on his son Demetrius for support in a decisive trial of strength in Anatolia. Ptolemy was campaigning in Syria, but Seleucus, aided by Lysimachus, the ruler of Thrace, brought Antigonus to battle at Ipsus. The huge armies formed up conventionally, with spear-wielding infantry phalanxes in the center,

SELEUCID RUINS
Cities such as Apamea in Anatolia, founded by Seleucus's son, Antiochus I, promoted Hellenistic culture in the century following Alexander's death.

flanked by light infantry and cavalry. The most notable imbalance between the forces was their respective numbers of elephants: Seleucus had five times the number that Antigonus fielded. Demetrius opened with a cavalry charge that swept away the left of the Seleucid line, but Seleucus deployed a chain of elephants to cover the exposed flank and block Demetrius's cavalry from returning to support the Antigonid center. Exposed to a rain of arrows and javelins from Seleucid skirmishers, much of the Antigonid mercenary infantry switched sides in the middle of the battle. When Antigonus was killed by a javelin, his army collapsed. A new division of Alexander's old empire followed the battle. Lysimachus added Anatolia as far as the Taurus mountains to his kingdom; Seleucus gained northern Syria while Ptolemy held the south; and Cassander, another general, retained control of Macedonia. Demetrius, meanwhile, who survived the battle, kept support from parts of western Asia and Greece, and his descendants formed the Antigonid dynasty.

c.367–283 BCE

PTOLEMY I

The Macedonian soldier Ptolemy was one of Alexander's closest aides. He was quick to seize control of Egypt after Alexander's death, but had to fight hard to preserve the realm from other claimants. He earned the name Soter (Greek for "savior") for defending the island of Rhodes against a siege by Antigonus's son Demetrius in 304 BCE. The dynasty Ptolemy founded ruled Egypt until 30 BCE—longer than any other state that succeeded Alexander.

ROYAL COIN
A four-drachma piece issued by Ptolemy I, ruler of Egypt.

SELEUCIDS VERSUS PTOLEMIES

Raphia

DATE June 22, 217 BCE	
FORCES Antiochus III: 62,000 infantry, 6,000 cavalry, 102 elephants; Ptolemy IV: 70,000 infantry, 5,000 cavalry, 73 elephants	
LOCATION Southwest of Gaza, southern Palestine	**CASUALTIES** No reliable estimates

The battle at Raphia, one of the largest between the successor states of Alexander's empire, involved the Seleucid ruler Antiochus III and Ptolemy IV of Egypt. Antiochus was the aggressor, challenging Ptolemy for control of Coele Syria—roughly the area of modern-day Israel, Lebanon, Syria, and Jordan. Although Antiochus successfully invaded Coele Syria in 219, he failed to follow up with a decisive attack on Egypt. His delay allowed Ptolemy to strengthen his forces, training 30,000 Egyptian hoplites. When Antiochus marched toward Egypt in 217, his forces were matched by those of Ptolemy in number and quality. Each side had a substantial force of elephants, although the Egyptians' African elephants were smaller than the Seleucids' Indian beasts. Early in the battle the Indian elephants advanced on the African elephants and put them to flight, while a cavalry charge led by Antiochus broke up the cavalry on Ptolemy's left. The battle turned, however, when both sides' phalanxes clashed. Superior in numbers, well trained and officered, and inspired by Ptolemy himself in their midst, the Macedonian-Egyptian infantry carried the day.

> "Showing himself to his troops, [Ptolemy] inspired his own men with increased alacrity and spirit."
>
> *Polybius*, The Histories, c.200–c.118 BCE

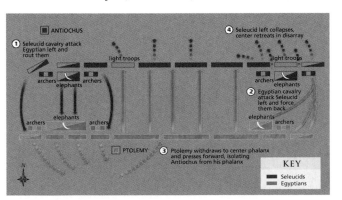

ANTIOCHUS
1. Seleucid cavalry attack Egyptian left and rout them
light troops
archers   elephants   archers
archers   elephants   archers

4. Seleucid left collapses, center retreats in disarray
light troops
archers   elephants
2. Egyptian cavalry attack Seleucid left and force them back
elephants   archers

PTOLEMY
3. Ptolemy withdraws to center phalanx and presses forward, isolating Antiochus from his phalanx

KEY
Seleucids
Egyptians

> "With their tusks firmly interlocked [the elephants] shove with all their might, each trying to force the other to give ground, until the one who proves the strongest pushes aside the other's trunk; and then, once he has made him turn and has him in the flank, he gores him with his tusks as a bull does with his horns."

WITNESS TO WAR

POLYBIUS

This account of an elephant fight at Raphia was written by the Roman historian Polybius. The use of massed elephants—inspired by Indian armies' use of the animals—was one of the most striking features of Hellenistic warfare.

TRIREME

In the Greek and Hellenistic periods oared warships were classified by the number of banks of oars they had—triremes three, biremes two, quinqueremes five. The trireme, the most successful warship, was a fairly light vessel that usually carried 14 fighting men—10 armored infantry and four archers—as well as its 200 crew. Even so, a trireme fleet was immensely expensive to run. A fleet of 100 triremes required 20,000 sailors, which, even at the low pay accepted by the poorest classes, still meant a heavy wage bill. The preferred method of attack with a trireme was to ram an enemy vessel and pierce the side of its hull, after which it would either sink or be boarded.

ROWING TIERS
This cross-section shows two different ways of staggering the oarsmen's seating arrangement.

OAR POWER
A trireme was typically propelled by 170 rowers, with a helmsman to steer and a lookout at the prow.

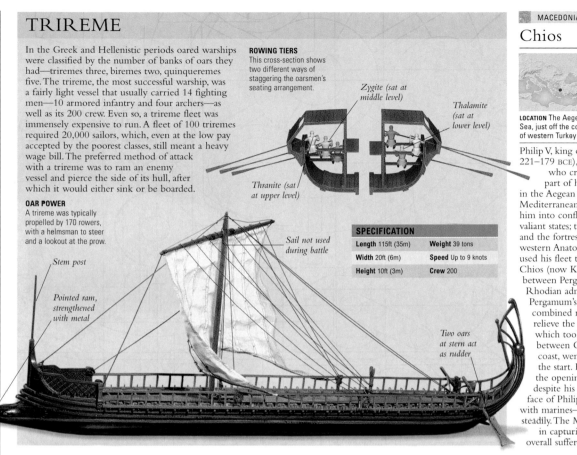

Zygite (sat at middle level)

Thalamite (sat at lower level)

Thranite (sat at upper level)

Stem post

Pointed ram, strengthened with metal

Sail not used during battle

Two oars at stern act as rudder

SPECIFICATION			
Length 115ft (35m)		**Weight** 39 tons	
Width 20ft (6m)		**Speed** Up to 9 knots	
Height 10ft (3m)		**Crew** 200	

MACEDONIANS VERSUS GREEKS

Chios

DATE 201 BCE	
FORCES Macedonians: 53 heavy warships; Rhodes and Pergamum: 65 heavy warships	
LOCATION The Aegean Sea, just off the coast of western Turkey	**CASUALTIES** Macedonians: 9,000; Rhodes and Pergamum: 130

Philip V, king of Macedonia (ruled 221–179 BCE), was an aggressive ruler who created a large fleet as part of his expansionist policy in the Aegean and the eastern Mediterranean. His ambitions brought him into conflict with two small but valiant states; the island of Rhodes and the fortress city of Pergamum in western Anatolia. In 201 BCE Philip used his fleet to attack the island of Chios (now Khios), which lies between Pergamum and Rhodes. The Rhodian admiral Theophiliscus and Pergamum's king Attalus mounted a combined naval operation to relieve the island. The battle, which took place in the strait between Chios and the Asian coast, went badly for Philip from the start. He lost his flagship in the opening encounter and—despite his enemies' caution in the face of Philip's larger vessels, packed with marines—his losses mounted steadily. The Macedonians succeeded in capturing Attalus's flagship, but overall suffered a costly defeat.

ROME VERSUS MACEDONIA

Cynoscephalae

	DATE 197 BCE
	FORCES 26,000 on either side
LOCATION Thessaly, northern Greece	**CASUALTIES** Macedonians: 8,000 killed, 5,000 captured; Romans: 700 killed

In 200 BCE Rhodes, Pergamum, and Athens appealed to Rome for help against the expansionism of Philip V of Macedonia. In 197 Philip, leading his army south through Thessaly, unexpectedly ran into a Roman army marching north under consul Titus Quinctius Flamininus. Both armies turned sideways to form a hasty battle line. The Macedonian infantry formed its traditional dense phalanx, bristling with sarissas, while the Romans positioned themselves in maniples (units of 120 men) spaced out in a chessboard pattern, three lines deep. The Macedonian phalanx was almost invulnerable from the front, but at a crucial moment in the battle the more flexible Roman infantry moved around to attack from the flank. As the phalanx broke up, the Macedonian infantry was slaughtered or forced to surrender.

ROME VERSUS THE SELEUCIDS

Magnesia

	DATE December 190 or January 189 BCE
	FORCES Rome and Pergamum: 40,000; Syria: 72,000
LOCATION East of Smyrna (present-day Izmir), Anatolia	**CASUALTIES** Rome and Pergamum: 350; Syria: 53,000

In 192 BCE an expansionist Rome declared war on the Seleucid ruler of Syria, Antiochus III, the loser at Raphia. In the winter of 190–189 BCE, Lucius Cornelius Scipio and his famous brother, Scipio Africanus, led an army of Romans and their allies from Pergamum into Anatolia. Antiochus advanced to meet them with a much larger force that included elephants and scythed chariots. The chariots' attack proved useless, but Antiochus led a cavalry charge that broke through the Roman left. However, while he wasted time attacking the Roman camp to the rear, his infantry phalanx showed its vulnerability—just as it had done at Raphia. Disrupted by panicking elephants and attacked from the flank by Roman cavalry, the tight Syrian formation broke apart. The Romans slaughtered tens of thousands of men.

ROME VERSUS THE GREEKS

Pydna

	DATE June 22, 168 BCE
	FORCES Romans: 37,000; Macedonians: 42,000
LOCATION Near Mount Olympus, northern Greece	**CASUALTIES** Romans: fewer than 1,000 killed; Macedonians: 20,000 killed, 11,000 captured

Pydna was the battle that sealed Rome's domination of Greece. It involved a Roman force led by Lucius Aemilius Paullus Macedonicus and the Macedonian army under King Perseus. The two forces camped on either side of a stream: following initial clashes, Perseus marched his whole army across the water to give battle. At first the Macedonian phalanx had the better of it, advancing with sarissas lowered and shields interlocked and preventing the Roman legionaries from closing to hand-to-hand combat. As the Macedonians advanced, however, they began to lose formation. Paullus seized the initiative, ordering small units to infiltrate the enemy ranks and strike at their unprotected sides and backs. In close combat the Macedonians' unwieldy sarissas were useless. Many threw them away and drew daggers instead, but these were no match for the Romans' brutally efficient short swords. Whether the Macedonians stood and fought or turned and ran, the legionaries cut them down. The Romans' victory was total.

ROMAN DESTRUCTION
The ruins at Corinth bear witness to Rome's ruthlessness in Greece in the 2nd century BCE. Rome razed the city for resisting its power.

CELTIC BRONZE AND IRON WEAPONS

THE CELTS SPREAD THROUGHOUT western Europe in the 1st millennium BCE; they were the Gauls who stormed Rome in 390 BCE and the Britons that Caesar fought in 55 BCE. Their warfare was noisy and flamboyant, with warriors crying out challenges to single combat while the whole army shouted war cries and clashed weapons on shields, to the accompaniment of hornblowers and trumpeters. It took the icy efficiency of the Roman legions to defeat the Celts' wild rage for battle.

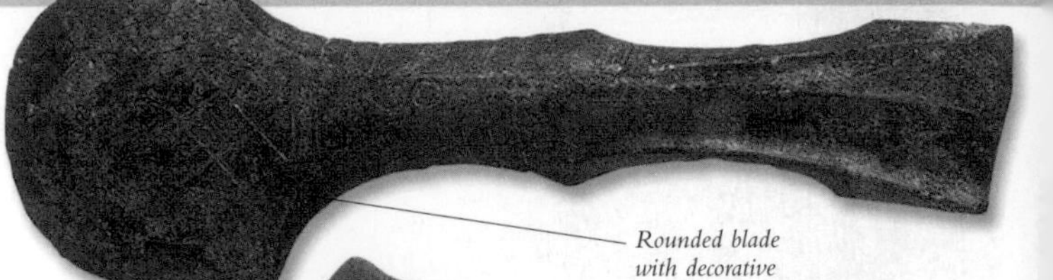

WEAPONS OF WAR

The Celts used chariots long after most other peoples had abandoned them. Julius Caesar describes Celts as "driving all over the field, hurling javelins" and then "jumping down from the chariots to fight on foot." Celtic metalworking skills were highly developed and the quality of their swords, both in bronze and in iron, was often outstanding. Swords were costly, however, and not available to all Celtic soldiers; many warriors had to make do with a spear for stabbing or throwing, or a slingshot.

Rounded blade with decorative markings

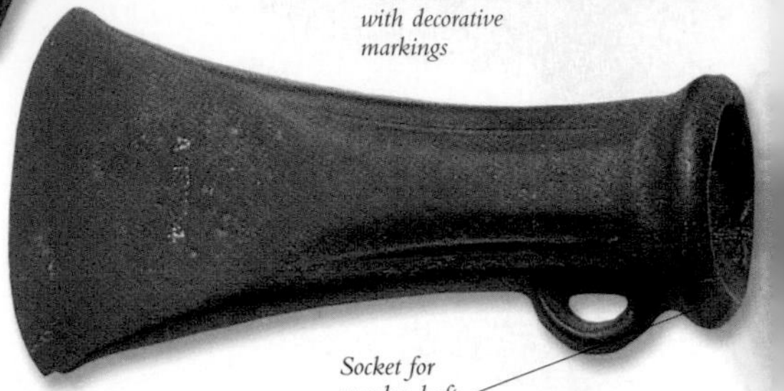

AX HEADS
The top ax head dates from the 2nd millennium BCE, the lower two from 750–650 BCE. Attached to wooden hafts, they could have been tools or weapons.

Socket for wooden haft

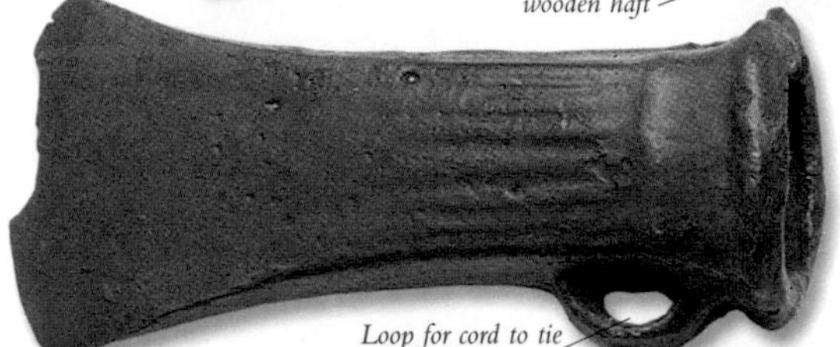

Loop for cord to tie axehead to haft

Tip for lightweight spear

GUNDESTRUP CAULDRON
A detail from a silver vessel, believed to be of Celtic origin, found in a peat bog at Gundestrup in Denmark. It shows cavalry, infantry with shields and spears, and battle trumpets.

Finely tapered point

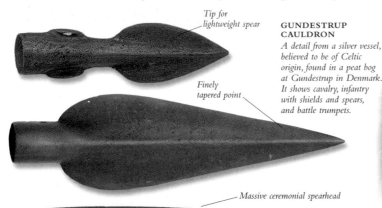

Massive ceremonial spearhead

SPEARS
Spears, often thrown as javelins, were the standard weapon of Celtic warriors, from the Bronze Age through to the Iron Age.

Sharp point, even though sword used more for slashing than stabbing

SWORDS
The Celts were renowned for their swords, from bronze blades such as these to the famous Hallstatt longswords (750–400 BCE), with their hard iron cores and soft iron cutting edges.

Double-edged blade

DEFEATED GAUL

*Vercingetorix Before Caesar is
a 19th-century representation of
the Gaulish leader's surrender to
the Romans at Alesia (see p.46).
By the 1st century* BCE *the Romans
consistently defeated Celtic armies.
The Romans' organization and
discipline was superior, and their
body armor was more effective.*

CEREMONIAL SHIELD

*This beautifully decorated
shield, consisting of a bronze
sheet set with colored glass
studs, was recovered from
London's Thames River.
Dating from about the 2nd
century* BCE, *it was probably
for ceremonial use.*

BATTLE DRESS

Celts often used their
appearance to unsettle an
enemy. They were of large stature,
wore their hair in outlandish styles,
and, in the words of the Roman
historian Polybius, some threw off their
clothes before battle and "stood in front of
the whole army naked, with nothing but their
arms." This use of nudity for shock effect was an
exception, however; depending upon their
shields for protection, Celts' habitual war dress
was a cloak, tunic, and pants, along with
decorative gold armbands and bracelets.

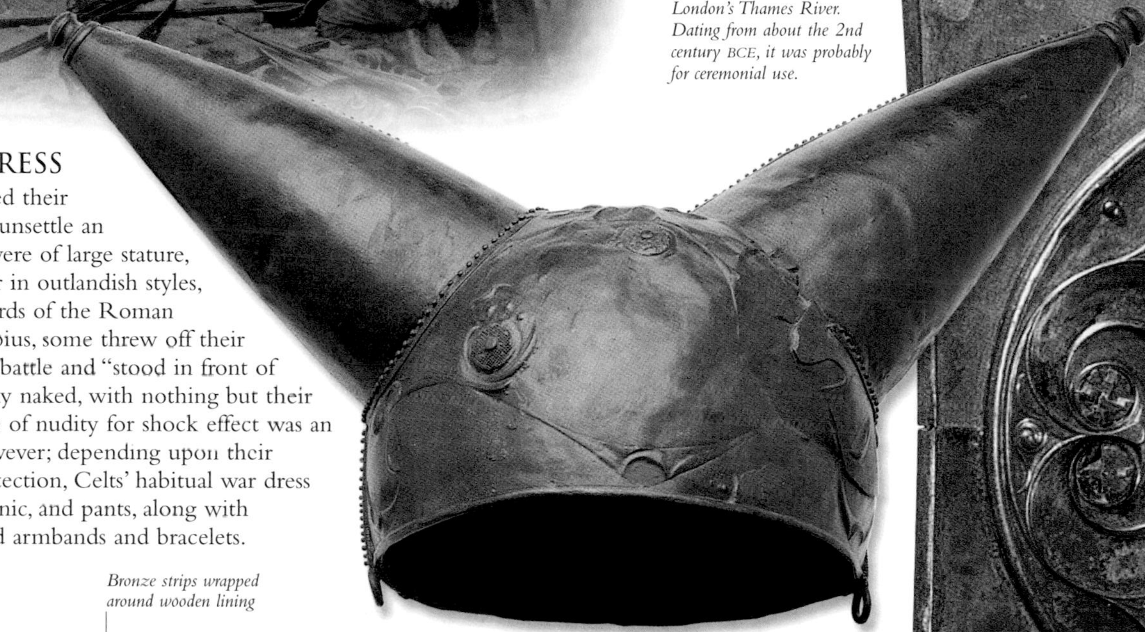

*Bronze strips wrapped
around wooden lining*

BRONZE HELMET

*Like the bronze shield (right), this Celtic
helmet was found in the Thames River. It is
uncertain whether this type of horned helmet
would have provided much protection in
battle; it too may have been ceremonial.*

*Sockets may have held
precious stones*

DAGGER AND SHEATH

*This iron dagger, protruding from its wood
and bronze sheath, is from 6th-century*
BCE *Britain. It probably belonged to a
tribal chieftain.*

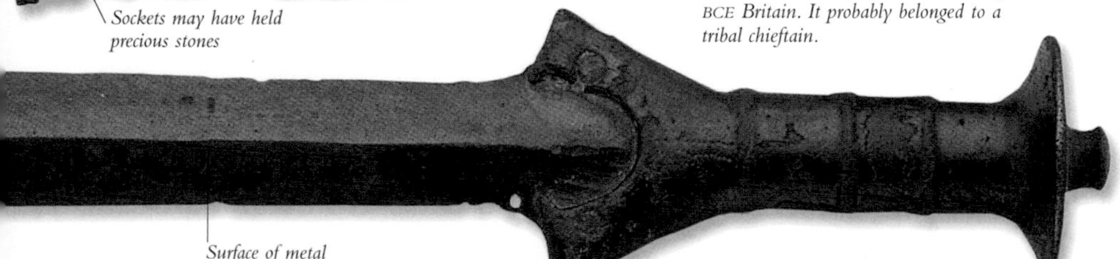

*Surface of metal
would have been a
shiny gold color*

*Grip would have been of
wood, bone, or horn,
wrapped in leather*

THE CONQUESTS OF THE LEGIONS

BETWEEN THE 5TH AND 1ST CENTURIES BCE, the Roman Republic grew from a small city-state into an imperial power dominating the Mediterranean region. It did this almost exclusively by force of arms. Constantly at war, the Romans defeated the other peoples of Italy, then fought a life-or-death struggle with the rival power of Carthage, and finally established Rome's dominance over the Hellenistic kingdoms of the eastern Mediterranean.

RAMPANT REPUBLIC
In the 2nd century BCE the Roman republic underwent its fastest period of growth. It established provinces in newly conquered areas, ruled by governors who maintained order and collected taxes.

KEY

■	Roman Empire c.200 BCE	■	Ptolemaic Empire and possessions
■	Roman gains by c.120 BCE	■	Seleucid Empire
■	Massalia and possessions	ASIA 133	Roman province and date of foundation
■	Independent Greek states and cities	Volcae 121	People and date of conquest by Rome

ETRUSCAN SOLDIER
The Roman army was influenced by Etruscan arms and armor.

LEGIONARIES
A relief (above) on a 2nd-century BCE cinerary urn. Romans saw legionary service as an opportunity to prove themselves to fellow citizens.

SABINE WOMEN
In legend, the Romans came into conflict with the Sabines by abducting their women. In this painting, Sabine women halt a fight between Sabine and Roman men.

THE EARLY REPUBLIC

Although Rome's early history is cloaked in legend, it appears that the Romans first fought their neighbors in war bands led by warrior aristocrats. During the 6th century BCE Rome evolved a citizen army, possibly through the influence of the Etruscans. But it was not until the 4th century BCE, perhaps provoked by shock defeats at the hands of the Gauls and Samnite mountain tribesmen, that the Romans developed the legion. In its early form this was still a militia, with citizen conscripts serving for the duration of a campaign and then returning to their normal lives. Each citizen legion, numbering 4,500–5,000 men, was twinned with a similar-sized legion drawn from Rome's Italian allies. The whole force was commanded by a consul (an elected politician). Perhaps surprisingly, many of these amateurs were excellent commanders.

LEGIONS AT WAR

In time of war the Romans often fielded two consular legions as a single, 10,000-strong army, with consuls alternating command on a daily basis. Instead of leading the charge from the front when battle was joined, in the manner of Alexander the Great, Roman commanders generally stayed just behind the line, urging troops on and directing reserves to where they were needed. Roman cavalry and light-infantry skirmishers had important battlefield roles, but the heart of the army was the heavy infantry. This was organized into maniples of 120 men, in turn subdivided into 60-man centuries under the command of centurions. For battle, the maniples were arranged three rows deep in a chessboard formation: between each maniple was a gap equal to the size of the maniple itself, and the maniple in the row behind covered the space. This manipular formation was far more flexible than the old phalanx and could fight as independent small units or rapidly tighten up in mass formation. Advancing to attack, the legionaries would throw their javelins into the enemy ranks and then close to use their short swords to deadly effect.

DEATH BLOW
This 3rd-century CE terracotta relief suggests the ruthless pleasure that Romans took in killing their enemies.

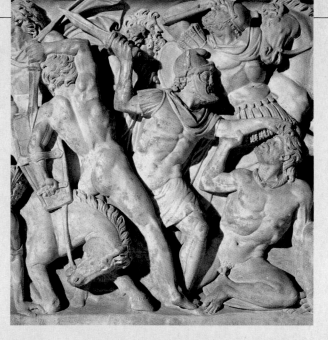

BRONZE HELMET
The Romans developed many legionary helmets. This "Coolus type" helmet is from the 1st century CE.

A PROFESSIONAL ARMY

The citizen soldiers of the manipular legion were rigorously trained and subject to fierce discipline, including the punishment of decimation (the killing of every tenth man by his colleagues) for legions that disgraced themselves. Yet the system had drawbacks. Raising a new army each time war broke out was inefficient, while military service disrupted Rome's economy. By the 1st century BCE the Roman legions had evolved into a professional army of career soldiers, recruited from the poor and equipped by the state. The legions became permanent formations, consisting almost exclusively of heavy infantry. Career legionaries developed stronger allegiance to their legion and their commander than to the Roman state—a key factor in precipitating the civil wars of general against general that ravaged Rome in the 1st century BCE. But the continuity of a professional army also allowed the development of military skills, guaranteeing further Roman conquests as the republic became an empire.

SUPPLY LINE
Roman roads such as the Via Appia, leading south from Rome, allowed rapid movement of soldiers and equipment.

MARIUS
Gaius Marius (c.157–87 BCE) was an overweight veteran who became consul a record eight times. It is likely that he played a key role in replacing Rome's militia system with a professional army.

EARLY ROME

A SERIES OF WARS FOUGHT between the 5th and 3rd centuries BCE enabled the Romans—originally just one of many Italian peoples—to dominate the whole of Italy south of the Po River. Etruscans, Latins, Samnites, Celts, and Greeks all fought the Romans, occasionally beating them, but Rome always recovered and, in the process of conquering Italy, created an army that would build one of the world's mightiest empires.

Lake Regillus

DATE Between 509 and 493 BCE

FORCES
Romans: unknown;
Latins: unknown

CASUALTIES
No reliable estimates

LOCATION Possibly near Frascati, north of Rome

According to the Roman historian Livy, at the battle of Lake Regillus the Romans under Appius Postumius and Titus Aebutius fought a force of Latins—Rome's immediate neighbors, in revolt against the rising power of the Roman Republic—led by Octavius Mamilius. The two sides almost certainly fought in a style learned from the Greeks, with armored infantry in a phalanx stabbing with spears, and lighter skirmishers using javelins or slingshots. The battle reached its climax when the Roman horsemen dismounted to join in the hand-to-hand fighting. This secured a Roman victory and a further step toward Rome's control of Latium, the ancient region of west-central Italy.

TEMPLE OF THANKSGIVING
The Temple of Castor and Pollux in the Roman Forum is said to have been built in gratitude for the support of the heavenly twins at the battle of Lake Regillus.

Allia

DATE
July 18, 390 BCE

FORCES
Celts: 30,000;
Romans: 10,000–15,000

CASUALTIES
No reliable estimates

LOCATION
18km (11 miles)
outside Rome

In the first decade of the 4th century BCE, Roman confidence was high. The capture of the fortified Etruscan city of Veii in 396, after a struggle lasting nine years, constituted a major victory and sealed the reputation of Rome's first great general, Marcus Furius Camillus. This success made the Romans' defeat at Allia—at the hands of a Celtic tribe, the Senones—all the more shocking. The Celts (also known as Gauls) had been migrating across the Alps into northern Italy for some years, seeking land to settle and towns to plunder. In 390, led by their chief Bran (Brennus to the Romans), the Senones pushed farther south, crossing the Apennine mountains and besieging the Etruscan city of Clusium.

CELTIC HEADGEAR
This 4th-century BCE iron, bronze, and gold Celtic chieftain's helmet belies the Roman view of the Celts as barbarians and savages.

In response to an appeal for aid, the Romans sent envoys to Clusium. Their mission was to negotiate with the Celts, but their arrogance so enraged the tribesmen that the Celts abandoned the siege to march on Rome instead. A hastily assembled army advanced along the Tiber River to block the Celts' path, neglecting—it was later said—to make the proper sacrifices. The battle was fought with the river on one side and the other flank open, allowing the Celts to use their superior numbers to outflank the Roman line. The Roman phalanx was ineffective against tribesmen who fought in a looser formation. Intimidated by the Celts' wild appearance and unnerving war cries, the Romans fought with less than their usual resolve and were put to flight. Many sought safety by crossing the river, but drowned under the weight of their armor. Many more were cut down as they ran.

When Brennus's army reached Rome it found the city gates open and the dirt-and-wood walls undefended. The fortified capitol held out, but the Celts occupied the rest of the city. They agreed to leave only after payment of a large tribute in gold. Rome never forgot its humiliation. Under Camillus's guidance, the city erected new walls of stone, while military reforms moved the army away from dependence on the phalanx toward the more flexible legion.

PLUMED WARRIOR
The distinctive style of Samnite armor, shown in this 4th-century BCE fresco, was adopted by Roman gladiators.

Trifanum

DATE
338 BCE

FORCES
Romans and Samnites:
unknown; Latins and
Campanians: unknown

LOCATION
Campania,
southern Italy

CASUALTIES
No reliable estimates

The battle of Trifanum involved an alliance of Romans and Samnites—hardy tribespeople of the Apennine mountains—against the Latins and the Campanians of southern Italy. This was a turnaround: in 343 BCE the Campanians had asked for and received Rome's support against Samnite raids. The resulting First Samnite War (343–341) failed to subdue the Samnites, but extended the Romans' dominion over Campania. The Campanians were unhappy with this outcome. At the same time, Rome's Latin allies were discontented with their role in the alliance. In 340 the Latins and Campanians together rose in revolt. In 339, at the battle of Vesuvius, the Roman army narrowly escaped disaster and could do no better than fight to a draw. In 338, however, a Roman army under Titus Manlius Torquatus, accompanied by Samnite auxiliaries, faced the Latin-Campanian alliance at Trifanum. Torquatus was a tough commander—he is said to have executed his own son for disobeying orders—and his leadership had largely saved the day at Vesuvius. At Trifanum his forces triumphed, crushing the Latins and Campanians so completely that the rebellion collapsed. The defeated were treated leniently, being brought back into a subservient alliance with Rome.

> "The Latins were so utterly worsted that when the consul and his victorious army was preparing to ravage their territory, they made a complete surrender."
>
> *Livy*, The History of Rome, c.29 BCE–17 CE

Caudine Forks

DATE
321 BCE

FORCES
Romans: unknown;
Samnites: unknown

LOCATION
Apennine mountains,
southeast Italy

CASUALTIES
No reliable estimates

The battle of the Caudine Forks took place during the Second Samnite War (327–304 BCE). A Roman army led by consuls Spurius Postumius and Titus Veturius Calvinus was ambushed in a mountain pass in the Apennines. Samnite general Gavius Pontius blocked both ends of the pass with felled trees, while his men occupied the heights on each side, from where they rained down missiles. In a hopeless position, the Romans surrendered. The Samnites released them only after the Romans had accepted peace terms and succumbed to the humiliation of "passing under the yoke" (an arch formed by Samnite spears). The Roman Senate rejected the terms once the men had been freed.

Sentinum

DATE
295 BCE

FORCES
Romans 38,000;
Samnites and Gauls:
c.60,000

LOCATION
Umbria,
central Italy

CASUALTIES Romans:
8,500; Samnites and
Gauls: 25,000

In the Third Samnite War (298–290 BCE), Rome faced a dangerous alliance of Samnites, Etruscans, Umbrians, and Gauls. The Romans mobilized two consular armies, led by consuls Publius Decius Mus and Quintus Fabius Maximus Rullianus. Each army consisted of two Roman legions and two legions from Rome's allies. This powerful force marched out to locate and destroy the Samnites and their allies. A diversionary attack against their homelands drew the Etruscan and Umbrian forces away, leaving the Samnites and Gauls to face up to the Romans at Sentinum (near present-day Sassoferrato). Decius's army took up position opposite the Gauls, while to his right Fabius's army prepared to fight the Samnites, under their leader, Egnatius. As usual, the consuls positioned the two Roman legions at the center of the line of each army, flanked on each side by the allied legions, with the cavalry at either end. When fighting began, the legions led by Fabius soon gained the upper hand over the Samnites. Decius and his army had a more difficult time, however, and were surprised by the Gauls, who sent war chariots careering into the Roman cavalry. Milling horses disrupted the legion's infantry formations, which began to crumble under the attack of sword-wielding Gallic warriors. At this desperate juncture, Decius rode out alone into the midst of the Gauls in a suicidal act of self-sacrifice. Emboldened by the courageous death of their consul, the legions fought with renewed vigor. By this time the Samnites were fleeing, their leader, Egnatius, and thousands of his people cut down by the pursuing Romans. The Gauls successfully disengaged, limiting their losses, but Rome had won another important victory.

SAMNITE GEAR
Although the Samnite wars ended in defeat for the Samnites, two of whom are shown on this vase, they continued to fight Rome in the 2nd and 1st centuries BCE.

Beneventum

DATE
275 BCE

FORCES
Romans: unknown;
Pyrrhus's army:
unknown

LOCATION Beneventum,
Campania,
southern Italy

CASUALTIES
No reliable estimates

After the battle of Asculum (see Heraclea, below), Pyrrhus crossed to Sicily to support the Greek city of Syracuse in its conflict with Carthage. Returning to southern Italy in 275, he encountered a Roman army led by Manius Curius Dentatus. Pyrrhus's infantry and elephants pressed the Romans back to the walls of their camp, but the Romans goaded the elephants to turn back into the Greek phalanx. In the resulting confusion the Romans counterattacked and carried the day. Pyrrhus soon returned to Greece, and, before the end of the year, Tarentum had fallen to Rome.

Heraclea

DATE
280 BCE

FORCES
Romans: 35,000;
Greeks: 30,000

LOCATION
Apulia,
southeast Italy

CASUALTIES
Romans: 7,000–15,000;
Greeks: 4,000–11,000

The expansion of Roman power into southern Italy posed a threat to the independence of the many Greek cities established there. One of these, Tarentum, invited Pyrrhus, king of the Greek state of Epirus and the most experienced general of his day, to help them against the Romans. He brought with him some 20,000 infantry and 3,000 cavalry, as well as war elephants, and took control of southern Italy. The Romans responded by sending an army, commanded by Publius Valerius Laevinus, to confront Pyrrhus. The forces met at Heraclea, by the Siris River. While Pyrrhus's elephants—beasts the Romans had never before encountered in battle—frightened off the Roman cavalry, the Greek infantry phalanx drove the Romans back across the river in a vicious fight with no quarter given. The slaughter was so great on both sides that Pyrrhus reputedly said, "One more such victory and I am lost"—hence the term "Pyrrhic victory." After the battle Pyrrhus marched north toward Rome, expecting the Romans to sue for peace. Instead, Rome and its allies assembled another army to face him. Pyrrhus prudently withdrew to build up his forces, amassing a coalition of about 70,000 men from southern Italy, including the Samnites, his own soldiers, and recruits from the Greek cities. Rome once more took the offensive, marching south into Apulia. In another fierce fight at Asculum, Pyrrhus was victorious, but again at heavy cost—he himself was badly wounded. The Romans lost on the day but retained their forces in fighting shape.

> "The elephants more particularly began to distress the Romans, whose horses, before they came near, not enduring them, went back with their riders…"
>
> *Plutarch,* "Life of Pyrrhus," c.75 CE

MIGHTY BEASTS
This 17th-century CE painting of the battle of Heraclea overestimates the carrying capacity of Pyrrhus's elephants. A crew of three was usual: one to steer, two to fight.

319–272 BCE

PYRRHUS

Pyrrhus, king of Epirus, was an inspired soldier of fortune who amassed power and wealth fighting in the wars between Alexander the Great's successors in Greece. His outstanding talents as a general made warring rulers vie for his services, for which he ensured that he was well recompensed. As a professional military man, he was startled by the ferocity of Roman warfare and by the Romans' refusal to do a deal when clearly beaten. In 272 BCE, while fighting in the streets of the Greek city of Argos, Pyrrhus was knocked out by a tile thrown from a rooftop and promptly decapitated by a passing enemy soldier. He left behind two highly praised books: his memoirs and a study on the art of war.

THE PUNIC WARS

THE EXPANSION OF ROME IN THE 3rd century BCE brought it into conflict with Carthage, the dominant power in the central Mediterranean. In the First Punic War (264–241 BCE) Romans and Carthaginians fought for control of Sicily in a series of naval battles. Defeated in Sicily, Carthage sought revenge in the Second Punic War (218–201). The Carthaginian general Hannibal came close to destroying Rome, but once more the Romans ultimately triumphed. Finally, in the Third Punic War (149–146), Rome completed the destruction of Carthage.

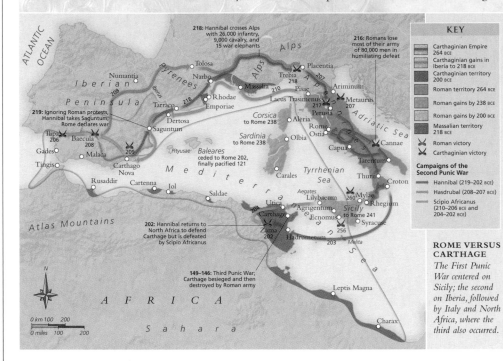

218: Hannibal crosses Alps with 26,000 infantry, 9,000 cavalry, and 15 war elephants

219: Ignoring Roman protests, Hannibal takes Saguntum; Rome declares war

216: Romans lose most of their army of 80,000 men in humiliating defeat

202: Hannibal returns to North Africa to defend Carthage but is defeated by Scipio Africanus

149–146: Third Punic War; Carthage besieged and then destroyed by Roman army

KEY

- Carthaginian Empire 264 BCE
- Carthaginian gains in Iberia to 218 BCE
- Carthaginian territory 200 BCE
- Roman territory 264 BCE
- Roman gains by 238 BCE
- Roman gains by 200 BCE
- Massalian territory 218 BCE
- Roman victory
- Carthaginian victory

Campaigns of the Second Punic War
- Hannibal (219–202 BCE)
- Hasdrubal (208–207 BCE)
- Scipio Africanus (210–206 BCE and 204–202 BCE)

ROME VERSUS CARTHAGE
The First Punic War centered on Sicily; the second on Iberia, followed by Italy and North Africa, where the third also occurred.

FIRST PUNIC WAR

Ecnomus

DATE 256 BCE	
FORCES Romans: 330 ships, 140,000 crew; Carthaginians: 350 ships, 150,000 crew	
LOCATION Off the southeast coast of Sicily	**CASUALTIES** Romans: 24 ships sunk; Carthaginians: 30 ships sunk, 64 captured

In terms of the number of sailors and soldiers involved, Ecnomus was one of the largest naval battles in history. In 256 BCE the Romans decided to attack Carthage itself. A large fleet, under the command of consuls Lucius Manlius Vulso and Marcus Atilius Regulus, set out to ferry an army across to North Africa. Two squadrons in wedge formation in front and a reserve squadron in line behind protected a squadron of galleys towing transports. This fleet met the Carthaginians, whose ships were stretched out in line off the Sicilian coast. In a pincer movement, the Carthaginian right wing attacked the Roman reserve squadron while their left drove into the transport squadron. But the front two Roman squadrons broke through the center of the Carthaginian line and then turned back to rescue the struggling rear squadrons—no mean feat of commanding and maneuvering. In the words of the Greek historian Polybius, "It was now the turn of the Carthaginians to be in difficulties." The Romans routed them and, after refitting in Sicily, their fleet sailed across to Africa unopposed.

FIRST PUNIC WAR

Mylae

DATE 260 BCE	
FORCES Romans: 110 warships; Carthaginians: 130 warships	
LOCATION Off the north coast of Sicily	**CASUALTIES** Carthaginians: 31 warships captured, 14 sunk

Early in the First Punic War, Roman armies dominated Sicily, but the Carthaginians controlled the seas around the island. Rome had no navy, and so built a fleet of quinqueremes and triremes in 60 days. Mylae put this new fleet to the test. To make up for their inexperience at sea, the Romans depended on an innovation: the corvus, a boarding bridge with an iron spike on its underside. Each time a Carthaginian galley closed with a Roman vessel, the corvus was dropped so the spike drove through its deck. Roman legionaries then swarmed across to capture the ship. The result was a shock defeat for the Punic forces.

BOARDING PARTY
The corvus, shown here, exemplified Roman engineering and innovation.

FIRST PUNIC WAR

Drepana

DATE 249 BCE	
FORCES Romans and Carthaginians: 130 warships each	
LOCATION Off the west coast of Sicily	**CASUALTIES** Romans: 93 ships lost, 8,000 men killed, 20,000 captured;

Despite their triumph at Ecnomus, the Romans' expedition to Africa ended in catastrophe. A large fleet sent to evacuate the Roman army was wrecked by a storm, claiming around 100,000 lives. By 249 BCE, however, Rome had built another fleet, which set out to blockade the Carthaginians at Lilybaeum, one of Carthage's last strongholds in Sicily. Seeking a good omen before the operation, Roman consul Appius Claudius Pulcher spread grain in front of sacred chickens on his ship's deck. When the chickens refused to eat, Claudius had the birds thrown overboard. This sacrilege proved unwise. Carthaginian admiral Adherbal sailed out of port before Claudius's fleet arrived, then doubled back from behind a headland to trap the Romans as they closed on the harbor. The Carthaginians

OFFICER'S CREST
Roman legionary officers wore this simple bronze helmet with its horsehair crest in the late 1st century BCE.

rammed and boarded most of the Roman galleys—fewer than 30 escaped—but this was to be Rome's last defeat in the First Punic War. In 241 a decisive Roman victory off the Aegates Islands cut the supply route for the Carthaginian army in Sicily. Carthage had no choice but to give Rome full control of the island.

SECOND PUNIC WAR

Trebia

DATE
218 BCE

FORCES
Romans: 40,000;
Carthaginians: 30,000

LOCATION
South of Milan,
northern Italy

CASUALTIES
Romans: 30,000 killed;
Carthaginians: 5,000
killed

At the start of the Second Punic War, the Carthaginian Hannibal marched an army from Spain through Gaul and across the Alps, into northern Italy. He lost many of his men and animals—including most of his 37 elephants—traversing Alpine passes deep in snow, but his arrival in Italy was a shock to the Romans. Hannibal was victorious in his first encounter with Roman forces, near the Ticinus River. The battle was little more than a cavalry skirmish, but with two significant outcomes: the Roman general Publius Cornelius Scipio (father of Scipio Africanus) was badly wounded, and Hannibal's success encouraged more

Gallic warriors to join his forces. A few weeks later the Carthaginians faced a Roman army across the Trebia River. Hannibal sent light horsemen to harass the Romans, provoking them into attacking across the swollen river. Meanwhile his brother Mago led a concealed force of infantry and cavalry to strike the Romans' rear. Most of the Roman forces fled or

ROMAN DEFEAT
Scipio Africanus (center) saves his father at the battle of Ticinus, the first encounter between Hannibal and the Romans on Italian soil, a few weeks before Trebia.

were massacred, although the legionary infantry hacked its way through the Carthaginian center and escaped to safety.

247–182 BCE

HANNIBAL

Hannibal was the son of Hamilcar Barca, a Carthaginian general in the First Punic War. Hannibal inherited his father's obsession with revenge against Rome and provoked the Second Punic War by besieging Saguntum, in eastern Spain, in 219. He showed his military genius time and again in the campaigns in Italy from 218 onward, but even he could not prevent the final defeat for Carthage at Zama in 202. He spent his later years in exile, first at the court of the Seleucid king Antiochus III and finally in Bithynia, where he poisoned himself rather than face Roman captivity. Roman accounts of Hannibal mention his cruelty and greed, but there is much evidence to the contrary, such as the respect he showed for the bodies of fallen Roman generals and the care he took of his men and his animals.

SECOND PUNIC WAR

Lake Trasimene

DATE
June 217 BCE

FORCES
Romans and
Carthaginians: 40,000
soldiers each

LOCATION
Near Perugia,
central Italy

CASUALTIES
Romans: c.30,000 killed

In the spring of 217 BCE Hannibal outmaneuvered the Romans again. By marching his forces across the Apennines and through a supposedly impassible swamp around the Arno River, he bypassed the armies positioned to block his advance on Rome. Consul Gaius Flaminius

responded by rushing his army south in pursuit. This is exactly what Hannibal had anticipated. He positioned his men where the road to Rome passed through a narrow gap between Lake Trasimene on one side and steep hills on the other. As Flaminius's army marched through the defile they ran into Hannibal's infantry, drawn up across the road. Hannibal's cavalry and light infantry then charged down from the hills above. The cavalry attacked the rear of the Roman column, while the light infantry clashed with the Roman flank. Flaminius was killed in the ambush along with thousands of his men, who were cut down in the fighting or drowned fleeing into the lake. Thousands more surrendered in return for their lives being spared.

> **"The Romans, before they could discover their foe, learned from the shouts raised on all sides that they were surrounded."**
>
> *Livy*, The History of Rome, c.29 BCE–17 CE

HANNIBAL'S ARMY

The army that Hannibal led into Italy in 218 BCE had few Carthaginians in its ranks. Since Carthage had too small a population to form a citizen army, it relied on allies or tributaries to provide most of its forces. Various Spanish tribes supplied the core of the army,

along with Libyans and Numidians from North Africa. In addition, large numbers of Celts (Gauls) enlisted as the operation went on. Rather than standardizing these forces, Hannibal exploited their different fighting styles—Numidian horsemen fought as javelin throwers, for example, while Spanish tribesmen were fearsome wielders of slingshots. Hannibal welded these troops into a disciplined force, hardy on the march and responsive to his command.

MIXED FORCE
A 16th-century portrayal of Hannibal's army reflects the variety and exoticism of his forces.

LAKESIDE SLAUGHTER
Many of Flaminius's men were driven into Lake Trasimene, which reputedly turned red with blood. As a result, the stream that crosses the lake was named Sanguineto—"blood river."

SECOND PUNIC WAR

Cannae

DATE August 2, 216 BCE

FORCES Romans: 80,000 infantry, 6,000 cavalry; Carthaginians: 40,000 infantry, 10,000 cavalry

LOCATION Apulia, southeast Italy

CASUALTIES Romans: 50,000 killed; Carthaginians: 6,000 killed

After the disaster at Lake Trasimene, the Romans elected Quintus Fabius Maximus as dictator to lead the war effort. Fabius's policy was to avoid pitched battles, instead shadowing and harassing Hannibal's army, although these tactics were alien to the Roman way of making war. In July 216 BCE, when Hannibal captured a major Roman supply depot at Cannae in southern Italy, a massive Roman army set out to destroy his forces. Under the command of consuls Lucius Aemilius Paullus and Gaius Terentius Varro, the Roman force consisted of 16 legions: eight Roman and eight allied. After some initial skirmishes, both sides established camps on the north side of the Aufidus River. On August 1, Hannibal deployed his forces in front of the Romans but

they declined to fight. The following day, on Varro's orders, the Romans forded the river and drew up ready to fight on the south bank—a relatively narrow battlefield between the river and some hills, in which the Carthaginians would find it hard to use their cavalry. Without hesitating, Hannibal sent his own army across the river, shielding its movement with a screen of skirmishers. The Roman infantry legions were massed in a deep, tight formation at the center of their line, with Roman cavalry flanking them on the river side and allied horsemen on their left. Hannibal's line consisted of lightly armored Celtic and Spanish infantry at the center, flanked by African infantry. At the edge of the river, Hannibal's armored cavalry charged into the Roman horsemen. With no room to maneuver, most

PUNIC ARMOR
A 3rd- or 2nd-century-BCE Carthaginian gold breastplate, representing the distinctive style of a culture that was wiped out by Rome.

combatants dismounted and fought hand to hand. Hannibal's men, superior in armor and weaponry, cut the Romans apart. In the center, meanwhile, the Roman legionaries forced back the Spanish and Celtic infantry, but— as Hannibal had intended— became drawn into the retreating Carthaginian line. Hannibal's African troops closed in from the sides, while his horsemen remounted and rode around to the rear, charging into the back of the already retreating enemy. The Carthaginians butchered about 50,000 Romans, including Paullus. It was one of the most costly day's fighting in the history of warfare.

> "Thus it came about, as Hannibal had planned, that the Romans were caught between two hostile lines of Libyans—thanks to their impetuous pursuit of the Celts. Still they fought, though no longer in line, yet singly, or in maniples…"
>
> *Polybius*, The Histories, c.200–c.118 BCE

FIELDS OF WAR
A column overlooks the battlefield of Cannae, the site of the Roman army's severest defeat ever.

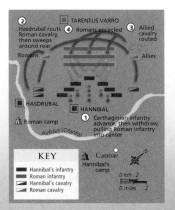

2 Hasdrubal routs Roman cavalry, then sweeps around rear

TARENTUS VARRO

4 Romans encircled

3 Allied cavalry routed

Romans

Allies

HASDRUBAL

HANNIBAL

Roman camp

1 Carthaginian infantry advance, then withdraw, pulling Roman infantry into center

Aufidus (Ofanto)

Cannae
Hannibal's camp

0 km 2
0 miles 2

KEY
Hannibal's infantry
Roman infantry
Hannibal's cavalry
Roman cavalry

Siege of Syracuse

DATE
213–211 BCE

FORCES
Romans: unknown;
Syracusans: unknown

LOCATION
East coast
of Sicily

CASUALTIES
No reliable estimates

Events after Cannae show the importance of sieges in ancient warfare. Hannibal found it difficult to capture any fortified cities, let alone Rome itself, because he had no siege equipment. Some cities did, however, side with the Carthaginians. Among these was the Greek city of Syracuse, on the east coast of Sicily, which rebelled against Rome in 213 BCE. A Roman force led by the general Marcus Claudius Marcellus consequently laid siege to the port city by sea and land. The elderly inventor Archimedes was one of the leaders of Syracuse's defense. He organized siege artillery to protect the city's walls, concentrating the fire of different catapults and ballistas upon the besiegers. The Romans had ingenious devices of their own, including *sambucae* (scaling ladders mounted on galleys). Roman

soldiers used pulleys attached to a ship's mast to lower these ladders against the city walls, but Archimedes' defensive devices managed to smash them. The siege dragged on for many months. The Romans were unable to tighten the blockade sufficiently to keep all supplies out, but Carthage's attempts to relieve the city also failed. In 212, however, while the inhabitants participated in a festival to the goddess Artemis, the Romans managed to get over the walls

DEATH OF ARCHIMEDES
This mosaic shows the Greek inventor Archimedes (c.290–c.212 BCE) about to be killed by a Roman soldier during the assault on Syracuse.

and into the outer city. Archimedes was among those killed. It was another eight months, however, before a Syracusan traitor opened the gates of the inner citadel to the besiegers, who then sacked the city.

Metaurus

DATE
June 22, 207 BCE

FORCES
Romans: 40,000;
Carthaginians: 30,000

LOCATION
Marche region,
central Italy

CASUALTIES
Romans: 2,000;
Carthaginians: 10,000

The Carthaginians' only major attempt to reinforce Hannibal's army in Italy came in 207 BCE, when Hannibal's brother Hasdrubal marched an army from Spain across the Alps. A Roman force led by Gaius Claudius Nero, strengthened at the last minute by 6,000 crack troops from Apulia, was sent to face Hasdrubal. Outnumbered, Hasdrubal attempted a night withdrawal across the Metaurus River, but his forces lost their way in the darkness and were still south of the river when the Romans caught up with them just after dawn. The battle was evenly balanced until Nero led his troops around the back of the Roman line to attack the Carthaginians from the flank. Hasdrubal's forces disintegrated in panic; he himself was among thousands killed in a battle that marked a turning point in the war.

Zama

DATE
202 BCE

FORCES
Romans: 35,000;
Carthaginians: 45,000

LOCATION
Present-day Tunisia,
North Africa

CASUALTIES
Romans: 1,500 killed;
Carthaginians: 20,000
killed, 15,000 captured

Up to 203 BCE Hannibal successfully maintained an army in southern Italy, but elsewhere the war was turning in Rome's favor. The Roman general Scipio Africanus conquered Carthaginian Spain and, in 204, invaded Carthage itself, forcing it to sue for peace. During the armistice, however, Hannibal's army—now numbering 18,000 men, mostly Italians—returned to Africa. Carthage broke off negotiations with Rome and assembled a new army built around the

core of Hannibal's Italian veterans. As the Romans were laying waste to Carthaginian territory, Hannibal was forced to bring them to battle, even though the majority of his infantry were raw recruits and his cavalry were outnumbered, since most of the horsemen of the Numidians—former allies of Carthage—had joined the Roman side. At the start of the battle Hannibal depended on elephants to break up the Roman infantry, but Scipio had arranged his maniples in columns so that they could move aside and let the charging beasts pass harmlessly through gaps in the line. Scipio's advancing infantry dispersed Hannibal's inexperienced footsoldiers, but the Italian veterans proved equal to the legionaries. However, when Scipio's cavalry, which had driven off Hannibal's horsemen, returned to charge the veterans from the rear, the rout was complete. Scipio's tactics owed much to Hannibal's earlier successes, but this was no comfort to Carthage, which was forced to accept a humiliating peace.

236–183 BCE

SCIPIO AFRICANUS

Publius Cornelius Scipio was one of Rome's greatest generals. He became commander of Roman forces in Spain in 210, aged just 25, and within four years had conquered the whole region. His triumphs in Africa from 204 to 202 won the Second Punic War and earned him his nickname. With his brother Lucius he defeated Antiochus III of Syria at Magnesia in 190, but after accusations of corruption he retired to his country estate.

Siege of Carthage

DATE
149–146 BCE

FORCES
Romans: unknown;
Carthaginians:
unknown

LOCATION Carthage
(part of present-day
Tunis, Tunisia)

CASUALTIES
No reliable estimates

The Third Punic War was a sad postscript to the epic struggle between Rome and Carthage. Fifty years after the battle of Zama, important figures in Rome such as senator Cato the Elder argued that Carthage was still a threat and should be destroyed. A war between Carthage and Numidia (present-day Algeria) offered a pretext for Roman intervention, and in 149 BCE an expeditionary force was sent to besiege Carthage. Yet the siege of a city surrounded by 20 miles (32km) of walls and capable of resupply by sea was no easy matter. Despite breaching the walls with rams, the Romans at first achieved little against a vigorous defense organized by the Carthaginian commander

PUNIC MAUSOLEUM
This monument in Dougga, Tunisia, honors a Numidian prince. Numidia's shift of allegiance from Carthage to Rome played a role in the Second and Third Punic wars.

Hasdrubal. However, in 147, when Scipio Aemilianus—the adopted son of Scipio Africanus—took charge of the Roman forces, the siege gained momentum. As starvation and disease decimated the city's population, resistance weakened. In spring 146 the Romans penetrated the city walls. After fierce fighting, the survivors—numbering about 50,000—surrendered. The Romans enslaved them and destroyed their city.

IMPERIAL ROME

A SERIES OF CIVIL WARS in the 1st century BCE brought down the Roman Republic and led to the founding of the Roman Empire. Under the first emperor, Augustus, and his successors, military attention shifted to the frontiers of the empire. In the east, Rome sought to extend and defend territory against successive rulers of Persia, while in the west it fought the barbarian, or Germanic, tribes.

AN OUTSTANDING ARMY

The legions of the early Roman Empire were an outstanding force, formidable in battle and in all aspects of siege warfare and engineering—building roads, bridges, and fortifications. From the 1st to the 4th century CE there were always about 30 legions, each consisting of ten 480-strong cohorts. These troops were augmented by large numbers of auxiliaries, mostly recruited from conquered peoples within the empire. Yet, despite their advantages, including the support of field artillery in the form of catapults and ballistas, the legions were occasionally beaten, especially by enemies who relied on missile weapons and refused to engage in close combat.

HADRIAN'S EMPIRE
The emperor Hadrian (r. 117–138 CE) gave up some of Rome's eastern provinces, but strongly defended the rest with a large army and navy.

HADRIAN'S WALL
In 122 CE Hadrian ordered the building of a wall to discourage raids by northern tribes into Roman Britain. The wall stretched 117 km (73 miles) across Britain.

THE LEGIONS' DECLINE

From the late 2nd century CE, the Roman Empire once more slipped into an era of civil wars that sapped the strength of its armies. In the 3rd century, barbarian raids and migrations also began to overrun the empire's borders. The Roman army responded by building up its cavalry, which probably more than doubled in number between the 2nd and 4th centuries. It also extended the recruitment of auxiliaries to include entire barbarian war bands under their own commanders. For infantry, thrusting spears and longer swords replaced the classic *pilum* (throwing spear) and *gladius* (short two-edged sword), while soldiers wore chain mail and iron helmets. During the 5th century the classic Roman army ceased to exist, mutating into the Byzantine army in the east, with its emphasis on armored cavalry, and supplanted in the west by the war bands of peoples such as the Franks, Lombards, and Saxons.

CONQUERING FORCE
The reliefs on Trajan's Column in Rome clearly depict Roman military operations. Here the Dacians of southeast Europe fight Roman auxiliaries.

LEGION INSIGNIA
Imperial legions were proud of their identity. This plaque shows the emblem of the Twentieth Legion, which took part in suppressing the Iceni revolt in Britain (60–61 CE).

IMPERIAL ROMAN ARMOR

This weaponry and armor comprised a legionary's equipment in the second half of the 1st century CE. The iron helmet replaced earlier bronze headgear, but by this time helmet crests were probably only worn for special ceremonies or as a sign of rank. The throwing spear (*pilum*) and the short two-edged sword (*gladius*) were the Roman infantry's basic weapons for at least 500 years (200 BCE to 300 CE).

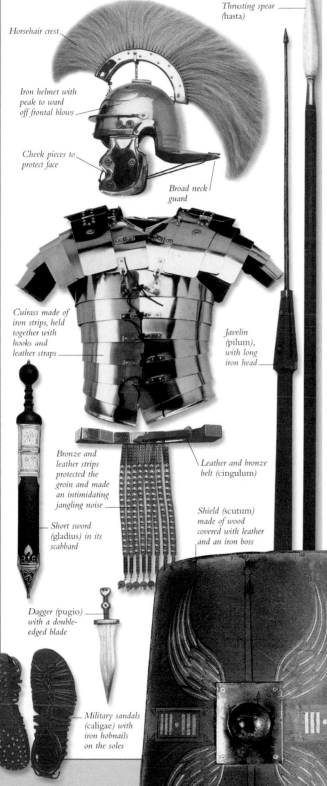

Thrusting spear (hasta)

Horsehair crest

Iron helmet with peak to ward off frontal blows

Cheek pieces to protect face

Broad neck guard

Cuirass made of iron strips, held together with hooks and leather straps

Javelin (pilum), with long iron head

Bronze and leather strips protected the groin and made an intimidating jangling noise

Leather and bronze belt (cingulum)

Short sword (gladius) in its scabbard

Shield (scutum) made of wood covered with leather and an iron boss

Dagger (pugio) with a double-edged blade

Military sandals (caligae) with iron hobnails on the soles

SLAVE WAR

Slave War

DATE
73–71 BCE

FORCES
Romans: unknown; Spartacus's army: unknown

LOCATION
Across southern Italy

CASUALTIES
No reliable estimates

In 73 BCE, about 80 gladiators escaped from their prison in Capua, southern Italy. Under the leadership of the Thracian Spartacus, this small band attracted a growing army of recruits, mostly slaves who had run away from their masters. Spartacus shaped the group into an effective guerrilla army, which in 72 BCE trounced two consular armies, as well as smaller Roman forces. Each victory brought more captured weaponry and armor to Spartacus's force, which plundered country estates across southern Italy. The Senate entrusted the brutal Marcus Licinius Crassus with restoring order. In 71 BCE Crassus succeeded in bringing Spartacus to battle. It is said that the ex-gladiator slit the throat of his horse before the fight to show his men that he would not flee. With the majority of his army, Spartacus died fighting. Crassus had 6,000 prisoners crucified.

GLADIATORIAL COMBAT
Gladiators in action in a Roman amphitheater. Most gladiators were prisoners, including captives taken in war.

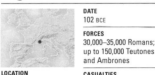

INVASION OF THE TEUTONES

Aquae Sextae

DATE
102 BCE

FORCES
30,000–35,000 Romans; up to 150,000 Teutones and Ambrones

LOCATION
Present-day Aix-en-Provence, France

CASUALTIES
Up to 100,000 Teutones killed or captured

In the last decade of the 2nd century BCE, Germanic tribes threatened the Roman Empire in Gaul. After the Romans' defeat at Arausio in 105, Gaius Marius took command in southern Gaul. Facing the Teutones and Ambrones at Aquae Sextae, he drew up his battleline at the top of a slope while sending 3,000 men to hide in woods. When the enemy were almost upon them, the Roman legionaries threw their *pila* and charged, battering with their shields and stabbing with their swords. The barbarians were pushed back to the foot of the hill, at which point the 3,000 concealed troops emerged to attack them from the rear. The barbarians were slaughtered.

ROMAN–PARTHIAN WARS

Carrhae

DATE
53 BCE

FORCES
39,000 Romans; 7,000 Parthians

LOCATION The Syrian desert, east of the Euphrates River

CASUALTIES
24,000 Romans killed; 10,000 captured

Carrhae was a disaster for the Roman Empire in the east. In 53 BCE Marcus Licinius Crassus led an army into Syria to attack the Parthians, rulers of Persia. Parthian armies consisted entirely of cavalry, mostly mounted archers, but also armored lancers. When Crassus met the Parthian forces under Surenas, their leader, he advanced with his legions in a tightly packed square. Parthian horsemen galloped around the square, shooting a hail of arrows into the troops, the fire of their composite bows powerful enough to pierce armor. When the Romans attempted to engage them they rode off at speed, then turned back to envelop their pursuers. Crassus's son Publius was killed leading a charge against the lancers, and the Parthians paraded his head on a spear. Crassus himself was one of many Romans who survived the battle only to be killed while retreating.

"All Gaul is divided into three parts…"

Julius Caesar, The Gallic War, *1.1*

GALLIC WARS

Gaius Julius Caesar was the first general to leave a detailed account of his own campaigns. That he was not only a military commander but a statesman who achieved supreme political authority over the whole Roman world makes his account of the Gallic Wars a text of almost unparalleled significance. Caesar's work has remained an unrivaled literary epitaph, yet beneath his artfully polished prose it is hard now to discern that its content was as much self-serving propaganda as unvarnished truth.

> "As a nation the Gauls are extremely superstitious; and so persons suffering from serious diseases, as well as those who are exposed to the perils of battle, offer, or vow to offer, human sacrifices, for the performance of which they employ Druids. They believe that the only way of saving a man's life is to propitiate the gods' wrath by rendering another life in its place…. Some tribes have colossal images made of wickerwork, the limbs of which they fill with living men; they are then set on fire and the victims burned to death."

Julius Caesar, The Gallic War, *6.16*

Although Caesar provides a great deal of important evidence about the Celtic tribes' social and political organization, much of it is quite generalized. His narrative dwells in some detail on Gallic customs that a Roman audience would find barbarous and threatening. Caesar no doubt played on inherited folk-memories of the Gaulish sack of Rome in 396 BCE (see p.36). So deeply fixed were these that each year guard dogs were crucified on the Capitol in recurring vengeance for their ancestors' failure to alert the people of Rome to the presence of the marauding Celtic host. That Julius Caesar had in effect exceeded his authority when he crossed into Gaul in 58 BCE made it all the more expedient that he should invoke the shadow of the predatory Celt in retrospective justification of his invasion.

> "Himself a man of boundless energy, he terrorized waverers with the rigors of an iron discipline. Serious cases of disaffection were punished by torture and death at the stake…. By this terrorism he quickly raised an army…. 'We must strive by every means,' he [Vercingetorix] said, 'to prevent the Romans from obtaining forage and supplies. This will be easy, since we are strong in cavalry and the season is in our favor. There is no grass to cut, so the enemy will be forced to send out parties to get hay from the barns, and our cavalry can go out every day and see that not a single one of them returns alive."

Julius Caesar, The Gallic War, *7.4–7.5, 7.14*

Caesar clearly regarded Vercingetorix, the Celtic chieftain, as a worthy foe against whom to test the mettle of his legions. This was no mere inflation of the martial prowess of his opponent that in victory would reflect favorably Caesar's own achievement; the Roman general would have been well aware that it was his own determination to conquer the whole of Gaul that had united the tribes behind a single war-standard.

66 **To baffle the extraordinary bravery of our troops the Gauls resorted to all kinds of devices…. They made our terraces fall in by undermining, at which they were expert because they have extensive iron mines in their country and are thoroughly familiar with every kind of underground working. They made frequent sorties by day and night, either to set fire to the terrace or to attack our soldiers at work…** 99

Julius Caesar,
The Gallic War,
7.22.1–4

RECONSTRUCTED
FORTIFICATIONS AT ALESIA

In imitating Roman battle tactics, the Gauls proved themselves able students. Celtic raiding parties harried the Roman supply lines and Vercingetorix adopted surprisingly effective countersiege techniques, while biding his time for the arrival of a relief force. When Caesar found his own forces under siege and short of provisions, the situation became critical. It was a true mark of his military genius that he succeeded in the maneuver that the Celts least expected: attacking their own relief force from behind.

66 **Caesar put on speed to get there in time for the fight. The enemy knew that he was coming by the scarlet cloak that he always wore in action…. The Romans dropped their spears and fought with their swords. Suddenly the Gauls saw the cavalry in their rear and fresh cohorts coming up in front. They broke and fled, but found their retreat cut off by the cavalry.** 99

Julius Caesar,
The Gallic
War,
7.87.3–88.3

66 **[Caesar] fought pitched battles at various times with three million men, of whom he destroyed one million in the actual fighting and took another million prisoners.** 99

Plutarch, Life of Caesar, *chapter 15*

TROPHY OF THE ALPS
This monument in the Alps celebrates a victory by Augustus, Caesar's heir, over rebellious Gallic tribes.

CAESAR'S GALLIC WARS

Alesia

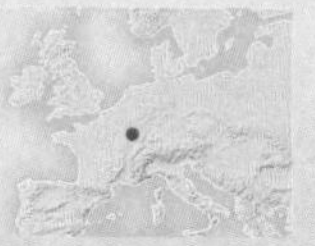

DATE
July–October 52 BCE

FORCES
Romans: 45,000;
Gauls: unknown

LOCATION
Near Dijon,
east-central France

CASUALTIES
No reliable estimates

In 53 BCE a rebellion broke out among the Gauls, threatening to undo the conquests of Julius Caesar, whose legions had subjugated the Gallic tribes. The charismatic Gallic chieftain Vercingetorix formed an army that defied Caesar in a campaign of

SIEGE LINES

A reconstruction of the awesome fortifications that Caesar's army built at Alesia. The two lines, facing inward and outward, totaled 22miles (35km).

guerrilla warfare. Caesar's pursuit of Vercingetorix ended when he found the Gallic army camped on high ground outside the town of Alesia in the summer of 52. Caesar set his legionaries to work building a line of fortifications to enclose both the town and camp, consisting of 23 forts, linked by ditches and a rampart mounted by a palisade, with towers at intervals of 80ft (25m). Before this astonishing siege line was complete, Vercingetorix's cavalry managed to break out, although they suffered heavy losses. Caesar suspected that the cavalry had been sent to organize a relief force, and so had another ring of fortifications built facing outward. As food ran out in besieged Alesia, the Gauls sent their women, children, and old people out of the town. Caesar, however, refused to let them through his lines and they slowly starved to death in the no man's land between the armies. The siege was in its third month when, as Caesar

had anticipated, a large Gallic relief force arrived. The force made three assaults on the siege line, each time assisted by a sortie from Alesia. The last attack came close to success when Vercingetorix's men cleared Roman troops from a section of wall with a hail of javelins, arrows, and slingshots. But Caesar threw reinforcements into the threatened sector before leading a mixed force of infantry and cavalry to put the Gauls to flight. The Gallic relief force dispersed in disarray. Vercingetorix, with all hope lost, rode down to the Roman camp. He surrendered by laying his sword at Caesar's feet. Each Roman soldier received a Gaul to sell as a slave.

died 46 BCE

VERCINGETORIX

A chieftain of the Arverni, Vercingetorix united warriors from central and western Gaul into a disciplined army that matched the Romans in willpower. Exploiting his forces' superior knowledge of terrain, he harassed Caesar's legions, using ambush and scorched-earth tactics. His dignified surrender at Alesia was rewarded with humiliation by the Romans, who led him in chains through Rome in celebration of Caesar's triumph and, after six years' imprisonment, executed him.

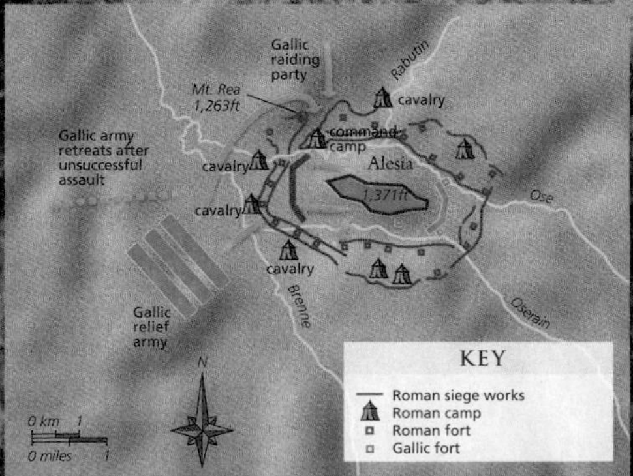

KEY

⎯ Roman siege works
▲ Roman camp
▫ Roman fort
▫ Gallic fort

ROMAN CIVIL WARS

Dyrrachium

DATE
July 48 BCE

FORCES
Caesar's army: 40,000;
Pompey's army: 90,000

LOCATION
Modern-day
Albania

CASUALTIES
1,000 of Caesar's
troops; fewer on
Pompey's side

In 49 BCE Caesar led his army across the Rubicon stream into Italy, in defiance of an order by Pompey and the Senate (see box opposite). Civil war resulted. Pompey fled from Italy, allowing Caesar to occupy Rome, where he was declared dictator. But Pompey had control of the Roman navy and superior land forces. In January 48, Caesar sailed seven legions across the Adriatic in merchant vessels, evading Pompey's warships and landing near his opponent's base at Dyrrachium. Although greatly outnumbered, Caesar's forces laid siege to Pompey's army, which was positioned around a natural harbor. After a competition in fortification building, in which Caesar tried to wall Pompey in and Pompey's engineers sought to block these attempts, fighting broke out in which Caesar's forces came off worst. The dictator retreated to northern Greece.

ROMAN CIVIL WARS

Pharsalus

DATE August 9, 48 BCE

FORCES Caesar: 22,000
infantry; 1,000 cavalry;
Pompey: 45,000
infantry; 7,000 cavalry

LOCATION
Thessaly,
northern Greece

CASUALTIES Caesar: 230
killed, 2,000 wounded;
Pompey: 15,000 killed
or wounded

Pompey followed Caesar from Dyrrachium into Thessaly, where the two armies set up camps on the plain of Pharsalus. After much hesitation, on August 9, Pompey arranged his numerically superior troops for battle. Caesar at once led his forces out to take up the challenge. Pompey concentrated his cavalry on Caesar's right flank (the dictator's left flank stretched to the Enipeus River) with the goal of sweeping away Caesar's horsemen and attacking his infantry from the flank and rear. To counter this, Caesar placed six cohorts under his personal command behind the right

FIELD ARTILLERY
Roman troops used the ballista—also known as the scorpion—to propel missiles such as bolts or stone shot.

flank. Sure enough, more than 6,000 of Pompey's horsemen caused havoc by crashing into Caesar's small contingent of cavalry, but at this point Caesar led his six cohorts into the fray. Stabbing with their pila, the cohorts drove the horsemen from the field. Caesar then urged them forward to attack Pompey's infantry from the flank. He also ordered the third line of his infantry to charge through the other two and deliver a shock frontal assault on the enemy, throwing their pila and plunging in with their swords. Under this pressure Pompey's infantry broke and fled, and were ruthlessly pursued and cut down by Caesar's men. Pompey escaped but was assassinated two months later.

100–44 BCE

JULIUS CAESAR

Gaius Julius Caesar achieved prominence in 59 BCE when he formed an alliance with Pompey and Crassus, the most powerful figures in Rome. As commander of Gaul and Illyria he extended Roman rule as far as the Rhine and twice invaded Britain. He was an archetypal Roman commander: daring, quick to seize initiative, and always present at the hottest point on the battlefield. His accounts of his campaigns are classics of military history. When some senators threatened to bring Caesar to trial at the end of his command, he refused to submit and kept the support of his legions. In the ensuing civil war his opponents set Pompey against him. Caesar was completely victorious and in 44 BCE was declared dictator for life, but he was assassinated by his former supporters that same year.

3000 BCE–476 CE

ROMAN CIVIL WARS

Philippi

DATE October 3 and 23, 42 BCE

FORCES Republicans: 80,000 infantry, 20,000 cavalry; Antony and Octavian: 85,000 infantry, 13,000 cavalry

LOCATION
Philippi,
northeast Greece

CASUALTIES
No reliable estimates

In the confused power struggle after the assassination of Julius Caesar in 44 BCE, Mark Antony and Octavian (the great-nephew of Caesar and the future Emperor Augustus) formed an uneasy alliance to hold power in Rome. However, Marcus Junius Brutus and Gaius Cassius Longinus—the leaders of the assassination plot against Caesar—remained in command of republican forces in the eastern Mediterranean. In September 42, Antony and Octavian led an army into Macedonia and discovered the republican army in two fortified camps at Philippi. Octavian became ill, so Antony

took sole command. He planned a surprise attack across a swamp to take the camp commanded by Cassius. This operation was wholly successful—believing all was lost, Cassius committed suicide. Brutus, however, seized the opportunity presented by Antony's absence by attacking and temporarily overrunning his camp, forcing the sickly Octavian to hide to escape capture. With honors even, the opposing armies remained in position. Three weeks later, suffering serious supply problems, Brutus decided to risk a pitched battle. It was a disastrous decision. While Octavian kept Brutus occupied from the front, Antony once more led his men through the swamp to envelop the republicans' left. Brutus escaped the rout that followed, but soon followed Cassius's example and fell on his sword.

The alliance between Octavian and Antony was destined to continue, in fragile fashion, for a decade after this victory.

EMPEROR AUGUSTUS
Octavian, shown here in this statue in Turin, Italy, became Rome's first emperor after winning the power struggle following Caesar's death.

ROMAN CIVIL WARS

Actium

DATE
September 2, 31 BCE

FORCES Octavian: 400 warships; Antony and Cleopatra: 230 warships

LOCATION Off the coast of Acarnania, western Greece

CASUALTIES Antony and Cleopatra lost 150 ships

In 32 BCE Octavian induced the Roman Senate to declare war on Antony, who had offended Octavian by divorcing his sister and establishing himself in Egypt with the Ptolemaic queen Cleopatra. Once the alliance between the two men ended, Antony also posed a serious threat to Octavian's power. Armies from Rome and Egypt confronted one another at Actium in Greece the following year.

Octavian refused to give battle, but used his navy—commanded by his deputy Agrippa—to blockade his enemy. Antony and Cleopatra decided to attempt a breakout by sea. They hoisted their sails (usually left on shore for battle), hoping for a wind to speed them to safety. When they encountered Agrippa's fleet, Antony's ships split to the left and the right, opening up a gap through which Cleopatra's squadron escaped into open sea. Antony's flagship was lost in the fierce fighting, but he transferred to another ship and also escaped with a few remnants of his fleet. Antony and Cleopatra committed suicide when Octavian invaded Egypt the next year.

ROMAN WARSHIP
This Roman relief depicts a warship manned by legionaries. The tower on the deck enabled soldiers to throw missiles down onto enemy ships.

WARFARE IN THE ANCIENT WORLD

JUDAEAN REVOLT

Siege of Masada

DATE
73–74 CE

FORCES
Romans: 5,000;
Jews: 960

CASUALTIES
Jews: 953

LOCATION Mountaintop
near the southwest
coast of the Dead Sea

Masada was the site of the Jews'
dramatic last stand against the
Romans. Situated on the top of a
steep-sided, rocky hill near the
coast of the Dead Sea, Masada's
fortifications dated back to the 2nd
century BCE, but major development
took place the following century
under Herod I, the Roman-appointed
king of Judaea, the southern province
of Palestine. In 66 CE Judaea rebelled
against Roman rule. The suppression
of the revolt, by the emperor Vespasian
and his son Titus, culminated in the
siege of Jerusalem in 70. Once
Jerusalem had fallen, the uprising was
effectively at an end, but a small
group of Jewish rebels, led by Eleazar
ben Yair, held out in Masada. The
Romans could not ignore the rebels'
defiance, and in November 73 Flavius
Silva, the governor of Judaea, led the
Tenth Legion to besiege the fortress.
Since the approach to the fortress was
along treacherous paths exposed to
the defenders' fire, the Romans
encircled the hill with walls, towers,
and camps. They realized, however,
that a blockade would be too slow for
their purposes. Large storehouses and
water cisterns in the fortress meant
that those inside would be able to
survive a siege that lasted several
years. Instead, the Romans devised a
remarkable plan to take the fortress by
assault. They began building a massive
siege ramp up the western side of the
hill. The construction work proceeded
under constant attack from catapult
artillery from the fortress, to which
the Romans replied in kind. When
complete, the siege ramp was nearly
2,000 ft (600m) long and rose to a
height of over 660 ft (200m). The
Romans then pushed a siege tower
up the ramp, containing a ram on its
lower floor and ballistas on the top
floor to give covering fire. The ram
soon breached the wall, but when
legionaries stormed the fortress they
found that Eleazar had incited his
followers to commit mass suicide.
Only two women and five children
were found alive—they had hidden in
a water conduit during the assault.

MOUNTAINTOP FORTRESS
*The ruins of the city of Masada, which
in 73 CE included two palaces with
heavy walls, towers, and aqueducts.*

ROMAN SIEGE TACTICS

The *testudo*, or tortoise, was a
formation that Roman legionaries
adopted during sieges. Soldiers
behind the front rank held their
shields over their heads so that a
unit could advance to the wall of a
fortress or city and attack it with
crowbars or picks, sheltered from
the rain of missiles that defenders
would pelt down on them. Other
methods of making a breach
included using battering rams and
digging mines under walls.

GERMANIC WARS

Teutoberg Forest

DATE
September 9 CE

FORCES
Romans: 15,000;
German tribes:
unknown

LOCATION
Near Osnabrück,
northwest Germany

CASUALTIES
Most Romans
were killed

In the last two decades of the 1st
century BCE the frontier of the
Roman empire in northern Europe
extended eastward from the Rhine
river—the boundary of Roman
Gaul— to the Elbe river in eastern
Germany. The conquest of the fierce
Germanic tribes was far from
complete, however, and there were
sporadic revolts in the first decade
of the new century. In the summer
of 9 CE, the Roman general Publius
Quinctilius Varus was conducting
operations in central Germany, east of
the Weser River, with an army of three

legions—the Seventeenth, Eighteenth,
and Nineteenth—accompanied by
German auxiliaries. The commander
of auxiliaries from the Cherusci tribe
was a prince called Arminius, who had
served the Romans for some years,
winning their trust. When Varus heard
rumors that Arminius planned to
lead a rebellion, he refused to believe
them. In the late summer the Roman
army headed back toward its winter
quarters, encumbered by a long train
of baggage and camp followers,
including many of the soldiers' families.
Arminius and his auxiliaries soon
abandoned them, proving that the

TEUTOBERG FOREST
*Unlike today, the Teutoberg forest
of 2,000 years ago was a marshy
woodland with narrow passes, in
which the Romans easily got lost.*

rumors were well founded.
Without German scouts to
guide them or warn of ambush,
the Romans entered the
sinister, marshy Teutoberg forest.
Arminius's warriors
harassed the Roman
column mercilessly
over a period of
days, taking a steady
toll with hit-and-
run attacks. Finally
the weakened army
was completely
overrun. Most of the
Roman soldiers and
their families were
killed, and Varus
committed suicide.
According to the Roman
historian Tacitus, Roman
soldiers coming upon the site

of the massacre four years later found
"whitening bones…broken weapons
and bits of horses, while the skulls
of men were nailed to tree trunks."
News of the disaster shocked the
elderly Emperor Augustus, who
reportedly wandered around his
palace shouting, "Varus, give me back
my legions!" Although Roman forces
soon returned to punish the Germanic
tribes, plans to advance the frontier
of the empire eastward
were abandoned.
The lands
beyond the
Rhine would
remain
permanently
outside the
Roman Empire.

ROMAN MASK
*This mask, found
at the Teutoberg forest
battle site, is of a kind
worn by Roman soldiers
in tournaments.*

AGRICOLA'S SCOTTISH CAMPAIGN

Mons Graupius

DATE	
Late summer 84 CE	

| **FORCES** Caledonians: 30,000; Romans and auxiliaries: 25,000 | |

| **CASUALTIES** | |
| **LOCATION** Aberdeenshire, northeast Scotland | Caledonians: 10,000; Romans and auxiliaries: 360 |

Gnaeus Julius Agricola, the Roman governor of Britain, led a force of legionaries and local auxiliaries into Scotland to forestall an uprising by Caledonian tribes. When he met the Caledonian army, led by Calgacus, Agricola let his auxiliaries do the fighting, keeping his Roman troops safely in reserve. The key role was played by cavalry, which dispersed the Caledonians' chariots and then attacked their footsoldiers from the rear. The Caledonians were hacked down as they fled the field.

BOUDICCA'S REVOLT

Revolt of the Iceni

DATE	
60 CE	

| **FORCES** Romans: 10,000; Britons: unknown | |

| **CASUALTIES** | |
| **LOCATION** Near present-day Towcester, England | Romans: 400 killed; Britons: tens of thousands killed |

Following the emperor Claudius's invasion in 43 CE, much of Britain had become a Roman province. However, in 60 the Romans faced a major uprising in eastern Britain led by Boudicca, queen of the Iceni, who had been brutally treated by Roman officials. The Iceni were joined in their rebellion by the neighboring Trinovantes. With the bulk of the Roman legions away on campaign in Anglesey, in northwest Wales, the rebel army sacked the towns of Camulodonum, Londinium, and Verulamium. The governor of Roman Britain,

VERULAMIUM
Remains of the settlement at Verulamium (near present-day St. Albans), which Boudicca's forces sacked in 60–61 CE.

CONQUERING CLAUDIUS
Claudius took credit for conquering Britain, although he spent only two weeks there during the 43 CE invasion.

Suetonius Paulinus, swiftly marched back from Anglesey at the head of the Fourteenth and Twentieth legions, which he positioned in a defile between wooded hills. Boudicca's warriors, who greatly outnumbered the Romans, advanced to attack. The legionaries waited, still and silent, until the Britons were almost upon them. Then, on command, they threw their pila and charged with swords drawn. As the front ranks of the Britons fell, the warriors behind pushed forward in a confused mass. Thousands were cut down by the Romans as defeat turned into rout. Boudicca died, probably by taking poison.

TRAJAN'S DACIAN CAMPAIGNS

Dacian Campaigns

DATE	
101–106 CE	

| **FORCES** Romans: unknown Dacians: unknown | |

| **CASUALTIES** | |
| **LOCATION** Dacia (present-day Romania) | No reliable estimates |

The Dacians were a warlike people who dominated a region east of the Danube River in the Balkan Peninsula. In the last decades of the 1st century CE, led by Decebalus, they carried out raids across the Danube into Roman territory. These only ended with a peace treaty favorable to the Dacians. The emperor Trajan's invasion of Dacia in 101 was a punitive expedition, intended to

reassert Roman superiority. An army of nine legions, accompanied by large numbers of Germanic auxiliaries, crossed the Danube over a bridge of boats. Little is known about the campaign, but there was clearly much fighting, with Trajan's auxiliaries usually in the front line. In 102 Decebalus sued for peace, but once the Romans had gone he rebuilt his army and resumed attacks on Roman outposts. In 106 Trajan returned, this time determined on conquest. His

soldiers built a permanent bridge across the broad expanse of the Danube—typical of the legions' feats of engineering—and his army thrust into the Carpathian mountain region to besiege the Dacian capital, Sarmizegethusa. Despairing of any relief, the besieged Dacians committed mass suicide. Decebalus escaped but slit his own throat when tracked down by Roman scouts. Dacia was absorbed into the empire. Subsequent campaigns by Trajan in Arabia, Assyria, and Mesopotamia ensured that Rome reached its greatest extent under his rule.

TRAJAN ON HORSEBACK
Trajan's exploits in Dacia are famously depicted on Trajan's Column in Rome, erected to celebrate the emperor's victory in the Balkans.

THE SHIFT TO THE EAST

LATE IN THE 3RD CENTURY CE the emperor Diocletian (ruled 284–305) responded to threats of revolt or invasion throughout the Roman Empire by sharing his rule with several subordinates. During the following century the number of co-emperors varied, while the empire's center shifted east from Rome to Constantinople. The western part of the empire relied increasingly for military support on the Germanic and Gothic tribes that settled in its territories. By the late 5th century the commanders of these tribes saw no further need to recognize an emperor, and the western empire ceased to exist.

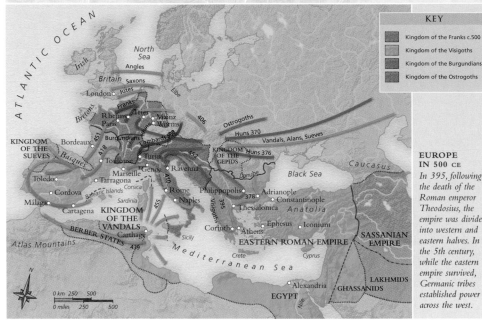

KEY

- Kingdom of the Franks c.500
- Kingdom of the Visigoths
- Kingdom of the Burgundians
- Kingdom of the Ostrogoths

EUROPE IN 500 CE
In 395, following the death of the Roman emperor Theodosius, the empire was divided into western and eastern halves. In the 5th century, while the eastern empire survived, Germanic tribes established power across the west.

Milvian Bridge

DATE
October 28, 312 CE

FORCES
Constantine: 50,000;
Maxentius: 75,000

CASUALTIES
No reliable estimates

LOCATION
Near Rome,
central Italy

In the early 4th century CE as many as six emperors vied for power in the divided empire. In 312 Constantine, ruler of Britain and Gaul, invaded Italy to attack Maxentius, ruler of Rome. After a series of victories in northern Italy, Constantine's legions marched on Rome. Maxentius set out to meet them. He had already ordered the destruction of the stone Milvian Bridge over the Tiber, to block the enemy's approach, so his men crossed the river on a pontoon bridge. They would have been safer remaining inside Rome's newly built Aurelian Walls. Constantine, allegedly inspired by a vision from God in the sky, led his troops to victory. The pontoon bridge collapsed as Maxentius's army withdrew. Maxentius himself was drowned.

CONSTANTINE I
By 323 CE Constantine was sole ruler of the Roman Empire. The first Christian emperor, he promoted the Church across the empire.

Argentoratum

DATE
357 CE

FORCES
Romans: 13,000;
Alemanni: 35,000

CASUALTIES
Romans: 243 killed;
Alemanni: 6,000 killed

LOCATION On the west bank of the Rhine, eastern France

In 356 CE the emperor Constantius II sent the 24-year-old Caesar Julian to fight the Alemanni, a confederation of German tribes led by King Chnodomar that was raiding across the Rhine. After a year of indecisive fighting, Julian met Chnodomar's army as it crossed the Rhine near Argentorate (present-day Strasbourg). Julian's forces were heavily outnumbered, since reinforcements from Rome had failed to arrive, and at first the battle went badly for them. Their cavalry almost bolted when Alemanni light infantry got among them, creeping low and stabbing at the horses, but the Roman infantry stood firm, subjecting the Alemanni to a sustained missile barrage from field artillery, bows, and slingshots. When it came to hand-to-hand combat, the Romans and their auxiliaries—many of whom were also German tribesmen—put the Alemanni to flight, pursuing them to the Rhine, where many drowned.

WATCH TOWER
Fearful of barbarian invasions, the Romans erected watch towers— like this reconstruction—along land borders, rivers, and coasts.

Ctesiphon

DATE
363 CE

FORCES
Romans: 83,000;
Persians: unknown

CASUALTIES
No reliable estimates

LOCATION Near present-day Baghdad, east-central Iraq

After becoming emperor in 361 CE, Julian, the nephew of Constantine I, invaded Sasanian Persia, Rome's major enemy in the east. He advanced down the Euphrates, accompanied by a fleet of more than 1,000 supply boats, and then marched across to the Tigris, his boats following along canals. In front of the Persian capital, Ctesiphon, the Sasanian king Shapur II briefly gave battle before retreating to leave the Romans outside the city's walls. Julian was unable to take Ctesiphon or provoke a decisive battle, however, so he burned his boats and withdrew across country. The retreat was harsh: Persian mounted bowmen harassed the Romans and then, countering a night attack, Julian himself was killed. Hostilities ended only when the Romans agreed to a humiliating peace.

PERSIAN VICTORY
This relief shows Emperor Valerian kneeling before King Shapur I after the Sasanian victory at Edessa in 260. Julian aimed— in vain—to reverse such losses.

Adrianople

DATE
August 9, 378 CE

FORCES
Romans: 60,000;
Goths: 100,000–200,000

LOCATION
Present-day Edirne,
western Turkey

CASUALTIES
Romans: 40,000;
Goths: no reliable
estimates

The pressure on the Roman Empire
from barbarian migration or invasion
increased as the 4th century
progressed. In the 370s the Huns—
central-Asian nomadic horsemen—
began to move westward, attacking
the Germanic Goths living northwest
of the Black Sea. Although they were
fierce warriors, the Ostrogoths (the
Greuthungi) and Visigoths (the
Tervingi) fled the Huns, their whole
tribes migrating in search of refuge. In
376 the Visigoths sought and
received permission from Valens,
the Roman emperor in the
east, to cross the Danube
into Thrace, in northern
Greece. Valens refused a
similar request from
the Ostrogoths, but
they crossed into the
empire regardless.
Inevitably, this influx
of barbarians—
possibly numbering
two million in total—
led to friction with

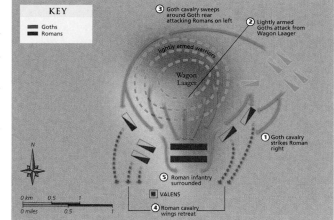

KEY

- Goths
- Romans

③ Goth cavalry sweeps
around Goth rear
attacking Romans on left

② Lightly armed
Goths attack from
Wagon Laager

lightly armed warriors

Wagon
Laager

① Goth cavalry
strikes Roman
right

⑤ Roman infantry
surrounded

■ VALENS

④ Roman cavalry
wings retreat

0 km   0.5   1
0 miles   0.5   1

Roman officials. Soon the Visigoths,
led by Fritigern, and the Ostrogoths,
led by Alatheus and Saphrax, were at
war with Rome and rampaging
through Thrace, joined by
bands of Sarmatians, Alans,
and even Huns. By
August 378 the Goths
had established a
camp outside
Adrianople from

IMPERIAL COIN
*Valens ruled the
eastern half of the
Roman Empire from
375 until his death
at Adrianople in 378.*

which their horsemen went raiding
and foraging in the surrounding area.
Without waiting for reinforcement
from the western emperor, Gratian,
Valens marched an army out from
Constantinople to attack the Goths.
When his marching column
approached their camp—a circle of
wagons protected by a ditch—the
Goths' horsemen, including Alatheus
and Saphrax, were away on a raid.

Fritigern called for a parley, which
Valens, his men tired from marching
in the heat and not yet in battle
formation, accepted. As negotiations
were starting, however, fighting broke
out between the two sides. Valens
ordered a general attack, even
though his infantry were still not
fully prepared. At this point, the
cavalry of Alatheus and Saphrax
returned, in the words of the
Roman historian Ammianus
Marcellinus, "descending from the
mountains like a thunderbolt."
Charging down upon the Roman
right flank they routed the cavalry
and wheeled to attack the infantry
from the rear. Fritigern's footsoldiers
then emerged from behind their
wagons to strike the legionaries
from the front. As his soldiers
were slaughtered in their tens of
thousands, Valens was first wounded,
then killed. In typical fashion, the
Romans recovered from this disaster
and, under Valens' successor,
Theodosius, fought back vigorously
against the Goths. Fritigern died
resisting the Romans five years
later. Many Goths ended up as
"federate" allies of the Romans,
providing armies to fight for
the empire instead of against it.

> **"The plain was covered with carcasses, strewing the mutual ruin of the combatants, while the groans of the dying or of men fearfully wounded were intense."**
>
> Roman historian *Ammianus Marcellinus*, **330–395 CE**

Frigidus

DATE
September 5, 394 CE

FORCES
Theodosius's army:
unknown; Arbogast's
army: unknown

LOCATION
North of Trieste,
northeast Italy

CASUALTIES
No reliable estimates

The increasing prevalence of
barbarians fighting both in the ranks
of Rome's armies and as its allies
added further confusion to the
already complex power struggles in
the declining western
Roman Empire. In
388 CE Arbogast, a
Germanic Frank in the
service of the eastern
Roman emperor
Theodosius I,
suppressed a rebellion
in Gaul. However,
when the western
Roman emperor
Valentinian II tried to
oust the Frank from the
power base he had
established in Gaul,
Arbogast murdered him
and set up a scholar
named Eugenius in his
place. Theodosius set out
to crush Arbogast. The
army he led into western

Europe included 20,000 Goths
among its ranks, as well as the Vandal
general Stilicho and the chief of the
Visigoths, Alaric. Theodosius's army
met Arbogast's in northeastern Italy
by the Frigidus, a tributary of the
Isonzo River. The first day's fighting
went badly for Theodosius: the Franks
repulsed a Roman attack, inflicting
heavy losses. On the following day,
however, a gale-force following wind
came to his aid, blinding the enemy
with dust and almost knocking them
over where they stood. Along with
the brilliant generalship of Stilicho,
the gale helped Theodosius to win a
total victory. Eugenius was beheaded
and Arbogast fell on his sword.
Theodosius himself died
soon after the battle, but
Stilicho went on to
become supreme
commander in the
west, until he was
murdered on the
orders of the western
emperor Honorius.
Alaric became one of
the empire's gravest
enemies, sacking
Rome just before
his death in 410.

VANDAL GENERAL
*This diptych portrays
Stilicho (365–408 CE)
with a Roman soldier's
spear and shield.*

Chalons

DATE
June or July 451 CE

FORCES
Romans: unknown;
Huns: unknown

LOCATION Near
Châlons-sur-Marne,
northeast France

CASUALTIES
No reliable estimates

In the 5th century CE the incursions
of the Huns, led by Attila, struck
terror into the settled populations of
the Roman Empire. It seemed that no
army could resist the Huns' swarms
of horsemen, who darted around the
battlefield, showering their enemy

with bone-tipped arrows, before
closing in to finish off survivors with
swords and lassos. In 451, however,
the Roman general Aetius caught up
with Attila in Gaul, at a site
sometimes called the Catalaunian
plains. Both armies were a mix of
peoples. Aetius's force included Alans
and Franks, as well as an army of
Visigoths under their king, Theodoric.
Attila had Ostrogoths and Gepids
alongside his Huns. The details of the
battle are unclear, but it was certainly
a bloody affair in which the Visigoths
distinguished themselves, despite
Theodoric being killed. The Huns
were forced to withdraw to their
wagon-circle camp, which Aetius and
his allies failed to assault. It was,
nonetheless, a serious defeat for Attila.

c.406–453 CE

ATTILA THE HUN

Known to those who feared him
as the "scourge of God," Attila
became sole ruler of the Huns in
443. Joined by warriors from other
barbarian peoples, he led his
horsemen in forays deep inside the
Roman Empire. He was a raider,
intent on pillage and destruction,
rather than a conqueror.

THE POPE AND THE HUN
This tapestry depicts a meeting between Pope
Leo I and Attila in 452, in which the pope paid
the Hun leader not to attack Rome.

ASIAN EMPIRES

IN THE 1ST CENTURY CE, while the Roman Empire underwent a period of consolidation, China's Han Empire (206 BCE–220 CE) was at the height of its power, possessing arguably the most formidable army in the world. The Han general Pan Chao (32 CE–102 CE), for instance, led forces deep into central Asia. Empires in China and India were similar to Rome in that both struggled to protect their borders against "barbarian" invaders, and, in China, political rivalries were never far from the surface.

EVOLVING ARMIES

As in the Middle East, warfare in China was at first dominated by a chariot-riding aristocracy. Chariots appeared under the Shang dynasty (c.1500–1050 BCE) and proliferated under their successors, the Zhou. In the 8th century BCE centralized power collapsed in China, leading to the Spring and Autumn Period, characterized by small battles between local lords. Gradually, the consolidation of larger kingdoms led to the Warring States Period (476–221 BCE). This was a time of military innovations that saw the world's first crossbows. Cavalry began to replace chariots in the 4th century BCE, a move credited to King Wu Ling of Zhao, who persuaded aristocrats to abandon their long robes and adopt the pants and short gowns required for horseriding. In 221 BCE, Qin Shi Huangdi united China through a series of spectacular military campaigns. The dynasty he founded, the Qin, was swiftly succeeded by the Han.

TERRA-COTTA WARRIOR
This armored soldier is one of thousands of life-sized clay figures buried in the tomb of Emperor Qin Shi Huangdi, who ruled China between 221 and 210 BCE.

CHINESE WEAPONS

ARMOR, PRE-5TH CENTURY BCE   *Leather scales*

The crossbow, introduced about 450 BCE, was the archetypal Chinese missile weapon, but other types of bow were also used. For close combat, soldiers relied on spears and swords. Instead of shields, they depended on leather, metal, or quilted armor. There is dispute over when iron weapons supplanted bronze in China, but both were in use in the Han Empire.

SCABBARD AND DAGGER, 7TH–6TH CENTURY BCE

Bronze blade

Ornate design

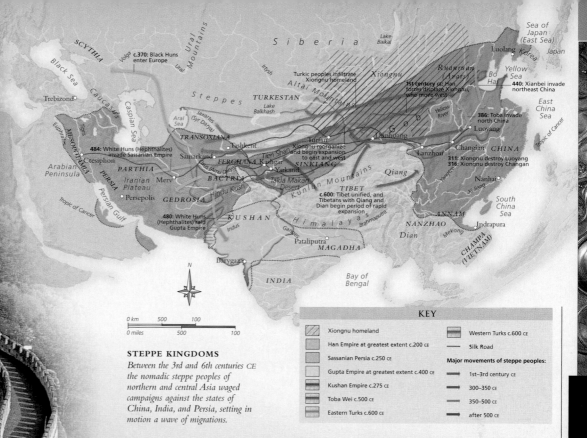

STEPPE KINGDOMS

Between the 3rd and 6th centuries CE the nomadic steppe peoples of northern and central Asia waged campaigns against the states of China, India, and Persia, setting in motion a wave of migrations.

KEY

Xiongnu homeland	Western Turks c.600 CE
Han Empire at greatest extent c.200 CE	Silk Road
Sassanian Persia c.250 CE	**Major movements of steppe peoples:**
Gupta Empire at greatest extent c.400 CE	1st–3rd century CE
Kushan Empire c.275 CE	300–350 CE
Toba Wei c.500 CE	350–500 CE
Eastern Turks c.600 CE	after 500 CE

MAURYAN CHARIOT

The Mauryans maintained their Indian Empire by means of a standing army, which included elephants and chariots.

NOMADIC INFLUENCE

For much of its existence, the major challenge to China's Han dynasty came from the nomadic horsemen of the steppe—the plains that stretch through central Asia to northeast China. When different steppe tribes came together they were able to field cavalry armies that repeatedly overran China's long land border. One of the Hans' responses to this threat was the construction of frontier defenses, which coalesced into the Great Wall. Another was the recruitment of nomadic horsemen into the imperial army. But these measures were not enough: in the 3rd century CE the Han Empire disintegrated, largely under the pressure of nomadic invasions. Nomadic warriors had a similar impact on northern India. There the Mauryans (c.310–185 BCE) and the Guptas (320–540 CE) established sizeable empires and developed their own art of warfare, most strikingly using elephants in battle. Yet India was always prone to attack by nomadic invaders from the north, including the Scythians and Parthians and the mysterious White Huns, who swept away the Gupta Empire in the 6th century CE.

GREAT WALL

In the 300s BCE, Chinese states began building fortifications to keep out steppe nomads. Under the Qin and Han dynasties these fortifications became a continuous wall over 2,000 miles (3,200km) long.

died c.234 BCE

ASOKA

Asoka was one of the last Mauryan emperors of northern India. For much of his life he was noted for his bravery and ruthlessness—qualities admired among the Mauryan warrior aristocracy. In order to attain the throne, he is said to have had all his brothers murdered, including the rightful heir, Susima. It was only after the massacres that resulted from the Kalinga Wars (see p.56) that Asoka apparently converted to Buddhism and adopted a creed of nonviolence. It is not clear how he maintained his empire without resorting to force.

FOUR LIONS

This four-lion capital tops the Asoka Pillar in Sarnath, India, erected to record a visit by the emperor in the 3rd century BCE.

CHINESE WARFARE

DURING NEARLY 1,000 YEARS between the battle of Chengpu (632 BCE) and the battle of the Fei river (383 CE), the Chinese experienced almost constant warfare. Wars ranged from power struggles between rival kingdoms to resistance to "barbarian" invasion by steppe nomads. In addition, at times when China was at its strongest, wars were fought to project power far beyond its borders. Among the consequences of these experiences were sophisticated developments in military theory and practice.

WARFARE IN THE ANCIENT WORLD

SPRING AND AUTUMN PERIOD

Chengpu

DATE	632 BCE
FORCES	Chu: unknown; Jin: unknown
LOCATION Possibly Henan or Shandong province	**CASUALTIES** No reliable estimates

Chengpu was a classic battle from the era of chariot warfare in China. It occurred during the country's Spring and Autumn Period (770–476 BCE), when the state of Chu, which dominated an area stretching south of the Yangtze River almost as far north as the Yellow River, fought a three-cornered contest with the states of Jin to the

CHARIOT ORNAMENT
This 4th-century BCE gold-inlaid bull's head decorated the shaft of a chariot.

north and Wu on the coast. The main players at Chengpu were King Cheng of Chu and Duke Wen of Jin. Between them, Cheng and Wen fielded more than 1,000 chariots; Wen alone is said to have had 700 of the vehicles, which were usually drawn by four horses. The battle began with a chariot attack by both wings of the Jin army, the left wing of which, under the command of Xu Chen, had clad their chariot horses in tiger skins. Whether or not as a result of this gesture, Xu Chen's chariots swept through the Chu right wing, and then threatened to attack the Chu center from the flank. Meanwhile, the Jin right wing, facing stiffer opposition than their comrades on the left, decided to fake a disorderly retreat. As the chariots of the Chu right wing set off in pursuit, a band of Jin chariots led by Luan Zhi rode

WALL FORTRESS
The Chu built defenses against outside attack that later linked up to become the Great Wall of China. Jiayuguan Fortress, shown here, was one of the strongpoints on the Great Wall.

across their path, dragging tree branches to stir up a dust cloud. The trick worked: the swirling dust blinded the Chu to the Jin chariots' about-face and the launch of a devastating counterattack. With both wings of their army shattered, the Chu had no choice but to withdraw rapidly to avoid envelopment. They lost more than 100 chariots to the Jin—a serious blow.

WARRING STATES PERIOD

Guai Ling

	DATE 341 BCE
	FORCES Wei: unknown; Qi: unknown
LOCATION Modern-day Shanshi or Hopeh province, China	**CASUALTIES** No reliable estimates

This battle of the Warring States Period (476–221 BCE) involved the rival northern states of Wei and Qi. It began when Wei's forces besieged the Zhao city of Handan, leading Zhao's ruler to appeal to Qi for help. On the advice of the master tactician Sun Ping, instead of sending an army to Handan, Qi sent its forces into Wei. The Wei general Pang Juan hastily ended the siege and pulled his army back to defend Wei—right into the path of thousands of Qi crossbowmen, who slaughtered the Wei and took Pang Juan prisoner. Sun Ping's tactics were much admired by a later guerrilla leader, Mao Zedong.

c.400–c.320 BCE

SUN-TZU

Sun-Tzu was the author of the world's first book of military theory, *The Art of War*. Everything about his life is obscure, including when he lived, but his thoughts have remained fresh throughout the centuries. He regarded the goal of war not as the destruction of the enemy but as the achievement of political objectives and a secure peace. He also advocated the use of subtlety, arguing that "all war is based on deception."

WARRING STATES PERIOD

Changping

	DATE 260 BCE
	FORCES Qin: unknown; Zhao: unknown
LOCATION Shansi province, northeast China	**CASUALTIES** Qin: unknown; Zhao: 400,000 (reportedly)

The Warring States Period was an era of continual conflict in China as various feudal kingdoms vied with one another. By the 3rd century BCE there were seven feudal kingdoms: Qi, Chu, Yan, Han, Zhao, Wei, and Qin. As the century progressed, Qin slowly asserted its dominance over the other states. The secret of its success was its cavalry. Qin was the most westerly of the warring states and

MODEL ARMY
These terra-cotta soldiers, found in the tomb of Emperor Shi Huangdi, reveal much about the dress of 3rd-century BCE Qin warriors.

the one most in contact with marauding nomadic horsemen, and it was probably through encounters with these raiders that Qin developed the best Chinese cavalry. After Qin had defeated Wei in about 280 BCE, Zhao remained its most formidable opponent. The battle of Changping was the final showdown between the massive armies of the two kingdoms. Besides cavalry, there were large infantry forces on both sides. Some soldiers wore armor and some did not; some carried crossbows, while others wielded iron spears or pikes. There were also chariots, although these were chiefly used as command platforms for generals. The battle was a desperate attempt at escape by the Zhao army, whom the Qin had been besieging for two months. The attempt utterly failed: the Qin massacred the Zhao, taking no prisoners alive. Even if the reported figure of 400,000 Zhao dead was a vast exaggeration, it was still a decisive victory. Within 40 years, under Shi Huangdi, Qin had completed the suppression of the warring states and established a unified Chinese empire.

Xiongnu Invasion

DATE
201–200 BCE

FORCES
Xiongnu: 300,000;
Chinese: unknown

LOCATION
Mongolia and
northwest China

CASUALTIES
No reliable estimates

After the collapse of Qin rule in 202 BCE the Han dynasty was founded under the emperor Han Gaozu, whose assertion of central authority prevented a reversion to the civil disorder of the Warring States Period. His new empire faced an immediate

GOD OF WAR
Guandi, the Confucian war god, was revered for preventing conflict as well as for aiding victory.

threat, however: the Xiongnu nomads from Mongolia. In 201, united under the leadership of Modu, they invaded northwest China with an army of horsemen said to be 300,000 strong. The following year Gaozu led an army out against the invaders, but his forces were no match for the Xiongnu's fast-moving mounted archers. Surrounded by the enemy in a frontier fortress, Gaozu was forced to make a humiliating peace, which included the marriage of his daughter to Modu.

WAR SCENE
A brick relief from the Han period showing infantry, horsemen, and chariots in battle.

Red Cliffs

DATE
208 CE

FORCES
Cao Cao: 220,000; Liu
Bei and Sun Quan:
50,000

LOCATION
Yangtze River,
central China

CASUALTIES
No reliable estimates

Toward the end of the Han period, Cao Cao, the Han general and effective ruler of the empire, faced a major challenge to his authority in southern China from the warlords Liu Bei and Sun Quan. In 208 CE Cao launched a campaign against his southern rivals, resulting in the battle of the Red Cliffs, one of the most famous events in Chinese military history. Although details of the battle are unclear, it seems that Liu Bei and Sun Quan's leading commander, Zhou Yu, negated the effect of Cao's numerically superior forces by drawing him into a naval engagement on the Yangtze River. The southerners were experienced in river warfare, but Cao's northerners were used to fighting only on land. Cao captured a fleet of ships and apparently chained them together for greater stability. But what was gained in stability was lost

EVE OF BATTLE
A 14th-century illustration depicting the Han general Cao Cao in melancholy mood on the eve of the battle of the Red Cliffs, in which he suffered a massive defeat.

in maneuverability: the chained ships were easy prey for the fire arrows of the southern archers and the burning ships sent sailing into their midst. After this disaster the remnants of Cao's army retreated north in disarray.

Fei River

DATE
November 383 CE

FORCES
Eastern Jin: 80,000;
Fu Jian: 870,000

LOCATION
Fei River, Yangtze
valley, central China

CASUALTIES
No reliable estimates

The background to the battle of Fei river was the disintegration of China through barbarian invasion and civil war in the 3rd and 4th centuries CE. Unable to resist the attacks by nomadic horsemen, the Jin emperors were driven out of northern China and established themselves south of the Yangtze River as the Eastern Jin. The Eastern Jin were not free of threats, however, and the greatest of these came from Fu Jian, a vigorous and effective war leader of Tibetan origin. In around 370 CE Fu Jian established control over northern China, setting up a state known as the Qianqin, or Former Qin. He was soon applying military pressure to the

BRONZE SWORD
This bronze sword belonged to an earlier period of Chinese warfare, but the techniques of hand-to-hand fighting remained the same.

Eastern Jin, capturing the important city of Xiangyang in 379. When a Jin army failed to retake the city in 383, Fu Jian seized on it as the right moment to launch a major campaign to conquer the south. He assembled an army that reportedly numbered 600,000 infantry and 270,000 cavalry. Even if these figures are exaggerated, it must have been a massive force, recruited from the many peoples under Fu Jian's rule or from those owing him allegiance. As this multinational army advanced south into the Yangtze valley, it confronted the forces of the Eastern Jin across the Fei River. The Jin, outnumbered by as many as 10 to one, faced nearly impossible odds. No reliable account of the battle survives, but according to one version of events the Jin sent a messenger to Fu Jian's field commander, Fu Rong, offering him the chance of a pitched battle if he would just pull back from the river bank to allow the Jin forces to cross unimpeded. Seeing this as a perfect chance to crush the Jin, Fu Rong ordered his vast army to withdraw, intending to turn and deliver a crushing attack once the Jin had crossed the river. As his army moved back, however, word began to spread among the soldiers that they were retreating because they had been defeated. In fact, the Jin army, once it had crossed the river, immediately began harassing the rear of Fu Jian's

> ## "Those skilled in warfare move the enemy, and are not moved by the enemy…. Know the enemy's plans and calculate their strengths and weaknesses."
>
> *Sun-Tzu*, The Art of War, 4th century BCE

forces. A panic set in that Fu Rong was unable to control: he was swept along with his men as they fled the scene of battle. Whether this account is true or not, the Former Qin empire certainly disintegrated in the years after 383, while the southern Chinese states maintained their independence. The Eastern Jin continued to rule China south of the Yangtze until 420.

ARMORED HORSE
Chinese heavy cavalry protected their warhorses with battle armor made of linked leather segments. This statue of an armored warhorse was discovered in a tomb dating from the 5th or 6th century ce.

INDIAN WARFARE

INDIAN EMPIRES SUCH AS THE Maurya and Gupta practiced warfare on an impressive scale, with large standing armies comprising infantry, cavalry, elephants, and possibly chariots. The *Arthasastra*, a manual of political and military advice compiled at the court of Chandragupta Maurya in the 4th century BCE, discusses the correct tactical use of the different components of an army, the training of cavalry, the conduct of battles and sieges, and the construction of fortifications. Yet accounts of battles fought in Ancient India are scant, the most detailed being Greek reports of the battle of Hydaspes, in which Alexander the Great defeated the Punjabi ruler Porus (see p.27). Although the status of warriors was high in Ancient India, the influence of Buddhism provided a counterweight, pulling many people—including the Mauryan emperor Asoka—toward pacifism.

WARFARE IN THE ANCIENT WORLD

MAHABHARATA WAR

Mahabharata War

DATE
c.1300 BCE

FORCES
Kauravas: unknown;
Pandavas: unknown

CASUALTIES
All the Kauravas were killed; only five Pandavas survived

LOCATION Kurukshetra, Haryana state, northwest India

One of the classic literary texts of Ancient India, the *Mahabharata* tells of the power struggle between rival cousins the Kauravas and the Pandavas. Most authorities accept that the war was not a real historical event; nonetheless, the account is a rare source of information about how wars were fought in India before the 4th century BCE, the probable date of its composition. According to the work, armies fought mostly on foot, with bows; horses were scarce and were used only to draw the chariots in which the nobility fought. The course of the 18-day battle that settled the war has similarities with the Greek epic the *Iliad*: there is plenty of divine intervention and even a hero who, like Achilles, is killed because a protective magic spell misses one part of his body.

MAHABHARATA RELIEF
Relief at Angkor Wat, Cambodia, depicting a scene from the Mahabharata. *Indian warfare heavily influenced Cambodia.*

MAURYAN WARS

Chandragupta's Wars

DATE
c.310–303 BCE

FORCES
Chandragupta's army: 600,000 infantry; 30,000 cavalry; 9,000 elephants

LOCATION
Northern and central India and Afghanistan

CASUALTIES
No reliable estimates

Chandragupta Maurya is said to have based his military ambitions upon the example of Alexander the Great, whom he apparently met when Alexander invaded India. It was probably with the aid of some of Alexander's Macedonians, serving as mercenaries, that Chandragupta first took over the Magadha kingdom of northern India, and then extended his rule over the rest of the north and center of the subcontinent. The expanding Mauryan Empire came into conflict with Seleucus, who, after Alexander's death, had gained control of his Asian conquests. In a war lasting from 305 to 303 BCE, Chandragupta fought Seleucus over control of much of present-day Afghanistan. It was little surprise that Chandragupta was the victor: an ambassador named Megasthenes, sent by Seleucus to Chandragupta's court, reported on the vast size of the Mauryan army. Chandragupta rigidly controlled this army—soldiers were paid by the state, and he had a monopoly of ownership on horses and elephants, which were thus a permanent part of the standing army. Elephants provided a shock force on the battlefield, as well as acting as living battering rams for breaking through fortifications.

MAURYAN WARS

Kalinga Wars

DATE c.262 BCE

FORCES
Mauryans: unknown;
Kalingans: unknown

CASUALTIES
Mauryans: 10,000 killed; Kalingans: 100,000 killed

LOCATION
East-central India

Like his grandfather Chandragupta and his father, Bindusara, Emperor Asoka fought campaigns to extend the boundaries of the Mauryan Empire. Asoka eventually ruled all but the southern tip of India, and his empire extended north as far as southern Iran. One of the states he conquered was Kalinga, a kingdom on India's east coast. Around 262 BCE, in the eighth year of Asoka's rule, he called on the Kalingan king to acknowledge Mauryan overlordship. When the king refused, Asoka sent an army to enforce his authority, but this first Mauryan army was routed by the Kalingans. Enraged by this unexpected setback, Asoka gathered the largest forces he could muster for a second invasion. This time the Kalingans had no answer to the Mauryan military might, and their sturdy resistance was completely overwhelmed. Asoka devastated Kalinga in brutal revenge for the earlier affront to his imperial power: Mauryan inscriptions record that 100,000 Kalingans were killed in the war and its immediate aftermath. Yet the spectacle of the bloodbath that he had unleashed apparently sickened the emperor and prompted a total change of heart. He adopted the Buddhist faith and turned against warfare, ruling in peace up to his death in 234 BCE. Ironically, his new policies—including a costly welfare state based on Buddhist teaching—led to the Mauryans' destruction. In 185 BCE a military coup overthrew the last of the Mauryan emperors. It would be 1,700 years before so much of the Indian subcontinent was again unified.

THE DHAMEK STUPA
After his conversion to Buddhism, Asoka erected stupas (religious monuments) like this one, and founded monasteries, irrigation programs, and even a health service—all of which sprang from his rejection of warfare after the Kalinga Wars.

Campaigns of Samudragupta

DATE
c.330–375 CE

FORCES
Guptas: unknown

CASUALTIES
No reliable estimates

LOCATION
Southern, central and northern India

After the decline of the Mauryan Empire in the 2nd century BCE, India went through a long period of political fragmentation. But the memory of the Mauryans was not lost. In the 4th century CE a ruler came to power in Magadha—the state from which the Mauryan Empire had originated—who consciously took the Mauryans as a model to imitate. Chandragupta I claimed descent from his namesake, the founder of the Mauryan Empire, and set about extending his rule over as wide an area as possible. In about 330 his son Samudragupta succeeded to what had become the Gupta Empire. As so often occurs in Ancient Indian history, the evidence for the military activities of Samudragupta is very limited—all of it being based on a single inscription found on a partly destroyed pillar in Allahabad, in the northern state of Uttar Pradesh. Yet Samudragupta does appear to have been a formidable war leader who achieved substantial conquests: it is recorded that he performed a horse sacrifice in celebration of his victories over 21 kings. The list of his triumphs

ROYAL MINT
A gold coin from the reign of Chandragupta I, father of Samudragupta and founder of the Gupta Empire.

GUPTA TEMPLE
This Gupta-period temple at Deogarh, Uttar Pradesh, testifies to the wealth and power of the Gupta Empire.

includes the defeat of the kingdoms of Kota and Andhra in southeastern India. Samudragupta forced the kings of Kota and Andhra to pay him tribute, while other kingdoms he took over entirely, with the result that he built an empire stretching from the Bay of Bengal to the Arabian Sea and north as far as the Himalayas. Gupta rule over some of this wide area was, however, probably little more than nominal.

White Huns

DATE
c.450–530 CE

FORCES
White Huns: unknown

CASUALTIES
No reliable estimates

LOCATION Northern India (present-day Punjab and Bihar)

Northwest India was subject to repeated invasions by central-Asian peoples. In the 1st century BCE the Scythians and the Parthians arrived in India and established kingdoms there. In the 1st century CE the Kushans established an empire that ruled much of northern India, as well as Afghanistan and part of central Asia, for almost two centuries. And in the 5th century it was the turn of the White Huns to follow this well-worn path. The Byzantine Greeks called the White Huns Hephthalites, and the Byzantine historian Procopius described them as "of the stock of the Huns," but "the only ones among the Huns who have white bodies." One inference is that the White Huns may have been of mixed Mongolian and Indo-European stock. Their style of warfare was similar to other nomadic steppe people, however: White Hun warriors were fast-moving horsemen who preyed upon and terrorized settled civilizations. The White Huns appear to have developed a power base along the Oxus River in modern Tajikistan and Uzbekistan, from where they waged war upon Persia's Sasanian Empire. In 484 CE they defeated a large Persian army and captured the Persian ruler Firuz, plunging the Sasanian Empire into crisis. At first the White Huns were less successful in India, suffering a defeat at the hands of the Gupta emperor Skandagupta in 457. They nonetheless established themselves in the Punjab and maintained their pressure on the Gupta Empire, overrunning it after Skandagupta's death in 467. Their progress along the Ganges reportedly left Buddhist monasteries in flames and cities in ruins; apparently, the population of the Gupta capital, Pataliputra, was reduced to that of a village. In the early 6th century the White Hun kings Toramana and Mihirakula extended their rule to the south and east. In 530, however, Mihirakula was decisively defeated by a coalition of Hindu princes. Within 20 years the White Huns' Indian kingdom had fallen. Around the same time, Chosroes I of Persia destroyed their central-Asian empire, too. It is unclear what happened to the White Huns after their states disintegrated, but they may be the ancestors of the Rajputs, the fierce warriors whose kingdoms were prominent in India from the 8th to the 12th centuries.

HUN COIN
The White Huns' coins reveal an artistic sophistication at odds with their reputation as barbaric nomads.

> "The Hephthalites have no cities, but roam freely and live in tents. They do not live in towns; their seat of government is a moving camp."
>
> *Sun Yung and Hui Sheng*, Buddhist pilgrims, 6th century CE

WARFARE IN THE MIDDLE AGES

476–1492

CAVALRY AND CITADELS

ALTHOUGH "THE MIDDLE AGES" IS A EUROPEAN TERM, referring to the period between the ancient times of the Roman Empire and the modern times ushered in by the Renaissance, it makes sense in military terms to apply it to the rest of the world, too. New military technologies spread—if at differing speeds—across most of the globe, and civilizations from Europe and the Middle East to China and India endured waves of invasion, often by the same nomadic forces.

HORSEBORNE EMPEROR
Charlemagne, shown here in an 8th-century statue, relied on cavalry to expand his empire.

The Middle Ages were marked by the failure of states and empires either to absorb or to achieve any decisive superiority over the "barbarian" peoples who pressed against their borders. This failing left them exposed to damaging incursions or outright conquest. Under the Tang and Sung dynasties, China was the most technologically advanced society of its time, yet it came under constant pressure from steppe horsemen before finally succumbing to Mongol invaders in the 13th century. Relatively backward western Europe, meanwhile, struggled to resist waves of raiders and settlers from the 8th to the 10th centuries, as did the Byzantine Empire. Most western European states found it impossible to sustain professional standing armies and were far from establishing a monopoly of armed force. This weakness made it hard to distinguish between war and simple violence, as local lords or mercenary commanders fought in pursuit of their own motives. But while much warfare was conducted purely to amass plunder or to settle vendettas, the great Arab conquests of the 7th and 8th centuries were fired by

belief in Islam, which inspired a religiously driven campaign of conquest that was mirrored in the Christian crusades from the late 11th century.

DOMINANT CAVALRY

Warfare throughout most of this period was dominated by cavalry, ranging from Turkish horsemen armed with bows who wore little or no armor and specialized in hit-and-run tactics, to the heavily armored knights of western Europe and the Byzantine Empire. Everywhere cavalry was the high-status division of an army, literally looking down on the footsoldiers. Although the diffusion of the stirrup throughout Europe from about the 9th century did something to increase the stability of the mounted warrior, it was only one factor in the move toward more heavily armored cavalry—other developments included better-designed saddles and the breeding of stronger warhorses. The improving skills of metalworkers, in both the Christian and the Islamic worlds, made swords more deadly and enabled European knights to adopt plate armor from

567 Lombards invade Italy from the north	**642** Most of China united under the Tang dynasty	**702** Arabs convert the Berbers of North Africa	**800** Charlemagne adopts the title "emperor"		**1071** Battle of Manzikert *(p.77)*	**1095** Pope Urban II calls for a crusade against the Turks
570 Birth of the prophet Muhammad		**711** Arabs conquer most of Spain	**845** Viking ships sail up the Seine River	**c.1000** Vikings explore the coast of Newfoundland	**1066** Battle of Hastings *(p.71)*	**1128** Military religious order the Knights Templar gain papal approval	**1180** Start of the Gempei Wars in Japan

500   **700**   **900**   **1100**

507 The Frankish king Clovis defeats the Visigoths at the Battle of Vouillé	**636** The first major Arab–Islamic victory at the Battle of Yarmuk	**778** Battle of Roncesvalles *(p.67)*	**c.790** Vikings begin raiding the British Isles	**911** France grants Normandy to the Viking chief Rollo	**960** Sung dynasty replaces the Tang in China	**1085** Beginning of the Reconquista in Spain	**1177** The Khmer defeat the Cham at Angkor in Cambodia	**1187** Battle of Hattin *(pp.84–85)*

ARAB CAVALRY, 11TH CENTURY   **KHMER KING JAYAVARMAN VII (r.1181–c.1215)**   **FRENCH KNIGHTS, 12TH CENTURY**

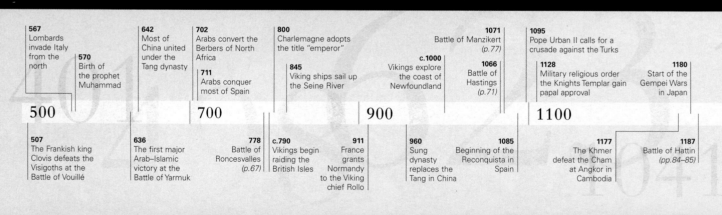

the 13th century. Bows were a key weapon of cavalrymen in many armies—including those in Japan and the Byzantine Empire—but western-European knights spurned missile weapons, committed as they were to ideals of warfare that involved the charge with couched, or forward-pointing, lance and hand-to-hand combat. Although no elite warrior could be without a horse, in practice horsemen often dismounted to fight. Infantry rediscovered a more respected place on European battlefields in the later part of the Middle Ages, when the intelligent deployment of footsoldiers with crossbows and longbows challenged the effectiveness of the cavalry charge. The 14th and 15th centuries were marked by the growing success of disciplined infantry such as Swiss pikemen, who fought in phalanxes reminiscent of Ancient Greece.

FORTS AND SIEGES

Widespread insecurity and political fragmentation during the Middle Ages were reflected in the construction of formidable stone castles and the fortification of cities. In turn, these feats of engineering ensured that sieges were a prominent feature of medieval warfare, in China as much as in western Europe or the Islamic world. Since siege engines were, at best, no more effective than those of the ancient world, sieges were often protracted and messy affairs, with heavy losses to disease and hunger among both the besiegers and the besieged.

GUNPOWDER

The gradual introduction of gunpowder weapons offered the potential for a significant change in siege warfare. The Chinese had explored the military potential of gunpowder by the 11th century at the latest, and by the end of the 13th century they had primitive guns firing stone or iron balls. It did not take long for these innovations to spread to the rest of Asia and Europe. By 1326 the Italian city of Florence was ordering metal cannon for defensive duties, and cannon played a marginal part in the battle of Crécy, between French and English forces, in 1346. Although Europe did not invent gunpowder weapons, it showed great aptitude for developing and improving them. The manufacture of gunpowder in granular form— "corned" powder—made it far more powerful, while the evolution of cannon progressed from iron strips held together with hoops to cast-bronze pieces firing wrought-iron shot. Cannons also increased in mobility, as soldiers mounted them on two-wheeled carriages or limbers, from where they raised and lowered the weapons by means of trunnions (axlelike devices). By the second half of the 15th century the French army was operating with an artillery train, while handguns were beginning to become practical weapons. Gunpowder artillery had far from revolutionized warfare by 1500, but it had already made the stone walls of the medieval castle obsolete.

MISSILE WARFARE
Trebuchets——stone-throwing machines operated by ropes or, on later models, a counterweight system—were a major part of medieval armies' siege artillery.

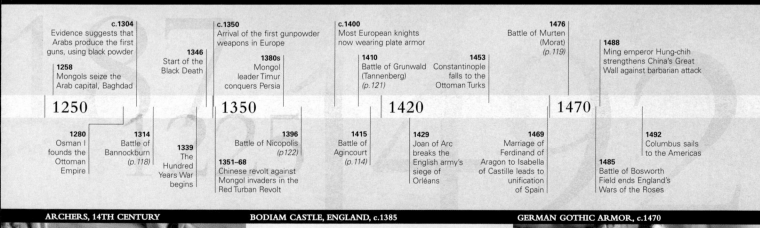

c.1304 Evidence suggests that Arabs produce the first guns, using black powder	**c.1350** Arrival of the first gunpowder weapons in Europe	**c.1400** Most European knights now wearing plate armor	**1476** Battle of Murten (Morat) *(p.119)*	
1258 Mongols seize the Arab capital, Baghdad	**1346** Start of the Black Death	**1380s** Mongol leader Timur conquers Persia	**1410** Battle of Grunwald (Tannenberg) *(p.121)*	**1453** Constantinople falls to the Ottoman Turks	**1488** Ming emperor Hung-chih strengthens China's Great Wall against barbarian attack
1250	**1350**	**1420**	**1470**	
1280 Osman I founds the Ottoman Empire	**1314** Battle of Bannockburn *(p.118)*	**1339** The Hundred Years War begins	**1396** Battle of Nicopolis *(p122)*	**1415** Battle of Agincourt *(p.114)*	**1429** Joan of Arc breaks the English army's siege of Orléans	**1469** Marriage of Ferdinand of Aragon to Isabella of Castille leads to unification of Spain	**1492** Columbus sails to the Americas
		1351–68 Chinese revolt against Mongol invaders in the Red Turban Revolt			**1485** Battle of Bosworth Field ends England's Wars of the Roses

ARCHERS, 14TH CENTURY   **BODIAM CASTLE, ENGLAND, c.1385**   **GERMAN GOTHIC ARMOR, c.1470**

INVADERS AND FEUDAL LORDS

AFTER THE DISINTEGRATION of Imperial Rome in the 5th century the empire continued in the east, centered on Constantinople. In western Europe the Franks extended control over Gaul in the vacuum left by the Romans, but waves of intruders—Vikings, Saracens, Magyars—made life insecure for the settled population. It was not until the 11th century that the pressure from raiders and invaders would begin to subside, allowing western Europe to enter a more aggressive phase.

IVORY HORSEMEN
Byzantine cavalrymen carried a lance and a sword as well as a small shield to protect their necks and backs.

EUROPE c.600
In the 500s Byzantines won back parts of the west, but then faced invasions from peoples such as the Lombards and the Avars.

KEY

Lombard kingdom and duchies

Frankish overlordship

→ expansion of the Slavs (from 580s)

BYZANTINE SURVIVAL

The Byzantine Empire was named after Byzantium, the ancient city refounded as Constantinople in 330. After an early phase during which it attempted to restore control in the west, the empire was largely on the defensive, often relying on the formidable walls of Constantinople to resist invaders. The heart of the Byzantine army was its armored cavalry, the cataphracts, who carried heavy swords, bows, and sometimes lances. From the 7th century cavalry recruitment was based on the duty of farmers to serve the empire, although this system evolved to one in which regional lords provided agreed to numbers of horsemen. Byzantine use of cavalry was sophisticated; for example, in response to raiding by Arabs and Turks, frontier watchtowers provided early warning of intruders, allowing cavalry to track down and destroy the raiding parties.

BYZANTINE HERO
General Belisarius (far right) led Byzantium's 5th-century resurgence, with victories over the Persians, Vandals, and Ostrogoths.

KNIGHTS AND FORTS

Like the Byzantines, Charlemagne's Franks saw armored cavalry as the core of the army—the prestige arm expected to predominate on the battlefield. The knight's horse and armor have been calculated as being equivalent in value to 20 cows. No state in early medieval Europe could afford to maintain such expensive warriors, so the knight had to be self-supporting, owning land to provide the income to equip himself for war. Recent historians have warned against seeing this period in terms of "feudalism"—with knights holding land in return for military service—but landowners certainly had the duty to present themselves armed and mounted when their lord required. A major military feature missing from European landscapes until the 10th century was the castle. Before that there were simple places of refuge such as hill forts and fortified monasteries that people went to in time of danger. When castles did begin to be built, most were of earth and wood, like the famous motte-and-bailey design—an earthen mound topped by a tower and surrounded by ditches, a rampart, and a palisade.

AFTER ROME

In much of the former western Roman Empire there were long periods of general insecurity, during which warfare was extensively decentralized, with local lords organizing protection for their people. The strongest kingdom to emerge in the wake of the Roman Empire was that of the Franks: the Frankish rulers of the Merovingian dynasty controlled most of what is now France by the time they converted to Christianity at the end of the 5th century. Under the Carolingian dynasty from 751, the Franks' military conquests expanded the area under their rule so substantially that, by 800, their powerful king, Charlemagne, was ready to assume the title of emperor, which the pope formally bestowed upon him in Rome. After Charlemagne's reign his successors had difficulty maintaining both his power and the unity of their realms. In the 10th century, however, in what is now Germany, the Saxon emperor Otto the Great was able to revive imperial power, winning some notable victories over Magyar invaders from western Asia.

FRANKISH WARRIOR
This crude 7th-century carving of a Frankish warrior gives prominence to his "scramasax" (dagger). Frankish weapons were prized across Europe.

RAIDERS AND SETTLERS

Between the 5th and 10th centuries, western Europe experienced waves of armed raids, invasions, and migrations that threatened the stability of states and the safety of established communities. While Muslims and Vikings raided around the coasts, peoples such as the Avars, Bulgars, and Magyars pressed across Europe's long land border to the east. The Vikings were especially feared, the raids of their warships terrorizing communities along coasts and up rivers far inland from the late 8th century. However, many raiders and invaders evolved into settlers, as in the Muslim states of Spain and the Magyar kingdom of Hungary. The Scandinavians, for a long time a plague to Christian western Europe, eventually established realms in eastern England, Ireland, and northern France. Intermarrying with local people, the French Northmen became known as Normans, and their fearsome warrior bands adopted the fighting practices of their settled neighbors, becoming mounted knights like the Franks. In the 11th century Norman armies—hardly to be distinguished from those of any other European state—conquered not only Anglo-Saxon England but also southern Italy and Sicily.

VIKING BELIEFS
In this Viking picture stone the god Woden is welcomed to Valhalla. Beneath him is his longship full of armed warriors.

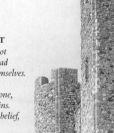

VIKING HELMET
Viking soldiers did not wear uniforms and had to dress and arm themselves. Iron helmets with noseguards, like this one, were worn by chieftains. Contrary to popular belief, Viking helmets had no horns.

THE STIRRUP

Stirrups came into use in Europe around the 9th century, but central Asian horsemen had already used them for about 800 years. It was once held that they revolutionized warfare, giving cavalry the stability to stage attacks with couched lances. However, many examples exist of heavy cavalry performing perfectly well without stirrups. More important was the adoption of a saddle with a raised pommel at the front and cantle at the back.

Top attaches to a strap that hangs from the saddle

Rider rests ball of foot here

MEDIEVAL IRON STIRRUP

NORMAN CASTLE
Begun in the 11th century, Rochester Castle in southeast England is one of the earliest Norman stone fortresses.

476–1492

BYZANTIUM SURVIVES

IN THE EARLY 6TH CENTURY the Byzantine emperor Justinian (483–565) recovered the lost regions of the Roman Empire in much of the western Mediterranean. His success, however, was short-lived: Italy, for example, had succumbed to the Lombards by the 580s. The Byzantine Empire retained its vigor, triumphing over the Persians in the 620s, but over the next 100 years Islam-inspired Arab conquests delivered a blow from which Constantinople never completely recovered. The Byzantine army remained a well-organized fighting force, and its armored cavalry was second to none, but from the 7th century Byzantium's stance was defensive. Even its most expansive phases were chiefly a search for more defensible frontiers.

JUSTINIAN'S CONQUESTS

Tricamarum

DATE December 15, 533	
FORCES Byzantines: 5,000 cavalry, 10,000 infantry, 20,000 sailors; Vandals: up to 50,000	
LOCATION West of Carthage, modern-day Tunisia	**CASUALTIES** No reliable estimates

In summer 533, Emperor Justinian sent an expedition to reconquer former Roman north Africa, which the Vandals had occupied since the 5th century. Led by the Byzantine general Belisarius, an army sailed from Constantinople on board 500 transports, under the escort of 92 warships. The force landed in Tunisia and advanced on the

BYZANTINE ARMY
Byzantine cavalry and infantry advancing to battle. Horsemen fought with bows, lances, and swords.

Vandal capital, Carthage, which it seized on September 15 after brushing aside the warriors of the Vandal king Gelimer. Gelimer, however, built up a new army in neighboring Numidia and returned to the offensive. As the Vandals drew nearer to Carthage, Belisarius came out to meet them, despite having doubts about the loyalty of his light-mounted archer horsemen, who were made up of Huns. His heavy cavalry, in contrast, which had advanced ahead of the infantry, charged at the Vandals as soon as they saw them, giving the enemy no time to prepare for battle. After intense hand-to-hand fighting the Vandals began to waver. Once they saw that a Byzantine victory was probable, the Huns joined in, delivering a thundering charge that shattered the Vandal forces. Gelimer escaped the rout but surrendered the following year.

c.505–565

BELISARIUS

Born in Illyria in the Balkans, Belisarius rose to prominence in the early 530s through his victories over Persia and his bloody suppression of a revolt in Constantinople. However, after conquering Ostrogothic Italy in 540 he was recalled by Emperor Justinian on suspicion of aspiring to rule the western empire. Although he fought many subsequent campaigns, Belisarius never fully regained Justinian's trust and was even briefly imprisoned in 562. The English historian Edward Gibbon (1737–94) praised him as "daring without rashness, prudent without fear."

JUSTINIAN'S CONQUESTS

Siege of Rome

	DATE 537–538
	FORCES Byzantines: 5,000 and 7,000 reinforcements; Ostrogoths: up to 50,000
LOCATION Rome, central Italy	**CASUALTIES** No reliable estimates

In 535 Emperor Justinian sent Belisarius to reconquer Italy from the Ostrogoths, who had ruled the country since 493. Belisarius first took Sicily, then marched north via Naples to enter Rome in December 536. Led by Vitiges, the Goths organized a counteroffensive, advancing to besiege Rome the following March. The siege lasted a year and nine days. The Goths' attempts to assault the city walls failed, wilting in the face of disciplined fire from Belisarius's experienced archers. Efforts to blockade the city also failed, for Belisarius received both troop reinforcements and food supplies during the siege, and sent his cavalry out on punitive raids into the surrounding country. Demoralized and decimated by disease, the Goths lifted the siege in March 538. Byzantine forces sallied from the city to attack them as they withdrew.

JUSTINIAN'S CONQUESTS

Taginae

	DATE June 552
	FORCES Byzantines: 20,000; Ostrogoths: 15,000
	CASUALTIES Ostrogoths: 6,000 killed
LOCATION Umbria, central Italy	

By 551, under the energetic leadership of Totila, the Ostrogoths had recovered most of Italy from the Byzantines. Justinian appointed an aged eunuch, Narses, to command an army to take on Totila. In the summer of 552 Narses marched around the head of the Adriatic coast into Italy and advanced south toward Rome. Totila blocked his path in a narrow mountain pass in the Apennines. The Gothic heavy cavalry, armed with lances, charged at their enemy, but came under concentrated crossfire from archers, both mounted and on foot, whom Narses had placed in advanced positions on the flanks. Thrown back in confusion, the Goths were then enveloped by the Byzantine armored cavalry. Totila was among those killed in the ensuing slaughter. Within two years, after another decisive victory at Casilinum, Narses had regained Italy for the empire.

JUSTINIAN'S CONQUESTS

Dara

	DATE 530
	FORCES Byzantines: 25,000; Persians: 40,000–50,000
LOCATION Byzantine fortress town of Dara, Armenia	**CASUALTIES** Byzantines: unknown; Persians: 8,000 killed

Twenty-two years before Taginae, Byzantine forces under Belisarius demonstrated their abilities with a victory over a numerically superior Persian army on the border between the two empires. The battle began with a prolonged exchange of arrow fire. Then the Persian armored cavalry charged with their lances, first on the right flank and then on the left. Each time they pushed back the Byzantine horsemen, only to be enveloped by mounted Hun archers whom Belisarius had positioned in between his heavier cavalry. Once the Persian horsemen had been savaged, the Persian infantry fled. Most escaped, as Belisarius restrained his cavalry from a potentially dangerous pursuit.

GREEK FIRE

The Byzantine weapon "Greek fire" was invented by the chemist Calinicus in around 670. A petroleum compound (the exact mix remains unknown), it was a primitive version of the incendiary device napalm. Soldiers sprayed with a pump or poured it into cartridges, which they launched at the enemy.

FIRE ATTACK
Greek fire was chiefly used in naval warfare, sprayed over enemy warships.

Nineveh

DATE
December 12, 627

FORCES
Byzantines: unknown;
Persians: unknown

CASUALTIES
No reliable estimates

LOCATION
Near present-day
Mosul, northern Iraq

In the early 7th century the fortunes of the Byzantine Empire were at a low ebb. The Persian armies of King Chosroes II had conquered Egypt, Syria, Armenia, and Anatolia, and were camped outside Constantinople. Emperor Heraclius resolved on a counteroffensive, and in 622 he sailed with an army to the north coast of Asia Minor. In a series of campaigns over the following years he harassed the Persians, building up his army's training and experience. In the spring of 627 he swept into Mesopotamia. In December he encountered a Persian army, led by the commander Razates, on a plain near the ruined ancient city of Nineveh. Battle was joined in the early morning and continued for 11 hours without a break. Heraclius, always in the thick of the fighting, eventually came face to face with Razates and severed his head with a single blow. The routed survivors of the Persian army fled, but the Byzantines pursued them to the gates of their capital, Ctesiphon, and then withdrew without attempting a siege. The defeated Chosroes, however, was overthrown in a palace coup and his successors sued for peace. Unfortunately for Heraclius, this great victory was almost immediately followed by a wave of Arab conquests, between the early 630s and 651, that negated all his gains.

HERACLIUS'S VICTORY
A 13th-century depiction of the battle of Nineveh, in which the Byzantine emperor killed three Persian generals, as well as the Persian commander, in single combat.

Pliska

DATE
July 26, 811

FORCES
Byzantines: numbers unknown; Bulgars: numbers unknown

LOCATION Near modern-day Shumen, northeast Bulgaria

CASUALTIES
No reliable estimates

By the early 9th century, while the Arab caliphate showed signs of weakening, the Byzantine Empire attempted to reassert itself. In 811 Emperor Nicephorus led an expedition against the Bulgar Khan Krum. The Byzantines captured the Bulgar capital, Pliska, but were then ambushed and slaughtered at a mountain pass. Nicephorus was decapitated and his skull used by Krum as a drinking cup.

Kleidion

DATE
July 29, 1014

FORCES
Byzantines: unknown;
Bulgars: 20,000

CASUALTIES
Byzantines: unknown;
Bulgars: 14,000
blinded

LOCATION North of Thessaloniki, northeastern Greece

Under the rule of Samuel, from 976 the Bulgars extended their territory at the expense of the Byzantine Empire, taking over Macedonia and much of Greece. Byzantine emperor Basil II fought back in a series of successful campaigns. By 1007 he had recovered the lost territories and was envisaging the conquest of the Bulgar state. To block a Byzantine invasion, Samuel built towers and palisades to defend key passes and valleys leading into the Bulgarian heartlands. In 1014 a large Byzantine army approached the pass of Kleidion, on the Strymon River. The Bulgars positioned forces behind fortifications they had constructed at the entrance to the pass. Basil accepted a plan proposed by one of his generals, Nicephorus Xiphias, to lead a small force through mountainous country and attack the Bulgars from the rear. The ploy worked to perfection. Panicked by the sudden appearance of Xiphias's men, the Bulgars turned to face them. Basil's main army was then able to overrun the unmanned fortifications,

BASIL THE BULGAR SLAYER
A coin shows the heavily bearded features of Basil II (r. 976–1025), an energetic ruler who was capable of extreme cruelty.

trapping the enemy in the pass. About two-thirds of the Bulgars were captured and on these, according to Byzantine historian John Skylitzes, Basil took dreadful vengeance. For every 100 prisoners, 99 were blinded and one was left with a single eye to lead them back to their king. Samuel apparently died of shock at the sight of his mutilated army. Four years later the Byzantines completed the conquest of Bulgaria.

FRANKISH POWER

AFTER THE COLLAPSE OF ROMAN RULE the Franks became the dominant force in Gaul. By the late 8th century, under Charlemagne, their authority extended over much of the former western Roman Empire. In 843, however, the Carolingian Empire was divided between Charlemagne's three grandsons. While Franks continued to rule the western regions, in the 10th century the German, eastern portion came under Saxon dominance. Saxon king Otto I did his best to reestablish Charlemagne's Empire, but France remained an independent kingdom.

Vouillé

DATE
Spring 507

FORCES
Franks: unknown;
Visigoths: unknown

LOCATION
Near Poitiers, west-central France

CASUALTIES
No reliable estimates

A series of military campaigns enabled Clovis (d. 511), king of the Salian Franks, to extend his authority well beyond his original territory in northeastern Gaul. Around 486 he defeated Syagrius, ruler of northwestern Gaul, while in about 496 he defeated the Alamanni, after which victory he converted to Christianity. The pretext for Clovis's invasion of the Visigothic kingdom, which culminated in the battle of Vouillé, was the Visigoths' Arian faith—a version of Christianity that originated with the 4th-century theologian Arius. But just as important for Clovis was the conquest of Visigothic territory in Gaul. In 507 Clovis led an army across the Loire River, and Alaric II, the Visigoth leader, advanced to defend his kingdom. When both sides met, Clovis triumphed over the Visigoths, Clovis reportedly slaying Alaric in person. The Franks took the Visigoth capital, Toulouse, and most of southwestern Gaul to add to their growing domain.

KEY

- Frankish kingdom in 751
- conquest of Pepin
- conquest of Charlemagne
- regions recognizing Charlemagne as overlord, at least nominally
- states of the Church, part of Charlemagne's empire
- division of Charlemagne's empire, with date of final conquest
- marches

EMPIRE OF THE FRANKS
Charlemagne expanded Frankish rule eastward, bringing France, Germany, and Italy together for the first time since the fall of Rome.

Poitiers

DATE
c.732

FORCES
Franks: 15,000–75,000;
Muslims: possibly 50,000

LOCATION Between Poitiers and Tours, west-central France

CASUALTIES
No reliable estimates

In 732 Abd ar-Rahman, the governor of newly conquered Muslim Spain, invaded neighboring Aquitaine with a substantial army, predominantly of Arab and Berber cavalry. Duke Eudo, the ruler of Aquitaine, fled to Austrasia in the eastern part of the Frankish kingdom. Abd ar-Rahman pursued the duke, threatening the safety of the Christian shrine of St. Martin at Tours. Charles Martel, the governor of Austrasia and effective ruler of the Franks, confronted the invaders somewhere between Poitiers and Tours. Both sides hesitated to commit to battle, but after a six-day stand-off the Muslims attacked. The Frankish knights fought dismounted, forming a tightly packed square that they defended with sword, spear, and shield against the Muslim cavalry. The Franks held formation, at one point surrounding and killing Abd ar-Rahman himself, and the Muslims eventually gave up and withdrew. This victory was traditionally seen as a

"The northern peoples remained immobile as a wall, holding together like a glacier in the cold regions, and in the blink of an eye annihilated the Arabs with the sword. The people of Austrasia, greater in number of soldiers and formidably armed, killed…Abd ar-Rahman when they found him, striking him on the chest."

WITNESS TO WAR

ANONYMOUS

The writer of the anonymous *Chronicle* of 754 described the resistance of the Franks to the Muslims at the battle of Poitiers.

turning point in history, the moment at which Christian Europe stemmed the tide of Arab conquest. More recently, historians have emphasized that the battle had little importance for the Muslim world, even if it was of great significance to the Franks.

CLASH OF ARMS
An illuminated manuscript depicts a cavalry clash at Poitiers. For much of the battle, however, the Franks fought dismounted.

Charlemagne's Saxon Campaigns

DATE
772–799

FORCES
Franks: unknown;
Saxons: unknown

CASUALTIES
No reliable estimates

LOCATION
Saxony and
Westphalia, Germany

In the 770s the Saxons rebelled against Frankish overlordship and carried out raids into Frankish territory. Almost every year, Charlemagne sent forces to subdue them. Occasionally the Saxons were successful, as in 782, when Charlemagne's cavalry came to grief against a well-prepared defensive line. But mostly the size of Charlemagne's forces and his ability to invade Saxon territory from several directions at once gave him the upper hand. Widukind, the Saxon leader, surrendered in 784 and submitted to baptism, but campaigns against the Saxons continued until the end of the 8th century.

742–814

CHARLEMAGNE

Charlemagne was the grandson of Charles Martel and the son of the Franks' first Carolingian king, Pépin. The first three decades of his reign was a period of conquest and expansion. By the time he was crowned emperor by Pope Leo III on Christmas Day 800 Charlemagne had conquered Lombardy (northern Italy), subdued the Saxons, and defeated the Avars and Slavs. He dedicated the later years of his reign to consolidating the defenses of an empire that stretched from northeastern Spain to Denmark. The secret of Charlemagne's military success was his ability to mobilize and supply large forces for annual campaigns over long distances, and later to provide permanent garrisons for fortresses on distant borders.

Roncesvalles

DATE
August 15, 778

FORCES
Franks: unknown;
Basques: unknown

CASUALTIES
No reliable estimates

LOCATION The
Pyrenees, Navarre,
northeast Spain

In 778 Charlemagne made his first expedition into Spain but found his way checked by Muslims. While the Frankish army was returning across the Pyrenees, stretched out in a long column through a narrow mountain pass, lightly armed Basques ambushed the rearguard. Among the slain was a count named Roland. The ambush became the subject of an Old French epic poem, "The Song of Roland." In the poem, the Basques have become Muslims, and Roland Charlemagne's nephew. Roland refuses to blow a horn to call for help, feeling that this would show a lack of knightly valor.

FRANKISH KNIGHTS
Cavalry were the core of Frankish armies. The charge with forward-pointing lance, shown here, was common by the 11th century.

Lechfeld

DATE
August 10, 955

FORCES
Germans: unknown;
Magyars: unknown

CASUALTIES
No reliable estimates

LOCATION On the Lech
River, near Augsburg,
Bavaria

In the 9th century the Magyars, horsemen from central Asia, began to mount destructive raids into the former Carolingian Empire. In 955 they invaded Bavaria and besieged Augsburg. Otto I, the Saxon king of Germany, led a force of up to 10,000 heavy cavalry to relieve the city. The Magyars, who greatly outnumbered the Germans, unhesitatingly gave battle. Their faster-moving horsemen

CRUEL VICTORY
A 19th-century painting of the battle of Lechfeld bathes Otto I in light. After the battle, hundreds of Magyar prisoners had their noses and ears cut off.

quickly outflanked the Germans but became distracted by the chance to plunder the enemy camp. Otto led a charge on the captured camp, routing the dismounted Magyars, before turning his forces to attack the main body of the enemy. Riding through their volley of arrows, his cavalry smashed into the Magyars and drove them from the field. There were no more Magyar raids. The victory confirmed Otto's authority in Germany.

FRANKISH WEAPONS

The trade in Frankish weapons, from Iceland to Russia, suggests the regard in which they were held in early medieval Europe. During the 9th century short Frankish swords disappeared from use, while the edges of longer swords began to taper from hilt to tip, increasing their maneuverability.

FRANKISH SWORDS AND HELMET FROM THE 6TH AND 7TH CENTURIES

Double-edged iron blade

Missing grip would have been made of wood covered with leather or bone

Parallel edges gave the sword power but made it heavy

Cheek guard

VIKINGS AND NORTHMEN

THE VIKINGS ENTER HISTORY in the late 8th and 9th centuries as sea raiders, terrorizing Europe from Dublin to Constantinople. These outstanding shipborne warriors were also traders, explorers, and settlers, and the period of hit-and-run raids was followed in some areas by permanent settlement. Over time, improved political organization in Scandinavia turned raiding into the more ambitious warfare waged by the kings of Denmark and Norway. In 911, in return for a promise of good behavior, the Frankish king Charles III granted Vikings territory in northern France. Thus Normandy was founded and Vikings became Normans ("Northmen"), in which guise their military enterprises continued, with conquests ranging from England to Sicily.

KEY

- areas settled by Vikings
- areas of Viking influence
- → Viking voyages, trade routes, and raids
- • Viking settlement
- 844 date of Viking voyage, raid, or settlement
- ---- frontiers c.1000

VIKING REACH
The Vikings' superb longships allowed their navigators to explore lands near and far, including North America, Russia, and the Byzantine Empire.

WARFARE IN THE MIDDLE AGES

▨ **VIKING RAIDS**

Lindisfarne

DATE	
	793
FORCES	
	Vikings: unknown; Anglo-Saxons: unknown
LOCATION	**CASUALTIES**
Northeast coast of England	No reliable estimates

"It is nearly 350 years that we and our forefathers have inhabited this most lovely land, and never before has such terror appeared as we have now suffered from a pagan race...." Such was the response of the scholar Alcuin of York to the shocking news of the sack of Lindisfarne by Scandinavian warriors in 793. Up until this date the Anglo-Saxon kingdoms of England, established by invading Saxons, Angles, and Jutes in the 5th century, enjoyed a comfortable sense of security from outside attack. Nothing showed this more clearly than the siting of the Lindisfarne monastery, a famed center of Christian learning, on

VIKING HELMET
Many Viking helmets had "goggles" to protect cheeks, as well as a nosepiece.

an island just off the coast of Northumbria. When Viking warships came to raid across the North Sea, Lindisfarne was an appallingly exposed target. The 11th-century chronicler Simeon of Durham related how the raiders "laid everything waste with grievous plundering, trampled the holy places with polluted feet...and seized all the treasures of the holy church." Some monks were put to the sword; some were drowned; some were taken away

VIKING SPEARS
Vikings used short-headed spears for stabbing or throwing; long-headed spears were often cavalry weapons.

in chains, probably to be sold as slaves. With such rich plunder to be had it is not surprising that the Vikings felt encouraged to return. In the 790s attacks such as that on Lindisfarne were only scattered incidents. But from the 830s raids resumed with greater frequency around the coasts of mainland Europe, with Utrecht and Antwerp among the first targets. In the 840s inland France was ravaged as the Vikings sailed or rowed their warships up the Seine and the Loire rivers. In 845 a fleet of 120 ships led by the Viking Ragnar attacked Paris for the first time. The Frankish king Charles the Bald had no option but to buy them off with 7,000 pounds of silver. Soon, however, Vikings began to winter in France; responding to population growth in Scandinavia they began to envisage settlement rather than plunder.

MEDIEVAL RUINS
The ruined church and priory at Lindisfarne, both built at a later date, evoke the atmosphere of the 793 disaster.

VIKING RAIDS

Raid on Constantinople

DATE	Summer 860
FORCES	Vikings: 200 ships; Byzantines: unknown
LOCATION	Constantinople (modern-day Istanbul)
CASUALTIES	No reliable estimates

On June 18, 860, without warning, a fleet of warships sailed down the Bosphorus toward Constantinople, burning and pillaging every town, village, and monastery that it passed before anchoring opposite the walls of the Byzantine capital. The warriors on these ships called themselves "Rus," but they were almost certainly Vikings who had brought their longships along trade routes from the Baltic. Byzantine chroniclers recorded with horror the acts the raiders committed, but the Vikings made no attempt to assault Constantinople's formidable city walls. Instead, in a pattern familiar to western Europeans, they took their plunder and disappeared. In the 10th and 11th centuries Vikings would return, however, giving rise to the Varangian Guard, the elite troops of the Byzantine emperor's household.

VIKING LONGSHIPS

The sleek and graceful longship was the key both to the Vikings' raids and their voyages of discovery. Its strengths were speed and versatility. Capable of sailing the open seas instead of hugging coasts, it allowed its crew to arrive without warning. Its shallow draft meant it could land on beaches, with no need of harbors, and because it had a prow at both ends it could make a rapid getaway when required. It had a square sail but the Vikings could row it, too, giving it great maneuverability. Its shape and draft also meant that it could progress up shallow rivers, and it was light enough to be carried overland, at least for short distances—vital for inland journeys that involved moving from one river to another.

SPECIFICATION

Origin	Norway	**Date**	c.800
Length	71ft (22m)	**Crew**	30 oarsmen
Width	16ft (5m)	**Speed**	Up to 10 knots

THE OSEBERG SHIP
This ship was reconstructed from remains discovered in a burial mound in 1904. It is the earliest known Viking vessel to have a mast.

Stout pine mast

Sail of woven cloth

Elaborately carved stern prow

Oars used when there was no wind

HULL *The Viking longship was clinker-built, with a hull made of overlapping planks. The wood used was oak.*

RUDDER *The longship was steered by a rudder-paddle mounted aft on the starboard side.*

DANISH SETTLEMENT OF ENGLAND

Edington

DATE	May 878
FORCES	Possibly 5,000 on each side
LOCATION	Near Chippenham, southwest England
CASUALTIES	No reliable estimates

In 865 a Danish Viking force caused an upheaval within the Anglo-Saxon kingdoms of England. Within five years Northumbria, Mercia, and East Anglia were all under Danish rule. At the start of January 878, Danish forces led by King Guthrum infiltrated Wessex, the remaining Anglo-Saxon kingdom, and surprised its king, Alfred, at his royal manor at Chippenham. With only his personal bodyguard to defend him, Alfred had to

ALFRED JEWEL
This jewel bears the inscription "Alfred had me made" on its rim, suggesting it belonged to Alfred the Great.

flee to an area of marsh and woodland, where he established a fort from which to harass Guthrum's forces. Surprisingly, in May 878 Alfred was able to summon a substantial army to join him and march on Chippenham, which Guthrum had made his base. The two armies met at Edington. Alfred's contemporary biographer, Asser, tells how the king fought "fiercely with a compact shield wall against the entire Viking army [until] he destroyed the Vikings with great slaughter." In the wake of this defeat Guthrum was forced to withdraw from Wessex. An agreement in 885 formally divided England between an Anglo-Saxon area and the Viking Danelaw.

CAVALRY SWORDFIGHT
The Vikings adapted to land warfare in the 9th century, as this carving from a burial site in Oseberg, Norway, shows.

VIKING RAIDS

Siege of Paris

DATE	November 885– September 886
FORCES	Vikings: possibly 700 ships and 30,000 men; Franks: unknown
LOCATION	Paris, France
CASUALTIES	No reliable estimates

Although the Franks built fortified bridges to block major rivers, they could not stop the Vikings penetrating deep inland, and in November 885 Viking forces reached Paris. After their first attempts to seize the city failed, they settled down to a siege. The defense of Paris was led Count Odo and Bishop Gozelin, who used ballistas and stone-throwing mangonels to repel attacks on the city walls. Although the Vikings took one of the strongpoints outside the city, they could not break inside. A first relief expedition, led by Duke Henry of Saxony, was seen off, but in the late summer of 886 the Frankish emperor Charles the Fat arrived with a larger army. Instead of fighting the Vikings he paid them a large indemnity to lift the siege and gave them permission to ravage Burgundy, which was refusing to acknowledge his imperial authority.

VIKING RAIDS

Maldon

DATE
August 991

FORCES
Vikings: 3,000; Anglo-Saxons: possibly a similar number

LOCATION
Maldon, Essex, southeast England

CASUALTIES
No reliable estimates

During the 10th century the Anglo-Saxon kings, successors of Alfred the Great, conquered Danish England to rule the whole country. From the 980s, however, a new wave of Norse raiders arrived to prey upon the English coastal population. One of these raids, in Maldon, Essex, became

DEATH MARSH
The marshland by the Blackwater River in Essex, where the battle of Maldon was fought.

the subject of an Anglo-Saxon poem. In the summer of 991 a fleet of warships headed by Olaf Tryggvason (the future king of Norway) sailed along the coast of Essex. The earl of the county, Byrhtnoth, set out with his *thegns* (personal retainers) and a local militia to confront them. The raiders made camp at Northey island, connected to mainland Essex at low tide by a causeway. Byrhtnoth took up position at the end of this causeway. When the tide went out, the raiders advanced to the mainland but found their way blocked. Seeing that a real battle was impossible in such a confined space, Tryggvason called on Byrhtnoth to let the raiders on to the mainland so they could fight properly. This Byrhtnoth did, perhaps confident that he could defeat the enemy. A fierce fight ensued, in which the earl was killed by a spear. Most of his army fled, but the thegns fought on around Byrhtnoth's body until they were all dead.

VIKING WEAPONS

Axes, swords, and spears of iron were the main Viking weapons. Their long double-edged swords, made by skilled Norse craftsmen, were designed to deliver slashing blows rather than for stabbing. Viking warriors probably wielded them in much the same way as their fearsome battle axes. Horsemen and infantry used long-headed spears to thrust at enemies from behind a shield wall. The Vikings also employed missile weapons such as throwing spears, bows, and throwing axes.

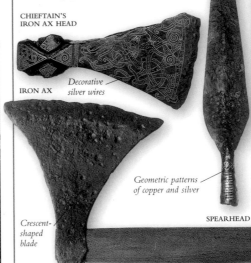

IRON SWORDS

CHIEFTAIN'S IRON AX HEAD

IRON AX

Decorative silver wires

Geometric patterns of copper and silver

Crescent-shaped blade

SPEARHEAD

VIKING SETTLEMENT IN IRELAND

Clontarf

DATE
April 23, 1014

FORCES
c.7,000 on both sides

CASUALTIES
Brian Boru's forces: 1,600–4,000 killed; Vikings and Leinstermen: up to 6,000 killed

LOCATION
Just north of Dublin, Ireland

The Vikings established themselves in Ireland during the 9th century, with Dublin as their major trading center.

Outside Viking areas, fractious Gaelic tribes competed for power. In 1002 Brian Boru, king of Munster, claimed leadership of the Gaels as High King of Ireland. Mael Morda, king of Leinster, was among those who resisted this claim. Mael allied himself with Sigtrygg Silkbeard, the Viking ruler of Dublin. In the spring of 1014 Brian raised an army, including a Viking contingent, to attack Dublin. In response, the Dublin Vikings and Leinstermen sailed to Clontarf, behind Brian's camp, where they drew up in a battle line to face Brian's army. (Brian himself apparently did not fight, since it was Good Friday.) The Vikings on both sides were generally better armed and armored than the Gaels, but Brian's army carried the day. Put to flight, their enemies could neither reach their beached ships nor cross the Liffey River back into Dublin. Most were slaughtered. Brian Boru was also killed, however, when fleeing Vikings attacked his camp. Sigtrygg, who had remained in Dublin, kept control of the Viking settlement, but the Vikings ceased to be an independent force in Ireland's power struggles.

VIKING CHAINMAIL
By the 11th century most Norse warriors wore knee-length coats of mail, made of interwoven metal links.

DANISH INVASIONS OF ENGLAND

Ashingdon

DATE
October 18, 1016

FORCES
Danes: unknown; Anglo-Saxons: unknown

LOCATION Ashingdon, Essex, southeast England

CASUALTIES
No reliable estimates

In 1013 the Danish king Sweyn Forkbeard invaded England and drove the Anglo-Saxon ruler Aethelred II into exile. When Sweyn died in 1014 Aethelred returned to the throne, but died himself as Sweyn's son Cnut led an army against the king at London. Aethelred's son Edmund Ironside contested Cnut's subsequent rule, and, after a number of indecisive engagements, both sides met at Ashingdon. The battle was evenly fought until Edmund's Mercian contingent fled the field, possibly in an act of treachery. The rest of the English battle line broke, to be heavily cut down by Cnut's army. The Anglo-Saxon Chronicle records that "all the nobility of England were there destroyed." Edmund survived the battle only to die six weeks later, leaving Cnut as king of all England.

995–1035

KING CNUT

Cnut came to England in 1013 with his father, King Sweyn of Denmark. The Danish fleet hailed him as king of England in 1014, but he had to fight to secure the throne, first against Aethelred and then against Edmund. In 1019 Cnut succeeded his elder brother as king of Denmark and in 1028 conquered Norway. He strengthened his hold on the English throne by marrying Aethelred's widow, Emma of Normandy, although he also had a Danish wife. Cnut was generally respected as a wise and powerful ruler.

(see battle plan)

NORMAN CONQUESTS
Civitate

DATE
June 18, 1053

FORCES
Normans: 3,000 cavalry; Imperial and papal forces: chiefly infantry

LOCATION
Apulia, southern Italy

CASUALTIES
No reliable estimates

The Normans retained the ruthless enterprise of their Viking ancestors—nowhere was this more clearly shown than in southern Italy, where the Norman Hauteville family built up such a power base that, in 1053, Pope Leo IX invited the Holy Roman Emperor Henry III to lead an army against them. In a battle of cavalry against infantry, the Normans trounced their enemies, with the young Robert de Hauteville, later known as Robert Guiscard ("the cunning"), distinguishing himself. The Normans took the pope prisoner, holding him for 10 months. Robert went on to establish Norman rule in Apulia, Calabria, and Sicily, and to mount an invasion of the Byzantine Empire.

NORMAN ARROWS

ANGLO-SAXONS VERSUS NORSE
Stamford Bridge

DATE
September 25, 1066

FORCES
Anglo-Saxons: 10,000; Norse: 5,000

LOCATION 8 miles (13km) east of York, north-central England

CASUALTIES
Norse: 4,000 killed; Anglo-Saxons: no reliable estimates

In January 1066 Harold Godwinson became king of England. His right to the throne was contested by William of Normandy, while he also faced the hostility of his brother Tostig, ejected from the earldom of Northumbria the previous year. Tostig invited the Norwegian king Harald Hardrada to join him in an invasion. They crossed the North Sea in 300 ships, defeated an army led by the earls of Mercia and Northumbria, and occupied York. Moving north with astonishing speed, King Harold came upon the invaders at Stamford Bridge. According to a Norse account, the English attacked first, but a frenzied counterattack led by Harald almost won the day. The battle turned, however, when Harald was killed by an arrow in the throat. Harold offered Tostig peace, but he rejected it, encouraged by the arrival of Norse reinforcements. But these arrivals were exhausted, and after more savage fighting—in which Tostig was cut down with most of his men—King Harold was victorious.

NORMAN CONQUESTS
Hastings

DATE
October 14, 1066

FORCES
Normans: 7,000–15,000; Anglo-Saxons: 9,000

LOCATION
6 miles (10km) north of Hastings, southeast England

CASUALTIES
(Possibly) Normans: 2,000; Anglo-Saxons: 4,000

Three days after Stamford Bridge, William of Normandy, who had crossed the Channel with up to 700 ships, landed at Pevensey, southern England. King Harold rode south with his housecarls, the elite royal bodyguard, and dispatched messengers

BAYEUX TAPESTRY
Harold's housecarls fight to the death with sword and ax in this scene, while Norman cavalry press forward with spears and shields.

KEY
- English line
- Norman archers
- Norman spearmen
- Norman cavalry
- feint retreat

to order the shires to send levies. On October 14, outside Hastings, Harold's men formed up in a tight infantry phalanx at the top of Senlac ridge. The Normans had a more varied force, with archers, armored infantry, and several thousand cavalry. In the early stages of the battle the English shield wall held firm, rendering arrow fire ineffective and repulsing charges by Norman infantry and cavalry with their spears and axes. At one point a rumor spread that William had been killed and he had to show himself to rally his men. Then the tide of battle turned because the English lost formation, possibly in the excitement of imminent success or, according to one account, because of several feigned retreats the Normans made (see battle plan).

The English right wing collapsed, but a shrinking body of weary housecarls fought on until Harold died, possibly shot in the eye by an arrow. Fleeing Anglo-Saxon soldiers turned and ambushed a number of pursuing Norman horsemen, but the battle was won and the English throne William's.

1027–1087
WILLIAM THE CONQUEROR

The bastard son of Robert, Duke of Normandy, William acceded to the dukedom at the age of seven and was lucky to survive childhood—three of his guardians were killed. He asserted himself with the necessary savagery once he came of age, however. William showed diplomatic skill in winning papal blessing for his invasion of England and ruthlessness in stamping his rule on the country after Hastings.

WARRIORS OF ISLAM

FROM THE ESTABLISHMENT OF A Muslim state in the 620s, the expansion of Islam was astonishingly swift. Within a century the Islamic caliphate controlled much of Asia, North Africa, and part of Europe. These conquests were achieved without innovative technology or tactics, but were the triumph of a militant ideology, inspiring believers with a fighting spirit and an urge to conquer in the name of their faith.

VAN CASTLE
This ancient fortress in eastern Anatolia was taken over by the Muslim Abbasids in the 9th century CE and later rebuilt and strengthened by the Seljuk and Ottoman Turks.

KEY

Muslim lands by 634	649 date of Muslim conquest
Muslim lands by 656	Byzantine Empire c.610
Muslim lands by 756	Sassanian Empire c.610
Muslim raid, with date	Frankish Empire c.610
Muslim victory, with date	Abbasid caliphate at its greatest extent c.800
Muslim defeat, with date	further expansion of Islam

RAPID RISE
In the century after Muhammad's death Islam created an empire to rival Ancient Rome's, reaching as far as northern Spain and central Asia.

PROPHET AND CALIPHS

Although in principle war between Muslims was forbidden, war against unbelievers was permitted by the tenets of Islam and encouraged by its early history. The prophet Muhammad (c.570-632), founder of Islam, was also a military leader who fought and was wounded during the war between the north Arabian cities of Medina and Mecca. During the brief rule of Abu Bakr, the first of the "caliphs" who led the Muslims after Muhammad's death, Arab Muslim forces had already begun to push outside Arabia. By the foundation of the Umayyad caliphate in 661, with its capital in Damascus, the Arabs ruled Egypt, Persia, Palestine, and Syria. Within a century they penetrated to the east as far as Afghanistan and as far west as Spain and central France. The unity of Islam was an ideal not realized, the founding of the Umayyad dynasty itself sowing the seeds of the split between Sunni and Shia Muslims that has persisted to this day. In the 750s the Umayyads were bloodily overthrown by the Abbasids, who moved the caliphate's center to Baghdad. Rival caliphs were proclaimed in Cordova and in Egypt (the Shiite Fatimids) in the 9th and 10th centuries. Internal disputes necessarily hobbled Islam's expansion.

Iron helmet with decorative spike

Chain mail

ARMORED WARRIOR
By the period of the Crusades (1099–1291), Muslim warriors were wearing chain mail and distinctive spiked helmets such as the example shown here.

FIGHTING TECHNIQUES

Arab armies were originally notable largely for their use of camels, which gave them great mobility, carrying equipment and supplies as well as soldiers. Yet the Arabs proved quick learners: adapting much from the military techniques of the Byzantines, they developed effective cavalry and even learned the art of naval warfare. But over time Arabs ceased to be simple warriors of Islam. From the 9th century, their aristocracy lost its taste for warfare. Instead, Muslim rulers co-opted men from the Turkish tribes of central Asia to fight in their armies. These soldiers were slaves, even if of an unusual kind: some slave-commanders became wealthy and privileged members of society. This preference for slave soldiers was to become a feature of Muslim armies. A saying of the vizier Nizam al-Mulk (1018–92) summed up the attitude of Muslim rulers: "One obedient slave is better than 300 sons, for the latter desire their father's death, the former long life for his master." But the passing of military power to non-Arabs was inevitably followed over time by a transfer of political power.

CERAMIC CAVALRYMAN
This bowl was made in 9th-century Persia. Persian arms and armor—for example, helmets—influenced Islamic warfare.

BERBERS AND TURKS

By the 11th century the Arabs had ceased to be the effective rulers of the Muslim world. In the west, the Almoravids and their successors, the Almohads drew their support from the Berbers, taking control of Morocco and Muslim Spain. In the east, Islamicized Turks seized most of northern and central Asia, including Arabia. The Turks were superb horsemen who traditionally fought as mounted archers, firing their composite bows in hit-and-run skirmishing style. When they also learned to engage at close quarters with lance, mace, and saber, they became a formidable enemy. In the 10th and 11th centuries the Ghazni Turks, who had been the sword arm of the Abbasids in central Asia, formed their own empire, ruling from eastern Persia to Afghanistan. During the 11th century they were superseded by another Turkish group, the Seljuks, who became the dominant force in Muslim Asia. Under the warrior leaders Toghril and Alp Arslan, the Seljuks extended their rule to the Mediterranean and began to Islamicize Anatolia (modern-day Turkey).

SELJUK SOLDIERS
The Seljuk Turks emerged as a dominant force in the Islamic world in the 11th century, decisively defeating the Byzantines at Manzikert in 1071.

NEW WAVES

By the 12th century there were signs that the Islamic tide was ebbing. In Spain the Christian Reconquista (see p.88) was well under way. Disunity among the Seljuks had allowed Christian crusaders to seize Jerusalem and establish new states in the eastern Mediterranean. In the 13th century most of Spain was lost by Islam, while Muslim Asia felt the full fury of Mongol attacks under Genghis Khan and his successors. Muslims ruled much of northern India but were solidly resisted by Hindu Rajput kingdoms and, from the 14th century, by the empire of Vijayanagar in southern India.

Yet Islam retained a power of renewal, capable of fresh waves of military aggression. The slave soldiers of Egypt, the Mamelukes, proved capable of defeating both the Mongols and the crusader states, while in Anatolia in the early 1300s the Turkish sultan Osman I began the slow build-up of the Ottoman Empire.

INDIAN ARMY
Soldiers such as these, depicted in a frieze at a palace of the Hindu Vijayanagar kingdom in southern India, held back the spread of Islam beyond north and central India.

DOME OF THE ROCK
One of Islam's holiest sites, this shrine was built in Jerusalem in the late 7th century, some 50 years after the Arabs' capture of the city in 638. It was designed by Byzantine architects.

476-1492

ARAB ADVANCE

WITHIN TWO DECADES OF THE formation of the first Muslim state in 622, Arabs had conquered the Sassanian Persian Empire, the eastern Mediterranean, and Egypt. Although the Byzantine Empire held out, largely due to the impregnability of Constantinople's walls, within another century Muslim armies had conquered the North African coast and most of the Iberian peninsula. In the 9th century Sicily underwent an Islamic invasion, and even parts of Italy were occupied. The Muslim *jihad* (holy war) had brought much of the globe under Islamic rule.

CAMPAIGNS AGAINST THE BYZANTINES

Yarmuk

DATE
August 20, 636

FORCES
Byzantines: up to 80,000; Arabs: up to 40,000

LOCATION Yarmuk River, south of Sea of Galilee, Palestine

CASUALTIES
Byzantines: possibly 70,000

In 634 Arab forces invaded Palestine and Syria, taking major cities from the Byzantines, including Damascus. In 636 the Byzantine emperor Heraclius responded by raising a large army that advanced through Syria, forcing the Muslims to abandon Damascus. Arab forces led by the inspired general Khalid al-Walid confronted the Byzantines by the Yarmuk River.

> "The battle fought at al-Yarmuk was of the fiercest and bloodiest kind....the Greeks and their followers tied themselves to each other by chains, so that no one might set his hope on flight. By Allah's help some 70,000 of them were put to death, and their remnants took to flight…"

WITNESS TO WAR
AL-BALADHURI

The Arab historian al-Baladhuri (d. c.892) described the battle of Yarmuk in his work *The Origins of the Islamic State*, which he based on oral history and earlier writings. His account of the battle also tells how the Arabs were welcomed by many people in Syria and Palestine, who resented Byzantine rule.

A lengthy period of skirmishing ensued, but on August 20 a sandstorm blew up, the wind coming from behind the Arabs' backs. Al-Walid mounted a tremendous charge against the enemy encampment. Blinded by sand and dust, most of the Byzantines were slaughtered. The Arabs reoccupied Damascus and, in February 638, captured the holy city of Jerusalem.

MUSLIMS VERSUS SASSANIANS

Qadisiyya

DATE
June 1, 637

FORCES
Arabs: 30,000; Persians: 50,000

LOCATION Near al-Hirrah, south of Baghdad, Iraq

CASUALTIES
No reliable estimates

When Arab armies, inspired by their new Muslim faith, headed north from Arabia in the 630s, they advanced into a power vacuum created by the exhaustion of the two great regional empires, Byzantium and Sassanian Persia. Although the Sassanians coped with early Muslim Arab incursions, in 637 a large army commanded by Saad ibn abi-Waqqas advanced toward the Persian capital, Ctesiphon. Meeting a numerically superior Sassanian army at a canal of the Euphrates River, the Arabs' aggression and determination secured an outstanding victory. They were able to continue their advance, crossing the Tigris River and staging an unopposed triumphal entry into Ctesiphon. Sassanian resistance continued in other parts of the empire until another Arab victory, at Nahavand in 641, destroyed the last remnants of the once great Persian army.

CAMPAIGNS AGAINST THE BYZANTINES

Siege of Constantinople

DATE
717–718

FORCES
Arabs: 160,000–200,000
Byzantines: unknown

CASUALTIES
Arabs: possibly 130,000–170,000

LOCATION
Constantinople (modern Istanbul, Turkey)

Forty years after the Arabs' first, unsuccessful siege of the Byzantine capital (674–678), they returned for a second attempt. An 80,000-strong army led by Maslama crossed into Europe to besiege Constantinople from the land, while 1,800 war galleys sailed into the sea of Marmara, south of the city. The Byzantine emperor Leo III led the defense with skill and determination—Maslama found Constantinople's walls unassailable. Meanwhile the Arab galleys proved unable to sail up the Bosphorus strait in the face of sorties by the Byzantine navy, armed with its famous incendiary weapon, "Greek fire." With the Bosphorus open to their shipping, the Byzantines kept Constantinople supplied from the Black Sea, and it was the besiegers rather than the besieged who suffered during the

UNDER SIEGE
Unlike the Byzantine fortress in this Persian depiction, Constantinople's walls proved impervious to successive waves of attackers right up until the 15th century.

STRATEGIC POSITION
The Arabs desired Constantinople for its position between the Aegean and the Black seas and its control of vital trade routes.

harsh winter of 717–718. The Arabs were reduced to eating their donkeys and camels; disease killed thousands. In the spring the arrival of an Egyptian fleet reinforced the Arab army, but further assaults on the city failed. In July the Bulgars—temporary allies of their Byzantine neighbors—attacked Maslama's demoralized forces, inflicting heavy casualties. The next month the Arabs abandoned the siege. Part of their army retreated back through Anatolia. The rest tried to withdraw by sea, but a storm devastated the fleet and only five galleys survived.

MUSLIM WAR OF SUCCESSION

Karbala

DATE
October 10, 680

FORCES
Umayyads: 4,000;
Husayn: 70

CASUALTIES
Husayn: 70

LOCATION 55 miles
(88km) southwest of
Baghdad, central Iraq

Internal divisions within Islam always threatened to put a brake on its military expansion. In 661, after the murder of the prophet Muhammad's son-in-law Ali, the wealthy Umayyad family claimed the caliphate—the secular and religious leadership of the Muslim world. Some Muslims resented the Umayyad accession, however, regarding the descendants of Ali as the only legitimate claimants. Tension mounted until 680, when Mu'awiyah, the first Umayyad caliph, died and the leadership passed to his son, Yazid. Opponents of the Umayyads rose up in the ancient Iraqi city of Kufah, inviting Ali's second son, Husayn, to join them and lead their resistance movement. Husayn set off for Kufah from Mecca in Arabia, accompanied only by his family, personal retinue, and harem. Yazid, meanwhile, sent Umar, son of Saad ibn abi-Waqqas, the victor of Qadisiyya, to intercept Husayn with a substantial army.

CAMEL WARRIORS
One account of Husayn's death tells how horses trampled on his body. Arab warriors did fight on camels, but they were more commonly used for transport, aiding the movement of armies.

The Umayyad general came upon Husayn at Karbala. For eight days Husayn appealed to his opponents' sense of faith and humanity, but to no avail: he, along with all his men, was slaughtered. His head was cut off and sent to Yazid as proof that the job had been done. Karbala was an ambush rather than a battle, but it had profound results. It secured the Umayyad caliphate, but at the same time made a martyr of Husayn, and confirmed the split between Shiites— believers in the succession from Ali—and Sunnis within Islam. The Shiite version of Islam is the dominant belief in Iran and Iraq to the present day, while Husayn's death is remembered on Ashura, a day of public mourning.

MUSLIM INVASION OF SPAIN

Covadonga

DATE
c.718

FORCES
Visigoths: 300;
Muslims: unknown

CASUALTIES
Unknown

LOCATION
Asturias,
northwest Spain

By 710 the Arabs had conquered North Africa from Egypt to Morocco. The Arab governor of this vast region, Musa ibn Nusair, sent an exploratory force across the straits into southern Spain, which, in 711, defeated the Visigothic king of Spain, Roderic. The Visigothic kingdom collapsed very quickly as a result of this defeat because most of the high aristocracy was

NATIONAL HERO
Pelayo, the victor at Covadonga, was later celebrated as a hero of the Spanish Reconquista and the founder of Asturias.

killed, and in that sense the battle was similar to Hastings (see p.71). By 721, the Muslims had subdued all Visigothic resistance except in the remote northern areas of the peninsula, most notably in the mountains of the Asturias. When the Arabs tried to expand their control into the region they were defeated by a local aristocrat called Pelagius (Pelayo). As a result, an independent Christian kingdom of the Asturias came into being and in time formed the core of the later kingdom of Castile. Nothing is known for certain of Pelayo's victory at a place called Covadonga, but within half a century several legends had grown up around it, alleging that the Arab army numbered 187,000 men (of whom 124,000 were killed) and that God had turned the Muslims' missiles around in mid-flight and sent them back against them. The importance of Covadonga, probably little more than a skirmish, lies in the fact that it acquired an almost religious status as the first step in the Spanish Reconquista (see p.88).

MUSLIM INVASION OF SICILY

Siege of Palermo

DATE
831

FORCES
Arabs: 10,000 (before reinforcements);
Byzantines: unknown

CASUALTIES
No reliable estimates

LOCATION
North coast
of Sicily

From the mid-7th century, Sicily, then part of the Byzantine Empire, came under attack from Arab sea raiders, who plundered its cities and terrorized its population. There was no Arab attempt to occupy the island, however,

ARAB VICTORY
This Byzantine illustration is of the Arab conquest of Messina, in northeastern Sicily, which fell to the invaders in 842.

until the powerful Muslim Aghlabid state established itself at Kairouan in North Africa at the start of the 9th century. Separated from Sicily by a narrow stretch of sea, the Aghlabids were inevitably tempted to mount an invasion. A pretext came when the Byzantine admiral Euphemius, the loser in a power struggle in the Sicilian port of Syracuse, asked the Aghlabids to help him regain the city. In June 827 the Aghlabid ruler Ziyadat Allah I sent a fleet of 70 ships to land 10,000 men and 700 horses on the island. At first Byzantine resistance was too strong, but the Aghlabid forces were eventually joined by troops from Muslim Spain, and together seized Palermo in 831. The city became the seat of an emirate, or province, and was used as a base for Muslim incursions into southern Italy. It remained in Muslim hands until the Normans took it in 1071.

ISLAMIC IMPACT

ONE RESULT OF THE MUSLIM ARAB VICTORIES in the 7th and 8th centuries was the Islamicization of the mainly Turkish peoples of central Asia. Consequently the Turks became warriors of Islam, putting their traditional fighting skills at the service of the faith in "slave" armies employed by Arab rulers. Soon these Turkish slave soldiers themselves became rulers of large areas of Asia, overawing the Arabic Empire known as the Abbasid caliphate. In the 10th and 11th centuries Turkish leaders such as Mahmud of Gazhni and Alp Arslan headed a new wave of Muslim military expansion. Mahmud took the armies of the faith deep into India, while Alp Arslan turned Anatolia, the heartland of the Byzantine Empire, into the territory of the Seljuks of Rum.

ABBASID EXPANSION

Talas

DATE
751

FORCES
Arabs: unknown;
Chinese: unknown

LOCATION Present-day Kyrgyzstan, Central Asia

CASUALTIES
No reliable estimates

In the 8th century China's Tang dynasty, extending its influence west into central Asia, clashed with the Arab Abbasid caliphate, pressing eastward from Persia. In 751 a Chinese army commanded by the Korean general Gao Xianzhi met an Abbasid army by the Talas River. For cavalry support, the Chinese infantry relied chiefly on horsemen from various Turkish tribes. But early in the battle many of these riders defected, leaving the Chinese footsoldiers exposed to encirclement by Arab cavalry. General Gao Xianzhi escaped the defeat, but Chinese influence west of the Pamir mountains (in modern-day Tajikistan) was at an end and the Turkish peoples of central Asia came fully under Islamic influence.

GHAZNAVID CONQUESTS

Peshawar

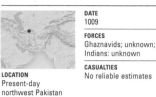

DATE
1009

FORCES
Ghaznavids; unknown;
Indians: unknown

LOCATION
Present-day
northwest Pakistan

CASUALTIES
No reliable estimates

Mahmud of Ghazni, the son of a Turkish slave who had become ruler of what is now Afghanistan, extended his father's empire through military raids and conquest. His favorite target was Hindu India, which he invaded 17 times between 1000 and 1030. At Peshawar in 1009 he was confronted by an alliance of Hindu princes led by Anang-pal. The Indian army depended heavily on the shock effect of massed elephants, but Mahmud panicked the beasts, making them turn back on their own side. After this victory Mahmud adopted elephants as part of his own army.

MAHMUD'S MAUSOLEUM
Mahmud's tomb is one of the few monuments of the Ghaznavid Empire to have survived centuries of warfare in Afghanistan.

SELJUK CONQUESTS

Dandanqan

DATE
1040

FORCES
Turks: unknown;
Ghaznavids: unknown

LOCATION
Near Merv, modern-day Turkmenistan

CASUALTIES
No reliable estimates

In the 1030s the Seljuk Turks, led by Toghril Beg, began to raid areas of northern Khurasan, part of the Ghaznavid Empire. The Ghaznavids, led by Mahmud's son Masud, found the hardy Seljuk forces difficult to counter. In 1040 Masud's army, which included Arab and Kurdish cavalry and Turkish palace soldiers as well as 12 elephants, set out from the city of Merv. Encountering the Seljuks at Dandanqan, they were first fatally weakened by fire from skirmishing mounted archers and then cut apart at close quarters. Masud fought tirelessly with mace, sword, and poison-tipped short spear, but his army was defeated and Khurasan fell to the Seljuks. Under Toghril Beg the Seljuks went on to take control of Abbasid Persia.

INDIAN FORTRESS
The 12-century fortress of Jaisalmer in Rajasthan was built by a Hindu Rajput prince who resisted Muslim rule in India.

GHURID CONQUESTS

Tarain

DATE
1192

FORCES
Ghaznavids: unknown;
Turks: unknown

LOCATION
Near Thanesar,
northwest India

CASUALTIES
No reliable estimates

In the late 12th century Muhammad of Ghur established Muslim rule through much of northern India. Like Mahmud of Gazhni, Muhammad was based in Afghanistan and used Turkish slave soldiers as the core of his army. In 1191 he suffered a setback when, at Tarain, he was defeated by the Hindu Rajput leader Prithviraj III. Although he was badly wounded in the encounter, Muhammad returned the following year for a rematch on the same battlefield. This time, making maximum use of his Turkish mounted archers, he defeated the Hindu army. Prithviraj was captured and put to death. After Muhammad's death in 1206 his slave commanders Qutb ud-Din and Muhammad Bakhtiyar extended Muslim rule in India.

Manzikert

DATE
August 19 or 26, 1071

FORCES
(Possibly) Byzantines: 50,000; Seljuks: 40,000

CASUALTIES
Unknown

LOCATION Near Manzikert (now Malazgirt), Armenia

In 1071 the Byzantine emperor Romanus IV decided to strike a decisive blow against the Seljuk Turks, who had been carrying out incursions into Armenia and Anatolia. He set out east across the Bosphorus with a large army—although the loyalty of many of its mercenaries and feudal levies was questionable. Alp Arslan, the Seljuk leader, led a force north from Syria to meet the Byzantines. Romanus, meanwhile, divided his forces, sending the larger part against the Seljuk-held fortress of Khelat while he himself occupied the fortress town of Manzikert. The first he knew of the proximity of the Seljuks was when a Byzantine reconnaissance force was virtually annihilated. Undeterred, Romanus drew up his forces on a plain outside Manzikert and began to advance. The Turks, however, proved an elusive enemy. Their mounted archers maintained harassing fire on the Byzantines from

BYZANTINE PERSPECTIVE
An illumination from an 11th-century Byzantine chronicle depicts a cavalry battle between Byzantine (left) and Arab forces.

the flanks, but their center refused battle. After an exhausting day chasing shadows, Romanus was far from his camp as evening fell and decided to turn back. This was the moment the Seljuks had been waiting for. They swarmed down from the hills around the plain and surrounded Romanus and his vanguard. The rearguard, made up of the Anatolian levies, fled the

field rather than aid the emperor. Almost all the troops who stayed with Romanus were killed, while he himself was taken prisoner. The Seljuks soon occupied Armenia and most of Anatolia. The following century, with the help of the crusades, the Byzantines were able to regain part of Anatolia, but the Byzantine Empire never truly recovered from the defeat at Manzikert.

> **"It was like an earthquake: the shouting, the sweat, the swift rushes of fear, and not least the hordes of Turks riding all around us."**
>
> A Byzantine chronicler on the Seljuk assault at Manzikert

KEY

- Byzantine frontier in Asia c.1025
- Byzantine forces
- Seljuk Empire c.1095
- Seljuk forces
- Byzantine territory overrun by Seljuks by 1095
- eastern boundary of territory regained by Byzantines 1180
- major battle

1030–1072

ALP ARSLAN

Alp Arslan, the conqueror of Georgia, Armenia, and Anatolia, succeeded his uncle Toghril Beg as Seljuk leader in 1062. Chroniclers differ in their descriptions of Alp Arslan's character, some stressing his cruelty and contempt for human life, others his efficiency and justice as a ruler. He was undoubtedly a superb leader of an army in the field, displaying a mix of caution, trickery, and absolute ruthlessness. He was killed by a prisoner while on campaign in Persia the year after his great victory at Manzikert.

THE CRUSADES

IN THE LATE 11TH CENTURY, responding to a call from Pope Urban II for a holy war against the Muslims, a military expedition captured Jerusalem and founded Christian states in the eastern Mediterranean. For the next 200 years Muslim armies sought to drive the Christians out, while more crusades were mounted to relieve them. Other crusades were declared—against Christian heretics in France, Muslims in Spain, and pagans around the Baltic Sea—but it is with the expeditions to the Holy Land that the word is forever associated.

KNIGHT'S CROSS
The pectoral cross of Godfrey of Bouillon, the knight who was prominent in the capture of Jerusalem in 1099 and became the first Latin ruler in Palestine.

KEY

Western Christendom c.1100	⟶ Second Crusade 1147–49
Orthodox Church c.1100	⟶ Third Crusade 1189–92
Islamic lands c.1100	⟶ Louis IX's Crusade 1248
⟶ First Crusade 1096–99	⟶ Louis IX's Crusade 1270
	—— border of crusader states

BUILT IN STONE
Reinforcing their precarious occupation of hostile territory, the crusaders built many elaborate stone castles like this one at Mamure in southern Turkey.

TAKING THE CROSS

There were many motives for going on a crusade, from the papal promise of eternal salvation to greed for land and plunder. It was not an enterprise to be taken lightly. Getting to Palestine—a journey of some 2,500 miles (4,000km) from Europe—was in itself a considerable undertaking. The overland route through Turkish-controlled Anatolia proved a death trap for many crusaders. From the Third Crusade (1189–92) the preferred route was by sea, which involved expensive reliance on the fleets of Italian cities such as Genoa, Pisa, and Venice. A large-scale crusade such as that of the French king Louis IX in 1248 was an extremely ambitious undertaking, costing six times the French crown's annual income. Exactly how many Christians went on crusade is unknown, but the Fifth Crusade is believed to have involved about 3,000 cavalry, 20,000 infantry and archers, and 30,000 assorted pilgrims and camp followers.

DIVIDED LOYALTIES

Raiding and sieges were the two most common forms of warfare in the crusader lands. The Europeans made no special effort to change their style of fighting—centered on the charge with lance by heavily armored knights—to suit local conditions. Crusader armor, generally heavier than that of Muslim armies, could become unbearably hot, so the cloth surcoat, worn over armor, was adopted to keep the metal cooler. Warfare was often far from a straightforward fight between Muslim and Christian. Each side fought their co-religionists as well as the infidel. In the search for survival, the Christian states formed alliances with Muslim neighbors and even, in the 13th century, with the pagan Mongols. Whenever strong Muslim leaders such as Saladin (1137–93) or the Mameluke Egyptian ruler Baybars (d. 1277) emerged, the Christians fell back on the strength of their stone fortifications. Baybars could field an army of around 40,000, at least twice or three times the combined strength of the crusader states. The crusaders were, however, generally skilled and aggressive fighters, even if they sometimes lacked discipline.

SALADIN'S ARMY
A European representation of the army of Saladin, one of the crusaders' most impressive Muslim foes. He was respected by many Christians as a chivalrous warrior.

RICHARD I THE LION-HEART

Richard, the son of Henry II of England and Eleanor of Aquitaine, embarked on a crusade to Palestine in 1190, just a year after acceding to the English throne. His encounters with Saladin became the stuff of legend, but he failed to retake Jerusalem and quarreled with fellow crusaders Philip II of France and Leopold V of Austria. While returning from the crusade he fell into Leopold's hands and was imprisoned, returning to England in 1194 after paying a hefty ransom.

ROYAL TOMB
Richard was buried in Fontevrault Abbey, France, after being killed by a crossbow bolt during the siege of Chalus Castle.

SIEGE WAR
A medieval image of the storming of Jerusalem in July 1099 shows crusaders using a wheeled siege tower and a stone-throwing catapult.

THE MILITARY ORDERS

From the 1120s military orders such as the Hospitallers and the Templars established themselves in the crusader states. Like monks, members of these orders followed religious rules but were dedicated to war in defense of Christendom, becoming the elite of Christian armies in the east. The Templars were accused of heresy and suppressed in 1312, but other orders continued to play an important role in European warfare, such as the Order of Santiago in Spain and the Hospitallers in wars against the Ottoman Turks.

TEMPLE KNIGHTS
A seal of the Knights Templar, who took their name from their quarters in crusader-run Jerusalem, in the former Jewish Temple.

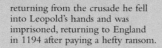

476–1492

THE FIRST AND SECOND CRUSADES

IN 1095 POPE URBAN II called on Christian knights to embark on an expedition to seize the holy city of Jerusalem, held by Muslims for more than 400 years. Some 100,000 people across east and west Europe answered the pope's call, fired by the hope of material gain and Urban's promise of a place in heaven to those crusaders who died on the battlefield. Against all the odds, this large-scale foray into distant, hostile territory succeeded, and Christian states became established in Palestine and Syria. Their existence, however, was always precarious, and the mounting of Muslim counterattacks necessitated other crusades to defend the gains of the first. Instead of a one-time event, crusading became an established part of medieval Christian life.

THE FIRST CRUSADE

Dorylaeum

DATE
July 1, 1097

FORCES
Turks: 3,000;
Crusaders: 4,000

CASUALTIES
No reliable estimates

LOCATION Modern-day Eskisehir, central Anatolia, Turkey

The participants in the First Crusade assembled outside Constantinople in late 1096 and early 1097. Among their main leaders were the Norman duke Bohemond, Count Raymond of Toulouse, the German prince Godfrey of Bouillon, and Adhemar, bishop of le Puy. The army set out across Turkish-held Anatolia the following spring, with Bohemond's Normans in the vanguard. Near Dorylaeum they were ambushed by the army of Kilij Arslan, the Seljuk sultan of Rum. The fast-moving Turkish mounted archers evaded every effort of the Norman knights to engage them. The crusader Fulcher of Chartres wrote how,

CATAPULTED HEADS
On the way to Dorylaeum the crusaders besieged Nicaea, during which they catapulted severed Turkish heads into the city to demoralize the defenders.

"crushed one against the other, like sheep penned up in a fold, we were shut in by the Turks on every side." The Normans were saved by the arrival of another crusader column, led by Count Raymond, which charged the Turks. Kilij Arslan, surprised by the size of the crusader forces, prudently pulled his horsemen away as Turkish casualties mounted.

THE FIRST CRUSADE

Siege of Jerusalem

DATE
June 7–July 18, 1099

FORCES
Crusaders: 1,300 knights and 12,000 footsoldiers

LOCATION
Jerusalem, Palestine

CASUALTIES
No reliable estimates

By the time the First Crusade reached Jerusalem, its numbers had dwindled. Under the vigorous leadership of Count Raymond of Toulouse and Godfrey of Bouillon,

however, they prepared an assault, building wheeled siege towers equipped with catapults. Under a barrage of stones and Greek fire, the crusaders wheeled the towers up to the walls. Once knights from a tower had captured a section of wall, others could join them using siege ladders. The defenders were soon overcome. A great massacre of the city's Muslim and Jewish inhabitants followed, which left the streets knee-deep in bodies.

ASSAULT ON JERUSALEM
The crusaders saw their goal as the liberation of Jerusalem from Muslim rule, but once they took the city they perpetrated a massacre of appalling barbarity.

THE FIRST CRUSADE

Antioch

DATE
October 21, 1097–
June 28, 1098

FORCES (June 1098)
Turks: 75,000
Crusaders: 15,000

CASUALTIES
No reliable estimates

LOCATION Coast of Ancient Syria (now in southern Turkey)

In October 1097 the crusaders laid siege to the large, heavily fortified city of Antioch. The defense of the city was energetically conducted by its Turkish governor, Yagi Siyan, who mounted damaging sorties against the crusaders. Through the winter the besiegers found themselves more seriously threatened by hunger and hardship than the besieged. Relief forces for both sides, meanwhile, either turned back or were driven off. Finally, on June 3,

> "The Turks…pressed us on one side, and excruciating hunger on the other, but of succor and help we had none."
>
> *Gesta Francorum,*
> Fulcher of Chartres, 1101

1098, a Turkish traitor admitted the crusaders to one of the towers on the city walls. After massacring the inhabitants, the crusaders besieged the citadel, which remained in Turkish hands. A Muslim relief army said to be 75,000 strong now appeared, led by Emir Kerboga of Mosul, and the crusaders were themselves besieged inside Antioch. They were on the verge of defeat when the discovery of a sacred relic—the Holy Lance—restored morale and inspired Bohemond to lead a sortie against Kerboga. With around 1,000 mounted knights and 14,000 footsoldiers, he crossed the Orontes River and attacked the far superior Muslim forces so decisively that they fled, suffering heavy casualties. Bohemond then took possession of Antioch as the base of his own principality.

SIEGE SCENE
A 15th-century representation of the siege of Antioch reflects crusader accounts of the city's strong walls and great wealth.

Harran

DATE
May 1104

FORCES
Crusaders: 3,000 knights, 9,000 infantry; Muslims: unknown

LOCATION
Present-day southeast Turkey

CASUALTIES
No reliable estimates

In spring 1104 Bohemond of Antioch joined with Baldwin of Edessa to capture the fortress of Harran. A relieving Muslim army came upon the Christians outside the city. Bohemond and Baldwin split their forces, the Edessenes facing the Muslim attack while the Antiochenes hid in ambush. But the Muslims used the well-tried stratagem of fleeing, luring Baldwin's men straight into the maw of the main Muslim force. By the time Bohemond entered the battle, the Edessenes had been cut apart.

Edessa

DATE
1144

FORCES
Muslims: unknown; Christians: unknown

LOCATION
Modern Sanliurfa, southeastern Turkey

CASUALTIES
No reliable estimates

The fall of Edessa, the most isolated of the crusader states, set the stage for the Second Crusade. In 1144 Zengi, the Muslim atabeg of Aleppo, invaded the state. Edessa's ruler, Joscelin II, had neglected its defenses and Zengi found little resistance as he advanced on the city. Muslim catapults and siege engines soon weakened Edessa's fortifications and sappers undermined the city wall, opening a breach through which Zengi's army poured to massacre its inhabitants.

Siege of Ascalon

DATE
January 25– August 19, 1153

FORCES
Christians: unknown; Egyptians: unknown

LOCATION
Coastal Palestine, south of Jaffa

CASUALTIES
No reliable estimates

In 1153 Baldwin III of Jerusalem besieged the Egyptian port of Ascalon. The city's land fortifications were strong and the Christians lacked the resources to prevent the Egyptians from reinforcing by sea, but a crusader siege tower fell against the city wall, causing a section to collapse. Further battering by siege engines proved too much for the Muslims, and on August 19 they surrendered in return for safe passage.

Second Crusade

DATE
1147–1149

FORCES
Around 20,000 German and 15,000 French crusaders

LOCATION
Anatolia and the Near East

CASUALTIES
No reliable estimates

In the wake of the capture of Jerusalem in 1099, the crusader states depended for their survival largely upon dissension between different Muslim states, which spent far more energy fighting one another than attempting to evict the infidels. In 1127, however, Imad al-Din Zengi, the atabeg of Mosul, took control of Aleppo and began extending his rule over northern Syria and northern Mesopotamia. In 1144 he captured Christian-ruled Edessa, the first crusader state to fall to a Muslim counterattack. Zengi died in 1146, but his son Nur ed-Din proved an even more dangerous enemy for the Christians. Meanwhile, in response to the fall of Edessa, Pope Eugenius III called for a new crusade. Armies led by

HEAVY WEAPONRY
This 12th-century cruciform hilted sword would have been typical of the heavy blades that the crusaders wielded to great effect against their Muslim opponents.

CHRISTIAN HORDE
The Christian army sent against Damascus was unusually large by the standard of these mostly small-scale encounters.

King Louis VII of France and Emperor Conrad III of Germany set out from Europe, but got into serious trouble crossing Anatolia. Conrad's army, hungry, thirsty, and exhausted, was ambushed by Turks and massacred near Dorylaeum. The emperor escaped with a few survivors and eventually arrived in Palestine by sea. After following the Anatolian coast to Attalia, King Louis also took to the sea with most of his knights safely reaching his destination, but his footsoldiers and remaining cavalry were decimated by the Turks.

SAFETY HELMET
The "pot helm" was the most common headgear for crusader knights. It offered solid protection but could lead soldiers to overheat in the hot sun of the Levant.

DAMASCUS
Looking to strike a spectacular blow against the Muslims, Louis and Conrad agreed with Baldwin III, king of Jerusalem, to attack the famous city of Damascus. The decision was highly questionable, since Damascus was hostile to Nur ed-Din, and the Christians should have courted its friendship. Yet in July 1148 the largest Christian army ever seen in the east advanced on the city, provoking its ruler, Emir Unur, reluctantly to call on Nur ed-Din to send an army to save him. At first the Christians progressed well, driving the Damascene forces back inside the city walls. But they soon came under attack from Muslim skirmishers in the orchards around the city and from sorties by Unur's forces. Put on the defensive, the Christians quarreled over who would rule Damascus when it was captured. When news of Nur ed-Din's approach was received, controversy spread to more pressing matters. The local barons belatedly tried to explain to Louis and Conrad the complexities of local politics. There was also nervousness as to what might happen if their army found itself caught between Nur ed-Din and the Damascus garrison. Ignominiously, the great expedition retreated just four days after arriving outside Damascus. It was a bitter blow to Christian prestige and a major boost to Muslim morale.

"Let this one cry be raised by all the soldiers of God: It is the will of God!"

Robert the Monk, History of Jerusalem, reporting on Urban II's sermon at Clermont, 1095.

FIRST CRUSADE

With these words, Pope Urban II set off the most powerful force of Christian renewal since the days of the Emperor Constantine, or, depending on one's point of view, gave religious sanction to the murder and dispossession of countless thousands of Levantine Muslims and Jews. Ever since the Patriarch Sophronius died of a broken heart after the Muslim capture of Jerusalem in 638, successive Christian prelates had alternately chafed at Muslim restrictions on pilgrims or dreamed of the glory that the restoration of the cross to Jerusalem would bring. The shattering of the Byzantine army by the Seljuk Turks at Manzikert in 1071 and a subsequent appeal for help from Emperor Alexius I was all that Urban needed to preach a new holy war, a crusade, to liberate the Holy Land.

" [When] the Arabs, coming against the Count of Flanders, saw that the affair was not to be conducted at a distance with arrows, but at close quarters with swords, they turned in flight. The Count followed them for two miles, and in this space he saw the bodies of the killed lying like bundles of grain reaped in the field. The ambushes which Bohemund had encountered were scattered and put to flight... "

Raymond d'Aguilliers, History of the Franks on a battle outside Antioch

From early 1096, enthusiastic crowds flocked to "take the cross" and embark on armed pilgrimage to the Holy Land. The first waves of crusaders were more a disorganized and marauding peasant rabble than an effective military force. But when the nobility of Europe, inspired by a potent trinity of eternal salvation, martial glory, and earthly plunder, embarked on the journey to Jerusalem, the prospects for the crusade grew brighter. Christianity's shock troops, the mounted knights, pushed through Asia Minor and on into northern Syria. Their opponents employed unfamiliar tactics, using light cavalry to harass, encircle, and entrap the more lumbering crusader columns. But when the Christian army succeeded in pinning down their foes in the open, the impact of their heavy-cavalry charge was irresistible.

RICHARD THE LIONHEART ER THE BATTLE OF HATTIN

" ...they hurled not only stones and arrows, but also burning wood and straw. The wood was dipped in pitch, wax, and sulfur; then straw was fastened on by an iron band, and, when lighted, these firebrands were shot from the machines. [They were] all bound together by an iron band...so that wherever they fell, the whole mass held together and continued to burn. Such missiles, burning as they shot upward, could not be resisted...by high walls. "

Raymond d'Aguilliers, History of the Franks on the siege of Antioch, 1097–98

At Antioch, the crusaders became bogged down in the characteristic squalor and frustrated violence of a medieval siege. Deciding not to risk the losses that would ensue from storming the city's impressive fortifications, the Christian army was caught in a waiting game. They hoped that Antioch's starving defenders would surrender before their own dwindling supplies gave out entirely. Meanwhile, they sought to undermine Muslim morale—if not the walls—by hurling a creative array of incendiary devices against the infidel.

" Some of our men (and this was more merciful) cut off the heads of their enemies; others shot them with arrows, so that they fell from the towers; others tortured them longer by casting them into the flames. Piles of heads, hands, and feet were to be seen in the streets of the city. It was necessary to pick one's way over the bodies of men and horses... Indeed, it was a just and splendid judgment of God that this place should be filled with the blood of the unbelievers... "

Raymond d'Aguilliers, History of the Franks on the capture of Jerusalem

CRUSADER CASTLE
The imposing crusader fortress at Byblos was built following the town's capture by Raymond de St. Gilles in 1103.

The siege of Jerusalem (June–July 1099) was a much briefer affair than that of Antioch. Aware that they could not risk the weakening of their forces that a long investment of the Holy City would entail and eager to grasp the ultimate prize of its liberation, the crusaders held back from a major assault for little more than a month. When their siege towers succeeded in capturing a section of the walls, the Muslim defenders' will to resist buckled. What ensued was a massacre of such bloody ferocity that it shocked even the crusaders' chroniclers, whose tolerance for wanton slaughter was normally quite elevated. It also forever poisoned all hope of coming to an accommodation with neighboring Muslim powers.

" Anyone who had not even a village there has a city here, thanks to God. Why go back to the west, when we can find all this in the east? "

Fulcher of Chartres, Gesta Francorum

WARFARE IN THE MIDDLE AGES

MUSLIMS VERSUS CRUSADER STATES

Hattin

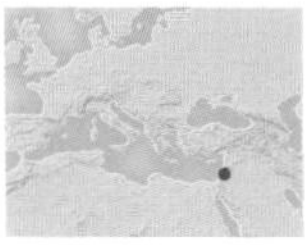

DATE
June 30–July 4, 1187

FORCES
Muslims: 30,000;
Christians:
15,000–20,000

LOCATION
Near Lake Tiberias,
northern Palestine

CASUALTIES
Unknown

After establishing his rule in Egypt and Syria the Muslim sultan Saladin set out to destroy the crusader states of Palestine. In late June 1187 he crossed the Jordan River with a large army, part of which advanced to seize the Christian-held city of Tiberias. The crusader states had gathered an army at Acre, commanded by the newly installed king of Jerusalem, Guy de Lusignan. When they learned of Saladin's offensive, they advanced toward the springs of Saforie. After a harsh debate between Guy and Count Raymond of Tripoli, who favored a defensive strategy, the army set off to relieve Tiberias. Crossing barren hills in intense heat, the Christians faced constant harassment from Muslim archers. Parched with thirst, the army halted on a dry plateau by a double hill known as the Horns of Hattin. That night, Saladin's army encircled the Christian forces and started fires in the brush around the camp. The next morning, by now almost dying of thirst, the Christians tried to break through the Muslim encirclement,

but their footsoldiers were corralled and slaughtered by the enemy. Count Raymond broke out during a cavalry charge, but most Christian riders were struck down by Muslim archers. The remaining knights fell back to one of the Horns, where they resisted bravely until they were forced to surrender. King Guy was among those taken prisoner.

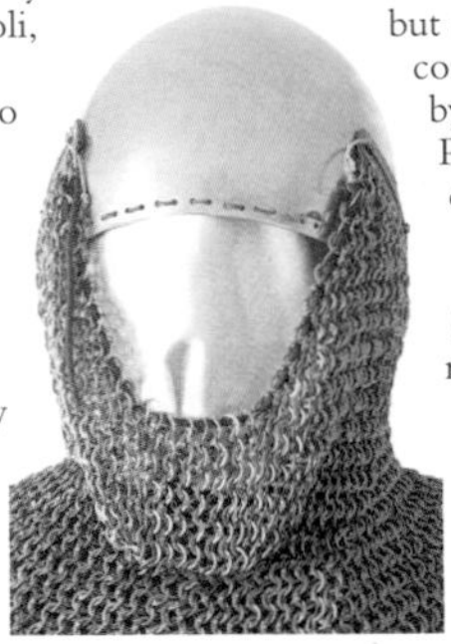

HEAD GEAR
Most knights in the crusades period wore a chain-mail coat and a coif (head covering), topped by a steel cap and possibly a helmet.

SALADIN
1137–1193

Saladin was a Kurdish warrior who seized control of Egypt in 1171, replacing the Fatimid caliphate with his own Ayyubid dynasty. A series of campaigns gave him control of Damascus and Aleppo, after which he focused on the jihad against the Christians. He was a cautious military leader who waited for an opportunity to strike decisively but who avoided battle if there was a serious risk of defeat.

PIOUS RULER
Saladin deserved his reputation for piety but did not shrink from bloodshed.

MUSLIM RESURGENCE
Saladin followed victory at Hattin, illustrated here in a 15th-century French manuscript, by taking Jerusalem and reversing much of the crusaders' earlier successes.

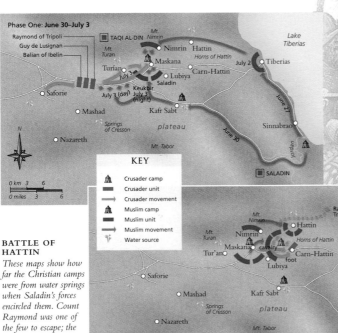

BATTLE OF HATTIN
These maps show how far the Christian camps were from water springs when Saladin's forces encircled them. Count Raymond was one of the few to escape; the remaining knights got as far as Carn Hattin but were overwhelmed.

Phase One: June 30–July 3

Raymond of Tripoli
Guy de Lusignan
Balian of Ibelin
TAQI AL-DIN
Mt. Nimrin
Mt. Turan
Turian
Maskana
Nimrin
Hattin
Horns of Hattin
Lake Tiberias
July 2
Tiberias
July 3
Saladin
Lubiya
Carn-Hattin
Keukbir July 3 (night)
July 3 (day)
Saforie
Kafr Sabt
Mashad
Springs of Cresson
plateau
Sinnabrao
Nazareth
Mt. Tabor
June 30
June 27
Jordan
SALADIN

KEY
- Crusader camp
- Crusader unit
- Crusader movement
- Muslim camp
- Muslim unit
- Muslim movement
- Water source

0 km 3 6
0 miles 3 6

N

Phase Two: July 4

Mt. Nimrin
Mt. Turan
Nimrin
Maskana
cavalry
Tur'an
Lubiya
foot
Hattin
Horns of Hattin
Carn-Hattin
Raymond of Tripoli escapes
Lake Tiberias
Tiberias
Saforie
Kafr Sabt
Mashad
Springs of Cresson
plateau
Sinnabrao
Nazareth
Mt. Tabor
Jordan

DECLINE OF THE CRUSADES

AFTER SALADIN'S TRIUMPHANT CAPTURE of Jerusalem in 1187, Pope Clement III called a Third Crusade. Europe's most powerful rulers, Frederick Barbarossa, Richard the Lionheart of England, and Philip Augustus of France all responded, but Frederick died on the way to Palestine and Richard and Philip met with very mixed fortunes. Further crusading efforts were directed to attacking Byzantium (the Fourth Crusade) and Egypt (the Fifth and Seventh Crusades), and to doing deals with Muslim rulers. Emperor Frederick II, leading the Sixth Crusade, even got Jerusalem back by clever diplomacy, but was promptly excommunicated for his pains. By the end of the 13th century, the crusader states of Palestine had disappeared from the map.

THE THIRD CRUSADE

Siege of Acre

DATE
August 28, 1189–
July 12, 1191

FORCES
Christians: unknown;
Muslims: unknown

LOCATION
Acre, modern Israel

CASUALTIES
No reliable estimates

In 1189 a small Christian force led by Guy de Lusignan boldly laid siege to Acre two years after its fall to Saladin. The siege was supported by a blockade of Pisan and Genoese ships. In April 1191 they were joined by King Philip of France and, in June, by King Richard of England, whose arrival gave the Christians the edge. Saladin's forces failed to fight their way through to relieve the city. As breaches began to open in the walls, the besieged finally surrendered, a great victory for the Christians after so many reverses.

GOD'S ACRE

Crusaders disembark at Acre in 1191. The ability to resupply the crusader states by sea was vital after the long land route through Anatolia became too dangerous.

THE THIRD CRUSADE

Arsuf

DATE
September 7, 1191

FORCES
Crusaders: under 50,000; Muslims: unknown

LOCATION
Coastal Palestine

CASUALTIES
Muslims: 7,000 killed; Crusaders: 700 killed

On August 22, 1191, Richard the Lionheart marched south out of Acre, shadowed by Saladin's army. Richard moved in short daily marches, keeping a disciplined formation that minimized casualties. Templars led the army, with Hospitallers at the rear, while crossbowmen and infantry covered the landward flank. Knights were under strict orders to hold formation, whatever the provocation from Muslim hit-and-run attacks. On September 7, however, Richard decided to give battle. At a prearranged trumpet signal, the Christian knights charged, scattering Saladin's men in a few minutes. For all the discipline and organization of his army, Richard failed to take Jerusalem the following year.

THE FOURTH CRUSADE

Constantinople

DATE
July 1203–April 1204

FORCES
Christians: unknown;
Muslims: unknown

LOCATION
Constantinople,
(modern Istanbul)

CASUALTIES
No reliable estimates

In 1201 Pope Innocent III called for a new crusade—the Fourth. Enrico Dandolo, the Doge of Venice, agreed to provide ships for 25,000 crusaders. When the crusaders failed to raise the fee, Dandolo offered to transport them in return for help in seizing Zara, a former Venetian dependency then held by Hungary. In 1202 Zara was duly captured and sacked. The crusaders had with them Alexius, a claimant to the Byzantine throne, who offered them various inducements, including a payment of 200,000 marks, to install him as Byzantine ruler. Reaching Constantinople in June 1203, the crusaders launched an assault on the city the following month. The Venetian fleet penetrated the Golden Horn and attacked the sea walls, directed in person by the 95-year-old Dandolo. The emperor Alexius III fled, hastening the fall of the city. The crusaders' candidate was installed on the throne as Alexius IV. The Venetians and crusaders settled down to wait for their 200,000 marks. But the money was not forthcoming. Instead, Alexius IV was overthrown in a palace coup and his successor, Alexius V, prepared to defend the city. The crusaders' first attack, on April 6, 1204, was repulsed with heavy losses, but six days later, during an assault on the sea walls, fire broke out in the city and the defenders scattered in panic. For the next three days Constantinople was a scene of looting and massacre on a massive scale.

ASSAULT ON ZARA

The crusaders' capture of Zara in 1202 saw them fighting the Hungarians, fellow Christians.

THE SEVENTH CRUSADE

Harbiyah

DATE	
October 17, 1244	
FORCES 1,500 Christian knights plus Muslim allies; 5,000 Egyptians plus Khwarizmians	
LOCATION Near Gaza	**CASUALTIES** 5,000 Christians killed, 800 taken prisoner

In 1244 Khwarizmian horsemen from central Asia swept through Syria and Palestine, attacking Christians and Muslims alike. They seized Jerusalem and then allied with the Egyptians. The Templars made a pact with the Muslim rulers of Homs and Damascus to resist them. A combined Muslim–Christian army advanced toward Egypt, where it was met by a horde of Khwarizmians and a disciplined body of Egyptians, including Mameluke slave soldiers. The Khwarizmian horsemen charged and broke the Muslim forces on the Christian–Muslim left, leaving the Christians trapped. Although they fought bravely, the Christians, including the Templars' Grand Master, were massacred. Only 33 Templars and 26 Hospitallers escaped.

THE SEVENTH CRUSADE

Mansurah

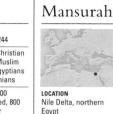

DATE	
February 8, 1250	
FORCES Christian: 20,000 cavalry, 40,000 infantry; Egyptians: 70,000 soldiers	
LOCATION Nile Delta, northern Egypt	**CASUALTIES** Heavy on both sides

In 1249 French King Louis IX landed in Egypt, quickly capturing the city of Damietta. Advancing toward Cairo, in December he met a large Egyptian army, commanded by Fakhr ad-Din,

holding the far side of the Bahr as-Saghir canal. At dawn on February 8 the king's brother Robert of Artois led a vanguard of knights across the ford. He launched an immediate surprise attack on the Egyptian camp, in which many Egyptians, including Fakhr ad-Din, were slaughtered. The remaining Egyptians fled to the nearby town of Mansurah. Imprudently, Artois gave chase. A Mameluke commander, Ruk ad-Din Baybars, swiftly set an ambush. The Christian knights charged into the town unopposed; then, trapped in the narrow streets, they were butchered. But outside the town the Christians prevailed. It was an illusory victory. Decimated by disease and harassed by Egyptian forces, the crusaders tried to withdraw to Damietta. At Fariskur on April 6 they were overrun; almost all were either killed or, like King Louis, taken prisoner.

ROYAL PRISONER
King Louis IX was taken prisoner by the Muslims and kept in chains in a house in Mansurah.

1215–70

LOUIS IX

Louis IX of France set off on his first crusade (the Seventh) in 1248, hoping to defeat Egypt, the most important Muslim power, and retake Jerusalem. The crusade ended in disaster, with Louis a prisoner of the Muslims and his brother, the Count of Artois, dead. Louis was released in return for a huge ransom and the return of Damietta to the Egyptians. His long and peaceful reign in France ended in 1270 when he embarked on another crusade (the Eighth), this time landing in Tunisia, where he died in an epidemic.

SAINT AND KING
This portrait by 15th-century Italian artist Vivarini emphasizes King Louis's saintly aspect. He was canonized in 1297.

FALL OF THE CRUSADER KINGDOMS

The Fall of Acre

DATE	April 6–May 28, 1291
	FORCES Muslim cavalry: 60,000, infantry: 160,000; Christian knights: 1,000, infantry: 16,000
LOCATION Acre (modern Israel)	**CASUALTIES** No reliable estimates

In 1260 Baibars seized control of Egypt. With its vast wealth at the disposal of such a skillful, single-minded Muslim warrior, the crusader states

CRUSADER CASTLE
The Hospitaller castle of Krak des Chevaliers was considered one of the world's strongest fortresses. In 1271, after a long siege, it fell to Baibars, who used it as a base for his attacks on the last crusader strongholds on the coast.

were doomed. He conquered their cities and castles one by one, employing plentiful siege engines: Antioch fell in 1268, Krak des Chevaliers in 1271. Baibars's death in 1277 brought some respite, but Egypt's new ruler, Qalawun, and, from 1290, his son al-Ashraf Khalil continued the conquest. By then, the port city of Acre was the last fortress still in Christian hands. In 1291 al-Ashraf laid siege to Acre. Built on a peninsula, the city was defended by a double line of walls reinforced with 12 towers. It was open to resupply by sea, but the number of defenders was insufficient to man the walls. Day after day the

Muslims battered the walls with their siege engines, while their engineers mined under the walls. By May 18 part of the outer wall had collapsed and al-Ashraf ordered a general assault. According to a Christian eyewitness, "They came on foot, in numbers which were beyond comprehension; first came those who carried massive shields, and next came those who threw the Greek fire, and after were those who fired darts and feathered arrows so thickly that it was as if rain was falling from the sky…" The Muslims fought their way into the city, killing or taking prisoner all who failed

to flee by boat. By the evening only the Templars held out. On May 28, mined by al-Ashraf's engineers, this last stronghold collapsed and Acre was in Muslim hands.

KNIGHT AND CROSS
This knight wears the white surcoat and red cross of a Templar. The Knights Templar had a key role in Acre's defense and managed to save some of its civilians as the city fell.

476–1492

THE SPANISH RECONQUISTA

FROM THE 8TH CENTURY, Muslim rulers controlled most of Iberia. After the caliphate of Cordova disintegrated in the early 11th century, however, the Christian kingdoms of Castile, León, Aragon, and Portugal began a "Reconquista," pushing the Muslims back, and eventually driving them out entirely.

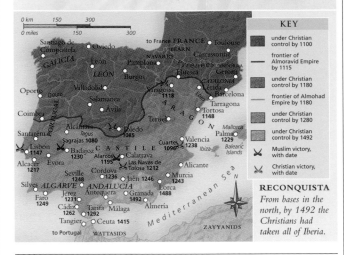

KEY

under Christian control by 1100

frontier of Almoravid Empire by 1115

under Christian control by 1180

frontier of Almohad Empire by 1180

under Christian control by 1280

under Christian control by 1492

Muslim victory, with date

Christian victory, with date

RECONQUISTA
From bases in the north, by 1492 the Christians had taken all of Iberia.

THE SPANISH RECONQUISTA

Siege of Toledo

DATE
Fall 1084–
May 25, 1085

FORCES
Unknown

CASUALTIES
Unknown

LOCATION
Toledo, central Spain

By the 11th century the Muslim emirate of Spain had broken up into numerous small kingdoms known as *taifas*. King Alfonso VI of León and Castile took advantage of this disunity to force neighboring *taifa* kings to pay him tribute. When in 1081 a faction in Muslim Toledo demanded that these payments cease, Alfonso besieged the city. At first the siege was half-hearted, but in the fall of 1084 Alfonso established a stricter blockade around Toledo. He also laid waste to the surrounding countryside to sharpen the mounting famine. The Toledan ruler, al-Qadir, appealed to the other Muslim kingdoms for help, but none came to his aid. On May 6, 1085, al-Qadir agreed to surrender, and on May 25 Alfonso entered Toledo. It was the largest city yet to be captured by the Spanish Christians, and its rulers, the Dhul-nunids, were the first Muslim dynasty to be dethroned by a Christian attack. Toledo was also strategically vital—the Muslim geographer al-Himyari called it "the center of all the country." Its conquest meant the Spanish Christians could strike anywhere into Moorish territory.

WARRIOR OF FAITH
After his remains were found at Compostela in about 800, St. James became the patron of the Reconquista. He allegedly appeared in battle to help the Christians, earning the nickname "Matamoros" (Moor-killer).

SPANISH RECONQUISTA

Siege of Valencia

DATE
July 1093–
June 16, 1094

FORCES
Christians: unknown;
Muslims: unknown

LOCATION Valencia,
Mediterranean coast
of Spain

CASUALTIES
Unknown
30,000 prisoners

After a decade fighting as a mercenary for both Christian and Muslim rulers in eastern Spain, by the 1090s Rodrigo Diaz "El Cid" (see panel) had become a powerful figure in his own right. The Muslim king of the city of Valencia was effectively his client. But in 1086 Spain was invaded from the south by the Almoravids, an expansionist Muslim power based in Marrakesh, Morocco. Their ruler, Yusuf ibn Tashufin, defeated Alfonso VI at Zallaka in 1086, and also conquered all of Muslim Spain. Valencia came under a new ruler, Ibn Jehhaf, owing allegiance to the Almoravids. In July 1093 El Cid placed the city under siege, building a

> **"The city was cut off from the entire Moorish race and stood alone amidst a sea of death."**
>
> *Ibn Alcama, Moorish historian and eyewitness to the siege of Valencia, in his* History of El Cid's conquest of Granada, 1110

fortified camp at Juballa, just outside the city. The Almoravid garrison left the city but Ibn Jehhaf refused to capitulate. In response, El Cid tightened the siege, razing the city's suburbs. By April 1094 there were severe food shortages in the city, with reports of cannibalism. El Cid pressed ever closer, battering the defenses with siege machines. In June, Valencia was forced to surrender and El Cid entered the city. But his position was far from secure. An Almoravid army advanced to counter-attack. In December 1094 El Cid ambushed and defeated this force at Cuerte, 5 miles (7km) outside Valencia. He held the city as an independent ruler until his death in 1099. It was recaptured by the Almoravids in 1102.

EL CID'S SWORD
El Tizona, the Cid's sword was captured from a Muslim king. In the 20th century Spanish dictator General Franco tried, but failed, to acquire it.

---

c.1040–1099

EL CID

In his early twenties Rodrigo Diaz de Vivar, nicknamed "El Cid" (from the Arabic, meaning "Lord"), served in the army of the future Sancho II of Castile. In 1081, however, he fell out with Alfonso VI of Castile and was exiled. He then served as a mercenary in eastern Spain, fighting for both Christians and Muslims—ironically, in view of his status as an icon of the Reconquista. Christian rule over Valencia did not long survive El Cid's death in 1099. In 1102 his widow, Ximena, who had held the city after he died, burned it rather than let it fall intact to the Muslims.

MOUNTED CID
El Cid was also called "Campeador," or champion, for his valor in battle.

SPANISH RECONQUISTA

Siege of Saragossa

DATE
Winter 1118

FORCES
Christians: unknown;
Muslims: unknown

LOCATION
Zaragoza,
northeastern Spain

CASUALTIES
No reliable estimates

Alfonso I, "the Battler" of Aragon, was determined to push the Muslim Almoravids out of Spain and welcomed French crusading knights to help his cause. Alfonso's expedition to Saragossa in 1118 was proclaimed a crusade, and Gaston de Béarn, who had participated in the conquest of Jerusalem (see p.80), joined his army. Gaston's experience of siege warfare in the Holy Land was vital, and he supervised the construction of siege towers and 20 catapults, which rained missiles on the city's defenders. After several months a Muslim relief force arrived, commanded by the Almoravid general Tamim. Alfonso routed him in a pitched battle on December 8. Saragossa capitulated under pressure of the renewed siege and the Christian army occupied it on December 19.

Siege of Lisbon

DATE
June 28–October 24, 1147

FORCES
Crusaders: 13,00 men, 164 ships;
Muslims: unknown

LOCATION
Lisbon, Portugal

CASUALTIES
No reliable estimates

In western Iberia victory over the Almoravids at the battle of Ourique in 1139 allowed Afonso Henriques to become the first king of Portugal. In 1147 he persuaded a fleet of German, Flemish, and English crusaders on their way to the Holy Land to stop off and help him conquer the Muslim city of Lisbon. The crusaders landed outside the city on June 28 and, after a series of skirmishes, occupied the suburbs on July 1. At first the siege went badly: five mangonels (catapults) used to batter the walls were destroyed and a siege tower got stuck in waterlogged ground. The Germans and Flemish dug mines under the city walls, opening a breach on October 16, but the defenders repulsed an assault. On October 19, however, the English completed a second siege tower. As the tower was rolled toward the walls, the Muslims agreed to surrender the city in return for an undertaking that it would not be sacked. When the crusaders entered Lisbon under truce on October 24 they nonetheless engaged in massacre and pillage.

Las Navas de Tolosa

DATE
July 16–17, 1212

FORCES
Christians:
60,000–80,000;
Muslims: 100,000

LOCATION
Sierra Morena,
southern Spain

CASUALTIES
Possibly 60,000 dead

In the mid-12th century the Almohads, a Muslim revivalist movement, swept through Almoravid Morocco and Spain and then won a great victory over a Christian army at Alarcos in 1195. Alfonso VIII of Castile, faced with this Moorish offensive,

ALFONSO'S TRIUMPH
Alfonso VIII's victory at Las Navas de Tolosa opened the way for the Christian reconquest of most of the Iberian peninsula by the mid-13th century.

persuaded Pope Innocent III to proclaim a crusade against them. On June 20, 1212 a large crusader force marched southward from Alfonso's capital, Toledo, including an Aragonese contingent led by Peter II and knights from Portugal and France. The Spanish military orders of Calatrava and Santiago and Spanish city militias provided vital

parts of the army. Alfonso's force was further reinforced by Sancho VII of Navarre. Caliph al-Nasir waited for the Christians on the high plain of Las Navas de Tolosa, believing they would have to force the well-defended Losa canyon. But a local shepherd guided Alfonso's army along a secret path that enabled it to surprise the Muslims on the plain. The lightly armored Almohads hoped to weaken the heavier Christian cavalry and then to close in for the kill. At first al-Nasir's tactics succeeded. But when all seemed lost Alfonso ordered a charge of his cavalry reserve that broke the Almohad army, who were massacred as they fled. The Christian victory at Las Navas de Tolosa effectively destroyed Almohad power in Spain.

Map: Las Navas de Tolosa campaign

Toledo Christian stronghold from **1085**

Tagus

Montes de Toledo

Guadiana

Malagón **June 24**

Piedrabuena **July 5–6**
Benavente **July 5–6**
Caracuel **July 5–6**

Calatrava la Vieja **July 1**
Alarcos **July 1**
Salvatierra
Fresheda

Las Navas de Tolosa **July 16**

Sierra Morena

Ferral

Vilches **July 19**

Úbeda **August 3** sacked by crusaders
Baeza

Guadalquivir

Jaén **July 16** Muslim forces withdraw to Jaén

KEY
→ Christian forces
⚔ Christian victory
→ Muslim forces
⊠ Muslim fortress

N

0 km 50 100
0 miles 50 100

The Fall of Granada

DATE
February 1482–
January 2, 1492

FORCES Spanish: 26,000
rising to 60,000;
Granada Moors:
53,000 at start of siege

LOCATION
Kingdom of Granada,
southern Spain

CASUALTIES
No reliable estimates

By the 15th century Granada was the last enclave of Muslim rule in Spain. In 1479 Isabella of Castile and Ferdinand of Aragon were established as joint rulers of Christian Spain. Determined to complete the Reconquista, in February 1482 an army commanded by Ferdinand invaded Granada. Most of his horsemen were *caballeros a la jinete*—light cavalry well suited to fighting in dry, arid conditions. The Spanish army possessed a contingent of Swiss pikemen and was well supplied

with gunpowder weapons. It had 91 artillery pieces in 1485, as well as a corps armed with primitive arquebuses. Ferdinand systematically conquered cities and fortresses around Granada, in an eight-year campaign that hardened his fighting men into an experienced and disciplined army. Infighting among the ruling Moorish dynasty of Granada, the Nasrids, prevented any concerted Muslim counterattack. Under siege from April 1491, the city of Granada submitted

on New Year's Day 1492. Ferdinand and Isabella entered the city the next day. The terms of surrender guaranteed the Moors the right to practice their religion, but this toleration did not last—in 1502 the Moors were forced to choose between baptism and exile.

ALHAMBRA
Granada's Alhambra was the last Moorish stronghold in Spain to fall to the Christians. Its splendors are a reminder of the Muslim achievement in the Iberian peninsula.

476–1492

MONGOL POWER

THE 13TH-CENTURY CONQUESTS of the Mongols have never been surpassed. Under the leadership of Genghis Khan and his successors, the steppe horsemen struck east and west, conquering China and the Muslim states of central Asia, and penetrating deep into Europe and the Middle East. Although their attempts to extend Mongol rule into Japan and Southeast Asia failed, they only once suffered a decisive defeat—at the hands of the Mameluke general Baibars at Ain Jalut, Palestine, in 1260.

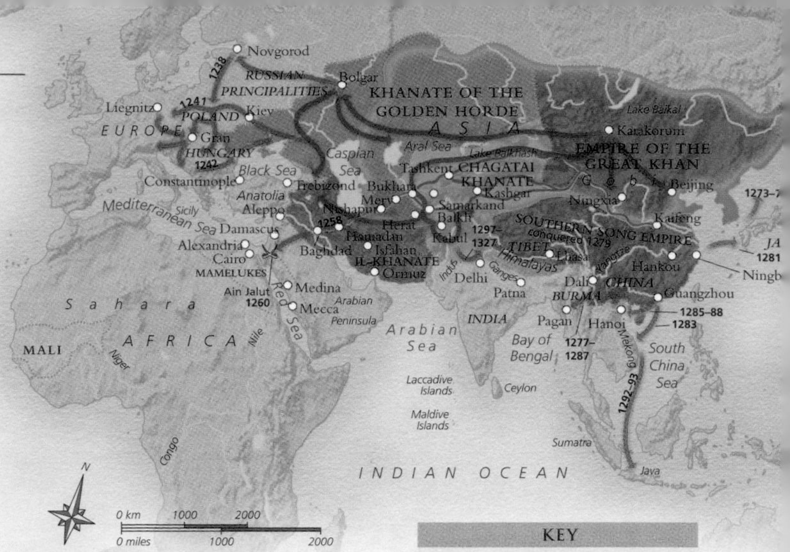

THE MONGOL EMPIRE
The Mongols ruled an area stretching from modern-day Korea to the eastern edge of Europe. By 1300 this empire was divided into four khanates.

KEY
→ campaigns of Genghis Khan 1206–1227
  empire of Genghis Khan 1227
→ campaigns of Genghis Khan's successors
▨ empires of Genghis Khan's successors
— Silk Road

MODERN NOMADS
Like their Mongol ancestors, these Mongolians from Bogdo Suma, ride their small horses on the steppe.

MOUNTED WARRIORS

The Mongols—tribes from the grasslands north of the Gobi desert who united under Genghis Khan—followed the tradition of steppe warriors: swift-moving mounted archers who rained arrows on their enemies while keeping out of range of retaliation. They delighted in tricks familiar to the Huns almost a thousand years earlier, such as pretending to flee and then rounding on their pursuers. They also, however, had armored lancers who engaged the enemy at close quarters to achieve a decisive victory. The Mongols' ability to fight over immense distances was due to the endurance of their small steppe horses, but also to their lack of a supply chain. Like most armies of their time, they brought a train of camp followers with them, but they lived by plunder and foraging. Their resilience and endurance were matched by their indifference to the suffering of others. They were merciless toward those who defied them, massacring entire populations of cities without remorse.

REIGN OF TERROR
The Mongols cultivated a reputation for brutality. Some towns that they destroyed, such as this one in Afghanistan's Bamian valley, were never rebuilt.

MONGOL ARMIES

The Mongol armies were far from being a single horde. Each *tumen*, or unit, of 10,000 men was subdivided into thousands, hundreds, and tens of warriors. This modern-seeming structure, with low-level commanders empowered to make decisions on the battlefield, was a steppe tradition handed down from the time of the Huns. Genghis Khan oversaw a meritocratic army in which fighters of proven ability achieved high command, whatever their birth. The Mongol forces were also open for subject peoples to join. Turkish, Arab, and Chinese recruits brought skills that the Mongols lacked—most notably in siege warfare—and contributed to the numerical strength of Mongol armies. This was vital for, while all Mongols were warriors, their manpower would not have sufficed across an entire continent.

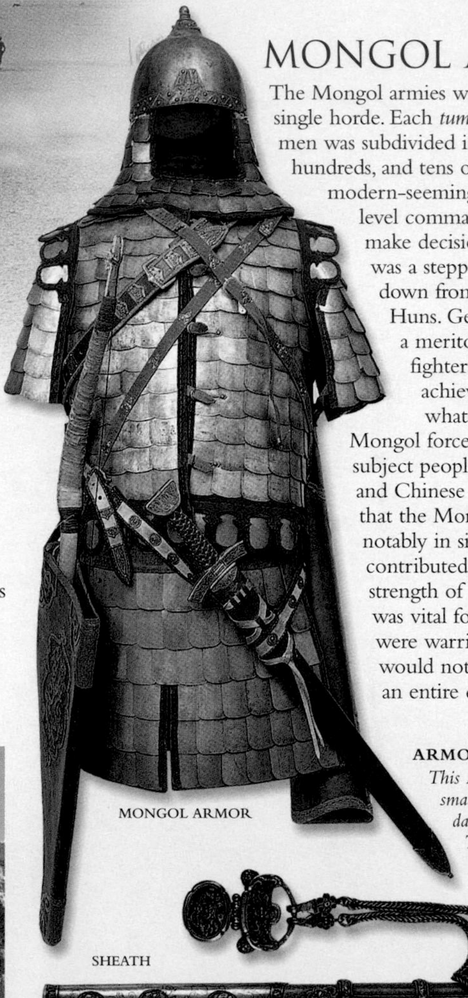

MONGOL ARMOR

ARMOR AND WEAPONS
This Mongol armor, made of small overlapping steel plates, dates from the 14th century. The composite bow, fired on horseback, was the key Mongol weapon, backed up by swords and daggers.

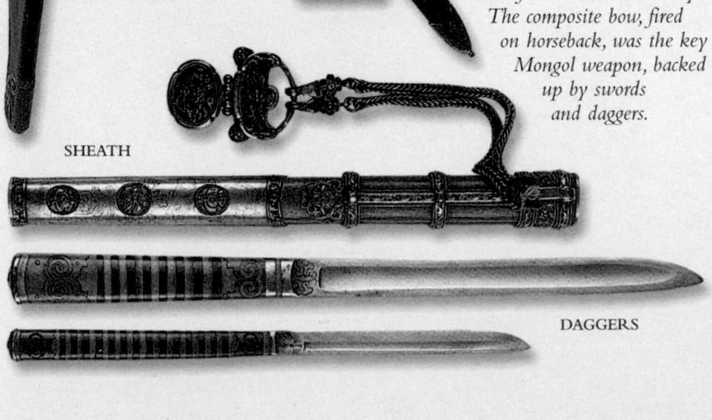

SHEATH

DAGGERS

c.1162–1227

GENGHIS KHAN

Temujin, later known as Genghis Khan ("lord of the earth"), was the son of a tribal chief in the north of what is now Mongolia. When he was 13 his father was murdered, and Temujin had little choice but to learn the art of survival. Rising to power through a mix of diplomacy and aggression, he united the warring tribes under his leadership, which a *kuriltai* (tribal council) acknowledged in 1206. His subsequent conquests appear to have been driven by a belief in his mission to rule all peoples.

MACE, SPEAR, AND BOW
This 14th-century image of Mongols at war accurately portrays their weaponry, but their small, sturdy horses were very different from these noble steeds.

TRIUMPH AND DIVISION

Genghis Khan began the Mongol conquests in 1211 with an invasion of northern China, an area with a long history of nomadic incursions. At first the Mongols failed to seize the region's walled cities, but soon learned the arts of the siege with the help of Chinese engineers. Genghis then turned west, taking the great central Asian cities of Bokhara and Samarkand. The drive westward continued under his son Ogetai, who subjugated Russia. By the time of Ogetai's death in 1243, Mongol armies had reached Poland, Hungary, and the eastern Mediterranean. By about 1250 Karakorum, the Mongol capital, was the diplomatic center of the world, receiving ambassadors from the king of France, the Byzantine emperor, and the princes of Russia. More triumphs followed. In 1258 Mongol forces captured and destroyed the Islamic capital Baghdad; two years later Genghis's grandson Kublai Khan embarked on the conquest of southern China. Kublai Khan's campaign introduced strong Chinese influences into the Mongol army. Sea warfare and sieges replaced the warfare of the steppes, and Kublai founded a short-lived dynasty of Chinese emperors, the Yuan. In the west, Mongol khanates ruled as far as the Black Sea and the Persian Gulf, but succession disputes since the mid-1200s steadily undermined Mongol unity. By 1294, the year of Kublai's death, the great wave of Mongol conquests was already at an end.

CHIEF AMONG CHIEFS
Genghis presides over a kuriltai, a council of tribal leaders. A kuriltai after Genghis's son Ogetai's death—to which all leaders had to return to attend—saved western Europe from Mongol invasion.

MONGOL CONQUESTS IN ASIA AND EUROPE

THE MONGOL ARMIES' SPEED OF MOVEMENT and outstanding skill in battle and siege allowed them to project their power west across most of Asia and central Europe. In 1241, after the battle of Leignitz and a subsequent rout of the Hungarians at the Sajo River, the Mongols were able to send scouting parties as far west as Vienna and the Alps. It was only the timely death of the great khan Ogodei, requiring the Mongols to go home to debate the succession, that saved western Europe from invasion. The Islamic world had a similar escape in 1259. The Mongol Hulegu, who had destroyed Baghdad, conquered Syria and Palestine, and was poised to invade Egypt, withdrew following the khan Mongke's death and the ensuing conflict over his successor.

▪ MONGOL CAMPAIGNS IN RUSSIA

Kalka River

DATE	1223
FORCES	Mongols: 40,000; Russians and Cumans: 80,000
LOCATION Ukraine, north of the Black Sea	**CASUALTIES** No reliable estimates

In 1222 Mongols crossed the Caucasus mountains into the territory of the Turkish Cuman peoples. An alliance of Russians and Cumans met the far smaller Mongol force at the Kalka River. The Mongols' peace envoys were murdered; in response the Mongols drove the Cumans from the field and all but annihilated the Russians.

KHAN'S COIN
A coin issued by the great khan Ogodei showing a mounted archer.

▪ MONGOL CAMPAIGNS IN RUSSIA

Vladimir

DATE	1238
FORCES	Mongols: 150,000 horsemen; Russians: unknown
LOCATION East of Moscow, Russia	**CASUALTIES** No reliable estimates

In 1237 the Mongols launched an invasion of the Russian principalities. The nominal Mongol leader was Genghis Khan's grandson Batu, but effective control lay in the hands of Subotai, one of the generals at Kalka River. The Mongols attacked in midwinter, riding their horses across the many frozen rivers

COMMANDER BATU
Batu, commander-in-chief of the western Mongol Empire, had overall responsibility for the invasion of central Europe.

BURNING VLADIMIR
The Mongols' destruction of captured cities was a deliberate policy to spread terror and cow enemies into submission.

that might otherwise have impeded their progress. The Russians believed that if they stayed within their walled cities they would be safe. But fortifications were no deterrent to the Mongols. In early 1238 they sacked the cities of Ryazan, Moscow, and Vladimir, burning each one to the ground. In March, at the Sil River, the Mongols wiped out a Russian army led by Yuri II, the grand prince of Vladimir, before moving south into Ukraine.

▪ MONGOL CAMPAIGNS IN EUROPE

Leignitz

DATE	April 9, 1241
FORCES	Mongols: 20,000; Germans and Poles: 40,000
LOCATION Leignitz (modern Legnica, southwest Poland)	**CASUALTIES** Germans and Poles: 30,000

In 1241 Subotai led a Mongol invasion of central Europe. One branch of his army, commanded by Ogodei's grandson Kaidu, swept through Poland. At Leignitz it encountered a force of Germans, Poles, and Teutonic Knights. Aware of approaching European reinforcements, Kaidu gave battle at once. His archers unleashed a hail of arrows that put part the coalition army to flight, then Mongol lancers and the more heavily armored Christian knights clashed. The Mongols gave way before the knights' charge, but swiftly turned to surround them. The Christians' losses, including many nobles, were great.

GORY PRIZES
After the battle of Leignitz the Mongols collected ears from the fallen enemy as trophies, and mounted heads on lances.

MONGOL CAMPAIGNS IN PERSIA

Fall of Baghdad

DATE
January 11–
February 10, 1258

FORCES
Mongols: 150,000

LOCATION
Baghdad, Persia
(now central Iraq)

CASUALTIES
Baghdad's citizens:
80,000

In 1256 Hulegu, the Mongol khan of Persia and the brother of the great khan Mongke, set out to conquer the Muslim Abbasid caliphate in Baghdad.

> "The Mongol army swarmed in like ants and locusts from all directions, forming a circle around the ramparts of Baghdad and setting up a wall....They prosecuted the battle in unison, set up catapults opposite the Ajami Tower, and breached it... Fierce battle was joined for six days and nights…"

WITNESS TO WAR
RASHID AD-DIN

The Persian politician and historian Rashid ad-Din (1247–1318) served under the Mongol ruler of Persia, Abagha, and was the author of the *Jami' at-tawarikh* ("Universal History").

Although real power in the Islamic world had long since shifted to Cairo and Damascus, al-Mustasim, the 37th caliph, remained a figure of major symbolic importance to Muslims. He haughtily rejected Hulegu's demands to acknowledge Mongol suzerainty. Hulegu responded by destroying the fortress of the Mongol warrior sect the Assassins at Alamut. Then, in late 1257, he marched on Baghdad from the east, while another force, led by the Mongol general Baichu, advanced south from Anatolia. On January 11, 1258, the Abbasid army confronted Baichu about 30 miles (50km) outside Baghdad. Baichu apparently lured the enemy on to marshy ground, then sent his engineers to breach the dykes of the Euphrates River behind them. Trapped between the Mongols and flooded ground, the bulk of the Arab army was destroyed in the subsequent battle. Hulegu reached Baghdad and directed his soldiers to build bridges of boats across the Tigris River up and down stream of the city. Within four days the Mongols had encircled Baghdad by land and blocked any possible escape by water. Hulegu had brought with him a formidable siege train, with large catapults that

set to battering the city's eastern walls. By the end of the first week of February the walls had begun to collapse. The Mongols were already in the suburbs when al-Mustasim surrendered on February 10, emerging from the city with all his chief officials and military commanders.

Hulegu ordered them to disarm and then had them massacred, with the exception of the caliph himself, who was kept alive for five more days, until he revealed the location of his hidden treasure. The massacre of the city's population continued for over a month, until the stink of decaying corpses in the streets persuaded Hulegu to move on.

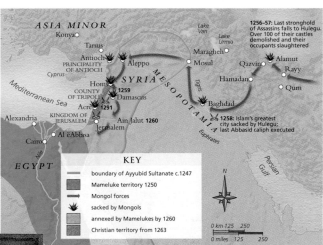

CRUEL SACKING
The only residents of Baghdad spared from the massacre of 1258 were Christians, seen by the Mongols as allies.

MONGOL CAMPAIGNS IN PALESTINE

Ain Jalut

DATE
September 23, 1260

FORCES
Mongols: 20,000;
Egyptians: possibly
30,000

LOCATION
Eastern Galilee,
Palestine

CASUALTIES
No reliable estimates

After the destruction of Baghdad, Hulegu captured the Syrian cities of Aleppo and Damascus, leaving Egypt as the sole unsubdued Muslim state in the region. Hulegu sent envoys to Cairo, calling on the Egyptian sultan Saif ad-Din Qutuz to accept Mongol

suzerainty. Qutuz had them executed. At this crucial moment, however, Hulegu was forced to return eastward to discuss the succession after the death of Mongke, the great khan. He left behind only a small part of his forces under his general Kitbuqa. Qutuz seized the opportunity and led an Egyptian army into Palestine with his Mameluke (slave soldier) general Baibars in the van. They found the Mongol forces at Ain Jalut in eastern Galilee. The numerically superior Egyptians hid part of their cavalry behind hills while Baibars led the rest out to confront the Mongols. When the Mongols charged, Baibars retreated into the hills, behind which the rest of the Egyptian cavalry emerged to hit the enemy from the

flanks. Although the trap worked, the battle was still close fought—Kitbuqa's men were superb fighters. In the end a few Mongol horsemen cut a way through to escape, while Kitbuqa was beheaded. The Egyptians went on to retake Damascus and Aleppo, although Qutuz did not benefit from his victory—Baibars assassinated him and took control of Egypt.

MONGOL CAVALRY
This 13th-century Persian illustration from Rashid ad-Din's Universal History *accurately depicts Mongol armored cavalry in action, bearing lances and round shields.*

CONQUESTS OF TIMUR

THE GREAT WARRIOR TIMUR'S career of conquest, which terrorized cities from Delhi to Damascus, was an unexpected late reprise of the era of Mongol triumph. Although himself more Turk than Mongol, Timur took the Mongol conquerors as his model, leading armies of equal fighting skill and exceeding his mentors in ferocity. His capital, Samarkand, became a place of beauty and learning, but the effect he had on most of the lands he occupied was purely destructive—the most striking feature of his campaigns was his use of terror. Timur's last expedition to the West took him as far as the Aegean at Izmir, and he died while attempting to conquer China. The vast Timurid Empire he left behind swiftly crumbled after his death.

CONQUEST OF PERSIA

Sack of Isfahan

DATE
1387

FORCES
Timur: 70,000; Persians unknown

LOCATION
Southern Persia

CASUALTIES
70,000 civilians killed

In 1387 the Shah Hodshah, who ruled southern Persia from Isfahan, died. Timur advanced on the city to make his successor pay homage. The new ruler promptly fled, leaving Isfahan to the mercies of the Timurid army. The city opened its gates and its leaders agreed to pay tribute. Timur then departed with his

PRIZED QUIVER
Timur's lieutenants may have carried richly decorated quivers like this one.

REIGN OF TERROR
Timur's troops are shown here terrorizing Isfahan. One man is being killed by having molten metal poured down his throat.

army, leaving an occupation force to collect the agreed upon payment. When they were asked to hand over their valuables, however, the citizens revolted, killing several thousand of Timur's occupation force. Timur turned back with his army and stormed the city. He then ordered his 70,000 soldiers each to bring him the severed head of one of the citizens. This order was duly fulfilled, some men who balked at killing in cold blood buying a head off a less scrupulous colleague to meet their quota. The heads were then piled in a pyramid on the walls of Isfahan.

TIMUR VERSUS GOLDEN HORDE

Terek

DATE
1395

FORCES
Timur: 100,000; Golden Horde: unknown

LOCATION
Central Asia

CASUALTIES
Possibly 100,000 dead

Timur's hardest-fought campaigns were against Tokhtamysh, leader of the Mongol Golden Horde that dominated much of western Asia. In 1391, at Kandurcha, they fought a three-day battle that may have left 100,000 dead. Although Timur held the field, he did not have the strength to pursue his enemy. In 1395, the two armies met again, this time by the Terek River. As hand-to-hand fighting raged, Tokhtamysh urged his men to seek out and kill Timur himself. They very nearly succeeded. Timur had his sword broken while resisting his attackers and was only saved by his bodyguards forming a living wall around him. But it was Tokhtamysh who finally fled the field, and this time Timur's pursuit was merciless.

INVASION OF INDIA

Panipat

DATE
December 16, 1399

FORCES Sultan of Delhi: 10,000 cavalry, 40,000 infantry; Timur: unknown

LOCATION
North of Delhi, India

CASUALTIES
Possibly 100,000 dead

As an intolerant follower of Islam, Timur was scandalized by the Muslim sultan of Delhi's failure to keep his Hindu subjects in proper submission. He decided to invade northern India, although his generals emphasized the hazards of India's mountains and rivers. The advance into India partly confirmed these fears. The section of the army led by Timur crossed the Hindu Kush, experiencing hardship— the aging leader was pulled down icy slopes on a sledge. But they reached

FIRE WEAPON
Mounted on a war elephant, a soldier hurls an incendiary device filled with flammable liquid at Timur's horsemen. The depiction of the cavalry's armor and lances is authentic.

the Indus and descended toward Delhi in an avalanche of destruction. By the time they approached the sultan's city, Timur's army was so cluttered with plunder and slaves that he ordered all Hindu captives killed, so that his men could concentrate on the battle ahead. Those murdered may have numbered 100,000. Timur met the sultan's army at Panipat, on a plain between the Himalayan foothills and the desert of Rajasthan. The Indian army lined up behind its war elephants, from which soldiers hurled incendiary devices down onto the enemy. The sultan's soldiers also fired rockets—metal fireworks—at Timur's men, but nothing disconcerted the battle-hardened invaders. Timur said contemptuously that the elephants were "driven off like cows." The sultan's defeated army fled and the gates of Delhi were opened to the conquerors, who sacked the city.

CONQUEST OF SYRIA

Aleppo

DATE
October 30, 1399

FORCES
Timur: unknown;
Mamelukes: unknown

LOCATION
Aleppo, Syria

CASUALTIES
No reliable estimates

In the 13th century the Mameluke rulers of Egypt had defeated the Mongols at Ain Jalut (see p.93), taken control of Syria, and driven the

ALEPPO CITADEL
The 10th-century citadel of Aleppo was the center of military power in the region. It was razed by Timur's forces but restored to its old glory by the Mamelukes in 1415.

Christians out of Palestine. But by the end of the 14th century they were by no means powerful enough to stand up to the army of Timur, who was drawn to western Asia by revolts against the corrupt and brutal rule of his son Miran Shah in Persia. Having implacably punished those responsible, Timur advanced on Syria. In front of Aleppo the Mameluke army attempted to make a stand, but was annihilated by Timur's forces with contemptuous ease. Aleppo was taken and sacked, leaving the great city of Damascus open to the conqueror. Timur was surprisingly lenient with the Damascenes, perhaps because they did not oppose the entry of his army. But, in the absence of systematic mass executions, his soldiers still pillaged and burned much of the city.

1336-1405

TIMUR

Timur was born into a Turkic tribe in Uzbekistan, although he claimed distant descent from Genghis Khan, whom he sought to emulate. Through fighting and intrigue he made himself emir of Samarkand and leader of the Chagatai Mongols by 1370. Unlike Genghis, he always commanded his armies in person, taking an interest in every detail of logistics and equipment. His ambition was insatiable. He was in his 60s when he undertook his invasions of India and Anatolia, and he had embarked on the conquest of China when he died, apparently of drinking too much iced water.

INVASION OF ANATOLIA

Ankara

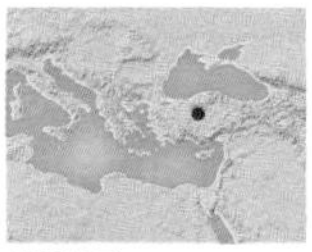

DATE
July 20, 1402

FORCES
Timur: unknown;
Ottomans: unknown

LOCATION
Near Ankara,
central Turkey

CASUALTIES
Ottomans: at least
15,000 killed

Timur's conquest of Syria brought him to the borders of Ottoman-ruled Anatolia. Rivalry between these two ethnically related powers turned to open war after Timur seized the Ottoman city of Sivas in 1400. Ottoman ruler Bayezid I, victor in the crushing defeat of the Christians at Nicopolis in 1396 (see p122), was engaged in a siege of Constantinople, but he pulled his army away to face

the threat from Timur. In the summer of 1402 Bayezid advanced east toward Sivas while Timur headed west toward the Ottoman city of Ankara. The two armies missed one another. Timur laid siege to Ankara while the Ottomans had to turn around and come back to find him. It was a weary and thirsty Ottoman army that eventually confronted Timur's battle line, which had Indian war elephants arrayed at its center. Accounts of the battle are confused, but Timur's forces seem to have been placed between the Ottomans and the only available water supply. Bayezid, forced to take

THUNDERBOLT SULTAN
Sultan Bayezid I (1360–1403) was known as "The Thunderbolt" because of the speed of his victories. His defeat at Ankara was a shock to the Ottomans.

the offensive, came under attack from the rear. Some of the Ottoman troops, ethnically related to Timur's men, deserted. At the end of the day Bayezid fled with a few hundred warriors, but was pursued and caught. He died the following year without having regained his liberty.

> "Bayezid took to flight and went with at least a thousand horsemen to a mountain. Timur surrounded the mountain so that he could not move and took him."
>
> *Johann Schiltberger*, eyewitness of Bayezid's capture, 1402

EAST ASIAN WARFARE

FOR MUCH OF THE MEDIEVAL PERIOD, China was the world's richest and most powerful empire, enjoying a significant lead in technological progress and large-scale organization. At times it extended its rule deep into central Asia, Korea, and Southeast Asia, as well as exerting a dominant influence over the early development of Japan. But with its long land border, China was always exposed to invasion and its sheer size made it liable to division and civil war.

CHINA UNDER THE SUNG

In the 7th century the Tang dynasty united China, ending 400 years of chaotic civil conflict. Under Emperor Taizong (626–649), punitive expeditions defeated Tibetans and central Asian Turks, carrying warfare far beyond China's traditional frontiers. These successes were partially reversed in the 8th century by Muslim armies in the west. The Tang depended heavily on non-Chinese troops, such as Turkish cavalry, and it was a revolt by Turkish soldiers in 755 that undermined the Tang Empire. Two centuries of insecurity followed until, in 960, the Sung dynasty replaced the Tang. The Sung concentrated on resisting seminomadic horsemen to the north and west, building up a vast standing army of Chinese peasant infantry equipped with crossbows and halberds.

PRECIOUS HORSES
The Chinese mounted frequent expeditions to central Asia in their search for thoroughbred horses to equip their cavalry.

GUNPOWDER WEAPONRY

Gunpowder was invented in China in the 9th century. Under the Sung, its incendiary and explosive properties were developed to create burning arrows, firecrackers, grenades, and flamethrowers. During the 13th century, the flamethrowers—tubes packed with gunpowder—were used to fire projectiles. These proto-guns could be used to fire lead shot or bundles of arrows, as in the device shown below.

Turban-style headgear

Bamboo tube

Bundle of arrows

PROJECTILE WEAPON

NOMADIC INVASIONS

All the efforts of Sung emperors could not prevent the north of China from being overrun. For a time the Chinese played off two tribal federations, the Khitan and the Jurchen, against one another, but in the early 12th century the Jurchen defeated first the Khitan and then the Sung. The Jurchen founded their own Jin dynasty in northern China, which was in turn overthrown by the Mongols a century later. Meanwhile, the Sung withdrew to the southern capital of Hangzhou, depending largely on naval control of the Yangtze River for defense. Their navy numbered hundreds of ships, including armored vessels with paddle wheels driven by treadmills. Siege catapults were mounted on the ships as artillery. The Mongol leader Kublai Khan was forced to employ naval power and use Muslim-developed siege machinery to conquer the Sung. By 1279 he ruled over all China.

MONGOL WARRIORS
Waves of invading horsemen entered northern China over the centuries, but only the Mongols went on to conquer the south.

SAMURAI REVOLT

This painting depicts a scene from The Tale of Heiji, *which tells the story of the failed seizure of power by the Minamoto clan of samurai in 1160.*

MONGOL DOMINANCE

Kublai Khan absorbed and developed Chinese ways of making war. He turned the Sung River fleet into an oceanic force for overseas campaigns against Japan and Java and carried out land invasions of Southeast Asia. He had limited success against areas with established military traditions, such as Southeast Asia. Mongol rule swiftly declined and in the 14th century native control was restored to China under the Ming dynasty. Korea's history mirrors that of China, as it repeatedly fought Khitan incursions, ambushing and decimating a Khitan army in 1018. Resistance to Mongol invasion in 1238 stimulated a sense of national consciousness. In the 14th century General Yi Song-gye rose to power after distinguishing himself against Japanese raiders, establishing the Choson dynasty which ruled Korea for 500 years.

Laequered sheath

War mask with nose piece

Opening for warrior's pigtail

Helmet of riveted plates

Cord to attach scabbard

SAMURAI GEAR

A samurai carried a long and a short sword, both of layered steel with an iron core. The helmet, or kabuto, and face mask gave the head comprehensive protection.

EUROPEAN VERSION

A 15th-century European artist— with no knowledge of the distinctive ships, clothes, or weaponry of the East, represents Kublai Khan conducting a siege

THE EMERGENCE OF THE SAMURAI

Japan developed a distinctive style of warfare in the course of almost ceaseless civil conflicts caused by the lack of a strong central authority. The principal warriors, the samurai, were armored horsemen, usually fighting dismounted with bows and swords, and placing a heavy emphasis on one-to-one combat. With their origins in the imperial palace guard in 10th-century Kyoto, the samurai developed into a widespread warrior class, and then into warring clans vying for supreme power. The triumph of the Minamoto clan in the late 12th century created the shogunate, a system of military rule under puppet emperors. The rule of the shoguns allowed spells of internal peace and of organized resistance to Mongol invasions in 1274 and 1281, but in the 14th century civil strife returned. It was another 300 years before Japan was effectively pacified.

KUBLAI AND THE MING

THE SLOW-MOTION FALL of China's Sung Empire took a century and a half to complete, from the loss of northern China to Jurchen steppe horsemen in the early 12th century to the final triumph of Kublai Khan's Mongol armies in the 1270s. In order to accomplish these military triumphs, however, the invaders from the steppe were forced to adopt Chinese military techniques, including the use of siege engines and gunpowder weapons, and fighting in large-scale naval warfare. Eventually, however, the Mongols lost control of China to the Ming.

JURCHEN–SUNG WAR

Kaifeng

DATE
September 1126–
January 1127

FORCES
Jurchen: unknown;
Chinese: over 500,000

LOCATION
Northern China

CASUALTIES
No reliable estimates

In 1122 the Jurchen, tribal horsemen from beyond the Great Wall, invaded the Chinese Sung Empire. Despite the vast size of the Chinese forces—a standing army of around 500,000 plus huge peasant militias—the Jurchen swept through northern China and eventually laid siege to the Sung capital, Kaifeng. Although the Sung used their latest weapons—explosives and gunpowder-tipped arrows—the city fell after a siege of four months. Emperor Hui Zong was captured, but his Sung successors continued to rule over southern China, while the Jurchen established the Jin dynasty in the north.

MONGOL CONQUEST OF CHINA

Fall of Zhongdu

DATE
February 1214–
May 1215

FORCES
Mongols: unknown;
Chinese: unknown

LOCATION
Modern Beijing

CASUALTIES
No reliable estimates

In 1211 Mongol leader Genghis Khan (see p.93) turned his attention to the conquest of the Jin Empire. At first his campaign was frustrated by the Mongols' ignorance of siegecraft and inability to capture fortified Chinese cities. But, with typical resourcefulness, the Mongols developed a siege train, probably employing Chinese experts to provide the necessary skills. In February 1214, equipped with mangonels and rams, they besieged the city of Zhongdu (Beijing). After the Mongols defeated a Jin relief army in March, there was little hope for the city's defenders, yet they held out for over a year. Food shortages had reportedly reduced both besiegers and besieged to cannibalism by the time the city fell in May 1215.

Quiver of arrows

WARRIOR
Most Mongol horsemen fought as mounted archers, using hit-and-run skirmishing tactics, although there were also heavier Mongol cavalry with lances and swords.

MONGOL CONQUEST OF CHINA

Siege of Kaifeng

DATE
1232–33

FORCES
Mongols: unknown;
Chinese: unknown

LOCATION
Northern China

CASUALTIES
No reliable estimates

In 1231 the Mongols undertook the final destruction of the Jin Empire, supported by the Sung, long-standing enemies of the Jin. In 1232 the Mongols, led by Subotai, laid siege to the Jin capital, Kaifeng. It was an extraordinary confrontation: both the Mongols and the Jurchen Jin were steppe horsemen, yet fought a classic siege in the style developed by settled civilizations. The Mongols used siege engines and dug sapping trenches toward the walls. The Jin, meanwhile, employed the latest Chinese gunpowder technology. Their most powerful device, a "Heaven-Shaking Thunder-Crash Bomb," created an explosion that could be heard 30 miles (50km) away and scorched an area 300ft (100m) square. The device had a devastating effect: "The attacking soldiers were all blown to bits, not even a trace being left behind." The Jin also had proto-flamethrowers: bamboo tubes full of gunpowder mounted on a lance, which sent out a 6ft- (2m-) long jet of sparks and fire. This was all to no avail. Kaifeng was taken by assault after a year-long siege.

MONGOL CONQUEST OF CHINA

Xiangyang

DATE
1268–73

FORCES
Mongols: unknown;
Chinese: unknown

LOCATION
Hebei, southern China

CASUALTIES
No reliable estimates

Once in control of the Jin Empire, the Mongols turned south to attack the Sung, who had been foolish enough to help them achieve dominance over northern China. Overcoming the Sung was, however, no mean task. The economic and manpower resources of the southern empire were vast. The terrain of the Sung lands was totally unsuited to the fast-moving mounted warfare of the steppe tradition, being a mix of agricultural land and forest, traversed by large rivers and canals—hot and short on fodder for horses. But Genghis Khan's grandson Kublai had the relentless will to complete the final conquest of China. He began the campaign as lieutenant to Great Khan Möngke; after Möngke's death in 1259 he continued the conquest as great khan himself. The pivotal struggle of the war took place from 1268 around the fortified cities of Fancheng and Xiangyang. Kublai's troops were commanded by his brilliant general Bayan, grandson of the famed Subotai. The Sung armies were commanded by Lu Wenhuan. A hard-fought series of battles and skirmishes took place around the two cities, including river engagements in which the Mongols proved they had adapted to naval warfare, fielding a fleet equipped with shipborne catapults. Handheld weapons firing projectiles were probably employed by both sides—the first ever use of firearms in battle. In 1272 two Muslim engineers arrived from Mongol-ruled Persia. Under their direction siege engines were built so powerful that no city walls could resist them. Fancheng and Xiangyang fell and Lu Wenhuan surrendered. Kublai then took the vast and wealthy Sung capital, Hangzhou, in 1276. The final battle of the war was a naval battle in the South China Sea during which the last Sung emperor, still a child, was drowned.

BRIDGE OF BOATS
An illustration from a 16th-century Persian history of the Mongols shows Kublai's men crossing the Yangtze River on a pontoon bridge.

1214–1294

KUBLAI KHAN

The grandson of Genghis Khan, Kublai was a Mongol great khan who came fully under the spell of Chinese civilization. Well before becoming the first emperor of the Chinese Yuan dynasty in 1271, he had established Beijing as his capital, rather than fixing himself in the Mongol steppe. His ambition for conquest was insatiable, leading him to campaign as far afield as Japan in the north and Vietnam, Burma, and Java in the south.

RISE OF THE MING

Red Turban Revolt

DATE
1356–68

FORCES
Mongols: unknown;
Chinese: unknown

CASUALTIES
Unknown

LOCATION
Eastern China

The Yuan dynasty that Kublai Khan founded never won general acceptance in China, the Mongols being seen as an alien rulers. The Yuan, moreover, failed to maintain efficient government and an effective military system. In the mid-14th century, banditry and revolt spread through large areas of China, and in 1351 a group known as the Red Turbans became the focus for a widespread anti-Mongol uprising. Their leader, Zhu Yuanzhang, came from humble peasant origins and was living in a Buddhist monastery in south China when he was recruited into a local Red Turban band in 1352. Within four years he rose to command his own section of the Red Turbans, led them in the seizure of the city of Nanjing, and established an oasis of orderly government there. In a series of campaigns against rival rebel or bandit leaders, Zhu seized most of southern China, before taking on the Yuan emperor Ch'en-liang, still ruling from Beijing, in a struggle focused on control of the Yangtze River. In 1363 a major naval battle was fought at Lake Po-yang, on the middle Yangtze. The

CHINESE FIRELANCE
Early Chinese gunpowder weapons like this one worked by stuffing projectiles such as darts into a bamboo tube or lance: the exploding gunpowder would hurl these with lethal force.

ZHENG HE

Under the expansionist Ming Yongle emperor, Muslim eunuch Zheng He projected Chinese power around the coasts of Southeast Asia and the Indian Ocean. He built a fleet of huge nine-masted junks which, with numerous smaller vessels, embarked on seven voyages between 1405 and 1433, sailing as far as Sumatra, India, Persia, Arabia, and the east coast of Africa. The last of his voyages involved 63 ships and over 30,000 men. Zheng brought back curios such as a giraffe for the emperor's zoo, but the serious purpose of his enterprise was to make rulers in these distant lands—already linked to China by trade—acknowledge the Chinese emperor as their suzerain and pay tribute. In 1436, however, the Hongxi emperor banned all further ocean voyages as the Ming dynasty turned from power projection to a defensive concentration on its internal affairs.

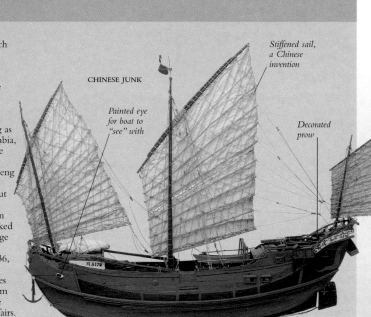

CHINESE JUNK

Stiffened sail, a Chinese invention

Painted eye for boat to "see" with

Decorated prow

Yuan fleet included three-decked warships that were larger than any vessels Zhu could muster, but Zhu's smaller ships were more maneuverable. Both sides had cannon mounted on board—the Chinese had discovered how to fire projectiles from gunpowder weapons. Zhu was victorious, incorporating many of the captured Yuan ships into his own fleet, which went on to take the coastal cities along the South China Sea.

In 1368 the last Yuan emperor fled as Zhu's army advanced on Beijing. Zhu founded the Ming dynasty as Emperor Hung Wu. Ming armies fought the Mongols for the next 20 years until their final victory in 1388.

MING DEFENSES
Built under the Ming dynasty at the most westerly extremity of the Great Wall, this fortress was an attempt to protect China against renewed invasions by steppe horsemen.

> **"But when the nation began to rouse itself, we, as simple peasants of Huai-yu, conceived the patriotic idea to save the people…"**
>
> *Manifesto of Accession, sent by Zhu Yuanzhang to Byzantine emperor,* 1372

476–1492

SOUTHEAST ASIA

MEDIEVAL WARFARE IN SOUTHEAST ASIA was heavily influenced by Indian models. War elephants were widely used, in part because horses were largely unsuited to the area's climate and vegetation. Armies were more Chinese-influenced in the northern portion of what is now Vietnam. Although most wars were between states within the region, incursions from the north by Chinese forces were also frequent.

CHINESE–ANNAMESE WAR

Bach Dang

DATE
938

FORCES
Chinese: unknown;
Annamese: unknown

LOCATION
Near Haiphong,
northern Vietnam

CASUALTIES
No reliable estimates

Annam (present-day northern Vietnam), which had been under Chinese rule from the 2nd century BCE, seized the opportunity presented by the decline of the Tang dynasty in the 10th century CE to assert its independence. A force under Liu Hung-tsao sailed south to uphold Chinese authority. The Vietnamese general Ngo Quyen, anticipating that this fleet would sail up the tidal Bach Dang River, had a line of iron-tipped stakes driven into the riverbed so that they were just submerged at high tide, then sent shallow-draft boats out at high tide to provoke a fight and retreated, drawing the Chinese ships into a pursuit. As the tide went out, the Chinese fleet was impaled on the spikes. Ngo Quyen then attacked to complete the rout, in which Hung-tsao was killed. The area became independent as Dai Co Viet in 946.

CAMPAIGNS OF KUBLAI KHAN

Ngasaunggyan

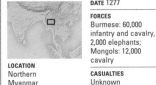

DATE 1277

FORCES
Burmese: 60,000
infantry and cavalry,
2,000 elephants;
Mongols: 12,000
cavalry

LOCATION
Northern
Myanmar

CASUALTIES
Unknown

This battle, between Kublai Khan, the Mongol ruler of China, and the Burmese king Narathihapate is chiefly known from the account of the Venetian traveler Marco Polo. Although his version is at variance with Burmese chronicles, it is probably substantially correct. In 1273, Kublai sent envoys to Pagan, the Burmese capital, demanding tribute. Narathihapate had the envoys killed, apparently because they showed disrespect by failing to take off their shoes. A force, probably consisting mostly of Turkish cavalry, was sent from the southern Chinese province of Yunnan to punish the Burmese. The two armies met on a plain. The Burmese advanced with their war elephants in the van, causing the enemy's horses to shy away. The Mongol commander ordered his men to dismount and fire their bows on foot. The rain of arrows panicked the elephants, which turned and charged back into the Burmese ranks. Kublai's cavalry then remounted and charged the Burmese, striking out with sword and mace. After a fierce fight, Narathihapate's army was put to the flight. The city of Pagan was eventually captured by the Mongols and the kingdom destroyed.

PAGAN TEMPLE
Pagan became a Mongol provincial capital in 1287 and was razed to the ground by the emergent Shans in 1299.

KHMER–CHAM WARS

Sack of Angkor

DATE
1177

FORCES
Cham: unknown;
Khmers: unknown

LOCATION North of
Tonle Sap lake, north-
central Cambodia

CASUALTIES
No reliable estimates

The 12th century brought prolonged warfare between the kingdoms of the Cham, in what is now southern Vietnam, and their neighbors, the Khmers, in what is now Cambodia. The Cham, a people of Indonesian origin, had established the powerful Champa state and repeatedly waged war against Annam (northern Vietnam) as well as Angkor. The Khmer kingdom of Angkor is now known chiefly for its remarkable Hindu temples, but it too was a state whose rulers were expected to be warriors, and Angkorian armies fought not only Champa and Annam but also against the Thais to the west. Most of the details of this warfare can be derived only from temple inscriptions and reliefs. It appears, however, that in the 1170s Champa gained the upper hand over Angkor. The two countries' armies were similar, consisting of war elephants carrying a single warrior armed with spear or bow, a few cavalry, and a mass of infantry levies, who may have fought in nothing but loincloths. The Chams also possessed crossbows, possibly due to their contact with China. These weapons were used by their horsemen and may have given them the edge over Angkor. In 1177 Cham invaders sacked Angkor's cities and subjugated the country. With Angkor's king, the usurper Tribhuvanadityavarman, dead, Jayavarman assumed leadership of the Khmer resistance. In 1178 it seems that a naval battle was fought, either on the Mekong River or on Lake Tonle Sap, in which the Cham were decisively defeated. By 1181 Jayavarman had restored Angkor's independence and over the next two decades he completely turned the tables on the Cham. By 1203 Jayavarman had defeated and occupied Champa, but the cycle of warfare continued—neither of the antagonists

c.1125–1219

JAYAVARMAN VII

One of the greatest Khmer rulers, Jayavarman was seemingly reluctant to assume power. He did not assert his right to the throne after the death of Dharanindravarman, his father, in 1160, and it was only after Angkor's humiliation by the Cham in 1177 that he emerged as a Khmer leader. King from 1181, he not only restored Khmer power through his military activities but also constructed some of Angkor's most impressive temples.

had the resources to make a victory permanent. Indeed, the 13th century turned out to be a period when Champa's star was once more in the ascendant, while Angkor struggled against rising pressure from the Thais.

KHMER WARRIORS
Reliefs such as this one at Bayon, Cambodia, of a war elephant and footsoldiers provide much information about Khmer warfare.

DAI VIET INDEPENDENCE WAR

Lam Son Uprising (Tot Dong)

DATE
1426

FORCES
China: unknown;
Vietnamese: unknown

LOCATION
West of Hanoi,
northern Vietnam

CASUALTIES
No reliable estimates

In 1405 the Chinese Ming dynasty invaded Dai Viet (northern Vietnam) on the pretext of settling a succession dispute. Within a year the previously independent kingdom had been reduced to a province of China. Ming rule was harsh and provoked a resistance movement led by Le Loi, a Vietnamese landowner, who in 1416 established himself with a few followers in a mountainous region, from where he gradually built up an army of several thousand soldiers. From 1424 he began a guerrilla campaign, attacking isolated garrisons. Some 100,000 more troops were sent from China, but Le Loi's forces also grew as Vietnamese flocked to his banner. By 1426 the rebels were strong enough to take on the Chinese—commanded by the experienced general Wang Tong—in open battle. Using elephants to unnerve Wang Tong's cavalry, Le Loi routed the enemy at Tot Dong. Restricted to a few strongpoints, the Chinese forces were in a precarious situation. Le Loi offered to help Wang Tong evacuate his troops in return for a guarantee of Vietnamese independence. In 1427 the Chinese accordingly left and Le Loi became ruler of Dai Viet.

SAMURAI WARFARE

IN THE MEDIEVAL PERIOD JAPANESE warfare was highly stylized. Battles were preceded by an exchange of oratory as samurai picked out individuals to fight in single combat, while fighting often began with a series of archery duels. Strict rules of honorable conduct applied—for example, the severed heads of samurai killed in battle were supposed to be mounted on spiked boards and returned to their own side. Yet there was no doubt of the samurai's fighting prowess, as shown when the Mongols tried and failed to invade Japan in 1281.

SHOGUN AGE
The Taira clan gained supremacy in mid-12th-century Japan, but their rule was short-lived and civil war again broke out.

KEY

―――	daimyo boundaries
◼	Taira
◼	Northern Fujiwara
◼	Minamoto Yoritomo
◼	Minamoto Yoshinaka
▨	area of Yoritomo control 1190
→	Minamoto campaigns

476–1492

First Battle of Uji

DATE
1180

FORCES
Taira: unknown;
Minamoto: unknown

CASUALTIES
No reliable estimates

LOCATION
Uji, near
Kyoto, Japan

In 1160 the Taira clan took power in Japan, executing many of their Minamoto rivals. Twenty years later the Minamoto fought back against the rule of Taira Kiyomori, setting off a series of conflicts known as the Gempei Wars. The Minamoto were allied to Buddhist warrior-monks, rough fighters who upheld the interests of their temples in the chaotic conditions of the time. The monks' chief weapon was the *naginata*, a long-handled, swordlike implement. The first battle of the Gempei Wars occurred when a force including Minamoto Yorimasa was pursued by the Taira to the south bank of the Uji River. They set out to prevent the Taira crossing, while waiting for reinforcements. Warrior-monks fought in single combat on the broken bridge over the river to hold the Taira back. The Minamoto were finally driven back to the Byodo-In temple, where, as his sons held the enemy at bay, Yorimasa dashed off a poem before committing ritual suicide.

> "Like a fossil tree
> From which we
> gather no flower
> Sad has been my
> life Fated no fruit
> to produce."

Minamoto Yorimasa,
poem written before
his *seppuku*, 1180

Kawasaki

DATE
1057

FORCES
Abe Sadato: 4,000;
Minamoto: unknown

CASUALTIES
Unknown

LOCATION
Northern
Japan

Minamoto Yoshiie (1041–1108) came to be seen as embodying the pure spirit of the samurai. At the time of the Early Nine Years War (1051–63), he was a young man fighting alongside his father, Minamoto Yoriyoshi. The Minamoto clan had been entrusted with defeating a rebellion by the Abe clan in Dewa Province, northern Japan. The first major battle of the war took place at Kawasaki. Abe Sadato had established his forces in a strong defensive position. The Minamoto attacked during a snowstorm, but were driven off and pursued. In the hard-fought retreat, Yoshiie showed his outstanding qualities as a samurai, earning the name Hachimantaro—son of the war god Hachiman. He played a major role in the eventual defeat of the Abe, capturing several forts, and successfully besieging their stockade at Kuriyagawa. Victorious, he carried Sadato's severed head back to the Japanese capital, Kyoto, to prove that the job was done.

SAMURAI SWORD
This 17th-century short sword is the kind that samurai would use when committing ritual suicide, or seppuku, for which they became famed.

MOUNTED BOWMEN
This scene of early samurai warfare highlights the importance of the bow as a weapon. Prowess as an archer was valued more highly than swordsmanship.

HONORABLE SUICIDE
Minamoto Yorimasa, shown here in a 19th-century Japanese representation, became revered more for the manner of his death than for any feat on the battlefield.

GEMPEI WARS

Kurikara

DATE	June 1183
FORCES	Taira: 100,000; Minamoto: 50,000
LOCATION Central Japan, north of Kyoto	**CASUALTIES** No reliable estimates

Kurikara is the battle that marked the point the Gempei Wars turned in favor of the Minamoto. Led by Taira Koremori, son of the clan leader Taira Munemori, the Taira army advanced north to meet the forces of Minamoto Yoshinaka. The Taira forces, although numerous, consisted mostly of poorly trained levies. They passed through the countryside like a plague of locusts, consuming the meager rice stocks of a desperate peasantry. After capturing the Minamoto fortress of Hiuche, the Taira made the mistake of dividing their forces. While Taira Koremori led the larger part into the mountain pass of Kurikara, a smaller contingent split off to march farther north into Noto province—where they achieved a

FACE MASK
Samurai wore masks such as this both for protection and to make themselves look fierce. This type of half-mask with nose piece was called a mempo.

small and strategically worthless victory. The main Taira army reached the top of the pass, from where they saw Yoshinaka's army in the valley below. Yoshinaka had erected a crowd of banners in a prominent spot to give the impression that his forces were

more numerous than they actually were. In this way he deterred the Taira from an immediate attack. While they rested and watered their horses in the mountain pass, Yoshinaka sent a detachment sweeping around to the enemy's rear. To distract the Taira's attention from this move, he initiated a prolonged archery duel that kept them occupied until near sunset. As the light failed, the Minamoto mobile contingent suddenly attacked the Taira from the rear. To increase the panic, Yoshinaka had burning torches tied to the horns of a herd of oxen, which were driven into the narrow pass. The Taira forces fled in disorder, many falling to their deaths from the edges of mountain paths. Of those who made it down into the valley, many were slaughtered. After this resounding victory, Yoshinaka pursued the remnants of the Taira army toward the capital, Kyoto. Taira Munemori fled the city, taking most of the imperial family with him. Yoshinaka entered in triumph and installed the Minamoto candidate for the imperial throne, Go-Shirakawa, as emperor.

GEMPEI WARS

Awazu

DATE	1184
FORCES	Yoshinaka: unknown; Noriyori and Yoshitsune: unknown
LOCATION Awazu, Tokushima Prefecture, Japan	**CASUALTIES** No reliable estimates

Minamoto Yoshinaka's rule, after his victory at Kurikara, was so vicious that his own clan took up arms against him. He was driven out by his cousins Minamoto Yoshitsune and Minamoto Noriyori. After an initial defeat at the second battle of Uji, Yoshinaka faced his foes at Awazu. Fighting alongside him were his trusted companion Imai Kanehira and his wife, Tomoe Gozen. Yoshitsune and Noriyori won after a hard fight. Yoshinaka was killed by an arrow after his horse was immobilized. Tomoe Gozen also died, though only after claiming the head of a samurai opponent. Facing defeat, Imai Kanehira committed *seppuku* in original fashion by plunging headfirst off his horse with a sword in his mouth.

GEMPEI WARS

Dan no Ura

DATE	April 25, 1185
FORCES	Minamoto: 850 ships; Taira: 500 ships
LOCATION Between Honshu and Kyushu, Japan	**CASUALTIES** No reliable estimates

The sea battle at Dan no Ura sealed the Minamoto victory in the Gempei Wars. The two fleets each carried a number of samurai. The battle began with an exchange of long-range arrowfire, followed by hand-to-hand fights with sword and dagger. Helped by the treachery of a Taira general and an opportune turn of the tide, the Minamoto triumphed. Most of the Taira committed suicide, leaping into the ocean to drown. Taira Munemori was fished out of the sea, to be taken back to Kyoto for execution.

GEMPEI WARS

Ichinotani

DATE	March 1184
FORCES	Minamoto: 10,000; Taira: unknown
LOCATION West of Kobe, western Honshu	**CASUALTIES** No reliable estimates

Minamoto Yoshinaka's death left his clan free to concentrate on their struggle with the Taira, whose leaders had retreated to the fortress of Ichinotani. Led by Minamoto Yoshitsune, an army advanced down

the coast toward the fort. Yoshitsune positioned his main army facing the Taira defensive line. The battle opened in traditionally ritualistic fashion: Minamoto samurai approached the Taira line, shouting out their lineage and military record, waiting for a Taira warrior to propose single combat. As this prelude to full battle was played out, Yoshitsune led a mounted detachment to the rear of the fortress, where it backed on to a steep cliff. The Taira had neglected their defenses on this side. But Yoshitsune's forces rode down the cliff and stormed into the rear of the Taira position. The Taira staged a fighting retreat to their boats on the beach. One account of the battle tells how the Minamoto samurai

HEAD SEVERING
After a battle it was a samurai convention to cut off the heads of enemy dead with a dagger. Some of these men carry naginata *blades, along with bows and swords.*

Kumagai Naozane, grieving for his 16-year-old son killed earlier in the battle, found himself in a position to kill the 16-year-old Taira Atsumori—which he did, after much soul-searching. Most of the Taira escaped by sea, but the Minamoto pursued them along the coast. Yoshitsune drove the Taira out of their last stronghold at Yashima. Dispirited, the Taira fell back to the shore of the Shimonoseki Strait. There Yoshitsune found them in April 1185 for the decisive battle of Dan no Ura.

SAMURAI AT SEA
This scroll depicting the battle of Dan no Ura shows long-oared ships closing with grappling hooks ready to enable the samurai warriors to engage in close-quarter combat.

First Mongol Invasion

DATE
November 1274

FORCES
Mongols: 40,000;
Japanese: 10,000

LOCATION
Hakata Bay,
Japan

CASUALTIES
No reliable estimates

In 1274 the Mongol leader Kublai Khan dispatched a fleet of 900 ships from Korea, carrying a combined force of Mongol, Chinese, and Korean troops. The army landed at Hakata Bay, after having slaughtered the defenders of Tshushima and Iki

islands. It was the first time samurai had encountered a foreign force and they were startled by the enemy's unceremonious form of warfare, ignoring calls for single combat and instead, as a Japanese chronicle puts it, "rushing forward all together in a mass, grappling with any individuals they could catch and killing them." This shock was augmented by the Mongol use of massed bowmen and gunpowder bombs flung by catapults, forcing the Japanese to retreat inland toward Dazaifu. Japan seemed in danger of falling to the invaders, but the Mongols reembarked and disappeared almost as soon as they had come, presumably having only constituted a reconnaissance in force. The oft-repeated story that they were scattered by bad weather seems unlikely.

> "On this past first day a typhoon sank most of the foreign pirates' ships. Several thousands were killed or captured. Not one enemy boat remains at Iki or Tshushima."

Japanese courtier Kadenokoji Kanenaka on the second Mongol invasion, 1281

1159–1189

MINAMOTO YOSHITSUNE

The most brilliant general of the Gempei Wars, Yoshitsune was a son of Minamoto Yoshitomo. When his father was assassinated in 1160, the infant Yoshitsune was sent away to be brought up in a monastery. In 1180, he joined the revolt against the Taira led by his elder brother Minamoto Yoritomo. He was largely responsible for the victories that resulted in the defeat of the Taira in 1185. Yoritomo reacted to Yoshitsune's military success with fear rather than gratitude. Declaring Yoshitsune guilty of treason, Yoritomo had him pursued and harried until, cornered by his enemies, he committed suicide in June 1189.

SAMURAI ARMOR

This 12th-century samurai warrior's battle dress is in the great armor, or O-yoroi, style. The samurai of the period were in essence mounted archers.

Ornamented face mask, or mempo

Ornate armored sleeve, or kote

Iron strip attached to the top breast plate

Skirtlike guard, or haidate, to protect loins

Lacquered iron plates laced with silk and leather

Style of boots reflected samurai's rank

476–1492

Second Mongol Invasion

DATE
June–August 1281

FORCES
Mongols: 150,000;
Japanese: 40,000

LOCATION
Hakata Bay,
Japan

CASUALTIES
Mongols: allegedly
100,000

For seven years after his abortive invasion of 1274, Kublai Khan bided his time. By 1281, when he mounted a renewed serious invasion, the Japanese had prepared coastal defenses to meet it, including the building of a

12.5 mile- (20km-) long stone barrier at Hakata Bay. This time the Mongols had 4,400 warships in two fleets, the smaller one sailing from Korea and the larger from northern China. The Korean fleet arrived first at Hakata Bay, but the ferocity of the Japanese response and the strength of their coastal fortifications restricted the Mongols to offshore islands, where they were repeatedly raided by samurai in small boats. The fleet withdrew to rendezvous with the ships from China at Iki island, but aside from an attack on the island of Takashima they had achieved nothing when a typhoon—known to the Japanese as the "divine wind" (*kamikaze*)—scattered and sank the invasion force. The Mongols made no further attempts to conquer of Japan.

Minatogawa

DATE
June 5, 1336

FORCES
Imperial army: 2,700;
Ashikaga: unknown

LOCATION
Minato River,
near Kobe, Japan

CASUALTIES
No reliable estimates

In 1331 Japanese emperor Go-Daigo led a revolt against the Hojo shoguns. Among the imperial supporters was Kusunoke Masashige, who defied the Hojo from his mountain fortresses. The capture of their capital, Kamakura, in 1333 brought the Hojo's downfall, only for another clan, the Ashikaga, to

launch a bid for power. In 1336 their army marched on the imperial capital. Go-Daigo's commander, Nitta Yoshisada, called on Kusunoke to come to Kyoto's defense. Kusunoke protested at the decision to confront the Ashikaga, but reluctantly went along with it. The imperial forces took up position astride the Minato River. The Ashikaga advanced by land and sea, Tadayoshi and Shoni Yorihisa commanding the land forces, Ashikaga Takauji and Hosokawa the seaborne forces. Facing a frontal assault led by Shoni and threatened by Hosokawa from the rear, Nitta retreated. This left Kusunoke's small band hopelessly exposed. After six hours' fighting, with his situation hopeless, Kusunoke committed suicide along with his relatives and retainers.

SAMURAI SWORDS

FROM THE 12TH CENTURY Japanese military life was dominated by the samurai, an elite warrior class with its own code of honor. Samurai were expected to cultivate an ascetic lifestyle, and be willing to die at any moment in the service of their lord. Central to a samurai's armory were his swords, which were often of superb quality. A long sword (*katana*) was worn pushed through his sash together with a short sword (*wakizashi*). Both were carried with the sharp edge uppermost in order to deliver a sweeping cut straight from the scabbard. Not until 1868 was the samurai class abolished.

BLADES AND SCHOOLS

As forging techniques improved, so did the style of the sword. Early swords were straight, but by the 8th century warriors found that a curved sword could be drawn from the scabbard more quickly and provided a better cutting angle. With the rise of the samurai the military arts, inspired by the teachings of Zen Buddhism, became the highest form of study. A local lord would sponsor a fencing school where his retainers could learn to use the sword—a skill acquired through years of grueling training. Wooden and bamboo swords were used for practice, and only from the 17th century was padded armor worn to reduce the risk of injury in training.

DAGGERS

The samurai carried a tanto, a small dagger that he kept hidden in his armor. The tanto scabbard contained a kozuka (small knife) and a kogai (skewer).

TANTO

LACQUERED TANTO SCABBARD

KOZUKA

KOGAI

SHORT SWORDS

The wakizashi, or short sword, was an additional fighting weapon, but was also used by samurai for seppuku, *ritual suicide by disemboweling.*

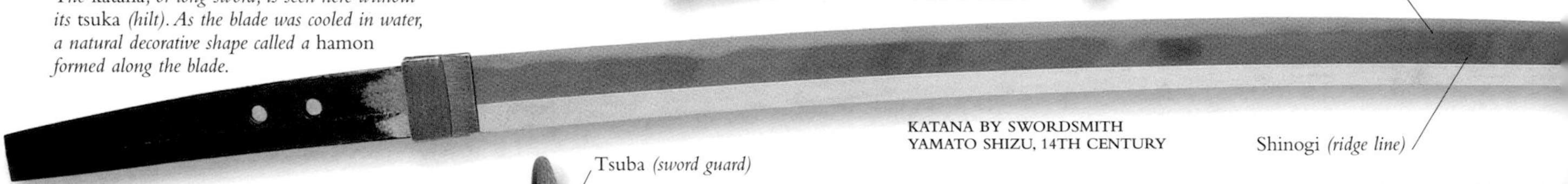

SWORDSMITHS

This print shows swordsmiths practicing their art. Blades were forged through a complex process of heating and folding iron ore, hammering it into shape, and cooling it in cold water to harden the metal.

WAKIZASHI, 17TH CENTURY

Hamon (*crystalline wave pattern*)

LONG SWORDS

The katana, or long sword, is seen here without its tsuka (hilt). As the blade was cooled in water, a natural decorative shape called a hamon formed along the blade.

KATANA BY SWORDSMITH YAMATO SHIZU, 14TH CENTURY

Shinogi (*ridge line*)

Tsuba (*sword guard*)

Menuki (*ornaments*)

KATANA ATTRIBUTED TO SHIZU GROUP OF SWORDSMITHS, 15TH CENTURY

SWORD STATUS

The long sword was carried out of doors only and samurai alone were permitted to own one. The short sword was worn at all times. The hilts were often ornate status symbols, made of wood, wrapped in sharkskin and braid, and containing ornaments. The butt of the hilt could be used as a punching weapon if an opponent was too close for the samurai to draw his sword.

Sageo (*cord*) fastened the scabbard to the belt

LACQUERED SCABBARD (SAYA) WTH CORD (SAGEO), 15TH CENTURY

ORNATE WAKIZASHI

SHORT-BLADED SPEAR (YARI)

BATTLE ARMOR

As the samurai sword was used for delivering wide cuts, armor had to permit free and rapid movement while providing some protection. Even so, a good blade could cut through most armor. Numerous laquered metal plates were laced together with silk and leather to cover the chest, arms, and shoulders. From the 16th century, armor became sturdier, partly to provide more protection against musket fire. The style and complexity of armor evolved over time until the whole body was protected, as in this elaborate 19th-century example (right).

FIGHTING SKILL
This 19th-century print shows a samurai raising his long sword to deflect a cut. He does this by pushing the flat side of the blade forward in order not to damge his cutting edge.

WAKIZASHI BY SWORDSMITH SESHU JU NAGATSUNA, DATED 1792

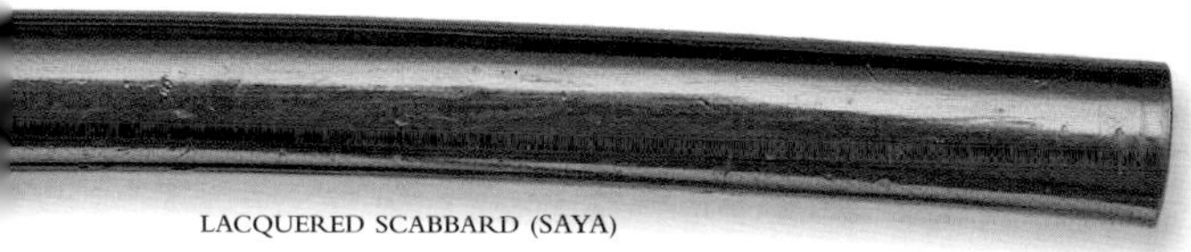

LACQUERED SCABBARD (SAYA)

Monuchi *(the part of the blade used for cutting)*

Mune *(flat back of blade)*

Kissagi *(point)*

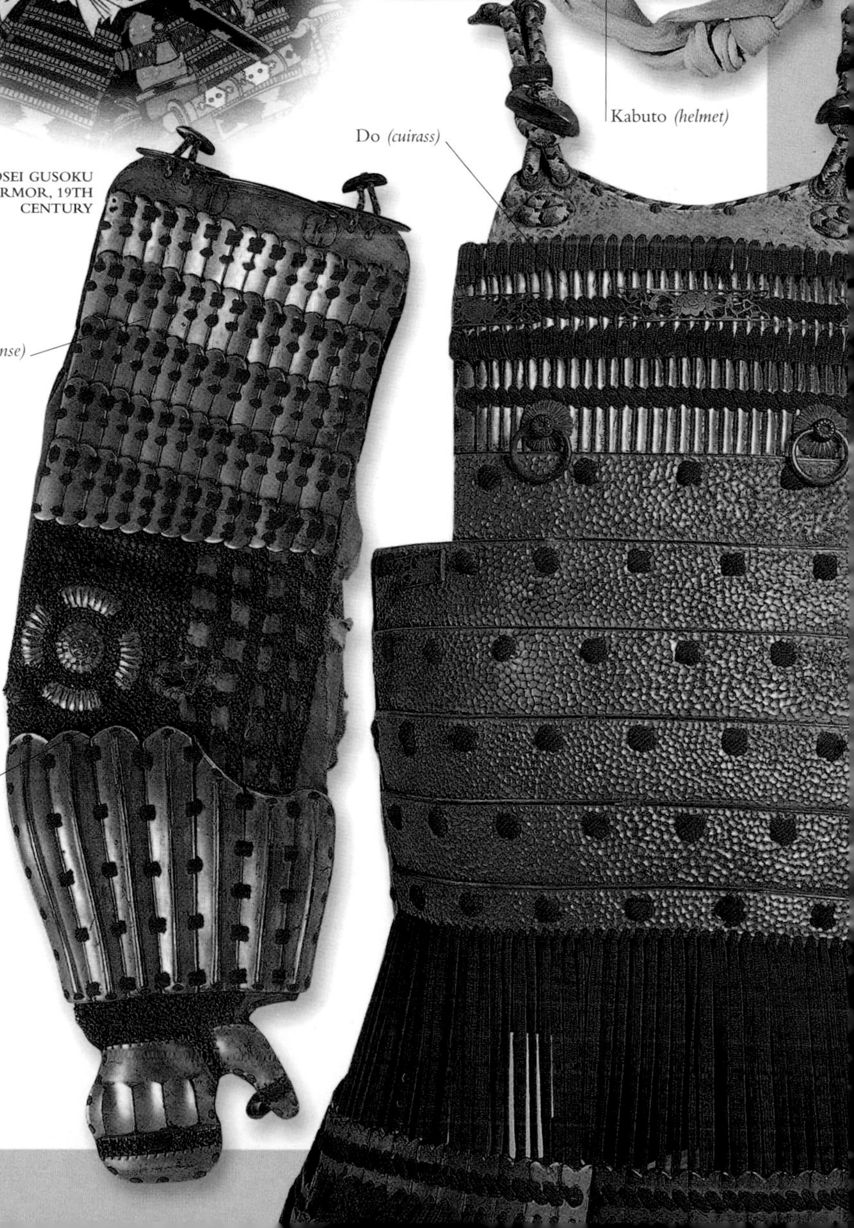

Ikada *(plate in mail)*

Kabuto *(helmet)*

Do *(cuirass)*

TOSEI GUSOKU ARMOR, 19TH CENTURY

Kote *(arm defense)*

KNIGHTS, CASTLES, AND BOWMEN

DESPITE ATTEMPTS TO DIRECT fighting energies outward during the Crusades, there was more or less constant warfare in Europe in the period 1100–1500. Fighting wars was regarded as the proper activity of able-bodied young men of high status. Combined with the fragmented nature of European political authority—the territorial claims of rival kingdoms, competing cities, dukedoms, popes, and emperors vying for power—this ensured that conflicts smoldered and flared across the continent.

CHIVALROUS COMBAT

Europeans had a clear idea of what warfare was supposed to be: a matter of chivalrous combat between knights on horseback, inspired by an ideal of honor and valor. Preferably they would charge one another with lances. The reality, outside jousting tournaments, was rather different. For much of the period raiding and pillaging were the norm, as in the "chevauchées" with which the English laid waste areas of France during the 100 Years War. Pitched battles were avoided as much as possible—regarded as too risky in every way. Knights had a healthy desire for safety, leading to the adoption of all-over armor, with gauntlets and greaves, and moveable visors on helmets. Horses too had to be armored, making horse and rider a weighty package that could get into difficulty on soft ground.

IRON CONE HEAD
The basinet was common headgear for 14th-century knights. Germans called it a Hundsgugel ("hound's hood").

TRICKS OF DEFENSE
The late-14th-century Bodiam Castle, England, has stretches of curtain wall protected by flanking towers.

KEY
	frontier of Holy Roman Empire 1250
	Kingdom of Germany
	Kingdom of Italy
	under effective Hohenstaufen control 1250
	Papal States 1178
	added by 1219
	added by 1278
	Venetian Republic and possessions
●	member of Lombard League 1167
—	frontiers 1250

0 km 100   200
0 miles   100   200

EMPIRE OF FREDERICK II
The Holy Roman Empire was stymied by the medieval papacy, which was at the height of its spiritual authority.

RAISING ARMIES

Raising and maintaining armies was a constant strain on the resources of Europe's states. The cheapest way of waging war was to use those deemed to owe obligation of military service, who provided their own arms and were paid from plunder. But rulers increasingly found themselves obliged to come up with payment, and the employment of mercenaries became common. Mercenary companies were led by ambitious entrepreneur-soldiers, known as *condottieri* in Italy. Some of these earned fame and fortune. But mercenaries were always changing sides or simply plundering if unemployed. By 1450 use of mercenaries was evolving toward the formation of professional standing armies.

MEDIEVAL FOOTSOLDIERS

Ordinary footsoldiers with bows, pikes, and halberds could prove effective against charging knights, as long as they were well disciplined. For a knight, losing on the battlefield was more likely to mean being taken prisoner and ransomed than being killed (one of the purposes of chivalrous behavior was to minimize casualties), but footsoldiers could expect no such treatment. Many knights hated archers, whose style of fighting at a distance they considered unfair. The Church attempted to ban the use of crossbows in 1159 and knights would sometimes take savage revenge on captured bowmen.

SALLET HELMET

SINGLE-HAND SWORD

FOOTSOLDIER GEAR
A late-medieval infantryman wore a padded coat for protection and carried a small buckler shield for punching. His main weapon was the glaive, a long spiked pole.

GLAIVE

BUCKLER SHIELD

ARMOR WITH GAUNTLETS

EATING KNIFE AND DAGGER

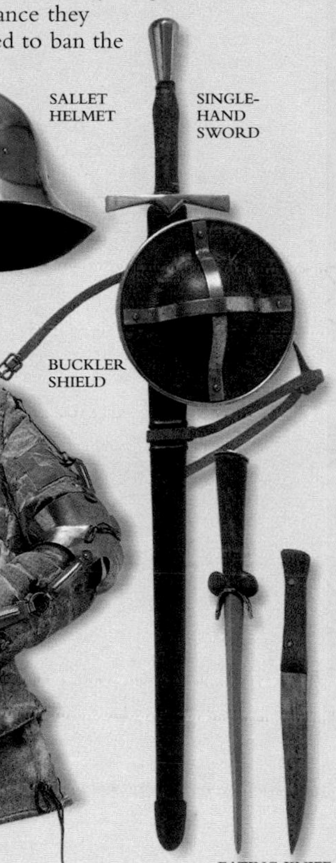

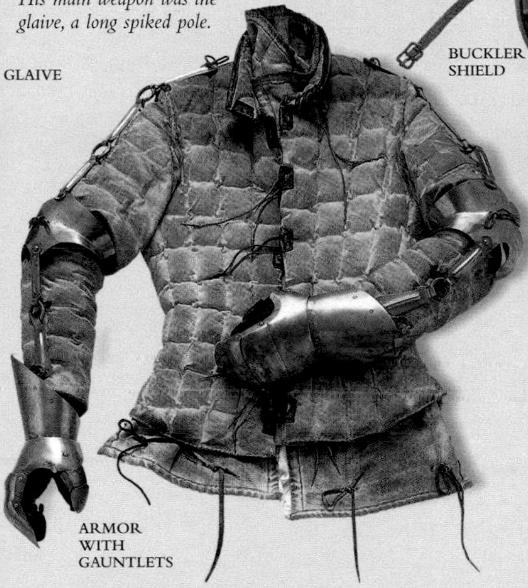

CASTLES AND SIEGES

The general insecurity in Europe meant that this was a time of fortification. Both city walls and castles were formidable structures in stone. Castles evolved from being a simple ring wall surrounding an inner tower to a series of concentric walls with a fortified gatehouse and towers built into the walls. A panoply of siege equipment was deployed against such defenses, including missile-hurling mangonels and trebuchets, ballistas, rams, and siege towers. From the 14th century these were joined by cannon, which would eventually force a rethink in fortification design.

Ratchet for keeping tension on skeins

Sliding section of tiller

BALLISTA
The giant crossbow was a machine inherited from the Ancient Greeks. It used the tension of twisted ropes to shoot a large bolt.

Bolt

Bow cord

Wooden wheel, reinforced with metal

Winch for pulling back bow

BOLT

TREBUCHET

The trebuchet was a large stone-throwing machine operated either by pulling on ropes or, from the 13th century, by a counterweight system (the weight was wound up and then dropped to power the missile). Some trebuchets could hurl a 220lb (100kg) stone a distance of more than 1,300ft (400m). Unlike simpler stone catapults, which might be built by carpenters on the site of a siege, trebuchets were transported with the army.

Sling pouch

Rope to pull arm down again

SPECIFICATION			
Origin Italy		**Height** 15ft (4.5m)	
Length 12ft (4m)		**Caliber** 220lbs (100kg)	
Used from 11th century		**Weight** 2 tons plus	

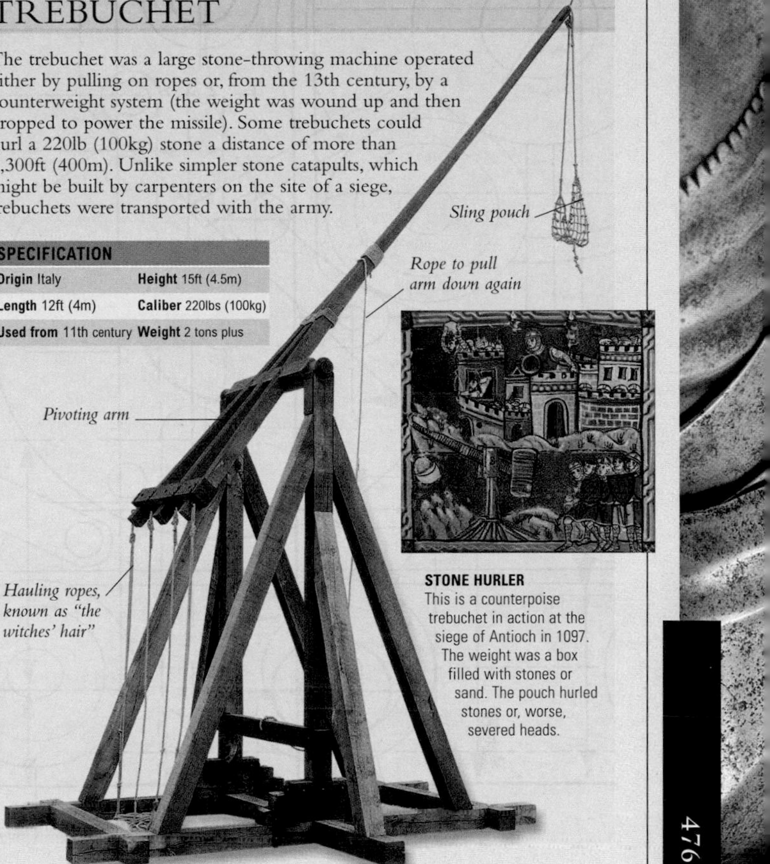

Pivoting arm

Hauling ropes, known as "the witches' hair"

STONE HURLER
This is a counterpoise trebuchet in action at the siege of Antioch in 1097. The weight was a box filled with stones or sand. The pouch hurled stones or, worse, severed heads.

BOWMEN

The two most effective archery forces in medieval Europe were Genoese crossbowmen and English archers with longbows. The crossbow was a relatively slow-loading weapon, although it compensated for this with its high penetrative power. The longbow could be used much more quickly—shooting about 12 arrows a minute—but it required a specialist to use it effectively. In 1337 all sports except archery were banned in England in a bid to maintain the supply of skilled archers. Early firearms were no match for bows in battlefield effectiveness.

LONGBOWMEN
Welsh archers are shown here in a depiction of the battle of Crécy. Shooting a longbow required strength and years of training.

476-1492

POPES AND EMPERORS

IN THE 12TH AND 13TH CENTURIES Europe was riven by a three-way power struggle between the papacy, France, and the Hohenstaufen Holy Roman Emperors. The arena in which this struggle was most bitterly contested was politically fragmented Italy, where pro-imperial Ghibellines and pro-papal Guelfs vied for power. Initially the Hohenstaufens were based in Germany, but in the 13th century their focus shifted to lands inherited by marriage in southern Italy and Sicily. The papacy called in the French, in the person of Charles d'Anjou, to evict the Hohenstaufen from these territories in the 1260s, although the Angevins were themselves defeated by the Aragonese in the war of the Sicilian Vespers (1282–1302).

WARS OF THE LOMBARD LEAGUE

Siege of Crema

DATE	June 1159–February 1160
FORCES	Barbarossa's forces: unknown; Cremese: unknown
LOCATION Crema, near Milan, northern Italy	**CASUALTIES** No reliable estimates

In 1158 Frederick Barbarossa led an army to Italy to establish his overlordship in Milan and other cities in Lombardy. Crema was a small but well-fortified city allied to Milan. In June 1159 Frederick ordered its citizens to dismantle their city walls, a move urged upon him by neighboring Cremona, Crema's direst enemy. When Crema refused, a bitter siege ensued, characterized by barbarous cruelty on both sides. Frederick had prisoners decapitated; the Cremese responded by hacking prisoners to bits on the city walls in full view of their comrades. Frederick is said to have put Cremese children in siege catapults and hurled them against the walls. Every known technique of siege warfare was employed. The besiegers used a "cat"—a mobile roof—to cover engineers who mined under the walls. The defenders responded with tunnels of their own, leading to underground warfare. When a ram breached the fortifications, the Cremese built an earthen wall behind the breach and blocked it again. Decimated by hunger and disease, the citizens eventually surrendered. They were allowed to leave before the entire city was razed to the ground.

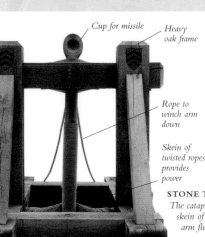

Cup for missile

Heavy oak frame

Rope to winch arm down

Skein of twisted ropes provides power

STONE THROWER
The catapult used the pulling power of a skein of twisted ropes. When released, the arm flew up and hurled the missile.

WARS OF THE LOMBARD LEAGUE

Legnano

DATE	May 29, 1176
FORCES	Imperial: 3,500 cavalry; Lombard League: 4,000 cavalry; infantry: unknown
LOCATION 20 miles (30km) from Milan, northern Italy	**CASUALTIES** Unknown

During 1176 Frederick Barbarossa was on campaign in Italy, again attempting to impose his authority on the pope and the city states of Lombardy. He was riding south from Como toward Pavia with a force of more than 3,000 German cavalry when he was intercepted by the Milanese and their allies from other cities of the Lombard League. The Milanese forces were a citizen army, with the richer citizens providing the cavalry and the less wealthy the infantry. All were well equipped with armor and weapons thanks to the city's wealth gained from trade and agriculture. The citizen cavalry were less skilled than their imperial opponents, but the Milanese footsoldiers were highly disciplined and motivated. With only cavalry at his disposal, Frederick was heavily outnumbered, but he rejected advice to avoid battle, "considering it unworthy of his imperial majesty to flee." At first the German cavalry carried all before them. They swept aside the Lombard mounted vanguard and then delivered a crushing attack on the main body of Lombard cavalry, putting the citizen horsemen to flight. This left the Lombard infantry exposed to a cavalry charge. The footsoldiers stood shoulder to shoulder around their *carroccio*, a large wagon surmounted by a banner and manned by priests, which acted as a sacred rallying point for troops to defend. Forming a shield wall with grounded pikes bristling outward, they faced the thunderous charge of the imperial heavy cavalry. Had their line been broken, they would have been massacred, but they held firm and the repeated attacks of the German knights shattered against the long pikes. Frederick, in the thick of the fighting, was unhorsed and fell from sight just as the Lombard cavalry, which had regrouped, smashed into the flank of the wavering German army. The Germans broke and fled, pursued by the Milanese, who took many prisoners as well as capturing Barbarossa's lance and shield and the imperial standard. At first believed dead, Frederick turned up safe in Pavia three days after the battle.

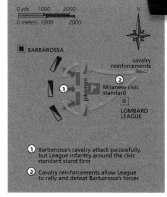

0 yds 1000 2000
0 meters 1000 2000

BARBAROSSA

cavalry reinforcements

pikemen

Milanese civic standard

LOMBARD LEAGUE

1 Barbarossa's cavalry attack successfully, but League infantry around the civic standard stand firm

2 Cavalry reinforcements allow League to rally and defeat Barbarossa's forces

SACRED WAGON
The Milanese forces' carroccio, the wagon carrying their standard and priests, dominates the scene of carnage in this 19th-century depiction of the battle of Legnano.

---

c.1123–1190

BARBAROSSA

Frederick I Hohenstaufen, known as Barbarossa because of his red beard, became Holy Roman Emperor in 1152. He fought six campaigns in Italy, finally making peace with Pope Alexander III and Milan in 1177 after his defeat at Legnano. In Germany, he came out on top after a long power struggle with Henry the Lion of Saxony. Having participated as a young man in the Second Crusade of 1147, he again departed for the Holy Land in 1189, only to drown on the way in a Turkish River. Sometimes cruel, he was nonetheless a skillful general and an ambitious political leader.

GILDED HEAD OF BARBAROSSA

Bouvines

DATE July 26, 1214

FORCES French: 1,450 cavalry, 6,000 infantry; German and Flemish: 1,500 cavalry, 7,500 infantry

LOCATION Bouvines, south of Tournai, northeastern France

CASUALTIES German and Flemish knights: 300 captured or killed

In 1213 an alliance of Otto IV of Germany, Count Ferdinand of Flanders, and King John of England made war against Philip II of France. An army led by Otto came up against the French at Bouvines in 1214. While armored cavalry clashed in couched-lance charges, infantry also fought savagely and Otto's army was reduced to a formation of mercenary footsoldiers. Victory gave Philip control of Flanders and ruined John's hope of regaining territory in France.

CLASHING ARMOR
Knights fought in very close combat at Bouvines. As well as lances, they used daggers to stab through gaps in armor.

Benevento

DATE February 26, 1266

FORCES Angevin: 3,000 knights; Manfred: 3,500 knights, several thousand archers

LOCATION Benevento, east of Naples, southern Italy

CASUALTIES Angevin: unknown, but heavy; Manfred: unknown, but heavier

When Holy Roman Emperor Frederick II died in 1250, his illegitimate son Manfred gained control of southern Italy and Sicily. Like Frederick, Manfred used these territories as a power base from which to challenge papal influence in Italy. In 1264 Pope Urban IV hit back by offering the crown of Sicily to Charles d'Anjou, brother of French king Louis IX. Louis provided funds to help Charles raise an army, partly because Manfred's friendly relations with Muslim Saracens offended his Christian principles.
In the winter of 1265-66 Charles landed at Rome and led his army south, meeting Manfred's forces on a plain near Benevento. Manfred opened the battle by sending forth thousands of Saracen archers as skirmishers. Deluged in deadly arrow fire, the French infantry fell back in disorder. The foremost section of French knights responded by charging the Saracens, who swiftly scattered. Some German knights then charged with couched lances into the flank of the disorganized French cavalry. The battle developed into a vast melée, as more and more knights charged into the thick of the fighting. Battle was so closely joined that the Saracen archers could not fire, unable to mark out friend from

ROYAL LANCE
Charles d'Anjou, wearing a crown, thrusts his lance in the battle of Benevento. Manfred himself was slain in the battle.

CROSSBOWS

The crossbow was the most powerful handheld missile weapon of its day. It was wound by the crossbowman holding it steady by pressing his foot in a stirrup attached to the end of the stock. The string was then hooked over a nut. It was slow to reload but required no special skill to shoot.

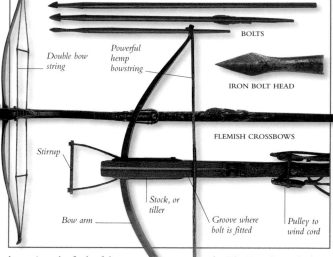

foe. The French wreaked havoc by attacking their enemies' horses, rather than the heavily armored riders. At a crucial moment, Manfred called on his reserves to charge, but many betrayed him, riding away from the field. Manfred charged regardless, disappearing into the mass of wheeling, hacking knights. Gradually overwhelmed, his forces fell apart and were slaughtered piecemeal.

Bay of Naples

DATE June 5, 1284

FORCES Aragonese: 40 galleys; Angevins: 30–40 galleys

LOCATION Southern Italy

CASUALTIES At least 10 Angevin galleys captured

In the war of the Sicilian Vespers, the Aragonese fought Charles d'Anjou for control of southern Italy. In June 1284 Aragon's admiral Roger de Lauria, blockading Naples, succeeded in luring the Angevin fleet out of the port to fight. Commanded by Charles d'Anjou's brother Charles of Salerno, the Angevin fleet pursued Lauria's ships into open sea. When they were well away from port, Lauria turned on them, aided by reinforcements that had crept up unseen from nearby Castellamare. Some of Charles's fleet fled. The rest were deluged with arrows by Lauria's crossbowmen. Reportedly, the Aragonese also threw soap onto the enemy decks to make them too slippery for soldiers to stand. Charles held out until his ship was holed, then surrendered.

HERESY AND REVOLT

THE LATER MIDDLE AGES saw increasingly powerful sovereigns seeking to impose real authority and religious uniformity upon vassals and subordinates who had hitherto owed them only nominal allegiance. Throughout Europe, warfare frequently erupted in the form of challenges to these newly assertive religious and political authorities. In France the repression of the Cathar heretics (also known as Albigensians) from 1209 sparked complex and brutal conflicts that ultimately led to the extension of French royal authority over previously independent Languedoc. In Britain English kings fought to extend control over Scotland and Wales, as well as facing internal challenges from rebellious barons or rival claimants to the throne.

WARFARE IN THE MIDDLE AGES

ALBIGENSIAN CRUSADE

Muret

DATE September 12, 1213	
FORCES Crusaders: 900 cavalry, 1,200 infantry; Toulouse/Aragon: 4,000 cavalry, 30,000 infantry	
LOCATION 12 miles (20km) south of Toulouse, France	**CASUALTIES** Toulouse/Aragon: at least 7,000 killed

Simon de Montfort, leading a crusade against the Albigensian heretics in southern France, was besieged inside Muret by the far superior forces of Count Raymond of Toulouse and King Pedro II of Aragon. With his only hope lying in attack, Simon led his knights out of the town and rode in a wide arc toward the enemy camp. With their armor and helmets glittering in the sun, they charged at full tilt into the Toulouse cavalry with a noise "like a whole forest going down under the ax." Next, Peter of Aragon's cavalry corps was crushed in similar fashion, the king himself cut down by a sword blow. Then de Montfort scattered Raymond's cavalry that was defending the camp. All that remained was to slaughter the infantry besieging the town walls.

THE PERFECT HERESY
The Albigensian heresy pervaded all levels of society, appealing to rich town-dwellers such as these as much as to rural peasants.

ALBIGENSIAN CRUSADE

Toulouse

DATE October 8, 1217– July 1, 1218	
FORCES Crusaders: unknown Toulousains: unknown	
LOCATION Toulouse, France	**CASUALTIES** No reliable estimates

In 1209 Pope Innocent III declared a crusade against the Albigensians, or Cathars, heretical Christians who were especially numerous in Languedoc, southern France. Barons and knights from northern France proceeded to suppress the heretics with great thoroughness, massacring the entire population of Béziers in July 1209—papal legate Arnaud-Amaury allegedly gave the order: "Kill them all, God will know his own." The major beneficiary of the crusade's early successes was Simon de Montfort, who gained extensive lands including Béziers and Carcassone. His growing power brought him into conflict with Raymond VI, Count of Toulouse, and with King Peter of Aragon, who had his own interests in southern France. After victory at Muret, de Montford's position seemed unassailable. Raymond fled and Simon took control of

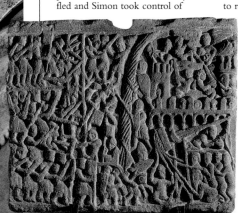

Toulouse. However, in 1216 the citizens of Toulouse rebelled and Simon sacked the city in retaliation. Count Raymond saw the opportunity to regain his lands. In September 1217 he reentered Toulouse to a rapturous reception. The Toulousains rebuilt the city's fortifications, which Simon had destroyed, and toiled night and day to have defenses ready before the appearance of the crusader army. Simon arrived outside the city on October 8 and ordered an immediate attack on the half-finished works. The whole population

SIEGE SCENE
A relief on Simon de Montfort's tomb in, Carcassonne, depicts the use of siege engines at Toulouse.

responded with any missile they could find. A chronicler described rocks, arrows, staves, and stones falling on the attackers "dense as fine rain." Toulousain knights made a sortie to

EVICTED CITIZENS
In August 1209 crusaders expelled the Cathars of Carcassonne. They had to leave behind their possessions, as well as their homes.

take the crusaders on at close quarters but the attack was driven back. Although reinforced by knights from northern France, through the following winter and spring Simon repeatedly failed to storm the city. Supplies, moreover, got through to the city along the Garonne River. In June 1218, Simon had a massive siege tower built with a platform higher than the city battlements. The defenders decided that they must destroy the tower or face defeat. On June 25 they swarmed out of the city to attack the machine. Simon and his knights rode into the attack, driving the Toulousains back but advancing dangerously close to the defenders. Simon was hit on his iron helmet by a rock fired from a mangonel (allegedly operated by Toulousain women). The blow, wrote a chronicler, "shattered his eyes, brains, back teeth, forehead and jaw." With Simon dead, the siege was soon abandoned.

---

c.1160–1218

SIMON DE MONTFORT

Anglo-French knight Simon IV de Montfort went on the Fourth Crusade in 1202–04, distinguishing himself by refusing to take part in attacks on fellow Christians. His role as leader of the Albigensian crusade after 1209 earned him the undying hatred of the people of Languedoc. His death at the siege of Toulouse is shown here. His second son, also Simon de Montfort, led the Barons' Revolt in England.

SECOND BARONS WAR

Evesham

DATE
August 14, 1265

FORCES
De Montfort: 7,000;
Prince Edward: 20,000

CASUALTIES
No reliable estimates

LOCATION Evesham,
Worcestershire,
England

In 1258 a group of barons led by Simon de Montfort, Earl of Leicester, forced English King Henry III to agree to the Provisions of Oxford. This obliged the king to devolve government to a baronial council and hold regular parliaments. When Henry reneged on this agreement in 1261, civil war followed. At the battle of Lewes in 1264 the king and his son Edward Longshanks were defeated by de Montfort and taken prisoner. Edward, however, escaped to raise an army in western England, while Earl Simon made an alliance with Welsh prince Llewelyn. Assembling an army in Wales, he set out to join up with much larger forces commanded by his son, also called Simon. Edward knew that he must prevent the junction of the two de Montfort armies. Marching

CLOSE ENCOUNTER
Prince Edward and Simon de Montfort—sporting a crusader's cross—clash in an imaginary episode of the battle of Evesham.

rapidly eastward from Worcester, at dawn on August 2 he surprised and defeated the younger Simon's forces in their camp at Kenilworth. Unaware of this disaster, Earl Simon stopped in the vale of Evesham on the night of August 3-4. Allowing his men no rest, Edward advanced through the night and positioned his forces to block the only two roads out of Evesham. When Simon saw he was surrounded by far superior forces, he reportedly said: "May God have mercy on our souls, for our bodies are theirs." With typical bravado he led his men in a charge uphill against the center of Edward's army, but his forces were engulfed and Simon was slain. The battle was so one-sided that chronicler Robert of Gloucester called it "the murder of Evesham, for battle it was none."

ANGLO-SCOTTISH WARS

Stirling Bridge

DATE
September 11, 1297

FORCES
Scottish: 15,000;
English: 50,000–60,000

CASUALTIES
No reliable estimates

LOCATION
Abbey Craig, north of
Stirling, Scotland

In 1297 the Scots were in rebellion against the annexation of their country by English King Edward I. A Scottish army led by William Wallace and Andrew de Moray took up position on a slope above the Forth River, to face a far larger English force under the Earl of Surrey. The English began to cross the river by a narrow bridge in front of the Scottish lines. Wallace and De Moray hurled their spears down the slope. Floundering in marshy ground, thousands of English knights were slaughtered. The rest of the English army, on the other side of the river, fled the field.

SCOTTISH HERO
William Wallace was captured and executed by the English in London in 1305.

476–1492

GLYNDWR'S REBELLION

Owain Glyndwr's Rebellion

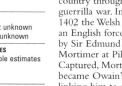

DATE
1400–09

FORCES
Glyndwr: unknown
English: unknown

CASUALTIES
No reliable estimates

LOCATION
Wales

Wales was conquered in the 1280s by English King Edward I, who built a string of castles to stamp English rule upon the country. Although on the surface most Welsh people appeared to accept this situation, discontent smouldered. In September 1400 a Welsh landowner, Owain Glyndwr, caught in a dispute with an unruly

English neighbor, burned down the township around Ruthin castle. This sparked a general Welsh uprising. Declared Prince of Wales, Owain took control of most of the country through a guerrilla war. In June 1402 the Welsh routed an English force led by Sir Edmund Mortimer at Pilleth. Captured, Mortimer became Owain's ally, linking him to a revolt against King Henry led by the Percy family in northern England. The Percys were defeated at Shrewsbury in July 1403, however, before they could link up with Glyndwr. Owain next sought support from France and in 1405 a force of French crossbowmen and

> **"The Welsh habit of revolt against the English is a long-standing madness… from the sayings of the prophet Merlin they still hope to recover England."**
>
> *A scribe at Edward III's court*

infantry landed at Milford Haven and advanced with the Welsh to Worcester. Confronted by King Henry and a force of armored knights, the Welsh withdrew and the disappointed French soon went home. The rebels still held most of Wales, but Prince Henry, the king's son, ground down the rebellion by military action coupled with inducements to tempt rebels back to allegiance. Harlech Castle was the last stronghold to resist the English. In 1409, starving and without hope of resupply, its tiny Welsh garrison surrendered. Owain disappeared into the Welsh hills. His subsequent fate is uncertain.

CONTESTED CASTLE
Carreg Cennen, near Brecon, south Wales, was an English-built castle besieged by Glyndwr's forces in 1403.

WARS OF THE ROSES

Bosworth Field

DATE
August 22, 1485

FORCES
Henry Tudor: 5,000;
Richard III: 8,000

CASUALTIES
No reliable estimates

LOCATION Near Market
Bosworth,
Leicestershire, England

On August 7, 1485, Henry Tudor landed at Milford Haven, Wales, intent on asserting his claim to the English throne. His army met the forces of King Richard III at Bosworth Field (the exact site of which is unknown). Richard's army was numerically superior but riddled with disloyalty. A third army, led by Lord Stanley, who had promised both sides that he would fight for them, intervened on the side of Henry Tudor. At the key moment in the battle, the king led a charge toward the position where Henry stood, hoping to kill the pretender and thus carry the day. Richard succeeded in killing Henry Tudor's standardbearer, but with much of his own army changing sides or holding aloof from the battle, he was surrounded and cut down. Henry Tudor came to power as Henry VII.

THE HUNDRED YEARS WAR

THE SERIES OF WARS fought between the kings of England and France between 1337 and 1453 is conventionally known as the Hundred Years War. Provoked by King Edward III of England's claim to the French throne, they ended with King Charles VII of France driving the English almost completely out of France.

HUNDRED YEARS WAR

Sluys

DATE
June 24, 1340

FORCES
English: 150–250 ships; French and Genoese: around 190 ships

LOCATION
Sluys, Zeeland, southern Netherlands

CASUALTIES 166 French and Genoese vessels captured or sunk

In the earliest phase of the Hundred Years War, Edward III sought to exploit alliances with Flemish nobles to attack the French. Little was achieved, however, and in the summer of 1340 a fleet commanded by Edward III crossed the Channel intent on asserting his claim to the French throne. A French fleet, reinforced by Genoese mercenary galleys, gathered to oppose them, commanded by Admiral Hugues Quiéret (for the

French) and Egidio Bocanegra, known as Barbavera (for the Genoese). The two fleets met in an inlet off the coast of Flanders. The French fleet was still in anchorage, against the advice of Barbavera, and the ships were formed into three or four lines, the vessels lashed together with ropes. King Edward's fleet entered the inlet on the morning of June 24. Ships on both sides were packed with soldiers, for at this time battles at sea were the same as battles on land except that, in the words of chronicler Froissart, "battles on sea are more dangerous and fiercer…for on the sea there is no recoiling or fleeing." The English fleet was arranged with one ship full of men-at-arms between each two ships of archers. After maneuvering to get the wind and sun behind them, the English vessels closed on the French and battle was joined. The English got by far the better of a series of encounters decided by the exchange

COGS OF WAR
Most of the vessels at Sluys were cogs— clumsy single-masted sailing ships. Their function in battle was to carry the soldiers on board into fighting range of the enemy.

of arrow fire and by hand-to-hand fighting between soldiers in vessels grappled side by side. After a battle that, according to Edward, lasted "all that day and the night after," the French fleet was almost entirely

destroyed. Quiéret was killed, although Barbavera escaped. Froissart puts the French loss of life at more than 30,000, although this is almost certainly an exaggeration. Edward failed to capitalize on this victory, however; the subsequent land campaign achieved little more than an unsuccessful siege of Tournai. The cost of the expedition, moreover, had been exorbitant and prevented any further major invasions for much of the 1340s.

HUNDRED YEARS WAR

Crécy

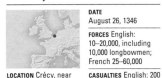

DATE
August 26, 1346

FORCES English: 10–20,000, including 10,000 longbowmen; French 25–60,000

LOCATION Crécy, near Abbéville, Picardy, northern France

CASUALTIES English: 200 dead; French: probably 4,000 dead

In July 1346 Edward III took an army across the Channel to Normandy. Cutting a destructive swathe through French territory, he marched south toward Paris and then turned northeast. The army of French king Philip VI caught up with the English near the French coast. Edward took up position on a slope alongside the village of Crécy. During the morning

> **"The English archers then advanced one step forward, and shot their arrows with such force and quickness that it seemed as if it snowed."**
>
> *Jean Froissart*, Chronicle, c.1369

of August 26 he arranged his forces in three "battles," one nominally commanded by his 16-year-old son, Prince Edward. Each battle included knights, squires, and sergeants fighting dismounted (as armored infantry), longbowmen, and some Welsh light infantry. The French army arrived tired and disorganized from a long march, wet from a thunderstorm, and facing into the low sun behind the

KNIGHT'S HELMET
The iron helm, with its narrow eye slits, provided protection at the cost of weight and poor vision.

English position. But Philip could not restrain his knights' enthusiasm for an immediate attack on the outnumbered English. Reluctantly, his Genoese mercenary crossbowmen advanced up the slope. They fired their first volley too early to be effective and were then decimated by the English longbows, which outstripped them in range and rate of fire. As the crossbowmen fell back, French knights led by the Comte d'Alençon charged through them up the slope, into the dense fire of the English archers. A few reached the English line, engaging in fierce fighting with Prince Edward's battle, but most were killed or wounded. In a memorably quixotic gesture, Philip's aged and blind ally King John of Bohemia had himself led into the battle to die. He lay among thousands of nobles and commoners left on the battlefield the following morning.

Battle map

0 km 0.5 1
0 miles 0.5 1

baggage and wagon park — Wadicourt
KING EDWARD
DUKE OF NORTHAMPTON
Welsh and Irish footmen
windmill church
Maye
Crécy
Genoese crossbowmen
KING PHILIP
Estrées ② French cavalry charge into path of retreating Genoese
EDWARD, PRINCE OF WALES
ALENÇON
① English longbowmen disperse Genoese crossbowmen
Fontaine

KEY
■ English forces
□ Longbowmen
■ French forces

1330–1376

BLACK PRINCE

Prince Edward, the eldest son of English King Edward III, was one of the most successful commanders of the Hundred Years War. He was known as the Black Prince after the color of his armor. As a youth he acquitted himself well at Crécy. His subsequent victories included Poitiers in 1356 and Najera in 1367. He was also a noted practitioner of the *chevauchée*—campaigns of pillage and destruction that laid waste large areas of France. His last act of war was a notorious massacre at Limoges in 1370. He died before Edward III and so never became king.

Siege of Calais

DATE
August 4, 1346–
September 4, 1347

FORCES
English: possibly
30,000; French:
unknown

LOCATION
Calais, northern
France

CASUALTIES
No reliable estimates

After the victory at Crécy, Edward III marched north to besiege the port city of Calais. With his army he had some 20 primitive cannons, which he deployed against the city's stone walls. Basically metal tubes mounted on carts, they proved ineffective. The noise unnerved the citizens of Calais but their projectiles failed to breach the walls. The English had to starve the city into submission, a long and costly procedure, since reinforcements and supplies had to be ferried across the English Channel. After 13 months, with Philip VI failing to mount a relief of the city and its people reduced to eating rats and mice, Calais surrendered. Its captain, Jean de Vienne, and six wealthy burghers came out of the city with halters around their necks to plead for mercy. The capture of Calais was a valuable prize for Edward, but his finances were exhausted and Europe was entering the nightmare of the Black Death. A truce was agreed that lasted eight years.

IVORY TOWERS
A medieval ivory carving depicts the siege of a moated castle. Crossbows were much used by both besiegers and besieged.

Poitiers

DATE
September 19, 1356

FORCES English: 12,000,
including 4,000 men-
at-arms; French:
20,000–40,000

LOCATION 2 miles (3km)
east of Poitiers,
central France

CASUALTIES French:
2,500 killed, 2,600
prisoners: English
1,000 killed

In the late summer of 1356 Edward the Black Prince led an army from Aquitaine on a raid through central France. In September, slowed by a baggage train loaded with booty, the English were intercepted by a French army led by King Jean II. Edward took up a strong defensive position on a slope outside Poitiers, seeking to avoid battle against superior forces. Early on September 19 he attempted to slip away. Spotting the English retreat, the French launched their attack, forcing Edward hastily to return to the field. As the chronicler Froissart relates, the English were positioned behind a hedge "lined with archers and the men-at-arms drawn up behind among the vine and thorn bushes, all on foot; the hedge had but one gap in it, where four knights might ride abreast…." The French sent 300 of their best knights to charge through this gap. The rest dismounted to follow on foot behind this mounted spearhead. When the French cavalry reached the gap in the hedge, the longbowmen shot their horses. English men-at-arms waded into the chaos of fallen horses and riders, hacking right and left. The next wave of French knights, led by the dauphin, advanced through a hail of arrows and engaged the English in savage hand-to-hand fighting. After Edward threw his reserves into the front line, the English barely prevailed. Exhausted and with many wounded, they prepared to face a further French onslaught, the archers pulling arrows from bodies to replenish exhausted quivers. Fortunately, the next French formation, commanded by the young Duc d'Orléans, was so unnerved by the fate of the dauphin's forces that it fled the field. This left the final French force, personally commanded by the king, to advance on the English. Seizing the initiative, Edward ordered his entire army to charge the French, and sent a force of 200 horsemen around the French flank to attack from the rear. There was fierce fighting as the two forces clashed; English archers, out of arrows, resorted to fighting with knives. But the cavalry charge from the rear broke the French. At last only the king and his entourage fought on, surrounded by dismembered bodies, until they too were overpowered and forced to surrender.

KING AT BAY
French King Jean II makes a last stand at Poitiers. The king was taken prisoner and held by the English until 1360, when he was ransomed for three million gold crowns.

MODEL KNIGHT
This 14th-century bronze model of a mounted knight represents the medieval ideal of a noble warrior.

HUNDRED YEARS WAR

Najera

DATE	April 3, 1367
FORCES	French and Castilian: probably 30,000; English: perhaps 20,000
LOCATION South of the Ebro, northern Spain	**CASUALTIES** French and Castilian: 7,000 killed; English: 100 killed

England and France officially made peace in 1360, but this brought no end to the suffering of the French people. The "free companies," mercenary soldiers, refused to disband and sought profit from general plunder. After their reign of terror, it was a great relief to the French population when the renowned French soldier Bertrand du Guesclin took a large company of mercenaries from France into Castile to support Enrique of Trastamara in a civil war with his English-backed brother, King Pedro the Cruel. Pedro was deposed and Enrique placed on the throne. In February 1367 Edward, the Black Prince, led an army across the Pyrenees to restore Pedro's rule. Du Guesclin and his Castilian allies met the Black Prince's army at Najera. As so often, English archers dominated the battlefield, routing the Castilian cavalry. Du Guesclin's mercenaries, were undaunted by the bowmen and put up staunch resistance. But in the absence of real support from their Castilian allies they were inevitably defeated. Du Guesclin was taken prisoner and Pedro restored to his throne. The Black Prince allowed du Guesclin to be ransomed for 100,000 francs and he returned home to become constable of France in 1370.

HUNDRED YEARS WAR

Lancaster's raid

DATE	July–December 1373
FORCES	English: 5,000–10,000 men; French: unknown
LOCATION France	**CASUALTIES** English: roughly half of force lost

When war resumed in 1368, French King Charles V sought to apply constant pressure to the English but avoided pitched battles. With du Guesclin as his constable, Charles reversed many of the French losses. In 1373 the English mounted a fresh expedition to France, led by John of Gaunt, Duke of Lancaster, who took his men on a five-month pillaging march from Calais down through Champagne and Burgundy, and into Aquitaine. The French took refuge within their walled towns and harassed the English forces, picking off stragglers and laying ambushes. When winter set in, the English began to die of hunger, exposure, and exhaustion. By the time he reached Bordeaux, Lancaster had lost half his men and almost all his horses without fighting a battle.

ENGLISH DUKE
John of Gaunt (1340–1399) never matched the military successes of his father King Edward III.

HUNDRED YEARS WAR

Agincourt

DATE	October 25, 1415
FORCES	English: 6,000; French 20,000–30,000
LOCATION Near Hesdin in the Pas-de-Calais, northeastern France	**CASUALTIES** French: 3,000–5,000 killed; English: 300–400 killed

In August 1415 Henry V of England sailed for Normandy with around 10,000 men, seeking to exploit a civil war in France to reassert the English kings' claim to the French throne. The campaign began with the siege of Harfleur. By the time the city was taken on September 22, Henry's forces had been depleted by casualties and disease. Exhausted, hungry, and harassed by hostile local people, his army began to melt away as they marched north to English-held Calais. Henry found the road blocked by an army led by the constable of France, Charles d'Albret. Early on October 25 (St. Crispin's Day), Henry drew up his forces, now probably 6,000-strong, at a point where the Calais road passed through a gap between thick woods.

ARMOR AND BOWMEN
Armored men-at-arms and archers were the two key components of the forces that contested the battle of Agincourt.

THE LONGBOW

The English adopted the longbow after encounters with Welsh archers in the 13th century. It was not a technological novelty, but its use en masse to defeat mounted knights was a masterly tactical innovation.

Best made of yew, a longbow could be fired 10 times a minute and hit a target more than 650 feet (200 m) away. It took years of training to acquire the strength and skill to use a longbow effectively.

His archers, placed on the flanks and interspersed with dismounted men-at-arms in the center, hammered pointed stakes into the ground in front of them. The far more numerous French were forced by the narrow battlefield to arrange their men in three "battles," one behind the other. Most of their men-at-arms were on foot. When the French attacked, the few mounted knights reached the English line first, but were held off by the archers' stakes. Under heavy arrow fire and milling around on soft, muddy ground, the cavalry were soon in desperate trouble. Their colleagues advancing on foot, plodding through the mud in heavy armor, reached the English line exhausted and having suffered heavy casualties. As close combat developed, the English archers exchanged their bows for axes and swords, and joined the men-at-arms in a savage melée. At one point, Henry was told that his camp to the rear had been attacked. Fearing encirclement by the French, he ordered that the prisoners be killed—in a last stand the English would not have had the manpower to guard them. The French plan to surround Henry had backfired. A mounted charge by a few hundred English cleared the remnants of the French army from the field. The French dead included d'Albret, three dukes, seven counts and more than 90 other noblemen.

KING HENRY V
The king is shown here enthroned and carrying a shield with a fleur-de-lys motif, a symbol of his claim to the French crown.

Siege of Orléans

DATE
October 12, 1428–May 7, 1429

FORCES
English and French: 5,000; French: variable

LOCATION
Loire valley, central France

CASUALTIES
No reliable estimates

Shortly after the death of Henry V in 1422, his infant son Henry VI was declared king of France as well as of England. The regent, the Duke of Bedford, ruled from Paris, with the aid of his Burgundian allies, while the French dauphin, the future Charles VII, cowered south of the Loire. In 1428, Bedford sent an army south to seize the Loire River crossing at Orléans. The English concentrated on a two-towered fortress guarding a stone bridge south of the city. On

> "Everyone marveled at this, that she acted so wisely and clearly in waging war, as if she was a captain who had the experience of 20 or 30 years..."
>
> *Duc d'Alençon, testimony at Joan of Arc's rehabilitation,* 1456

October 23, they seized it after mining efforts forced the French to abandon the position. The leader of the English army, the Earl of Salisbury, was killed by a cannon as he climbed one of the two towers to observe the French defenses. Thus the siege was instituted under the leadership of the Earl of Suffolk. The English had insufficient forces to blockade Orléans. They constructed a series of earth-and-wood fortified positions around the city, but the French were able to filter in supplies and troop reinforcements. By December, Jean

the Bastard, commanding the defense of the city, probably had stronger forces than the English, although the latter had been reinforced by around 1,500 Burgundians. The French, however, remained largely passive. When, with the aid of a Scottish contingent, they intercepted an English supply convoy approaching Orléans from Paris on February 12, they were fought off by the convoy's able commander, Sir John Fastolf. The arrival of Joan of Arc at Charles VII's court at Chinon, however, began a transformation of morale in the French camp. The defection of the Burgundian contingent in March also undermined the English position. In April 1429 Charles allowed Joan to attempt the relief of Orléans. Under her inspiration, an army some 5,000 strong marched to Orléans and safely passed the English strongpoints. Overcoming the resistance of the senior French commanders, she successfully urged a series of sorties that took a chain of strongpoints by assault. By May 7 the

DESTINY'S COURT
Château Chinon, where Charles VII held court in 1429. On March 4, Joan of Arc, the daughter of a tenant farmer, arrived there. Her miraculous visions helped rally the French cause and inspire them to victory.

c.1412–1431

JOAN OF ARC

Seventeen-year-old Joan of Arc came to the French court in February 1429 convinced that voices were urging her to save France. Her role has been disputed, some arguing that she was a master tactician, others relegating her role to the purely inspirational. Either way, she turned the tide of the war. An attack on Paris in September failed and in May 1430 Joan was captured by the Burgundians. Handed over to the English, she was burned as a heretic.

FLIGHT OF ARROWS
Bodkin arrowheads such as these would have pierced vulnerable points in armor. In the hands of skillful longbowmen they wrought lethal destruction on the French.

English were left in occupation of only a few bastions northwest of the city. They then formed up for battle in the open, but the French refused to be drawn into a direct assault, and the English abandoned Orléans. Joan was wounded by an arrow in the fighting, but went on to inspire further French successes along the Loire valley, culminating in the battle of Patay on June 19, in which an English army led by Lord John Talbot and Sir John Falstolf was routed with heavy losses. By July 16 the French had triumphed as far north as Rheims, where the dauphin was crowned king of France.

COUNTERPOISE TREBUCHET
As the weight on one end of the pivot arm dropped, the sling on the other end flew up launching a missile up to 1,000 feet (300 m).

Châtillon

DATE
July 17, 1453

FORCES
English: 6,000 men; French: 7,000–10,000 with 300 cannon

LOCATION
Western France

CASUALTIES
No reliable estiamtes

The closing stages of the Hundred Years War brought an almost unbroken series of French victories. During a truce in 1444–49, Charles VII avoided the problem of unemployed soldiers rampaging around the country by paying them to serve the state in *compagnies d'ordonnances*—the beginnings of a standing army. He also employed the brothers Jean and Gaspard Bureau to develop a well-organized mobile artillery train which played a vital role

in the war's final years. From 1449, the French took city after city from the English, battering stone walls with cannonfire. They also used cannon as field artillery to decisive effect at the battle of Formigny in April 1450. By the summer of 1451, France had driven the English out of Normandy and conquered Aquitaine. Loyal to the English king, however, the nobles of Aquitaine appealed for help. An English army led by John Talbot, Earl of Shrewsbury, landed in October 1452 and regained Bordeaux.

GREAT HELM
The conical or globular skull of a basinet helmet gave good protection to the neck and side of the face.

> "The artillery caused grievous harm to the English, for each shot knocked five or six men down..."
>
> *An eyewitness to the battle of Châtillon,* 1453

In July 1453, Talbot went to the aid of the town of Châtillon (Castillon), under siege by Jean Bureau who was battering its walls with his artillery. Aware the English were coming, Bureau turned his cannon around. Talbot, at the head of the English cavalry, was deceived into thinking the French were withdrawing and charged the earthworks Bureau had thrown up to

THRUSTING SWORD
This blade has a diamond-shaped profile to give extra stiffness. Its acute point could burst apart links in chain mail.

protect his forces. Fire from the French cannon and archers threw the cavalry into disarray. An eyewitness wrote, "The artillery caused grievous harm to the English, for each shot knocked five or six men down…" Talbot was killed after his horse was shot from under him and the English army eventually fled in disorder. The French went on to retake Aquitaine.

MEDIEVAL ARMOR

BY THE 15TH CENTURY EUROPEAN KNIGHTS HAD OPTED FOR FULL STEEL PLATE ARMOR, WHICH, WITH ITS RIGID SURFACE, PROVIDED BETTER PROTECTION THAN CHAIN MAIL.

There were two main centers for the manufacture of plate armor: southern Germany and northern Italy. The style of armor made in Germany, such as the suit shown here, is called "Gothic." Suits of armor were extremely expensive custom-made objects and their decorative detail was intended to be admired, which is why knights at this period stopped wearing cloth surcoats over their armor. Although it looks cumbersome, the armor was painstakingly shaped to fit the body and its weight of about 55lb (25kg) was evenly distributed. As a result, the knight could move perfectly freely, including mounting and dismounting his horse unaided. It did, however, take a considerable time to put the armor on.

ROMANTIC KNIGHT
Dürer's famous engraving, The Knight, Death and the Devil, made in 1513, displays a splendid suit of Gothic armor.

INVULNERABLE KNIGHT

Encased in plate armor, the knight had no need to carry a shield. The armor would resist any slashing blow from a sword, forcing enemies instead to stab at weak points at joins between the plates. To block this ploy, a knight might wear chainmail under the plate armor—a weighty combination—or have chain sewn into the joins. A heavy blow from a mace might still injure the knight without piercing the armor, but the curved helmet was well designed to deflect blows and was much better for this purpose than the flat-topped helmets of the period of the crusades. A knight in this armor was truly vulnerable only to two types of weapon: powerful steel crossbows and firearms. The increasing use of handguns in the 16th century, however, eventually led to the abandonment of full suits of plate armor.

CHAIN AND PLATE
The knights shown here are wearing chainmail under cloth surcoats with plate armor on their arms and legs, a combination that was common in the 14th century.

SPECIFICATION	
Origin Northern Germany	**Height** Up to 6ft (2m)
Style Gothic	**Thickness** 0.1in (2mm)
Date Late 15th century	**Weight** 55lbs (25kg)

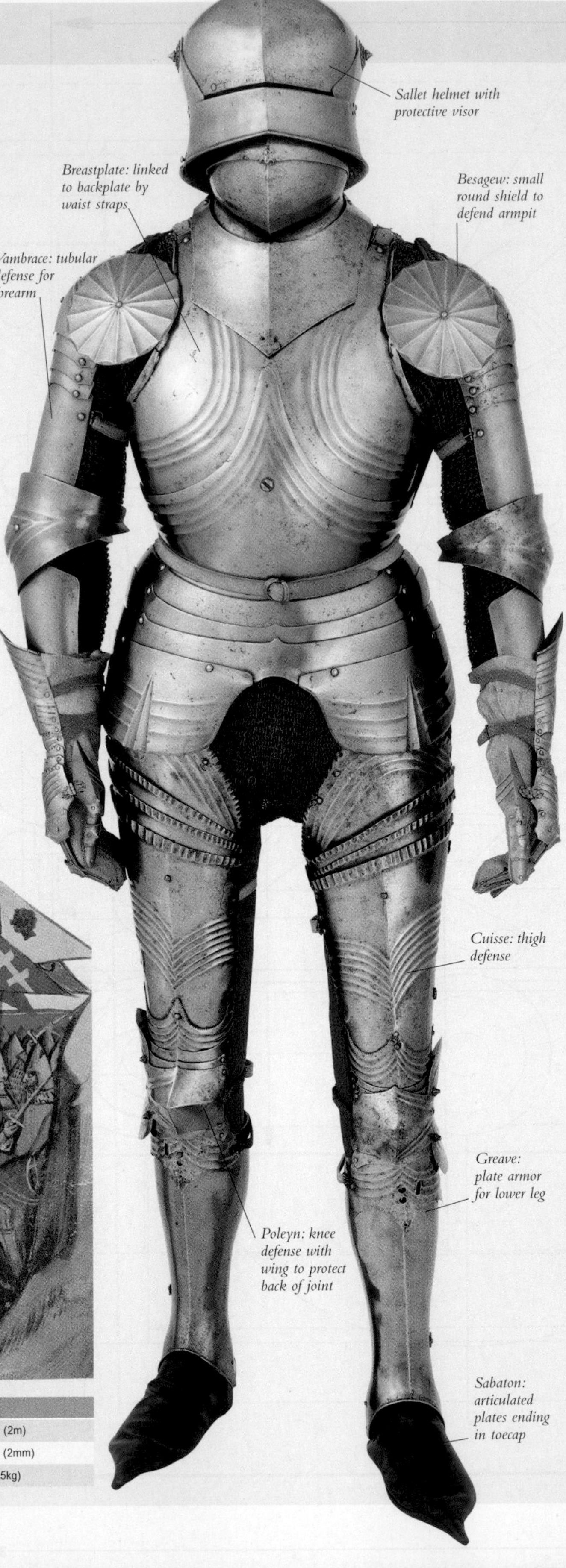

Sallet helmet with protective visor

Breastplate: linked to backplate by waist straps

Besagew: small round shield to defend armpit

Vambrace: tubular defense for forearm

Cuisse: thigh defense

Poleyn: knee defense with wing to protect back of joint

Greave: plate armor for lower leg

Sabaton: articulated plates ending in toecap

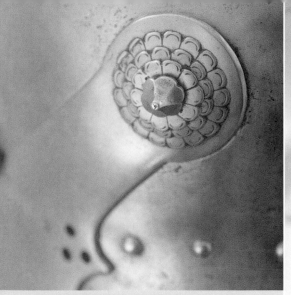

BESAGEW *These small round shields were attached to chain mail at the shoulder to defend the armpit. Although uncommon in the 14th century, this feature reappeared in 15th-century Gothic armor.*

VISOR ROSE *Any joint was a potential weak spot in the knight's armor. Features such as this rose at the hinge on the sallet helmet's visor would help deflect the force of any blows.*

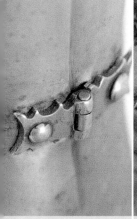

HINGE *at the join between the greaves and sabonet.*

BUCKLE *Sections of plate armor were laced or buckled to a padded undergarment or arming doublet.*

CHAIN MAIL *was used to protect exposed joints such as by the armpits. Occasionally full mail coats were worn under plate.*

CUISSE *This rear view of the knight's upper leg armor shows the intricate work necessary to join the plates together while permitting freedom of movement.*

GAUNTLET *This was the armor to defend the hand, which evolved out of a mail mitten. By the 15th century the gauntlet had developed into a complex series of intricately articulated plates, with separate finger plates to allow movement.*

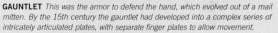

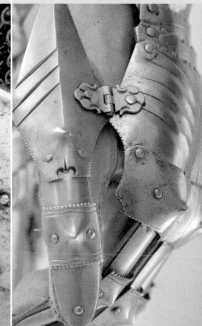

TRIUMPH OF THE INFANTRY

A NUMBER OF BATTLES IN THE 14th and 15th centuries showed that non-noble footsoldiers could defeat high-status mounted knights in pitched battle—a profound shock to those who held medieval views of warfare and society. Clever tactical innovation and disciplined ferocity were usually the secret. The advice given by Flemish general William of Jülich to his footsoldiers at Courtrai was: "Do not allow the enemy to break through your ranks. Do not be afraid. Kill both man and horse." The relative decline in the effectiveness of armored cavalry through this period was also seen in the success of bowmen and the introduction of gunpowder weapons, although mounted soldiers were to remain a key element in warfare into the 19th century.

FRENCH–FLEMISH WAR

Courtrai

DATE
July 11, 1302

FORCES Flemish: 8,000–10,500 footsoldiers; French: 2,500 knights/squires plus infantry

LOCATION
Courtrai (Kortrijk), Belgium

CASUALTIES 1,000 French knights killed; several hundred Flemish dead

In 1302 Guy, Count of Flanders, rebelled against his feudal overlord, Philip of France and soon controlled almost all of Flanders. Philip sent his brother, Robert of Artois, to bring them to heel. Guy's army consisted of Flemish merchants, artisans, peasants, and a few nobles, all on foot, armed with pikes or wooden clubs known as *goedendags* ("good-days"). The French knights were impatient to charge and, riding through their footsoldiers, they crossed the ditches and advanced on the Flemish infantry with couched lances. The enemy did not flinch, standing with pikes firmly planted in the ground and *goedendags* raised to strike. The knights ran into the line of pikes with a frightful impact and were hacked to pieces in the ensuing melée.

"Each made his confession on the spot, and then they crowded together, one against another. Thus they formed as it were a stone wall to endure the frightful ordeal."

Chronicler Louis de Velthem on the Battle of Courtrai

HORSE TRAP
A caltrop was a spiked metal device scattered on the ground to injure horses and their riders.

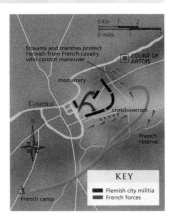

ANGLO–SCOTTISH WARS

Bannockburn

DATE
June 24, 1314

FORCES
English: 25,000; Scottish: 9,000

LOCATION
South of Stirling, Scotland

CASUALTIES English: up to 15,000 dead; Scottish: 4,000 dead

In 1314 King Edward II of England sent an army northward to confront the forces of Robert Bruce (King Robert I of Scotland), whose raids and ambushes threatened to drive the English from Scottish soil. Robert was besieging English-held Stirling as Edward's army neared. The Scottish king moved his forces to a carefully chosen battlefield on a slope above a stream called Bannockburn. Forest and marsh restricted the width of the battlefront to about a mile. There were some initial skirmishes on June 23, in one of which Robert clashed with the English knight Henry de Bohun, killing him with a battle ax. The main battle was joined on June 24. The Scottish formed up in their traditional infantry formation, the schiltron. This resembled the Greek phalanx, with footsoldiers shoulder to shoulder making a wall of shields from which their pikes thrust

LOCAL HERO
Robert Bruce, whose statue at Stirling Castle is shown here, remains a hero for Scottish nationalists.

outward. Unlike the phalanx, though, the schiltron infantry faced outward in all directions—to the rear and flanks as well as the front, like the 18th-century infantry square. The English knights foolishly deployed in front of their archers, preventing them from shooting, and charged across the burn at the Scots. The schiltrons held firm. Even when a knight broke through the bristling shieldwall, he was surrounded and hacked down. The bottom of the valley was soon filled with a confused mass of English knights and footsoldiers floundering in the marshy ground. Into this mass the schiltrons advanced to deadly effect. English longbowmen tried to fire on the Scots but to little effect. King Edward took an early decision to flee the field, further undermining the morale of his men. His army soon followed, suffering heavy casualties as it fled. The decisive victory enabled Robert to reestablish Scottish independence. It also gave the Scots a false confidence in the offensive power of their schiltrons. At Halidon Hill in 1333, the English inflicted a severe defeat on the Scots by using their longbowmen to pour arrow fire into the dense Scottish formations.

CONFUSED MELÉE
This medieval illustration epitomizes the chaos and confusion of Bannockburn as mounted knights fell prey to the schiltrons.

SWISS WARS OF INDEPENDENCE

Morgarten

DATE
November 15, 1315

FORCES Austrian: 8,000 with 2,500 armoured cavalry; Swiss: 1,500 infantry and archers

LOCATION
By the Aegerisee, Switzerland

CASUALTIES
Most Austrians killed

In 1315 Leopold of Austria led an army into Switzerland to enforce Habsburg authority over the Swiss. He was ambushed in a mountain pass by a much smaller Swiss force that hurled boulders and tree trunks down on the Austrians, throwing them into confusion. Leopold's knights could not deploy in the confined space and were virtually annihilated when the Swiss charged down the slopes, stabbing and hacking them with their halberds.

CAVALRY AT BAY
Infantry with pikes and clubs hold an armored cavalry force in check. Pikes were longer than knights' lances.

BURGUNDIAN WAR
Murten

DATE
June 22, 1476

FORCES
Swiss: 25,000;
Burgundian:
15,000–20,000

LOCATION
Murten (Morat), west
of Bern, Switzerland

CASUALTIES Burgundian
7,000–10,000 killed;
Swiss losses small

Duke Charles the Bold of Burgundy was an innovative and ambitious leader who created a well-trained standing army, equipped with field artillery. Yet in the footsoldiers of Switzerland he faced the 15th century's most potent military force. In June 1476 the Burgundian army besieged Swiss-held Murten. They created strong defensive field fortifications of trenches and palisades. But the Swiss infantry, supported by cavalry supplied by Austria and Germany, arrived so swiftly that they took the Burgundians completely by surprise. Not stopping to deploy in battle order, the Swiss attacked immediately, finding the trenchworks only lightly held. When the majority of the Burgundian army began to arrive in haste from their camp, they were overrun and slaughtered by the Swiss pikemen.

FALL OF THE BOLD
Six months after Murten, on January 5, 1476, Charles the Bold was again defeated by the Swiss at Nancy, and this time was killed. This painting of the event is by French artist Delacroix.

HUSSITE WARS
Kutna Hora

DATE
December 21–22, 1421

FORCES
Sigismund's forces:
unknown; Hussites:
unknown

LOCATION
Kutna Hora, Bohemia,
Czech Republic

CASUALTIES
No reliable estimates

In 1419 the pope declared a crusade against the Hussites, Czech religious reformers inspired by the teachings of Jan Hus, executed in 1415. One radical branch of the Hussites, known as the Taborites, formed a religious-military community at their stronghold of Tabor. Mostly peasants, though including people from all levels of Czech society, the Taborites became a disciplined military force, bonded by their shared religious beliefs and governed by strict rules of conduct. Under the inspired leadership of Jan Zizka they adopted the latest available weaponry, including handguns and long, thin cannons they called "snakes." Their war wagons provided them with a flexible means of conducting mobile warfare. Their most remarkable operation was at Kutna Hora in the winter of 1421. There Zizka's Taborite army was encircled by King Sigismund's numerically superior forces. Although Sigismund's armored cavalry was kept at bay by the Taborite artillery, the Hussites apparently faced imminent destruction. But Zizka organized his wagons into a column and charged the enemy lines. The battle wagons advanced with all guns blazing and punched through to safety. Sigismund failed to mount a pursuit, considering the Hussites defeated. Zizka, however, soon mounted a counteroffensive, despite still having numerically inferior forces. His normal tactic was to mount raids that would draw his opponent into attacking his wagon fort, then, at the right moment, sortie with cavalry, bowmen, and pikemen to savage the enemy. Relentlessly pursued by Zizka's apparently unbeatable army, Sigismund's demoralized force was driven back out of Bohemia.

c.1376–1424
JAN ZIZKA

Czech general Jan Zizka learned his fighting skills in the service of King Wenceslas IV of Bohemia. After the battle of Tannenberg in 1410, he returned to Prague and was converted to the strict beliefs of Jan Hus. When the suppression of the Hussites began in 1419, he became the leading organizer of the Hussite armed camp at Tabor. His revolutionary tactics, built around the use of wagon forts, achieved some outstanding successes against superior forces.

HALBERDS
The halberd was a highly effective infantry weapon, a combination of a pike and an ax. It was the main weapon of Swiss armies in the 14th century,

GERMAN
HALBERD
c.1500

SWISS
HALBERD
c.1400

HUSSITE WAR WAGONS

Drawing wagons into a circle for defense dated back to ancient times. However, the Hussites developed the wagon fort, or "wagenburg," into a formidable defensive system. The wagons, reinforced with iron as armor, were chained together to make a continuous barrier. They might also be surrounded by a palisade. Crossbows and hand guns were fired through loopholes; other wagons had cannon mounted on them. Pikemen were ready to repel any enemy soldiers who made it through this hail of fire.

Notch to rest gun

Wooden pavise shield

Iron barrel

14th-century handgun

Wooden prop

Heraldic badge to identify the lord of the marksman

SHIELDED GUNNER
Early handguns were often mounted behind portable shields. Arranged in groups behind earthworks or war wagons, they could unleash a withering fire.

NORTHERN WARS

A SERIES OF CONFLICTS fought at Europe's northern edge from the 13th to the 15th century eventually saw the rise of Lithuania, Muscovite Russia, Poland, and Prussia as important states. Much of the fighting had a religious edge, between Catholic and Orthodox Christians and between Christians and non-Christians. The Teutonic Knights, a military order founded in Palestine, carried the spirit of the Crusades into these northern lands. Ultimately Poland and Lithuania united and held back the tide of German expansion.

KEY

- frontier of Kievan Rus c.1100
- Holy Roman Empire, 1100
- added to Holy Roman Empire by 1380
- Sweden
- added to Sweden by 1323
- under Danish control c.1225
- possessions of the Hungarian Angevins
- frontiers 1380

NORTHERN WARS
A German-led wave of migration from 1100 to 1350 transformed eastern and Baltic Europe and led to conflicts with Poland, Lithuania, and Russia. The Teutonic Order led crusades in the east

Saule

DATE September 22, 1236

FORCES Livonians: unknown; Lithuanians: unknown

LOCATION Saule (Siaulai), Lithuania

CASUALTIES Livonian Knights: around 50 killed

The Livonian Brethren of the Sword was a military order established in 1204 to protect Christian colonists around the Baltic from pagan attack. In September 1236, the Livonian leader Volquin Schenk led an expedition into pagan territory but was routed by the Lithuanians. Their leader, Mindaugas, used light cavalry armed with javelins, which were hurled at short range—highly effective against unwieldy Livonian heavy cavalry. Chronicler Petrus von Dusburg records the Livonians were "cut down like women."

MEMORY OF WAR
The Siaulai monument marks the victory that enabled Mindaugas to unite Lithuania.

Neva

DATE July 15, 1240

FORCES Swedes: unknown; Novgoroders: unknown

LOCATION Confluence of Neva and Izhora rivers, Russia

CASUALTIES No reliable estimates

In July 1240 a Swedish army led by Birger Jarl attacked the prosperous Russian city of Novgorod. The Swedish army included Norwegian and Finnish contingents; the invasion was ostensibly launched to punish the Novgoroders for encroaching on the lands of their Finnish allies, but the Swedes also sought to gain control over the mouth of the Neva River and bar Russian access to the Baltic. Prince Alexander Yaroslavovitch, the son of Prince Yaroslav of Vladimir, led a small Russian army up the Volkhov River to defend Novgorod. He approached the Swedish camp under cover of thick fog, and launched a surprise attack before the Swedes could assail the city itself. The Swedish army was soundly defeated, and survivors were able to flee across the Izhora River only because of the poor light. After the battle Alexander was given the nickname "Nevski" ("of the Neva") in honor of his victory. The success at the Neva saved Russia from an all-out

SAINTLY PRINCE
Alexander Nevski (1218–63), victor of the battles of Neva and Lake Peipus, was declared a saint by the Orthodox Church.

invasion from the north at a time when it faced attack from the Mongols in the east. After his victory, Alexander argued with the rulers of Novgorod, who thought that his growing influence posed a threat to them, and he was exiled from the city.

Lake Peipus

DATE April 5, 1242

FORCES Tuetonic Knights: unknown; Nevski's fores: unknown

LOCATION Near Lake Peipus, Russian–Estonian border

CASUALTIES No reliable estimates

In spring 1242, the Teutonic grand master Gerhard von Malburg led his Knights across the frozen ice of Lake Peipus to attack Pskov. Before they could reach it, they encountered

Alexander Nevski, recalled from exile to defend the city. The armies clashed on the ice on April 5. The Teutonic Knights, possibly outnumbered 60 to one, attacked in a wedge and hours of hand-to-hand fighting ensued. The Knights finally retreated in the face of a fresh cavalry charge. In addition, their heavy armor caused the ice to crack, and many of them drowned as they retreated across it. Their defeat put a stop to Teutonic plans to conquer Russia.

ICE BATTLE
Alexander Nevski leads the Russian charge across the ice in this representation of the battle of Lake Peipus.

MUSCOVITE–MONGOL WAR

Kulikovo

DATE
September 8, 1380

FORCES
Muscovite Russians:
30,000–80,000;
Mongols:
30,000–125,000

LOCATION On Kulikovo
Pole (Snipe's Field), by
Don River, Russia

CASUALTIES
No reliable estimates

By the mid 14th century, civil wars had weakened the authority of the Mongol Golden Horde, which had dominated Russia for a century. Prince Dmitri of Moscow took advantage of this by ceasing regular tribute payments. In response the Mongol

> **"…they were routed by the Christians, and some were struck down with weapons, and others drowned in the river, a countless number of them."**
>
> *The Chronicle of Novgorod*

general Mamai raised an army, which included Genoese crossbowmen. He allied with Jogaila of Lithuania and Oleg of Ryazan, planning to launch a massed combined attack against the Muscovites. But Dmitri managed to intercept the Mongols at Kulikovo, near the Don River, before they could link up with their allies, who were just 25 miles (40km) away. Before the battle a champion from each side met in single combat, but both died. The ensuing fighting was fierce and both

sides suffered heavy casualties. Dmitri eventually won the day by launching a flanking counterattack, and Mamai fled the field. After the battle Dmitri was given the soubriquet "Donski" ("of the Don"). Kulikovo was the first battle in which a Russian army was victorious over the Mongols.

MUSCOVITE TRIUMPH
Dmitri Donski is shown here both before and after the victory that marked the end of Mongol rule over Russia.

TEUTONIC KNIGHTS VS. POLAND

Grunwald

DATE
July 15, 1410

FORCES
Polish–Lithuanians:
39,000; Teutonic
Knights: 27,000

LOCATION Grunwald
(Tannenberg), East
Prussia

CASUALTIES Teutonic
Knights: 13,000 killed,
14,000 prisoners

In July 1409, a Polish–Lithuanian army approached the headquarters of the Teutonic Knights at Marienberg, seeking to crush the independent state the Knights had established in Prussia. The Teutonic grand master Ulrich von Jungingen planned to cut them off at Grunwald with a force of heavy cavalry and infantry. The Polish–Lithuanian army was led by King Ladislav II Jagiello

of Poland, assisted by Grand Duke Witold of Lithuania. At first the Polish–Lithuanians simply let the Teutonic Knights get hotter and hotter on the open plain opposite them. However, at noon they attacked, breaking the Teutonic infantry, who were caught in retreat by advancing cavalry from their own side.

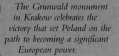

POLISH VICTORY
The Grunwald monument in Krakow celebrates the victory that set Poland on the path to becoming a significant European power.

The Knights rallied, forcing the Lithuanians on the right flank to retreat. They seemed to be getting the better of the fighting until Ladislav launched a reserve force from a forest behind the main army. A Teutonic flanking counterattack failed and the Knights were crushed.

1360–1410

ULRICH VON JUNGINGEN

In 1407 Ulrich von Jungingen was elected as the 23rd grand master of the Order of the Teutonic Knights, in succession to his brother Konrad. It was an unfortunate choice as he was arrogant and irascible and embarked on an aggressive policy that led to war with Poland and Lithuania in 1409. He fatally underestimated the Poles and Lithuanians, especially their footsoldiers. That he led his men bravely is not in doubt; at one point in the battle of Grunwald he personally charged the strongest Polish unit. But he was killed in the final stages of Grunwald, along with most of his knights. Von Jungingen's successor as grand master, Heinrich von Plauen, struggled to keep the Order's holdings from complete extinction; land had been lost both to Poland and Lithuania and the loss of life at Grunwald meant the Teutonic Knights had to rely on hiring mercenaries, an expense they could ill afford.

THIRTEEN YEARS WAR

Chojnice (Conitz)

DATE
September 18, 1454

FORCES
Polish: 20,000;
Teutonic Knights:
15,000

LOCATION Chojnice
(Conitz), northern
Poland

CASUALTIES Polish 3,000
killed, 300 knights
prisoner; Teutonic
Knights: 100 killed

The Thirteen Years War began in 1454 when leading Prussian cities allied with Poland against the Teutonic Knights. Chojnice had been under siege by the Poles and their Prussian allies since April 1454. The mercenary Bernard Szumborski, hired by the Teutonic Knights, led an army to relieve the city. The Polish army, led by their king Casimir IV, was almost wholly composed of heavy cavalry, their commanders believing infantry and artillery would be unnecessary. The Poles wheeled around to face the Teutonic force. Initially their tactics of massed cavalry charge were successful, breaking the Teutonic lines and taking Szumborski prisoner. But the Poles were thrown into disarray when a force of Teutonic Knights broke out of the besieged city and attacked their rear, forcing them to retreat. In the panic Szumborski succeeded in escaping and helped to organize the pursuit of the fleeing Polish army. The Poles were completely defeated at Chojnice, but they eventually triumphed over the Teutonic Knights in 1466.

TWO-HANDED SWORD
Double-edged two-handed swords were heavy weapons used for combat on foot. Only plate armor could resist a blow.

RISE OF THE OTTOMANS

IN ABOUT 150 YEARS, the Ottoman Turks grew from a small band of *ghazis*, or holy warriors, settled on land in northwest Anatolia, into the rulers of an empire straddling Europe and Asia. They destroyed the Byzantine Empire and conquered the great city of Constantinople, while also extending their dominion over the Christian Balkans. The secret of their success was partly a cunning diplomacy that took full advantage of the weaknesses and divisions of their enemies. But it was also their successful blending of traditional Turkish warrior spirit with the latest technology borrowed from Europe, exemplified by the use of cannons at the siege of Constantinople. By the mid-15th century, their advance looked set to overwhelm central Europe.

OTTOMAN–BYZANTINE WARS

Siege of Nicomedia

DATE
1333–37

FORCES
Osman's forces: unknown; Byzantines: unknown

LOCATION
Modern Izmit, Turkey

CASUALTIES
No reliable estimates

In the early 14th century an ambitious Anatolian Turkish warrior, Osman, was establishing himself as the leader in a continuous war of raids conducted against the Byzantine Empire. By 1301 he controlled land around the city of Nicaea (Iznik) and, as his success against the Byzantines grew, more Turkish warriors were attracted to his banner. Soon after Osman's death in 1326, his army captured the major city of Brusa (Bursa), which became the first Ottoman capital. When Byzantine emperor Andronicus III sent an army to relieve Nicaea in 1328 it was soundly defeated by Osman's son, Orkhan. In 1331 Nicaea fell to the Ottomans, leaving Nicomedia (Izmit) the only major Byzantine stronghold in Anatolia. When Orkhan laid siege to the city in 1333, Andronicus sought to buy him off by paying a hefty sum in tribute. It was to no avail. Four years later the Ottomans took the city anyway, making it their new capital.

SULTAN OSMAN
Osman I began life as a ghazi, a warrior-raider, and founded an emirate that would grow to control Anatolia and the Balkans.

OTTOMAN–SERBIAN WAR

Kosovo

DATE
June 15, 1389

FORCES
Ottomans: 30,000; Serbs and allies: 15,000–20,000

LOCATION
Kosovo Polje, near Pristina, Kosovo

CASUALTIES
No reliable estimates

The Christian world began to wake up to the threat posed by the Ottomans in 1365, when Sultan Murad I moved his capital from Asia to Edirne (Adrianople) in Europe. The following year Pope Urban V called for a crusade against the Ottomans, but the response was largely ineffectual; Murad exploited divisions between Christians in the Balkans to extend his influence. In 1386 the Ottomans occupied the southern Serbian city of Nis. The Serbian ruler, Tsar Lazar, assembled a force of Serbs, Bosnians, Wallachians, Hungarians, Albanians, and Saxon mercenaries to take on the Ottomans. Murad marched north, attracting the support of some disaffected Serbs. Accounts of the battle at Kosovo Polje are confused. It appears that Lazar himself was killed quite early in the fighting. Murad was also killed, stabbed by a Serb who was pretending to surrender. The Ottomans carried the day, largely through the treachery of Serbs who betrayed their own side and through the bold fighting skills of Murad's son Bayezid. The outcome of the battle was that Serbia became a loyal ally of the Turks.

CAVALRY TURK
An Ottoman sipahi— a feudal cavalryman—is depicted on an Italian Renaissance plate.

CRUSADE OF NICOPOLIS

Nicopolis

DATE
September 25, 1396

FORCES
Christians: 16,000; Ottomans: 20,000

LOCATION
Nikopol, Bulgaria

CASUALTIES Heavier for Ottoman victors than defeated Christians

Sultan Bayezid, Murad's successor as Ottoman leader, was an energetic warrior who earned the nickname "Thunderbolt" and laid siege to Constantinople itself. Fearing he would be next to face Bayezid's army, King Sigismund of Hungary appealed to the French court for a crusade against the Turks. As France and England were at peace, there were many knights eager for a chance to show their valor. The Comte de Nevers, son of the Duke of Burgundy, and other notables set off for Hungary with some 8,000 men. There they met up with Sigismund's army and advanced down the Danube into Ottoman-controlled Bulgaria. A force of Knights Hospitaller sailed from Rhodes to join them. The Christian army laid siege to the Ottoman stronghold of Nicopolis, believing Bayezid to be far away. But the sultan hurried north by forced marches and took up position a few miles outside Nicopolis. Brushing aside appeals for caution from King Sigismund, the French knights insisted on opening the battle with a charge. Many were unhorsed by sharpened stakes planted in their path or arrow fire, but they fought on with great valor on foot, only to be enveloped by Ottoman *sipahis*. Sigismund then led the reserves into the battle and looked on the point of carrying the day when Bayezid's Serbian allies, under Stefan Lazarevich, weighed in with a cavalry charge that put the knights to flight. Only a few escaped by boat or on foot. About 3,000 were taken prisoner and most of those were slaughtered next day.

> **"Then each [warrior] was ordered to kill his own prisoners, and for those who did not wish to do so the king [Bayezid] appointed others in their place."**
>
> *16-year-old Johann Schiltberger, who was spared because of his age*

CRUSADE OF VARNA

Varna

DATE
November 10, 1444

FORCES Hungarians and allies: 30,000; Ottomans: possibly 60,000

LOCATION Black Sea coast of Bulgaria

CASUALTIES Probably half of Hungarians and allies killed

Murad II, sultan from 1421, resumed the Ottoman campaign of conquest in southern Europe that had faltered after Timur's defeat of Bayezid in 1402 (see p.94). His progress was halted, however, by a spirited fightback led by Hungarian general János Hunyadi. Pope Eugenius IV declared the campaign a crusade, but it won little support outside the Balkans. Hunyadi, King Ladislas of Hungary and Poland, and Vlad Dracula of Wallachia found themselves facing superior Ottoman forces on the Black Sea coast. Hunyadi took up a strong position, using wagons to make a defensive line, and for a time the battle was evenly balanced. Then Ladislas ill-advisedly waded into the thick of the fighting and was killed. After the Ottomans displayed the king's head on a spear, the battle was lost for the Christians.

c.1387–1456

JÁNOS HUNYADI

Between 1437 and 1443, Hunyadi, the Hungarian national hero, inflicted a series of defeats on the Turks that drove them out of Transylvania and carried the war south of the Danube. After the death of King Ladislas at Varna, Hunyadi ruled Hungary as regent. He lost to the Ottomans again at the second battle of Kosovo in 1448, but defeated them decisively at the battle of Belgrade in July 1456, a month before his death.

OTTOMAN–BYZANTINE WARS

Constantinople

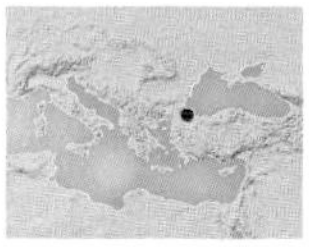

DATE
April 6–May 29, 1453

FORCES
Ottomans: 80,000;
Byzantine: 7,000

CASUALTIES
No reliable estimates

LOCATION
Constantinople,
modern Istanbul

Sultan Mehmet II, who succeeded his father, Murad II, in 1451, was determined to achieve the conquest of Constantinople, which was almost all that remained of the once-great Byzantine Empire. He built fortresses on the Bosphorus and the Dardanelles, isolating the city from relief or supply by sea. To deal with the apparently impregnable thousand-year-old city walls, he ordered the building of the largest cannon yet seen. In April 1453 teams of oxen hauled this and other smaller pieces to face the formidable walls. A massive Ottoman army blockaded the city by land while a fleet of around 120 ships sailed into the sea of Marmora, although they were stopped from entering the inlet of the Golden Horn by a boom laid across the entrance. The bombardment of the outer walls began on April 12, the heavy pieces firing about seven rounds a day. Soon breaches began to appear, but the defenders repulsed all assaults by the janissaries. To increase the pressure, on April 22 the Ottomans hauled ships from the

BOSPHORUS CASTLE
Mehmet II built Rumeli Castle on the European bank of the Bosphorus in 1522 to block the sea passage to Constantinople.

Bosphorus overland and launched them inside the Golden Horn. The defenders, already thinly spread, now had to man the relatively weak sea wall. A combined land and sea assault was begun on the morning of May 29. Some janissaries found a way into the city by an undefended side gate. The last Byzantine emperor, Constantine XI, died leading a doomed counterattack. That afternoon, as his soldiers plundered and massacred, Mehmet rode into the city to pray to Allah in the cathedral of St Sophia.

CANNON WAR
This, the largest of Mehmet II's cannons, had a barrel over 25ft (8m) long and fired a stone ball weighing more than 1,100lb (500kg).

"All through the day the Turks made a great slaughter of Christians through the city. The blood flowed in the city like rainwater in the gutters after a sudden storm, and the corpses of Turks and Christians were thrown into the Dardanelles, where they floated out to sea like melons along a canal."

WITNESS TO WAR
NICOLO BARBARO

Nicolo Barbaro, a Venetian surgeon and member of a noble family, witnessed the siege and the slaughter that followed the capture of Constantinople, which he describes here. His account takes the form of a diary. Genoese and Venetians, as well as a few Spanish and other Christian soldiers, fought alongside the Byzantine Greeks in defense of the city. As the city was falling, Barbaro, along with many of his countrymen, managed to escape aboard a galley to the relative safety of the Venetian colony at Pera.

476–1492

THE CONQUEROR ARRIVES
A Romanian fresco depicts Mehmet II's army arriving triumphantly before the walls of Constantinople.

EARLY MODERN
WARFARE

1492–1750

FIREARMS AND FLEETS

THE GROWING IMPORTANCE OF GUNPOWDER WEAPONS was a vital factor in land warfare from the 16th century onwards, while ocean-going sailing ships armed with cannon revolutionized naval battles. Louis de la Tremouille, a 16th-century biographer of the French knight, bemoaned these changes: "What is the use any more of the skill-at-arms of the knights, their strength, their hardihood, their discipline … when such weapons may be used in war?"

Spain's success in the 1500s against the Aztec and Inca empires in the Americas demonstrated European military prowess—its steel weapons, cavalry, and ruthless attitude to warfare. But the Spanish conquest did not typify Europe's relationship to the rest of the world in this period. Powers outside Europe had little difficulty keeping up with the new gunpowder technology, as peoples as diverse as the Japanese and the Ottoman Turks showed. Throughout most of the 16th century, indeed, Christian Europe was on the defensive against the Muslim Ottomans. Although Europeans fought around the world—in the West Indies, the Indian Ocean, and the Pacific—it was mostly against one another, in an extension of the wars that almost continuously ravaged Europe itself. Much of this warfare had a religious edge after the split between the Protestant and Catholic versions of Christianity divided Europe at the Reformation, although dynastic conflicts reinforced or cut across religious divides.

CHANGES TO LAND WARFARE

The challenge posed by cannons meant that, by the early 1500s, siege warfare in Europe was already being transformed through the construction of new types of fortification. Instead of tall stone walls, early-modern fortresses had bastions, or projections, jutting out in front of ramparts, from which defenders with cannons and other missile weapons could cover all approaches. Earth ramparts, furthermore, blocked cannonfire from striking the relatively low walls. Besiegers, therefore, had to adopt painstaking new tactics, digging zigzag sap trenches toward the walls to prevent exposure to direct fire, while using mortars to lob munitions into the fortress or city. On the battlefield, commanders sought ways of deploying firearms and cannons to good effect alongside more traditional resources. The Spanish *tercios*, the most effective infantry of the 16th century, combined a disciplined mass of pikemen with

CANNON POWER
Artillery helped Russia to victory over Sweden in the battle of Poltava in 1709.

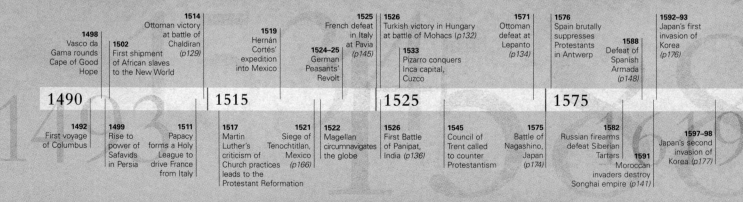

1490			1515			1525			1575		

Above the line:

- **1498** Vasco da Gama rounds Cape of Good Hope
- **1502** First shipment of African slaves to the New World
- **1514** Ottoman victory at battle of Chaldiran *(p129)*
- **1519** Hernán Cortés' expedition into Mexico
- **1524–25** German Peasants' Revolt
- **1525** French defeat in Italy at Pavia *(p145)*
- **1526** Turkish victory in Hungary at battle of Mohacs *(p132)*
- **1533** Pizarro conquers Inca capital, Cuzco
- **1571** Ottoman defeat at Lepanto *(p134)*
- **1576** Spain brutally suppresses Protestants in Antwerp
- **1588** Defeat of Spanish Armada *(p148)*
- **1592–93** Japan's first invasion of Korea *(p176)*

Below the line:

- **1492** First voyage of Columbus
- **1499** Rise to power of Safavids in Persia
- **1511** Papacy forms a Holy League to drive France from Italy
- **1517** Martin Luther's criticism of Church practices leads to the Protestant Reformation
- **1521** Siege of Tenochtitlan, Mexico *(p166)*
- **1522** Magellan circumnavigates the globe
- **1526** First Battle of Panipat, India *(p136)*
- **1545** Council of Trent called to counter Protestantism
- **1575** Battle of Nagashino, Japan *(p174)*
- **1582** Russian firearms defeat Siberian Tartars
- **1591** Moroccan invaders destroy Songhai empire *(p141)*
- **1597–98** Japan's second invasion of Korea *(p177)*

BATTLE OF MARIGNANO, 1515   INDIAN CANNON, 18TH CENTURY   DEFEAT OF THE SPANISH ARMADA, 1588

a smaller number of soldiers armed with matchlock arquebus guns. As more effective flintlock muskets came into use, throughout the 17th century the balance shifted, with the proportion of pikemen in European armies decreasing. By the early 18th century the widespread use of bayonets was making pikes redundant and every infantryman could be armed with a musket. Cavalry evolved in the course of the 16th century, from knights charging with couched lance to horsemen fighting with pistol and sword, though their role as high-status shock troops remained unchanged. Armor reached its peak of development in the 16th century, but then began to wane in popularity because of its increasing ineffectiveness against firearms. It was still worn throughout most of the 17th century, but generally covered smaller areas of the body in greater thickness.

NAVAL POWER

Sea warfare in the Mediterranean in the 16th century was little different from the naval battles of the ancient world, with oared galleys seeking to ram and board one another—even if some of the galleys now mounted cannons in their bows. But there were startling innovations in Korea, where ironclad "turtle ships," equipped with cannons, proved formidable vessels, repelling Japan's attempts at invasion. The most significant development, however, was the ocean-going fleets of Spain, France, England, and the Netherlands. These countries' sailing ships, increasingly specially

built for war, were equipped with a profusion of cast-iron guns—one 17th-century warship, for instance, might have as many cannons as a whole land army. Although boarding still happened, naval battles between sailing ships developed into standoff cannon duels.

COSTLY PROFESSIONALISM

Only states with considerable resources could build such fleets of warships, while on land bastion fortresses and large armies were also costly. In late-17th-century Russia, for example, the armed forces took up 60 percent of the government's revenue in peacetime and 90 percent when at war. By the late 1600s all the major European powers had adopted standing armies in place of mercenaries- - although private companies such as the British East India Company still managed armies in far-off colonies. The stress on drill, which had been found to increase the effectiveness of infantry, came to the fore. Countries founded military academies and established clear ranks in their armies. They issued soldiers with uniforms and standardized weapons, and subjected them to draconian discipline. By the 1700s European armies and navies were impressive professional forces.

NEW FIREARMS
Small-arm technology developed rapidly in the early-modern period. This 17th-century wheel-lock pistol was ready to fire at any time, unlike earlier matchlock weapons that required a constantly lit length of match in order to work. Both were superseded by the flintlock.

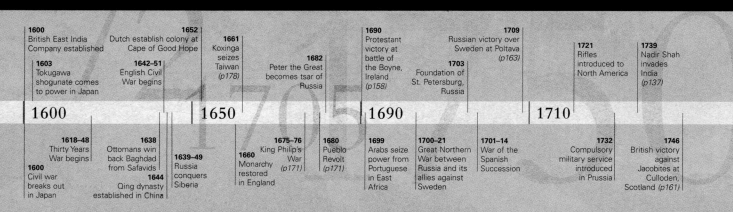

1600 British East India Company established	**1652** Dutch establish colony at Cape of Good Hope	**1661** Koxinga seizes Taiwan *(p178)*	**1682** Peter the Great becomes tsar of Russia	**1690** Protestant victory at battle of the Boyne, Ireland *(p158)*	**1709** Russian victory over Sweden at Poltava *(p163)*	**1721** Rifles introduced to North America	**1739** Nadir Shah invades India *(p137)*
1603 Tokugawa shogunate comes to power in Japan	**1642–51** English Civil War begins				**1703** Foundation of St. Petersburg, Russia		

1600   1650   1690   1710

1618–48 Thirty Years War begins	**1638** Ottomans win back Baghdad from Safavids		**1675–76** King Philip's War *(p171)*	**1680** Pueblo Revolt *(p171)*	**1699** Arabs seize power from Portuguese in East Africa	**1700–21** Great Northern War between Russia and its allies against Sweden	**1701–14** War of the Spanish Succession	**1732** Compulsory military service introduced in Prussia
1600 Civil war breaks out in Japan	**1644** Qing dynasty established in China	**1639–49** Russia conquers Siberia	**1660** Monarchy restored in England					**1746** British victory against Jacobites at Culloden, Scotland *(p161)*

JAPANESE SHOGUN IEYASU (1543–1616)   BATTLE OF THE BOYNE, 1690   TSAR PETER THE GREAT (1672–1725)

ISLAMIC EMPIRES

IN THE 16TH AND 17TH CENTURIES the Islamic empires—the Ottoman Turks across Europe and Asia, the Safavids in Persia, the Moguls in India—were among the world's most dynamic powers, with large and sophisticated armed forces. Their fighting style was characterized by a combination of the traditional aggression and mobility of Asian cavalry with the latest gunpowder technology; Mogul emperor Akbar, for example, was an early user of mobile field artillery.

MUSLIM TROOPS

The Ottomans were capable of the bureaucratic organization needed to create a standing army and could also raise feudal cavalry from their landed class. Their most renowned troops, the Janissaries, were originally Christian-born slaves who had been brought up as Muslim soldiers. The Janissaries formed a disciplined elite infantry, skilled in firearms, that provided the emperor's bodyguard. However, cavalry predominated in the Ottoman army, and artillery was also a formidable element. Not least of Ottoman achievements was the creation from scratch of a powerful navy that for a time reigned supreme on the Mediterranean.

SAFAVID HORSEMAN
Armed with sword and bow, a Persian soldier gets the better of an Uzbek enemy.

OTTOMAN DRUMS
The Janissaries of the Ottoman army are shown here parading with the drums that were used to urge the soldiers into battle.

KEY

■	Ottoman Empire and vassals, 1512
■	conquests of Selim I, 1512–20
■	conquests of Suleiman I, 1520–66
■	Ottoman conquest, 1566–1639
■	Austrian Habsburg possessions
■	Spanish Habsburg possessions
■	Venetian Republic and possessions
✗	Ottoman victory
✗	Ottoman defeat
▣	Knights of St. John
○	siege, with date
---	vassal border
—	frontiers 1600
—	Holy Roman Empire

GROWTH OF AN EMPIRE
In the 16th and 17th centuries the Ottoman Empire grew to encompass almost the entire Mediterranean.

SAFAVIDS

Safavid Persia did not have as strong an army as the Ottomans until the great Shah Abbas (1571–1629) introduced reforms around the start of the 17th century. Using European advisers he created standing forces of well-organized artillery and musket-armed infantry. He also set up a force of cavalry responsible directly to himself, rather than relying on tribal horsemen. These reforms turned the Safavids into a dangerous rival to the Ottomans, as Shah Abbas showed when he routed the Turks at Sis in 1606. The prolonged warfare that ensued over the following three decades exhausted both empires.

DECLINE

In the 16th century Europeans regarded Islamic armies with the highest respect. But by the second half of the 17th century the Muslim empires were in decline, suffering from decaying political and social structures and losing ground rapidly to the Europeans in technology and organization. Typically, the Janissaries, once so admired, became a weakness in Ottoman forces through their political intriguing and their conservatism, which obstructed military reform.

INDIAN SPLENDOR
The wealth of 18th-century India, shown in this garment of silk, gold, and silver, was reflected in large and richly accoutred armies.

EARLY MODERN WARFARE

OTTOMAN GLORY AND DECLINE

FROM THE FALL OF BYZANTIUM in 1453 through to the late 16th century the Ottoman Turks had probably the most effective fighting forces in the world, on both land and sea. They conquered Egypt, dominated the Mediterranean, and managed a campaign against the Austrian Empire on one frontier while also fighting the Persian Safavids on the other.

After their crushing naval defeat at Lepanto in 1571 (see p.134), however, the Ottomans never recovered their dominance at sea. By the late 17th century their overall decline as a military power was extremely apparent. A last attempt to take the Austrian capital, Vienna, in 1683 only narrowly failed, but the rout of the Ottoman army at the battle of Zenta marked the end of an era.

 OTTOMAN WARS OF EXPANSION

Chaldiran

DATE
August 23, 1514

FORCES
Ottomans: 60,000;
Safavids: up to 50,000

LOCATION
Between Tabriz
and Lake Van

CASUALTIES
Probably fairly even

Ismail I, founder of the Safavid dynasty in Persia, attracted the special hatred of Sultan Selim I, not only as a Shi'ite heretic but also for supporting Selim's brother Ahmed in the power struggle after their father's death. In 1514 Selim led a large army eastward into Safavid territory. The Safavids retreated, burning the land behind them so that the Ottoman forces

OTTOMAN CONQUEROR

Sultan Selim I achieved remarkable conquests during his brief reign (1512–20).

almost starved. When the two armies met on the plains of Chaldiran, however, it was the Ottomans who triumphed—their mix of infantry, cavalry, and artillery beating the Safavid horsemen. The Ottomans went on to occupy Tabriz, but a mutiny by the Janissaries meant that Selim was forced to withdraw without achieving a decisive conquest.

 OTTOMAN WARS OF EXPANSION

Rhodes

DATE
June–December 1522

FORCES
Ottomans: 100,000;
defenders: 7,000

LOCATION
Rhodes, eastern
Mediterranean

CASUALTIES
Ottomans: 50,000 killed;
defenders: 5,200 killed

In 1522 Sultan Suleiman I (known as "The Magnificent") laid siege to the Christian fortress of Rhodes, which was defended by the Knights of St. John led by Villiers de l'Isle Adam. The Ottomans made breaches in the mighty walls with fire from over 100 cannons, as well as by tunneling and exploding charges under the wall foundations. But the defenders

resisted repeated assaults, repelling the Ottomans with very heavy casualties. However, denied any help by the Christian powers, after six months the Knights eventually surrendered the fortress in return for safe conduct.

KNIGHTS' FORTRESS

Rhodes had exceptionally strong fortifications, withstanding an Ottoman siege in 1480 before succumbing in 1522.

 OTTOMAN CONQUEST OF EGYPT

Raydaniya

DATE
January 22, 1517

FORCES
Ottomans: 40,000;
Mamelukes: c.40,000

LOCATION
Sinai desert,
east of Cairo

CASUALTIES
Ottomans: 6,000 killed;
Mamelukes: 7,000 killed

Mameluke-ruled Egypt was a rich prize inviting conquest. In the summer of 1516 Selim's army trounced the Egyptians at Marj Dabik in Syria, Ottoman gunpowder weapons putting the famed Mameluke cavalry to flight. Egyptian historian Ibn Zabul relates that the Mamelukes appealed to the Ottomans to stop using cannons and the "contrivance artfully devised by the Christians," the arquebus. Now led by Tuman Bey, the Mamelukes hastened to assemble their own cannons, creating

a fortified position at Raydaniya to block the advance on Cairo. The experienced Ottoman gunners dominated an initial exchange of cannon fire. When the Mameluke cavalry charged they were harassed by Ottoman light cavalry from the flanks and repulsed by Janissary arquebusiers. The Ottomans went on to capture Cairo after hard street fighting; Tuman was hanged from one of the city gates.

CAIRO CONQUERED

The wealth of Egypt and, above all, the city of Cairo, seen here, gave the Ottomans the resources to become a world power.

WEAPONS OF THE OTTOMAN EMPIRE

A **16TH-CENTURY AMBASSADOR** to the Ottoman empire, Baron de Busbecq, remarked that "no nation has shown less reluctance to adopt the useful inventions of others," citing the Ottoman use of "large and small cannons." The same observation could be applied to their adoption of muskets and pistols. The combination of these firearms, intelligently deployed, with traditional edged weapons was what helped make Ottoman armies so formidable.

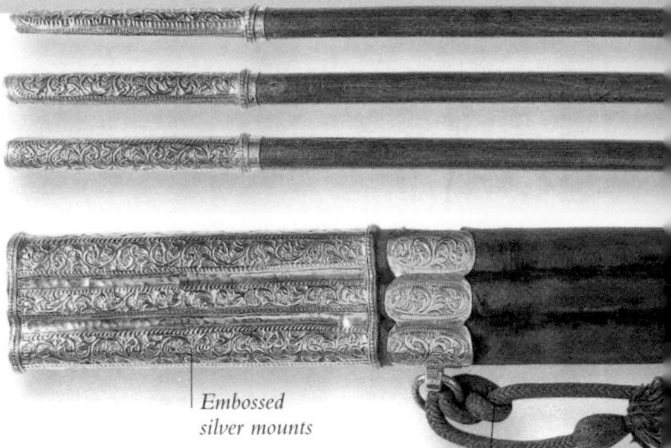

Flint-cock

Pan cover

Embossed silver mounts

Saddle-bar and ring, for use when mounted on horseback

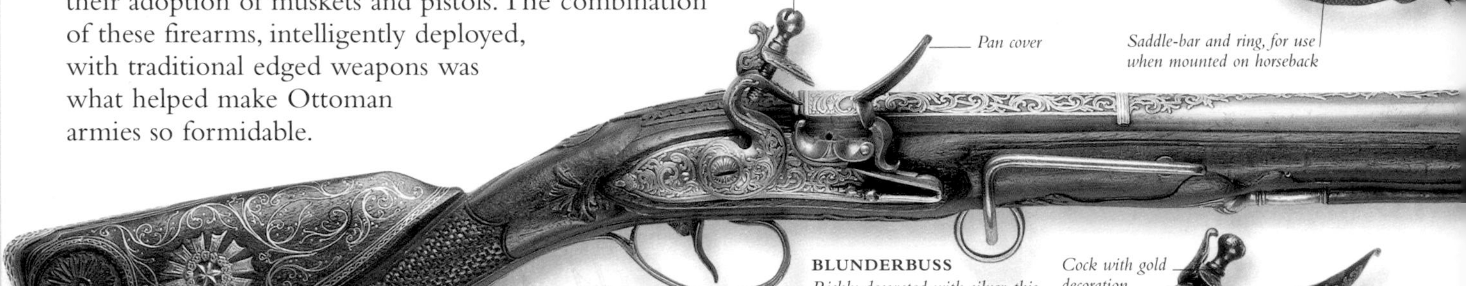

BLUNDERBUSS
Richly decorated with silver, this blunderbuss is inscribed "made by the Dervish Amrullah."

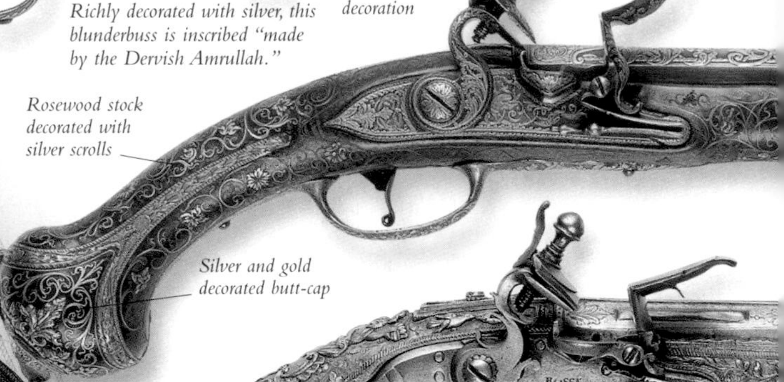

Cock with gold decoration

Rosewood stock decorated with silver scrolls

Walnut stock carved and inlaid with silver

Silver and gold decorated butt-cap

SMALL ARMS

In the 16th century Ottoman footsoldiers amazed Christian troops with the accuracy of their musket shooting. Flintlock pistols were as popular with the Ottoman *sipahi* (cavalry) as with their European counterparts. But fellow Muslims were sometimes appalled by the use of such unheroic contrivances. Egyptian Mameluke chieftain Kurtbay beseeched the Ottoman sultan to prevent the army from shooting with firearms because a musket could be effective "even if a woman were to fire it." By the 18th century, however, the Ottomans had begun to fall behind their European rivals in the quality and tactical deployment of firearms.

Cast and chiselled silver gilt

Italian-made lock inscribed with the maker's name

TURKISH DAGGER
The style of Ottoman daggers, both in design and decoration, probably originated in medieval India or Persia.

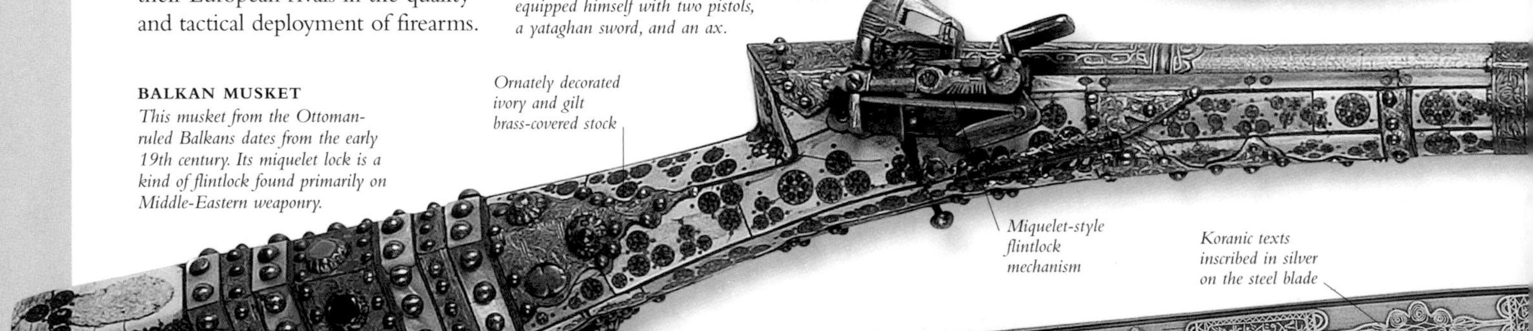

Ornate blade inlaid in gold

OTTOMAN PIRATE
This Ottoman sea fighter has equipped himself with two pistols, a yataghan sword, and an ax.

BALKAN MUSKET
This musket from the Ottoman-ruled Balkans dates from the early 19th century. Its miquelet lock is a kind of flintlock found primarily on Middle-Eastern weaponry.

Ornately decorated ivory and gilt brass-covered stock

Miquelet-style flintlock mechanism

Koranic texts inscribed in silver on the steel blade

Steel head

JAVELINS
Thrown spears were a favored weapon of
the Asiatic tribal world from which the
Ottomans emerged. They may have been
used by the Ottomans' tribal auxiliaries.

Case for three
javelins

Flared muzzle

Large-bore barrel
firing scatter shot

Blued-steel barrel

Ram rod inserted in
barrel to ram home
powder and shot

FATAL DAGGER
Sultan Murad I is stabbed to
death by a Balkan Christian
at the end of the battle of Kosovo
in 1389. Note the exaggerated form
of the sultan's kilij scimitar.

FLINTLOCK PISTOLS
Ottoman flintlock pistols were often a direct
copy of European designs of the time. They
were distinguished only by their decoration.

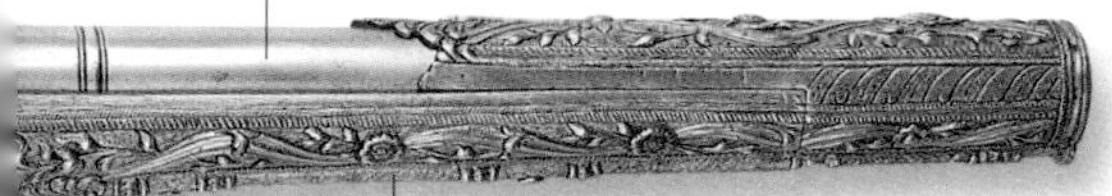

Polished
steel barrel

Smooth-bore barrel
giving only limited
accuracy of fire

SWORDS AND DAGGERS

Ottoman edged weapons were understandably
much feared by their enemies, for they could
sever a head with a single stroke. The Ottomans
are credited with generalizing the use of curved
sword blades in the Muslim world. In addition
to being practical weapons, they often displayed
the wealth and status of their owners through
decoration with precious metals and stones. The
owner's piety was emphasized by Koranic
inscriptions in elaborate calligraphy.

Silver gilt
inlaid with
precious
stones

JEWELED GRIP
Coral and turquoise
have been used to
turn this quama
sword grip into a
lavish display of
the owner's wealth
and rank.

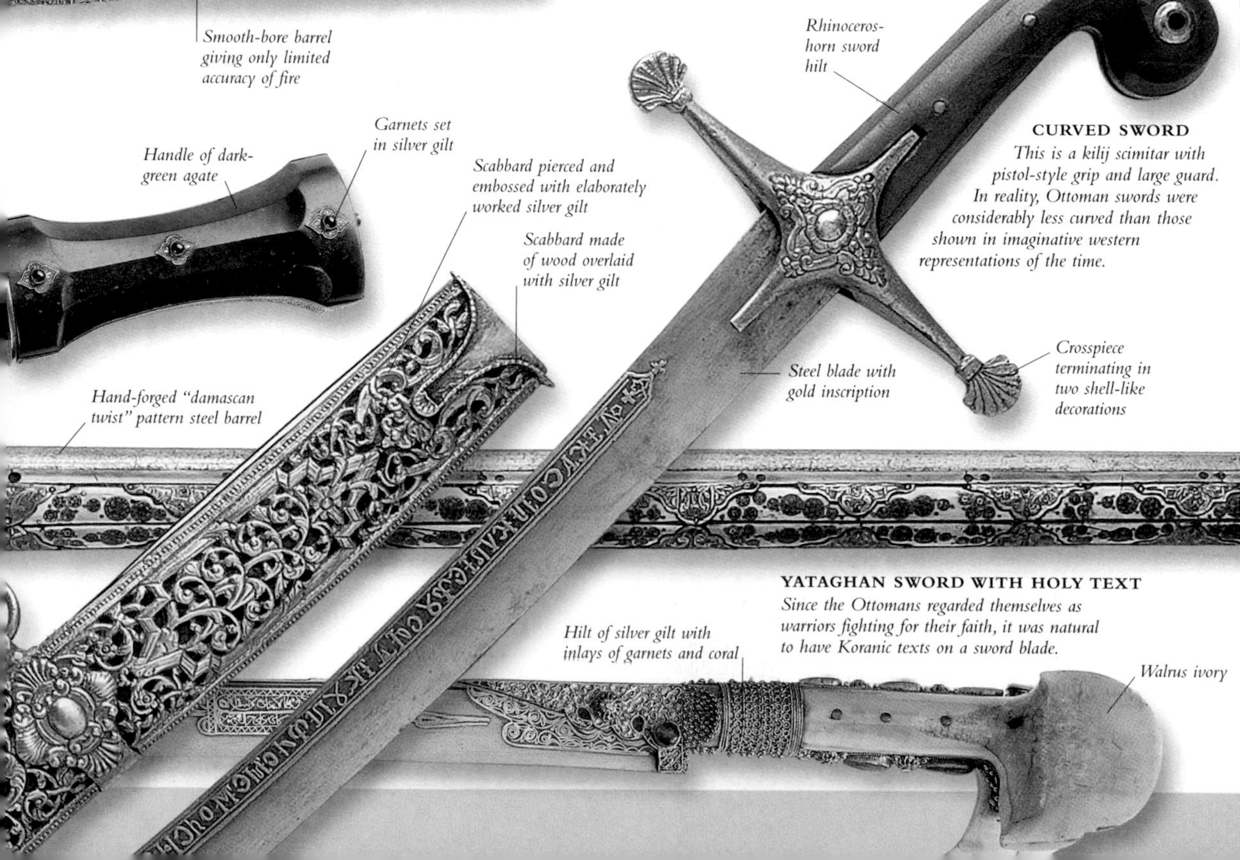

Rhinoceros-
horn sword
hilt

CURVED SWORD
This is a kilij scimitar with
pistol-style grip and large guard.
In reality, Ottoman swords were
considerably less curved than those
shown in imaginative western
representations of the time.

Handle of dark-
green agate

Garnets set
in silver gilt

Scabbard pierced and
embossed with elaborately
worked silver gilt

Scabbard made
of wood overlaid
with silver gilt

Hand-forged "damascan
twist" pattern steel barrel

Steel blade with
gold inscription

Crosspiece
terminating in
two shell-like
decorations

YATAGHAN SWORD WITH HOLY TEXT
Since the Ottomans regarded themselves as
warriors fighting for their faith, it was natural
to have Koranic texts on a sword blade.

Hilt of silver gilt with
inlays of garnets and coral

Walrus ivory

■ OTTOMAN CONQUEST OF HUNGARY

Mohacs

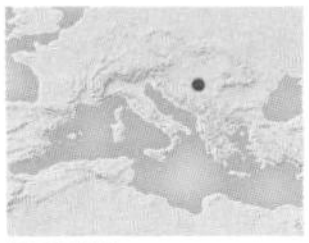

DATE August 29, 1526

FORCES Hungarians: 12,000 cavalry, 13,000 infantry; Ottomans: 70,000–100,000

LOCATION Near Mohacs, southern Hungary

CASUALTIES Hungarians: 15,000 killed; Ottomans: probably similar

In April 1526 Suleiman I marched out of Constantinople with a vast army bent on conquering Hungary. During the Ottoman army's long advance, King Louis of Hungary failed to win support from other Christian rulers. He also failed to contest the crossing of the Drava River, which took Suleiman's army five days across an improvised bridge of boats. Instead, Louis took up position on the plain of Mohacs, blocking the road leading to the Hungarian capital, Buda. The heavily outnumbered Hungarians put their faith in the shock power of their armored cavalry troops. After a brief opening barrage from their handful of cannons, the Hungarian knights charged the Ottoman center. Two lines of Turkish feudal cavalry gave way in the face of this tremendous onslaught, but this brought the knights up against Ottoman cannons—chained together to form an unbreakable line—and the Janissary infantry. The Hungarians fought desperately to break through to Suleiman himself, but were cut down by Ottoman firepower and by flanking attacks from light cavalry. An Ottoman counterattack turned the battle into a rout. King Louis was among those killed in the flight, crushed beneath his falling horse. Hungary became an Ottoman tributary and neighboring Austria lay open to attack—although, when Suleiman returned to besiege Vienna for the first time in 1529, it proved to be his first military failure.

JEWELED HELMET
This 16th-century ceremonial helmet from the Ottoman court, cast in iron and decorated with gold and jewels, reflects the spectacular wealth acquired through conquest.

VICTORIOUS ARMY
The Ottoman army at Mohacs was primarily a cavalry force, but in the hands of disciplined infantry, arquebuses as well as cannons, were crucial to victory.

1492–1750

Tunis

DATE
June–July 1535

FORCES
Imperial forces:
60,000; Ottoman:
unknown

LOCATION
Tunis, North Africa

CASUALTIES
No reliable estiamtes

Khair ad-Din, also known as Barbarossa, the admiral of the Ottoman fleet, was raiding Christian shipping and coastlines from his base at Algiers. In 1534 he captured Tunisia, including the capital Tunis, which became a new base for Turkish piracy. Holy Roman Emperor Charles V assembled a crusading army to retake the city. He crossed the Mediterranean protected by the fleet of Genoese admiral Andrea Doria, who decisively defeated Barbarossa's forces at sea. After a siege, during which many died of dysentery, the imperial forces took the fortified port of La Goleta. They went on to Tunis, which they sacked, killing an estimated 30,000 inhabitants.

Siege of Malta

DATE May 18–
September 7, 1565

FORCES Defenders:
13,000–14,000;
Ottomans:
30,000–60,000

LOCATION
Malta

CASUALTIES Defenders:
5,000 killed; Ottomans:
24,000 killed

Forced out of Rhodes in 1522, the Knights of St. John created a new fortified island headquarters in Malta. In 1565 Suleiman sent a large Ottoman army under Mustafa Pasha to take the island. The entrance to the harbor at Malta was guarded by the ultramodern star-shaped fort of St. Elmo. Heroically defended by the knights and resupplied by sea, St. Elmo held out until June 23, when it was finally taken by assault. The capture of the fort cost the Turks around 8,000 dead with 1,500 defenders killed. The fighting then shifted to the fortifications inside the Grand Harbor, at Senglea, Birgu, and Fort St. Angelo. Intensive bombardment by the Ottoman artillery opened breaches in the walls,

but repeated assaults were repulsed in savage fighting. A clever attempt to take the fortifications from their weaker seaward side was mounted by Hassan, pasha of Algiers and son of admiral Barbarossa, but his boats were blocked by a hidden boom just under the water's surface. The arrival of a Spanish fleet carrying a relief force under Garcia of Toledo finally convinced Mustafa Pasha that it was time to withdraw.

KNIGHTS' CROSS
Used for swearing their oath of fealty, this cross, made from silver and adorned with precious stones, was carried from Rhodes by the Knights of St. John in 1522 and taken with them to Malta.

"The darkness of the night then became as bright as day, due to the vast quantity of artificial fires. So bright was it indeed that we could see St. Elmo quite clearly. The gunners of St. Angelo… were able to lay and train their pieces upon the advancing Turks, who were picked out in the light of the fires."

WITNESS TO WAR
FRANCISCO BALBI, SPANISH SOLDIER

The "artificial fires" were torches and incendiary weapons that were used by both sides, and included burning hoops; pots filled with an inflammable mixture known as "wildfire," which were thrown like grenades; and primitive flamethrowers called "trumps," which shot jets of burning liquid from a tube.

Siege of Vienna

DATE July 16–
September 12, 1683

FORCES Ottomans:
150,000–200,000;
Viennese garrison:
12,000; Sobieski's relief
army: 75,000–80,000

LOCATION
Vienna, Austria

CASUALTIES
No reliable estimates

In 1683 the Ottomans made a second attempt to seize the Austrian capital, which they had failed to capture 154 years earlier. Led by Grand Vizier Kara Mustafa, the Ottoman army had few heavy cannons and depended on mining to breach the walls. They did not attempt an assault on the city until September 1. The outer fortifications were breached and the garrison was running short of ammunition when, on the afternoon of September 12, a relief force of Poles, Germans, and

Austrians led by Polish king Jan Sobieski struck the Ottoman camp. Kara Mustafa's army precipitately fled, only escaping destruction because nightfall prevented an immediate pursuit. The sultan, Mehmed IV, had his grand vizier executed, strangled by a bowstring around the throat.

SIEGE CITY
The Ottomans made themselves comfortable in a vast camp outside Vienna; the grand vizier brought with him 1,500 concubines.

Zenta

DATE
September 11, 1697

FORCES
Austrians: 50,000;
Ottomans: unknown

LOCATION
Northern Serbia

CASUALTIES
Austrians: 300 killed;
Ottomans: 30,000 killed
or taken prisoner

Sultan Mustafa II marched north from Belgrade in an overambitious attempt to invade Hungary. Austrian imperial forces under Eugène of Savoy attacked the Ottomans as they were crossing the Tisza River on a bridge of boats. Eugène split the Ottoman army, waiting until the cavalry had crossed before destroying the pontoon. He then crushed the stranded infantry. As well as destroying the Turkish army, Eugene captured 87 cannons, 6,000 camels, and the sultan's treasure chest.

EUGÈNE OF SAVOY
Victory at Zenta made Eugène of Savoy the most renowned military commander in Europe. He later fought at Blenheim.

OTTOMAN WARS OF EXPANSION

Lepanto

DATE October 7, 1571

FORCES Ottomans: 88,000 (16,000 soldiers); Holy League: 84,000 (20,000 soldiers)

LOCATION In Gulf of Patras off modern-day Navpaktos, Greece

CASUALTIES Ottomans: 15,000–20,000 killed; Holy League: 7,566 killed

In 1570 the Ottomans attacked the island of Cyprus. Pope Pius V organized a Holy League, including the Habsburg domains, Genoa, and Venice, to come to the island's aid. By the time a large seaborne force, led by Don Juan of Austria, had assembled at Messina, Cyprus had been lost. The fleet sailed anyway, and on October 7 it came upon the Ottoman fleet off Lepanto (Navpaktos). The opposing forces spread out across 5 miles (8km) of sea and met head-on, with little plan but to ram and board one another in a fierce melée—though most of the Holy League galleys had a few cannons mounted in their bows. Six ships of twice the normal size, known as galleasses, led the Christian fleet into battle and broke through the Turkish front line. As opposing galleys locked together, the Christian troops, armored and carrying firearms, largely got the better of unarmored Turks firing bows or crossbows. Don Juan's flagship rammed the flagship of Ottoman commander Ali Mouezinzade, who was shot in the head by an arquebus. Around 50 Ottoman galleys escaped, as the rest were sunk, captured, or ran aground, and some 15,000 Christian slaves were freed. The Ottomans subsequently showed their resources by building a new fleet for the following year, but the battle was understandably celebrated in Christian Europe as a great victory.

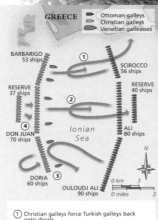

GREECE

● Ottoman galleys
● Christian galleys
● Venetian galleasses

BARBARIGO 53 ships

SCIROCCO 56 ships

RESERVE 37 ships

RESERVE 40 ships

Ionian Sea

DON JUAN 70 ships

ALI 80 ships

DORIA 60 ships

OULOUDJ ALI 90 ships

N

0 km 3
0 miles 3

① Christian galleys force Turkish galleys back onto shoals

② Christian center defeats Turks, and forces them back on their reserve

③ Christian right withdraws from action, and Turkish left withdraws as center collapses

④ Christian reserve fleet covers center and right, and pursues left after center collapses

D. IOAN. AB AVSTRIA.
FR. PHILIPPI REGIS HISP. CATHOLICI.

DON JUAN OF AUSTRIA

The growing reputation of Spanish military commander Don Juan (1547–78) was cemented by his show of leadership at the battle of Lepanto.

THE LAST BATTLE
This painting of the battle of Lepanto captures the some of the chaos of the fighting. It was the last great naval action fought by oared galleys.

MOGUL INDIA

THE MOGUL EMPIRE BROUGHT a golden age of political stability and a cultural flowering to India. The Moguls—Muslims originating from central Asia—conquered Delhi and the north of India from 1526, expanding rapidly southward and establishing a dynasty that endured until 1858. But from the death of Aurangzeb in 1707, their rule fractured, and for the last century of their existence the Moguls were effectively puppets of the British or the French. Much of the Mogul expansion was at the expense of existing Hindu regimes, but, although Muslim, the Moguls' acceptance of other faiths was greater than any to be found in contemporary Europe. The abandonment of this tolerance was to prove one of the key factors in their decline.

MOGUL CONQUEST OF INDIA

First Panipat

DATE
April 21, 1526

FORCES
Moguls: 12,000;
Lodi: 100,000 and 1,000 elephants

LOCATION
90km (55 miles) north of Delhi, north India

CASUALTIES
Lodi: 20,000–50,000 killed

Zahiruddin Muhammad, known as Babur (literally, the "tiger"), was a direct descendant of the great Mongol rulers Timur and Genghis Khan (see pp.92-95) and the ruler of a small principality in Ferghana, central Asia. In 1525, having lost his ancestral home to the rival Uzbegs and "tired of wandering about like a king on a chessboard," Babur invaded northern India in search of a new kingdom. "Placing his hand on the reins of confidence in God," he faced Sultan Ibrahim Lodi at Panipat, a few days' march from Delhi.

Ibrahim, ruler of central-northern India, commanded 1,000 elephants and 100,000 men. Fatally, however, he lacked gunpowder weapons. Ibrahim was provoked into attacking on a narrow front against a line of stockades and wagons roped together, from the shelter of which Babur's cannons and matchlocks poured out deadly fire. Babur's mounted archers reduced the unwieldy Indian army to a panicked mob. Sultan Ibrahim himself died in the rout, and Babur seized his domains, which formed the core of the Mogul empire. With his capital at Agra, he extended his rule to cover most of northern India (including Delhi) before his death in 1530.

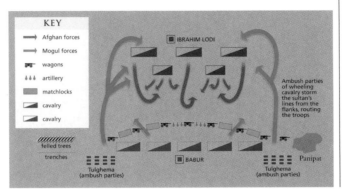

KEY

→ Afghan forces
→ Mogul forces
🐘 wagons
↓↓↓ artillery
▪ matchlocks
▰ cavalry
▱ cavalry
∿∿∿ felled trees
∷∷∷ trenches

IBRAHIM LODI

Ambush parties of wheeling cavalry storm the sultan's lines from the flanks, routing the troops

BABUR

Tulghema (ambush parties)

Tulghema (ambush parties)

Panipat

MOGUL CONQUEST OF INDIA

Second Panipat

DATE
November 5, 1556

FORCES
Moguls: 20,000;
Afghans/Hindus: 100,000 and 1,500 elephants

LOCATION
55 miles (90km) north of Delhi, north India

CASUALTIES
Moguls captured 1,500 elephants

Under Humayun, Babur's son, the Mogul empire suffered a series of reverses. His son, Akbar, reestablished the dynasty's fortunes. In 1556, at Panipat, scene of Babur's great victory, Akbar faced a combined Afghan-Hindu army. Their opponents' war elephants initially made strong headway. In the heat of battle, however, the Hindu general Hemu was hit by a stray arrow, causing panic among his troops. As the Hindu-Afghan army fled, it was slaughtered. Akbar built a victory pillar with their severed heads.

FALL OF VIJAYANAGAR

Talikot

DATE
23 January 1565

FORCES
Hindus: up to 600,000;
Muslims: up to 700,000

LOCATION 80 miles (130km) north of Vijayanagar, India

CASUALTIES
Sources claim Hindus lost hundreds of thousands

Although by the mid-16th century the Moguls dominated north and central India, in the south the Hindu kingdom of Viyajanagar ("city of victory") held sway. For three centuries this Hindu bastion had resisted the southward push of various Muslim dynasties. Vijayanagar possessed a strong military aristocracy, the Nayaks, but in the 1560s its king, Rama Raja, had alienated them and proved inept

JEWELED DAGGER
The opulence of Indian weapons was a sign of wealth and power, but equally attracted the attentions of invaders intent on plunder.

diplomatically. Although his Muslim opponents had been weakened by the fragmentation of the Bahmani sultanate in 1527, Rama Raja contrived to unite all the successor sultanates of central and western India against him. In 1565 this alliance of Ahmadnagar, Bidar, Berar, Golconda, and Bijapur decisively defeated the Hindu ruler in a battle at Talikot, in the northern part of his kingdom. In the aftermath of Talikot, Rama Raja was beheaded and Vijayanagar was destroyed. Contemporary sources speak of hundreds of thousands of Hindus killed, but while this is doubtless an exaggeration, Hindu political power was irrevocably shattered in southern India. The Muslim sultanates were able to expand as far as Mysore but they were, in their turn, absorbed by the Moguls under Aurangzeb (1658–1707). Yet his intolerance of Hinduism sparked opposition that would, within decades, fatally weaken the Mogul empire.

MOGUL VICTORY
A war elephant can be seen in one of Akbar's battles of the 1560s. They formed a part of many Indian armies.

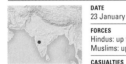

Haldighati

DATE
June 18, 1576

FORCES
Moguls: 80,000;
Mewaris: 20,000

LOCATION
30 miles (45km) north
of Udaipur, India

CASUALTIES
Unknown, but heavier
on Mewari side

By the mid-1570s Mogul emperor Akbar had defeated all the Rajputs (Hindu warrior princes) except Pratap Singh of Mewar. His forces swelled by Pratap's rival Man Singh of Amber, Akbar marched south to face Pratap. Resplendent on Chetak, his white Arab charger, Pratap fought bravely, being wounded seven times, but was forced to withdraw. The battle was indecisive; Mewar came to terms only in 1614.

EQUINE HERO
Pratap Singh comforts his stallion, Chetak, as it lies mortally wounded. The horse had earlier saved his life.

Nadir Shah's invasion of India

DATE
1738–39

FORCES
Nadir Shah: unknown;
Indians: unknown

LOCATION
Northern India

CASUALTIES
Up to 20,000
in sack of Delhi

After Nadir Shah's accession to the Persian throne in 1736 (see box), he occupied himself first with the conquest of Afghanistan. In late 1738 he crossed the Khyber pass into northwestern India. Brushing aside Indian resistance at Karnal (February 24, 1739), Nadir entered Delhi unopposed on March 20, 1739. The sacking of the city and the massacres that accompanied it were so

PEACOCK THRONE
The jeweled throne, made for Mogul emperor Shah Jahan, was seized by Nadir Shah in 1739.

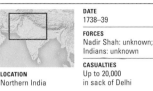

> "Nadir Shah had not the wisdom to think of both the present and the future."
>
> *Napoleon Bonaparte*, letter to Fatih Ali, Shah of Persia, 1805

comprehensive they gave rise to a new word, *nadirshahi*, meaning holocaust. As many as 20,000 may have perished. On his return, the treasures he had acquired, including the Koh-i-Noor diamond and the jewel-encrusted Peacock Throne, meant he could afford not to levy taxes in Persia for three years. But Nadir's rule became increasingly tyrannical and paranoid, and in 1747 he was assassinated. His successor, Ahmad Shah Durrani, invaded India in 1757, sacking Delhi, but leaving the Moguls on the throne. Yet his control over India was threatened by new powers rising in the wake of the Mogul decline, including the Sikhs in the Punjab and the Marathas, a Hindu confederacy. In 1761, Panipat saw another great battle as Ahmad Shah defeated a Maratha army, but continuing revolts led him to abandon India in 1772.

NADIR SHAH

Nadir Shah is often seen as the last great Asian conqueror. Entering the service of the Safavid Persian ruler Tahmasp, he won a brilliant series of victories against the Afghans, and in 1736 took the Persian throne for himself. His invasion of India in 1738–39 extended Persian control to its greatest extent for over a thousand years. Prone to paranoia (he had his own son blinded), he was assassinated in 1747, and his realm quickly disintegrated.

Campaigns of Shivaji Maharaj

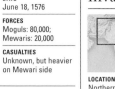

DATE
1646–80

FORCES
Maratha confederacy:
unknown; Mogul:
unknown

LOCATION
Central India

CASUALTIES
No reliable estimates

As Mogul power diminished in central and southern India, the Hindu Maratha confederacy rose to fill the vacuum. Led by the brilliant, romantic figure of Shivaji Maharaj (1627–80), the "mountain rats" refused to confront the enormous Mogul army openly, instead preferring guerrilla warfare. (One chronicler refers to Shivaji's "fox play.") Taking advantage of a civil war within the Mogul empire, Shivaji seized a string of forts in the Western Ghats, a mountainous regions on the west coast near Mumbai. In 1674 he felt sufficiently secure to declare himself king. To distance himself from the increasingly intolerant regime of the Mogul emperor Aurangzeb,

Shivaji espoused a policy of religious tolerance. He "made it a rule...not to desecrate mosques or the Book of Allah, nor to seize the women." Muslims as well as Hindus served in his forces. Although Shivaji died in 1680 and the Moguls sought to exploit a civil war between his sons, Aurangzeb was never truly able to subdue the Marathas, who grew in strength and in 1771 took Delhi.

SHIVAJI STATUE
The Maratha leader's army was mainly made up of horsemen who could rapidly withdraw to the highlands if threatened. Such tactics were brilliantly successful, allowing the Marathas to conserve their limited strength.

RAIGAD FORT
Mountain refuges such as the fort at Raigad were considered to be impregnable to direct Mogul attack and formed the backbone of Maratha military power.

1492–1750

WEAPONS OF MOGUL INDIA

WHEN THE MOGULS INVADED INDIA in the 16th century, they brought with them arms and armor that belonged to the Islamic culture of Asia—a world with which northern India had, of course, been in touch for many centuries. Also found in Indian armies from the 16th century onwards were European-derived gunpowder weapons. Indians took such a liking to the matchlock musket that they were still using it in the 19th century.

UNIQUE TO INDIA

POWDER FLASK
This Hindu powder flask was used with a matchlock musket.

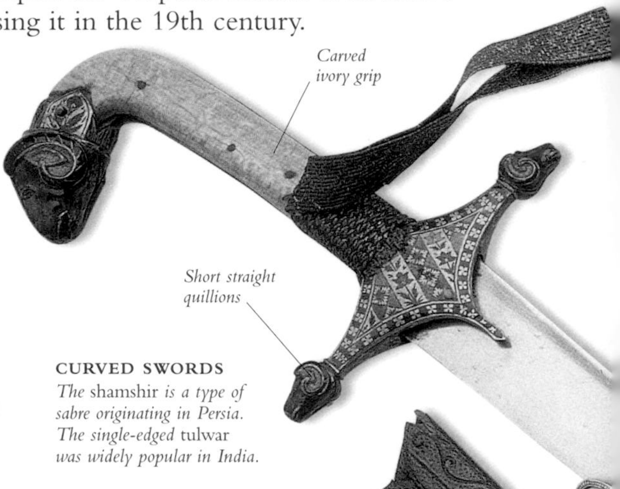

However, some Indian states did develop unique weapons. One of the most original was the *chakram*, a band of steel formed in the shape of a quoit. Sikh soldiers wore several *chakram* looped around their tall, conical turbans. *Chakram* were launched either by being whirled around the forefinger or held between forefinger and thumb and thrown underarm. The Hindu dagger known as the *katar* was also unique to India; a soldier gripped its H-shaped handle and punched the blade into an enemy's body at close quarters. The *bhuj*, a single-bladed battle ax with a long handle, also originated in India.

Carved ivory grip

Short straight quillions

CURVED SWORDS
The shamshir is a type of sabre originating in Persia. The single-edged tulwar was widely popular in India.

CONTRASTING DAGGERS
The all-steel khanjar has a recurved double-edged blade. The katar was a thrusting dagger held in the fist.

KHANJAR

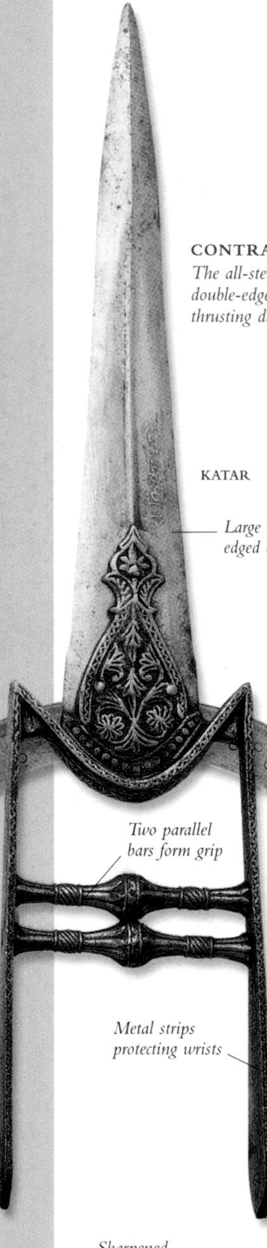

KATAR

Large double-edged blade

TULWAR

Gold damascened steel hilt

Wooden scabbard bound in leather

Two parallel bars form grip

BABUR AT THE HEAD OF HIS ARMY
Here, Moguls carry bows and arrows, lances, axes, swords, and shields. Note Babur's neck-protecting headgear.

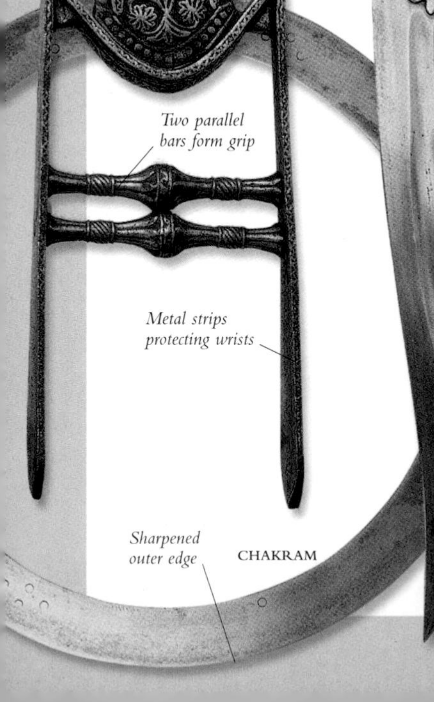

Metal strips protecting wrists

BHUJ

THROWING RING
The chakram steel quoit, used mainly by Sikhs, had a razor-sharp outer edge.

EDGED WEAPONS
The bhuj was a distinctive Indian battle ax; the pesh-kabz was an armor-piercing dagger.

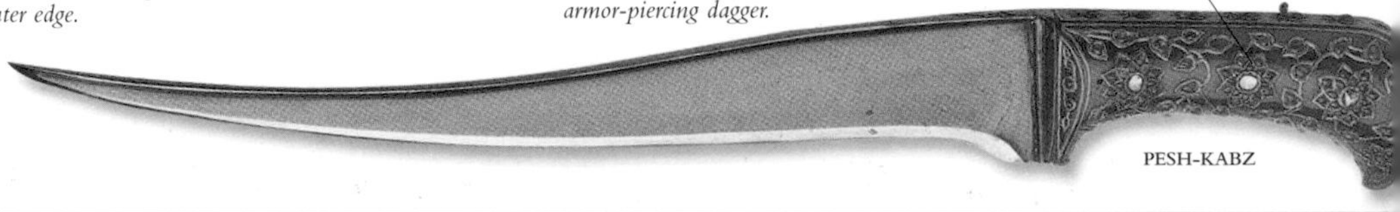

Persian-influenced decorative detail

Sharpened outer edge CHAKRAM

PESH-KABZ

MOGUL HELMET
This Indian helmet, known as a top, has chain mail curtains called aventails descending to the wearer's shoulders.

Head inlaid with silver and gilt

Aventile to protect neck

BATTLE AXES
All-steel axes known as tabars were popular weapons in India for many centuries. Some had a hollow handle with a dagger concealed inside.

Rounded cutting edge

HINDU SHIELD

ORNATE EQUIPMENT
The elaborate decoration on Indian weapons and armor is often their most distinctive characteristic. Decoration was a display of wealth and status in societies that were far from taking a straightforward functional view of warfare. It was probably this decorative quality that prompted Sir Thomas Roe, English ambassador to the Mogul court in the 17th century, to describe Mogul forces as "an effeminate army, fitter to be a spoil than a terror to enemies".

SHIELDS
Indian shields were known as sipars or dhals. Both Hindu and Muslim shields were ornately decorated, the former often painted with scenes depicting Hindu gods.

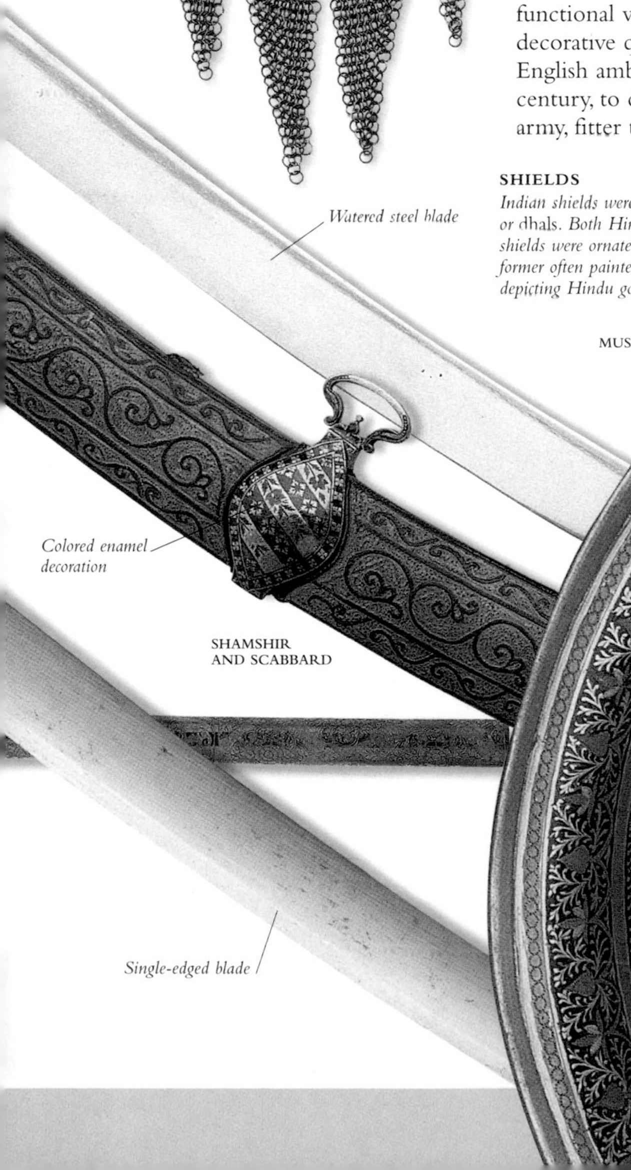

Watered steel

Guilded decoration

Watered steel blade

MUSLIM SHIELD

Colored enamel decoration

SHAMSHIR AND SCABBARD

Single-edged blade

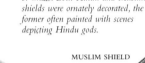

EARLY MODERN WARFARE

AFRICAN EMPIRES

MANY OF THE ASPECTS OF WARFARE familiar in Eurasia were also found in Africa—for example, armored cavalry, walled cities, and, from the 16th century, firearms. Although Ethiopia survived as a Christian outpost, most of northern Africa was an extension of the Muslim world. Islamic rulers in the Sahel region south of the Sahara used cavalry to dominate agricultural societies, founding empires such as Mali and Oyo. Morocco, on the north coast, was a major power center supporting armies that defeated both Christians and fellow Muslims.

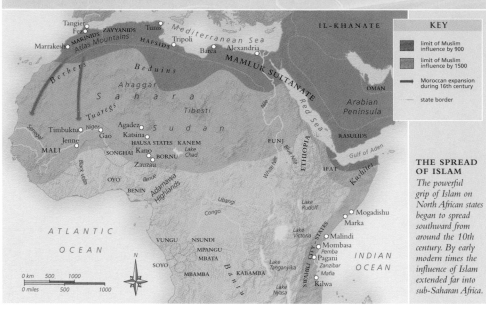

KEY

- limit of Muslim influence by 900
- limit of Muslim influence by 1500
- Moroccan expansion during 16th century
- state border

THE SPREAD OF ISLAM

The powerful grip of Islam on North African states began to spread southward from around the 10th century. By early modern times the influence of Islam extended far into sub-Saharan Africa.

Ethiopia fights Ahmed Gran

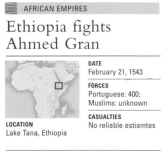

DATE
February 21, 1543

FORCES
Portuguese: 400;
Muslims: unknown

CASUALTIES
No reliable estiamtes

LOCATION
Lake Tana, Ethiopia

From the 1520s Christian Ethiopia was threatened by Muslim forces led by the sultan of Adal, Ahmed Gran. In 1541 Portuguese soldiers led by Cristovao da Gama arrived to help their fellow Christians. In August 1542 Ahmed defeated the Ethiopians and Portuguese; Cristovao was beheaded. In February 1543 the Ethiopians and Portuguese encountered Ahmed Gran again at Lake Tana. Half of the Portuguese were killed, but Ahmed was shot dead. With this inspired leader gone, the threat to Ethiopia evaporated.

CIRCULAR SHIELD

Ethiopian shields were made of hide. This ornate example is covered with velvet and silverwork.

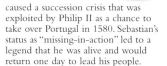

Alcazarquivir

DATE August 4, 1578

FORCES Portuguese: 16,500–18,000; Moroccans: unknown

CASUALTIES Portuguese: 7,000 killed, 8,000 taken prisoner; Moroccans: unknown

LOCATION Morocco

The battle of Alcazarquivir, or al-Kasr al-Kebir, was a significant defeat for European forces at the hands of an African power. In 1576 a new ruler, Abd al-Malik, took control of Morocco with the backing of the Ottoman Turks. His evicted predecessor, Muhammad al-Mutawakkil, appealed to the king of Portugal, Sebastian, for support in regaining his throne. Young King Sebastian, who was obsessed by dreams of conquest and noble crusading adventures, obtained approval from the pope for a crusade against the infidel in Morocco. On a more practical level, however, he failed to win the military backing of his

KING SEBASTIAN

Sebastian of Portugal was only 24 when he led the ill-advised invasion that cost him his life.

powerful neighbor Philip II of Spain. Sebastian assembled a force of Portuguese noblemen and German, Spanish, and Dutch mercenaries. This makeshift force, led by Sebastian in person, landed on the Moroccan coast and unwisely headed inland, away from the ships that could have provided supplies and reinforcements. Abd al-Malik met them with a well-equipped, Ottoman-style army composed of Moors from Andalucía,

Turks, Arabs, and Berbers, and including cavalry trained to fire arquebuses from horseback. What followed is sometimes known as the battle of the Three Kings, because all three leaders died: Moroccan pretender al-Mutawakkil; Abd al-Malik, who died of natural causes early in the battle; and Sebastian, who disappeared, never to be seen again. The Portuguese forces were routed, almost all either killed or taken prisoner. Sebastian's death

caused a succession crisis that was exploited by Philip II as a chance to take over Portugal in 1580. Sebastian's status as "missing-in-action" led to a legend that he was alive and would return one day to lead his people.

PREPARING FOR BATTLE

The Christian forces, depicted here before the battle of Alcazarquivir, were armed with a host of weapons: lances, pikes, swords, and firearms.

Moroccans defeat Songhai Empire

DATE
March 1591

FORCES Moroccans:
5,000–25,000,
including 2,000–4,000
musketeers; Songhai:
10,000–18,000 cavalry,
30,000–100,000 infantry

LOCATION
Niger River,
West Africa

CASUALTIES Unknown

Moroccan ruler Ahmed al-Mansur
sent an army south across the Sahara
to attack Songhai, the dominant power
on the Niger River. Advancing toward
Gao, they met a much larger Songhai
force, but the Moroccans had firearms;
the Songhai did not. The Songhai drove
cattle into the Moroccan lines, hoping
to panic their enemy, but this had no
effect. When the Moroccans opened
fire with their muskets, most of the
Songhai soon fled. The Songhai capital
Timbuktu was occupied shortly after.

MUD MOSQUE
*The 14th-century Great Mosque at
Jenne, Mali, lay at the heart of the
Songhai Empire at the time of the
Moroccan conquest.*

1549–1603

AHMED AL-MANSUR

The death of his brother Abd
al-Malik at Alcazarquivir in 1578
brought Ahmed to power in
Morocco and allowed him to take
credit for the victory over the
Christians, hence the name al-
Mansur, meaning "the victorious."
Ahmed set up a Moroccan standing
army around a core of Turkish
mercenaries, who were familiar with
muskets, arquebuses, and cannons.
He recruited professional soldiers
from among renegade Christians
and Moorish refugees who had
fled Christian rule in Spain. It was
this force that enabled him to put
into effect his plan for the conquest
of Songhai in 1591, extending
Moroccan influence farther south
than had ever been achieved before.

Slave Wars

DATE
From the 14th
century onward

FORCES
Not applicable

LOCATION
West Africa

CASUALTIES
Not applicable

As in most of the world throughout
much of history, warfare in Africa
was associated with the acquisition
of slaves. This might occur either
as an accidental by-product of war—
through the taking of prisoners—
or as the goal of military raids and
conquests. From the 14th century,
for example, the Islamic empires of
the Upper Niger basin, such as Mali
and Songhai, developed military
superiority over neighboring peoples
through the use of cavalry. Riding
fine Barbary horses
and wearing coats
of mail, these forces
took thousands of
prisoners in more or
less constant raiding.
These prisoners were
eventually carried
along trans-Saharan
trade routes to serve
as slaves in the Muslim
world around
the Mediterranean.
In the 15th century
Portuguese sailors
established trade contact
with states along the
west coast of Africa, and
one of the commodities
they found it useful to
buy was slaves. The
symbiotic relationship
between the slave trade
on the West African
coast and warfare
developed significantly
in the 17th and 18th
centuries. By 1700
around 30,000 slaves a
year were being shipped
out of Africa, and by
1780 around 80,000
a year. Many of these
slaves were captured
during the raids and
conquests of West
African kingdoms such
as Asante, Dahomey, and

BENIN BRONZE
*A bronze plaque that once
decorated the palace of the
ruler of Benin, West Africa,
shows a Portuguese soldier
with a matchlock musket.*

Oyo, which were able to increase
their military dominance by using
the income from the slave trade to
buy firearms. By the mid-18th
century the Asante standing army,
consisting of infantry armed with
muskets, was a formidable force
capable of extending Asante rule
over a wide area. Tribute and the slave
trade made Asante's rulers extremely
wealthy. With rare exceptions, during
this period European nations present
in Africa did not attempt any military
intervention against native states.
With their firearms and armored
cavalry, the African kingdoms would
have made formidable opponents.

EUROPEAN STRONGHOLD
*Cape Coast Castle, like all European
forts in West Africa, was designed for
protection against rival European trading
nations, not against African states.*

POWER AND RELIGION

SIXTEENTH- AND SEVENTEENTH-CENTURY Europe was profoundly shaped by warfare. Technological developments gave aspirant empire-builders an increased ability to project their will by military means. Governments and societies were transformed through the need to raise revenues and construct states able to withstand these novel pressures. From 1648 dynastic ambition and territorial aggrandizement, rather than religious zeal, became the prime motives for war.

GUNPOWDER AND SQUARES

The increasing adoption from the early 16th century of smaller, portable firearms presented a profound challenge to early modern armies and signaled the end of the supremacy of the mounted knight. In the 1520s the Spanish *tercios*—blocks of pikemen supported by soldiers with firearms—emerged as the most effective means of deploying guns in battle, a position that they held for over a century, until the Spanish defeat at Rocroi in 1643. The preeminence of the *tercio* was not, however, unchallenged. The Dutch prince and brilliant strategist Maurice of Nassau employed smaller formations of disciplined infantry who fired muskets in volleys.

KEY

	Austrian Habsburg possessions 1683
	Spanish Habsburg possessions 1683
⚔	civil war or widespread disturbance
⚒	local revolt or unrest
⚲	civic autonomy suppressed by territorial rulers
	frontiers 1683
—	Holy Roman Empire 1683

0 km 400 800
0 miles 400 800

POLITICAL CONSOLIDATION
The 17th century saw the breaking of Spain's previously dominant position and an increase in English and French power.

ACT OF FAITH
The massacre of 2,000 French Protestants on St. Bartholomew's Day, 1572, set off a bloody religious conflict that plagued France for nearly 30 years.

MATCHLESS MUSKETS

Throughout the 17th century, the successive appearance of the matchlock, wheel-lock, and then flintlock saw a steady improvement in the musket's rate of fire: a well-trained musketeer of the mid-18th century could discharge three or four rounds per minute. In turn, this increased effectiveness fostered innovations, not all of them successful. The *caracole* was a maneuver in which horsemen trotted up to the enemy lines, performed a half-turn, fired their pistols, and then retreated. By 1680 cavalry had largely abandoned any real attempt to use gunpowder weapons in battle.

OUT OF THE WINDOW
The Defenestration of Prague, which sparked the Thirty Years War, is shown here. Catholic officials accused of violating Bohemian Protestants' rights were hurled from a window in Prague castle.

ROYAL SWORD
The sidering of this 17th-century sword possibly depicts Gustavus Adolphus, the Swedish king who almost won the Thirty Years War for the Protestant side.

HORSE ARMOR

Despite the enormous changes in warfare in the course of the 16th and 17th centuries, cavalry retained its role as one of the essential components of the early modern army. Horse armor, such as that shown here, was expensive and uncommon; full equestrian armor even more so, and the shaffron, or head armor, was the most common single piece. Possession of such armor was a sign of high status and by 1600 it was more commonly seen in royal equestrian portraits than on the battlefield.

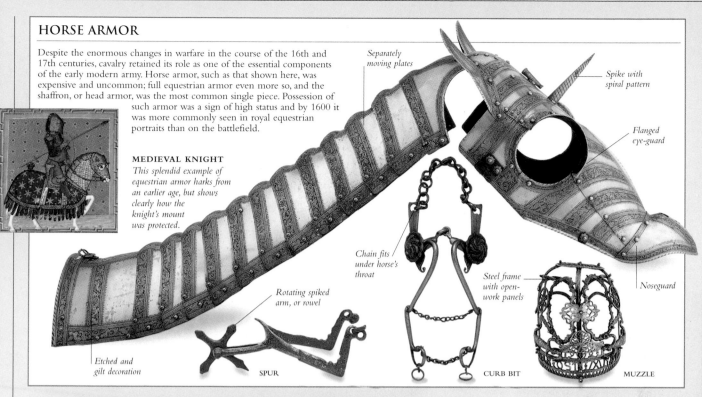

Separately moving plates

Spike with spiral pattern

Flanged eye-guard

Noseguard

MEDIEVAL KNIGHT
This splendid example of equestrian armor harks from an earlier age, but shows clearly how the knight's mount was protected.

Chain fits under horse's throat

Steel frame with open-work panels

Rotating spiked arm, or rowel

Etched and gilt decoration

SPUR

CURB BIT

MUZZLE

DRILLS AND GRENADIERS

The 17th century saw the increasing professionalization of armies. By 1700 uniformed infantry, armed with flintlock musket and socket bayonet and performing maneuvers with perfect discipline, had become a standard feature of European warfare from St. Petersburg to Lisbon. Permanent regiments had been founded, each with its own colors. Specialization became marked: units such as the grenadiers, who were trained in assaulting fortified positions, became more and more important.

DUTCH VICTORY
The Dutch flag is seen flying above this warship at the battle of Texel in 1673. The Dutch won, bringing an end to war with England.

1594–1632

GUSTAVUS ADOLPHUS

Swedish King Gustavus Adolphus was hailed as the "Protestant Alexander." His genius was to coordinate the deployment of cavalry, infantry, and artillery. This required a new kind of soldier—a professional, disciplined, and highly trained figure. Part of the success of this new model lay in its revival of the role and importance of cavalry.

TAX AND WAR

By 1750 the demands of war placed a far greater stress on the state than they had in 1500. The French army had five times as many guns at the battle of Neerwinden in 1693 as at Rocroi 50 years earlier. The strain on those states that failed to modernize their revenue-raising ability in parallel was intolerable: the attempt by the French crown to raise taxes without any corresponding increase in political participation by the urban elites was a primary contributor to the French Revolution (see p.196).

BATTLE IN BOHEMIA
The battle of White Mountain in 1618 marked the start of the Thirty Years War. The Protestant defeat near Prague was a severe blow to their cause.

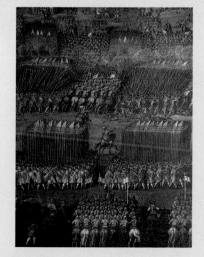

FRANCE'S ITALIAN WARS

IN 1494 CHARLES VIII OF FRANCE invaded Italy, displaying the power of his standing army and his cannons on wheeled carriages. This action set off a chain of wars lasting until the mid-16th century, in which the leading protagonists were France, Spain, the Swiss, and the Italian city-states. These conflicts saw the evolution of fresh military tactics and technologies, from the development of bastion fortresses to new ideas for the use of handguns. But the battles were above all heterogenous, with armored knights charging with lances, infantry fighting in pike phalanxes, and crossbowmen operating alongside arquebusiers and cannons. The outcome was the European dominance of Spain and the Holy Roman Empire, combined in the person of Emperor Charles V.

FRANCE'S ITALIAN WARS

Cerignola

DATE
April 28, 1503

FORCES
French and Swiss: 10,000;
Spanish: 6,000

LOCATION Italy, 18 miles (30km) from the Adriatic coast of Italy

CASUALTIES
No reliable estimates

Cerignola is often said to be the first battle won by infantry firearms. The experienced Spanish commander Gonzalo Fernández de Cordoba was attempting to block a French takeover of southern Italy, and had decided that a small army of pikemen and arquebusiers held the secret of battlefield success. Facing a superior force of French armored cavalry and Swiss pikemen, he entrenched his men on the slope of a hill, protected by a ditch and an earthen rampart, and placed his arquebusiers behind the rampart with the pikemen at their rear. The French and Swiss decided on a frontal assault, assuming that the shock

of their charge would break the flimsy Spanish line. Stalled at the ditch, they were shot down by the arquebusiers, who were highly effective at such close range. The French leader, the Duc de Nemours, was among those shot dead. At the right moment, Fernández ordered his pikemen and light cavalry to counterattack, completing the destruction of the enemy. Although

BRUTAL BATTLE
An artist's impression of the battle of Cerignola conveys the brutality of war fought with pike, sword, and arquebus.

everything the arquebusiers had done could have been achieved by archers, the Spanish victory confirmed growing confidence in firearms as the missile weapons of the future.

SPANISH TERCIOS

The Spanish *tercio*, or "third," was a formation of pikemen and arquebusiers some 3,000 strong. Based on tactical innovations in the combined use of pikes and firearms, the tercios were first named as such in 1534, and their discipline made them feared throughout Europe until the early 17th century. The arquebusiers were usually placed outside the pike squares, moving inside for protection if threatened with close-quarters attack.

FRANCE'S ITALIAN WARS

Ravenna

DATE
April 11, 1512

FORCES
Spanish: 16,000;
French: 21,000

LOCATION
Ravenna, Italy

CASUALTIES
Spanish: 9,000 killed;
French: 4,500 killed

In 1511 Pope Julius II formed a Holy League to fight the French. In 1512 predominantly Spanish Holy League forces under Ramon de Cardona and engineer Pedro Navarro advanced to confront a French army led by Gaston de Foix that was besieging Ravenna. The Spanish took up a defensive position behind earthworks, and for two hours the rival field artillery battered one another's lines. Eventually the nerve of the Spanish cracked; they charged and were cut down by French heavy cavalry. The Landsknechte, German mercenary pikemen employed by France, delivered frontal assaults on the Spanish earthworks, where a bloody battle ensued. Eventually, attacked by French armored cavalry from the flank, the Spanish staged a fighting withdrawal. The edge was taken off the French victory by the loss of de Foix, who was killed in the pursuit.

1489–1512

GASTON DE FOIX

Made Duc de Nemours after his father's death at Cerignola in 1503, Gaston de Foix was appointed to lead the French forces in Italy in 1511 at the age of 21. He displayed electrifying boldness and energy, storming Brescia in February 1512 before defeating the Spanish army at Ravenna in the battle that cost him his life. Rarely has a military commander built such a reputation in a single campaign.

FRANCE'S ITALIAN WARS

Novara

DATE
June 6, 1513

FORCES
French: 12,000;
Swiss: 5,000

LOCATION
Northern Italy,
west of Milan

CASUALTIES
No reliable estimates

The Swiss pike-wielding phalanx was the most admired infantry unit of the late 15th and early 16th centuries. The Swiss were much in demand as mercenaries, and by the time of Novara they had joined the Holy League fighting against France. A French army commanded by Marshal Louis de la Trémoille crossed the Alps, captured Milan, and then laid siege to the Swiss-held city of Novara. Alerted in June to the approach of a Swiss relief army, La Trémoille withdrew from the siege lines to prepare for battle, but he had not counted on the speed of Swiss movement. Marching through the night, the Swiss caught the French

OPEN-FACED HELMET
The combed morion helmet was adopted by arquebusiers in the 16th century. The open style was convenient when taking aim.

utterly unprepared with an attack at dawn on June 6. Advancing at a trot, dense columns of pikemen smashed through the French lines into the heart of their camp, slaughtering the infantry and forcing the cavalry to flee as best they could. La Trémoille retreated into France with the remnants of his shattered army. Despite this striking victory, overall the Italian wars revealed the limitations of pike formations on the offensive when faced with field fortifications and gunpowder weapons.

Marignano

DATE
September 13–14, 1515

FORCES
French: 30,000;
Swiss: 20,000

LOCATION Modern-day
Melegnano, 9 miles
(15 km) from Milan

CASUALTIES
French: 5,000;
Swiss: 6,000–10,000

François I of France invaded Italy in
the summer of 1515. In alliance with
Venice, he intended to recover Milan
from the Swiss. Crossing the Alps with
around 50 bronze cannon by routes
that had been presumed impassable,
he arrived in Lombardy in June.
François attempted—with considerable
success—to bribe the Swiss to go
home. In mid-September those Swiss
remaining marched out to attack. They
counted on a swift approach to catch
their enemy off balance and then upon
the shock effect of their dense pike
phalanxes to smash through the enemy
line. But at Marignano resistance from
François's Landsknecht mercenaries and
counterattacks by armored cavalry—
led by the king in person—broke the
Swiss attack. The close-fought battle
continued long after dark and resumed
at dawn, but remained undecided until
François's Venetian allies belatedly
arrived on the field. Faced by these
fresh troops, the Swiss withdrew. They
subsequently evacuated Lombardy,
signing a perpetual peace with France.

ROYAL TOMB
*A relief from the tomb of François I
shows the mounted king trampling the
Swiss pikemen. For François the Italian
wars still belonged to the age of chivalry.*

Pavia

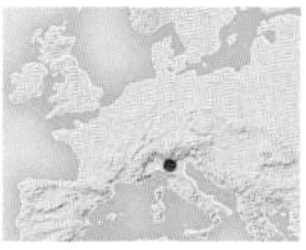

DATE
February 24, 1525

FORCES
French: 20,000;
Imperial: 23,000

LOCATION
Pavia, south of Milan

CASUALTIES
French: 8,000;
Imperial: 1,000

CANNON CAPTURED
*Imperial troops capture
French artillery at the
battle of Pavia. The
French cannons were
ineffectual because
François I and his
knights charged
between the guns
and the enemy.*

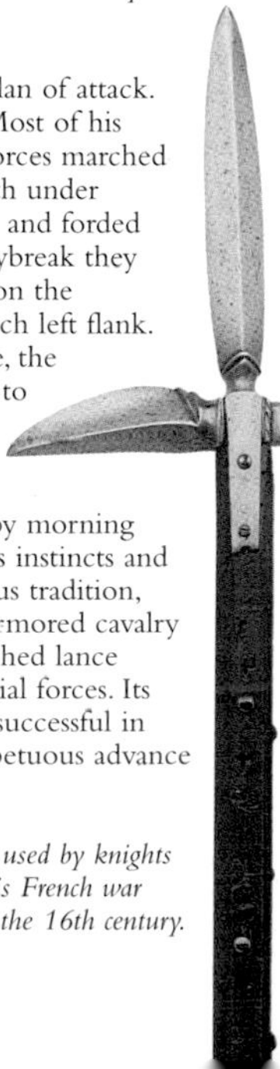

When François I of France invaded
Italy for the second time, his main
opponent was Charles V, king of
Spain and Holy Roman Emperor.
In autumn 1524 François marched
his army across the Alps and made a
triumphal entry into Milan. He then
laid siege to the imperial-garrisoned
town of Pavia. When an imperial relief
force, commanded by the Marchese di
Pescara, arrived in late January 1525,
the armies dug in to face one another
across a stream, occasionally exchanging
artillery fire. On the night of February
23–24 Pescara set in motion a bold
plan of attack.
Most of his
forces marched
several miles north under
cover of darkness and forded
the stream; by daybreak they
were positioned on the
unprotected French left flank.
Taken by surprise, the
French struggled to
turn their forces.
The situation
was rendered
more confusing by morning
fog. Following his instincts and
fulfilling chivalrous tradition,
François led an armored cavalry
charge with couched lance
against the imperial forces. Its
shock effect was successful in
itself, but the impetuous advance
of the French knights
blocked their artillery
from firing on the
enemy. François's
Swiss mercenary
infantry was
tardy to come
up in support and
much of the French
army, unclear what
was happening, failed
to join in at all. As the
battle fell apart into
small unit engagements
across the field, the
imperial pikemen and
arquebusiers proved as
effective fighting in the
open as they previously
had defending earthworks.
The French knights
gradually succumbed,
the Duc de la
Trémoille was shot
through the heart, and
François was unhorsed
and taken prisoner.
Mercenaries of the
Landsknecht Black
Band were the last to
cede as the rest of the
French army fled.

WAR HAMMER
*War hammers were used by knights
fighting on foot. This French war
hammer dates from the 16th century.*

STEEL MACE
*Made in Italy in the 16th
century, this skull-crushing
flanged mace would have
been used by a knight in
hand-to-hand combat.*

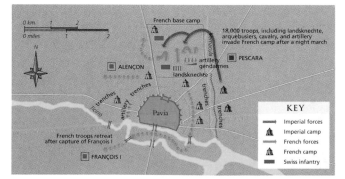

KEY
- Imperial forces
- Imperial camp
- French forces
- French camp
- Swiss infantry

WARS OF RELIGION

A SERIES OF INTERLOCKED CONFLICTS set Protestants against Catholics in the late 16th and early 17th centuries. The Dutch revolted against Spanish Habsburg rule, in France Protestants and Catholics fought a series of civil wars, and Protestant England came into conflict with the Catholic Spanish. This warfare was significant in history for the widespread use of muskets and the demonstration of the power of sailing ships with cannons.

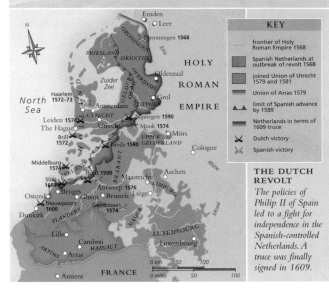

KEY

	frontier of Holy Roman Empire 1568
	Spanish Netherlands at outbreak of revolt 1568
	joined Union of Utrecht 1579 and 1581
	Union of Arras 1579
	limit of Spanish advance by 1589
	Netherlands in terms of 1609 truce
	Dutch victory
	Spanish victory

THE DUTCH REVOLT

The policies of Philip II of Spain led to a fight for independence in the Spanish-controlled Netherlands. A truce was finally signed in 1609.

FRENCH RELIGIOUS WARS

Dreux

DATE
December 19, 1562

FORCES
Huguenots: 15,000;
Royalists: 19,000

LOCATION
Dreux, east of Paris,
France

CASUALTIES
Huguenots: 4,000;
Royalists: 4,000

In 1562 open warfare broke out in France between Calvinist Huguenots, led by Prince Louis de Condé and Admiral Gaspard de Coligny, and Catholics led by the Duc de Guise and Montmorency. The first full-scale battle of the French Religious Wars occurred when the Huguenot army, marching north to join up with an English force at Le Havre, ran into Guise and Montmorency who had just sacked the city of Rouen. The battle opened with Coligny leading a powerful cavalry charge that threw the Catholic forces into confusion. Believing the battle won, Condé led his own cavalry into the melée. But Guise then sent in his Swiss mercenary pikemen, followed by the French gendarmes. Condé was taken prisoner, but Coligny succeeded in extricating a large part of the Huguenot army from the field. The battle was not a clear Catholic victory, as Montmorency was also captured.

CAVALRY CHARGE
Pike-wielding cavalry from both sides are depicted here charging on each other and at artillery positions at the battle of Dreux.

DUTCH REVOLT

Jemmingen

DATE
July 21, 1568

FORCES
Spanish: c.15,000;
rebels: c.15,000

LOCATION Ems estuary,
Friesland, modern-day
Netherlands

CASUALTIES
Spanish: c.100 killed;
rebels: 6,000–7,000
killed

> "These troubles must be ended by force of arms without any use of pardon, mildness, negotiations, or talks until everything has been flattened."

The Duke of Alba on the Dutch rebellion, 1573

When the predominantly Protestant population of the Netherlands rose in revolt against his rule, Catholic Spanish king Philip II, ordered the Duke of Alba and his veteran army to crush the rebellion. Alba was an outstanding commander who is credited, among other things, with introducing the heavy musket to replace the arquebus as the standard Spanish infantry firearm. Alba's opponent was William of Orange, who, having fled his country to avoid arrest, raised a German mercenary army and sent it into the northern Netherlands under the command of his brother, Louis of Nassau. Alba's army caught up with Louis on the peninsula of Jemmingen. Although the two forces were evenly matched in numbers, they were dissimilar in discipline and firepower. Trapped with their backs to the Eems estuary, the rebel army was crushed, with no quarter given. Thousands tried to swim the estuary but few made it. The citizens of Emden found out about the disaster when the hats of drowned Orangists drifted down to their city on the tide. The Duke of Alba had a bronze statue erected in Antwerp to celebrate his victory, cast from rebel cannons captured at Jemmingen.

DUTCH REVOLT

Brill

DATE
April 1, 1572

FORCES
Dutch: 600; Spanish:
unknown

LOCATION Brill, east of
Rotterdam, modern-
day Netherlands

CASUALTIES
None

The Dutch Watergeuzen, or Sea Beggars, were a fleet originally assembled by Louis of Nassau to support his forces at Jemmingen. After the Dutch defeat there, they turned to preying indiscriminately on merchant shipping to make a living. On April 1, 1572, around 600 Sea Beggars boldly seized the town of Brill in Zeeland. The Spanish counterattack was muted because at that time French Huguenots had allied with William of Orange and were threatening to invade the Netherlands. Thousands of unemployed fishermen and other sailors swarmed to join the Sea Beggars, and rebels were soon in control of Flushing (Vliessingen) and other ports along the Zeeland coast. In their fast-moving cannon-armed "fly-boats," the Sea Beggars were unbeatable in coastal waters, defeating Spanish squadrons on the Zuider Zee in November 1573 and in the Schelde estuary in January 1574. Their attacks on Catholic merchant shipping became a valuable source of financing for the rebel cause.

MATCHLOCK MUSKET

To fire a matchlock, the musketeer tipped powder followed by a ball and wad down the barrel. He then put finer powder in the priming pan. When he pulled the trigger, the smouldering rope plunged into the priming pan, igniting the powder which in turn set off the charge in the barrel. The heavy weapon had to be leaned on a forked rest to fire.

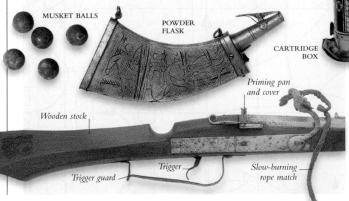

MUSKET BALLS

POWDER
FLASK

CARTRIDGE
BOX

*Priming pan
and cover*

Wooden stock

Trigger

Trigger guard

*Slow-burning
rope match*

Siege of Antwerp

DATE
September 1584–
August 1585

FORCES
Rebels: unknown;
Spanish: unknown

LOCATION
Antwerp, modern-day
Belgium

CASUALTIES
No reliable estimates

Alexander Farnese, the Duke of Parma, took command of Spanish forces in the Netherlands in 1578. The peak of his achievement was the siege of Antwerp. The rebels opened the dykes to flood the Spanish out of their siege lines, but the dykes remained above water, and on these the Spanish built forts, fighting off rebel sorties. During the winter of 1584–85, Parma's engineers constructed a bridge 2,625ft (800m) in length across the Scheldt River. On this structure Parma mounted 200 siege guns. On April 5 the rebels sent fire ships packed with explosives down the Scheldt and blew a large hole in the bridge, killing 800 Spanish troops. But they had no way of exploiting the breach they had made. The siege held and on August 17 the starving city surrendered.

WELL FORTIFIED
Ignoring Antwerp's extensive land fortifications, the Duke of Parma cut the city off from supply by sea.

Coutras

DATE
October 20, 1587

FORCES
Royalists: 10,000;
Huguenots: 6,500

LOCATION Western
France, northeast
of Bordeaux

CASUALTIES
Royalists: 3,000 killed;
Huguenots: up to
200 killed

By 1587 the French Religious Wars had evolved into the "War of the Three Henrys": King Henry III of France, at that time leaning toward the Catholic side; Henry of Navarre, the leader of the Protestant Huguenots (and future King Henry IV); and French Catholic leader Henry of Guise. At Coutras, an army led by Navarre unexpectedly encountered an army under Henry III's favorite, the Duc de Joyeuse. Trapped in the fork of two rivers, Navarre drew up his forces skillfully, his infantry—mostly arquebusiers—on each flank protected by natural obstacles and his

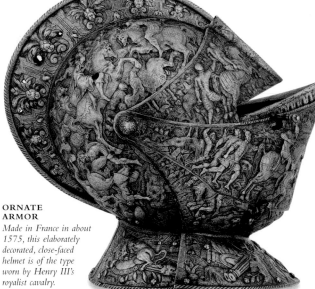

ORNATE ARMOR
Made in France in about 1575, this elaborately decorated, close-faced helmet is of the type worn by Henry III's royalist cavalry.

light and heavy cavalry in the center. His three cannons were placed on the left flank. Joyeuse's cavalry was also drawn up in the center, but it was stretched out in a line, glittering in elaborately decorated heavy armor, ready to charge with couched lance. Henry's cavalry, relatively lightly

MERCIFUL HENRY
Though the clemency of Henry of Navarre after the battle is celebrated in art, many of his men showed no mercy to prisoners.

armored, were armed with pistol and sword and arranged in compact squadrons six lines deep, with infantry arquebusiers between the squadrons to augment their firepower. The issue was decided in the center as de Joyeuse's cavalry lowered lances and charged. The fire of arquebuses had already taken its toll on the royalist cavalry before they smashed into the Huguenot cavalry and broke apart. Thousands of royalists were slaughtered in the rout that followed. No quarter was given—the Duc de Joyeuse was shot through the head after surrendering—until Henry of Navarre intervened to restore order and the rules of chivalry.

Raid on Cadiz

DATE
April 29–May 1, 1587

FORCES
English fleet: 23 ships
Spanish: unknown

LOCATION
Cadiz, southern Spain

CASUALTIES
33 Spanish ships lost

Aware that King Philip II of Spain was assembling a fleet for the invasion of England, Queen Elizabeth I ordered Sir Francis Drake to disrupt Spanish preparations. Drake, whose privateering attacks had helped provoke hostilities, boldly sailed his ships into the port of Cadiz, defying on shore cannons and war galleys. Maneuvering skillfully to avoid fireships and fend off galleys, Drake sank or set fire to a range of vessels from a galleon to merchantmen, before escaping with few casualties. Reading a report of the incident, Philip concluded, "The loss was not very great, but the daring of the attempt was very great indeed."

NAVAL HERO
A statue of Sir Francis Drake who boasted that at Cadiz he had "singed the King of Spain's beard."

ANGLO–SPANISH CONFLICT

Spanish Armada

DATE
May–October 1588

FORCES
Spanish Armada:
130 ships;
English fleet:
c.170 ships

LOCATION
Most battles fought in
the English Channel

CASUALTIES
Spanish lost 63 ships

In the mid-1580s hostility between England and Spain broke into open warfare. When Queen Elizabeth I of England sent a force to support Dutch rebels against Spain, Spanish king Philip II received the pope's blessing for an invasion of England. The Spanish fleet (or "Armada") sailed from Lisbon in late May 1588, commanded by the Duke of Medina Sidonia. Its goal was to establish naval superiority in the English Channel. Bad weather forced the Armda to take refuge in La Coruña, and it did not appear off the coast of Cornwall until July 19. An English fleet under Lord Howard of Effingham, with Sir

Francis Drake as second-in-command, set out from Plymouth and engaged the Spanish from July 21. In a series of battles along the Channel the English long-range guns inflicted damage on the Armada but failed to disrupt its formation. Both sides had run short of ammunition by July 26, when the Spanish anchored off Calais. On the night of July 27–28 the English sent fireships packed with gunpowder into the Armada's anchorage. Panicking, the Spanish ships cut their anchors and drifted north in loose formation. This allowed the English fleet to get among them, sinking or damaging many ships. Carried by the wind into the North Sea, Medina Sidonia decided to head for home by sailing around the British Isles. The voyage was a disaster, as September storms wrecked ship after ship on the coasts of Scotland and Ireland. The English fleet also suffered its heaviest losses after the action, with thousands of sailors dying of typhus. The victory was less decisive than the English wanted to believe.

VICTORY MEDAL
This 17th-century English medal commemorates the victory over the Armada.

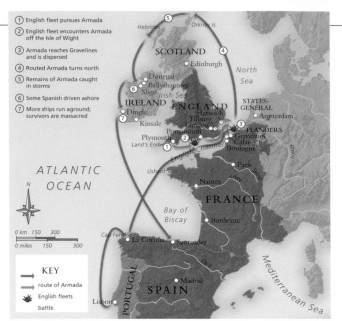

① English fleet pursues Armada
② English fleet encounters Armada off the Isle of Wight
③ Armada reaches Gravelines and is dispersed
④ Routed Armada turns north
⑤ Remains of Armada caught in storms
⑥ Some Spanish driven ashore
⑦ More ships run aground; survivors are massacred

KEY
→ route of Armada
⚓ English fleets
⚔ battle

"I am come amongst you…being resolved in the midst and heat of the battle to live or die amongst you all, to lay down for my God and for my kingdom, and for my people, my honor and my blood, even in the dust."

Elizabeth I, speech to troops at Tilbury, AUGUST 8, 1588

1527–1598

PHILIP II OF SPAIN

King of Spain from 1556, Philip's life-long goals were the expansion of Spanish power and the defense of Catholicism against Protestants and Muslims. He annexed Portugal in 1580 and saved the southern Netherlands for Catholicism, but failed to suppress the Dutch revolt, or to prevent Henry of Navarre from becoming king of France, or to restore Catholic rule in England.

ENGLISH FIREPOWER
Keeping the estimated 1,800 cannon of the English fleet supplied with shot through this lengthy naval engagement was a serious problem.

HUGUENOT CONFLICT

Siege of La Rochelle

DATE
June 27, 1627–
October 28, 1628

FORCES
Royalists: c.25,000;
French: unknown

LOCATION
La Rochelle, France

CASUALTIES 18,600
die in La Rochelle;
2,000 English killed

The French Wars of Religion came to an end after Henry of Navarre took the French throne as Henry IV, adopting the Catholic faith but reconciling the Protestant Huguenot faction by the 1598 Edict of Nantes. Under his successor, Louis XIII, however, the Huguenots were once more alienated. Duc Henri de Rohan and his brother Soubise led a Huguenot revolt from 1625, while Louis's chief minister, the Duc de Richelieu, declared the suppression of Huguenot dissidence his first priority. The rebels won backing from English King Charles I, who sent a fleet of 80 ships under his favorite, the Duke of Buckingham. In June 1627 the fleet landed 6,000 soldiers on the Ile de Ré, just off

OCEAN BARRIER
An imaginative picture shows Richelieu inspecting the sea wall built to isolate the city. The real structure was 4,600ft (1,400m) long, built on top of a line of hulks that had been filled with rubble and sunk.

La Rochelle, which although a Protestant stronghold, had hesitated to join the revolt. With the English installed on the Ile de Ré, however, Richelieu deployed an army around the city, and at the start of September the siege began. Meanwhile, on the Ile de Ré, the English laid siege to the small fort of St. Martin but could not take it, as French boats boldly ran the blockade to ferry in supplies and reinforcements. By the fall Buckingham's forces were themselves short of supplies and decimated by disease. After a final assault on the fort went awry, they retreated

to their ships under attack from French forces that inflicted heavy casualties. With the English gone, the blockade of La Rochelle tightened. Cut off on land by a rampart 7 miles (12km) long with 11 forts and 18 redoubts, the city was also isolated by a massive sea wall built by 4,000 workmen. The appearance

"Its port was the last in France open to the English, and by closing it against England, our eternal enemy, the cardinal, completed the work of Joan of Arc…"

Alexandre Dumas on La Rochelle in The Three Musketeers, 1844

of an English fleet in September 1628 momentarily raised the city's hopes, but after bombarding French positions the English were forced to withdraw. With all hope gone and most of its people dead of starvation, the city surrendered on October 28. Some 5,400 of a population of 24,000 remained alive.

SPANISH–DUTCH WARS

Siege of Breda

DATE
August 28, 1624–
June 5, 1625

FORCES
Dutch: unknown;
Spanish: unknown

LOCATION
Breda, north Brabant,
Netherlands

CASUALTIES
No reliable estimates

By the early 17th century, the key commanders in the Spanish-Dutch war were Ambrogio Spinola and Maurice of Nassau. Maurice, son of William of Orange, is credited with major improvements in the organization of Dutch forces. Spinola, a Genoese,

entered the conflict by bringing troops from Italy at his own expense and was financially ruined by the war. Yet Spinola defeated Maurice repeatedly up to 1609, when a truce was agreed to, and again after 1621 when war resumed. The siege of Breda, a key Dutch border fortress, is considered the peak of Spinola's career. He surrounded the fortress with a ring of redoubts, rather than trench lines, and defended these against attempted breakouts and relief forces. Maurice of Nassau died of disease during the siege. The garrison and citizens suffered much hardship; at one point, when scurvy had taken hold, a mass cure was achieved by distribution of a placebo. By June 1625, however, conditions inside Breda were desperate. Informed of this from an intercepted message, Spinola proposed generous surrender terms. The Dutch were allowed to withdraw and the citizens remained unharmed. As was usual in this war of interminable sieges, this victory had little practical result.

SURRENDER
Here, Spinola accepts the surrender of the garrison of Breda. This famous painting by Velázquez emphasizes the chivalry of the occasion.

SPANISH–DUTCH WARS

The Downs

DATE
October 31, 1639

FORCES
Dutch: 117 ships;
Spanish: 77 ships

LOCATION Off the
southeast coast of
England, east of Dover

CASUALTIES
Spanish: 70 ships
destroyed or captured;
15,000 men killed

Dutch sea power was a thorn in the side of the Spanish, especially in the form of commerce raiding. In 1628 Dutch privateer Piet Heyn seized a Spanish fleet laden with silver from the mines in Peru, possibly the most valuable prize ever captured at sea. The Dutch navy also threatened to cut Spain's sea communications with the Spanish Netherlands. In 1639 the Spanish sent a large fleet of warships under Admiral Antonio de Oquendo toward the Spanish-held port of Dunkirk. Dutch admiral Martin Tromp, with only 13 heavily gunned ships, intercepted the Spanish fleet, attacking with such ferocity that they were forced to seek refuge in neutral waters off the English coast. Tromp

kept the Spanish under surveillance until reinforcements had arrived from the United Provinces. On October 31, hemmed in close to land, outgunned, and unable to maneuver, the Spanish were slaughtered. Like the Armada conflict of 1588, the battle demonstrated the inability of the Spanish to adapt to the notion of ships as mobile gun platforms—their vessels were packed with soldiers waiting for a chance to board enemy ships that never came. The Dutch victory ensured that Spain would be eventually forced to recognize Dutch independence, which it did in 1648.

POPULAR WARSHIP
The galleon, the preferred warship of all ocean-going navies in this period, typically carried around 30 guns.

SPANISH
GALLEON

THE THIRTY YEARS WAR

BETWEEN **1618** AND **1648**, a complex series of campaigns, collectively known as the Thirty Years War, were fought in Europe. This was part civil war within the Holy Roman Empire; part battle for European supremacy between France, Sweden, and the Habsburgs in Spain and Austria; and part holy war between Catholic and Protestant. The war's origins lay in the attempt by the Habsburg emperors Matthias and Ferdinand II to eradicate Protestantism in Bohemia. The intervention of Sweden in 1630 and France in 1635 ensured that few regions of central or western Europe were untouched by the fighting.

KEY

	Austrian Habsburg possessions 1683
	Spanish Habsburg possessions 1683
⚔	civil war or widespread disturbance
⚔	local revolt or unrest
—	frontiers 1683
—	Holy Roman empire 1683

Expansionist tendencies

→ Sweden
→ Russia
→ England
→ Austrian Habsburgs
→ France
→ United Provinces

30 YEARS WAR
The bitter conflict thwarted Habsburg plans to re-Catholicize Europe

THIRTY YEARS WAR

Magdeburg

DATE	May 20, 1631
FORCES	Imperial: unknown Swedes: unknown
LOCATION Central Germany, 80 miles (130km) west of Berlin	**CASUALTIES** 20,000–25,000 Magdeburg citizens massacred

In 1640 King Gustavus Adolphus of Sweden landed an army in northern Germany, seeking to assist the beleaguered Protestant cities there. Chief among these was Magdeburg, staunchly Lutheran and one of the Holy Roman Empire's richest cities, with a population of 30,000. Besieged by Imperial forces under Tilly and Pappenheim since November 1630, Magdeburg finally fell on May 20, 1631, after heavy artillery made two breaches in the walls, and the city was sacked by the drunken soldiers of the victorious Imperial army. Up to 25,000 of Magdeburg's citizens perished in the massacre or in the fires that swept through the blood-drenched streets.

PLUG BAYONET
Early bayonets, such as this, were jammed into the musket's muzzle, so the weapon could not then be fired.

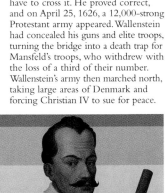

THIRTY YEARS WAR

White Mountain

DATE	November 8, 1620
FORCES	Catholic League: 20,000; Bohemians 24,000
LOCATION Bilá Hora, near Prague, modern-day Czech Republic	**CASUALTIES** No reliable estimates

By the early 17th century Calvinist Protestantism had become deep-rooted in Bohemia. In 1618 Holy Roman Emperor Ferdinand II tried to impose a Catholic king on the Bohemians, and a wholesale uprising ensued. In

UPHILL STRUGGLE
Tilly's professional army is seen here overpowering the motley Bohemian forces.

1620 a Bohemian army under Christian of Anhalt deployed on the slopes of a hill (White Mountain, or Bilá Hora in Czech) near Prague. Opposing him was the Imperial army under Count Tilly. Christian was totally unprepared when Tilly attacked uphill, and the Bohemian center was quickly overrun. The Protestant army disintegrated and soon afterward Tilly captured Prague, ending Bohemia's independence.

BURGONET HELMET
Burgonets had a peak, hinged cheek pieces and a crest.

THIRTY YEARS WAR

Dessau

DATE	April 25, 1626
FORCES	Imperial: 20,000; Protestants: 12,000
LOCATION 30 miles (50km) north of Leipzig, Germany	**CASUALTIES** Protestants: 4,000 dead

In 1625 the Danish king Christian IV intervened to help the beleaguered German Protestants against the Holy Roman Empire. To counter this new threat Emperor Ferdinand II employed the services of Albrecht von Wallenstein (see box), who pledged a large army to support the Imperial cause. At the strategic Dessau bridge Wallenstein lay in wait for the Protestant army, led by Ernst von Mansfeld. The bridge controlled movement into Silesia, and Mansfeld, calculated Wallenstein, would have to cross it. He proved correct, and on April 25, 1626, a 12,000-strong Protestant army appeared. Wallenstein had concealed his guns and elite troops, turning the bridge into a death trap for Mansfeld's troops, who withdrew with the loss of a third of their number. Wallenstein's army then marched north, taking large areas of Denmark and forcing Christian IV to sue for peace.

1583–1634

ALBRECHT VON WALLENSTEIN

Albrecht von Wallenstein, duke of Friedland, used his governorship of Bohemia to raise a large army to counter the Danish intervention in the war in 1625. Thereafter he won a string of victories, but his independent behavior caused jealousy among the German princes, and Emperor Ferdinand dismissed him in 1630. Recalled (at enormous cost) to face the threat of Gustavus Adolphus in 1631, he sought political power for himself and was assassinated in 1634.

First Breitenfeld

DATE
September 17, 1631

FORCES
Sweden/Saxony: 42,000; Imperial: 35,000

LOCATION
Just outside Leipzig, Germany

CASUALTIES
Imperial: 20,000 (of which 7,000–8,000 killed)

Following the sack of Magdeburg in May 1631, Swedish king Gustavus Adolphus sought to conclude a defensive alliance with John George, the elector of Saxony aimed at uniting the Protestant powers against Ferdinand II and his drive to impose Catholic conformity. In late August 1631, an Imperial army under Tilly invaded Saxony in an effort to force John George to abandon the Swedish cause. At Breitenfeld, north of Leipzig, Tilly and Pappenheim deployed their troops in 17 squares (tercios) to face the Swedish–Saxon force. The Swedish army was, for the time, relatively disciplined and Gustavus, a master

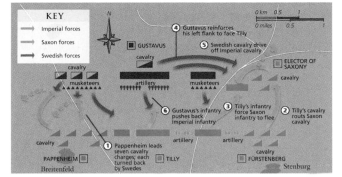

SWEPT-HILT CAVALRY SWORD
This sword is typical of early 17th-century cavalry swords. Its robust double-edged blade could be used for both cutting and thrusting.

Guard to protect hand

tactician, arrayed his forces in two long lines, creating a front that matched Tilly's, but giving him a crucial reserve force. Pappenheim's heavy cavalry charged seven times, but the Swedes drove them back each time. Tilly's cavalry, meanwhile, had routed the Saxon cavalry, while John George's infantry had also fled. It looked as if the Protestant cause was lost. At this point

SQUARE ATTACK
This contemporary engraving of the battle of Breitenfeld clearly shows the Imperial tercio formations.

Gustavus pushed his second line into the fray, fording the Loderbach stream at right-angles to the main front line. Tilly, inexplicably, chose not to attack, and the Swedes swept down on his left flank. The Swedish artillery joined in, devastating the remnants of the imperial army. It was a fine demonstration of the coordination of infantry, cavalry, and artillery that exemplified Gustavus's military genius and persuaded Protestant German princes to flock to his banner.

Lützen

DATE
November 16, 1632

FORCES Swedish: 12,800 infantry, 6,200 cavalry; Imperial: 13,000 infantry, 6,000 cavalry

LOCATION Saxony, Germany

CASUALTIES Swedish: 5–6,000 dead; Imperial 6–8,000 dead

Following his success at Breitenfeld, Gustavus Adolphus embarked on an "all or nothing" strategy, laying a trap for the Imperial commander Wallenstein at Nuremberg, where he positioned 500 artillery pieces. Wallenstein saw through the ploy and each side then embarked on a strategy of attrition throughout the summer of 1632. In November, Wallenstein, thinking that the campaign season was over, split his forces into two columns and retreated toward Leipzig for the winter. Gustavus caught up with him on the Lützen–Leipzig road. To the right of Wallenstein's army lay the castle of Lützen, while the Bavarian cavalry took its position on the weaker Imperial left flank. The Swedes, initially delayed by heavy mist, succeeded in surrounding this weak point in the imperial line. Disaster for Wallenstein's forces seemed imminent until the arrival of Pappenheim with the other Imperial column. The Swedish left, meanwhile, under Bernard of Weimar, had found itself in serious difficulties. Gustavus Adolphus led a cavalry charge to rally his beleaguered troops, but during it he was killed. Weimar was subsequently able to envelop the Imperial right, thus securing overall victory. At nightfall Wallenstein withdrew to Leipzig and then into Bohemia. Although the Swedes were left in possession of the field, the most serious consequence was the loss to the Protestant cause of Gustavus Adolphus, "the Lion of the North."

DESTINY'S CHARGE
Gustavus II Adolphus leads a cavalry charge at Lützen, the action that led to his death and so permanently damaged the Protestant cause.

THIRTY YEARS WAR

Nördlingen

DATE
September 6, 1634

FORCES Spanish: 20,000
infantry, 13,000 cavalry;
Protestants: 18,000
infantry, 9,000 cavalry

LOCATION Northwest
of Munich, Germany

CASUALTIES
Protestants: 17,000
dead, 4,000 prisoners

After the death of Gustavus Adolphus, the Swedish campaign lost its strategic direction at precisely the time the Catholic camp became more united.

> "At this unfortunate moment a barrel of powder blew up, and created the greatest disorder amongst the Swedes. The imperial cavalry charged… and the flight became universal."
>
> *Friedrich Schiller*, History of the Thirty Years War, 1789

Wallenstein's dismissal as commander helped heal a rift between the Imperial and Spanish branches of the Habsburgs. In September 1634 their combined army moved into Bavaria. Their encounter with the Swedish army at Nördlingen was characterized both by extraordinary bravery and great confusion. The Imperial and Spanish troops occupied the flatter ground in front of the town, with the vanguard on a hill commanding the road. The Swedish army took up position on a series of low hills one mile (1.5km) to the southwest. The Protestants planned to attack at daybreak simultaneously in the valley and on the hill, but fatally, their commanders did not consider the woods, which rendered the coordination of their forces nearly impossible. The battle descended into a series of intense but confused confrontations. At one point two brigades of Swedish infantry fired on each other. Isolated and eventually overcome, the Swedish forces were butchered. With Habsburg success threatening Europe with the specter of "universal monarchy," France entered the Thirty Years War.

SWEDES AT BAY
This scene of the battle of Nördlingen shows the situation before the collapse of the Swedish army.

THIRTY YEARS WAR

Second Breitenfeld

DATE
November 12, 1642

FORCES
Imperial: 20,000;
Swedish: 22,000

LOCATION
Just outside
Leipzig, Germany

CASUALTIES
Imperial: 5,000 killed,
5,000 prisoners

In 1636 Catholic France had entered the war in alliance with Protestant Sweden and Holland, more motivated by the desire to thwart Habsburg ambitions than by religious loyalties. A Spanish invasion of France in 1636 had been pushed back, and by 1642 the Swedish general Torstensson was ravaging the Habsburg lands in Austria. Intent upon capturing Leipzig, Torstensson encountered the Imperial forces under Archduke Leopold and

CAVALRY GUN
This wheel-lock carbine could be fired from horseback. It had much better range and accuracy than a pistol.

Count Piccolomini near the city. The battle was opened by a massive imperial cannonade of chain shot, intended to precede a sweeping cavalry attack. Torstensson realized that he must strike before the enemy formed in line of battle, and he moved quickly against the Imperial left flank, which broke almost at once, despite the Archduke's best efforts to maintain discipline. On the other flank, however, the Bavarian cavalry had repulsed their Swedish opposites, while the Archduke's infantry was beginning to press against the Swedish center. Torstensson brought his right wing across and pushed back the Swedish infantry. In the confusion, the Imperial cavalry found itself isolated by the withdrawal of the footsoldiers, leaving them little choice but to surrender or flee. Whole companies of troops simply threw down their arms and agreed on the spot to serve Torstensson. The Imperial army collapsed and fled. In the aftermath the irate Archduke, who had lost half his army, court-martialed the officers of one whole regiment. The higher officers were beheaded, and one in 10 of the soldiers summarily shot. The Imperial side's fortunes had reached their nadir.

> "Do you not know, my son, with what little wisdom the world is governed?"
>
> *Axel Oxenstierna*, the Swedish chancellor, in a letter to his son concerning the peace negotiations to end the Thirty Years War, 1648

1603–1651

TORSTENSSON

Lennart Torstensson was a skilled tactician and pioneer of new recruitment methods. Ill health— he was crippled by arthritis—meant he often had to lead his army in a litter. His suffering may have shaped his outlook on military discipline. Any failure or act of disobedience was instantly punished and his men heartily loathed him. His severity was matched only by his spectacular successes on the battlefield.

Rocroi

DATE
May 19, 1643

FORCES Spanish: 8,000 cavalry, 19,000 infantry; French: 7,000 cavalry, 15,000 infantry

LOCATION 55 miles (90km) northeast of Reims, France

CASUALTIES Spanish: 8,000 killed, 7,000 prisoners

In May 1642 a Spanish army under Don Francisco de Melo crossed into France, stopping to besiege Rocroi, a small fort north of Rheims. The French, under the Duc d'Enghien, advanced rapidly to face him. The Spanish troops were formed in their habitual *tercios* rather than the more advanced line formation favored by the French. Both sides formed up their cavalry on the flanks. The battle

STANDING ARMIES

The Thirty Years War proved decisive in the move toward the professionalization of armies. The very nature of warfare was changing. A new, more-disciplined and professional—and therefore more expensive—means of conducting war was emerging. One reason advanced for the repeated successes of Swedish forces is that they contained a small nucleus of career soldiers who fought across a number of campaigns. The Thirty Years War also saw the increasing use of drill manuals to provide formal training for soldiers.

MUSKETEER

GRENADIER

began at daybreak on May 19, and initially went well for the Spanish, whose horsemen defeated the cavalry of the enemy left. The French cavalry on the right wing, however, routed their adversaries. At this point the Duc d'Enghien charged through the enemy center, a move that allowed him to relieve the attack upon his exhausted infantry. The Spanish horsemen, caught between two assailants, broke and headed toward the marsh. Their flight left 8,000 Spanish infantrymen surrounded without any hope of escape. Despite heroic feats of endurance (the French

NO QUARTER
This graphic image depicts soldiers (possibly French) being savagely punished for indiscipline and crimes against civilians.

charged them four times), their resistance was destroyed by a combination of French artillery and relentless cavalry assault. But the *tercios'* surrender did not end the bloodshed; in the confusion d'Enghien was fired upon, and in revenge his men fell upon the helpless Spaniards, slaughtering over half of them. The defeat effectively marked the end of Spanish military power.

Jankov

DATE
March 5, 1645

FORCES
Swedish: 15,000; Imperial: 15,000

LOCATION
Near Prague, modern-day Czech Republic

CASUALTIES
No reliable estimates

After Second Breitenfeld, the Imperial forces were saved from disaster only by the outbreak of a Danish–Swedish War. But the Swedish general Torstensson was back in central Europe by the summer of 1645 and at Jankov, outside Prague, he was confronted by the Imperial army. The ensuing battle was a series of skirmishes over hilly and wooded terrain. The Swedes were outnumbered and Torstensson's tactical ability was crucial in defeating the Imperial forces, whose infantry offered little resistance. Only the Bavarian cavalry fought back against the Protestants, but, outnumbered and outgunned, they fell in large numbers. The loss of this elite force left Emperor Ferdinand militarily crippled and destroyed all Catholic hopes of enforcing a favorable peace.

Zusmarshausen

DATE
May 17, 1648

FORCES
Imperial: unknown; Franco–Swedish force: unknown

LOCATION
Near Munich, southern Germany

CASUALTIES
No reliable estimates

By 1648, the elector of Saxony had made peace with Sweden, leaving Emperor Ferdinand dangerously isolated. In the spring of 1648 the remaining Bavarian and Imperial armies found themselves outnumbered by a Franco–Swedish force. Little or no coordination existed between the two Imperial–Catholic forces, their respective commanders having fallen out over the question of precedence. The Imperial forces, moreover, were slowed down by an enormous train of camp-followers, who may have outnumbered the soldiers four to one. Melander, the Imperial field-marshal, tried

to move the infantry and artillery away from his pursuers, hoping that the Italian general Montecuccoli would be able to defend the rear with the cavalry. This the Italian did, with considerable doggedness, until, with Melander killed, he abandoned everything but the infantry, which he moved into Landsberg. The commander of the Bavarian army, which had retreated, was immediately

FRENCH MARSHAL
Henri, Vicomte de Turenne, was the leading French general in the final stages of the Thirty Years War.

arrested on a charge of treason. The battle at Zusmarshausen was followed not long after by the Treaty of Westphalia, negotiations for which had been dragging on interminably. The settlement, which finally ended the Thirty Years War, helped establish Sweden as a new force in Europe, and finally forced Spain to recognize the independence of the Dutch Republic. Its terms laid the foundations for a Europe based on the nation-state rather than on dynastic loyalties and overlapping religious and political jurisdictions.

PAPER PEACE
The seals on the Treaty of Westphalia, shown here, signaled an end to a generation of war and the advent of modern diplomacy.

THE ENGLISH CIVIL WAR

BETWEEN 1642 AND 1651 a series of wars erupted between supporters of the Crown and of Parliament in England, Wales, Scotland, and Ireland. The split between them stemmed from religious differences and from King Charles I's belief in his "divine right" to rule without recourse to Parliament. The first battle between Royalists and Parliamentarians was fought in 1642, and by 1646 Charles had been defeated. Conflict reignited in 1647–49, when the Scots allied with the Crown. Charles was executed in 1649, and his son Prince Charles became the Royalist figurehead. In 1649–51 the Royalists, and their Irish and Scottish allies, were decisively beaten, and Britain came under the rule of the most successful general of the English Civil War, Oliver Cromwell.

ENGLISH CIVIL WAR

Marston Moor

DATE July 2, 1644

FORCES
Royalists: 18,000;
Parliamentarians
and Scots: 27,000

LOCATION Marston Moor, 4 miles (6km) west of York, England

CASUALTIES Royalists: 4,150 killed; Scots and Parliamentarians: c.2,000 killed

Nearly two years after hostilities had started, the war was going badly for the Royalists in the north of England. Led by the Marquis of Newcastle, they had been driven back to York, where they were besieged by Parliamentary and Scottish forces led by Sir Thomas Fairfax and the Earl of Leven. A relief army, led by Prince Rupert of the Rhine, reached York on July 1, and the next day Royalists marched out of the city to give battle. Both sides deployed infantry in the center with cavalry on either flank. At about 2 p.m. there was a short artillery exchange, but neither side made a decisive move.

Rupert believed the battle would begin the next morning, but at 7:30 p.m., Parliamentary forces attacked. Their left flank, led by Cromwell, routed the Royalist right flank. Elsewhere, the Royalists were more successful, and Leven fled, believing the battle lost. However, Cromwell was able to attack the Royalists from the rear and relieve the beleaguered Parliamentary forces. Victory meant that the Parliamentarians would gain decisive control of the north of England.

BATTLE HORSES
The strength and maneuverability of Cromwell's Parliamentary cavalry was an important factor in the outcome of the battle.

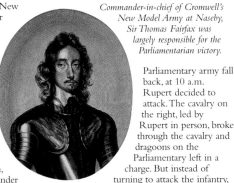

① Parliamentary cavalry scatter Royalist cavalry

Marston Moor

Wilstrop Wood

RUPERT

Tockwith

Moor Lane

Atterwith Lane

② Royalist cavalry routs Fairfax's cavalry

CROMWELL

EARL OF LEVEN

Ditch

Sike Beck

FAIRFAX

③ Parliamentary forces regroup and attack Royalist center

to York →

Broad Lane

Long Marston

to Wetherby

0 km   0.5   1
0 miles   0.5

KEY
- Royalist cavalry
- Royalist infantry
- Royalist musketeers
- Parliamentary cavalry
- Parliamentary infantry
- Parliamentary artillery

ENGLISH CIVIL WAR

Naseby

DATE June 14, 1645

FORCES
Royalists: 9,000;
Parliamentarians:
14,000

LOCATION Naseby, south of Leicester, central England

CASUALTIES Royalists: 400–1,000 killed; Parliamentarians: 150 killed

Parliament's establishment of the New Model Army in January 1645 created a well paid and disciplined force, although at first there was a wide gap in quality between its experienced cavalry and hastily organized infantry.

In May the Royalists sacked Leicester, drawing the New Model Army, led by Sir Thomas Fairfax, away from their siege of Oxford. Prince Rupert drew the Royalists up along a ridge north of Naseby, with infantry flanked on both sides by cavalry. Fairfax positioned the Parliamentary forces beneath the Naseby ridge in similar fashion, with 1,000 dragoons under Colonel John Okey behind a hedge on the left flank. The land in front of the Parliamentarians was waterlogged, and Cromwell advised Fairfax to withdraw to higher land. Seeing the

BATTLE PLAN
This plan of Naseby shows the exact position of the infantry and cavalry units commanded by Charles I and Fairfax.

NEW MODEL WARRIOR
Commander-in-chief of Cromwell's New Model Army at Naseby, Sir Thomas Fairfax was largely responsible for the Parliamentarian victory.

Parliamentary army fall back, at 10 a.m. Rupert decided to attack. The cavalry on the right, led by Rupert in person, broke through the cavalry and dragoons on the Parliamentary left in a charge. But instead of turning to attack the infantry, they charged on, losing touch with the battle. Meanwhile, the Royalist infantry was overwhelming the Parliamentary infantry. But Cromwell's cavalry, the "Ironsides," carried out a disciplined charge on the right flank that broke through the Royalist cavalry, and then charged the infantry. Also attacked by surviving Parliamentarian cavalry and dragoons from the other flank, the Royalists were crushed. King Charles's advisers stopped him from leading the reserves in a bid to save the day. The New Model Army had scored its first victory.

> "The foot on either side hardly saw each other till they were within carbine shot, and so only made one volley; ours falling in with sword and butt end of the musket did notable execution, insomuch as I saw their colors fall and their foot in great disorder."

WITNESS TO WAR
SIR EDWARD WALKER, ROYALIST

The infantry of both sides did indeed advance to "push of pike" so rapidly that the musketeers intermingled with the pikemen had time for only one volley before turning to using their muskets as clubs. The Royalist infantry were fewer than the Parliamentarians but fought with great determination in the face of inevitable defeat.

Drogheda

DATE
September 11, 1649

FORCES
Parliamentarians:
12,000; Royalists: 2,300

CASUALTIES
Parliamentarians: 150
killed; Royalists and
civilians: 3,500 killed

LOCATION Drogheda,
28 miles (45km)
north of Dublin

On January 17, 1649, the Marquis of
Ormonde settled an alliance between
the Royalists and the Irish, hoping
to turn Ireland into a Royalist
base from which a counterattack
could be launched against the
triumphant Parliamentarians. In
response Parliament appointed
Cromwell Lord-Lieutenant of
Ireland. Cromwell was able
to march into Dublin
unhindered, but met

with opposition on
arriving at Drogheda
on September 10.
The town was well
protected by a wall
23ft (7m) high and
6½ft (2m) thick; its
governor, Sir Arthur
Aston, felt confident of the town's
defenses and refused the order to
surrender. Cromwell immediately
ordered an artillery bombardment to
commence, and on September 11 the

UNUSUAL HELMET
*This type of iron hat
was occasionally worn
by horsemen during the
English Civil War.*

walls were breached. The
breach was too small to allow
many troops through, and so
Cromwell's men were repelled twice
as they attempted to storm it. The
third assault, led by Cromwell in
person, overwhelmed the defenders.

Cromwell's army surged through the
town, killing priests and friars on sight.
A church in which some defending
soldiers had sought refuge was set on
fire. Aston was bludgeoned to death
with his own wooden leg. Civilians
as well as soldiers were killed in the
slaughter; Cromwell's actions here and
later at Wexford ensured that he would
forever remain a figure of hatred for
Irish Catholics. He left Ireland in May
1650, two years before Parliamentary
control of the island was complete.

Iron wheel band

Gun barrel

DROGHEDA'S STRENGTH
*Even after the walls had been breached,
Drogheda held out for some time against
the onslaught of Cromwell's forces.*

*Wooden
carriage tail*

Hub

*Wooden
wheel rim*

FALCONET
*Small-caliber cannons such as this Civil
War falconet were designed for mobility. They
were attached to cavalry or infantry units,
rather than to the slow-moving artillery units.*

Preston

DATE
August 17–19, 1648

FORCES
Parliamentarians:
8,600; Scots: 17,600

CASUALTIES
Parliamentarians:
unknown; Scots:
1,000 killed

LOCATION
Preston, northwest
England

In January 1647 Parliament captured
Charles I. However, he escaped in
November and signed an alliance with
the Scots, who invaded England in July
1648. Led by the Duke of Hamilton,
they moved south through Lancashire.
On the morning of August 17,
Cromwell attacked Scots
guarding the road into
Preston and by nightfall
had secured the town. The
next day he pursued the
disorganized Scottish army.
Totally outmaneuvered
by a much smaller force,
Hamilton fled with
most of his cavalry.
The Scots surrendered
to Cromwell at
Warrington on
August 19.

ARMOR
*This pikeman's
breastplate with
tassets dates from
the Civil War.*

Dunbar

DATE
September 3, 1650

FORCES Scots: 20,000;
Parliamentarians:
11,000

CASUALTIES
Scots: 3,000 killed;
Parliamentarians:
20-40 killed

LOCATION Dunbar,
east of Edinburgh,
Scotland

The Scots, incensed at the execution
of Charles I, committed themselves to
restoring the crown in England. On
July 22, 1650, Cromwell led an army
of 16,000 into Scotland to preempt
any attack on England. The Scottish
army, led by General David Leslie,
was numerically superior,
but throughout August
Leslie avoided a direct
confrontation. This policy
was effective; by the end
of the month Cromwell's
army had lost 5,000 men
to sickness. He was
forced to withdraw to
the coast at Dunbar,
where he would have
the support of his fleet.
Leslie's army tracked
Cromwell's, and
by September 1
the Scots were
encamped on
Doon Hill above
Dunbar with
Cromwell's

men trapped between them and the
coast. On September 2 Leslie led
his army down the hill, planning to
attack Cromwell the next day. Only a
steep ravine separated the two armies.
Cromwell responded by ordering his
army across the ravine under cover
of darkness, and launching a surprise
attack at daybreak on September 3,
shouting to his men the words of a
psalm: "Now let God arise, and his

DAWN ATTACK
*Cromwell launched a surprise attack on the
Scots at Dunbar; moving his troops under
cover of night, he attacked at daybreak.*

enemies shall be scattered." At first
the Scots made, in Cromwell's words,
"a gallant resistance," but the English
commander had noticed that the
Scottish right wing was cramped
between the ravine and high ground.
He launched his reserve cavalry against
these poorly deployed troops, driving
into the flank. The Scottish cavalry
was forced back against the infantry
and lost all coherence. The battle
turned into a rout. Dunbar is often
considered the greatest example of
Cromwell's generalship. Although
the Royalists rallied under Prince
Charles, they were finally defeated
at Worcester in 1651.

1599-1658

OLIVER CROMWELL

Born into minor gentry, Cromwell
fought for the Parliamentary cause
from 1642, coming to prominence
as an inspiring, disciplined cavalry
leader. Courageous and charismatic,
he won the loyalty and admiration
of his men. It was his conviction
that a plain man who "knows what
he fights for" would win out against
"that which you call a gentleman."
He seized power as Lord Protector
in 1653, in effect a military dictator.

CANNONS

THE MUZZLE-LOADED, SMOOTHBORE CANNON, CAST IN BRONZE, BRASS, OR IRON, WAS THE BASIC FIELD-ARTILLERY WEAPON FROM THE LATE 15TH CENTURY THROUGH TO THE 19TH CENTURY.

Cannons were initially used primarily in sieges, but the development of lighter guns mounted on limbers (wheeled ammunition cases) created feasible battlefield weapons. Guns chiefly fired solid-iron round shot—the classic "cannonball" (early cannonballs were made of stone), although against advancing infantry at short range, a canister was used. This was a cluster of small balls inside a tin case. As the case exited the barrel, the balls were released to spray the area in front of the gun. A smaller version of canister shot was grapeshot, which was contained in a canvas bag rather than a metal case. Mortars, and, from the late 17th century, howitzers would fire explosive shells, which took the form of hollow-iron spheres packed with gunpowder and ignited by a fuse.

MANNING THE GUNS

Cannons were typically serviced by a crew of five or six artillerymen. The guns were pulled along by teams of horses or men to the battlefield, then disconnected from the limber. The barrel was swabbed out and then powder and shot rammed down the bore from the muzzle. The firer applied a smouldering portfire—a wooden holder with a length of quick burner attached to it—to a primer-filled tube in the vent to ignite the gunpowder propellant. After each shot a gun had to be "run up" to the original position from which the explosion's recoil had carried it—a process involving a lot of muscle power—and relaid on its target. This involved raising or lowering the gun barrel with handspikes and fixing it in position with quoins (wedges), until the elevating screw was introduced during the 18th century. In the late 17th century, when the art of creating shot for specific barrel sizes became more precise, types of cannon were classified according to the weight of the ammunition that they fired; this measurement became known as the gun's caliber.

FRENCH CANNON
A French cannon being captured by the Holy Roman Emperor Charles V's troops at Pavia in 1525. This battle that was unusual in that artillery proved ineffective.

RAMMER *The rammer (both pictures below) was used to stuff charge and shot down the barrel.*

ORNATE MUZZLE *Gunpowder and then a cannonball were placed into the barrel through this highly ornamental muzzle.*

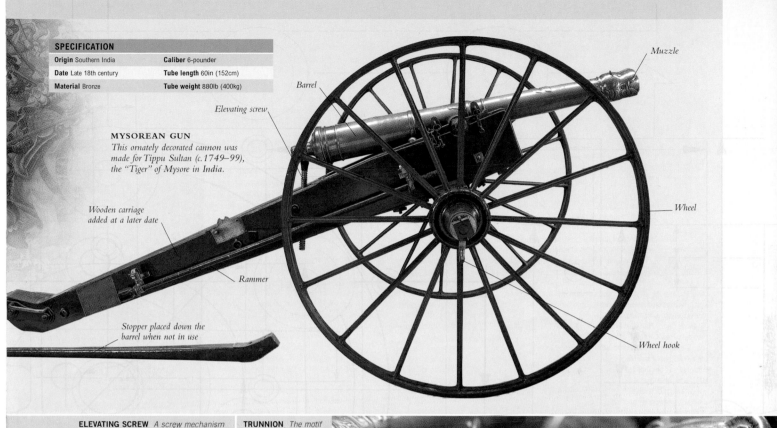

SPECIFICATION

Origin Southern India	**Caliber** 6-pounder
Date Late 18th century	**Tube length** 60in (152cm)
Material Bronze	**Tube weight** 880lb (400kg)

MYSOREAN GUN
This ornately decorated cannon was made for Tippu Sultan (c.1749–99), the "Tiger" of Mysore in India.

Muzzle

Barrel

Elevating screw

Wooden carriage added at a later date

Rammer

Stopper placed down the barrel when not in use

Wheel

Wheel hook

ELEVATING SCREW A screw mechanism was used for elevating and depressing the rear end of the gun barrel.

TRUNNION The motif of a tiger that decorates the barrel around this gun's muzzle is repeated on the two trunnions, or pivots, which were clamped in place firmly to attach the cannon to its wooden carriage. This method of attachment allowed for the vertical angle of the barrel to be changed by the gunner for firing at a target a specific distance away.

WHEEL HOOK The gun carriage would have been pulled by horses roped to a hook attached to the hub of each wheel.

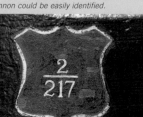

METALWORK The metal details of the gun carriage were constructed to be in keeping with the bronzework of the gun itself.

BARREL The designs on the barrel of the gun display the craft of an Indian master bronzesmith.

SERIAL NUMBER The 19th-century gun carriage bore a serial number by which the cannon could be easily identified.

CONSTRUCTION STAMP The builder of the gun carriage added a forger's mark to its side.

THE GREAT NORTHERN WAR

THE GREAT NORTHERN WAR (1700–21) saw Sweden and its warrior-king Charles XII (1697–1718) fight a series of campaigns against Denmark, Prussia, Saxony, Hanover, Poland, and Russia. The latter rose with unprecedented speed to become one of Europe's great powers. Russian prominence was achieved largely at the expense of Sweden and its Baltic Empire, which had been essentially trade-based. The Great Northern War became as much a fight for control of the wealth of Baltic trade as for territory. In this region towns were less strategically important than in France or Belgium. Armies were generally able to live off the land. As a result there were only three major sieges, producing a very different form of war from that seen in western Europe.

GREAT NORTHERN WAR

Narva

DATE
November 30, 1700

FORCES
Swedish: 8,000;
Russian: 40,000

LOCATION
Northeastern Estonia

CASUALTIES
Swedish:
light; Russian:
up to 10,000 killed

In May 1700 Sweden was attacked by an alliance of Frederick IV of Denmark, Peter I (the Great) of Russia, and Augustus the Strong, elector of Saxony and king of Poland, who were seeking to counter Sweden's growing influence in northern Europe. Sweden was, in many respects, a nation geared to war. The *Indelningswerk* system of recruiting, introduced during the 1670s and 1680s, supplied a professional army. This formidable force was settled on the land: each province provided a regiment; these regiments were settled in "files" (estates) made up of two farms. Each file provided one soldier. The system produced not only a national army but also a well-trained one, as regiments were called up for periods of training in peacetime. In contrast, Russian forces were badly in need of reform—a fact recognized by Czar Peter himself. The first stage of the war saw the small Swedish garrison at Narva (in modern Estonia) besieged by a force of about 50,000 Russians. When Charles XII moved to relieve the town, the Russians retired to an entrenched camp at Novgorod, a few miles away. Charles boldly attacked during a November snowstorm. His force of 8,000 Swedes broke into the entrenchments and, after a three-hour hand-to-hand battle, smashed the Russian left wing and defeated their cavalry, driving the Russians away. This triumph at Narva seemed to confirm Swedish dominance in the Baltic and Charles's status as a military genius. He occupied Warsaw and Cracow in 1701 and engineered the election of his client Stanislaus as king of Poland in 1704. Denmark was forced to make peace with Sweden in 1700, while Saxony did so in 1708, clearing the way for an attack on Russia. After Narva, Swedish predominance in eastern Europe seemed assured.

PETER'S TRIUMPH
Peter the Great used the nine years after the defeat at Narva to rebuild his army, which led to his triumph at Poltava, shown here.

1682–1718

CHARLES XII

Charles XII maintained a Swedish royal tradition of campaigning in person. He was profoundly devoted to the military life: he spoke of being married to the army. After the defeat at Poltava in 1709 he was for five years the unwelcome guest and, latterly, captive of the Ottoman sultan. Fittingly, he died on the field at Frederikshall in 1718. With his demise, Sweden's age of greatness came to a close.

Poltava

DATE
July 8, 1709

FORCES
Swedish: 17,000;
Russians: 80,000

LOCATION
Eastern Ukraine

CASUALTIES
Swedes: 10,000
killed/captured;
Russians: 1,300 killed

The defeat at Narva had shown the urgent need for Russian military reforms. Central organization was improved; while new regiments and military schools were established. In 1705 the system of recruiting infantry was extended; from then on, one soldier was provided by every 20 peasant households. In 1705–09 up to 168,000 men were recruited in this way. Guard regiments were established and training provided for all (including the nobles). Following a victory at Jolowcyzn in July 1708, Charles XII invaded the

REVENGE
This relief shows the recapture of Narva by the Russians in 1704, avenging their defeat there four years earlier.

Ukraine, hoping to deliver a decisive blow to the Russian army. His decision was to prove catastrophic to the Swedish cause. The winter of 1708–09 was extremely harsh. A Russian scorched-earth policy was partially successful. In January, near Hadyach hundreds of Swedish troops froze to death. Attacking the little fortress of Veprik, Charles's men found that the walls had frozen solid. Charles's ally, the Cossack leader (*hetman*) Mazepa, meanwhile, provided little assistance, and Baturin, the Cossack capital, was sacked by the Russians. More cautious advisers suggested to the Swedish king a tactical withdrawal to Poland.

Peter the Great enticed the Swedes to attack his fortified position at Poltava. With Charles injured and unable to oversee in person the battle, his generals proved inadequate. The Swedish attack was badly coordinated, hampered by inadequate reconnaissance and poor communications. Russian infantry and artillery inflicted heavy losses on the Swedes. At 10,000 men, however, Charles's losses paled beside the surrender of 15,000 Swedes at Perevolochna on July 11. Charles took refuge in the Ottoman Empire, where he was to remain until 1714. During this period, the Russian Czar was able to reconquer Poland and Sweden's Baltic provinces. The war ended only in 1721, but Swedish power was broken.

MOUNTED CZAR
This statue of Peter I emphasizes the majesty of the man who established Russia's greatness.

Ezel and Grengam

DATE Ezel: May 24, 1719;
Grengam: July 27, 1720

FORCES Ezel: 6 Russian
warships; Grengam: 61
Russian ships, 4 Swedish
frigates, 1 warship

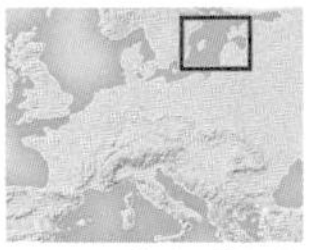

LOCATION Ezel: off Ezel
island, Estonia;
Grengam: off Grengam
island, Estonia

CASUALTIES Ezel: 2
Swedish ships sunk;
Grengam: 4 Swedish
frigates captured

More than any other activity, the creation of a fleet marked out Peter the Great's reign. In 1700 the Russian admiralty was established; in 1705 the navy began recruiting specialized seamen; in 1715 the prestigious Naval Academy came into being; and by 1724 there were 32 ships-of-the-line in the Baltic fleet. Using this fleet, Peter attacked the Swedes, whose will

to resist was much weakened after the death of Charles XII at Frederikshall in 1718. The Swedish navy was defeated in two major engagements at Ezel in 1719—the first victory of the Russian fleet on the open sea—and Grengam in 1720. At Ezel the Russian navy captured three ships in what Peter laconically described as "a good start for the Russian navy." At Grengam a Russian fleet composed largely of light galleys enticed the

heavier Swedish ships into shallow water; two frigates ran aground and were boarded and two more were captured in the subsequent pursuit. Denied its command of the Baltic, Stockholm was forced to the negotiating table. The Peace of Stockholm (1720)

SEA MAIL
Improved communications contributed to Russia's victory over Sweden. This frigate was reequipped by Peter the Great for a military postal service based at the fortress of Kronstadt.

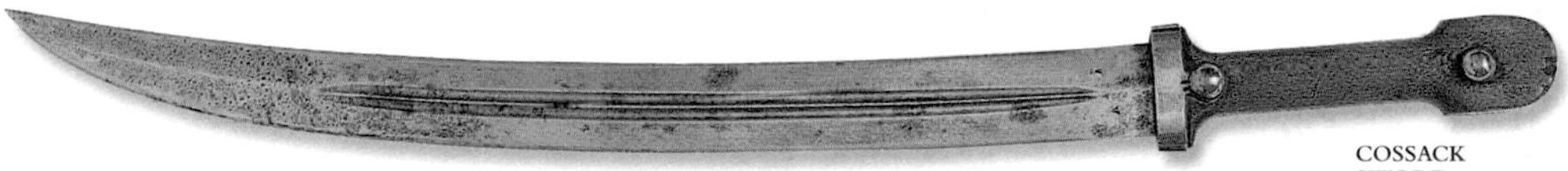

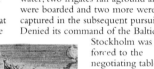

**COSSACK
SWORD**

STEPPE CLASS
The Cossacks were warrior horsemen armed with swords such as this shaska. They proved of little use as allies to Charles XII.

brought war between Sweden and Hanover to a close. The latter bought Bremen and Verden for one million thalers, while Prussia obtained part of Pomerania, including Stettin, for two million thalers. The Treaty of Rystad (1721). meanwhile, brought peace between Sweden and Russia and allotted the best part of Sweden's Baltic provinces to Peter, but Finland was restored to Sweden. Russia had now replaced Sweden as the great power in the Baltic and central and eastern Europe.

1492-1750

VICTORY BEACON
Peter the Great is shown here lighting a beacon to signal to his victorious fleet, in whose construction he had taken a great personal interest.

WARFARE IN THE AMERICAS

IN THE PRE-COLUMBIAN ERA—before the arrival of Europeans at the end of the 15th century—the Americas had their own history of warfare, most of it now difficult to reconstruct. Warfare was waged for conquest, to extract tribute, out of traditional rivalry between neighboring societies, or, perhaps above all, to win captives who might serve as slaves or as victims in ritual sacrifice. Battles were fought on foot, almost exclusively with weapons of wood and stone, but this simplicity of equipment did not prevent the creation of large empires such as those of the Aztecs and Incas.

PRE-COLUMBIAN WARFARE

In many pre-Columbian societies, being a warrior was synonymous with being a man—or at least, a man of any standing or repute. At the Aztec naming ceremony for a boy, a midwife would pronounce that he "belongs to the battlefield." The transition to manhood involved proving oneself as a warrior, especially by capturing high-status enemy fighters. The Aztecs were not exceptional in mostly aiming to cut at an enemy's legs, hoping to bring him down for capture rather than split his skull. But warfare was, nonetheless, at times totally destructive. Aztec codices speak of "wiping out all traces" of a particular society that had met with their displeasure.

AZTEC VICTIM
This image from an Aztec codex shows a warrior taking an enemy prisoner. Grabbing the enemy's hair was a traditional gesture enforcing submission.

YOUNG EMPIRES

Both the Inca and Aztec empires were creations of the 15th century, built by a series of wars in which other peoples were forced to accept tributary status. Their power was maintained by their swift and bloody suppression of any revolt against imperial authority. As imperial expansion ran out of steam, the levels of conflict naturally tended to decline, creating for the Aztecs the serious problem of a scarcity of enemies for their warriors to capture and their priests to sacrifice. They therefore instituted the extraordinary ritual of "flower wars," in which independent enclaves within the Aztec Empire, notably the Tlaxcala, were forced to make war on Aztec terms. These were not wars of destruction or invasion but Aztec prisoner-taking exercises.

FEATHER DEFENSE
Round shields, decorated like this one with jaguar skins and feathers, were carried by many warriors in pre-Columbian American societies.

KEY

■ Itzcoatl (1427–40)
■ Motecuzoma Ilhuicamina (1440–68)
■ Axayacatl (1469–81)
■ Ahuitzotl (1486–1502)
■ Motecuzoma Xocoyotl (1502–20)
→ Aztec transit route to Soconusco
■ independent northern states
● major post-Classic Maya center

AZTEC EMPIRE
By 1519 the Aztecs controlled most of central Mexico. A constant state of warfare served to provide tributes from neighboring states.

INCA EMPIRE
The Inca Empire emerged in less than a century. From 1470 the Incas ruled vast territories from their capital, Cuzco.

KEY

Expansion of the Inca Empire
■ by 1400
■ in reign of Pachacutec 1438–71
■ in reign of Tupac Yupanqui 1471–93
■ in reign of Huayna Capac 1493–1525
┈┈ border of Inca Empire 1525
── Inca road

EARLY MODERN WARFARE

EUROPEAN IMPACT

When Europeans arrived in the Americas after Columbus's voyage of 1492 their horses, steel weapons and armor, and gunpowder weapons (generally in small numbers) gave them clear-cut military advantages over all native peoples they encountered. They also had an attitude to warfare that was practical, ruthlessly aggressive, and decisive. And, above all else, they were unwittingly carrying diseases to which the Native Americans had no resistance. Even so, the conquest of the Aztec Empire by Hernán Cortés in 1521 was achieved only through alliance with subject peoples, and Francisco Pizarro's seizure of the Inca Empire was facilitated by an Inca civil war. In North America, where no such centralized empires existed, European settlers formed a different relationship with native peoples, sometimes in alliance, at other times hostile, but far from resting on absolute military superiority. American Indians adopted European imports such as the horse and firearms. In places such as Chile, where the Araucanians resisted, the Europeans had difficulty in establishing a foothold, let alone total control.

NATIVE DANDY
This 18th-century drawing depicts an Iroquois chieftain who has adopted European dress. The Iroquois fought alongside Europeans as well as against them.

AZTEC WEAPONS

Whether axes, clubs, or swords, Aztec weapons were made of wood studded on the edges or tip with razor-sharp flakes of obsidian or flint. These were supplemented by missile weapons such as bows and arrows and javelins, the latter given greater range by use of an *atlatl*, a lever that augmented the force of the hurling arm. For protection, warriors wore quilted armor, which was highly effective against arrows, and carried small shields. The inadequacy of the Aztecs' weaponry against people armed with metal was demonstrated even before the Europeans arrived when, in 1480, they were defeated by distant neighbors, the Tarascans, who had copper weapons.

Club known as a maquahuitl

Obsidian blades stud the edge of the club

Spear has spoon-shaped, bladed tip

Blades capable of inflicting deep cuts

INCA CONQUEST
Egged on by priests, conquistador Francisco Pizarro and his men overwhelm the Incas with pike and sword. The Incas also succumbed to the invaders' diseases.

PACIFYING JAPAN

FROM THE SECOND HALF OF THE 15th century, Japan was racked by war between feudal lords (*daimyo*). After European firearms were introduced in the 1540s, *daimyo* Oda Nobunaga established himself as the paramount power in the land. After Nobunaga's death in 1582 Toyotomi Hideyoshi went further, becoming ruler of virtually the whole nation. Hideyoshi began the disarming of the population but overreached himself in the 1590s by twice attempting to invade China through Korea. Tokugawa Ieyasu, who had not committed his men to Korea, was well placed to win power after Hideyoshi's death. The Tokugawa shogunate that he founded finally pacified Japan under firm central control, consigning the samurai to a life of leisure.

EARLY MODERN WARFARE

JAPANESE FEUDAL WARS
Okehazama

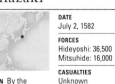

DATE
June 1560

FORCES
Yoshimoto: 25,000
Nobunaga: 3,000

CASUALTIES
Unknown

LOCATION Owari province, south-central Japan

This was the victory that made Oda Nobunaga's reputation. His territory was invaded by the army of Imagawa Yoshimoto, which set up camp in a steep, wooded valley. Nobunaga led his force through the woods and attacked from the north, putting the unprepared enemy to flight. In his tent, Yoshimoto was unaware what the noise outside signified. Nobunaga's men beheaded him almost before he realized he was under attack.

ODA NOBUNAGA
The first of the great unifiers of Japan, Nobunaga destroyed the power of the Buddhist warrior-monks.

JAPANESE FEUDAL WARS
Yamazaki

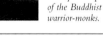

DATE
July 2, 1582

FORCES
Hideyoshi: 36,500
Mitsuhide: 16,000

CASUALTIES
Unknown

LOCATION By the village of Yamazaki, southwest of Kyoto

In 1582 one of Nobunaga's generals, Akechi Mitsuhide, forced Nobunaga to commit suicide and murdered his son and heir. In response, Toyotomi Hideyoshi, one of Nobunaga's most loyal supporters, force-marched an army toward Kyoto (where Mitsuhide had declared himself shogun) and occupied the Tennozan heights. There he fought Mitsuhide 13 days after Nobunaga's death. Hideyoshi's arquebusiers drove off all attempts to storm the heights, while his other men enveloped the enemy on both flanks. Defeated, Mitsuhide fled as far as the village of Ogurusu, where he was killed by bandits.

JAPANESE FEUDAL WARS
Nagashino

DATE
June 28, 1575

FORCES
Takeda: 15,000
Nobunaga: 38,000

CASUALTIES
Takeda: around 10,000 killed; Nobunaga: unknown

LOCATION Mikawa province, south-central Japan

Oda Nobunaga led a large army to relieve the castle of Magashino, besieged by Takeda Katsuyori. He took up a defensive position behind a stream, with his left wing anchored by a forest but his right wing open. In front of his forces he placed 3,000 arquebusiers, protected by a palisade. The Takeda charged, but Nobunaga's arquebusiers delivered rotating volleys to shattering effect. Those horsemen who reached the defensive line were held off by the long spears of Nobunaga's footsoldiers. His samurai emerged to engage the weakened Takeda with sword and spear in a melée that was especially fierce on the open right flank. Eventually the Takeda were put to flight and mercilessly pursued by samurai on horseback and archers on foot.

READY FOR BATTLE
Nobunaga's arquebusiers stand ready in the front line as the Takeda attack at Nagashino. Fire was opened at 165ft (50m).

> "While the enemy are still at a distance, the ko gashira distributes the bullets.... Subsequently the fuse will be inserted. This order will be given when they are about 1 cho (325ft) away. If the fuse is dropped in quickly or fitted badly, the fire will not continue and it may go out..."

WITNESS TO WAR
ZOHYO MONOGATARI

This advice to arquebusiers from a contemporary Japanese chronicle emphasizes the need to use firearms in a disciplined manner if they were to have proper effect.

JAPANESE FEUDAL WARS

Shiugatake

DATE
April 21, 1583

FORCES
Shibata Katsuie:
11,000; Toyotomi
Hideyoshi: 30,000

LOCATION On the
northern shore of
Lake Biwa

CASUALTIES
Shibata Katsuie: many
thousands killed

After his victory at Yamazaki, Toyotomi Hideyoshi fought to make himself the most powerful man in Japan. In April 1583 Shibata Katsuie, one of Oda Nobunaga's former followers, attacked a line of fortresses that Hideyoshi had built on high points north of Lake Biwa, including Shizugatake. Sakuma Morimasa, in command on the spot, was ordered by Shibata to withdraw when news arrived that Hideyoshi was heading for Shizugatake with a substantial army, but Sakuma decided to persist with the siege, believing Hideyoshi would take three days to arrive. Instead, he took less than 24

TOYOTOMI HIDEYOSHI
Sometimes called the "Napoleon of Japan", Hideyoshi was of humble birth but his military skills won him dictatorial power.

hours. Forced to adopt a hasty defensive posture, Sakuma was swiftly routed in a battle that gave seven of Hideyoshi's samurai, known as the Seven Spears of Shizugatake, a chance to distinguish themselves. Many of the routed troops were hacked down in a bloody pursuit through thick woods. Shibata Katsuie committed *seppuku* by the belly-cut, or *hara-kiri*.

JAPANESE FEUDAL WARS

Sekigahara

DATE
October 21, 1600

FORCES
Tokugawa Ieyasu:
80,000; Ishida
Mitsunari: 80,000

LOCATION
Northeast of Kyoto

CASUALTIES
Ishida Mitsunari: up to
60,000 killed

The death of Hideyoshi in 1598 set off an intense struggle for the succession in which Tokugawa Ieyasu faced an alliance led by Ishida Mitsunari. The two armies ran into one another at the village of Sekigahara, at a crossroads between three mountains. One of Ishida's allies, Kobayakawa Hideaki, was in a high flanking position. Ishida planned for Kobayakawa to attack Ieyasu from the flank and rear once battle was joined in the center. However, Kobayakawa had secretly agreed to betray Ishida. The battle was delayed by fog, but once it began Ishida gave the signal for Kobayakawa to attack Ieyasu's army. Instead, he attacked Ishida's flank, a blow from which the latter never recovered; the remnants of his army scattered, the reserve fleeing without a fight.

1542–1616

TOKUGAWA IEYASU

Until the defeat of Imagawa Yoshimoto in 1560, Tokugawa Ieyasu fought against Oda Nobunaga, but he then became Nobunaga's most loyal ally. He opposed Toyotomi Hideyoshi's rise to power after Nobunaga's death but managed a wary coexistence with Hideyoshi, cultivating his own power base at Edo (Tokyo). After his victory at Sekigahara, Ieyasu became shogun in 1603, founding a dynasty that ruled for 250 years.

JAPANESE FEUDAL WARS

Tennoji

DATE
May 7, 1615

FORCES
Toyotomi Hideyori:
55,000
Tokugawa Ieyasu:
150,000

LOCATION
Outside Osaka

CASUALTIES
Unknown

In 1614 Tokugawa Ieyasu's rule was contested by an alliance of *daimyo* gathered around Toyotomi Hideyoshi's son Hideyori. Thousands flocked to join Hideyori at his base in Osaka, including many *ronin* (masterless samurai). The battle of Tennoji was the climax of a long siege of Osaka Castle by Ieyasu's forces. Despite the odds against them, Hideyori and his allies chose to seek a decisive victory. Their plan was for forces under Sanada Yukimura to pin the enemy at the

front while Akashi Morishige attacked from the rear. Hideyori would then lead the castle garrison in a sortie to settle the issue. The plan went awry when impetuous ronin launched an all-out attack on Ieyasu's center, forcing Sanada to join in. For a while this boldness seemed to work. The aged Ieyasu, wading into the middle of the battle to firm up his wavering forces, was wounded by a spear thrust, but as the tide of battle turned, it was Sanada who was

killed. Akashi's encircling force was intercepted and never made its attack on the rear. Tokugawa forces penetrated Osaka Castle, driving Hideyori back into the keep, which they bombarded with cannons. His cause lost, Hideyori committed suicide.

THE SIEGE OF OSAKA CASTLE
Honda Tadatomo, one of Ieyasu's commanders, leads an attack on Osaka's defenders.

MANCHU CONQUEST

IN ABOUT 1610, NURHACI THE LEADER of a group of Jurchen hunters and pastoralists living north of the Great Wall, renounced his allegiance to the Chinese Ming dynasty. Within 30 years Nurhaci's successors had built up a powerful military organization of Jurchen, Mongol, and Chinese forces grouped into "banners." Calling themselves the Manchu, they were well placed to take advantage of the chronic decline of the Ming dynasty in China, where misgovernment and economic collapse provoked widespread revolts. The Manchu seized power in Beijing in 1644 with comparative ease, founding the Qing dynasty, but establishing their rule over all of China took hard fighting over many years.

MANCHU CONQUEST

Fall of Beijing

DATE	April–June 1644
FORCES	Manchu: around 170,000 men
LOCATION Beijing, northeast China	**CASUALTIES** No reliable estimates

By the 1640s, the Ming emperor Chongzhen was threatened from two sides: Chinese rebels led by Li Zicheng were in control of most of Shanxi, Henan, and Hubei provinces southwest of Beijing, while to the north of the Great Wall the Manchu had proclaimed a new dynasty. Li was one of thousands of ordinary Chinese who had drifted into revolt under the declining Ming Empire. The power of the Manchu had been rising for over 30 years. An able Ming general, Yuan Chonghuan, twice defeated attempted Manchu invasions of China in the 1620s, but the Manchu successfully invaded Korea in 1636–37, forcing the Koreans to switch allegiance from the Ming. Although many Chinese generals defected to the Manchu, Ming general Wu Sangui continued to block the crucial Shanhaiguan Pass. In the spring of 1644 Li led a large army across north China, gathering adherents as he went. In April his forces entered Beijing unopposed. Chongzhen, the last Ming emperor, hanged himself in a garden just outside the Forbidden City. Li's triumph was short-lived, however. Given the choice between low-born rebels and the well-organized Manchu, General Wu chose the Manchu. Now under a regent, Dogon, the Manchu banners flooded through the Shanhaiguan Pass and joined Wu in a showdown with Li. After a sharp battle south of the Great Wall, on June 6 the Manchu and Wu entered Beijing and the Qing dynasty took power.

MING TOMBS
This warrior statue (above) guards the entrance to the Ming tombs in Beijing (right). In 1635 Chinese rebel leader Li Zicheng looted some of the Ming burial grounds, a humiliating demonstration of the weakness of a declining dynasty.

MANCHU CONQUEST

Siege of Yangzhou

DATE	May 1645
FORCES	Numbers unknown
LOCATION Yangzhou, on the Grand Canal northeast of Nanjing	**CASUALTIES** Hundreds of thousands killed in Yangzhou massacre

After Emperor Chongzhen's suicide, surviving members of the Ming ruling family attempted to rally resistance to the Manchu invaders. One of them, the prince of Fu, was proclaimed emperor in Nanjing. In 1645 the Manchus sent a large army from Beijing and besieged the Ming-held city of Yangzhou. Ming troops defended the walls of the city with batteries of powerful cannons, but they held out for only a week. The Manchu had their own cannons, with which they shattered the walls, and their soldiers were almost suicidally fearless in the assault. When the city fell, it was sacked for 10 days in an orgy of killing.

YANGZHOU LAKE
The city of Yangzhou was a rich trading center with many fine buildings. It was extensively laid waste in the Manchu conquest.

SEIZURE OF TAIWAN

Koxinga seizes Taiwan

DATE	May 1661–February 1662
FORCES	Koxinga: possibly 200,000
LOCATION West coast of Taiwan, east of China	**CASUALTIES** No reliable estimates

Zheng Chenggong, known in the west as Koxinga, was a member of a wealthy family from coastal China. A Ming loyalist, he carried out attacks against the Qing with both land and sea forces. By the end of the 1650s, however, Qing armies were closing in on Koxinga's main base at the city of Amoy (Xiamen). Koxinga sailed his forces across to Taiwan and laid siege to the Dutch fortress of Zeelandia. The Dutch held out for nine months, despite being outnumbered 10 to one. After their surrender in February 1662 they were allowed to leave in peace. The Zheng family ruled over Taiwan until 1683, when the Qing finally launched a fleet of 300 warships and seized the island.

PIRATE AND TRADER
This is a Japanese image of Koxinga, who had a Japanese mother and a Chinese father. His wealthy family had made its money from trade and piracy.

MANCHU CONQUEST

War of the Three Feudatories

DATE
1673–81

FORCES
Numbers unknown

CASUALTIES
No reliable estimates

LOCATION
Various provinces,
southern China

In 1669 the 15-year-old Qing emperor Kangxi ousted the regent Oboi and took the reins of power. Kangxi's predecessors had accepted their inability to rule all of China, allowing three Chinese generals, known as "feudatories," to establish their own fiefdoms in the south and southwest of the country. Two of these, Shang Kexi and Geng Jimao, were Chinese

> "If my armies arrive and execute them all, this contradicts my desire to save the people."
>
> *Emperor Kangxi*, instructing his soldiers to spare rebels, 1681

bannermen—that is, they had joined the Manchu armies before the conquest of Beijing. The third was Wu Sangui, who had helped the Manchu to take power in 1644. This situation was unacceptable to the young Kangxi and he soon put pressure on the feudatories to renounce their domains. In 1673 Wu responded by proclaiming a new dynasty, the Zhou, and led an army from his southwestern base in Guizhou into Hunan. Geng and Shang Kexi's son, Shang Zhixin, both joined the rebellion, also pushing armies north toward the Yangtze. Kangxi had lost control of all of southern China, but the feudatories were riven by mutual suspicions and failed to coordinate their military operations. Kangxi's Manchu generals remained loyal and he was able to organize a counteroffensive. By 1677 both Geng and Shang had negotiated a surrender.

QING BANNER
This dragon banner belonged to a Qing cavalry formation. The "bannermen" were an elite group in Qing China, whether ethnically Jurchen, Mongol, or Chinese.

CHINESE–MONGOLIAN WAR

Jao Modo

DATE
1696

FORCES
Chinese: 80,000;
Zhungar: unknown

LOCATION
Mongolia, south of
Ulaanbaatar

CASUALTIES
No reliable estimates

In the second half of the 17th century the nomadic warriors of the Zunghar tribes in Outer Mongolia found an inspired leader in Galdan. In China, the Qing feared the rise of a new Mongol Empire and decided to take preemptive action. In 1696 three Chinese armies totaling 80,000 men marched westward. Qing Emperor Kangxi in person led an army across the Gobi desert, achieving a remarkable feat of logistical organization to keep them adequately supplied for an 80-day journey. The Qing forces drove the Zunghars back behind the Kerulen River and then brought them to battle at Jao Modo. With Chinese artillery playing an important role, the Zhungars were decisively defeated. Galdan died the following year.

SINO–RUSSIAN WAR

Albazin

DATE
1685–86

FORCES
Chinese: possibly
10,000;
Russian: a few
hundred

LOCATION On the Amur
River, northern
Manchuria

CASUALTIES
Unknown

With the defeat of the feudatories in 1681 and the capture of Taiwan from the Zheng family in 1683, Qing emperor Kangxi was free to turn his attention to establishing China's borders. Throughout the 17th century Russia had been expanding across Asia through a combination of military expeditions and the enterprise of hunters and traders, who around the middle of the century penetrated territory traditionally regarded by the Chinese as within their own sphere of influence. Qing attention focused on the stockaded Russian settlement of Albazin on the Amur River. Deciding that this constituted an unacceptable intrusion into his territory, Kangxi had a substantial force sent to attack the outpost. This included some of the Zhengs' followers recently defeated in Taiwan, who supplied valuable naval expertise for navigating the northern rivers. The expedition also had improved cannons developed under the supervision of Father Ferdinand Verbiest, a Jesuit missionary at the court of Kangxi. After some sharp fighting, the garrison at Albazin was obliged to surrender. The Russians were allowed to withdraw to Nerchinsk, but once the Chinese army had gone they returned to harvest crops they had planted and reoccupy the fort. The result was further intense fighting the following year. The Russians recognized, however, that in the long run they had little hope of sustaining outposts in the face of sustained military action. In 1689, under the Treaty of Nerchinsk, the Russians agreed to abandon Albazin and withdraw north of the Amur River.

CHINESE BLADE
A typical Chinese infantry weapon of the 16th and 17th centuries. Although the Manchu were horsemen, infantry and artillery dominated Chinese warfare.

IMPERIAL NAVY
Chinese troops disembark during a visit by Emperor Kangxi to Kiang-Han in 1699. Naval power played a part in the Albazin operation.

EMPIRES AND REVOLUTIONS

1750–1914

THE RISE OF MODERN WARFARE

BETWEEN 1750 AND 1914 European armies and those of countries founded by European settlement, such as the United States, achieved an unquestionable preeminence in military technology and organization. An ever wider gulf opened up between those forces that adopted western methods and armaments and those that did not—Japan being the only nonwestern country to cross this divide decisively. Mass armies, new firearms, and new forms of transportation and communication allowed western states to extend their rule over much of the planet.

Many wars in the 18th and 19th centuries crossed continents and created modern nations. The Seven Years War (1756–63), which opens this period, has been called the first true "world war," because its European combatants fought in India and North America as well as in Europe itself. Warfare was central to the creation of the United States, from the Revolutionary War (1775–83) against British rule through the wars against Mexico and American Indian peoples to the Civil War (1861–65). In Europe, the great convulsions of the French revolutionary and Napoleonic wars (1792–1815) were followed by a century of more limited but still decisive conflicts, which brought Germany and Italy into being as nation-states. Elsewhere, many wars occurred when western powers imposed their rule on Asian or African peoples, such as the British in India and east Africa and the French in Southeast Asia and west Africa.

MOBILE FIREPOWER
Artillery such as this field cannon played a pivotal role in the Civil War.

UNIFORM DISCIPLINE
By the mid-18th century European countries had uniformed, strictly hierarchical, and professional armies, for which the Prussians under Frederick the Great set the standard. Infantry armed with flintlock muskets and bayonets, and trained to fight in strict lines, squares, or columns, formed the core of the army. Often recruited from the dregs of society, the soldiers were disciplined by draconian punishments, although attempts were also made to inspire them with regimental pride. Cavalry remained the elite arm, executing functions such as screening, reconnaissance, and shock charge, while artillery had become a vital, fully mobile part of armies on the battlefield. Yet the Revolutionary War showed the potential vulnerability of a professional European army in difficult terrain and against an irregular enemy. As they became aware of the limitations of formally disciplined formations, the European powers recruited irregular skirmishing cavalry, often

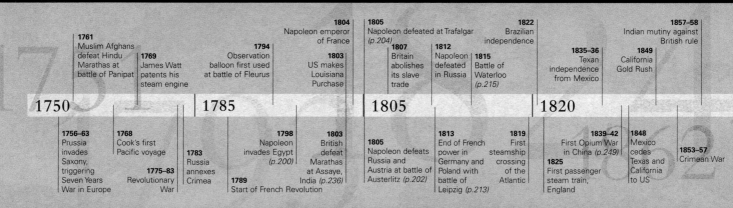

1761
Muslim Afghans defeat Hindu Marathas at battle of Panipat

1769
James Watt patents his steam engine

1794
Observation balloon first used at battle of Fleurus

1804
Napoleon emperor of France

1803
US makes Louisiana Purchase

1805
Napoleon defeated at Trafalgar *(p.204)*

1807
Britain abolishes its slave trade

1812
Napoleon defeated in Russia

1815
Battle of Waterloo *(p.215)*

1822
Brazilian independence

1835–36
Texan independence from Mexico

1849
California Gold Rush

1857–58
Indian mutiny against British rule

1750   **1785**   **1805**   **1820**

1756–63
Prussia invades Saxony, triggering Seven Years War in Europe

1768
Cook's first Pacific voyage

1775–83
Revolutionary War

1783
Russia annexes Crimea

1789
Start of French Revolution

1798
Napoleon invades Egypt *(p.200)*

1803
British defeat Marathas at Assaye, India *(p.236)*

1805
Napoleon defeats Russia and Austria at battle of Austerlitz *(p.202)*

1813
End of French power in Germany and Poland with battle of Leipzig *(p.213)*

1819
First steamship crossing of the Atlantic

1825
First passenger steam train, England

1839–42
First Opium War in China *(p.249)*

1848
Mexico cedes Texas and California to US

1853–57
Crimean War

HMS VICTORY, 1778–1812   **NAPOLEON BONAPARTE, 1769–1821**   **THE ALAMO, TEXAS, 1836**

from ethnic minorities in their empires, such as the Cossacks in Russia, and developed rifle sharpshooters and skirmishers.

CITIZEN ARMIES

Although there was no dramatic technological progress in warfare between the mid-18th and mid-19th centuries, in the 1790s the French Revolution ushered in a new type of army: the mass conscript force inspired by nationalism. It also brought a new dynamism to the battlefield, typified by Napoleon Bonaparte's use of rapid maneuvers and his search for decisive victories through the destruction of enemy forces. By the 19th century citizen armies raised by universal conscription had become the norm, at least in mainland Europe. Military service was regarded as a right and a duty, a school for patriotism and a force for national integration.

EXPLOSIVE TECHNOLOGY

Around 1850 a transformation of warfare began, linked to developments in precision machinery and mass production. The invention of the Minié bullet allowed the first effective rifled muskets to emerge—muskets with spiral grooves inside the barrel that made a bullet spin and so increased the weapon's range and accuracy. By the late 19th century mass-produced breech-loading rifles came into existence, firing metal cartridges that soldiers fitted into the breech (rear) of the gun instead of the muzzle.

Machine guns, revolvers, and repeater rifles were soon widely adopted. Gunpowder was superseded by various new forms of high explosive; artillery firing high explosive shells replaced solid shot. Railroads revolutionized the speed of mobilization and movement of mass armies, while communications were transformed, first by the telegraph and then by the telephone and the radio. At sea, ironclad steam-driven battleships ended the reign of the wooden ships of the line. Warfare tentatively rose into the sky with balloons and early aircraft, and dived under the sea with early submarines.

WAR AND PEACE

The Civil War showed how destructive modern warfare was likely to be if pursued to the limit by irreconcilable enemies. Responding to this changed reality, the western world was inspired by a new ideal of peace in this period, with self-conscious attempts to limit and even outlaw war, ranging from the first Geneva Convention in 1864, concerning treatment of the wounded, to the various agreements of the Hague Peace Conferences of 1899 and 1907. But this ideal was not enough: the creation of mass armies, backed by efficient arms industries and inspired by a virulent patriotism, paved the way for the mass slaughter of World War I.

REVOLUTION AND WAR
Liberty Leading the People is by the French artist Eugène Delacroix. The ramifications of the French Revolution were felt throughout Europe and beyond, and influenced the rise of mass armies based on universal conscription.

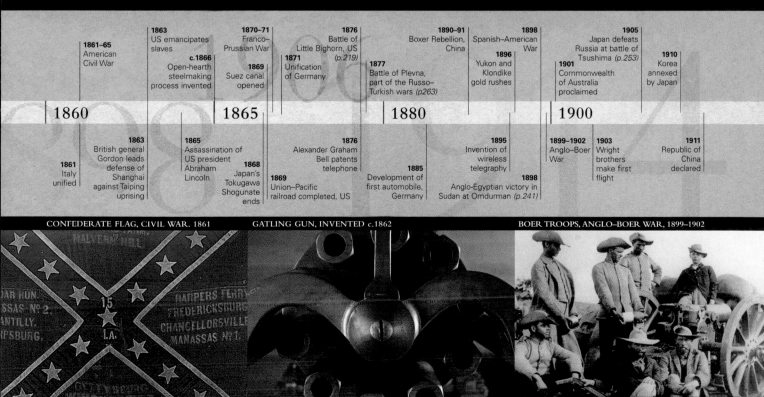

1861–65 American Civil War	**1863** US emancipates slaves	**1870–71** Franco–Prussian War	**1876** Battle of Little Bighorn, US *(p.219)*	**1890–91** Boxer Rebellion, China	**1898** Spanish–American War	**1905** Japan defeats Russia at battle of Tsushima *(p.253)*
	c.1866 Open-hearth steelmaking process invented	**1869** Suez canal opened	**1871** Unification of Germany	**1877** Battle of Plevna, part of the Russo–Turkish wars *(p263)*	**1896** Yukon and Klondike gold rushes	**1901** Commonwealth of Australia proclaimed	**1910** Korea annexed by Japan

1860 **1865** **1880** **1900**

1861 Italy unified	**1863** British general Gordon leads defense of Shanghai against Taiping uprising	**1865** Assassination of US president Abraham Lincoln	**1868** Japan's Tokugawa Shogunate ends	**1876** Alexander Graham Bell patents telephone	**1895** Invention of wireless telegraphy	**1899–1902** Anglo–Boer War	**1903** Wright brothers make first flight	**1911** Republic of China declared
		1869 Union–Pacific railroad completed, US	**1885** Development of first automobile, Germany	**1898** Anglo-Egyptian victory in Sudan at Omdurman *(p.241)*		

CONFEDERATE FLAG, CIVIL WAR, 1861 | GATLING GUN, INVENTED c.1862 | BOER TROOPS, ANGLO–BOER WAR, 1899–1902

Map labels:
James Bay · Wolfe 1759 · Gulf of St. Lawrence · 1758 Louisbourg · Fort Ticonderoga 1758: Montcalm captures fort 1759: Recaptured by Amherst · Montreal Sep 8. 1760: City surrenders to besieging British forces · Quebec Sep 13, 1759: Wolfe captures Quebec · Fort Beausejour 1755 · Fort St. John · Halifax · Amherst 1758 · NEW FRANCE · Fort William Henry 1755: Henry Johnson establishes fort 1756: Montcalm captures fort · St. Francis · Lake Champlain · Crown Point · MAINE · Gulf of Maine · Lake Superior · Fort Frontenac 1758: Captured by Bradstreet · Lake Huron · Fort Oswego 1756: Destroyed by French 1759: Captured by British · Lake Ontario · Albany · Fort Niagara 1759: Captured by British · NEW ENGLAND · NEW HAMPSHIRE · Boston · MASSACHUSETTS · Cape Cod · NEW YORK · CONN. · RHODE ISLAND · Lake Michigan · Fort Detroit · Lake Erie · Fort Augusta · Long Island · New York · NEW JERSEY · Philadelphia · PENNSYLVANIA · Fort Duquesne July 9, 1755: French defeat Braddock at Monongahela river and build fort 1758: Captured by British · Fort Necessity 1754 · Baltimore · Braddock 1755 · MARYLAND · DELAWARE · Alexandria · Ohio · Chesapeake Bay · Williamsburg · VIRGINIA · Norfolk · NORTH CAROLINA · N · 0 km 200 400 · 0 miles 200 400

KEY

- British town
- French town
- British fort
- French fort
- French ring of defense
- British line of attack
- French line of attack
- British victory
- French victory

THE SEVEN YEARS WAR

THE SEVEN YEARS WAR IS SOMETIMES described as the first true world war. All the great powers of Europe were involved, and fighting took place in Europe, North America, Asia, and Africa, as well as at sea. The war arose out of an Austrian attempt to regain the province of Silesia, recently occupied by Prussia. A transformation of European alliances left Prussia facing France, Austria, Russia, and others. Prussia's only ally was Britain, which provided some subsidies and a few troops while putting pressure on the French. But Britain's chief interest lay in the contest with France for maritime and colonial dominance. In Europe Prussia held out against its enemies, though at great cost, and Britain wrested power from the French in Canada and India.

ARMIES

In the mid-18th century European armies were still relatively small, and made up of mercenary troops fighting for wages. Prussia's survival in the war against huge odds was based on its strong military tradition. Many Prussian officers were recruited from descendants of the Teutonic Knights, a military order that had ruled medieval Prussia. The Prussian army was a well-drilled, national (not mercenary) army, with a system of selected conscription that provided ready-trained reserves. Strict discipline enabled them to move fast to attack the enemy at its weakest point with a barrage of howitzer fire. Soldiers knew their profession: officers were trained in military academies, gunners were expert mathematicians.

THE FRENCH AND INDIAN WAR
During the Seven Years War, the age-old rivalry between England and France became a battle for territory in the New World.

STYLISH UNIFORMS
In headgear like this, made for style rather than comfort, British soldiers climbed steep cliffs to attack Quebec.

CAVALRY WARS
Cavalry swords or sabers (with slightly curved, slashing blades) were used in the Seven Years War. These examples are French (left) and British (right). Their design was influenced by earlier Turkish weapons.

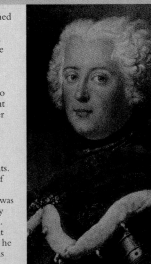

1712–1786

FREDERICK THE GREAT

Frederick II of Prussia, who reigned 1740-86, was highly cultured, a good musician, an art lover, and a friend of philosophers. Though he became a national hero for his successful military campaigns in Europe, his reputation as a great tactical genius has since come into question. He fought some brilliant campaigns, especially in 1757 after his capital had been sacked by foreign troops, and won great victories, but at such cost in manpower that he eventually employed reluctant foreign recruits. He understood the importance of mobility—he is credited with introducing horse artillery—and was a skillful strategist, but his military system was basically conventional. His biggest asset was the excellent quality of his soldiers. After 1763 he devoted his efforts to restoring his shattered country and army.

THE COLONIES

The campaigns of the war that were fought overseas resulted in overwhelming victory for Britain against its chief rival, France, which was fighting a costly war in Europe at the same time. Britain became the world's dominant maritime and imperial power, but this position came at a cost. Defense was expensive—Britain's national debt doubled during the Seven Years War—and efforts to persuade American colonists to pay for their own defense after the extensive campaigns pursued in North America provoked them to claim independence, which they eventually won. The Americans' success encouraged ideas of liberty and equality in Europe, especially France, but after the chaos of the French Revolution France reemerged as Europe's greatest military power under Napoleon. Prussia lay devastated in 1763, but recovered quickly. Russia, which saved Prussia by changing sides in 1762, was established as a great power.

THE FRENCH AND INDIAN WAR

THE SERIES OF CONFLICTS from the Seven Years War that took place in North America is known as the French and Indian War. Clashes had been going on for years between British and French settlers, who were trying to expand southward into the Ohio valley from "New France" (Canada). Both sides had allies among the American Indian nations. In 1758 a British expedition captured Fort Louisbourg on Cape Breton Island, then launched an ambitious attack on Quebec. When Montreal also fell, Britain controlled most of Canada. Thanks to their naval superiority, the British also captured the valuable Caribbean "sugar island" of Guadeloupe (returned at the 1763 Treaty of Paris), and gained Florida from France's European ally, Spain.

THE FRENCH AND INDIAN WAR

Quebec

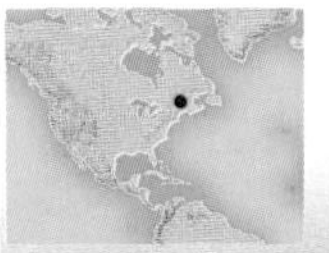

DATE
September 13, 1759

FORCES
British: 4,800;
French: 4,000

CASUALTIES
British: 658 killed;
French: 644 killed

LOCATION The plains of
Abraham outside
Quebec City

The capture of Louisbourg in 1758 opened up the St. Lawrence River and the capital of "New France," the city of Quebec, to the British forces. But the British feared that the French, under a greatly respected commander, the Marquis de Montcalm, could only be overcome by a long siege of the city, which the British could hardly sustain. A powerful British fleet conveyed about 8,000 troops under the 32-year-old General James Wolfe up the St. Lawrence. Several attempts at a landing below the city failed, but Wolfe seized Point Lévis on the opposite bank of the river, from which he was able to bombard the city. Some weeks later he decided to land the main body of his men at a cove discovered by his scouts upriver from Quebec. He led them up the Heights of Abraham by climbing the cliffs, about 165ft (50m) high. By moving at night they surprised the French; the actual pitched battle on level ground west of the city was brief, lasting less than an hour. Both commanders, Wolfe and Montcalm, were killed in the fighting. The city formally surrendered to the British a few days later.

DEFEAT OF NEW FRANCE
The taking of Quebec by the English, shown here in a near-contemporary engraving, heralded the end of France's attempt to dominate North America.

THE FRENCH AND INDIAN WAR

Pontiac's Rebellion

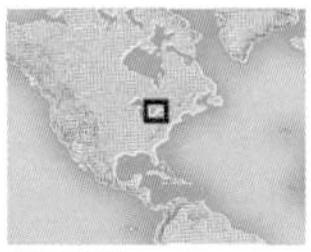

DATE 1763

FORCES
British/American
colonial militia; a
varying confederation
of native peoples

LOCATION
The Great Lakes
region

CASUALTIES Settlers
and traders: c.200;
Indians: unknown

Events in Canada convinced many American Indians that the British were a greater threat to their independence than the French, and they resented the British decision to discontinue the French custom of distributing gifts. Led by an Ottawa chief, Pontiac, the uprising began near Detroit, spread east, and became a loose association of nations including the Delaware, Shawnee, and Seneca. Attacks on British forts in the Great Lakes region resulted in eight being captured and the British supply line across Lake Erie was broken, but Fort Pitt (Pittsburgh) and Fort Detroit held out successfully. The rising disintegrated after the French surrender.

PRISONERS OF WAR
The peace treaty compelled the Indians to surrender all prisoners to Colonel Bouquet, who led the expedition that freed Fort Pitt.

THE FRENCH AND INDIAN WAR

Monongaleha River

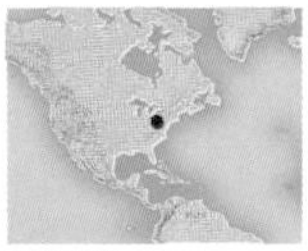

DATE July 9, 1755

FORCES
British and colonials:
1,500; French and
Indians: 900

LOCATION
Near the Forks of
the Ohio River

CASUALTIES British and
colonials: 876 killed;
French: 56 killed;
Indians: 40 killed

When the fighting began between British and French settlers in 1754, the 79-year-old General Edward Braddock was appointed British commander-in-chief in North America. His aide-de-camp was George Washington, who would later take command in the Revolutionary War and become the first president of the United States. Braddock planned a four-part offensive against the French in 1755 that included a march to take Fort Duquesne (now the city of Pittsburgh). About 9 miles (14km) south of the fort, the advance unit under Lieutenant Colonel Thomas Gage stumbled on the French and Indians on the banks of the Monongaleha River. After a brief engagement Gage retreated, only to collide with the main British force, which was coming up rapidly after hearing gunshots. While Braddock and his officers, who seem to have performed poorly in the battle, strove to reform their troops, the French and Indians inflicted heavy casualties from the surrounding woods. When Braddock himself was mortally wounded after the fighting had been going on for three hours, the British troops fled. Before withdrawing they burned about 150 wagons of their own equipment. As the demoralized British troops still outnumbered the French and Indian enemy, they were not pursued. However, the shocking defeat at Monongaleha sowed doubts about British military effectiveness.

WAR IN EUROPE AND INDIA

THE SEVEN YEARS WAR INCLUDED SEVERAL virtually separate conflicts around the world. The common denominator in the European and Indian Wars was that in both France was a major contestant and in both France was the loser. Prussia's great victories of 1757 ruined France's military reputation, after a century of almost continual military success, and it was not restored until the French revolutionary wars of the 1790s. In India, both the French and the English were a tiny proportion of the total population and depended on local alliances as much as superior military technology. As in North America, Britain's command of the sea, which deprived the French of reinforcements, ultimately dictated the British victory.

THE SEVEN YEARS WAR IN EUROPE

Rossbach

DATE	November 5, 1757
FORCES	French and Austrians: 42,000; Prussians: 21,000
LOCATION Near Leipzig, Germany	**CASUALTIES** French and Austrians: 7,700 killed; Prussians: 550 killed

After suffering defeat at Kolin in June 1757 and Gross-Jägersdorf in July, Frederick the Great of Prussia prepared to tackle the French–Austrian army at Rossbach in November, commanded by the Prince de Soubise. By the time of the battle Soubise's army was in poor shape and incapable of defeating a Prussian army half its size. The French and Austrians began well but came to grief when they attempted to march around the Prussian left, failing to notice that Frederick had turned his army around to meet them. A ferocious cavalry attack swept through the Franco–Austrian forces, swiftly followed by the Prussian infantry, which completed a devastating victory in about 15 minutes' fighting.

A LESSON LEARNED
The Prussian defeat of the French at Rossbach led eventually to reforms in the French army.

THE SEVEN YEARS WAR IN EUROPE

Leuthen

DATE	December 5, 1757
FORCES	Austrians: 60,000; Prussians: 36,000
LOCATION Silesia, modern-day Poland	**CASUALTIES** Austrians: 9,500 killed, 12,000 taken prisoner; Prussians: 2,300 killed

After Rossbach, Frederick was anxious to expel a second Austrian army, commanded by the empress's brother-in-law, Prince Charles of Lorraine, from Silesia, the immensely valuable province that he had seized from Austria in 1740. The battle of Leuthen is regarded as Frederick's outstanding performance, "a masterpiece of movement, maneuver, and resolve," according to Napoleon. The Austrians held a strong position centered on the village of Leuthen, with a front nearly 5 miles (8km) wide and their flanks protected by swampy ground. Frederick feigned an attack on the Austrian right, where all attention was concentrated while, partly hidden by a ridge, he advanced on their left.

MUSKET
Short Land Pattern Muskets, such as this example dated 1747, would probably have been used by dragoons.

South of Lobetinz, he completed a rapid redeployment with such parade-ground despatch that it attracted jeers from enemy observers. The move placed his troops facing the Austrians' southern flank. The Austrian reaction was too slow; their cavalry had been moved to what was assumed to be the threatened right. At Leuthen the Austrians stood 100 deep but could not stop the determination and courage of their attackers and were decimated by Frederick's "walking batteries" of robotic infantry. Silesia was saved, the defeated Austrians withdrew to Bohemia, and an angry Empress Maria Theresa removed Prince Charles from his post.

WINTER BATTLE
The battle of Leuthen was fought in snowy conditions. This painting depicts a Prussian charge with an officer and grenadiers at the village of Leuthen.

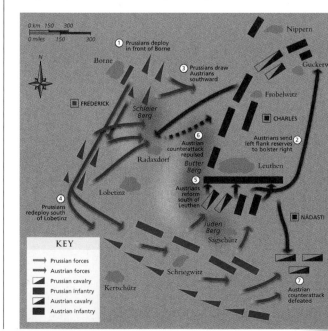

Nippern

① Prussians deploy in front of Borne

Borne

③ Prussians draw Austrians southward

Guckerwitz

■ FREDERICK

Schleier Berg

Frobelwitz

■ CHARLES

⑥ Austrian counterattack repulsed

② Austrians send left flank reserves to bolster right

Radaxdorf

Butter Berg

Leuthen

⑤ Austrians reform south of Leuthen

Lobetinz

④ Prussians redeploy south of Lobetinz

■ NÁDASTI

Juden Berg

Sagschütz

Schriegwitz

Kertschütz

⑦ Austrian counterattack defeated

KEY
→ Prussian forces
→ Austrian forces
Prussian cavalry
Prussian infantry
Austrian cavalry
Austrian infantry

Minden

DATE August 1, 1759

FORCES British and Hanoverians: 37,000; French: 44,000

CASUALTIES British and Hanoverians: 2,800 killed; French: 7,000 killed, 8,000 taken prisoner

LOCATION Westphalia, 44 miles (28km) west of Hanover

In July 1759 French forces under the Duc de Broglie and the Marquis de Contades captured the town of Minden and the bridge over the Weser River in Westphalia. The commander of the British and Hanoverian army, Prince Ferdinand of Brunswick, could not contemplate a frontal assault, since the French were well entrenched, but with raids on communications he attempted to provoke Contades into advancing. After some skirmishing and an artillery exchange at dawn, battle began. It was closely contested until a British brigade, acting on a mistaken order, advanced toward the French cavalry, which was protected by artillery crossfire. Such was the British momentum that they scattered the cavalry and continued against the infantry. The British cavalry was then ordered into action but, for unknown reasons, the commander Lord George Sackville failed to obey. Nevertheless, enough damage had been done, and after the British artillery had moved up front with surprising speed, the French retreated in disorder, losing many men and abandoning 40 guns. Sackville was discharged and the verdict read out to every British regiment "so that," said British prime minister William Pitt, "officers may be convinced that neither high birth nor great employment can shelter offences of such a nature."

Quiberon Bay

DATE November 20, 1759

FORCES British ships of the line: 23; French ships: 21

LOCATION Off the French coast between Lorent and St. Nazaire

CASUALTIES British: 2 ships lost; French: 8 ships lost or captured

The battle of Quiberon Bay was one of the most brilliant victories in British naval history. It was achieved by Sir Edward Hawke, who was famous for his success against the French off Cape Finisterre in 1747. The French had been planning to invade Britain and, although by this time such a plan was hardly practicable, they had collected transports at the mouth of the Loire. Hawke was sent to blockade Brest, where the French fleet of Admiral de Conflans was under orders to proceed to the Loire. A storm forced Hawke to seek shelter at Torbay in early November. A West Indies squadron joined de Conflans at Brest, and the enlarged French fleet left on November 14. Hawke turned in pursuit and caught them at the tricky entrance to Quiberon Bay. In poor light and sharp squalls, he boldly followed the French, who had pilots, into this dangerous bay. The French

> ## "All that could possibly be done has been done."
>
> *Edward Hawke*, November 1759

had lost four ships before nightfall but in the darkness two British ships were grounded. The French flagship, *Soleil Royal*, was also lost. Several French ships escaped into the Vilaine River, where they were long confined, and the remaining eight managed to escape to Rochefort. The battle negated any remaining possibility of an invasion and drastically weakened the French navy for the rest of the war.

HAWKE'S ATTACK
The British fleet fired on the French in Quiberon Bay on November 20, 1759. Even the French expressed admiration for Hawke's courage and seamanship.

Plassey

DATE June 23, 1757

FORCES British and East India Company troops: 3,000; troops of the Nawab of Bengal, including French gunners: 55,000

LOCATION Bengal on the Bhagirathi River, India

CASUALTIES British: 65; Bengalis: unknown

In 1756 the Nawab (governor) of Bengal, Suraj ud-Daula, captured the British settlement of Calcutta after a disagreement concerning defenses constructed without his permission. Irritated by British abuse of their trading privileges, the Nawab was also fearful of alien domination. A number of British prisoners (allegedly 146) were shut up overnight in a small cell. About 21 (far fewer than the number claimed by the British) died in this "Black Hole of Calcutta." Troops commanded by Robert Clive sailed from Madras and quickly recaptured Calcutta. The Nawab was forced to sign a treaty reconfirming British trading rights, but he was clearly unreconciled and plotting with the French. With the support of Hindu Bengalis, the British decided to replace him with Mir Jafar, a more compliant potentate. In the ensuing battle at Plassey Clive was outnumbered and also outgunned, as the Nawab had a unit of French artillery. However, many of the Nawab's commanders had been suborned by the British during preliminary "negotiations." Clive called a council of war where a majority opposed fighting but were overborne by the aggression of Major Eyre Coote. The battle itself was soon over, as most of the Nawab's commanders prevaricated. One exception was Mir Mudin, who made a disastrous cavalry charge and was killed. Ordinary soldiers unaware of their officers' disloyalty made a furious but unavailing charge, and the Nawab lost an artillery duel because rain dampened his powder. Clive then made a direct attack on the Nawab's defenses, and resistance crumbled. The victory made the British masters of Bengal, from where, eventually, they ruled most of India.

PUPPET LEADER
After the battle of Plassey, Robert Clive's dominance of Bengal was absolute. He installed the Indian general Mir Jafar (on the right) as nominal leader, but kept him under tight control.

ROBERT CLIVE

A clerk for the East India Company in Madras at 18, Clive later volunteered for military service. His capture of Arcot in 1751 made him famous and he stood unsuccessfully for Parliament before returning to Madras as a colonel in the regular army. The battle of Plassey made him effectively ruler of Bengal. He became a baron in the Irish peerage, but his difficult temperament made him many enemies. Accused of corruption as governor of Bengal in the 1760s, he was acquitted but later committed suicide.

THE EVOLUTION OF FIREARMS

EFFECTIVE FIREARMS evolved in the 1400s through two innovations: a wooden stock to help the firer hold the gun barrel and absorb the recoil, and "lock" mechanisms enabling a bullet to be fired on pressing a trigger. Until the 1800s most firearms were muzzle-loading. A soldier used a ramrod to push a ball and powder down the gun barrel and set off the charge by igniting the powder.

MATCHLOCKS

The earliest firing mechanism was the matchlock. Before stocks were carved to fit the shoulder, early matchlocks—known as arquebuses—were held against the chest when firing. From the mid-16th century the arquebus was superseded by the musket, which originally had to be propped on a forked rest to fire.

BRITISH MATCHLOCK MUSKET, c.1640

MATCHLOCK MUSKET
Matchlocks often failed to fire and were unusable in wet weather. The need for a flame in proximity to gunpowder was dangerous.

GERMAN PISTOL
Pistols such as this one were used by cavalry in the Thirty Years War (1618–48).

Cock holding iron pyrites

Serrated wheel wound against spring

Butt

Trigger releases wheel

GERMAN WHEEL-LOCK PISTOL, c.1640

WOODEN RAMROD

NORTH EUROPEAN WHEEL-LOCK PISTOL, c.17TH CENTURY

Brass and mother-of-pearl inlaid stock

WHEEL-LOCK PISTOL, 1590

Trigger guard

Cock or "dog"

EARLY PISTOLS
As expensive weapons, wheel-lock pistols were often ornately decorated. To fire, the cock with the iron pyrites was pulled down against the sprung wheel, which spun when the firer squeezed the trigger, firing sparks.

Ivory butt-cap

WHEEL-LOCKS

The wheel-lock mechanism, invented in the early 16th century, did away with the need for a match (actually a slow-burning cord) to ignite the priming powder. Instead, as in a modern cigarette lighter, a revolving toothed wheel caused a spark through friction with a piece of iron pyrite. Wheel-locks appealed to cavalry since firing a matchlock while riding a horse was tricky. But the mechanism was expensive and rather delicate, making it unsuitable for widespread use in military firearms.

PRUSSIAN FLINTLOCK CARBINE, c.1750

Iron barrel

Brass butt-cap

BRITISH MUSKET, c.1746

Flint held in jaws of cock

MATCHLOCK MECHANISM

This matchlock musket shows the match—a slow-burning rope—held by a curved lock called a serpentine. When the trigger was pulled the serpentine swiveled the match into the pan, igniting the priming powder that, in turn, set off the charge in the barrel.

Pulling trigger swivels rope into pan

Pan cover opened before firing

Slow-burning rope

GERMAN MATCHLOCK MUSKET, EARLY 17TH CENTURY

MUSKET FIRE

A soldier usually fired standing upright, managing about three shots a minute. Muskets were inaccurate—firing at any target over 330ft (100m) away was pointless—but devastating fired in volleys against advancing infantry.

FLINTLOCKS

From the late 1600s through to the 1830s the flintlock mechanism predominated. The priming powder was ignited by a flint, held in the gun's cock, striking against steel. The cock was set in a safety position—half-cock—when loading, and pulled back to full cock before firing. By the 18th century paper cartridges, containing the powder and ball for a single shot, were standard. The soldier bit off the end of the cartridge and rammed powder, ball, and paper down the barrel.

Box-lock type flintlock mechanism

DOUBLE-BARRELLED POCKET PISTOL, c.1785

CAUCASIAN PISTOL, 18TH CENTURY

Embossed silverwork

HOWDAH PISTOL, c.1850

PRUSSIAN CARBINE

This flintlock carbine was used by Prussian cuirassiers— heavy cavalry—during the Seven Years War (1756–63). Cavalrymen preferred carbines to muskets because they had shorter barrels and were lighter.

FLINTLOCK PISTOLS

The flintlock mechanism replaced the wheel-lock in pistols from the mid-17th century, before it replaced the matchlock in muskets. Even the best flintlocks often failed to fire, producing only a "flash in the pan."

Ramrod fits underneath barrel

Wooden stock stops before the end of the barrel to accommodate a bayonet

SOCKET BAYONET

MUSKET AND BAYONET

The Long Land Pattern flintlock was the standard British musket of the 18th century. A socket bayonet fit on the end of the barrel (bayonets had made pikes redundant).

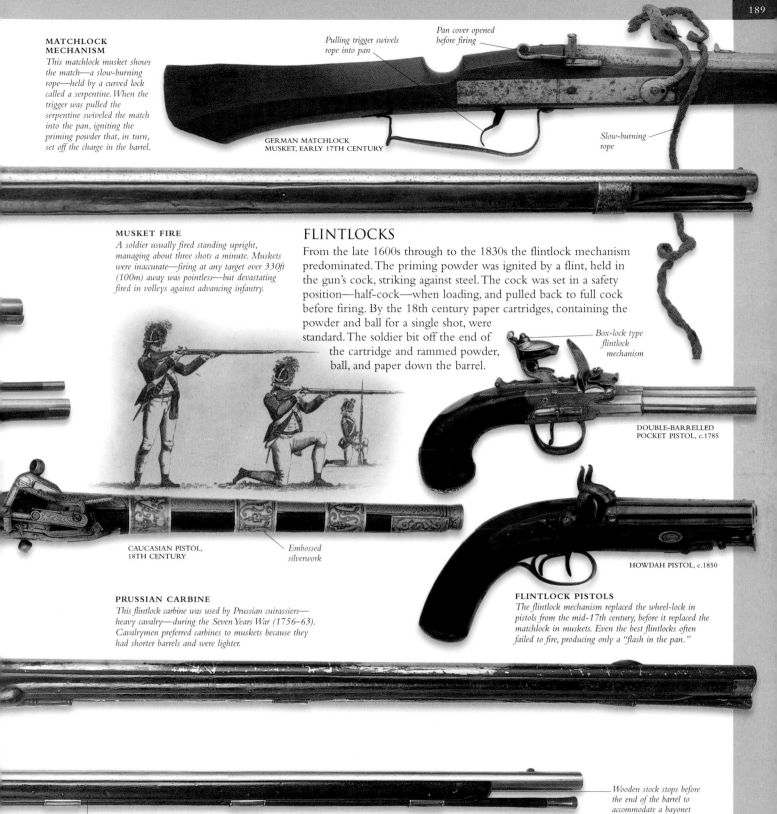

THE AMERICAN REVOLUTION

THE AMERICAN REVOLUTION, or Revolutionary War, had profound effects on world history. It foreshadowed the European revolutions of the 18th and 19th centuries, and to this day is synonymous with the struggle against oppression. It began as a protest against taxation and ended with the severance of Britain from its colonies, an event that shocked the world. The rupture was largely caused by pressure from the British, who miscalculated the colonists' loyalty to their mother country. In 1770 most colonists were happy to remain British, but they demanded some form of representative government.

SNIPER
An American sniper picks off a redcoat. The British considered such tactics cowardly.

KEY

■	the Thirteen Colonies **1763**
■	Indian Reserve **1763**
■	Quebec **1763–74**
■	Quebec under Quebec Act **1774**
■	other British possessions
■	Spanish territory
—	Proclamation line **1763**
✕	American victory
✕	British victory

REVOLUTIONARY WAR 1775–83
The early campaigns of The American Revolution ended in stalemate. British forces were superior in numbers and weaponry, but the patriots gained support as the struggle moved south.

TAXATION

The Seven Years War (see pp.184–87), which ended with British victory in 1763, had cemented Britain's bond with America. The war had been expensive, and the British believed that the colonists should pay their share of the costs. However, since 1620 the settlers had developed a liberal society with little or no interference from London. They resented restrictions and their protests resulted in many taxes being withdrawn. They made a strong constitutional point: that they should not pay British taxes without representation in the British Parliament.

BOSTON RIOTS
On March 5, 1770, a squad of soldiers went to support a sentinel being harassed by a large mob on King (now State) Street in Boston. They opened fire, killing three.

VIOLENT RESISTANCE

In 1773 Bostonians dumped a cargo of tea in the harbor in protest against the tax, and the British closed down the port in retaliation. British troops then went on to quell insurrections in Lexington and Concord, where fighting began in earnest. The popular image of well-drilled British soldiers with muskets fighting camouflaged, country-wise frontiersmen is a simplification; the British did indeed advance with bayonets fixed in an orderly line, and the Americans did employ hit-and-run tactics, but Washington's goal—largely successful—was to create a professional army along European lines. To this end he hired a Prussian officer to train his men.

THE FIRST SHOT
British forces, on a deliberately provocative mission to seize colonial arms, were attacked by a colonial militia of "Minutemen." It was during this engagement, at Lexington, Massachusetts, that the first shot of the war was fired.

WAR AT SEA

In spite of Britain's naval supremacy, the coastline of the Thirteen Colonies was so long and intricate that a successful blockade was impossible and the Americans were always able to land supplies. The colonies had a strong maritime tradition, and their lack of a war fleet was no disadvantage, since Britain was unable to gain any benefit from its weight of numbers and firepower. In duels between individual ships, Americans like John Paul Jones on the *Bonhomme Richard* (1779) did well.

EUROPEAN SUPPORT
France and Spain came to the colonies' aid in the war against the British. Here the French surprise a British fleet on its way to the Cape Verde Islands, 1781.

ARMIES AND ALLIES

This was a civil war as well as a struggle for independence, and many American loyalists fought for Britain and King George. Some American Indians fought on both sides. The French, after their defeat in the Seven Years War, exploited the chance to retaliate against the British, although their military efforts were comparatively minor. German (or "Hessian") mercenaries fought for the British, whose grave problems with logistics and supply often made them slow-moving and ineffective. George Washington's army was at first unreliable and ill-disciplined, but after the winter ordeal at Valley Forge (1777–78) morale improved steadily.

VALLEY FORGE
General Washington visits wounded soldiers at Valley Forge, where 2,500 men died from cold and lack of food.

MORTAR

A muzzle-loading artillery weapon in use since the 15th century (especially in sieges), the mortar had a short, stubby barrel, the length of which was little more than twice its diameter, and fired a missile in a high trajectory. It was particularly effective against "soft" targets, having a lower muzzle velocity than a howitzer but a faster rate of fire. It was also lighter and more easily transported. This 13in-(33cm-) gun, in use from about 1760 to 1860, was the largest in the British service.

Winch used to lift heavy bomb and lower it into muzzle

13in mortar bomb

Handle to wind winch cord

SPECIFICATION

Origin Britain		**Height** 28in (70cm)	
Length 28in (70cm)		**Caliber** 13in (33cm)	
First made 1760		**Weight** 2,800lb (1,270kg)	

Handles were called "dolphins"

Brass bed

INDEPENDENCE

Although there was no doubt as to who won the war, the military results were ambiguous, as was often the case in 18th-century wars. The comparative insignificance of cavalry and the scarcity of pitched battles contributed to military stalemate. While Americans shattered the old relationship with Britain, their leaders still respected British institutions, as their own form of constitution would demonstrate. In Britain the war had always been unpopular, and by the final battle at Yorktown in 1781 most British leaders were ready to accept the Declaration of Independence. With neither side able to command the resources to bring it total victory, hostilities ground to a halt gradually.

Eyepiece retracts for storage

MERCENARIES
Britain's Hessian troops, here on a night patrol, had little interest in the war, but they were generally reliable. Some 20,000 Hessians fought alongside the British.

This model was probably used by a British officer

TELESCOPE
A "perspective glass" (telescope) enabled its user to read the enemy's flag or signals from a distance.

1750–1914

BATTLES FOR INDEPENDENCE

FOR GEORGE WASHINGTON, the main goal of his underfinanced Continental Army was simply to stay alive. He therefore avoided pitched battles as much as possible, assisted by the enemy's slow movement and perhaps by the private sympathies of some British officers.

However, the British were disconcerted by American tactics, particularly those of Daniel Morgan's Virginia riflemen, who won at Cowpens. The most significant battles were Saratoga, which encouraged French participation, and Yorktown, which ended the war.

NEW JERSEY

Trenton and Princeton

DATE December 26, 1776–3 January 1777

FORCES
British: 1,200;
American: 2,400
(Trenton)

LOCATION
New Jersey

CASUALTIES British: 106
(plus 900 prisoners);
American: 4

The British held the initiative throughout the summer of 1776, but Washington, in command of the Continental Army since 1775, struck back at the end of the year. Gathering what troops he could, in just over a week of skillful maneuvers he secured two minor but convincing victories. First, he captured Trenton from its Hessian garrison, after crossing the ice-choked Delaware River on Christmas night. The Hessian commander was killed, while Washington took possession of badly needed supplies and went on to rout another enemy contingent at Princeton. Coming after a series of grim defeats, including the loss of New York, this double success, while relatively insignificant in military terms, helped to restore the Americans' flagging morale.

MASSACHUSETTS

Lexington and Concord

DATE
April 19, 1775

FORCES
British: 1,700;
American: 4,000

CASUALTIES
British: 273;
American: 95

LOCATION Lexington
and Concord,
Massachusetts

In an attempt to quell the rebellion, General Gage, the military governor of Massachusetts, sent a small force of British troops from Boston to Concorde to seize rebel arms and munitions. In spite of its secrecy, however, the rebels learned of the mission and the British were stopped at Lexington, where the first shot of the war (the "shot heard around the world") was fired. After a brief engagement, the British marched on Concord where they were again ambushed by the rebels. Largely young and inexperienced men, the British troops were disorganized by the Americans' guerrilla tactics, and after being routed they regrouped and fought constant skirmishes during the 20-mile (32km-) retreat to Charlestown (Boston), which was soon under siege.

LEXINGTON GREEN
British major John Pitcairn gives the order for his troops to fire on the first day of the American Revolution.

MASSACHUSETTS

Bunker Hill

DATE
June 17, 1775

FORCES
Colonial militia: 1,400;
British: 2,600

CASUALTIES
Colonial militia: 310
(plus 30 prisoners);
British: 1,053

LOCATION
Near Boston,
Massachusetts

In spite of its name, the battle of Bunker Hill was actually fought on Breed's Hill, on the western side of the narrow strait leading to the Charles River basin. After the outbreak of hostilities at Lexington, Boston was besieged by rebellious colonists, whose numbers were growing daily. Anticipating a British plan to capture the heights north of the city, the American commander General Artemas Ward ordered that Bunker Hill, on the Charlestown peninsula, should be fortified, but for some reason Breed's Hill was fortified instead. This may have been a mistake (it was fortified at night), but Breed's Hill was closer to the British ships and so provided a better attacking position. Nevertheless, the Americans were soon under attack from British soldiers under General William Howe, who had succeeded Gage as British commander in October. Howe had brought 9,000 reinforcements, and more followed later, among them Generals Burgoyne and Cornwallis. The British attacked in two lines and were twice driven back by the defenders. Although they finally achieved their objective and captured the hill, they lost over one-third of their number in the process—a serious blow to their confidence and morale. Moreover, Britain was

MEMORIAL
The Bunker Hill monument in Boston was erected in 1843. It stands 221ft (76m) high.

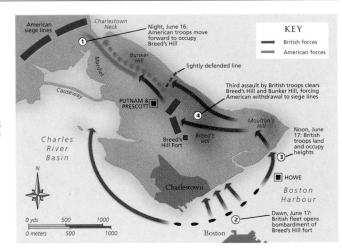

KEY
➤ British forces
➤ American forces

American siege lines

Charlestown Neck

Night, June 16: American troops move forward to occupy Breed's Hill

Bunker Hill

lightly defended line

Third assault by British troops clears Breed's Hill and Bunker Hill, forcing American withdrawal to siege lines

Marsh

Causeway

PUTNAM & PRESCOTT

Moulton's Hill

Noon, June 17: British troops land and occupy heights

Charles River Basin

Breed's Hill Fort

Breed's Hill

HOWE

Charlestown

Boston Harbour

0 yds   500   1000
0 meters   500   1000

Boston

Dawn, June 17: British fleet opens bombardment of Breed's Hill fort

under pressure elsewhere; rebels captured the forts at Crown Point and Ticonderoga (near Lake Champlain), and an American force had seized Montreal in November 1774, though an attack on Quebec was quelled. Meanwhile the Americans had acquired a regular army—as yet an unimpressive body of men—and found a first-rate general in George Washington, a Virginian who had been appointed commander-in-chief by the second Continental Congress the previous summer. John Adams and other leaders feared that the South—

so far little involved—might stand apart from the struggle, although a voyage to the South by British commander Sir Henry Clinton in 1776, designed to encourage the numerous loyalists to rise against the newly established American government, discovered that a loyalist counterrevolt in North Carolina had been crushed at the battle of Moore's Creek Bridge near Wilmington—and in June, when Clinton bombarded the harbor at Charleston in support of local loyalists, he was driven back and defeated.

"Don't fire until you see the whites of their eyes."

Colonel William Prescott (American) to his troops at Bunker Hill, 1775

SARATOGA

Saratoga

DATE September 19 and October 17, 1777

FORCES
British: 10,000;
American: 15,000

LOCATION
Saratoga County,
New York state

CASUALTIES
British: 800 (plus 6,000 prisoners);
American: 1,600

There were two engagements in the Saratoga campaign within a month of each other. In spite of Washington's much-needed success at Trenton and Princeton at the end of 1776, events in 1777 generally went against the Americans until Saratoga turned the tide. General Howe, having captured Philadelphia, defeated Washington but failed to destroy his army at the battle of Brandywine in September. This campaign went on simultaneously with another in the north where British general "Gentleman Johnny" Burgoyne, starting from Canada, attempted to cut off New England along the line of the Hudson River. He regained Crown Point and

BEMIS HEIGHTS

Benedict Arnold was wounded at Bemis Heights. He is here shown resting on a horse. On the right stands a group of Hessian riflemen.

Ticonderoga but lost about 1,000 men in a failed attempt to seize stores at Bennington, Vermont. Up the Hudson, American general Horatio Gates conducted delaying tactics, reducing Burgoyne's progress to a snail's pace. Approaching Saratoga in separate columns through the woods, the British were attacked at Freeman's Farm by Daniel Morgan, under the orders of Benedict Arnold, who commanded the American left. They drove Morgan off, but not without suffering heavy casualties. Arnold sent Morgan reinforcements, and when the British in turn attacked his line they were repelled with more losses. The British lines had not been broken because Gates had declined to reinforce Arnold, who was relieved of command after the British survived a final attack. But

> "And vain was their endeavor our men to terrify, though death was all around us, not one of us would fly!"
>
> *Contemporary American ballad*

Burgoyne had suffered losses he could not afford. He fortified his position while the Americans built field fortifications farther south. Burgoyne was anticipating reinforcements from General Clinton, but Clinton was in New York and could not leave because Howe, his superior, was off

SARATOGA NATIONAL PARK
Today a cannon stands above the Hudson River near the site of the American victory at Saratoga. The area became a national park in 1938.

in Pennsylvania. The failure to reinforce Burgoyne has been blamed on many people, including the British secretary for war, Lord George Germaine, but whatever the cause, the result was clearly a disaster. The second engagement, on October 7, took place at Bemis Heights, where Gates was encamped with more than 12,000 fresh and eager men. Burgoyne's attack was easily driven back. He had only about 5,000 fit soldiers left and supplies were running short. He started to retreat but was surrounded by Gates, whose force now outnumbered his by four to one. Ten days later Burgoyne had no alternative but to surrender. The capture of the British army with its weapons vastly increased American prestige and led to the alliance with France.

AMERICAN PISTOL
Made at Rappahanock Forge, this pistol was used by the American Light Dragoons. American firearms were generally of very high quality.

> "Love to my country actuates my present conduct, however it may appear inconsistent to the world, who very seldom judge right of any man's actions."

WITNESS TO WAR
BENEDICT ARNOLD

Benedict Arnold, second-in-command to Gates at Saratoga, was one of the most talented American generals. He captured Fort Ticonderoga and his march into Canada in the depth of winter is a military classic. Believing his ability was unappreciated, he later planned to betray the Americans to the British. His treachery was discovered, but he escaped and later fought for the British. The above quotation is from a letter Arnold wrote to Washington in which he justifies his treason.

THE NORTH SEA

Bonhomme Richard

DATE
September 23, 1779

FORCES
US frigate *Bonhomme Richard*; British frigate *Serapis*

LOCATION North Sea, off Flamborough Head, England

CASUALTIES
American: 150;
British: 128

John Paul Jones was commissioned into the Continental Navy in 1776. In command of a makeshift squadron, he sailed to "distress" the British in his frigate the *Bonhomme Richard*. Cruising south through the North Sea, they encountered a Baltic convoy escorted by HMS *Serapis*, commanded by Captain Pearson. Pearson held off the squadron while the merchantmen escaped, then engaged the *Bonhomme Richard*. The two ships fought for two hours until the *Serapis* caught fire and struck her colors. Jones, with only two guns still firing, was in worse shape; the *Bonhomme Richard* was sinking. He transferred to the *Serapis* and returned to France and a hero's welcome.

DUEL AT SEA
In the most famous naval duel of the century, Bonhomme Richard *and* Serapis *fought to a fiery standstill.*

GEORGIA

Savannah

DATE
October 9, 1779

FORCES
French and American: unknown; British and loyalist: unknown

LOCATION
Lower Savannah River, Georgia

CASUALTIES
No reliable estimates

In Savannah, Georgia, revolutionary sentiment was not strong, and in 1778 the city was occupied by British and loyalist forces. General Benjamin Lincoln, Southern commander of the Continental Army, set out to regain the key port in alliance with French admiral the comte d'Estaing, whose 22 ships-of-the-line mounted a blockade. The Continental Army surrounded Savannah on September 9, 1779, aware that the French blockade could not withstand a serious British assault. On October 9 the Continental Army attacked but was stopped short by British regulars under Colonel Maitland. As the attacking line started to crumble, Continental commander Count Pulaski was mortally wounded. Lincoln began an orderly withdrawal on October 16, and two days later d'Estaing abandoned his blockade and sailed for France.

THE CAROLINAS

Camden

DATE
August 16, 1780

FORCES
American: 4,100;
British: 2,239

LOCATION
Camden, South Carolina

CASUALTIES
American: 723
(including prisoners);
British: 324

In 1778 the British turned their attention to the South, which, they believed, contained a high proportion of loyalists and was economically important because it supplied cotton to British mills. They secured a foothold in Georgia, and in May 1780 captured Charleston. Pacification of the back country was more difficult, but a hastily gathered Southern army under General Gates was shattered at Camden, South Carolina, by General Cornwallis. Leading Gates's right flank was Baron de Kalb, a redoubtable German officer in French service, but the inexperienced men on his left broke when Cornwallis advanced against them. The British then executed a neat outflanking movement to encircle de Kalb, who was unhorsed and mortally wounded. Gates's reputation plummeted.

BARON DE KALB
Johann de Kalb died from his wounds at Camden. The title "Baron" was honorary: he was the son of a peasant.

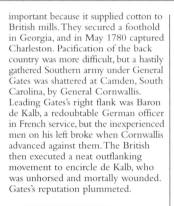

THE CAROLINAS

King's Mountain

DATE
October 7, 1780

FORCES
Loyalist militia: 1,100;
Rebels: 900

LOCATION
King's Mountain,
North Carolina

CASUALTIES
Loyalists: 320 (and 698 prisoners);
Rebels: 90

Following Gates's defeat at Camden, an unforgiving civil war between loyalists and rebels raged in the Carolinas. Major Patrick Ferguson took charge of the loyalist militia and advanced on Charlotte on September 26. Hearing of an approaching rebel force, Ferguson moved in the same direction and stopped at King's Mountain, a hill near the border. The rebels had no overall commander (each unit was commanded by a self-appointed "colonel"), but they demonstrated remarkable tactical cohesion. To surround the hill, they were split into half a dozen groups. When the rebels opened fire, Ferguson responded with a bayonet charge. The frontiersmen were forced to retreat down the hill, but rallied and attacked again. This pattern was repeated several times. The rebels constantly regrouped, and Ferguson's men suffered increasing casualties. When their commander, riddled with musket fire, fell dead from his horse, the loyalists lost heart and began to surrender, but many rebels, lusting for revenge, kept on firing regardless, until their officers finally regained control and took the remainder of the colonial militia into captivity. Several, accused of deserting the rebels' cause and joining the British, were subsequently hanged. The dead and wounded were left behind on the battlefield.

FRONTIERSMEN
Preparing to fight uphill, rebels open fire on loyalist troops on King's Mountain.

THE CAROLINAS

Cowpens

DATE
January 17, 1781

FORCES
American: 1,000;
British: 1,100

LOCATION Cowpens,
north of Spartanburg,
South Carolina

CASUALTIES
American: 73;
British: 150 (plus 830
prisoners)

This battle, fought near an area occupied by cattle pens, exemplified the failure of the British campaign in the Carolinas, in particular their failure to combat the Americans' guerrilla tactics, especially when waged in cooperation with the army of the bold and resourceful General Nathanael

MORTAR SHELL
*An 18th-century,
9-in mortar shell,
probably French, found
near a Virginia battlefield.*

Greene. With smaller resources, Greene kept the British commander, Cornwallis, off balance by rapid movement and guerrilla raids. Notwithstanding Cornwallis's superiority, Greene daringly divided his army into two, sending Brigadier Daniel Morgan into western South Carolina, where he encountered a British force about the size of his own. It was commanded by Colonel Sir Banastre Tarleton, who had taken part in the capture of Charleston, the battle of Camden, and other engagements. In pursuit of Morgan, Tarleton began his march at 2:30 a.m., arrived at Cowpens at 8 a.m., and ordered his tired and hungry "Tory Legion" into battle without breakfast. Greene had stationed his sharpshooters around the area, with the rest of his men out of sight behind a hill. They succeeded in

enveloping the British and rounded them up, appropriately, like cattle, suffering minimal casualties themselves. Only a handful of British soldiers escaped, including Tarleton, who was by repute one of the more brutal British commanders. Tarleton was later elevated to the rank of general.

1732–1799

GEORGE WASHINGTON

The American commander-in-chief and first president of the United States was a man of great abilities and an impressively powerful, if austere, character. Born to Virginia gentry of English descent, he inherited the family estate at Mount Vernon. As commander of the Virginia militia in the French and Indian War, he gained close experience of the British army, and was unanimously chosen to command the Continental Army. His generalship was not always faultless, notably with cavalry, but probably no other man could have held the American cause together for so many difficult years: patience was among his greatest virtues.

> "When I advance, I must either destroy Morgan's corps or push it before me over Broad River, toward King's Mountain."
>
> *Colonel Tarleton*, before Cowpens, 1781

VIRGINIA

Yorktown

DATE September–
October 1781

FORCES American:
8,845; French: 7,800;
British: 7,500

LOCATION
Yorktown, Virginia

CASUALTIES
American: 108; French:
186; British: 482 (plus
7,018 prisoners)

The Yorktown campaign, the last episode in the American Revolution, was remarkable for the smooth cooperation of American and French forces over a wide area. The forces included a French army from Rhode Island, an American army from New York, a French fleet from the West Indies, and Lafayette's force of regulars and militiamen from Virginia. The British commander, Cornwallis, after the failure of the Carolinas campaign, declined to

leave his base at the port of Yorktown because he hoped for supplies and support from the Royal Navy. He seemed not to recognize what was obvious both to Washington and Clinton (the British commander-in-chief in New York), that his 8,000 troops were vulnerable to a combined land and sea blockade. Washington hastened south to join Lafayette outside Yorktown, while the French fleet under de Grasse sealed off the sea approaches. A Franco-American attack forced the British to withdraw from their outer redoubts, and the siege of the town began in earnest on October 6. Clinton sent a relief squadron from New York but it was repulsed by de Grasse. After a prolonged artillery barrage, with his defenses crumbling, Cornwallis surrendered on October 19. The British held on to New York until 1783, while negotiations for an armistice were requested.

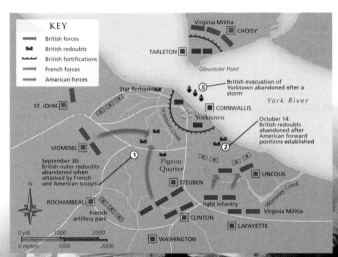

KEY
- British forces
- British redoubts
- British fortifications
- French forces
- American forces

PREPARING FOR BATTLE
Washington and his generals plan the disposition of their troops before the battle of Yorktown. Washington stands in the center with Rochambeau on his left.

FRANCE: REVOLUTION TO EMPIRE

IN 1789 IN FRANCE, the demands of commoners for political rights and an end to noble privilege erupted into full-scale revolution. By 1792 France had been declared a republic, which it remained until 1804, when Napoleon was crowned emperor. The revolution ignited a series of wars, which were both an ideological conflict between the revolution and its enemies and a continuation of the power struggle between European states.

Pan cover
Steel flint-cock
Wooden stock
Steel barrel
Trigger
Trigger guard
Ramrod

FLINTLOCK PISTOL
The pistol was primarily a cavalry weapon at the time of the Napoleonic Wars. This is the British army's New Land Pattern pistol, introduced in 1814.

CITIZEN ARMY

ARMED WOMEN
Women armed with pikes, axes, and muskets marched on the king's palace at Versailles in the French Revolution, 1789.

The dominance achieved by the French army in this period was rooted in the pre-revolutionary era. A royal war councillor, the Comte de Guibert, envisaged a "citizen army" that would fight decisive combined-arms campaigns based on mobility and aggression, and the royal army's inspector of artillery, Jean-Baptiste de Gribeauval, endowed France with mobile and accurate cannon commanded by trained artillery officers, including Napoleon Bonaparte. The most radical period of the revolution, from 1792 to 1794, made a citizen army a reality. The constitution of June 1793 declared, "All Frenchmen shall be soldiers; all shall be trained to arms." The following August 300,000 troops were raised by conscription, but it was declared the duty of every citizen to participate in the war effort.

INSTRUMENT OF POWER

Conscripts, revolutionary volunteers, and the old royal army were amalgamated into mass armies supplied by a rapidly expanding state armaments industry. Extreme revolutionary gestures such as the election of officers were soon abandoned in favor of formal discipline and hierarchy, but revolutionary and patriotic enthusiasm distinguished French troops from their enemies. Men of all social backgrounds were able to win rapid promotion on merit. This was the context for the rise of Napoleon, who turned the French army into a formidable agent of personal ambition. Creating self-contained, combined-arms formations, he followed an offensive strategy, seeking out and attacking the enemy in pursuit of victory.

MEDAL OF VICTORY
The British Waterloo medal celebrates the defeat in 1815 that marked the end of Napoleon's career.

1769–1821

NAPOLEON BONAPARTE

Born in Corsica, Napoleon was an artillery officer whose readiness to suppress street disturbances in Paris in 1795 earned him command of an army. His military successes gave him the chance to seize political power, culminating in the assumption of the title of emperor in 1804. Napoleon won almost all of the 50 battles he fought. A natural gambler, he even attempted a return to power from exile on Elba in 1815. Defeat at Waterloo led to his imprisonment on the British-held island of St. Helena, where he died.

ELITE GUARD
The Consular Guard, forerunners of Napoleon's Imperial Guard, formed resolute squares to hold off Austrian cavalry at Marengo in 1800.

MARSHAL OF FRANCE
Michel Ney, one of Napoleon's 26 marshals, was a mere sergeant-major at the outbreak of the French revolutionary wars.

SHOCK TACTICS

Napoleon's large armies moved swiftly by forced marches, living off the country. When battle was joined, success often depended on superior maneuver—for example, destroying a weaker part of the enemy's army and then turning with full force on the now outnumbered remainder. Napoleon's ruthlessly aggressive application of power on the battlefield—the cannonade by heavy artillery, the infantry attack in dense columns, the mass cavalry charge—ensured that casualty rates were high on both sides. At the battle of Borodino in 1812 there were 74,000 casualties in one day. Napoleon saw no need to conserve manpower, figuring more could always be raised by conscription.

KEY

→	British forces
✕	French victory
✕	French defeat
---	British blockade
----	frontiers 1797
—	Holy Roman Empire 1797
→	Egyptian campaign 1798–1801
→	The Peninsular War 1000–14
→	The war with Russia 1812
→	"The Hundred Days" March–June 1815

REVOLUTIONARIES
Soldiers of the Revolution vow to fight to the last at Montelegino in 1796.

A CONTINENT AT WAR
The Napoleonic wars were the last military campaigns to spread across all areas of Europe—and even to other continents—before the outbreak of World War I in 1914.

BRASS CANNON
Napoleon saw the gun as a crucial battle winner, not a support weapon. "It is with cannon that one makes war," he said.

FRENCH DEFEAT

Britain, France's most consistent enemy, remained dominant at sea throughout the Napoleonic wars, winning the fierce and costly warship battles. On land, Napoleon suffered a steady drain on his resources in the Peninsular War, where he faced Spanish guerrillas and British intervention. He overreached himself with the 1812 invasion of Russia and the retreat from Moscow destroyed his experienced army. Learning from the French, other states enlarged their forces—though only the Prussians began conscription—and improved their tactics. Never as brilliant as Napoleon, they nevertheless became increasingly capable of taking the French on and finally won out. The French monarchy was restored in 1814, and Napoleon's desperate gamble at Waterloo the following year was a doomed effort.

EMPIRES AND REVOLUTIONS

FRENCH REVOLUTIONARY WARS

THE WARS BETWEEN REVOLUTIONARY FRANCE and a varying coalition of European powers began in 1792 as resistance to an invasion intended to restore the authority of the French monarchy, but evolved into a crusade to spread the principles of the Revolution. A by-product of this was an aggressive expansion of France's borders. From 1793, under the inspired direction of Lazare Carnot, the hundreds of thousands of new recruits raised by mass mobilization—the *levée en masse*—were amalgamated with old regulars to form a national army full of revolutionary enthusiasm. In Napoleon Bonaparte they found a general of genius to lead them. But the limit to French power remained the sea, where Britain was dominant.

FRENCH REVOLUTIONARY WARS

Valmy

DATE
September 20, 1792

FORCES French:
30,000; Coalition:
30,000–40,000

LOCATION
Eastern France

CASUALTIES
French: 300 killed;
Coalition: 200 killed

In April 1792 France declared war on Austria and Prussia. Coalition forces (Prussian, Austrian, Hessian, and French emigrés) advanced into France in August. The Prussian commander, the Duke of Brunswick, took Verdun on September 3 and marched on Paris. Two French armies, commanded by Charles Dumouriez and François-Christophe Kellermann, failed to stop Brunswick from passing through the wooded heights of the Argonne and on into the west. With the road to Paris open in front of him, Brunswick chose to turn to engage the French, fearing to continue the advance with enemy armies across his lines of communication. Brunswick's army met French forces under Kellermann, drawn up on the heights of Valmy. Subjected to heavy artillery fire, the French soldiers stood firm. When the coalition infantry advanced, it was the turn of the French artillery to show its effectiveness in breaking up the assault. Brunswick soon decided that, since the French were not going to run away, his best course was to withdraw while his forces, already racked by disease, were still relatively intact. Although more a drawn stand-off than a serious battle, Valmy was hailed as a great victory and the salvation of the Revolution.

EPOCH-MAKING BATTLE
This painting shows French positions by the mill at Valmy coming under artillery fire. The German poet Goethe, who was present at the battle, described it as the beginning of "a new era in world history."

FRENCH REVOLUTIONARY WARS

Jemappes

DATE November 6, 1792

FORCES French: 40,000–
45,000; Austrians:
13,000–25,000

LOCATION
North of Mons,
eastern Belgium

CASUALTIES
French: 2,000–4,000
killed or wounded;
Austrians: 4,500 killed
or wounded

In early November 1792 Dumouriez advanced into the Austrian Netherlands (Belgium) with the Armée du Nord. He came upon an Austrian army led by Duke Albert of Saxe-Teschen at Jemappes, outside Mons. The Austrians were heavily outnumbered but occupying strong defensive positions. The battle began with a three-hour French artillery barrage that had little effect. Dumouriez then launched a series of frontal assaults, but the fire of Austrian cannon and Tyrolean *Jägers* armed with rifles, as well as cavalry counterattacks, repeatedly drove the French back. The Austrians were eventually swamped by force of numbers and retreated briskly. By the end of the year France had occupied the Austrian Netherlands.

FIELD ARTILLERY
Due to the reforming efforts of French general Jean-Baptiste de Gribeauval (1715–89), French guns were more accurate and mobile than those of their enemies.

FRENCH REVOLUTIONARY WARS

Toulon

DATE
August 27–
December 19, 1793

FORCES Some 18,000
British, Spanish,
and Piedmontese
inside Toulon

LOCATION
Toulon, on France's
Mediterranean coast

CASUALTIES
No reliable estimates

By August 1793 the revolutionaries were at war with Britain and Spain as well as Austria and Prussia, and large parts of France were in the hands of royalist rebels. After royalists invited an Anglo–Spanish fleet under Admiral Hood to occupy the port of Toulon, French forces laid siege to the town. A junior artillery officer, Napoleon Bonaparte, devised a plan to drive out the fleet by seizing high ground dominating the harbor, thus exposing the enemy to artillery fire. The French took Fort Mulgrave, the key to possessing this ground, on December 17. As Napoleon had predicted, the following day Hood was obliged to evacuate and pull out his fleet.

NAPOLEON AT THE SIEGE
Napoleon's reputation was made at the siege of Toulon. He was promoted from captain to brigadier-general in four months.

> "I have no words to describe Buonaparte's merit: much technical skill, an equal degree of intelligence, and too much gallantry…"
>
> *French officer Jacques Dugommier*, reporting on the siege of Toulon, 1793

FRENCH REVOLUTIONARY WARS

Fleurus

DATE
June 26, 1794

FORCES
French: 75,000;
Austrians and
Dutch: 52,000

LOCATION
Belgium, north
of Charleroi

CASUALTIES
French: 4,000 killed;
Austrians: 2,300 killed

From the fall of 1793 the French revolutionaries regained the initiative in their war against the coalition of foreign powers and against royalists in France. In June 1794 General Jourdan laid siege to the Belgian city of Charleroi. Austrian and Dutch forces, plus a sprinkling of British, under the Prince of Saxe-Coburg, advanced to relieve the city. Despite being fewer in number, the coalition forces attacked boldly near the town of Fleurus at daybreak on June 26. Saxe-Coburg's forces attacked in five columns, those on the left and right driving back the French at each end of their line. Jourdan, however, had the unprecedented advantage of aerial reconnaissance, as his hydrogen balloon, *Entreprenant*, floated above the battlefield. The crew of two, including the mastermind of the project, Charles Coutelle, stayed in the air for the duration of the battle, sliding messages about enemy movements down a cable to the ground. Aided by this impressive view of the battlefield, Jourdan was able to rally his forces on the right and left and launch an attack in the center. The coalition forces were

REVOLUTIONARY COMMANDER
General Jourdan, on a white horse, launched his reserves in a decisive counterattack against the coalition at the battle of Fleurus.

obliged to retreat, although the French, short of ammunition and exhausted, did not pursue. The victory was nonetheless decisive. The French occupied Belgium, which they were to hold for the next 20 years. By relaxing the fear of foreign invasion, the victory undermined the extremists of the ruling Committee of Public Safety, which fell in July 1794.

AIR WARFARE

The French established the world's first air force, the Compagnie d'Aéronautique, in 1794. A hydrogen balloon, the *Entreprenant*, was deployed at Maubeuge on June 2, 1794, and after success at Fleurus, three more balloons went into service. Napoleon did not take to the idea of aerial warfare and the company was disbanded in 1799.

FRENCH REVOLUTIONARY WARS

Arcole

DATE
November 15–17, 1796

FORCES
French: 20,000;
Austrians: 17,000

LOCATION
Southeast of Verona,
Italy

CASUALTIES French:
4,500; Austrians:
6,000

Appointed commander of the French Army of Italy in 1796, Napoleon Bonaparte proceeded to demonstrate his genius for rapid maneuver and decisive attack. In April and May he defeated Piedmont and drove the Austrians out of most of northern Italy. There followed a long siege of the remaining Austrian stronghold of Mantua, while the Austrians mounted a series of relief attempts. In November Napoleon confronted an Austrian army led by Josef Alvintzy near the junction of the Alpone and Adige rivers. The French army was short of everything from boots to food, but nonetheless took the offensive. The French crossed the Adige on November 14, after which the two armies were separated only by the Alpone. On November 15 and 16 repeated French attempts to cross this river by the bridge at Arcole were beaten back by Austrian firepower.

BRIDGE CROSSING
Heroic images such as this one of Napoleon crossing the Arcole served as propaganda to promote Napoleon's personal popularity.

On the 17th, however, French flanking moves convinced Alvintzy that he was threatened with encirclement and he retreated. Napoleon went on to rout the Austrians at Rivoli in January 1797, forcing Austria to sign the Peace of Campo Formio later that year.

FRENCH REVOLUTIONARY WARS

Cape St. Vincent

DATE February 14, 1797

FORCES
Spanish: 27 ships;
British: 15 ships

CASUALTIES British:
73 killed, 227 wounded;
Spanish: 255 killed,
341 wounded,
4 ships captured

LOCATION
Off Cape St. Vincent,
southwest Portugal

In 1796 Spain allied itself with France. The combined strength of the French and Spanish fleets threatened to end British naval superiority and open the way for an invasion of Britain. The British Mediterranean fleet under Admiral Sir John Jervis was given the task of preventing the Spanish from sailing north to join their French allies. On the morning of February 14, 1797, Jervis intercepted a Spanish fleet under Admiral José de Córdova off Cape St. Vincent. Despite having numerically inferior forces, the British sailed in to attack, their line of ships splitting the Spanish forces in two. Commodore

SHIP OF BONES
Prisoners of war from the French revolutionary navy constructed this model ship, the HMS Egmont, out of bones.

Horatio Nelson blocked the escape of the larger body of Spanish ships, at one point engaging seven of them unaided. Four Spanish ships were captured, two of them by Nelson, and a number of other vessels suffered serious damage. The surviving Spanish were blockaded in Cadiz; plans for an invasion of Britain were scotched.

> "The roar was like heavy thunder, and the ship reeled and shook as if she was inclined to fall in pieces. I felt a choking sensation from the smell and smoke of gunpowder..."
>
> *Midshipman George Parsons* on HMS *Barfleur* at Cape St. Vincent, 1797

NAPOLEON TAKES OVER

IN 1798 NAPOLEON BONAPARTE EMBARKED on a campaign in Egypt that brought him more military glory but was strategically negated by the strength of British seapower. Returning to France in the fall of 1799 he seized power in a coup d'état. By then France had suffered a number of reverses at the hands of the Second Coalition formed by Russia, Britain, Austria, and the Ottoman Empire, and in Italy Russian General Sovorov had all but driven out the French forces. Russia withdrew from the war, however, and Napoleon reversed the situation with victory at Marengo. By 1802 Napoleon had bludgeoned his enemies into accepting peace largely on French terms, and by the time war resumed in 1805 he had been crowned emperor of the French.

THE EGYPTIAN CAMPAIGN

Pyramids

DATE July 21, 1798
FORCES French: 25,000; Egyptians: 20,000–30,000 (6,000 Mameluke cavalry)
CASUALTIES French: 29 killed, 260 wounded; Egyptians: 4,000 killed (2,000 Mamelukes)

LOCATION At Embabeh, near Cairo, Egypt

On July 2, 1798, Napoleon landed at Alexandria, bent on the conquest of Egypt, then an Ottoman province governed by the Mamelukes. The French infantry advanced in a series of grueling marches toward Cairo, where an army of elite Mameluke cavalry and *fellahin* (peasant) infantry prepared to counter them. On July 20 French scouts discovered the enemy camped within sight of the Pyramids. The following day Napoleon's infantry drew up in

DEFEAT OF THE MAMELUKES
Routed by the fire of French muskets and artillery, flamboyantly dressed Mamelukes flee the field at the battle of the Pyramids.

squares six men deep, with artillery at each corner. Clad in gorgeous silks and heavily armed with sabers and pistols, the Mameluke cavalry hurled themselves against the squares with ferocious battle cries. According to Napoleon's official report, the cavalry "was allowed to approach within 50 paces and was then welcomed with a hail of case shot and bullets…" The French seized the initiative, advancing along the Nile bank supported by the guns of the river flotilla, and the Mameluke cavalry fled. Some tried to swim the river in search of safety and at least 1,000 drowned.

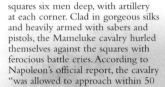

THE EGYPTIAN CAMPAIGN

Nile (Aboukir Bay)

DATE August 1–2, 1798
FORCES British: 14 ships; French: 13 ships
CASUALTIES French: 9 ships captured, 2 destroyed, 2,000 men killed or wounded; British: 213 killed, 677 wounded

LOCATION Aboukir Bay, Egypt

The French fleet that took Napoleon's forces to Egypt was commanded by Admiral Brueys. It was fortunate to reach Alexandria unscathed, as a British fleet under Admiral

Horatio Nelson had been hunting for it, hampered by a lack of frigates, the "eyes" of the fleet. On August 1, 1798, Nelson tracked the French down to their anchorage in Aboukir Bay. When the enemy was sighted, the British sailed in to attack, although only a few hours of daylight remained. The French were taken by surprise, with many men ashore fetching supplies. They were anchored in shallow water, but the British took the risk of sailing around the head of their line. Although one British ship ran aground, others led by

MARINE SWORD
The hilt of this French marine's sword of the Napoleonic period ends in the rooster's head, a French revolutionary symbol.

Goliath, anchored alongside the foremost French ships, raking them with broadsides. The French ships could not reply because all their guns were on the seaward side. Nelson, aboard *Vanguard*, led the other half of his fleet to anchor to the seaward side of the French ships, which were thus battered from both sides. The French put up a fierce fight, especially the three-deck 120-gun flagship *L'Orient*. Nelson himself was wounded in the head; Brueys was cut in two by a cannonball. *L'Orient* caught fire and at around 10 p.m. its gunpowder store exploded. The sound was heard nearly 20 miles (30km) away and two British ships were set on fire by blazing wreckage. The fighting continued all night and by dawn the French were routed. Only three ships escaped. Napoleon was cut off in Egypt.

FRENCH ON FIRE
The remaining ships of the French fleet under Admiral Brueys were ablaze by the closing phase of the battle of the Nile.

THE EGYPTIAN CAMPAIGN

Aboukir Bay

DATE July 25, 1799
FORCES French: 10,000; Ottomans: 15,000
CASUALTIES French: 220 killed, 750 wounded; Ottomans: c.2,000 killed

LOCATION North coast of Egypt

In September 1798 the Ottoman Empire declared war on France. To forestall a possible Ottoman descent on Egypt, in early 1799 Napoleon marched north to Acre, the capital of Ottoman Syria. The city held out through a 63-day siege, after which Napoleon marched his army, decimated by disease, back to Egypt. On July 11, 1799 the Ottoman army of Rhodes, led by Mustapha Pasha, landed on the Egyptian coast at Aboukir. In two weeks Napoleon marched a force of 10,000 men from Cairo to confront the Turks. After the French infantry had fought its way into the midst of the Turkish troops, Joachim Murat led a ferocious cavalry charge. Under the shock, the Turkish forces fell apart, fleeing back to their ships. Despite this victory, the next month Napoleon returned to France.

1750–1914

THE ITALIAN CAMPAIGN

Marengo

DATE June 14, 1800

FORCES Austrians: 31,000; French: 32,000

CASUALTIES Austrians: 9,400 killed, wounded or taken prisoner; French: 7,000 killed or wounded

LOCATION 1 mile (2km) east of Alessandria, northern Italy

In May 1800 Napoleon, now first consul, led the newly formed Army of Reserve across the Alps by the St. Bernard Pass. Cannon barrels were placed in hollowed-out tree trunks and dragged over the ice, snow, and rock. The French army came out on the Lombardy plain and marched west to engage the Austrians. In Turin, Austrian commander Baron Michael Melas decided his best course was to march east and break through Napoleon's forces, which lay across his line of communications. Not anticipating Melas's aggressive intentions, Napoleon confidently expected the Austrians to withdraw; when they attacked at Marengo his forces were scattered, with only some 22,000 immediately available to face Melas's 31,000. The French were driven back, at some

IDEAL HERO
In reality Napoleon crossed the Alps on a mule. This idealized image, painted by Jacques-Louis David, was imperial propaganda.

MOUNTAIN PASS
The St Bernard Pass was covered in snow and ice when the French Army of Reserve crossed it in May 1800.

points in disarray, and by the early afternoon Melas believed the battle won. At around 5 p.m., however, a contingent some 10,000 strong led by Desaix arrived on the battlefield and launched a decisive counterattack.

Although Desaix was shot through the heart, the combined force of French artillery, cavalry, and infantry broke the weary Austrians, who were routed. The next day Melas signed an armistice, agreeing to evacuate Lombardy.

THE DANISH CAMPAIGN

Copenhagen

DATE April 2, 1801

FORCES Danish: 18 ships; British: 33 ships (12 committed to battle)

CASUALTIES Danish: 470 killed, 550 wounded, 1,779 taken prisoner; British: 254 killed, 689 wounded

LOCATION Copenhagen, Denmark

In February 1802 Denmark, Russia, Sweden, and Prussia formed an armed neutrality league in reaction to British searches of neutral shipping. Britain responded by sending a fleet to the Danish capital under Admiral Sir Hyde Parker, who sent his second-in-command Nelson with 12 ships of the line to sail into the harbor. Nelson had to negotiate sand banks while engaging a defensive line of armed hulks and floating batteries, as well as Danish warships. When the battle was at its hottest, Parker ordered Nelson to withdraw, but he claimed not to see the signal, putting his telescope to his blind eye. After four hours of intensive cannon duels, Danish resistance ceased. Nelson said of the battle, "I have been in 105 engagements, but that of today was the most terrible of them all!"

THE THIRD COALITION

Ulm

DATE October 1805

FORCES Austrians: 45,000; French: 150,000

CASUALTIES Austrians: 10,000 killed or wounded, 30,000 taken prisoner; French: 1,500 killed or wounded

LOCATION Southern Germany

By 1805, when the Third Coalition of Britain, Austria, Russia, and Sweden was formed to fight France, Napoleon had created the impressive Grande Armée, almost 200,000 men organized in seven corps, each commanded by a marshal. Austria and Russia planned major offensives through northern Italy and across southern Germany into France. Through September General

Mack von Lieberich led an Austrian army as far as Ulm on the Danube, where he waited for a Russian army under Prince Mikhail Kutuzov to join him. Moving faster than their enemies considered possible, most of the Grande Armée reached positions in northern Germany by September 24. Napoleon then marched the majority of his forces in a sweeping arc behind

Mack's army, still paralyzed at Ulm. Some of Mack's forces attempted to break out of the encirclement, but largely in vain. After a few sharp engagements, Mack surrendered on October 20. Napoleon proclaimed, with good reason, "Never has a victory been so complete and less costly."

SURRENDER TO THE FRENCH
After the Austrian surrender to Napoleon as Ulm, depicted here, Austrian commander Mack was court-martialed and imprisoned.

Austerlitz

DATE December 2, 1805

FORCES French: 73,000; Allies: 70,000 Russians, 15,000 Austrians

CASUALTIES French: 1,300 killed, 7,000 wounded; Allies: 16,000 killed or wounded, 11,500 taken prisoner

LOCATION Moravia, modern-day Czech Republic

Hearing of the Austrian capitulation at Ulm (see p.201), the cautious Russian commander General Kutuzov withdrew eastward, allowing Napoleon to occupy Vienna. Pursuing the Russians put Napoleon's army in an increasingly precarious position. Winter was drawing in and they were advancing through country stripped bare by the retreating Russians. Napoleon gambled on bringing his enemies swiftly to battle before the Austrians could bring new forces into play. He found the battleground he wanted near the town of Austerlitz. There he gave the impression of preparing a withdrawal by evacuating the dominant

IMPERIAL EAGLE
Napoleon's regiments carried eagle standards in deliberate imitation of the Roman Empire.

Pratzen Heights. He also disposed his forces so that a weakness was visible on his right, where the line of the Goldbach stream was thinly held. Kutuzov would not rise to this bait, but emperors Francis of Austria and Alexander of Russia, both present at Austerlitz, favored bold offensives. Ignoring

Kutuzov, the Austrian generals devised a bold plan to break through the weak French right flank. At dawn on December 2 the Allies attacked, throwing their main weight against the French right. Reinforcements under Davout were rushed up to block this thrust and the Russian infantry was bogged down in swampy land around the Goldbach. As Napoleon had hoped, his opponents threw more forces to his right, drawing troops away from the center. At

CAVALRY CHARGE
The cavalry of the Russian Imperial Guard is shown here charging Soult's French infantry on the Pratzen Heights in the thick of the battle of Austerlitz.

"I was…under fierce and continuous canister fire….Many soldiers…incessantly engaged in battle from 7 a.m. to 4 p.m., had no cartridges left. I could do nothing but retreat…"

Russian lieutenant general Przhebishevsky, official report on Austerlitz, 1805

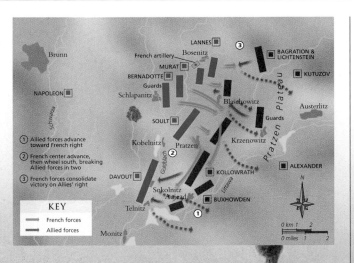

KEY
→ French forces
→ Allied forces

① Allied forces advance toward French right
② French center advance, then wheel south, breaking Allied forces in two
③ French forces consolidate victory on Allies' right

around 9 a.m. he ordered Soult to lead his corps up onto the Pratzen Heights. They emerged from fog that filled the valley onto the clear plateau, achieving complete surprise. Kutuzov threw in the Russian Imperial Guard cavalry to retake the high ground, to which Napoleon responded by sending in his Imperial Guard cavalry, driving the Russians off the heights. Soult was then able to send his men into the rear of

the enemy forces still stalled on the Goldbach. The Allies that escaped fled across the frozen Satschan lakes, some falling through the ice as it cracked beneath their weight. On the other flank, Russian commander Prince Bagration had no greater success and his men fell back in a rout. Napoleon had achieved his greatest victory. The Austrians sued for peace, while the Russians retreated into Poland.

1750–1914

FRENCH SUPREMACY

THE STRENGTH OF THE FRENCH ARMY and Napoleon's military genius enabled France to achieve an extraordinary dominance over Europe. The victories at Ulm and Austerlitz in 1805 were followed by the destruction of the Prussian and Russian armies in 1806–07 and another defeat for Austria in 1809. Napoleon reorganized European borders and political life at will. Only Britain remained unsubdued; in summer 1805 Napoleon had planned an invasion, but after the British naval victory at Trafalgar this project was never revived. Instead, France attempted to impose an economic blockade through the Continental System, banning trade between Europe and Britain. French attempts to make all countries conform to this blockade were to lead to the next round of fighting.

■ THE THIRD COALITION

Trafalgar

DATE October 21, 1805

FORCES
British: 27 ships of the line; French-Spanish: 33 ships of the line

LOCATION
South of Cadiz, off Cape Trafalgar

CASUALTIES British: 449 killed, 1,214 wounded; French-Spanish: 4,408 killed, 2,545 wounded

In October 1805 French Admiral Villeneuve, commanding a Franco–Spanish fleet off Cadiz, was ordered to sail to the Mediterranean. A British fleet commanded by Lord Horatio Nelson was waiting outside the port. Nelson planned to sail his ships in two columns perpendicular to the Franco–Spanish line, cutting it in the center

EXCHANGING BROADSIDES

Participants at the battle of Trafalgar described the astonishing noise and appalling injuries such as dismemberment and burns.

and toward the rear. In the ensuing melée superior British seamanship and gunnery would wreak havoc before the enemy could turn to join the battle. When Villeneuve sighted Nelson's fleet he turned back toward Cadiz but could not avoid battle. Nelson headed one of the British columns aboard *Victory*, Collingwood the other aboard *Royal Sovereign*. *Victory* sailed through the enemy line behind Villeneuve's flagship, *Bucentaure*, raking it with grapeshot. British vessels took heavy damage, however, from enemy broadsides that brought down rigging and masts. In the early afternoon *Victory* came alongside the French ship *Redoutable*. Marines firing down from the masts of the French ship killed many men on *Victory*'s deck, including Nelson, who had shown a reckless disregard for personal safety throughout. The last act of the battle came when the French ship *Achille* caught fire and exploded, with great loss of life. Eleven French and Spanish ships made it back to Cadiz.

1758–1805

LORD NELSON

Horatio Nelson first came to prominence at the battle of Cape St. Vincent in 1797 (see p.199). He repeatedly ignored direct orders, but headstrong boldness was crowned by success at the battle of the Nile in 1798 and at Copenhagen in 1801. Nelson established an admirable relationship of mutual trust with his captains, who were inspired to show initiative and daring by his example. His determination to lead from the front cost him an eye in 1794, his right arm in 1797, and his life at Trafalgar.

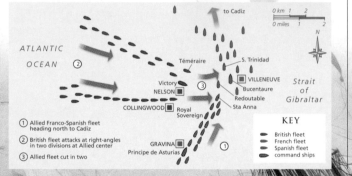

1. Allied Franco-Spanish fleet heading north to Cadiz
2. British fleet attacks at right-angles in two divisions at Allied center
3. Allied fleet cut in two

KEY
- British fleet
- French fleet
- Spanish fleet
- command ships

THE THIRD COALITION

Jena/Auerstadt

DATE October 14, 1806

FORCES
French: 121,000;
Prussians: 117,000

CASUALTIES French:
12,000 killed or
wounded; Prussians:
40,000 killed, wounded
or taken prisoner

LOCATION
East of Weimar,
Germany

In late 1806 Napoleon concentrated almost his entire Grande Armée against the Prussians, cutting off the Prussian army from Berlin. On October 13 a corps commanded by Lannes met a large Prussian force at Jena. Believing this to be the main army, Napoleon sent the bulk of his forces to join Lannes, while Bernadotte and Davout were ordered to outflank the Prussians to the north. In fact, the Prussian forces at Jena were the smaller part of their army, commanded by Prince Hohenlohe. The main army under the Duke of Brunswick was farther north at Auerstadt. The battle at Jena began with the French attacking while still moving up their forces and Hohenlohe desperately awaiting reinforcements. The Prussians were decimated as they stood on the defensive in virtual parade order. Given the French superiority of numbers, their eventual victory was assured. At Auerstadt, however, Davout found himself facing the bulk of the Prussian army, while Bernadotte wandered between the two battlefields. Davout fought a superb defensive battle. Brunswick was killed early on, leaving Prussian king William III in command.

When Davout began to push forward, the king ordered a retreat that swiftly turned into a rout. Over the following days the Prussians were unrelentingly pursued by French cavalry. Berlin was occupied on October 26.

CANNONS AT JENA
The Prussians were shot down in droves by French firepower as they stood in formation.

HEAVY CAVALRY
The French cuirassiers—heavy cavalry—wore steel helmets with elaborate ornament and steel breastplates over their uniforms. The straight sword was designed for thrusting.

THE THIRD COALITION

Eylau

DATE February 8, 1807

FORCES
French: 71,000;
Russians: 76,000

CASUALTIES
French: 25,000
killed or wounded;
Russians: 15,000
killed or wounded

LOCATION
Preussische-Eylau,
Poland

The Prussian defeat at Jena/Auerstadt left the Russians to bear the brunt of Napoleon's aggression. The French pursued the Russians and some Prussian remnants into Poland. In February the French and Russians stumbled into one another at Eylau, both sides calling in reinforcements as battle was engaged. Fighting in a snowstorm, the French came close to defeat when Augereau's corps, making a frontal attack on the Russian center directly into the fire of a 70-gun battery, was repulsed with massive casualties. Murat saved the day with a costly charge by 10,000 French cavalry, which swept through the Russian infantry and overwhelmed the cannons. When reinforcements under Ney arrived, Russian commander Bennigsen withdrew, although he had certainly not been defeated. It was not until the French victory at Friedland the following June that the Russians were crushed, forcing Emperor Alexander to sue for peace.

THE DANUBE CAMPAIGN

Wagram

DATE July 5–6, 1809

FORCES
French: 170,000;
Austrian: 146,000

CASUALTIES
French: 37,000
killed or wounded;
Austrians: 40,000
killed or wounded

LOCATION
Deutsch-Wagram,
east of Vienna

In 1809 Austria had the temerity to restart war with France. On April 9 Austrian forces commanded by Archduke Charles invaded Bavaria. When the French counteroffensive occupied Vienna, Charles's army was on the opposite side of the Danube. Napoleon started to move his men over the river, but a determined Austrian counterattack on May 21–22 drove the French back with heavy losses. It was not until July 4 that Napoleon resumed the offensive; battle was joined the following day. The Austrians mostly held their line in fierce but indecisive fighting up to nightfall. The following morning battle resumed with an Austrian attack that threatened to break the French left until Massena's corps repulsed it. On the other flank Davout captured the key village of Markgrafneusiedl. Napoleon then sent forward a body of 8,000 infantry under Macdonald, supported by cavalry and artillery, to deliver the final blow. Macdonald drove the Austrians back, but at massive cost: around three-quarters of his men were casualties. The Austrians withdrew, though not in disarray. Austria signed a peace treaty on French terms three months later.

STORMING THE WALLS
Early in the Wagram campaign French marshal Lannes took the Bavarian city of Ratisbon by storm, artillery giving support to infantry mounting the walls by siege ladders.

SHIP OF THE LINE

ITS ROLE AS HORATIO NELSON'S FLAGSHIP AT THE BATTLE OF TRAFALGAR MADE HMS *VICTORY* ONE OF THE MOST FAMOUS WARSHIPS OF ITS TIME.

Serving from 1778 to 1812, HMS *Victory* was one of the largest ships in the British fleet at the time of the Napoleonic wars. She was launched from Chatham dockyard in Kent in 1765, but it was another 13 years before her commission as the flagship of Admiral Augustus Keppel in the war against France. In 1778 and again in 1781 *Victory* led inconclusive actions near the island of Ouessant, off the coast of Brittany, northwest France. In 1793, during Britain's war with revolutionary France, she became the Royal Navy's flagship in the Mediterranean, heading the British destruction of the Spanish fleet—Spain was an ally of France at the time—off Cape Saint Vincent, Portugal. Considered too old after this triumph, *Victory* sailed home to serve as a prison hospital ship. But her finest hour was yet to come: in 1803 she was recommissioned as Admiral Horatio Nelson's flagship. Two years later, at the battle of Trafalgar, she fronted Nelson's successful attempt to break the French line off Cadiz, Spain, although many of her crew—including Nelson himself, who died in the ship's cockpit—fell to French sniper fire.

ARCHETYPAL WARSHIP

Victory was a typical example of a three-decked warship, the most powerful and prestigious vessels of the day. Made chiefly of oak, around 6,000 trees were felled for its construction, the British dockyards being some of the world's largest industrial enterprises. The ship was an expensive piece of military hardware, costing an estimated $90 million in today's money to build. Firing broadsides

UNDER FIRE *The Victory at Trafalgar. Its crew suffered the worst losses of any Allied ship, totaling 57 deaths.*

SPECIFICATION		
Origin Great Britain	**Date of launch** 1765	**Number of sails** 37
Length 186ft (57m)	**Tonnage** 2,361 tons	**Armament** 104 guns
Width 52ft (16m)	**Crew** 850 men	**Gundecks** 3

of solid shot from around 50 guns, *Victory* might use up hundreds of barrels of gunpowder in an engagement; a skilled crew could get a shot off every minute or two. Warships like *Victory* continued to dominate naval warfare until the second half of the 19th century, when the introduction of steam-driven, ironclad battleships, firing explosive shells from revolving turrets, revolutionized naval warfare.

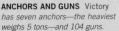

ANCHORS AND GUNS Victory has seven anchors—the heaviest weighs 5 tons—and 104 guns.

GUNDECK Besides housing the guns, most of the crew ate and slept on the ship's gundecks. The crew relied on lanterns when firing, as the deck filled with gunsmoke.

RESTORED WARSHIP
Today HMS Victory is in dry-dock at Portsmouth, on the south coast of England. It has been restored to the condition it was in before the battle of Trafalgar.

STERN *This housed the cabins of the captain, admiral, and other officers. Victory's stern was less decorated than earlier ships of its type.*

SHIP'S WHEEL *Aft on the quarterdeck, the wheel required four men to turn it in calm weather, but up to eight men in rough seas.*

FIRE BUCKETS *This row of leather buckets hangs from the edge of the poop deck. Victory's wooden construction and tar-coated rigging meant that fire posed a serious threat.*

GUN LOCK *Pulling the cord of the gun lock created a spark by which the gun's charge was ignited. The gun lock is brass, while the hammer and priming pan are both steel.*

SICK BAY *Forward on the upper deck, the sick bay had good lighting and ventilation, unlike the operating room deep in the ship.*

POWDER HORN *Each gun captain carried a cow horn filled with powder to prime the gun. The horn had a spring-loaded tip.*

HOLD *The hold is shown here almost empty, containing just a layer of gravel for ballast and a few barrels. However, when full it could store supplies for a six-month voyage. The officer in charge of the hold was the purser.*

SURGEON'S CABIN *This room was on the orlop deck, below the waterline.*

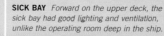

THE PENINSULAR WAR

IN 1807 FRANCE AND ITS SPANISH ALLIES invaded Portugal to close a breach in the Continental System by which Napoleon hoped to block Britain's trade with Europe. Then, in May 1808 the French emperor placed his brother Joseph Bonaparte on the Spanish throne. These two events sparked a war that became an ulcer draining the strength of Napoleonic France. After brutally repressing a popular uprising in Madrid, the French faced a nationwide Spanish insurrection that turned into a bitter guerrilla war, fought without quarter on both sides. Britain meanwhile, eager to protect its trading interests, landed forces in Portugal. Led by Arthur Wellesley, the future Duke of Wellington, they were to drive the French out of the Iberian peninsula.

PENINSULAR WAR

Vimeiro

DATE August 21, 1808

FORCES
British and Portuguese: 18,800; French: 13,000

LOCATION
North of Lisbon, Portugal

CASUALTIES
British and Portuguese: 700; French: 2,000

Encouraged by a French surrender to Spanish regulars at Bailen two weeks previously, in early August 1808 a British force led by Arthur Wellesley landed on the Portuguese coast near Coimbra and advanced south. Andoche Junot, the French commander in Portugal, gathered his forces and marched north to engage Wellesley, who was positioned on a ridge stretching from the village of Vimeiro to the sea. French columns made a series of attacks along the British line, but were repeatedly thrown back by concentrated enemy fire. Repulsed at Vimeiro, Junot felt his position was untenable. He negotiated surrender terms with senior British officers under which his troops and their equipment were repatriated to France by British ships—an agreement that caused an outcry in Britain.

SCOTTISH TROOPS
Highland regiments fought at Vimeiro. These soldiers, wearing ostrich feather caps, belonged to the Highland Light Infantry.

PENINSULAR WAR

La Coruña

DATE
January 16, 1809

FORCES
British: 15,000; French: 20,000

LOCATION On the coast of Galicia, northwest Spain

CASUALTIES
British: 800 killed or wounded; French: 1,000 killed or wounded

Stung by French setbacks in Iberia, in October 1808 Napoleon took personal command of a large army in northern Spain. The British forces in Portugal were now commanded by General Sir John Moore, as Wellesley had been recalled for an inquiry into Junot's repatriation. Moore advanced his army into Spain, only to learn that Napoleon had brushed aside the Spanish and occupied Madrid. The Spanish collapse forced the British to withdraw toward La Coruña, harried by the French. Marching through mountains in bitter winter weather, the British soldiers' morale disintegrated. But the rearguard fought successful holding actions and, when it arrived at La Coruña, formed a defensive line from the village of Elvina to the sea. On January 16 forces

GORGET
Gorgets were pieces of armor that protected the throat and symbolized the rank of officer in the British army. This one dates from c.1800.

RETREAT TO LA CORUÑA
About 4,000 British troops died during the midwinter mountain crossing in 1808.

under the French duke Nicolas-Jean-de-Dieu Soult made a frontal attack on the British line, twice capturing Elvina only to be driven out by the British both times. In the second counterattack, in which the British used bayonets for lack of ammunition, Moore was fatally wounded. He was buried that night on the ramparts of La Coruña. The following day the British forces were evacuated by sea.

PENINSULAR WAR

Talavera

DATE
July 28–29, 1809

FORCES
British: 24,000; French: 47,000

LOCATION 58 miles (94km) southwest of Madrid, central Spain

CASUALTIES British and Spanish: 6,500 killed or wounded; French: 7,400 killed or wounded

At the start of 1809 Napoleon left Spain with a substantial part of his army because impending war with Austria required his attention (see Wagram, p.205). Wellesley returned to Portugal in April with a force of around 28,000 British and Hanoverians (German subjects of the British crown), supplemented by 16,000 Portuguese. The French threatened from two directions: commander Soult in charge of an army in northern Portugal and Napoleon's brother, King Joseph, leading forces to the east of Lisbon. In May Wellesley drove Soult out of the city of Porto. Two months later, joined by 30,000 Spanish troops, he marched east from Lisbon, pursuing the other French army as it withdrew toward Madrid. At Talavera, the outnumbered French turned to fight their pursuers. In a series of bold attacks they almost

> "Our men suffered dreadfully on the route....The brain fever soon commenced, making fearful ravages in our ranks, and many men dropped by the roadside and died."

Sergeant Edward Costello, 95th Rifles, on marching to Talavera, 1809

SWORD AND SCABBARD
This c.1800 British light cavalry saber had a heavy blade that could sever an arm or split a skull with a single blow.

broke the British line, but Wellesley plugged what he called "an ugly hole" just in time. The hard-fought battle—which gained Wellesley the title Viscount Wellington of Talavera—was followed by the withdrawal of both sides. The French fell back on Madrid while the British marched back to Lisbon after learning that Soult was advancing from the north. Over the next two years the British remained on the defensive in Portugal, while the French suffered ever heavier losses at the hands of Spanish guerrillas.

PENINSULAR WAR

Salamanca

DATE July 22, 1812

FORCES British and Portuguese: 52,000; French: 48,000

CASUALTIES British and Portuguese: 4,800 killed or wounded; French: 14,000 killed, wounded, or captured

LOCATION South of Salamanca, western Spain

INFANTRY CLASH
The British 9th Infantry Regiment, shown here in combat with French forces at Bayonne, France, in 1814, played a crucial role in the battle of Salamanca.

From the start of 1812 Viscount Wellington took the offensive. After the capture of Ciudad Roderigo and Badajoz on the Portuguese–Spanish border, he was well positioned to strike into Spain. In June the British took Salamanca, but the army of the French marshal Auguste-Frédéric de Marmont hovered nearby. On July 22 Wellington began a withdrawal. Marmont tried to block the British, but his flanking movement thinly stretched his forces across the British front. Wellington now launched an attack led by General Edward Pakenham. After British infantry had broken the French squares, a cavalry charge scattered the rest of the French army. The battle was not a total rout, but British artillery and musket fire inflicted heavy casualties—Marmont, for example, was severely wounded—and allowed Wellington to go on to occupy Madrid.

> "The fire became stronger, there was a pause…General Pakenham approached and…said, 'There they are, my lads. Just let them feel the temper of your bayonets.'"
>
> *Sergeant Morley,* 5th Foot, at Salamanca, 1812

PENINSULAR WAR

Siege of Badajoz

DATE March 16–April 6, 1812

FORCES French garrison: 5,000; British: 40,000

CASUALTIES French: 5,000 killed, wounded, or captured; British: 5,000 killed or wounded

LOCATION Southern Spanish–Portuguese border

In March 1812 Wellington determined to take Badajoz from the French. The British dug trenches outside the city, where they were discomfited by wet weather and French shells. By April 6 three breaches had been made in the walls and a night assault was ordered.

INTO THE BREACH
British troops prepare to storm Badajoz. After the city fell the British avenged their heavy losses with looting, rape, and murder.

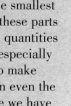

FULL HONORS
This service medal was awarded for action at Badajoz or Ciudad Roderigo.

The French had placed mines and sharpened stakes in the way and prepared lines of fire converging on the breaches. Some of the storming parties got lost in the smoke and the darkness, and not a single British soldier had penetrated the walls when troops under Sir Thomas Picton attacked the city's castle, using scaling ladders to mount the ramparts. The fall of the city swiftly followed.

> "The emperor wants me to take the offensive… but his Majesty does not realize that the smallest movement in these parts expends great quantities of resources, especially of horses….To make requisitions on even the poorest village we have to send a detachment of 200 men and, to be able to live, we have to scatter over great distances."

WITNESS TO WAR
AUGUST MARMONT

Marshal August Marmont, writing in 1812, attempted to enlighten Napoleon on the realities of warfare in Spain. The food shortages were due to armies stripping the land bare, while guerrillas preyed on foraging parties—hence the need for 200 men to make requisitions.

PENINSULAR WAR

Vittoria

DATE June 21, 1813

FORCES French: 50,000; British and allies: 70,000

CASUALTIES French: 8,000 men and 150 cannon; British and allies: 5,000 men

LOCATION South of Bilbao, northern Spain

Despite the defeat at Salamanca, the French continued to give Wellington a hard fight. But by the summer of 1813, by now in command of a large allied army of British, Spanish, and Portuguese forces, he was ready to embark on a drive across northern Spain toward the French border. King Joseph of Spain hurried to block Wellington's path, but the British commander ordered his army to attack in four columns, turning both flanks of the enemy and breaking through in the center. Joseph inevitably called for a retreat, which turned into a rout of his forces. The French abandoned their cannons along with wagonloads of supplies and treasure, all of which thoroughly distracted the victors from the pursuit. The following October Wellington's peninsular army invaded France.

WEAPONS OF THE NAPOLEONIC ERA

THE NAPOLEONIC WARS (1803–15) mostly involved the same weapons that had dominated European battlefields in the previous century: flintlock muskets and bayonets, swords and lances, a smattering of rifles, and cannons. Innovations, such as the British Congreve rockets for artillery, were marginal. Yet arms were produced in unprecedented numbers. The French empire manufactured almost four million small arms, while half a million musket balls might be expended in one battle.

NAPOLEON AT WATERLOO
The Napoleonic wars were fought between armies with near-identical weaponry.

MUSKETS AND RIFLES

The massed infantry in Napoleonic battles were armed with flintlock muskets. Standing in lines two or three ranks deep, with ranks firing alternately, they could unleash four volleys in the time it took an attacking column to cover the last 250ft (75m) of its advance. Rifles, firearms with grooved barrels invented in the 16th century, were still the weapons only of specialized regiments of sharpshooters.

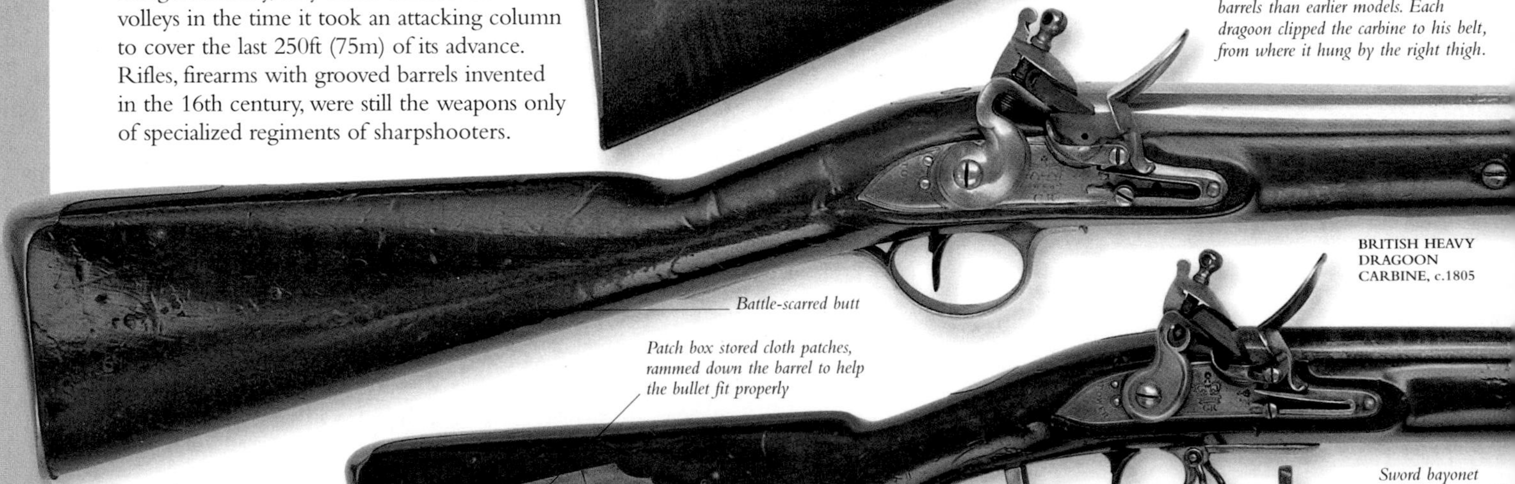

PISTOLS AND CARBINES

Although flintlock muskets were the dominant firearm of the Napoleonic wars, pistols and carbines—shorter and lighter than muskets—had their place. Captain Alexander Mercer, a British artillery officer at the battle of Waterloo (see p.215), described how the French sent out "a cloud of skirmishers, who galled us terribly by a fire of carbines and pistols at scarcely 40 yards from our front." Many cavalrymen went into battle with two loaded pistols, but these were only emergency backup for their principal weapon, the sword. In contrast, dragoons (cavalry who often fought dismounted) typically regarded the carbine as their main arm.

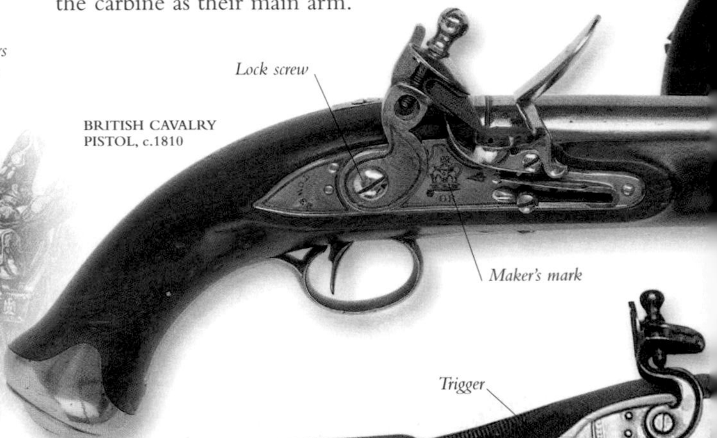

Lock screw

BRITISH CAVALRY PISTOL, c.1810

Maker's mark

Trigger

DRAGOON WEAPON
Napoleonic-era carbines had shorter barrels than earlier models. Each dragoon clipped the carbine to his belt, from where it hung by the right thigh.

BRITISH HEAVY DRAGOON CARBINE, c.1805

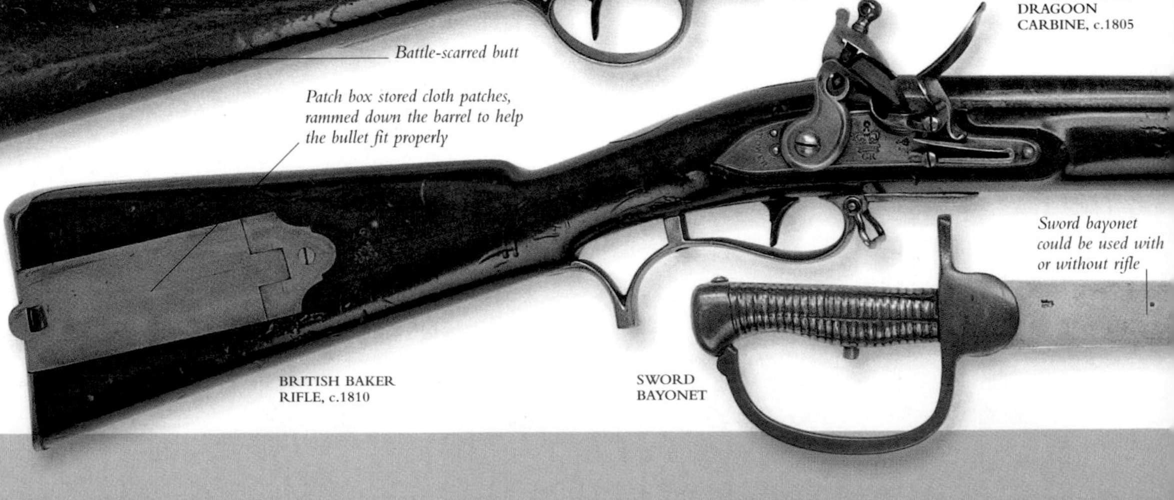

Battle-scarred butt

Patch box stored cloth patches, rammed down the barrel to help the bullet fit properly

Sword bayonet could be used with or without rifle

RIFLE
The Baker rifle armed British rifle regiments in the early 1800s. Its grooved barrel imparted spin to a bullet, greatly improving range and accuracy.

BRITISH BAKER RIFLE, c.1810

SWORD BAYONET

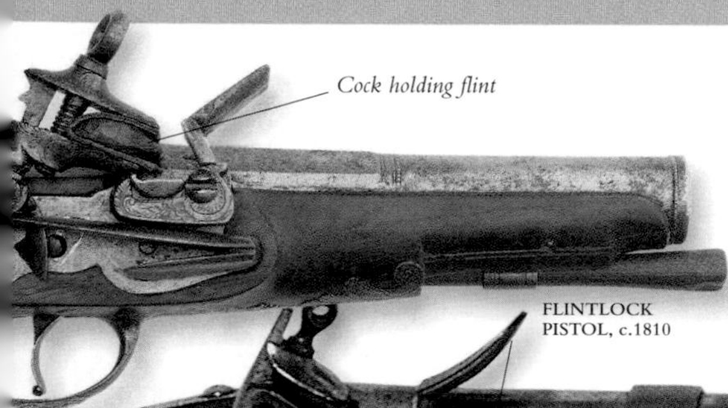

Cock holding flint

FLINTLOCK
PISTOL, c.1810

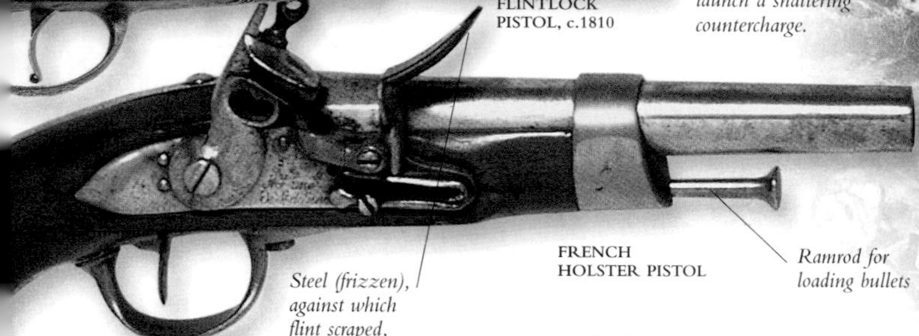

SWORDS DRAWN
At Waterloo, charging British cavalry are struck from the flank by Napoleon's lancers while his cuirassiers (heavy cavalry), in the foreground, prepare to launch a shattering countercharge.

FRENCH
HOLSTER PISTOL

Ramrod for loading bullets

Steel (frizzen), against which flint scraped, causing sparks

EDGED WEAPONS

The Napoleonic wars were the last major conflict in which swords played a significant role. They were not used for fighting on foot, but remained the weapon of choice for the cavalry charge—except for specialized light cavalry regiments armed with pennon- (or flag-) topped lances. Swords were highly effective against other cavalry and against infantry who were scattered or in flight, but they posed no threat to a tight infantry square bristling with bayonets.

FLINTLOCK PISTOLS
These muzzle-loading smooth-bore pistols were easy to carry, but mostly inaccurate and unreliable.

Brass barrel

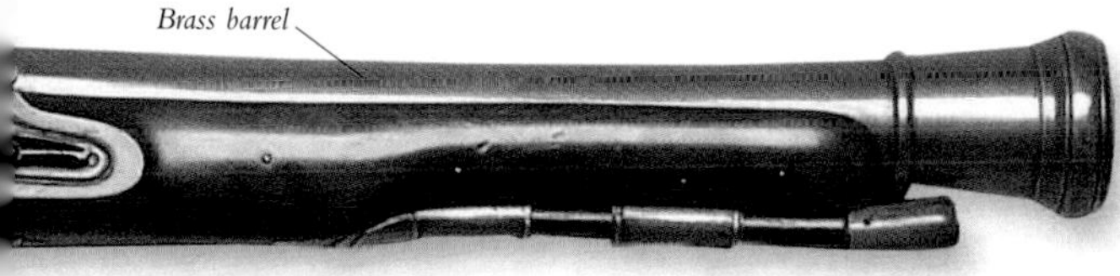

CLOSE QUARTERS
Blunderbusses were flintlock weapons with flared muzzle ends, designed to scatter the shot at point-blank range (although later experiments proved this did not actually happen). They were mainly used on warships, to repel enemy boarders.

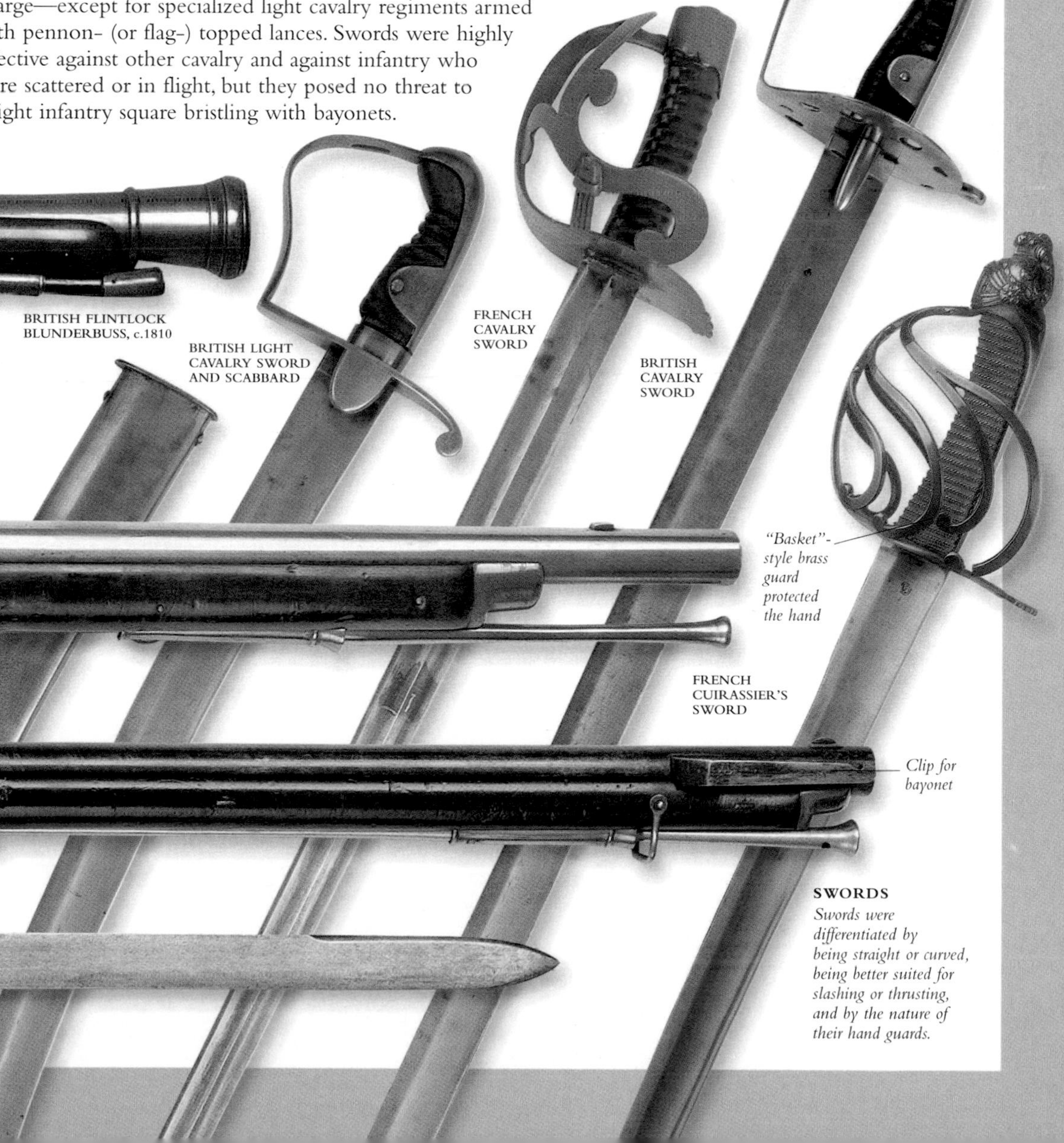

BRITISH FLINTLOCK
BLUNDERBUSS, c.1810

BRITISH LIGHT
CAVALRY SWORD
AND SCABBARD

FRENCH
CAVALRY
SWORD

BRITISH
CAVALRY
SWORD

"Basket"-style brass guard protected the hand

Bullets could be propelled up to 900ft (275m) through the grooved barrel

FRENCH
CUIRASSIER'S
SWORD

Clip for bayonet

SWORDS
Swords were differentiated by being straight or curved, being better suited for slashing or thrusting, and by the nature of their hand guards.

NAPOLEON VANQUISHED

IN THE SPRING OF 1812 Napoleon assembled an army of 614,000 men for an invasion of Russia, which had deserted his Continental System. The force included Austrians, Prussians, Poles, Italians, Swiss, and Danes—only a minority were French. Supported by a vast supply train of 25,000 vehicles, the army advanced into Russia on June 4, spread across a 300-mile (480km) front. Achieving coherent command over this vast area, with all messages carried on horseback, proved impossible, and supply problems mounted inexorably as the Russians fell back toward Moscow. After the battle of Borodino the French occupied Moscow, but the Russians' refusal to surrender led to a nightmare winter retreat from which Napoleon never recovered.

THE INVASION OF RUSSIA

Borodino

DATE	September 7, 1812
FORCES	French: 130,000; Russians: 120,000
CASUALTIES	French: 30,000 killed or wounded; Russians: 44,000 killed or wounded
LOCATION	75 miles (120km) west of Moscow

In the first three months of the invasion of Russia, Napoleon lost a third of his force to hardship and disease and fought only one substantial engagement, at Smolensk. At the start of September the veteran Russian general Mikhail Illarionovich Kutuzov decided to make a stand at Borodino,

CAVALRY CHARGE
Here, French dragoons charge the Russian fortification the Great Redoubt, securing a victory at the battle of Borodino.

improving a natural defensive position—hills between a river and a forest—with extensive field fortifications. Desperate for a decisive victory, Napoleon launched a series of frontal attacks on the Russian line. His infantry columns suffered appalling casualties against massed cannons, but the Russian

RUSSIAN CARTRIDGE CASE

counterattacks were similarly savaged by French firepower. The French took the fortification known as the Great Redoubt in the center of the Russian line but, with the way open to crush the Russian army, Napoleon refused to commit his 30,000-strong reserve, allowing Kutuzov to stage a withdrawal of his surviving forces.

THE RETREAT FROM MOSCOW

Berezina River

DATE	November 26–29, 1812
FORCES	French: 85,000; Russians: 65,000
CASUALTIES	French: 50,000 killed or captured; Russians: 10,000 killed or wounded
LOCATION	East of Minsk, Belarus

On October 19, 1812, having failed to make the Russians accept defeat, Napoleon ordered his army to retreat from Moscow. Short of food and fodder, tens of thousands of soldiers were left dead by the roadside. On November 23 the French arrived at the Berezina River to find a Russian army on the far bank and the only bridge destroyed. They were trapped between the icy raging torrent and another Russian army following at their heels. Rediscovering their ingenuity, the

ICY CROSSING
After the retreat from Moscow and the crossing of the Berezina River, shown here, Napoleon had fewer than 10,000 fit men.

"Crowds of poor wretches who were trying to cross the bridge were seen to fall into the stream and be sucked under the masses of ice."

Louis Constant, Napoleon's valet, on the crossing of the Berezina, 1812

French set about building two wooden bridges. About 400 French engineers worked chest-deep in the icy river; many died of exposure or were swept away. Between November 26 and 29 some 35,000 soldiers crossed the bridges while desperate actions were fought on both sides of the river to defend the bridgeheads. The French engineers then destroyed the bridges.

"The roads were like glass. The horses fell down and could not get up. Our worn-out soldiers no longer had strength to their arms. The barrels of their muskets were so cold that they stuck to their hands....The men fell frozen stiff all along the road....One must have seen these horrors in order to believe them!"

WITNESS TO WAR
J.-R. COIGNET

A French captain, Jean-Roche Coignet, describes the retreat from Moscow, when temperatures dropped to −22°F (−30°C). More than half a million men died in Napoleon's Russian campaign.

NAPOLEON VERSUS ALLIES

Leipzig

DATE
October 16–19, 1813

FORCES French:
195,000; Allies: 365,000

CASUALTIES
French: 70,000; killed,
wounded, or captured;
Allies: 54,000 killed or
wounded

LOCATION
By the city of Leipzig,
Saxony, Germany

Napoleon's Russian disaster encouraged
Prussia, Sweden, and Austria to ally
against him in 1813. Although France
had rebuilt its armies with fresh
conscripts, they were now thoroughly
outnumbered. After an indecisive
campaign in Germany, Napoleon
took up a defensive position on the
plain around Leipzig on October 14.
The Austrian army was the first to
attack him on October 16; by
October 18 the Prussians, Russians,
and Swedes had also arrived. Suffering
heavy casualties, Napoleon embarked
on a phased withdrawal across the
single bridge over the Elster River.
On the morning of the 19th, French
engineers blew up the bridge, leaving
15,000 troops on the wrong side.
Some drowned attempting to cross
the river; most were taken prisoner.

ALLIED VICTORY
*The battle of Leipzig, also known as
the battle of the Nations, was the largest
battle fought in Europe before 1914.*

NAPOLEON VERSUS ALLIES

The Defense of France

DATE
January 29–March 31,
1814

FORCES
French: 110,000;
Allies: 345,000

LOCATION
Eastern France

CASUALTIES
French: 30,000;
Allies: 50,000

By 1814 France faced almost certain
defeat. Napoleon attempted to repeat
the past success of his *levée en masse*
(mass conscription), but only 110,000
war-weary French responded to the

BREASTPLATE
*The steel cuirass of a
French heavy cavalryman
(a cuirassier) could
stop musket balls.*

call, many of them
as young as 16. His
enemies invaded
France along three
axes: the Swedish
army advanced from
Belgium, another
under the Prussian
general Gebhard von
Blücher marched into
Lorraine, and the largest
force, headed by the Austrian general
Karl Philipp Schwarzenberg, entered
from Switzerland. Napoleon attempted

to defeat the invaders
by engaging sections
of their forces in
turn. It is widely
agreed that he never
displayed his talents
more brilliantly than
in this impossible
situation. Between
January 29 and
February 18 he
scored a series of
limited victories
over Blücher and
Schwarzenberg. The
Allies offered a compromise
peace, but Napoleon insisted on
fighting to the end. Then, during
March, the Allies' numerical strength
began to tell. Blücher defeated

Napoleon at Laon on the 9th and
Schwarzenberg beat him at Arcis-sur-
Aube on the 20th. In a last gamble,
Napoleon maneuvered to the east of
the Allies, hoping to force them away
from Paris. But the Allies simply
ignored him and advanced to the
French capital, which surrendered
on March 30. Napoleon still wanted
to fight on, but his marshals refused.
On April 6 the emperor abdicated,
retiring to the Mediterranean island
of Elba. The monarchy was restored in
France in the person of Louis XVIII.

FIGHTING ON
*Napoleon leads his staff in the defense
of France, 1814. His defeat was due
to the Allies' superior numbers and
the exhaustion of the French people.*

EMPIRES AND REVOLUTIONS

NAPOLEON'S FINAL DEFEAT

IN 1815 NAPOLEON LEFT Elba and returned to France, landing at Cannes with an army of 1,100 men and four cannons. Resentment at the country's restored monarchy led all the troops sent by King Louis XVIII to oppose Napoleon to join him instead, and he entered Paris on March 20 without a shot fired. The Allies—chiefly Britain, Austria, Prussia, and Russia— declared the former emperor an outlaw and prepared to repeat the invasion of 1814. Assembling an army of loyal veterans and young volunteers, Napoleon gambled on an offensive against British and Prussian forces in Belgium before the Austrians or Russians could arrive. The end to the "Hundred Days" of his last bid for power was brief, however: three battles in three days.

THE HUNDRED DAYS

Ligny

DATE June 16, 1815

FORCES Prussians: 84,000; French: 70,000–80,000

CASUALTIES Prussians: 16,000 killed or wounded; French: 12,000 killed or wounded

LOCATION Northeast of Charleroi, southern Belgium

Advancing from Paris unobserved by the Allies, on June 15 Napoleon crossed the Belgian border and occupied Charleroi. In front of him were two Allied armies: the Prussians, led by Blücher, and a British, German, Belgian, and Dutch force under Wellington. Together they outmanned the French two to one, but Napoleon intended to take them on one at a time. On June 16 he advanced to attack Blücher with his main force, while sending Marshal Ney to take Quatre-Bras between the two enemy armies. Blücher drew up his forces along ridges on each side of the village of Ligny. At 2:30 p.m. the French attacked. Napoleon wanted to envelop the Prussians, but his plan rested on the arrival of the Count d'Erlon's corps. D'Erlon, however, received counterorders from Ney (see below), and arrived at Ligny late in the day from an unexpected direction, merely panicking the French soldiers who thought they were Prussian reinforcements. It was 8 p.m. before Napoleon threw forward his Imperial Guard to break the battered Prussian line. Blücher was unhorsed leading a cavalry countercharge and the Prussians withdrew under cover of darkness. Although defeated, they had not been crushed—a failing that was to rebound on Napoleon at Waterloo two days later.

ORDERING THE TROOPS
Following Blücher's unhorsing at Ligny, his chief of staff, August von Gneisenau, (center) took over operations.

THE HUNDRED DAYS

Quatre-Bras

DATE June 16, 1815

FORCES British and Dutch: 32,000; French: 24,000

LOCATION Northwest of Ligny, Belgium

CASUALTIES British and Dutch: 5,400 killed or wounded; French: 4,400

BRITISH BAKER RIFLE, c.1810

SWORD BAYONET

Napoleon was determined to take the crossroads at Quatre-Bras because he saw it as a means by which the armies of Blücher and Wellington could join up—French control would prevent the British-led force from coming to the Prussians' assistance. However, the Prince of Orange, commanding one of Wellington's corps, had recognized the crossroads' strategic importance. On the morning of June 16, the prince's 8,000 Dutch troops were holding Quatre-Bras when Marshal Ney approached with a force of 24,000. The disaster for Napoleon was Ney's delay in attacking: he waited until 2 p.m. before delivering a determined assault, by which time Wellington was nearing with reinforcements. Ney had hoped for support from 20,000 men under the Count

INFANTRY ARMS
The Baker rifle was the weapon of British rifle regiments during the Napoleonic wars. Many of Wellington's soldiers and officers in 1815 were veterans of the Peninsular War.

d'Erlon, but Napoleon instead ordered d'Erlon's corps to Ligny. Ney furiously countermanded, with the result that the count marched back and forth for most of the day between the two battles. By the evening Wellington had over 30,000 men at Quatre-Bras and Ney's increasingly frantic assaults came to nothing. At nightfall the crossroads remained firmly in British hands. The next morning, in the face of a strangely inactive enemy, Wellington disengaged, withdrawing north toward Brussels. Blücher also withdrew to the north, attempting to keep in touch with his allies. Napoleon joined Ney with most of his forces and pursued Wellington, while tasking Marshal Emmanuel de Grouchy with shadowing Blücher and stopping him from joining up with Wellington's army.

SMOKE OF BATTLE
In the gunpowder era, battlefields— including the one at Quatre-Bras—were partially obscured by smoke as soon as fire was opened.

Waterloo

DATE June 18, 1815

FORCES
Anglo–Dutch: 67,000,
Prussians: 53,000;
French: 74,000

CASUALTIES
Anglo–Dutch: 15,000,
Prussians: 7,000;
French: 25,000

LOCATION Outside
Waterloo village,
south of Brussels

Napoleon tracked the Anglo–Dutch army to Mont St. Jean, just south of the village of Waterloo. It was here that Wellington decided to fight. He took up a defensive position along a ridge, with most of his forces on the reverse slope for protection against artillery. He also manned two strongpoints, the chateau of Hougomont on the right and the farm of La Haye Sainte in the center. The French were in position to attack at dawn but, after heavy rain the day before, waited for the ground to dry before taking the offensive. Napoleon's heavy guns opened up shortly after noon—Wellington's infantry spent much of the battle lying down to avoid cannon fire. After an hour of this barrage four columns of French infantry marched against Wellington's center, pressing forward through shattering artillery fire, only to be stopped by volleys from muskets and finally hurled back by a cavalry charge. By then the Prussian army—aided by Napoleon's delay in opening the attack—had appeared on the French

right wing. Blücher had left a rear guard to cope with Marshal de Grouchy and marched most of his army across to join the battle. Marshal Ney, meanwhile, led French cavalry in a series of charges against the British infantry squares that were repulsed with heavy losses. The French almost turned the battle with the capture of La Haye Sainte, but when Ney begged for reserves to exploit this advantage, Napoleon,

> "The discharge of every gun was followed by a fall of men and horses like grass before the mower's scythe."
>
> *Captain Alexander Mercer,* Journal of the Waterloo Campaign, 1815

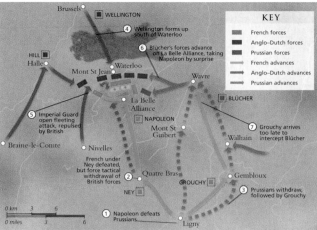

KEY

▬	French forces
▬	Anglo–Dutch forces
▬	Prussian forces
→	French advances
→	Anglo–Dutch advances
→	Prussian advances

Brussels
■ WELLINGTON
④ Wellington forms up south of Waterloo
HILL
Halle ■
⑥ Blücher's forces advance on La Belle Alliance, taking Napoleon by surprise
Mont St Jean   Waterloo
Wavre
■ BLÜCHER
La Belle Alliance
⑤ Imperial Guard open fleeting attack, repulsed by British
■ NAPOLEON
Mont St Guibert
Walhain
⑦ Grouchy arrives too late to intercept Blücher
Braine-le-Comte
Nivelles
French under Ney defeated, but force tactical withdrawal of British forces
② Quatre Bras
GROUCHY ■
Gembloux
■ NEY
③ Prussians withdraw, followed by Grouchy
① Napoleon defeats Prussians
Ligny

0 km   3   6
0 miles   3   6

BRITISH OFFICER'S KIT
The uniform of a Waterloo-era officer in the Royal Fusiliers.

Gilt epaulet
Gorget
Hat with cover
Shoulder belt holds sword
Silk sash
Leather Hessian boots
Officer's sword

1769–1852
DUKE OF WELLINGTON

Irish-born Arthur Wellesley was a practical tactician whose conduct in the Peninsular campaign made him a British national hero. He attributed his success always to being "on the spot" and "seeing and doing everything for myself." Although he never took unnecessary risks, he was a visible presence in the British lines throughout the battle of Waterloo.

heavily engaged with the Prussians, told him there were none. In a last gamble, at about 7 p.m., Napoleon ordered his Imperial Guard to march upon Wellington's infantry, only to receive volley after volley of musket fire before which the Guard wavered and then broke. After that it was a rout, the French fleeing with Blücher's cavalry in pursuit. It had been, as Wellington later said, "the nearest run thing you ever saw in your life".

SCOTTISH SERVICE
A Highland infantryman accompanies a cavalry charge against the French at Waterloo. A total of nine Scottish regiments fought at the battle.

WARS IN THE AMERICAS

IN THE 50 YEARS following the American Revolution, the old colonial masters were banished from everywhere in the Americas bar Canada and the Caribbean. Thereafter, struggles over internal control and disputes with neighbors led to conflicts right across the new American countries.

AMERICAN EXPANSION
In 1846–48 Mexico yielded nearly half its territory to the US. Westward expansion of the US was effected through land deals and Indian wars.

THE AMERICAS VERSUS EUROPE

HIDE SHIELD
Plains Indian shields were tough enough to stop arrows. The central symbol was thought to protect the wearer.

Inspired by both the American and the French revolutions, the emerging nations of Central and South America took advantage of Spain and Portugal's weakening military might to win their independence. After war against the British in 1812, the US cemented its nationhood, confidently asserting in the Monroe Doctrine its right to intervene wherever it chose. The US seized half of Mexico, drove the Spanish out of Cuba, and cleared the American Indians from productive land to become the "Colossus of the North." Despite the loss of most of their colonies, European powers continued to intervene in the Americas, but they would be increasingly excluded by the US, which saw it as its "manifest destiny" to dominate the New World.

CAPITAL BURNS
In 1814 Washington, D.C., was taken by British forces under Major General Ross. Many buildings, including the White House, were set alight.

KEY

—	Mexican frontier 1821	—	US forces in US–Mexican War 1846–48
✕	Seminole Wars 1816–58	✕	battle of US–Mexican War
—	"Trail of Tears" 1838–39		
—	Santa Ana during Texan Revolution 1835–36	✕	battles for the West 1850–90
✕	battle of Texan Revolution	—	flight of the Nez Percé

CIVIL WAR AND REVOLUTION

With the exception of Haiti, where the French were overthrown following a slave revolt in 1791, the revolutions of independence in the Americas were won by the countries' elites as the European powers lost their major colonies. This did not always solve questions of internal control, however, as by far the largest conflict—the American Civil War—showed. While the US united and gained in power, Latin America to the south remained weak and divided, no more so than in Mexico, where the overthrow of President Porfirio Díaz in 1911 initiated a bloody, decade-long revolution. The US played a major role in the conflict, supporting the metropolitan leaders against the rural guerrillas, and the merchant classes once more won through.

MEXICAN REVOLUTIONARIES
Bristling with bullets, northern guerrilla leader Francisco "Pancho" Villa (middle) poses with his men for the camera.

AMERICAN INDIAN WARS
This is the site in Oklahoma of one of the Red River battles of 1874–75, now cleared of both Indians and buffalo.

THE US FIGHTS BRITAIN

IN 1812, PRESIDENT MADISON declared war in response to Britain's high-handed patrolling of the seas, a move that played well with US expansionists who sought the annexation of Canada. Initially the Americans made progress, but the end of the Napoleonic Wars in Europe freed up British reinforcement, which blockaded the coast and burned down public buildings in Washington, D.C. With neither side able to force a victory, the peace treaty of 1814 restored the prewar status quo and the US forever relinquished its designs on Canada.

THE WAR OF 1812

Lake Erie

DATE
September 10, 1813

FORCES
US: 9 ships; Britain: 6 warships

LOCATION
Lake Erie is bordered by Ohio and Ontario

CASUALTIES
US: 27 dead, 96 wounded; British: 40 dead, 94 wounded

Control of Lake Erie was key to keeping supply lines to the US-controlled Northwest Territory open. For nine months, shipwrights in Erie built the ships that the US was to use in the battle for the lake, a remarkable feat of logistics given the town's mere 500 inhabitants. Commodore Oliver Perry gathered together his crews, many of them novice sailors, and readied them for action. They engaged the British fleet, under the command of Captain Robert Barclay, near Put-in-Bay, Ohio. After an initial reverse that saw his flagship *Lawrence* reduced to a defenseless wreck, Perry jumped onto her sister ship *Niagara* and sailed directly into the British line, firing broadsides. This bold move proved decisive and Barclay was forced to surrender. Perry's triumphant report to General Harrison included the famous line "We have met the enemy and they are ours." The victory ensured US control over Lake Erie and opened important supply lines. It was a major reverse to the British who were then forced to abandon Detroit.

JUMPING SHIP
Seen here is Perry's dramatic transfer to the Niagara *during the thick of the fighting.*

THE WAR OF 1812

Baltimore

DATE
September 12–15, 1814

FORCES
US 10,000 defenders; British: 5,000 troops

LOCATION
Baltimore, Maryland

CASUALTIES
Unknown, but not heavy on either side

By the fall of 1814, the lack of progress was taking its toll on both sides. With Canada still unconquered, American public opinion was turning against the war. Meanwhile, the British naval blockade was taking effect, especially in New England, where there was talk of negotiating a separate peace. The British attempted to inflict a decisive blow on American morale by targeting prowar Baltimore. On September 12, 3,000 British troops landed at North Point and marched on the city. The next day, British warships bombarded Fort McHenry. But the Fort's defenders, under Major George Armistead, held out. Having failed to force a surrender, the British sailed back to North Point to pick up their now retreating troops. Stalemate had been reached, with both sides now ready for peace. The defense of Fort McHenry inspired Francis Scott Key's *The Star Spangled Banner*, in which he mentions the "rockets' red glare," a reference to the new Congreve rockets that were used by the British.

THE WAR OF 1812

New Orleans

DATE
January 8, 1815

FORCES
British: 10,000 troops; US: 5–7,000 troops

LOCATION Mouth of the Mississippi, New Orleans

CASUALTIES
British: 700 killed, 1,400 wounded; US: 8 killed, 13 wounded

Weeks after the war officially ended with the signing of the Treaty of Ghent in Belgium, the news was still making its way across the Atlantic. Thinking he was still at war, British Admiral Sir Alexander Cochrane was eager to push on and capture New Orleans from the Americans, fitting out a flotilla of more than 50 ships to transport the troops from Jamaica. General Andrew Jackson, "Old Hickory" to his men, had arrived in late fall of 1814 to defend the city. In December, advance British troops had penetrated to within a day's march of the city, where they awaited reinforcements. Jackson used this time well, retreating 3 miles (5km) to the Rodriguez Canal, where he erected fortified ramparts protected on the right by the Mississippi River and on the left by an impassable swamp. The fresh troops finally arrived during the first week of January and assembled under the command of Sir Edward Pakenham, confident that they could breach Jackson's seemingly thin defensive line. Pakenham decided to attack at dawn to take advantage of early morning fog, but his forces on the west bank were delayed and the main columns had to advance across open fields with no cover. To make matters worse, they forgot their ladders, although many would not make it as far as the ramparts anyway. The British were sitting ducks, falling by the score as they marched, and within half an hour Pakenham and both of his senior generals lay dead. The British hurriedly withdrew. The victory came too late to affect the war, but future president Jackson was a hero and American national pride had been restored.

CHALMETTE BATTLEFIELD
An old cannon still points at the site in New Orleans where the British were gunned down in droves.

VICTORY DRUM
This US army drum of 1812 depicts an eagle battling a lion, a reference to the American victory over Britain.

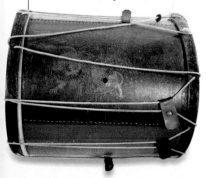

FAME AND POWER
Andrew Jackson (on the right) senses victory at New Orleans. His leadership in the battle won him fame and the presidency.

FIGHTING AMERICAN INDIANS

IN THE LATE 18TH AND EARLY 19th centuries, the eastern United States were systematically cleared of their aboriginal peoples. It was not until after the Civil War, however, that attention turned to the Plains Indians and the conflicts that so engaged Hollywood began. These were essentially guerrilla wars in which Indian horsemen used hit-and-run tactics, at first shooting arrows, later acquiring rifles. The conquest of the American Indian was characterized throughout by broken government promises and mass deportations to lands unwanted by the settlers. The Indians resisted, but they could not hold back the growing tide of whites who were pouring into the West, especially after the gold rush began in earnest in 1849.

THE INDIAN WARS

Tippecanoe

DATE
November 7, 1811

FORCES
Expeditionary force: 1,000; Shawnee: 1,000

LOCATION Near present-day Lafayette, Indiana

CASUALTIES
About 200 killed on both sides

In 1811 the governor of the Indiana Territory, Major General William Henry Harrison, was determined to clear the Northwest for settlers. Taking advantage of the absence of Tecumseh, leader of the Shawnee nation, who was away organizing resistance to white encroachment on Indian lands, Harrison marched up the Wabash River, camping near the Shawnee settlement of Prophetstown. The settlement had been left under the protection of Tecumseh's brother Laulewasikau, known as "the Prophet." Lacking his brother's talent for military strategy, the Prophet rashly attacked Harrison's camp. The warriors were easily repelled by Harrison's troops, who proceeded to attack and burn the Shawnee village. His reputation as a mystic in tatters, Laulewasikau fled to Canada—where a year later the Shawnee would fight alongside British troops in the war against the US—hotly pursued once more by Harrison. In truth, Tippecanoe was fairly inconclusive, but Harrison claimed it as a great victory, using it to further his career. Thirty years later he became the ninth US president.

FOREST FIGHTING
Harrison, on the left, is seen ordering his troops to fire. The battle was probably a lot less orderly than shown here.

THE INDIAN WARS

Second Seminole War

DATE 1835–36

FORCES Seminole: 4,000 remaining when they surrendered; US: unknown

LOCATION
Florida

CASUALTIES
US troops: 2,000; Seminoles: several thousand

The Indian Removal Act of 1830 was used by the US government to force the remaining eastern Indians west of the Mississippi River. In Florida the Seminole nation resisted. The US had wrested control of Florida from the Spanish in the First Seminole War, but the Seminoles had no intention of leaving. Led by the wily Osceola, the Seminoles began a bloody guerrilla resistance in what was to prove the longest of the Indian wars. Only after Osceola had been duplicitously taken hostage during peace talks were the Seminoles finally forced west.

THE INDIAN WARS

The Fetterman Fight

DATE
December 21, 1866

FORCES Lakota Sioux, Northern Cheyenne, and Arapaho: 1,000; US cavalry: 80

LOCATION
Just outside Fort Kearny, Wyoming

CASUALTIES
US cavalry: all 80 killed

Following the gold rush of 1849, increasing numbers of prospectors were traveling through Wyoming to the gold fields in Montana. In response, the government constructed the Bozeman Trail, a road protected by a series of forts that cut straight through traditional Sioux hunting grounds in the Bighorn Mountains. Incensed, Lakota Sioux leader Red Cloud organized an alliance of Plains Indians and began a campaign of hit-and-run raids on the new forts. Their most notable success occurred when a column led by Captain William J. Fetterman, sent to rescue a besieged wagon train, was ambushed by over 1,000 warriors, including a young Crazy Horse. Disobeying orders, Fetterman followed a decoy over Lodge Trail Ridge, where the Indians were lying in wait. The shooting started at around noon and was all over in half an hour. The bodies were found later that same day, stripped and mutilated. By 1868 Red Cloud had secured a peace treaty that would be honored by the government for precisely six years.

TO THE LAST MAN
Fetterman stares death in the face as Red Cloud's warriors, some armed with guns, encircle the remaining cavalry.

1822–1909

RED CLOUD

Makhpiya-Luta (Red Cloud) was a Sioux chief who inflicted several notable defeats on the United States. He established himself in wars against the Pawnee and Crow nations before orchestrating the successful resistance to the Bozeman Trail. Where others, including his son, refused to accept any accommodation with the white man, Red Cloud laid down his arms and kept his pledge of peace. Although he continued to defend his culture, by the time of his death in 1909 he had become a Christian and taken a European name.

THE INDIAN WARS

Red River War

DATE 1874–75

FORCES US troops: 3,000; Cheyenne, Comanche, Kiowa, Kataka: several thousand

LOCATION
Oklahoma and Texas

CASUALTIES
A few hundred dead on each side

In the 1870s white hunters were hunting the buffalo of the Southern Plains to extinction. Subsistence on meager reservation rations prompted talk of war among the previously peaceful Indians and on June 27, 1874, the Comanche chief Quanah Parker led 300 braves in an attack on the hunters at Adobe Walls. The attack failed, but the US army used it as an excuse to clear the area for white settlement. There followed as many as 20 pitched battles against Indians well equipped with ex-Civil War rifles. The turning point came with the destruction of five villages in Palo Duro Canyon on September 28, where over 1,000 horses were killed and the winter provisions were destroyed. The war ended in June 1875, when a half-starved Parker surrendered. Both Indians and buffalo would soon disappear from the Southern Plains.

Little Bighorn

DATE
June 25, 1876

FORCES US cavalry:
600; Cheyenne and
Dakota (Eastern
Sioux): 600

LOCATION The Little
Bighorn River,
Montana

CASUALTIES
US cavalry: all 600
killed

In defiance of Red Cloud's treaty, gold miners continued to settle in the sacred hunting grounds of the Black Hills. Outraged, the Sioux and Cheyenne fought back under the great warrior Sitting Bull, and troops were sent in when they refused to return to the reservations. General Alfred Terry took the main body of men up the Yellowstone River, while Lt.-Col. George Custer and the 7th Cavalry were to cross the Little Bighorn River and surround the enemy. Spotting a Sioux encampment, Custer ignored orders to wait and attacked. He had not counted on the rough terrain, however, and his troops lost all coordination. Major Charles Reno attacked first but was soon forced into a retreat. The Sioux then charged toward Custer's men, while a separate force led by Crazy Horse swooped in. Custer was trapped into his Last Stand. He ordered his men to shoot the horses and stack them up to form a wall, but it provided little protection and in less than an hour they were all dead. The Sioux victory was short-lived, however, as a buildup of troops forced Sitting Bull to surrender in 1881.

Geometric beadwork favored by Sioux

Buffalo rawhide covers wooden stirrup

SADDLE
Though Sioux usually rode bareback, a saddle and stirrups gave better stability. This "pad saddle" is stuffed with deer hair.

"The soldiers were divided, one party charging right into the camp. After driving these soldiers across the river, the Sioux charged [Custer's] soldiers below, and drove them into confusion; these soldiers became foolish, many throwing away their guns and raising their hands, saying, 'Sioux, pity us; take us prisoners.'"

WITNESS TO WAR

LAKOTA CHIEF RED HORSE

Chief Red Horse's account of Little Bighorn was recorded in pictographs in 1881. His description of the soldiers as "foolish" reflects the Sioux's martial values. By contrast, he was very impressed by Custer's bravery.

RIVER CROSSING
This photograph shows the site of Reno's crossing of the Little Bighorn River. Custer's battlefield is to the right.

Nez Percé War

DATE June–
December 1877

FORCES Nez Percé
warriors: 250;
US troops: 5,000

LOCATION
Idaho, Oregon, and
Montana

CASUALTIES Nez Percé:
(including women and
children): 239; US
troops: 266

The Nez Percé ("Pierced Nose" in French after their penchant for nose pendants) led a peaceful coexistence with the whites at first, until gold was discovered in their traditional land in the Columbia Plateau. In 1863 their reservation was reduced to a quarter of its size to permit mining. An escalation of raids by both whites and Indians led Nez Percé chief Joseph to decide that their future lay in Canada and in 1877 he took a small band of followers on an epic five-month trek north, pursued by the troops of General O. O. Howard. The Nez Percé were finally encircled in the Bear Paw Mountains, just 40 miles (65km) from the border. After a five-day battle both sides had fought to a stalemate, but Joseph's weary band gave up when they realized that more government troops were on the way. Although Joseph had won the respect of settlers, his people were nevertheless banished to Oklahoma, far from their ancestral lands.

Bow made of maple wood

A warrior carried about 20 arrows in his quiver

Quiver made of hide

BOY'S BOW
Nez Percé boys were expected to develop shooting skills from a young age and target-practiced on small game such as rabbits.

Wounded Knee

DATE
December 29, 1890

FORCES Sioux:
several hundred; US
cavalry: unknown

LOCATION Wounded
Knee Creek, South
Dakota

CASUALTIES Sioux:
c.150 killed, 30
wounded; US cavalry:
25 killed, 30 wounded

By the late 1880s the Sioux reservation had shrunk so much that the population was no longer able to feed itself. Reaching out for salvation, the half-starved Sioux turned to mysticism and the rites of the "Ghost Dance," designed to banish the white man from the earth. The government was sufficiently alarmed by this to send in the troops and arrest the leaders. While under arrest, Chief Sitting Bull was killed, prompting a group of several hundred Sioux led by the dying Chief Big Foot to leave the reservation. They surrendered quietly, however, to the 7th Cavalry on the night of December 28. The following morning a scuffle broke out while the Indians were being disarmed. A trooper fell to the ground and the soldiers moved in. It was a "battle" between Indians armed with clubs and knives and soldiers with machine guns. The resultant massacre of men, women, and children effectively concluded the conquest of the North American Indian. In 1973, however, Wounded Knee was occupied by 200 members of the American Indian Movement. A three-month siege ensued before they surrendered.

MASSACRE REMEMBERED
A memorial records the Wounded Knee massacre. The name became a byword for the wrongs inflicted on American Indians.

EMPIRES AND REVOLUTIONS

WAR IN SOUTH AMERICA

THE 19TH CENTURY BEGAN WITH Spain in possession of most of South America. Less than 30 years later, after a series of wars of liberation, the Spanish had been completely driven out by the continent's emerging nations. Sadly, the newly independent countries betrayed Simón Bolívar's dream of South American unity and soon began to turn on each other in an often bloody struggle for territory and power.

LIBERATION

The wars of liberation were fought between rebels and those loyal to the Spanish crown. Venezuelan Simón Bolívar and Argentine José de San Martín were the heroes of the conflicts. Upper Peru was renamed Bolivia in the former's honor in 1826.

KEY

	Spanish territory in South America 1810
VICEROYALTY OF NEW GRANADA	Spanish administrative region
1821	date of independence of new state

Principal campaigns of liberators

	Bolívar 1812–14
	O'Higgins 1817–18
	San Martín 1817–18
	Bolívar 1819
	San Martín 1820–22
	Sucre 1821–22
	Bolívar 1822
	Bolívar 1823–26
	Sucre 1824
✕	victory for armies of liberation
✕	defeat for armies of liberation

Chacabuco

DATE	February 12, 1817
FORCES	Rebels: 3,000; Royalists: 1,500
LOCATION Just north of Santiago, Chile	**CASUALTIES** Rebels: 12 dead, 120 injured; Royalists: 500 dead, 600 captured

After the declaration of Argentine independence in 1816, José de San Martín, the leader of the independence movement in the south, turned his attention to the liberation of Chile. In January 1817 San Martín and Bernardo O'Higgins, the Chilean liberation leader, led a force of 5,000 troops on a grueling 20-day trek across the Andes, during which about 2,000 men succumbed to the cold and high altitude. Despite these heavy losses, San Martín was able to surprise the royalists, whose Spanish general Rafael Maroto could muster only 1,500 men to confront the advancing army. By midday on February 11 Maroto's forces had come together at Chacabuco, just north of Santiago, and San Martín resolved to attack at dawn the next

PLAIN OF VICTORY
The Andean peaks of Mount Fitzroy and Mount Torre overlook the plains on which the bloody fighting took place.

JOSÉ DE SAN MARTÍN
This image shows San Martín heroically leading the charge at Chacabuco. He was a selfless soldier of high personal integrity.

day. Initially the Spanish infantry repelled O'Higgins' forces, but a grenadier charge led by San Martín against the Spanish cavalry gave O'Higgins time to regroup and attack the Spanish flank. The outnumbered royalists were routed and the victorious rebel forces were welcomed into Santiago as liberators. Victory enabled San Martín to join up with Admiral Cochrane at the coast and the liberation of Chile had begun. There would be reverses to come, including a heavy defeat at Cancha-Rayada, but after the final victory at Maipú, Chile's freedom was assured, and Bernardo O'Higgins became the country's first independent ruler.

Boyacá

DATE	August 7, 1819
FORCES	Rebels: 3,000; Royalists: 3,000
LOCATION Outskirts of Bogotá, Colombia	**CASUALTIES** Royalists: 100 dead, 1,800 captured

In July 1819, the struggle for control of New Granada (present-day Colombia and Venezuela) was in full swing. The rebel army, under the leadership of Generals Bolívar and de Paula Santander, defeated the Spanish

BOYACÁ SURRENDER
The royalist army surrender to Bolívar's rebels after Boyacá. The bridge (bottom left) was a key objective in the battle.

forces in preliminary skirmishes at Gámeza on July 12 and the Vargas River on July 25, before capturing Tunja on August 5. The final battle took place just outside Bogotá two days later. Santander cut off the Spanish advance force near a bridge over the Boyacá River as Bolívar's men simultaneously attacked the bulk of the Spanish troops a mile away. Bolívar attacked the Spanish left while the veteran British Legion launched a frontal assault and repulsed the Spanish cavalry. The result was a decisive victory for the rebels, with about 1,800 prisoners taken, including the Spanish commander. Three days later Bolívar marched into Bogotá, where he was welcomed as the liberator of New Granada. He set up a provisional government before pushing on into Ecuador and the central Andes, there to unite with San Martín's southern army.

FOUNDATION OF COLOMBIA

Carabobo

DATE June 24, 1821

FORCES
Rebels: 6,500;
including British and
Irish volunteers;
Royalists: 5,000

LOCATION Plains near
Caracas, modern-day
Venezuela

CASUALTIES
Unknown but heavy
on both sides

Under instructions from the new liberal government in Spain, General Pablo Morillo signed an armistice with Bolívar in November 1820. Bolívar, however, broke the terms by attacking the royalist garrison at Lake Maracaibo, and the two sides confronted each other on the plains of Carabobo. The royalists, under the command of General Miguel de la Torre, were demoralized and depleted by desertion. Bolívar sent a column of *llaneros* (plainsmen) and British volunteers to strike the enemy from the right, while the cavalry attacked the center. There were heavy losses on both sides, including many rebel officers, but de la Torre's men were crushed. Bolívar declared that the victory marked the birth of the republic of Colombia.

1783–1830

SIMÓN BOLÍVAR

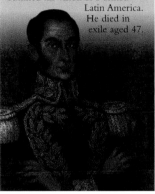

Bolívar, known as "The Liberator," was born in Caracas to aristocratic stock. While in Europe, his study of the ideas of the Enlightenment convinced him of the need for Latin American independence. On his return home in 1807, he assumed the leadership of the revolution, subsequently becoming president of Colombia and Peru. In his "Jamaica Letter," Bolívar outlined his vision of a united Latin America. He died in exile aged 47.

WAR OF PERUVIAN INDEPENDENCE

Ayacucho

DATE
December 9, 1824

FORCES
Rebels: 6,000;
Royalists: 9,000

LOCATION The high
plateau near
Ayacucho, Peru

CASUALTIES
Royalists: 2,000 killed

With New Granada to the north and Chile to the south under rebel control, Peru was the final enclave of Spanish rule in South America. Bolívar's brilliant Venezuelan lieutenant Antonio José de la Sucre led an army gathered together from all over South America against a numerically superior Spanish force that had ten times as many artillery pieces as the rebels. Against these odds, Sucre attacked the Spanish on a plateau near Ayacucho, Peru. He opened with a daring cavalry charge led by Colombian José María Córdoba, and within a short time thousands of royalists lay dead. The viceroy and his generals were taken prisoner, and the terms of surrender stipulated that all Spanish forces be withdrawn from Peru and Charcas (Bolivia). The last of the Spanish troops sailed from Lima in January 1826, thus ending Spain's presence in South America and confirming the independence of the new republics.

MEMORIAL
A dramatic monument to the battle of Ayacucho rises into the sky over La Quinua, Peru.

BATTLE OF CASEROS

Caseros

DATE
February 3, 1852

FORCES Rosas:
c.25,000; Coalition:
c.25,000

LOCATION 10 miles
(16km) northwest of
Buenos Aires

CASUALTIES Rosas:
1,400 dead, 7,000
captured; Coalition:
600 dead

Juan Manuel de Rosas, a bluff *gaucho* (cattle rancher) from Buenos Aires province, seized power in Argentina in 1835. His 17-year rule was characterized by an extreme cult of personality—his portrait adorned every public place and church. Opposition was crushed through a network of spies and secret police (the Mazorca). Rosas's autocratic manner aroused powerful opposition and in 1852 he was confronted by a coalition force of Argentinian, Brazilian, and Uruguayan troops under the command of General Justo José de Urquiza, a former friend and confidant of the dictator. The ensuing battle was the largest fought in the Americas before the American Civil War. Urquiza attacked first, leading the cavalry charge himself and blowing open the right flank. After that there was a prolonged period of hand-to-hand fighting, but the result was already beyond doubt. Many of Rosas's troops had surrendered before the battle had even begun and the rest had little stomach for the fight. Rosas himself fled, along with most of his cavalry, and found sanctuary in England. Urquiza's victory led to the adoption of a US-style constitution, a move that, ironically, would have been impossible before Rosas had united the country.

THE RED CULT

Soldiers of Rosas's federation are seen here in their distinctive red uniforms. All men were obliged to wear red in Rosas's honor.

PARAGUAYAN WAR

Paraguayan War

DATE May 1, 1865–
March 1, 1870

FORCES Paraguayans:
50,000; Argentinians,
Brazilians, and
Uruguayans: 26,000

LOCATION
Paraguay

CASUALTIES
Paraguayans: 300,000
(with civilians) killed

This was the bloodiest conflict in Latin American history. Paraguayan dictator Francisco López, ambitious to expand his rule, built up the largest army in South America and invaded Argentina and Brazil in 1865. In response, Argentina allied itself with Brazil and Uruguay and declared war on Paraguay. Paraguayan troops found themselves outnumbered ten to one and were soon driven back. Both sides suffered heavy losses in a series of fierce battles, including an early victory to Paraguay at Curupayti, and the war dragged on. Following the appointment of the Brazilian Marques de Caxias as commander-in-chief in 1868, Paraguayan defenses were finally breached and the capital, Asunción, was taken. López himself was killed on March 1, 1870. For Paraguay, a small nation of half a million people, this was a war of national suicide. Of the perhaps 200,000 people left alive, fewer than 30,000 were men. In addition, large chunks of territory were lost to Argentina and Brazil.

BLOODY CURUPAYTI

Argentinian troops are here seen taking the offensive at Curupayti. Troops carry ladders to storm Paraguayan earthwork defenses.

MEXICO AT WAR

WITH THE EXCEPTION OF ONE 35-year period of peaceful rule, known as the *porfiriato*, the century following independence in Mexico was marred by constant conflict. The central state was weak and the population deeply divided between Catholic conservatives and anticlerical liberals. These divisions, culminating in the 10-year-long revolution, led to endemic civil war. Mexico's problems were exacerbated by constant foreign intervention, including a catastrophic war with the United States that resulted in the loss of the northern states, and invasion by the French. The classic Mexican style of combat, used in the independence struggle and in the revolution a century later, was guerrilla warfare on horseback.

EMPIRES AND REVOLUTIONS

TEXAN INDEPENDENCE

Alamo

LOCATION San Antonio, Texas

DATE February 23–March 1836

FORCES Mexicans: 2,000–6,000; Texan volunteers: 184

CASUALTIES Mexicans: 1,000 killed or wounded; Texan volunteers: 184 killed

By 1830 about 30,000 US immigrants had settled in the Mexican state of Texas. Seeing this as a threat to its sovereignty, the Mexican government closed the border and imposed punitive restrictions on Texas, but it was only with the new constitution of 1836, which removed the state's remaining rights, that a revolt was provoked and Texas declared itself an independent republic, sparking the Texas War of Independence. A detachment of Texas volunteers drove a Mexican force out

of San Antonio and occupied the ruined chapel of the Mission San Antonio de Valero, named the Alamo by Spanish troops after the grove of cottonwood trees in which it stood. Texan leaders, including Sam Houston, urged them to withdraw from their exposed position, but they refused and a Mexican army, under the leadership of President Santa Anna

BREAKTHROUGH
This engraving depicts the dramatic moment when the Mexicans breached the Alamo's defences.

himself, crossed the Rio Grande River and laid siege to the chapel. The defenders, with frontier legends James Bowie and Davy Crockett in their number, held out for 13 days until the Mexicans finally breached the outer walls and overwhelmed them by sheer weight of numbers. Santa Anna ordered that no prisoners were to be taken, and no man was spared, with only a handful of women and children emerging alive. This setback was reversed a month later when Houston defeated Santa Anna at San Jacinto, assuring the independence of the "yanqui" settlers, although Mexico would not recognize this reality until Texas was annexed by the United States in 1845. For Texans, the Alamo and its defenders became symbols of heroic resistance.

> "It is very true I threw up my cap for liberty with great ardor, and perfect sincerity, but soon found the folly of it. A hundred years to come my people will not be fit for liberty."
>
> *Antonio López de Santa Anna*, disillusioned with his countrymen after his capture by Texans, 1836

1794–1876

SANTA ANNA

Antonio López de Santa Anna was an ambitious general who rose to prominence after supporting the campaigns of two presidents in the newly independent Mexico—only to help overthrow them both. Driven from the presidency after defeat in Texas, he fought the French at Veracruz two years later, losing a leg but regaining power. He was forced into exile when Mexico was defeated by the US in 1847. He returned home in 1874 and died two years later, aged 82.

REMEMBER THE ALAMO
The Alamo has been restored and is preserved as an historic site. The Texas flag is hoisted nearby.

MEXICAN–AMERICAN WAR

The Veracruz Campaign

DATE March–September 1847	
FORCES US: 25,000 regulars and 70,000 volunteers; Mexico: 20,000 regulars	
LOCATION Veracruz seaport, east coast of Mexico	**CASUALTIES** US: 6,000; Mexico: tens of thousands

In 1845 the US Congress voted to annex Texas, whose leaders enthusiastically agreed. President James Polk, eager to expand his country's territory, sent a delegation to Mexico City to negotiate a disputed Texas border area and to purchase New Mexico and California. When they were snubbed, he ordered troops into the disputed region and Mexico counterattacked. Polk had the war he sought. California and New Mexico were occupied with little resistance, but US commander Zachary Taylor seemed reluctant to push farther south. With the war stagnating, Polk ordered General Winfield Scott to take an army by sea and capture the key port of Veracruz. The port was taken easily and, after important victories over Santa Anna at Cerro Gordo and Chapaltepec, Scott's forces marched on to Mexico City, which fell on September 14, 1847. The price of defeat was heavy. Santa Anna was exiled and, under the peace treaty of Guadalupe Hidalgo, Mexico lost about half its territory, from Texas to California. Ever since, the war has been a sore point in Mexican history, as its name in the respective countries illustrates: in the United States it is known neutrally as the "Mexican–American War" while, tellingly, in Mexico it is still called the "War of the North American Invasion."

> "The fulfilment of our manifest destiny is to overspread the continent allotted by Providence."
>
> *John L. O'Sullivan*, the United States Magazine and Democratic Review, **1845**

COLT REVOLVER

The iconic Wild West weapon, the revolver, was patented in 1835 by Samuel Colt and first used a year later during the Texas revolt. It is named after its revolving cylinder, which enabled the firing of five or six shots rather than the handheld pistol's one or two. Its success in Texas led to the US government ordering 1,000 of them during the Mexican–American War. The Colt became the most popular gun ever made. The model shown here dates from the 1860s.

CYLINDER *The Colt's revolving cylinder is a design classic. It allowed the firing of up to six shots without reloading.*

Hammer · Loading gate · Six-shot cylinder · Loading lever · Pistol rammer · Cylinder release tab · Brass trigger guard · Trigger · Walnut grip

SPECIFICATION			
Origin United States		**Length** 13½in (34.3cm)	
Barrel 7½in (190mm)		**Caliber** .44in	
First Made 1836		**Weight** 4lb (113g)	

THE FRENCH EXPEDITION

The French Expedition

DATE January 1862–March 1867	
FORCES At Puebla: Mexicans: 2,000–4,000; French: 6,000	
LOCATION East coast of Mexico	**CASUALTIES** At Puebla: French: 1,000 killed; Mexicans: no reliable estimates

By 1860 Mexico was mired in a civil war between conservatives and liberals. The treasury was virtually bankrupt and liberal president Benito Juárez suspended payments on foreign debts, prompting Britain, Spain, and France to intervene to protect their investments. By January 1862 all three powers had landed troops at Veracruz, but the British and Spanish withdrew when it became clear that Napoleon III intended to conquer the whole country. French progress toward the capital was blocked by the fortified city of Puebla, where local forces confronted the invaders on May 5. The French unwisely launched a frontal assault on well-defended positions. The Mexicans, commanded by General Ignacio Zaragoza, drove the attackers back in a famous victory still celebrated as a national holiday. Nevertheless, Puebla was taken the following March with 30,000 French reinforcements, and the Habsburg Archduke Maximilian was crowned emperor of Mexico. A guerrilla war ensued until French troops withdrew in March 1867 and Juárez retook Mexico City. The hapless Maximilian was captured and executed.

THE MEXICAN REVOLUTION

The Mexican Revolution

DATE 1910–1920	
FORCES Various armies including government troops, Zapata's peasant guerrillas, Villa's guerrilla cavalry	
LOCATION Mexico	**CASUALTIES** About one million soldiers and civilians killed

In 1910 Francisco Madero, a young landowner, stood against long-standing dictator Porfirio Díaz in the presidential elections. Díaz's political machine duly delivered him victory, but from jail Madero called for armed resistance. The rebel movement took Ciudad Juárez and Díaz fled the country in May 1911. Madero was elected president but the forces of the revolution were now beyond his control. Southern peasant leader Emiliano Zapata, demanding land reform and suspecting that Madero would be no better than Díaz, declared his own revolution. Madero, a democrat at heart, vacillated and was assassinated by his own chief of staff, Victoriano Huerta. With tacit support from the US, Huerta attempted to impose his authority. Now he faced opposition not only from Zapata but from Pancho Villa's horseback ranch-hands in the north and from Venustiano Carranza, a dissident member of the elite. These forces, backed by the US, overthrew Huerta in 1914. Carranza now made a move against his two agrarian allies. Villa pressed on but was heavily defeated at Celeya in 1915 by Alvaro Obregón, Carranza's brilliant army commander, and forced to retreat. Carranza duly assumed the presidency and had Zapata killed in 1919. A year later Obregón rebelled, had Carranza murdered, and became president. The merchant classes emerged as the victors in the revolution. Villa was later killed in 1923.

FEMALE FIGHTERS
Women, too, fought as guerrillas during the revolution. Most were educated, middle class, and had their own horses and guns.

STAGED WARFARE
Government troops are seen here manning a cannon. Both sides launched some attacks especially for the newsreels.

THE AMERICAN CIVIL WAR

THE ELECTION OF ABRAHAM LINCOLN as president in 1860, committed to opposing slavery's spread in the United States, led 11 Southern states to secede from the Union and form the Confederacy. In April 1861 Fort Sumter, an outpost of Federal troops in South Carolina, was bombarded. A bloody war ensued, which lasted four years and cost 600,000 lives.

NORTH AND SOUTH

The Union had a population of 23 million to the Confederacy's nine million. It also had most of the country's railroads and industries. While the North manufactured almost 1.5 million Springfield rifle-muskets in the course of the war, the South was short of everything from boots to gunpowder, despite heroic efforts to create war industries and to procure weapons from Europe. Since the regular US Army numbered only 16,000, both sides had to create fresh armies from state militias and volunteers. The South eventually raised around 1.1 million soldiers to the North's 2.8 million. The Union was also overwhelmingly superior in seapower, enabling it to blockade Confederate ports and carry out amphibious operations along the coast, the most notable of which led to the capture of New Orleans in 1862. Given the disparity of forces, the South put its faith in outside assistance, hoping Britain or France would intervene in its favor. But the issue of slavery stood in the way, sapping foreign sympathy for the Southern cause.

BRAGG'S COAT
This dress coat and sword belonged to Confederate general Braxton Bragg. The coat is of brushed blue-gray wool with gold piping and golden rank insignia on the collar. Bragg's dress sword has an acid-etched steel blade.

KEY		
Union states 1861	Union forts	
Confederate states 1861	Confederate forts	
Union front line to December 1861	Union naval blockade	
Union front line to December 1862	Union victory	
Union front line to December 1864	Confederate victory	
Union movements	inconclusive battle	
Confederate movements	Apr 12, 1865 date of battle or attack	
	city destroyed by Union forces	

CIVIL WAR
The secession of the Southern states was resolved only after four years of fighting. The North's superior resources made the long resistance of the South a surprising but costly achievement.

1807–1870
ROBERT E. LEE

A US Army colonel when the Civil War started, Lee was offered overall field command of the Union forces but as a Virginian aristocrat chose to serve the Confederacy instead. His performance as commander in the Seven Days battle in the summer of 1862 revealed an outstanding military talent, characterized by adopting offensive tactics as the best means of defense against numerically superior forces. Despite a costly defeat at Gettysburg, Lee earned the devotion of his troops and the respect of his enemies.

IRONCLAD
The Union built flat-bottomed, paddle-wheeled gunboats to operate on the Mississippi. Protected by iron armor, they took on Confederate forts along the river.

1809–1865

ABRAHAM LINCOLN

With no military experience, Lincoln managed the problems of a war presidency with exceptional skill and determination. His subtle handling of the slavery issue kept four crucial slave states loyal to the Union, while his commitment to the war rallied waverers in the Union ranks. Once he had found the generals he needed in Grant and Sherman, Lincoln backed them to the hilt in pursuit of total victory. His assassination at the war's end was a tragedy for the United States.

EFFECTS OF MODERNITY

The Civil War has often been described as the first modern war, although it is perhaps better regarded as transitional between old and new. Its most notable "first" was the naval battle between the *Monitor* and the *Virginia* (*Merrimack*), the first encounter between ironclad steamships, in March 1862. Railroads and the telegraph were crucial in fighting a war over such huge distances, though both showed their weakness in depending on fixed lines that were easy to cut and hard to defend. Infantry warfare was based on the transitional technology of muzzle-loading rifle muskets with Minié bullets (which allowed fast loading and accurate fire). More advanced firearms such as breech-loading repeater rifles played a marginal role, being used by snipers and cavalry. Cannons fired solid shot or fused shells and were only slightly improved from Napoleonic times.

A WAR OF ATTRITION

Although more war deaths in the Civil War were caused by disease than by combat, the level of battlefield casualties was shocking. Massive losses were suffered in infantry assaults against defenders armed with rifle muskets and protected by field fortifications and batteries of cannons. Cavalry did not play a crucial role on the defense-dominated battlefield, although it was very important in raiding in depth. The difficulty of achieving decisive victory in battle led the Union to follow a coherent, if brutal, strategy of attrition, partly intended to undermine the will to fight of the South's civilian population. The war eventually cost the lives of 620,000 soldiers (360,000 on the Northern side and 260,000 Southerners) plus uncounted numbers of civilians—more than the losses in all the other wars in which the US has fought.

WAR PHOTOGRAPHY
Union General Joseph Hooker, captured on film by Matthew Brady, one of the first war photographers. Brady brought home the reality of the conflict to a public nurtured on more romantic views of warfare.

PRISON CAMPS
About 13,000 Union soldiers died of neglect and disease in the Andersonville prisoner-of-war camp in Georgia. Henry Wirz, its commander, was executed for war crimes.

UNION INSIGNIA
The crossed cannons were an artillery insignia in common use in the Union army. They were worn on soldiers' hats with the number of their artillery regiment positioned above the cross

MILITIAMEN
Individual states raised their own forces—state militias—which formed the core of the rival armies at the start of the war. Here, men of the 22nd New York State Militia are seen at Harper's Ferry.

1750–1914

NO EASY VICTORY

AT THE START OF THE Civil War, the North might sensibly have adopted the "Anaconda" strategy recommended by General Winfield Scott, squeezing the South between a naval blockade of its oceanic ports and the seizure of key river and railroad communications in the west. The South might have stood on the defensive while bidding for international support. But spirits roused on both sides demanded action, so aggressive operations were mounted all around—though with neither side able to find the quick victory it sought.

1824–1863

GENERAL THOMAS J. JACKSON

Known as "Stonewall," an epithet bestowed for his brigade's resolute stand at First Bull Run, Confederate General Jackson had a firm belief that divine providence directed his actions. Intolerant of any weakness, his guiding principle was to "move swiftly and strike vigorously" in pursuit of total victory. His death to friendly fire at Chancellorsville was a disaster for the South.

THE CIVIL WAR

First Bull Run

DATE
July 21, 1861

FORCES
Union: 30,000
Confederate: 25,000

LOCATION 25 miles (40km) southwest of Washington, D.C.

CASUALTIES Union: 2,700 dead; Confederate: 2,000 dead

The Confederates chose Richmond, Virginia, as their capital, only 100 miles (160km) from Washington. Succumbing to pressure from public opinion, the Union government ordered General Irvin McDowell to march south from Washington and seize Richmond. McDowell's soldiers were almost all without experience of war, as were the Confederates under Beauregard, who defended the rail junction at Manassas. Delays in assembling and moving the Union army allowed the Confederates to reinforce Manassas with troops moved by train from the Shenandoah Valley. They were still arriving when the battle began. McDowell achieved surprise

> "So thorough was the panic that no power on earth could have… made our men turn and fight."
>
> *Edwin S. Barrett*, Union soldier

with an attack on the Confederate left that drove them back on Henry House hill, but there Jackson's brigade stood "like a stone wall" and the tide of battle turned. In the late afternoon a counterattack by Confederates giving the spine-chilling "rebel yell" panicked the exhausted Union troops into headlong flight. The way to Washington was open, but the Confederates were in no shape to mount a pursuit. The battle was known in the South as Manassas.

CHAOS OF BATTLE
Here, Jeb Stuart's Confederate cavalry launch one of the very few mounted charges of the war at Bull Run.

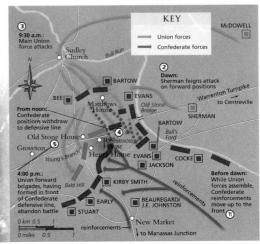

KEY
Union forces
Confederate forces

3 9:30 a.m.: Main Union force attacks

Dawn: Sherman feigns attack on forward positions **2**

From noon: Confederate positions withdraw to defensive line

4:00 p.m.: Union forward brigades, having formed in front of Confederate defensive line, abandon battle

Before dawn: While Union forces assemble, Confederate reinforcements move up to the front

Sudley Church, Bull Run, BARTOW, BEE, Matthews House, EVANS, Old Stone Bridge, Warrenton Turnpike, to Centreville, SHERMAN, BARTOW, Ball's Ford, Old Stone House, Robinson House, COCKE, Groveton, Young's Branch, Henry House, EVANS, JACKSON, KIRBY SMITH, Bald Hill, EARLY, BEAUREGARD/ J.E. JOHNSTON, STUART, reinforcements, New Market, to Manassas Junction, McDOWELL

0 km 0.5   1
0 miles   0.5   1

THE CIVIL WAR

Shiloh

DATE
April 6–7, 1862

FORCES
Union: 48,000
Confederate: 45,000

LOCATION By Tennessee River, south of Savannah, Georgia

CASUALTIES Union: 13,000; Confederate: 11,000

In February 1862 Federal General Ulysses S. Grant captured forts Henry and Donelson in Kentucky, forcing the Confederates to abandon Nashville. Grant then moved down the Tennessee River and disembarked at Pittsburg Landing, near a church called Shiloh, where he was to be joined by the Army of the Ohio under Buell. Confederate General Albert S. Johnston decided to hit Grant before the junction of the two armies. Grant had failed to dig any field fortifications and, surprised by a dawn attack, his troops were pushed back toward Pittsburg Landing in fierce close-quarters fighting. Johnston was killed, bleeding to death after a bullet severed an artery. The Army of the Ohio arrived during the night and was ferried across the river. Grant launched an aggressive counterattack at dawn; men fought over ground littered with the bodies of the dead and wounded from the previous day. The Confederates abandoned the field in late afternoon. The defeat at Shiloh severely weakened the Confederate position in the west.

SCABBARD

Ring to attach to sword belt

CAVALRYMAN'S BELT

Loop to connect scabbard

Sharp upper edge to blade

Brass-tipped scabbard end

UNION BLADE
This Union officer's sword is unlikely to have been bloodied. In the mid-19th century an unshakeable attachment to the romance of edged weapons prevailed, but their use in warfare had practically ceased.

CAVALRY SABER

1750–1914

THE CIVIL WAR
Seven Days Battles

DATE
June 26–July 2, 1862

FORCES
Union: 60,000;
Confederate:
100,000

LOCATION
East of Richmond,
Virginia

CASUALTIES
Union: 22,000;
Confederate: 15,000

In June 1862, when Robert E. Lee took command of the Confederate forces in Virginia, a Union army had advanced up the Jamestown peninsula to within a few miles of Richmond.

Recalling Stonewall Jackson's army from a successful campaign in the Shenandoah Valley, Lee launched a bold counteroffensive in the last week of June, combining a threatened envelopment of the Federal right with frontal attacks. The Federal forces outnumbered the Confederates and were better equipped. Their artillery took a heavy toll of Lee's infantry, especially in the slaughter at Malvern Hill on July 1. But the offensive totally unnerved the pessimistic Union commander George McClellan, who withdrew to a defensive position on the coast at Harrison's Landing, from which his army was evacuated in August.

> "Under repeated orders from General Magruder both brigades hurried through the swamp, the difficulties of which…cannot be exaggerated…. General Toombs reached the plateau first, and advanced directly toward the enemy's batteries…. These movements had been made under a murderous fire, which these brave troops endured without the opportunity of returning a shot."

WITNESS TO WAR
CONFEDERATE GENERAL D. R. JONES

The Confederate attack at Malvern Hill on July 1, 1862, was a costly failure. Union artillery firing canisters decimated ill-coordinated infantry. Lee, appalled by the carnage, asked General John Magruder why he had persisted in the attack, receiving the retort, "Because of your orders, twice repeated."

THE CIVIL WAR
Antietam

DATE
September 17, 1862

FORCES
Union: 80,000;
Confederate:
40,000

LOCATION
Sharpsburg,
Maryland

CASUALTIES
Union: 12,000;
Confederate: 11,000

This drawn battle (known in the South as Sharpsburg) was the costliest day's fighting of the war. After another Confederate victory at Second Bull Run on August 30, 1862, Lee gambled on an invasion of the North. Aware of Lee's plans through a captured document (General Order

BLOODY LANE
This sunken road at Antietam was valiantly defended by Confederate infantry before they were overwhelmed by Union firepower.

191), McClellan saw a chance to crush the Confederate army. He was too slow, however, allowing Lee to regroup his forces behind Antietam Creek. McClellan still had overwhelming superiority when battle was joined, but his caution stopped him from committing the full weight of his forces. The Confederate left barely held in the face of an onslaught across a cornfield, while in the center rebel infantry fought a costly delaying action in Bloody Lane. Thousands of Union troops were held up for hours, trying to cross a narrow bridge over the creek under rifle fire. Lee might still have been overwhelmed but for the arrival of a division under A. P. Hill, force-marched from Harper's Ferry, which struck the Union flank in the late afternoon. The following day McClellan allowed the Confederates to withdraw without pursuit, a failure that cost him his job. Strategically, Antietam was a Union victory, as it put an end to Lee's invasion of the North.

THE CIVIL WAR
Fredericksburg

DATE
December 13, 1862

FORCES
Union: 120,000;
Confederate:
75,000

LOCATION
Fredericksburg, south
of Rappahannock River

CASUALTIES
Union: 12,000;
Confederate: 5,300

After Antietam, General Ambrose Burnside took command of the Union Army of the Potomac. He

planned to capture Richmond through a rapid advance across the Rappahannock. But the pontoons for the river crossing were put at the rear of the marching column, causing a delay that was exacerbated as sharpshooters harassed the bridging operation. By the time Burnside's forces made it across the river, Lee was ready. The Confederate artillery, massed on Marye's Heights, dominated the battlefield. Repeated frontal assaults by Union infantry were cut down by cannon fire and by Confederate infantry firing from behind stone walls. A flank attack on the Confederate right at least succeeded in penetrating the defensive line, but was repelled by a fierce counterattack. Lee said of this victory, "It is well that war is so terrible; we should grow too fond of it." The next day, the Union army retreated back across the river.

REBEL DEAD
Confederate soldiers lie dead at the foot of Marye's Heights. They held the position against repeated attacks.

THE CIVIL WAR
Chancellorsville

DATE
April 30–May 6, 1863

FORCES
Union: 120,000
Confederate:
60,000

LOCATION
Virginia, south of
Rappahannock River

CASUALTIES
Union: 17,000;
Confederate: 13,500

After Burnside's failure at Fredericksburg, it was General Joseph Hooker's turn to lead the Army of the Potomac. He devised a brilliant plan: part of his forces would pin Lee at Fredericksburg while his main force advanced through the forests of the Wilderness to the Confederate left and his cavalry cut Lee's communications

WAR DAMAGE
These dead horses after Chancellorsville show how losing vital supplies as much as losing men damaged the war effort.

with Richmond. However, Hooker had underrated the boldness of his adversary. Lee left a small holding force at Fredericksburg and marched into the Wilderness, blocking Hooker at the Chancellorsville crossroads. Jackson was sent on a flanking move to attack Hooker's right, a blow delivered to devastating effect on the afternoon of May 2. Concussed by rebel artillery fire, Hooker ordered his forces to withdrew to a defensive line and then pulled back across the Rappahannock. For the Confederates, the taste of victory was soured by the loss of Jackson, who died of his wounds on May 10.

Gettysburg

DATE
July 1–3, 1863

FORCES
Union: 85,000;
Confederate:
75,000

LOCATION
Gettysburg, south
Pennsylvania

LOSSES
Union: 23,000;
Confederate: 28,000

After the victory at Chancellorsville
in May 1863, Lee planned a fresh
invasion of the North, rejecting the
alternative of going to the aid of
besieged Vicksburg (see p.230). In
June the Army of Northern Virginia
advanced through the Shenandoah
Valley into Pennsylvania unimpeded,
except for a check to Jeb Stuart's
cavalry at Brandy Station. Lincoln
responded by firing Hooker and
putting General George Meade in
command of the Army of the
Potomac, with orders to seek out
and destroy Lee's forces. When Lee
learned of the approach of the Union
army, he instructed his scattered forces
to concentrate at Gettysburg. Arriving
first, one of A. P. Hill's divisions
decided to enter Gettysburg on the
morning of July 1 because they had
heard that the town had shoes, of
which they were in dire need. Hill's
men came under fire from dismounted
Union cavalry. Marching to the sound
of the guns, infantry of both sides
began to pile in, and an unplanned
battle commenced. At first the
Confederates carried all before them,
but the Union
infantry and
artillery
succeeded in
holding a
defensive line
on high ground
south of the
town, which was
then reinforced
by freshly
arriving troops.
On July 2 Lee rejected the option of
outflanking this position and instead
ordered an assault on Cemetery Ridge.
In the late afternoon the Confederates
drove the Union troops back through
a peach orchard and wheat field in
desperate fighting, but failed to take
the commanding heights. In
particular the Union army
managed to occupy and hold the
strategic height of Little Round Top,
so denying the Confederates a
position from which their artillery
could have dominated the entire
Union army. This left it all to do

REBEL FLAG
*The Confederate flag
was designed to avoid
being confused with
the Stars and Stripes.
The flag of the 15th
Louisiana Regiment
bears the name of
Gettysburg among
its battle honors.*

FIGHTING FOR FREEDOM
*The Union government did not
sanction the formation of black
regiments until 1863, but by the end
of the war over 180,000 African-
Americans had served in Union forces.*

again the following day. At around
1 p.m. on July 3 the Confederate
artillery began a prolonged
bombardment to soften up the Union
center. Then, at around 3 p.m., some
14,000 Confederate infantry,
including a division commanded by
George Pickett, advanced across open
fields toward the enemy
lines. The Union
artillery opened up
with shot and shell,
shifting to canister
as the infantry drew
closer. At 200 yards
(200m) the Union
infantry joined in,
keeping up a rapid

fire of Minié bullets from behind
stone walls and earthworks. It was all
over in half an hour. Only a few
hundred of the attacking force
reached the Union line. Blaming
himself bitterly, Lee rallied his men,
declaring, "It is I who have lost this
fight, and you must help me out of it
the best way you can."
Meade failed to
mount a pursuit as
Lee led a weary and
demoralized march
back to Virginia.

ARMY DRUM
*Drummers were often,
though not always,
young boys. Music
improved morale and
could be used to convey
orders amid the chaos
of the battlefield.*

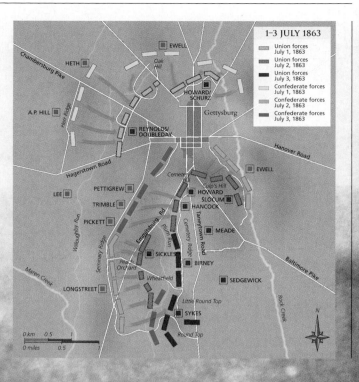

1–3 JULY 1863

- Union forces July 1, 1863
- Union forces July 2, 1863
- Union forces July 3, 1863
- Confederate forces July 1, 1863
- Confederate forces July 2, 1863
- Confederate forces July 3, 1863

EWELL · HETH · Oak Hill · Chambersburg Pike · A.P. HILL · Herr Ridge · HOWARD/SCHURZ · Gettysburg · REYNOLDS/DOUBLEDAY · Hanover Road · Hagerstown Road · Cemetery · EWELL · LEE · PETTIGREW · Colp's Hill · HOWARD SLOCUM · TRIMBLE · HANCOCK · PICKETT · Emmitsburg Rd · Taneytown Road · MEADE · Cemetery Ridge · Seminary Ridge · Willoughby Run · SICKLES · Plum Run · BIRNEY · Baltimore Pike · Peach Orchard · Wheatfield · SEDGEWICK · Maren Creek · Rock Creek · LONGSTREET · Little Round Top · SYKES · Round Top

0 km 0.5 1
0 miles 0.5 1

N

COST OF WAR
Some 7,000 died at Gettysburg, and thousands of
corpses were strewn across the battlefield after the
carnage. It took weeks to clear the field of bodies, which
quickly bloated grotesquely in the summer heat.

VICTORY THROUGH ATTRITION

THE UNION VICTORIES AT GETTYSBURG and Vicksburg in July 1863 placed the Confederacy irreversibly on the defensive. The South's last hope of avoiding defeat—by holding out until the North became weary of the fighting—was lost with Lincoln's reelection in 1864. The president found in Ulysses S. Grant a general who shared his commitment to victory at whatever cost.

Lincoln and Grant did not seek a war of attrition—they would have preferred the swift annihilation of rebel armies—but they did regard crippling the Southern economy and intimidating its population as a legitimate strategy. The late stages of the conflict exemplified Sherman's maxim: "War is cruelty. There is no use trying to reform it; the crueler it is, the sooner it will be over."

THE CIVIL WAR

Vicksburg

DATE
May 19–July 4, 1863

FORCES
Union: 70,000;
Confederate:
32,000

LOCATION
Vicksburg,
Mississippi

CASUALTIES
Union: 10,000;
Confederate: 9,000

The Confederate stronghold at Vicksburg, on the east bank of the Mississippi, controlled passage along the river. Surrounded by unhealthy swamps, it long defied capture. In April 1862, however, Grant sent ironclads (armor-plated ships) downriver, running the fortress's batteries, and ferried an army across from the west bank south of Vicksburg. Living off the land, he defeated the Confederate army of John Pemberton at Jackson and then drove it back into Vicksburg. After frontal assaults failed, Grant settled down for a siege. Starving and under constant bombardment from siege guns and river gunboats, Pemberton surrendered the garrison on July 4. The 30,000 Confederates taken prisoner were released on parole. Lincoln proclaimed that the Mississippi now "flowed unvexed" to the sea.

1822–1885

ULYSSES S. GRANT

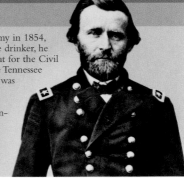

Grant resigned from the US Army in 1854, after serving in Mexico. A binge drinker, he might have lived in obscurity but for the Civil War. A string of victories on the Tennessee front persuaded Lincoln that he was the man to win victory—"He fights," was the president's comment. Union commander-in-chief from 1864, Grant directed the campaign of attrition that brought down the Confederacy and coined the phrase "unconditional surrender."

Hammer

Barrel band

Lock plate

**PERCUSSION
CAPS**

*Solid wood
stock*

Sling loop

.58 CALIBER RIFLE MUSKET
Civil War infantry used muzzle-loading muskets with rifled barrels, such as this Confederate copy of a Union Springfield. The charge was ignited by a percussion cap.

*Explosive
fulminate
of mercury*

THE CIVIL WAR

Wilderness and Spotsylvania

DATE
May 5–May 21, 1864

FORCES
Union: 120,000;
Confederate:
60,000

LOCATION
Spotsylvania County,
Virginia

CASUALTIES
Union: 32,000;
Confederate: 20,000

In spring 1864 Grant ordered a three-pronged offensive toward Richmond, Virginia, and a simultaneous attack against Atlanta, Georgia. The main thrust in Virginia was delivered by the Army of the Potomac, which crossed the Rapidan River and advanced into the area of dense vegetation known as the Wilderness. There, on May 5, they encountered Lee's Army of Northern Virginia. The terrain tended to break up the fighting into a confused melée. The scene was obscured by smoke from gunpowder and from fires lit by exploding shells in the dry brush. In two days' brutal fighting the Union forces suffered heavy casualties, but Grant refused to retreat. Instead, he sent his men forward

WAR FRENZY
The uniforms of the Yankees attacking this rebel position at Spotsylvania contrast with the homespun clothing of their opponents.

REBEL DEAD
At the Wilderness and Spotsylvania, Lee suffered over 20,000 casualties, losses he could ill afford.

on a flanking march that brought them up against Lee for a second time at Spotsylvania Courthouse on May 8. Dug into a V-shaped line of field fortifications, the Confederates held off a series of frenzied attacks for over 10 days. Unable to break through, Grant called off the battle on May 21 and set off on a flanking march aimed at Petersburg.

THE CIVIL WAR

Cold Harbor

DATE
June 3, 1864

FORCES
Union: 109,000;
Confederate:
59,000

LOCATION
6 miles (10km) north
of Richmond, Virginia

CASUALTIES
Union: 7,000;
Confederate: 1,500

By the start of June 1863 Grant was convinced that Lee's hungry and exhausted army was "really whipped." Grant had problems of his own, though. On top of the heavy losses suffered at Spotsylvania, volunteers who had joined the Union army at the start of the war for a three-year term were disappearing in droves. These pressures may explain Grant's decision to fling his troops into a desperate frontal assault on Confederate trenches at Cold Harbor. Poor reconnaissance—the Union side was unaware of the strength of the Confederate defenses—made matters worse. Federal troops advanced with names and addresses pinned to their uniforms, so high was their expectation of death. Even where the Yankees did reach the first trench line, the rebels fell back to a second line and butchered them from there. Grant admitted it was a disaster, saying, "I regret this assault more than any one I have ever ordered."

THE CIVIL WAR
March to the Sea

DATE November 15–December 21, 1864

FORCES
Union: 68,000;
Confederate: unknown

LOCATION
From Atlanta to
Savannah, Georgia

CASUALTIES
Union: losses minimal;
Confederate: no
reliable estimates

In early May 1864 Sherman led three armies in an advance on Atlanta, Georgia. The outnumbered Confederate Army of Tennessee fought a series of skillful delaying actions, holding off Sherman's advance so effectively that the Union forces did not arrive in Atlanta until late July. It took a further five weeks for Sherman to occupy the city. The Army of Tennessee under John B. Hood withdrew westward, believing that Sherman would be forced to pursue in order to protect Union supply lines.

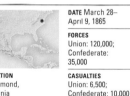

KETCHUM GRENADE
The Ketchum grenade was issued to Union forces. Rebels would try to catch a grenade in a blanket and throw it back.

Instead, Sherman detached one of his armies to cope with Hood and led the rest eastward. Advancing virtually unimpeded on a wide front, Sherman's men laid waste to the country, both out of necessity, since they were living off the land, and as a deliberate attack on the South's capacity to fight. The civilian and military infrastructure in their path was destroyed, damaging the Confederacy's ability to continue the war. Having marched 280 miles (450km), Sherman's army seized the port of Savannah on December 21, in time to offer it to Lincoln as a "Christmas gift." By then Hood's Army of Tennessee had been comprehensively defeated at the battle of Nashville (December 15–16, 1864).

EARTHWORK FORT
Fort McAllister, a fortress made of mud and sand situated outside the port of Savannah, repeatedly fought off Union ironclads but fell to an assault by Sherman's infantry.

1820–1891

WILLIAM T. SHERMAN

William Tecumseh Sherman was running a Louisiana military academy when the Civil War broke out. Of a depressive temperament, he found wartime command a torture to his nerves, but his political connections ensured promotion. He struck up a close working relationship with Grant based on a shared view of the necessary harshness of war, a principle Sherman applied ruthlessly in his March to the Sea.

THE CIVIL WAR
Siege of Petersburg

DATE June 18, 1864–April 2, 1865

FORCES Union: 96,000
(rising to 106,000);
Confederate: 55,000
(falling to 47,000)

LOCATION
25 miles (40km) south
of Richmond, Virginia

CASUALTIES
Union: 42,000
Confederate: 28,000

After the rebuff at Cold Harbor, Grant sent his Army of the Potomac across the James River to attack Richmond from the south. He failed, however, to seize the vital fortified town of Petersburg in mid-June. Lee rapidly strengthened the earthworks; Grant had no choice but to dig his own trenches and settle down for a long siege. The most notable attempt to pierce the Confederate defenses was made on July 28 when 320 kegs of gunpowder were detonated in a tunnel under the Confederate lines, making a crater 30ft (10m) deep and killing hundreds of rebel soldiers. But Union troops trying to break through the gap blown in the line found themselves trapped inside the crater under Confederate fire. For nine months shelling and raids failed to break the stalemate. While the Union troops were regularly reinforced and supplied, the Confederates grew ever hungrier and more demoralized.

PETERSBURG TRENCH
A captured trench outside Petersburg shows the spiked barriers that performed the same function as barbed wire in later wars.

THE CIVIL WAR
Defeat of Lee

DATE March 28–April 9, 1865

FORCES
Union: 120,000;
Confederate:
35,000

LOCATION
Richmond,
Virginia

CASUALTIES
Union: 6,500;
Confederate: 10,000

By late March 1865 Lee had decided his position in front of Petersburg was untenable. He needed to abandon the defense of Richmond and withdraw southward to join up with the army of Joseph E. Johnston, who was still resisting Sherman's advance through North Carolina. But a Confederate assault on Fort Stedman, on the right of the Union line at Petersburg, failed to create the opportunity Lee had hoped for to slip away. On March 29 Union cavalry under Philip Sheridan arrived at Petersburg after completing the devastation of the Shenandoah Valley and immediately went into action, sweeping around the west of the Confederate line. On April 2 Union infantry broke through the trenches in front of Petersburg. Lee managed an orderly withdrawal, but he could not evade pursuit. Sheridan's cavalry blocked his path at Appomattox Courthouse on April 8, and when Grant's infantry began to arrive in force the following day, the game was up. Lee surrendered the Army of Northern Virginia at 3:45 p.m. on April 9. The following day, Lincoln was assassinated. Sherman accepted Johnston's capitulation at Durham Station, North Carolina, on April 26. With the surrenders of Lee and Johnston, the Confederacy was finished and the long war was effectively over.

REUNITED
The Union flag flies over the Virginia State Capitol amid the ruins of Richmond, burned out at the time of its surrender.

"A house divided against itself cannot stand."

Abraham Lincoln's "House Divided" speech in Springfield, Illinois, JUNE 16, 1858

WITNESS TO WAR

AMERICAN CIVIL WAR

If the Civil War began in a clash of apparently incompatible views of how the liberty of states might be reconciled with the liberty of individuals, it was individuals on both sides who put flesh on the bones of those competing philosophies with their blood and their suffering. The Civil War is often cited as the first industrial war, but it was also among the first conflicts where a mass of letters and diaries survive from rank-and-file soldiers to give a human insight to a battlefield where modern technology and tactics created carnage on an unprecedented scale.

❝ We went into Pennsylvania and stayed for some time and had a hard Battle near Gettysburg…. We went in the 3 day [of July] and got nearly all of our Division killed & wounded…. Myself and Jon come through safely…. There was a ball passed through my sleeve though it did not hurt my arm. Me and Jon came very near being taken…. When I saw we were nearly surrounded I told Jon that we would run and try to get away from them and we made our escape by doing so, while several of our boys that was with us let the Yankees take them. ❞

Letter from James Booker at camp in Williamsport, Maryland, to his cousin Chloe Unity Blair, JULY 11, 1863, describing the battle of Gettysburg

Many soldiers on both sides presumed that the war would be brief. Indeed, in the Union army most had initially enlisted for only a 90-day period. By the time of Gettysburg, the key battle of the war, however, it had for the majority already been a two-year nightmare of march, countermarch, and countless fallen comrades. James Booker enlisted with his twin brother, John, in the 38th Virginia Infantry in May 1861. The 38th fought right through the war, seeing action at Sharpsburg and Gettysburg—where 40 percent of its soldiers were numbered among the casualties— and ended up just 2 miles (3km) from Appomattox at the time of Lee's surrender in April 1865. It was a long, harrowing road, and James's twin died in August 1864 of wounds suffered at Drewry's Bluff.

❝ The enemy massed their troops in front of the second Brigade & at daylight charged the second, drove them from their breastworks & following them closely captured many…. The air seemed filled with the laden messengers of death…. The Yanks have fought with more desperation than they ever fought before. ❞

Letter from *William Francis Brand* to *Amanda Catherine Armentrout*, about the battle of Spotsylvania, MAY 16, 1864

ARMY CAMP
The Army of the Potomac, shown here in an encampment, was the major Union force in the Eastern Front during the Civil War.

As well as the full-blooded butchery of battle, the Civil War figured the less dramatic but equally fatal engagements of scorched earth and siege. From the slow naval strangulation of Vicksburg to the final, heroic, and pointless Confederate resistance in the Petersburg trenches, soldiers daily faced death from disease, cold, starvation, and the pounding of enemy artillery. William Francis Brand, a miller, enlisted in the Confederate Army in April 1861, witnessing both the start and end of the war. He fought at Manassas, Cold Harbor, Cedar Mountain, Gettysburg, the Wilderness, and ended up at the siege of Petersburg in April 1865. Three times wounded, he lived to the age of 92.

110TH PENNSYLVANIA INFANTRY

Captain H. R. Hubbard, article in the *Mendon Dispatch,* c.1904, recounting his experiences at Andersonville Prison Camp

❝ Then came the scorching heats of summer, when the blood dried up in our veins, when almost disembodied spirits walked with creaking joints and rattling bones, when hundreds became insane or idiotic, and many others, who feared insanity, deliberately crossed the dead line and sat down, awaiting their turn to be shot. ❞

For those who were not killed or maimed in battle, there was another form of living death. The Civil War, which gave the world trench fighting that prefigured the sunken killing fields of World War I, also bequeathed it the prison camp. Andersonville, for Union prisoners, was a place of particular notoriety, so much so that its greatly loathed commander, Captain Wirz, was hanged for war crimes in Washington in November 1865.

❝ What a cruel thing war is…to fill our hearts with hatred instead of love for our neighbors. ❞

Confederate general Robert E. Lee

EMPIRES AND REVOLUTIONS

IMPERIAL CONFLICTS

THE INDUSTRIAL REVOLUTION tilted the balance of world power conclusively in favor of Europe and North America. It not only generated wealth on an unprecedented scale but also overcame many problems of supply, enabling ambitious expeditions and distant military bases. Economic and technological growth drove colonialism like never before, creating in nations a hunger for raw materials to feed their industries and dominate world markets. The aggressive expansion of western powers inevitably sparked resistance among indigenous peoples, from the United States to Australia and from Africa to India. Many of these uprisings proved futile, however, because of another consequence of the industrial revolution: mass-produced firearms.

MACHINE GUN
The Maxim gun, below, gave the British a huge advantage in colonial conflicts.

PATRIOTISM AND NATIONALISM

Many Europeans genuinely believed that imperial wars were a regrettable side-effect of an otherwise benevolent process—bringing civilization to "savages"—and not an exercise of power for the benefit of the home country. Empire-building drew upon strong feelings of nationalism that, in turn, stemmed from the French and American revolutions and the Napoleonic wars, conflicts that led to new demands for freedom and self-determination. Although people were often discontented with social and economic conditions, the mass of Europeans of all classes were inspired by loyalty to the flag. This loyalty was one reason why, in countries such as Britain, conscription was not necessary until 1914. The other reason was that, for many recruits, the army was the least unattractive of the few, unpromising, alternatives.

MAXIM AUTOMATIC GUN.

FOREIGN RECRUITS
The badge of a German unit that, in the late 1800s, defended British colonies in the Caribbean.

GUERRILLA WARFARE AND TACTICS

In spite of the overwhelming technological superiority of the western powers, conquest did not always come easily. In some cases—in Afghanistan, for example—it did not come at all. Imperial forces sometimes achieved victory only at heavy cost in money and lives, or after preliminary defeats. Although doomed in a pitched battle almost regardless of their numbers, non-European forces were often far more effective when they adopted guerrilla tactics, such as small-scale attacks on civil as well as military targets. Notable exponents of guerrilla warfare included the Berbers during the French conquest of Algeria (1830–47) and the Boers in the Second Boer War (1899–1902).

DESPERATE MEASURES
Facing a 500,000-strong British force, the Boers, with about 90,000 men, adopted guerrilla tactics in the Second Boer War.

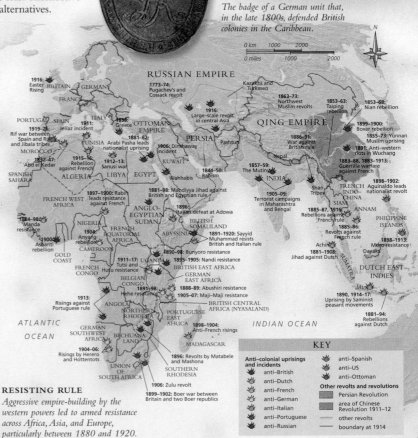

RESISTING RULE
Aggressive empire-building by the western powers led to armed resistance across Africa, Asia, and Europe, particularly between 1880 and 1920.

RUSSIAN EMPIRE
QING EMPIRE
OTTOMAN EMPIRE
PERSIA
INDIA
ATLANTIC OCEAN
INDIAN OCEAN

1916: Easter Rising
BRITAIN | GERMANY
FRANCE
PORTUGAL | SPAIN | ITALY
1919–26: Rif war between Spain and Riffi and Jibala tribes
MOROCCO
1837–47: Abd el Kedar
SPANISH SAHARA
ALGERIA | LIBYA | EGYPT
1911: Jellaz incident
1890: Greece
1881–82: Arabi Pasha leads nationalist uprising
TUNISIA
1915–16: Rebellion against French
1912–13: Sanusi war
KUWAIT
1906: Dinshaway incident
1844–50: Babism
Wahhabis
1773–74: Pugachev's and Cossack revolt
1916: Large-scale revolt in central Asia
Kazakhs and Turkmen
1863–73: Northwest Muslim revolts
1853–63: Taiping rebellion
1853–68: Nian rebellion
1886–91: War against British rule
Pashtun
Nepal
1857–59: The Mutiny
1899–1900: Boxer rebellion
1855–73: Yunnan Muslim uprising
1891: Anti-western riots in Wuchang
1883–88, 1883–1913: Guerrilla warfare against French
Shan Tribes
FRENCH INDO-CHINA
1898–1902: Aguinaldo leads nationalist revolt
1905–09: Terrorist campaigns in Maharashtra and Bengal
1881–98: Mahdiyya Jihad against British and Egyptian rule
1897–1900: Rabih leads resistance against French
FRENCH WEST AFRICA
1896: Italian defeat at Adowa
ANGLO-EGYPTIAN SUDAN
BRITISH SOMALILAND
1884–98: Manda resistance
NIGERIA
1904: Anyang rebellion
1900: Ashanti rebellion
GOLD COAST
CAMEROON
FRENCH EQUATORIAL AFRICA
ABYSSINIA
1891–1920: Sayyid Muhammad resists British and Italian rule
1890–98: Bunyoro resistance
1895–1905: Nandi resistance
1885–87, 1916: Rebellions against French rule
SIAM
ANNAM
1885–86: Revolts against French rule
Achin
1898–1913: Moro resistance
Dayaks
1881–1908: Jihad against Dutch
PHILIPPINE ISLANDS
FRENCH CONGO
1911–17: Tutsi and Hutu resistance
UGANDA
BRITISH EAST AFRICA
GERMAN EAST AFRICA
BELGIAN CONGO
1891–98: Hehe resistance
1888–89: Abushiri resistance
1905–07: Maji–Maji resistance
1913: Risings against Portuguese rule
ANGOLA
NORTHERN RHODESIA
PORTUGUESE EAST AFRICA
BRITISH CENTRAL AFRICA (NYASALAND)
1890, 1914–17: Uprising by Saminist peasant movements
JAVA
1881–94: Rebellions against Dutch
DUTCH EAST INDIES
GERMAN SOUTHWEST AFRICA
BECHUANA-LAND
SOUTHERN RHODESIA
MADAGASCAR
1898–1904: Anti-French risings
1904–06: Risings by Herero and Hottentots
1896: Revolts by Matabele and Mashona
UNION OF SOUTH AFRICA
1906: Zulu revolt
1899–1902: Boer war between Britain and two Boer republics

0 km 1000 2000
0 miles 1000 2000

KEY

Anti-colonial uprisings and incidents
- anti-British
- anti-Dutch
- anti-French
- anti-German
- anti-Italian
- anti-Portuguese
- anti-Russian
- anti-Spanish
- anti-US
- anti-Ottoman

Other revolts and revolutions
- Persian Revolution
- area of Chinese Revolution 1911–12
- other revolts
- boundary at 1914

ZULU WARRIORS

The rest of the world was not, of course, peaceful before the advent of European imperialism. Just as in Europe, individual nations in the Americas, Asia, and Africa used warfare to assert their interests and ways of life. In southern Africa, for instance, the Zulu leader Shaka turned his people into a nation of warriors that won an empire. Along with brutal violence, Shaka introduced superior strategies, such as the three-pronged assault based on the head of a buffalo, and tactics, adopting the traditional shield as an offensive weapon to throw an opponent off balance, and introducing a round-headed club and the *assegai* (a short, stabbing spear). The Zulu were eventually overcome by the British with their guns, but not before winning the enemy's admiration for their fighting ability.

1854–1934

MARSHAL LYAUTEY

A statesman and a soldier, Louis-Hubert-Gonzalve Lyautey was France's outstanding colonial administrator. He played a key role in the French conquest of Madagascar (1896–98) and later served as a commandant in Algeria. From 1912 to 1925 Lyautey was, with intervals, governor of the protectorate of Morocco, expanding its territory and combating the rebellion of the Rif people. He strove to create a system of colonial government that cooperated with local interests and was independent from Paris.

NATIVE SOLDIERS

Admiration often existed among both Europeans and indigenous peoples for the fighting qualities of their opponents. European armies frequently turned to traditional warrior peoples to provide a cutting edge to their own forces, while necessity often motivated large-scale recruitment among the local people. British India was won and maintained mainly by Indian troops known as sepoys. The sepoys' success was in large part due to their adoption of British drill, which turned the predominantly Hindu soldiers into excellent infantry. In North America, the local knowledge of the American Indians made them, with modern weapons, superior fighters in the forests. In the 19th century one of the most famous colonial military units was the Zouaves, members of the Zouaoua people of Algeria and Morocco, who helped the French conquer Algeria, as well as other parts of North Africa.

OFFICER'S HELMET
This typical British officer's helmet of the mid-1800s features a top-mounted ball, above which is a socket for a plume.

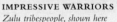

FIGHTING FOR FRANCE
The Zouaves, who served in the French army as light infantry, wore baggy pants, a braided jacket, and a fez. Their name and uniform were later adopted by native French units.

BRITISH INDIA

THE ORIGINS OF BRITISH RULE in India lie with the British East India Company. Although it was founded as a trading group, the decline of the Muslim Mogul Empire in northern India in the mid-1700s and the ensuing unrest forced the company to hire sepoys (Indian troops) to garrison its bases. What began as a unit of security guards became a private army as the company was drawn into the Indian power struggles, as well as into rivalry with French interests. In 1757, when the British defeated a French and Mogul army at Plassey, the way was open to expand British control over India. This control was challenged, however, first by the Maratha confederacy of Hindu princes and later by the sepoys themselves during the Indian Mutiny (1857–58).

SECOND MARATHA WAR

Assaye

DATE	
September 23, 1803	
FORCES	
British and Indian: 13,500; Marathas: 40,000	
LOCATION Present-day Maharashtra state, central India	**CASUALTIES** British: 1,500; Marathas: 6,000

The Maratha wars resulted from British attempts to exert influence over the Maratha confederacy. The first war (1775–82) ended with the British returning all the gains they had made in the fighting. The second war (1803–05) began when the governor-general of India, Richard Wellesley, offered protection to an ousted peshwa (Maratha chief minister), thus offending the other Maratha princes. Wellesley sent his younger brother, Arthur, the future duke of Wellington, against the French-trained forces of the powerful Maratha princes of Sindhia and Berar. Wellesley encountered the enemy unexpectedly, camped on the other side of the Kaitna River. Although his British and sepoy army was outmanned three to one, Wellesley decided on an immediate attack. Finding a ford, he crossed the river and attacked the enemy's left flank. The Marathas fought back fiercely, but the British captured their cannons and defensive position in the village of Assaye. In later years Wellington described the battle as his greatest military achievement.

SEIZING THE GUNS
British forces capture the Maratha guns at Assaye. The Duke of Wellington, who led the assault, described the battle as "the bloodiest for the numbers that I ever saw."

FIRST ANGLO–AFGHAN WAR

Retreat from Kabul

DATE	
January 6–13, 1842	
FORCES	
Afghans: unknown; British and Indian: 4,000	
LOCATION Between Kabul and Jalalabad, Afghanistan	**CASUALTIES** British: 3,800

Seeking to expand its territory into Afghanistan, and fearful of Russian influence, the British looked for an alliance with the country's ruler. In 1839, when their first efforts failed, the British decided to restore the unpopular Shah Shuja to the Afghan throne by force. This led to the First

BITTER END
Thousands of men, women, and children—along with British and Indian troops—died on the retreat from Kabul.

Anglo–Afghan War as resistance broke out across the country. By 1841 the position of British and Indian troops in Afghanistan was precarious. Sir William McNaghten, the head of the British mission in the Afghan capital, Kabul, opposed evacuation, but when he was murdered in December, the British decided to withdraw. In freezing temperatures they set out on January 6, 1842, only to be harassed by Afghan irregulars. All but a handful were massacred. The retreat from Kabul left bitter memories among the British, which the Second and Third Afghan Wars did little to heal.

FIRST AND SECOND SIKH WARS

Sikh Wars

	DATE 1845–46; 1848–49
	FORCES Sikh (including Muslims and Hindus): 66,000; British and Indian: 30,000
LOCATION Punjab, northwest India	**CASUALTIES** Sikh: 13,000; British and Indian: 6,000

Numbering about 50,000 infantry, 10,000 gunners, and 6,000 cavalry, the Sikhs were the most formidable opponents of the British in India. In 1845 the First Sikh War began after Sikh troops crossed the Sutlej River into British territory. The British commander in chief, Sir Hugh Gough, fought one bloody and indecisive battle against the Sikhs at Mudki and another at Firuzshah. At Sobraon, however, Gough was victorious—although at heavy cost. In 1848 another outbreak by mutinous Sikh troops led to the Second Sikh War. The main battle, fought at Chillianwala on January 13, 1849, on heavily forested terrain, was won by Gough's superior artillery. The Sikhs surrendered that March and the British annexed the Punjab.

DANGEROUS OPPONENTS
After the Sikh wars, Sikhs troops, shown here with a fighting elephant, became a formidable element in the British army.

THE INDIAN MUTINY

Delhi

DATE
July–September 1857

FORCES
British officers and loyal sepoys: unknown; rebel sepoys: unknown

LOCATION
Delhi, north-central India

CASUALTIES
No reliable estimates

The Indian Mutiny began in 1857 when rumors spread among the sepoys of the British East India Company that cartridges—the ends of which had to be bitten off before loading—for the newly introduced Enfield rifles were greased with pig and cow fat. Such cartridges offended Hindus and Muslims alike, but the sepoys' objections expressed a wider

BRITISH REVENGE
Two alleged mutineers, hanged in Delhi by the British when they retook the city. After the mutiny the territories and soldiers of the East India Company passed to the crown.

dislike of British modernization and the predominance of Christianity. When objectors in the Bengal Light Cavalry were arrested on May 9 in the town of Meerut, in northern India, their comrades decided to free them. Events got out of hand and ended in a massacre of British officers, their wives, and children. The violence spread rapidly and was especially fierce in Delhi, to where the Meerut sepoys marched and restored the elderly Mogul emperor to power. They sepoys then joined forces with the garrison in Delhi, leading to a two-month siege. When the British eventually recaptured the

garrison they enacted a terrible revenge, killing many of the rebels and many other able-bodied men. In one incident the emperor's three sons were murdered in cold blood by a British officer and their bodies

thrown on a garbage heap. British soldiers also set up artillery in the city's main mosque and destroyed nearby buildings, including the homes of rich families containing many cultural treasures.

ENFIELD RIFLE

The invention of the Minié bullet in 1849 led to the development of more effective rifles. Instead of a lead ball, the Minié bullet was long and conical, with a hollow base that expanded to grip the rifling (spiral grooves cut inside the gun barrel)

when fired, greatly increasing accuracy. Britain's Royal Small Arms Factory in Enfield, Middlesex, quickly utilized the new technology, producing in 1851 the .702-in Pattern Minié rifle, which British troops used to deadly effect in

the Crimean War (1854–56). In 1853 the factory manufactured a smaller-caliber version of the weapon, shown below. This firearm was extensively adopted by British and American soldiers: both sides in the American Civil War (1861–65) had Enfields.

SPECIFICATION

Origin England	**Range** 1,000 yds (914m)
Length 55in (140cm)	**Caliber** .577 inches
Date of Launch 1853	**Weight** 5¾lb (2.6kg)

STOCK
Made of walnut or beech

BARREL BANDS
These secured the barrel to the stock

MUZZLE-LOADING
This was a rifled musket: bullets were pushed down the barrel

BAYONET ATTACHMENT
A triangular cross-section bayonet could be fitted at the end of the gun

THE INDIAN MUTINY

Lucknow

DATE
June–November 1857

FORCES British and loyal sepoys: 1,712; Rebel sepoys: 6,000

LOCATION
Uttar Pradesh state, north-central India

CASUALTIES
British and loyal sepoys: 1,050; Rebel sepoys: unknown

Lucknow, the chief city of Oudh province and the headquarters of the British commissioner Sir Henry Lawrence, came under siege at the start of the Indian Mutiny. The fate of the British inhabitants of the frontier station of Cawnpore, less than 50 miles (80km) away, bore heavily on Sir Henry's mind. Cawnpore, too, had been swiftly besieged. The British had held out against bombardment for several weeks before surrendering on the promise of free passage to the city

of Allahabad. On leaving, however, the sepoys massacred them, men first, then women and children later. The troops at Lucknow consisted of one European battalion plus a number of sepoys. With many women and children to protect, Lawrence decided to make his base at the hospital buildings, close to the route that the anticipated reinforcements would take, even though it meant sacrificing the armory to the rebels. An unwise sally against the rebels resulted in ill-afforded British casualties and the loss of several outposts. Lawrence himself was fatally injured on July 4. Reinforcements finally arrived on September 25, enabling the garrison to enlarge the area it held. Then, on November 14, the British commander in chief, Sir Colin Campbell, reached Lucknow. Although his force was outnumbered ten to one, it evacuated the British, bringing the most famous episode of the Indian Mutiny to an end. A British force stationed outside Lucknow recaptured it the following May.

STILL STANDING
An early photograph shows the battle-scarred residence at Lucknow. The flag that flew over it during the siege remained flying until 1947.

SECOND ANGLO–AFGHAN WAR

Siege of Kandahar

DATE
September 1, 1880

FORCES
Afghans: 13,000; British and Indian: 10,000

LOCATION
South-central Afghanistan

CASUALTIES
No reliable estimates

During the Second Afghan War (1878–80) the British occupied Kandahar, Afghanistan's second city, where they were besieged by Ayub Khan, the governor of Herat and claimant to the Afghan throne. Sir Frederick Roberts, the outstanding British general of his time, was in command in Kabul. He marched about 300 miles (480km) between August 9 and 31, 1880. Ayyub Khan raised the siege before Roberts arrived, retiring a short distance to the west, where Roberts, having collected extra artillery from Kandahar, engaged and defeated him.

STAR OF INDIA
The British awarded this medal to Indian subjects who served the colonial government well.

GATLING GUN

FIRST USED DURING THE AMERICAN CIVIL WAR, GATLING GUNS WERE THE PRECURSORS OF A NEW TYPE OF MACHINE GUN.

By the second half of the 19th century improvements in engineering had made it possible to manufacture reliable multiple-fire weapons. The gun patented by Richard Gatling in 1861 employed multiple barrels, as would all early machine guns. It also took advantage of the new brass bullet-cartridge; earlier paper cartridges were dangerous, being liable to combust unpredictably. The barrels—at first six, later 10—were arranged around a cylindrical shaft. A hand-operated crank made the barrels revolve, and cartridges dropped into place from above as each barrel came around. A firing pin then struck and fired the bullet; the barrel turned and the process was repeated. As each barrel descended, its cartridge shell was ejected. The gun was produced in 1in to 0.65in calibers.

INFLUENTIAL DESIGN

After seeing very limited use in the Civil War, the gun was adopted by the US Army in 1866. Firing about 400 rounds a minute in practice, it was devastatingly effective against enemies such as Plains Indians or, for the British, the Zulus. It was also much used as a naval weapon. After a 15-year heyday, the Gatling gun and other rotating-barrel machine-guns were superseded from the 1880s by single-barrel guns such as the Maxim, which used the recoil of the barrel or combustion gases to produce continuous fire without the need for a crank. In the late 20th century Gatling-style guns reappeared in weapons systems on board military aircraft and ships, such as the US Mk 15 Phalanx system, which uses a rotating cluster of six 20mm barrels.

RICHARD GATLING
Richard Jordan Gatling (1818–1903) was a peace-loving individual who fondly believed that his new weapon would deter countries from going to war.

ZULU WAR
British soldiers crew a Gatling gun during the 1879 Zulu War. The gun increased Europeans' advantage in colonial wars.

CRANK *When rotated, the brass crank handle turns the barrels inside the cylinders. Each barrel is then loaded and fired once during a complete rotation.*

PLAQUE *The gun was manufactured at the armory of Samuel Colt—most famous for his revolver—in Hartford, Connecticut, which made hundreds of thousands of firearms for the Union side in the Civil War.*

MAGAZINE SLOT *Top: groove to help removal of a jammed magazine. Bottom: the 40-round magazine cartridge-feeder .*

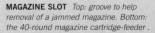

LOWERING GEAR *This wheel was used to raise and lower the barrels.*

TRAVERSING HANDSPIKE STOWAGE *on the side of the gun, used to damage the barrels and disable the gun to prevent its use by the enemy.*

WHEEL HUB *with a towing ring secured by a cottered crank (a wedge-shaped fastener). The towing ring enabled easier transportation.*

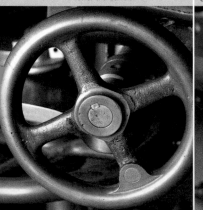

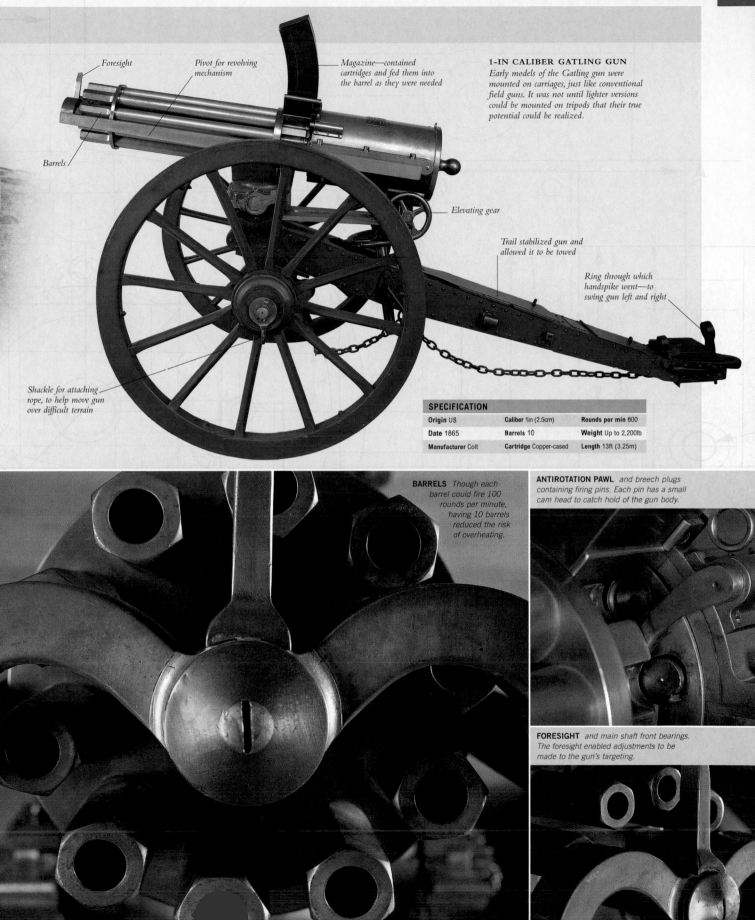

Foresight

Pivot for revolving mechanism

Magazine—contained cartridges and fed them into the barrel as they were needed

Barrels

1-IN CALIBER GATLING GUN
Early models of the Gatling gun were mounted on carriages, just like conventional field guns. It was not until lighter versions could be mounted on tripods that their true potential could be realized.

Elevating gear

Trail stabilized gun and allowed it to be towed

Ring through which handspike went—to swing gun left and right

Shackle for attaching rope, to help move gun over difficult terrain

SPECIFICATION		
Origin US	**Caliber** 1in (2.5cm)	**Rounds per min** 600
Date 1865	**Barrels** 10	**Weight** Up to 2,200lb
Manufacturer Colt	**Cartridge** Copper-cased	**Length** 13ft (3.25m)

BARRELS Though each barrel could fire 100 rounds per minute, having 10 barrels reduced the risk of overheating.

ANTIROTATION PAWL and breech plugs containing firing pins. Each pin has a small cam head to catch hold of the gun body.

FORESIGHT and main shaft front bearings. The foresight enabled adjustments to be made to the gun's targeting.

THE CONQUEST OF AFRICA

IN 1880 EUROPEAN CONTROL in Africa extended only to South Africa and a few small coastal regions. Within 20 years almost the whole continent had come under European rule. This scramble for African colonies was largely driven by European rivalries, and some events—such as the Zulu War—stemmed from the actions of ambitious officials on the spot. The pace of occupation soon quickened. Belgian King Leopold acquired the Congo as a vast personal estate in the 1870s. Ottoman weakness allowed France and Britain to take over much of North Africa by 1882. Germany seized a string of African territories in 1884. Finally, in 1885 the Berlin Conference sanctioned and accelerated the division of Africa between Britain, France, and the other European powers.

▪ REVOLT OF ABD EL-QADIR

Revolt of Abd el-Qadir

DATE
1832–47

FORCES
Algerian: around 10,000; French: up to 100,000

LOCATION
Algeria

CASUALTIES
No reliable estimates

In 1830 the French invaded Algeria, putting an end to Ottoman Turkish rule and deposing its ruler, the dey. They claimed to be acting to end the longstanding problem of Algerian piracy and to liberate the country from the Turks, but trade and prestige were more pressing motives. French rule was harsh, and widespread resistance broke out. In the west, this was led by Abd el-Qadir (1808–83), who united local tribes under his leadership, and was proclaimed amir of

Mascara (in western Algeria) in 1832. He was an astute, but not very successful, guerrilla leader, and the French accorded him conditional recognition in 1837. However, when it appeared the French were, despite this treaty, bent on total conquest, Abd el-Qadir declared a holy war. The French waged a brutal campaign, burning crops and seizing cattle, before occupying Mascara and destroying Abd el-Qadir's arms depots. The sultan of Morocco intervened, but the French defeated the Moroccan army in 1844. Abd el-Qadir finally surrendered in 1847 and was briefly imprisoned in France. A courteous foe, and a devout Muslim, he once released prisoners whom he could not feed. He later became a hero in France, receiving the *Légion d'Honneur* after saving 12,000 Christians from slaughter by a fanatical Muslim crowd in Damascus in 1860.

LEGIONNAIRES IN ACTION
The French Foreign Legion was founded in 1831 for the Algerian campaign. Here the legionnaires battle with Berber tribesmen.

▪ ANGLO–ASHANTI WARS

Second Ashanti War

DATE June 1873– February 13, 1874

FORCES
British and West African allies: 4,000; Ashanti: 20,000

LOCATION
Modern Ghana, West Africa

CASUALTIES British and allies: 1,700; Ashanti: unknown

By the 1870s the powerful Ashanti kingdom dominated the Gold Coast (modern Ghana), while the British controlled a string of coastal forts. Ashanti king Kofi Karikari's efforts to reestablish his authority on the coast

provoked a war. In November 1873 a British expedition under Sir Garnet Wolseley checked Ashanti progress. Then, in January, the British moved into the interior with 7-pounder guns and rocket launchers. The Ashanti had no guns, and their strongest ally was disease. On January 31 Wolseley won a battle at Amoafu and then burned down the Ashanti capital, Kumasi. Kofi agreed peace terms on February 13. His kingdom splintered, and by 1901 was a British protectorate.

RECRUITING GROUND
British officers check the equipment of local recruits for the Ashanti War. As well as soldiers, the British employed 6,000 porters for the march into the interior.

▪ REVOLT OF ARABI PASHA

Tel el-Kebir

DATE
September 13, 1882

FORCES
British: 11,000 infantry, 2,000 cavalry; Egyptians: 31,000

LOCATION 60 miles (100km) northeast of Cairo, Egypt

CASUALTIES
British: 460; Egyptians: up to 3,000

Following a British and French takeover of the government of Egypt—which was unable to pay its massive debts—a revolt erupted, led by Arabi Pasha. British citizens died in riots in Alexandria and on July 11, 1882, British gunships bombarded the port in retaliation. A British army under Wolseley defeated the Egyptians at Tel el-Kebir in a 30-minute battle. Britain then occupied Egypt.

EGYPT STAR
The Bronze Star was awarded to all British soldiers taking part in the Egyptian campaigns between 1882 and 1885.

▪ IMPERIAL CONFLICTS

Adowa

DATE
March 1, 1896

FORCES
Italians: 17,000; Ethiopians: 100,000

LOCATION
Northern Ethiopia

CASUALTIES
Italians: 7,300; Ethiopians: 10,000

In the 1890s the Italians, who already occupied Eritrea and Somalia, sought to add Ethiopia to their north African empire. Although Ethiopian emperor Menelik II had a large superiority in numbers, some of his forces were armed only with spears. The Italians, under General Oreste Baratieri, advanced into Tigray province but, held by Menelik at Amba Alagi in December 1895, they fell back to Adowa. Both sides were running low on supplies when, on February 29, 1896, Baratieri launched a night attack. But his plans had been betrayed by Ethiopian agents; moreover, the Italians were divided into small groups and, in the darkness and rough terrain, communications were poor. Menelik, who received reinforcements during the night, defeated the Italian contingents separately and won the greatest victory ever inflicted by an African force on a European army.

"Khartoum all right; could hold out for years.— C. G. Gordon. December 29."

Charles George Gordon, in a letter received by steamer by the relief expedition, five days before the fall of Khartoum January 21, 1885.

THE MAHDIST REVOLT

Siege of Khartoum

DATE March 13, 1884–January 26, 1885

FORCES Anglo–Egyptian: 2,000; Mahdist: about 100,000

LOCATION Khartoum, Sudan

CASUALTIES Anglo–Egyptian: 2,000; Sudanese: unknown

In 1881 Muhammad Ahmad, a Muslim religious leader in the Sudan, declared himself the Mahdi ("Expected One"). He began a holy war against Egyptian rule and gathered a large number of followers, the Ansar (dervishes), intent on establishing a purified form of Islam in the Sudan. In 1883 his forces exterminated an Egyptian army of 10,000 men led by a British officer,

GORDON'S LAST STAND
This romanticized view of Khartoum's fall shows Gordon facing down an oncoming mob of Mahdist Ansar. None of the garrison lived to give an impartial account of his end.

Colonel William Hicks. In Britain there was a clamor for action against the Mahdi, who now threatened Khartoum. British prime minister Gladstone reluctantly agreed to send General Charles George Gordon to Khartoum. Gordon had suppressed the Taiping Rebellion in China in 1863–64 and had served in Khartoum as the governor-general of the Khedive (the Egyptian ruler). The terms of his mission were unclear. Gladstone thought he was to evacuate the civilians from Khartoum, which he promptly did. The Khedive believed he should evacuate all the

Egyptian garrisons in the Nile valley. Gordon, however, became trapped in Khartoum as the Mahdi's Ansar advanced. The siege began in March. Gordon had no staff, and the Egyptian garrison was weak. Somehow it held out until January, when the falling level of the Nile weakened its defenses. The *Ansar* broke through, annihilated the garrison, and hacked Gordon to death. A relief expedition, led by Sir Garnet Wolseley, finally arrived three days later.

SUDAN SHIELD
Made of bamboo hoops and covered in cotton, this shield was of doubtful efficacy against bullets.

THE MAHDIST REVOLT

Omdurman

DATE September 2, 1898

FORCES British and allies: 26,000; Mahdists: 50,000

LOCATION About 5 miles (8km) north of Omdurman, Sudan

CASUALTIES British and allies: 430; Mahdists: 30,000

Gordon was not avenged for 13 years (see above). An Anglo-Egyptian army invaded the Sudan in 1898, led by General Hubert Horatio Kitchener, commander-in-chief of the Egyptian army and an admirer of Gordon, with whom he shared many characteristics. The Mahdi had died in 1885, but his movement flourished under his successor, the Khalifa al-Taashi. Kitchener stationed his men in an arc, with cavalry on the flanks, backed by gunboats on the Nile. His advance was spearheaded by the 21st Lancers. The one-sided battle was won by machine guns and artillery, against which spears and some old muskets offered little contest. The battle began at 6 a.m. with about 16,000 Mahdists, or Ansar, advancing against the center. The British artillery inflicted many casualties even before the Ansar came within range of the deadly Maxim guns, and none came within 50 yards (45m) of the British trenches. Kitchener advanced on Omdurman with the 21st Lancers, which

CAVALRY CHARGE
The 21st Lancers' charge swept away the last Sudanese resistance. Winston Churchill's vivid account of it in The River War *showed admiration for the Mahdists' spirit.*

DERVISH CHARGE
The British line lets off a volley against the onrushing mass of Mahdists. The slaughter inflicted on the Sudanese was appalling and the Mahdi's cause never recovered.

included Winston Churchill, doubling as war correspondent of *The Morning Post* and captain of cavalry, leading the van in one of the last British cavalry charges. They unexpectedly encountered a substantial and particularly ferocious band of Mahdists concealed in a wadi, and won three Victoria Crosses (the top British award for gallantry). That aside, there was almost no close-quarters fighting and the battle was over before noon. Kitchener occupied Omdurman, the Mahdist capital. The Khalifa escaped but was killed the following year.

ZULU WARS

EUROPEAN EXPANSION IN SOUTH AFRICA was facilitated by political divisions and warfare among the African groups they encountered. Small groups linked to single leaders, often fighting against their own neighbors, were unable to resist the organized forces of the British and Afrikaners. The rise, under Shaka, of a Nguni-speaking clan into a great warrior nation, the Zulu, posed the most significant threat to the Europeans.

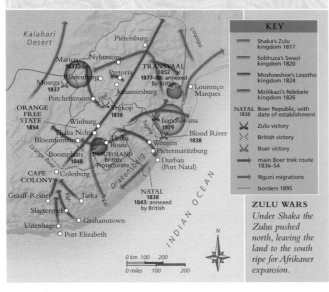

KEY

	Shaka's Zulu kingdom 1817
	Sobhuza's Swazi kingdom 1820
	Moshoeshoe's Lesotho kingdom 1824
	Mzilikazi's Ndebele kingdom 1826
NATAL 1838	Boer Republic, with date of establishment
⚔	Zulu victory
⚔	British victory
⚔	Boer victory
→	main Boer trek route 1836–54
→	Nguni migrations
	borders 1895

ZULU WARS
Under Shaka the Zulus pushed north, leaving the land to the south ripe for Afrikaner expansion.

ZULU WARS OF CONQUEST

Conquests of Shaka

DATE	
1818–28	
FORCES	
Zulus: 150,000; Others: unknown	
LOCATION	**CASUALTIES**
Natal, South Africa	Unknown, but in tens of thousands

Shaka, whose name comes from an intestinal beetle and is sometimes known as "Africa's Attila," earned his reputation as a protégé of Dingiswayo, paramount chief of the Zulu. A man of impressive physical strength and military stature, Shaka rose to power after the murder of Dingiswayo (1816) and an ensuing contest for power with Zwide, the king's assassin. At first Shaka escaped defeat only through his adroit use of spies and a policy of "scorched earth" retreats. In 1819, Shaka's young warriors outmaneuvered Zwide's exhausted and starving men in the Mhlatuze valley. Zwide escaped, but other survivors were incorporated in Shaka's army. From 1821 Shaka overran the whole of Natal, largely depopulating it in the process. The ripples spread, as defeated opponents carried the social dislocation farther into central Africa. By 1824 Shaka ruled about 500,000 people (his original tribe numbered about 2,000), and commanded 15 *impis*, or regiments. In 1827 he slaughtered thousands of people in a rage at the death of his mother. His attempts to contact European powers were thwarted, and he was considering an attack on European settlers in 1828, when he was murdered by his two half-brothers, one of whom, Dingaan, succeeded him.

ZULU WARRIORS
Three of Shaka's soldiers in battle dress. They carry the characteristic short stabbing spear and large shield.

THE ZULU–BOER CONFLICT

Blood River

DATE	
December 16, 1838	
FORCES	
Zulus: about 10,000; Voortrekkers: 470	
LOCATION	**CASUALTIES**
Natal, South Africa	Zulus: about 3,000; Voortrekkers: 3 wounded

The Dutch colony at the Cape of Good Hope, founded in the 17th century, had within 150 years given rise to a new nation, the Afrikaners, with few links to Europe and speaking a language no longer quite Dutch. The British captured the Cape in 1793, and from 1820 British immigration increased rapidly. The Afrikaners (also known as "Boers") resented British legal restrictions and more liberal attitudes to black Africans. In 1835, determined to regain freedom from British control, about 12,000 men, women, children, and their servants—the *voortrekkers*—embarked on the Great Trek. Both the high veldt and Natal appeared suitable for white settlement, their populations sparse as a result of the predations of Shaka. However, having been attacked in the

VOORTREKKER MEMORIAL
The monument to the battle of Blood River features a reconstruction of the voortrekkers's wagon laager. The Zulus failed to penetrate it.

high veldt, the *voortrekkers* pressed on to Natal. In February 1838, a party of about 100 led by Piet Retief went to discuss the cession of land with Shaka's successor Dingaan, only to be brutally massacred. The battle of Blood River was the response to this disaster. When scouts reported the approach of a Zulu host, the *voortrekkers*, led by Andries Pretorius, drew up their wagons in a defensive circle (*laager*) on a skillfully chosen site near Blood (then Ncome)

> "People will die, praises will remain, They will remain exposing them, They will remain mourning for them in the deserted kraals."
>
> *Magolwane ka Makhathini*, Izibongo (praise-poem) on King Dingaan

River. They were vastly outnumbered but, aside from their toughness and determination, the *voortrekkers* had European rifles and guns. The Zulu, led by Dambuza and Nhlela, made a series of attacks only to incur heavy casualties. Pretorius then took the offensive with a party of horsemen, and was one of the few *voortrekkers* hurt. The Zulus retreated, chastened.

THE ANGLO–ZULU WAR

Isandhlwana

DATE
January 22, 1879

FORCES
British: 1,700 regulars, 500 Africans; Zulus: 22,000

LOCATION
Natal, South Africa

CASUALTIES
British: 1,640; Zulus: about 6,000

In the late 1870s the British decided to consolidate all their possessions in southern Africa in one federation. The plan was pursued by Sir Bartle Frere, high commissioner in Cape Town. His ultimatum to Cetshwayo, the Zulu king, provoked a war. Lord Chelmsford led a substantial armed

ISANDHLWANA
The British camp that the Zulus overran was sited at the foot of the hill. The terrain offers little cover, save for a spur to the north.

expedition into Zululand. He then divided his forces, leaving the veteran troops of the 1st Battalion of the 24th Regiment at an unfortified advance camp at Isandhlwana. Scouting parties failed to establish the strength of the Zulus, some of whom had rifles. Led by Chiefs Ntshingwayo and Mavumengwana, the Zulus attacked and overwhelmed the British. No prisoners were taken and the 1st Battalion was slaughtered almost to the last man. Too late, Chelmsford arrived with reinforcements that evening at the scene of the disaster. For the Zulus it was not an unmitigated success, as they lost a large proportion of their young warriors.

THIN RED LINE
Zulus close in for hand-to-hand fighting with the British. The artist of this view of Isandhlwana has made the hill resemble the badge of the 24th Regiment.

THE ANGLO–ZULU WAR

Rorke's Drift

DATE
January 22–23, 1879

FORCES
British: 139; Zulu: 4,000

LOCATION Buffalo River crossing, west of Ishandhlwana, Natal

CASUALTIES
British: 32; Zulu: 550

When Lord Chelmsford arrived at Isandlwana (see above), he could hear gunfire and see a red glow to the west where he had left 140 men to guard

the crossing at Rorke's Drift. They included patients in the column's hospital, a few unruly soldiers of the Natal kaffirs, who fled on sight of the enemy, and a handful of European civilians. About 100 men defended the post, including Lieutenant Bromhead of the 24th and Lieutenant Chard of the Royal Engineers. As the senior, Chard took command to face an attack by a large Zulu force led by Prince Dabulamanzi, which included men

HOSPITAL ABLAZE
The evacuation of the hospital at Rorke's Drift. Two privates were awarded the Victoria Cross for holding off the attacking Zulus.

who had fought earlier the same day at Isandhlwana. With no chance of withdrawing, the British hastily created a 4ft (1.25m) rampart of grain bags and wagons. Charge succeeded charge and the British rifles inflicted many casualties, but their perimeter was steadily reduced to a circumference of about 500ft (150m). Hand-to-hand fighting, with long bayonets against spears, continued for several hours.

VICTORIA CROSS
Eleven Victoria Crosses were awarded to the defenders of Rorke's Drift, the largest number given for any single engagement.

Although the British were defending from a higher level, they eventually began to tire. However, after 10 hours' fighting, the Zulus retired shortly before dawn on January 23. The extraordinary defense of Rorke's Drift cost just 10 British lives.

1750–1914

THE SECOND BOER WAR

AFRIKANERS, OR BOERS ("FARMERS"), from Cape Colony founded the Orange Free State and Transvaal republics in the 1850s. Initial recognition by Britain was replaced by friction when gold and diamonds were discovered. Britain's annexation of the Transvaal in 1877 caused the First Boer (or Transvaal) War. In 1881 Transvaal regained its independence, but the European scramble for colonies in Africa prompted further British annexations that left it isolated. Transvaal's President Kruger withheld the vote from *uitlanders* (foreigners), who thronged the booming state, leading Cape governor Cecil Rhodes to organize the Jameson Raid to support a nonexistent *uitlander* rebellion. The outbreak of the Second Boer (or South Africa) War followed in October 1899.

THE BOER WAR

Boer Offensive

DATE October 1899– January 1900	
FORCES Varied throughout campaign	
LOCATION Natal and Cape Colony, southern Africa	**CASUALTIES** Heavier on British side

In 1899 Britain despatched 10,000 troops to quash a growing Boer revolt in Cape Colony. The Boer cavalry attacked before the reinforcements arrived, intending to spread the uprising and win a negotiated settlement. The Boers had no army, only mounted units called commandos. But they had been training for years, were disciplined, with elected officers and up-to-date artillery, as well as superior rifles (many provided by Germany). When the Boers invaded Natal, the outnumbered British forces withdrew to Ladysmith, which was cut off. Kimberley and

ARTILLERY BOERS
Afrikaner troops man a howitzer outside Ladysmith in 1899. The town was subject to bombardment by 22 guns. It was relieved after a four-month siege.

Mafeking were also besieged. Sir Redvers Buller, although over 60, had wide experience of colonial wars and, being popular with his men, was the obvious choice to command the South African corps. His reputation was ruined forever in "Black Week" of December 1899, when his forces, ill-provided with cavalry and divided into three columns (each to relieve one of the three besieged towns), all suffered defeat. Buller was later replaced as commander-in-chief. The war had become a civil war, with many Afrikaners in the Cape taking up arms against the British, but the Boers were thinly spread and by the beginning of 1900 their offensive was running out of steam.

THE BOER WAR

Colenso

DATE December 15, 1899	
FORCES British: 20,000; Afrikaners: 6,500	
LOCATION 22km (14 miles) south of Ladysmith, Natal	**CASUALTIES** British: 500; Afrikaners: 50

Of Buller's three columns (see above) one, bound for Mafeking, was defeated at Stormberg; the second, approaching Kimberley, at Magersfontein; the third, led by Buller himself in Natal, was defeated the same week by Louis Botha at Colenso. Botha had far fewer men but knew the land and was well dug in. As well as suffering heavy casualties, Buller's artillery was captured by the Boers.

MEDAL
The Queen's South Africa Medal was given to all the British soldiers who fought in the Boer wars.

THE BOER WAR

Spion Kop

DATE January 24, 1900	
FORCES British: 30,000; Afrikaners: 5,000	
LOCATION About 20 miles (30km) west of Ladysmith, Natal	**CASUALTIES** British: 2,000; Afrikaners: 200

Buller, the British commander in the Cape, made another attempt to relieve Ladysmith in January. He divided his large force into two, one part under General Sir Charles Warren. Speed was essential, but Warren took two days to cross the Tugela River, then hesitated for another two. Meanwhile, Boer general Botha reinforced his own men. Warren decided to take the commanding heights of Spion Kop. That night 2,000 men silently scaled the hill. They discovered that they could not dig in, had no sandbags, were in the wrong place, and, worst of all, were overlooked by Boer artillery. The

Fixed box magazine

Removable wooden shoulder-stock

MAUSER PISTOL AND HOLSTER
The Mauser C-96 was manufactured in Germany and supplied in large numbers to the Boers. It had a telescopic sight and a range of over 1,100yds (1,000m).

British came under heavy fire, to which they had no reply. Communications were poor, and Warren had little idea of what was happening. Reinforcements kept the hill in British hands, but at terrible cost. The Boers also lost heavily as they climbed the hill to engage at close quarters. By 4:30 p.m. both sides were exhausted and both believed they were losing. Each withdrew from the hill, but Botha rallied his men, who then retook the summit, now manned only by corpses and Mohandas Gandhi—the future Indian leader—with his Indian stretcher-bearers. The Boers allowed Buller to retreat. He finally relieved Ladysmith on February 28.

DEAD ON THE HILL
Corpses of British dead lie in heaps on Spion Kop. Boer snipers picked off hundreds.

THE BOER WAR

Paardeberg

DATE
February 18–27, 1900

FORCES
British and
Canadian: 6,000;
Boers: 5,000

LOCATION 23 miles
(37km) SE of Kimberley
Orange Free State

CASUALTIES British and
Canadian: 1,100;
Boers: 1,000

In December 1899 Lord Roberts of
Kandahar took over as British
commander-in-chief in South Africa,
with Kitchener as chief of staff. After
relieving Kimberley (February 15),
Roberts decided to strike at the Boer
capitals. Kitchener trapped 5,000
Boers in a bend of the Modder River,
where they were dug in on Paardeberg

Hill. Kitchener ordered a direct attack
on the Boer lines, despite a lack of
cover. The Boers opened fire at 100yds
(100m), inflicting over 1,000 casualties
and forcing a withdrawal. Roberts then
resumed command and subjected the
Boers to an eight-day artillery barrage,
after which they surrendered. Roberts
was undaunted by immense distances,
lack of fodder, and a typhoid outbreak
that caused 2,000 casualties. He was in
Bloemfontein on March 13, arrived at
Johannesburg on May 31, and Pretoria
on June 5. After a victory at Komati
Poort (September 25), he returned to
England, leaving Kitchener to clean up.

CROSSING THE VELDT
*British forces and supplies crossing the
Modder River near Paardeberg. Robert's
command of logistics has been criticized, but
he was an extremely effective commander.*

THE BOER WAR

Relief of Mafeking

DATE
May 17, 1900

FORCES
British: 2,000;
Boers:
2,000

LOCATION
Northern Cape,
South Africa

CASUALTIES
Unknown

Having relieved Kimberley in February
1900, Roberts detached a column to
undertake the relief of Mafeking, under
siege since the beginning of the war.
It was to join with Rhodesian and
Canadian cavalry on the way. In
Mafeking itself, Colonel Baden Powell
had organized the defense with the
élan that he would later bequeath to
the Boy Scout movement, but
conditions were growing grave. Food
was in such short
supply that the
Africans, whose
rations were smaller
than Europeans',
were digging up
dead horses to eat.
Baden Powell set
up a soup kitchen
that, oddly, ran at a
profit, while a press
correspondent
described the
horror of the
"human frameworks of both sexes and
all ages…standing in lines, each
holding an old blackened can…,

> "For 217 days the
> Boers tried to obtain
> Mafeking's surrender,
> but their strategy was
> futile owing to its
> noble defender."
>
> *William McGonagall,*
> The Relief of Mafeking

MAFEKING MONEY
*A £1 note issued during the siege of
Mafeking. The gun depicted is a 4½-in
howitzer improvised from a drainpipe and
nicknamed "The Wolf."*

awaiting their turn to crawl painfully
up to the soup kitchen…" When the
relief column approached, Botha sent
a force to intervene, but they were
brushed aside, while the numbers of
Boers besieging the
town had been
reduced. A final Boer
attack on the town on
May 11 failed, and
on May 17 Mafeking
was relieved. The
news set off almost
hysterical celebrations
in Britain, giving rise
to the term "to
maffick," or celebrate
extravagantly. Baden
Powell returned
home a hero and became the youngest
major-general in the British army.

THE BOER WAR

Guerrilla War

DATE
November 1900–
May 1902

FORCES
Varied throughout
campaign

LOCATION
South Africa

CASUALTIES
Unknown, but high
among Boer civilians

By mid-1900, with the conventional
war lost, the Boer commandos turned
to guerrilla warfare, harassing the
British at every turn. Railroad
communications were constantly
sabotaged, isolated outposts
captured, small detachments
ambushed. Boer leaders

such as De Wet—who surrounded
a whole brigade at Frederickstad—
Botha, De la Rey, Beyers, and the
young Jan Smuts operated with
impunity. The British, unable to keep
the outbreaks localized, adopted
harsher tactics. Kitchener, Roberts's
successor, most notoriously moved
civilians into concentration camps.
Chains of blockhouses successfully
protected targets such as the railroads.
The guerrilla leaders evaded the
British, but resources were running
out. De Wet discussed terms with
Kitchener in February, but the talks
broke down. The war continued
until Boer resistance was finally
worn out and peace was signed at
Vereeniging on May 31, 1902.

BOER COMMANDOS
*From 1900 the Boers fought on as
guerrillas. The British confiscated their
property and placed their families in
camps, where 28,000 died.*

BOER WAR RIFLES

Transvaal's President Kruger realized
that war with the British Empire
was inevitable, and that his
republic was unprepared. Despite
a legal requirement, many Boers
did not own a rifle, certainly not a
modern one. He ordered 37,000
rifles and 10 million cartridges
from Krupp, the German arms
manufacturer. The rifles were the
latest model of German Mauser,
the 95. Peter Paul Mauser
(1838–1914) was a brilliant
inventor who, with his brother
Wilhelm, invented the needle gun
(1863) and the breech-loading
rifle (1871) besides a pistol and
repeating rifle. The Mauser
magazine rifle first appeared in
1897. First adopted in Germany,
the Mauser was by far the most
successful rifle of its day. The
South African model 95 proved
extremely accurate at long range
and superior to the British Lee-
Metford. The Krag Jørgensen rifle,
designed at the Norwegian Arms
Factory, was also supplied in large
numbers to the Boers.

Front sight

*Four-groove
rifled barrel*

*Five-shot
magazine*

Rear sight

Butt stock

BOER RIFLES
Mauser model 1895 rifle made by Loewe
& Co. for the Orange Free State (left).
Krag Jørgensen model 1894 rifle manufactured
for export to the Boer Republics (right).

WARS OF IMPERIAL EXPANSION

OVER THE COURSE OF THE 19TH CENTURY the British and French extended their influence all around the globe, fighting a series of successful colonial wars in Asia, Africa, and Australasia. By the end of the century, their empires had reached their greatest extent. Meanwhile, the United States was asserting its dominance over regions it considered its own. While the US did not seek a formal empire in the European manner, the Philippines, Puerto Rico, Cuba, and Panama were all under US control by the beginning of the 20th century. All three great powers shared a belief in their mission to spread their own particular versions of civilization across the world.

IMPERIAL CONFLICTS

First Burma War

DATE
1823–26

FORCES
British and Indian: 50,000; Burmese: 60,000

LOCATION Burma and Assam, India

CASUALTIES British and Indian: 20,000; Burmese: 10,000

In 1823 Burmese forces crossed the border into British-controlled India, capturing Assam. They were pursuing exiled rebels from the Burmese-held former kingdom of Arakan. Britain responded by declaring war on Burma on February 24, 1824. Assam was quickly retaken, and an Anglo–Indian force of 11,000 men was sent under General Archibald Campbell to attack the Burmese capital, Rangoon, by sea, using a steamboat in war for the first time. Rangoon was taken and the Burmese forces fled into the jungle. From there, Commander Maha Bandula prepared to retake the capital and on December 1 stood before the city with 60,000 men, who were defeated two weeks later and forced to withdraw. Bandula was pursued and killed in April 1825 and the next month Campbell captured Prome, capital of Lower Burma. In February the following year the Burmese sued for peace and lost Arakan to the British East India Company. This was the first of three conflicts, after which Britain would hold hegemonic sway over the Bay of Bengal.

TASK FORCE
Seen here is the large British force landing at Rangoon on May 11, 1824.

Ornate dragon head

Painted bronze barrel

DRAGON CANNON
This bronze Burmese cannon is decorative but would have fired. It belonged to a royal household.

Replacement gun carriage

FRENCH CONQUEST OF VIETNAM

Cochinchina

DATE
1858–62

FORCES
French and Spanish force: unknown; Vietnamese: unknown

LOCATION
Southern Vietnam

CASUALTIES
No reliable estimates

Known to the Vietnamese simply as Nam Ky (southern region), Cochinchina was invaded by the French emperor Napoleon III in 1858. The excuse was provided by the murder of French missionaries, but Napoleon was intent on building his empire and the region was strategically important for trade. French forces landed in the port of Tourane (present-day Danang), and from there marched on Saigon, which was taken a year later. Resistance against the invaders continued for another three years, but Vietnamese leaders had long been torn between adherence to a strict Confucianism and modernization, and as a result the country was weak and lacking in modern equipment. The simple weapons of the Vietnamese proved no match for western arms and they had little choice but to surrender. In 1862, Emperor Tu Duc signed over Nam Ky to the French, who renamed it Cochinchina in 1867. By 1882 the French had control over the whole of Vietnam, which became, along with Laos and Cambodia, part of French Indochina.

PHILIPPINE–AMERICAN WAR

US Conquest of Philippines

DATE
1898–1902

FORCES US troops: unknown; Filipino rebels: unknown

LOCATION
The Philippines archipelago

CASUALTIES US troops: 4,234 killed, 2,818 wounded; Filipino: c.20,000 rebels killed

During the Spanish–American War of 1898, a US naval squadron entered Manila Bay on the morning of May 1 and trounced the Spanish fleet anchored there. By August US troops had occupied Manila itself, and December's Treaty of Paris, which ended the war, saw the islands bought from Spain by the US for $20 million. A month later there began an insurrection against the new masters by Filipino rebels who had fought the Spanish and believed they had been promised independence. Led by Emilio Aguinaldo, the rebels fought a two-year campaign, which was brutally put down and ended when the captured Aguinaldo appealed to his countrymen to accept US rule. In 1902 President Roosevelt declared the insurgency over, although sporadic fighting continued for four years.

BATTLE OF MANILA BAY
This picture captures the drama of the US fleet steaming into Manila Bay, guns blazing, and catching the Spanish off guard.

> "To die today for cowardly Spain! This implies not only want of dignity...but also gross stupidity in weaving a sovereignty of frightened Spaniards over the heads of brave Filipinos."
>
> *Emilio Aguinaldo*, criticizing those who argued for siding with Spain against the US, 1898

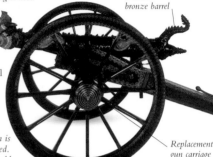

BRITISH VERSUS MAORI
Maori Wars

DATE 1860–72

FORCES At Gate Pa: British: 1,700; Maori: c.300

LOCATION North Island, New Zealand

CASUALTIES At Gate Pa: British: 120; Maori: fewer than a dozen

The First Maori War against British rule (1845–47) was suppressed by Governor George Grey, and the peace lasted 13 years. In 1860 the

BATTLE OF GATE PA
The Maori were outnumbered and outgunned but their wily strategy suckered the British into complacency and defeat.

Maori still owned most of North Island, but when Maori leader Te Teira sold his land in Taranaki without the consent of his people, war broke out. The war consisted of a series of sieges of Maori pas (fortified villages), and ended in Maori surrender, but hostilities broke out once more in Waikato. On April 27, 1864, the British mounted a siege on the Gate Pa, perhaps the strongest pa ever constructed. Maori general Rawiri Puhirake ordered his men to fire only occasional shots, leading the British to believe that Maori defenses had been destroyed. The British stormed in, only to be overwhelmed by Maori warriors. It was a great victory and led the British to seek peace, but guerrilla warfare continued until 1872, when vast tracts of Maori land were confiscated.

SPANISH–AMERICAN WAR
US Victory in Cuba

DATE February–August 1898

FORCES US troops: unknown; Spanish/Cuban forces: unknown

LOCATION The island of Cuba in the Caribbean

CASUALTIES US troops: 610 killed; Spanish forces: unknown

US intervention in Cuba came after three years of civil war. This was Cuba's second war of independence, led by the charismatic poet José Martí, and was notable for the use by the Spanish of concentration camps for the civilian population. By the 1890s the US had become Cuba's most important trading partner, and despite President McKinley's reluctance, gung-ho press coverage made intervention inevitable. The excuse to invade was provided on February 15, 1898, with the sinking of the USS *Maine* in Havana harbor. The cause was unclear, but the effect was an immediate declaration in the US Congress of war on Spain. The war was pitifully one-sided, no more so than in the battle of Santiago in July. Land forces including Roosevelt's 1st Volunteer Cavalry, a mixture of adventurers known as the "Rough Riders," and African American regiments, the so-called "Buffalo Soldiers," captured Kettle Hill, then seized San Juan Hill. Surrounded, Spanish Admiral Pascual Cervera led his fleet out of Santiago harbor, and every single Spanish boat was sunk by US naval squadrons. Five months later Cuba officially won independence. In reality, and fulfilling Martí's worst fears, the island would be dominated by her giant neighbor, and effectively became a US protectorate.

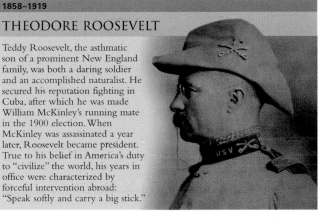

1858–1919
THEODORE ROOSEVELT

Teddy Roosevelt, the asthmatic son of a prominent New England family, was both a daring soldier and an accomplished naturalist. He secured his reputation fighting in Cuba, after which he was made William McKinley's running mate in the 1900 election. When McKinley was assassinated a year later, Roosevelt became president. True to his belief in America's duty to "civilize" the world, his years in office were characterized by forceful intervention abroad: "Speak softly and carry a big stick."

ROUGH RIDE IN CUBA
Theodore Roosevelt is seen here with saber drawn, leading a detachment of Rough Riders in a charge.

1750–1914

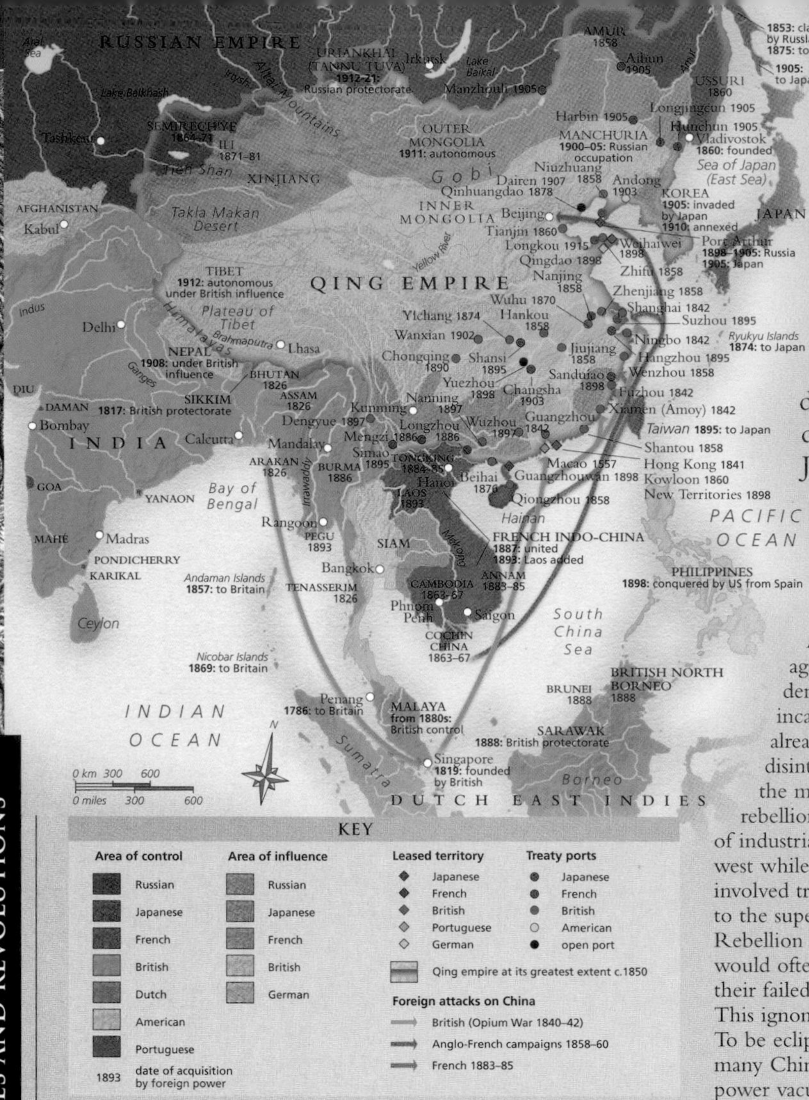

Map labels (Qing Empire and surrounding region):

RUSSIAN EMPIRE
URIANKHAI (TANNU TUVA) 1912–21: Russian protectorate
Irkutsk
Lake Baikal
AMUR 1858
Aihun 1905
1853: claimed by Russia
1875: to Russia
1905: to Japan
Altai Mountains
Manzhouli 1905
USSURI 1860
Longjingcun 1905
Harbin 1905
Hunchun 1905
Vladivostok
Sea of Japan (East Sea)
SEMIRECHYE 1864–71
ILI 1871–81
Tashkent
Lake Balkhash
OUTER MONGOLIA 1911: autonomous
Gobi
MANCHURIA 1900–05: Russian occupation
Niuzhuang 1858
Dairen 1907
Port Arthur 1898–1905: Russia 1905: Japan
1903
KOREA 1905: invaded by Japan 1910: annexed
Tien Shan
XINJIANG
INNER MONGOLIA
Beijing
Andong 1903
JAPAN
AFGHANISTAN
Kabul
Takla Makan Desert
Qinhuangdao 1878
Tianjin 1860
Longkou 1915
Weihaiwei 1898
Zhifu 1858
TIBET 1912: autonomous under British influence
QING EMPIRE
Qingdao 1898
Nanjing 1858
Zhenjiang 1858
Shanghai 1842
Indus
Delhi
Plateau of Tibet
Yellow River
Yichang 1874
Wuhu 1870
Hankou 1858
Suzhou 1895
NEPAL 1908: under British influence
Lhasa
Brahmaputra
Wanxian 1902
Ningbo 1842
Wenzhou 1858
Ryukyu Islands 1874: to Japan
DIU
Ganges
BHUTAN 1826
Chongqing 1890
Shansi 1895
Jiujiang 1858
Hangzhou 1895
DAMAN 1817: British protectorate
Bombay
SIKKIM
ASSAM 1826
Yuezhou 1898
Sanduao 1898
Fuzhou 1842
INDIA
Calcutta
ARAKAN 1826
Dengyue 1897
Kunming
Changsha 1903
Guangzhou
Xiamen (Amoy) 1842
GOA
Mandalay
Mengzi 1886
Longzhou 1886
Wuzhou 1897
Taiwan 1895: to Japan
YANAON
BURMA 1895 1884–5
Simao TONGKING 1884
Hanoi
Beihai 1876
Shantou 1858
Hong Kong 1841
MAHE
Madras
LAOS 1893
Guangzhouwan 1898
Kowloon 1860
New Territories 1898
Bay of Bengal
Macao 1557
PONDICHERRY
KARIKAL
Rangoon
Qiongzhou 1858
PACIFIC OCEAN
Andaman Islands 1857: to Britain
PEGU 1893
SIAM
Hainan
Ceylon
TENASSERIM 1826
Bangkok
FRENCH INDO-CHINA 1887: united 1893: Laos added
Nicobar Islands 1869: to Britain
CAMBODIA 1863–67
ANNAM 1883–87
PHILIPPINES 1898: conquered by US from Spain
Phnom Penh
Saigon
South China Sea
COCHIN CHINA 1863–67
INDIAN OCEAN
Penang 1786: to Britain
MALAYA from 1880s: British control
BRUNEI 1888
BRITISH NORTH BORNEO 1888
Mekong
SARAWAK 1888: British protectorate
Singapore 1819: founded by British
Borneo
Sumatra
DUTCH EAST INDIES

0 km 300 600
0 miles 300 600

KEY

Area of control
- Russian
- Japanese
- French
- British
- Dutch
- American
- Portuguese
- 1893 date of acquisition by foreign power

Area of influence
- Russian
- Japanese
- French
- British
- German

Leased territory
- Japanese
- French
- British
- Portuguese
- German

Treaty ports
- Japanese
- French
- British
- American
- open port

Qing empire at its greatest extent c.1850

Foreign attacks on China
- British (Opium War 1840–42)
- Anglo-French campaigns 1858–60
- French 1883–85

CHINA, JAPAN, AND EUROPE

WITH THE NEW INDUSTRIAL realities of the 19th century, military might depended increasingly on technological prowess. Those who industrialized would dominate; those who did not would be dominated. This was the key to the divergent fortunes of China and Japan. China succumbed to superior European arms, while Japan came to rival them.

Le Petit Journal
SUPPLÉMENT ILLUSTRÉ

ÉVÉNEMENTS DE CHINE

BOXER KILLING
Seen here is the assassination of German minister Baron de Ketteler in Beijing by the antiforeigner Boxers.

CHINA

A series of defeats for the Qing Empire against the better-equipped Europeans demonstrated that Chinese armies were incapable of defending China, and an already weak central power began to disintegrate. Losing out to foreigners at the margins of the empire and to internal rebellions, the regime initiated a program of industrial reform, based on learning from the west while staying faithful to Chinese values. This involved treating western learning as "substance" to the superior Chinese "essence." But, as the Boxer Rebellion showed (see p.251), Chinese "essence" would often manifest itself as hatred for foreigners. The Qing paid for their failed industrialization by being dominated by western powers. This ignominy was overshadowed, however, by the rising power of Japan. To be eclipsed by a small neighbor they considered inferior was more than many Chinese could bear. Soon, local warlords were stepping into the power vacuum left by the inept regime.

SHRINKING REALM
Even where the Qing resisted foreign encroachment, internal rebellions by Muslims and the Taiping left it virtually impotent in its own land.

JAPAN

For nearly three centuries Japan was controlled by a shogun of the Tokugawa clan, but increasing encroachments from Europe and the US led many who had been impressed by western warships to call for the country to modernize. The accession of the emperor Meiji in 1866 signified the end of the Tokugawa era as rival clans, the Satsuma and the Choshu, were given imperial permission to overthrow the shogun. Emperor Meiji took control of government and an astonishingly swift process of westernization began. Japan's thrust for industrialization was driven by a desire for military power, and in less than 30 years victories against China and then Russia left Japan a dominant force in East Asia, much to the chagrin of the incredulous Europeans.

THE OLD ORDER
A group of samurai is photographed shortly before the samurai class was abolished and the carrying of swords prohibited in 1868.

JAPAN BEGINS TO TRADE
Commodore Matthew Perry arrived in Edo (Tokyo) in 1853 and, backed by considerable naval might, enforced US trading treaties with Japan.

CHINA IN TURMOIL

THROUGHOUT THE 19TH CENTURY China's Qing dynasty was in terminal decline. Encroachments by European aggressors left China powerless to control its own economic policies and led to the loss of Vietnam to France and Hong Kong to Britain. Peasants were starving by their millions and the government was losing authority over its subjects, leading to open rebellion.

The ultimate indignity came with defeat against Japan and the loss of influence in Korea and Taiwan. By the end of the century, all major ports and trade routes were under foreign control. Japan, not China, was now the great economic and military power in East Asia, and the Qing Empire's days were clearly numbered.

1750–1914

FIRST OPIUM WAR

Opium War

	DATE September 1839–August 1842
	FORCES Chinese: 1 million; British and Indian: 10,000
LOCATION Numerous areas along the Chinese coast	**CASUALTIES** Chinese: 30,000; British and Indian: 10,000

By the 18th century a tremendous demand had developed in Europe for Chinese tea, silks, and pottery, but there was little desire in China for any of the goods Europe had to offer. The British East India Company solved the resultant trade imbalance through illegal sales to China of Bengali opium—the amount of opium imported into China jumping from about 200 chests in 1729 to 40,000 in 1838. Alarmed by the rising numbers of addicts, the Qing government sent commissioner Lin Zexu to Guangzhou with orders to confiscate all opium warehoused there by British merchants. A few days later drunken British sailors killed a Chinese villager and hostilities broke out when the British government refused to hand the accused over to the Chinese authorities. A British fleet was dispatched in June 1840, and outdated Chinese weaponry was no match for British gunboats. After a series of ignominious defeats, the

> ## "Let us ask, where is your conscience?"
>
> *Lin Zexu*, letter to British Queen Victoria, 1839

IMMORAL TRADE
A British ship enters the port of Lintin, China, laden with opium. Britain's policy was profit-led and morally blind.

Chinese were compelled to agree to the Treaty of Nanking whereby Hong Kong was handed over to British control, a humiliation that would be ended only when the island was given back to China in 1997. In addition, British subjects would now be tried under British law, not Chinese, for crimes committed on Chinese soil. Meanwhile, Lin was banished to Turkestan in disgrace. With all restrictions on British commercial activity lifted, the next three decades would see the opium trade more than double in value.

THE STORMING OF AMOY
The 18th Regiment of Foot captures the port of Amoy as British forces progress along the Chinese coast.

SECOND OPIUM WAR

Arrow War

	DATE October 1856– August 1860
	FORCES Chinese: 2 million; British and French: 50,000
LOCATION Eastern China	**CASUALTIES** Chinese: 6,000; British and French: 4,000

Despite the lifting of trade restrictions after the First Opium War, opium officially remained illegal, and on October 8, 1856 Chinese officials boarded the *Arrow*, a ship flying the British flag and suspected of drug smuggling. This provided the British with the pretext to mount an invasion. Using the murder of a French missionary as an excuse, French forces joined with British under the command of Admiral Sir Michael Seymour to occupy Guangdong. The Second Opium War had begun. The coalition sailed north and Seymour launched an attack on forts near Tianjin. Once more the Chinese were no match for the technologically superior Europeans, and the first phase of the war ended with the 1858 Treaty of Tientsin. A year later, China broke the truce by refusing to allow foreign legations in Beijing, prompting an Anglo–French assault on the city. Emperor Xianfeng fled and the Summer Palace was set alight on the orders of British commander Lord Elgin. Xianfeng now had little choice but to sign away further sovereignty in the Convention of Peking, which ratified the terms of the Treaty of Tientsin, provided a large indemnity to Britain and France, legalized the opium trade, and guaranteed the safety of Christian missionaries.

FIELD OF CORPSES
Corpses of Chinese soldiers lie strewn around the Taku Fort near Tianjin the day after its capture by Anglo–French forces on on August 22, 1860.

TAIPING UPRISING

Taiping Uprising

DATE 1850–64

FORCES Taiping army: more than 1 million; Government army: number unknown

LOCATION 17 provinces of eastern China

CASUALTIES Taiping, government, and civilian combined deaths: c.20 million

Rural China in the mid-19th century was fertile ground for cults preaching salvation from the "foreign" Manchu (Qing) regime. Hung Hsiu-chuan, the son of a poor farmer near Canton, was to provide the focal point for this discontent. After studying under a Southern Baptist preacher, Hung proclaimed himself to be Christ's younger brother, sent by God to rid the earth of demons. Soon afterward he founded the God Worshippers' Society among the impoverished peasants of Kwangsi, and proclaimed a new dynasty, the Taiping Tien-kuo (Heavenly Kingdom of Great Peace). Promising the overthrow of the Qing government, the Taiping ranks soon swelled from a few thousand to an army of over a million disciplined and fanatical soldiers, which swept north through the Yangtze River valley and captured the great central city of Nanking. There, Hung banned gambling, drugs, and prostitution, and declared men and women equal. There was dissent in the ranks, however, and Hung, now called Tien-wang or Heavenly King, faced repeated challenges to his authority. Yang, the Taiping minister of state, attempted a coup and he and thousands of his followers were murdered. Another general, Shih, fearing for his life, fled, taking tens of

thousands with him. In 1860, in an attempt to regain unity and power, the Taipings attacked Shanghai, where they were repulsed by the Chinese, western-trained "Ever-Victorious Army" under US General Frederick Ward. When Ward was killed, the Beijing authorities asked British General Charles Gordon to replace him, and it was under Gordon's command that government forces laid siege to Nanking in 1864. At least 100,000 Taiping soldiers preferred death to capture, and Hung himself took poison. The rebellion was finally quashed, but Qing authority had been fatally undermined in large parts of the country. Both the Chinese Communists and the Chinese Nationalists of the 20th century trace their origins to the Taipings.

PEOPLE'S HEROES
A memorial in Beijing depicts scenes of the Taiping Rebellion and of Lin Zexu destroying opium. The pioneers in the foreground are suitably respectful.

1835–1885

GENERAL CHARLES GORDON

Charles Gordon served in the Crimea before seeing service in China. After leading government forces in the suppression of the Taiping Rebellion, the emperor promoted Gordon to the prestigious rank of *titu* after his recapture of Nanking, earning him the nickname "Chinese Gordon." A varied career followed, involving service all over the British Empire. In 1885 he was killed in Sudan while defending Khartoum against the Mahdi (see p.241).

BATTLE OF TZAKI
This fresco depicts the repulsion of the Taiping by the Ever-Victorious Army at the battle of Tzaki, August 1862. The battle secured Shanghai for the Qing.

TONKIN WAR

Tonkin War

DATE August 1883–
June 1885

FORCES
At Fuzhou: French: 6
cruisers; Chinese: 6
cruisers

LOCATION
Northern Vietnam

CASUALTIES Chinese: 6
cruisers sunk with
heavy casualties

With the southern Vietnamese provinces of Cochinchina already under their control, in the 1880s the French began to encroach northward into areas under Chinese control. China responded by sending forces into the river delta that formed the core of Tonkin in northern Vietnam. Both sides accused the other of aggression, and French captain Henri Laurent Rivière was sent into Hanoi, the administrative center of Tonkin, to evict the "Black Flag Pirates," Chinese irregular troops who were occupying the city. Rivière expelled the Chinese but was killed in a counterattack. French reinforcements arrived and quickly won a series of battles, forcing the Chinese viceroy to negotiate an agreement under which the area would become a joint Sino-French protectorate. When the agreement was rejected in Paris, China declared war, confident that its newly equipped army would repel the invaders. Chinese ground forces led by Chang Chih-tung held off French incursions into southern China, but the hard reality about Chinese modernization was exposed in the battle of Fuzhou in August 1884. In the space of half an hour, an entire new fleet of Chinese cruisers was utterly destroyed by French naval firepower and torpedo boats. China had no choice but to surrender both Tonkin and, farther south, Annam to the French.

CRUISER CLASH
*Here, the French machine gunship
Revolver has blown up a Chinese cruiser
in Tuyen Quang province, Vietnam.*

SINO–JAPANESE WAR

Sino–Japanese War

DATE
August 1894–
April 1895

FORCES Japanese:
8,000; Chinese:
number unknown but
much larger

LOCATION Korea and
Manchuria

CASUALTIES No reliable
estimates

Just 20 years after it had begun to modernize, Japan was ready to flex its military muscles. Korea, a Chinese protectorate, had long been attractive to the Japanese, and the failure of a pro-Japanese coup there in 1894 prompted Japan to send in troops. War was declared on China and, although vastly outnumbered, Japan's modern army scored overwhelming victories on land and at sea. The battle of Yalu River in August 1894, the largest naval engagement, was typical of the conflict. The Chinese were ill-prepared, their munitions old and badly maintained. Two of their boats burst into flames as a result of too much paint and varnish having been applied to them. General ineptitude combined with superior Japanese tactical awareness to seal the Chinese fleet's fate. Japan's victory heralded the arrival of a new military power and led to its occupation of Korea, Taiwan, and northern Manchuria.

JAPANESE MODEL ARMY
*Japanese troops, clad in new, western-style
uniforms, attack Chinese positions in
Manchuria. Chinese flags fly on the hill.*

BOXER REBELLION

Boxer Rebellion

DATE
November 1899–
August 1900

FORCES Multinational
force: 18,000; Rebels:
number unknown

LOCATION Beijing and
surrounding area

CASUALTIES Foreigners:
229 killed; Rebels: no
reliable estimates

The "Boxers" was a name given to a secret society known as the I-ho chuan ("Righteous and Harmonious Fists") after their use of boxing rituals that they believed would make them impervious to bullets. The Boxers targeted foreigners—especially missionaries—and their strength in northern China grew along with foreign aggression in the area. Their message soon made its way to Beijing. In 1898, the new government persuaded the Boxers to support the Qing dynasty against foreign influence. By 1899, bands of Boxers were roaming the countryside around Beijing and, with the implicit backing of the Empress Dowager, Christians were attacked and churches burned. In June 1900 a multinational force was sent in to quell the rebellion. They were repelled by imperial troops and the Empress Dowager ordered the killing of all foreigners. Among others, a German minister and a Japanese diplomat were killed. A larger force finally captured Beijing in August, saving the foreigners and Chinese Christians who had been holed up inside the city's Catholic cathedral. The Empress Dowager fled to the country and left her princes to negotiate a bitter peace. All antiforeignism was to be suppressed and foreign troops would now be stationed at every important junction between Beijing and Shanghai. The Qing Empire's humiliation was total.

FOREIGN INTRUSION
*The sight of American troops
marching through the Fobidden City
in Beijing was a severe blow to
Chinese national pride.*

SWORD AGAINST BULLET
*These ornate Chinese swords date
from the time of the rebellion. Sadly,
neither swords nor faith made the
Boxers impervious to bullets.*

**CAPTURED
BOXERS**
*A group of impounded
Boxers contemplate
their fate. They were
captured by the
US Sixth Cavalry
near Beijing.*

THE RISE OF JAPANESE POWER

THE RESTORATION OF THE JAPANESE EMPEROR in 1868, after centuries of rule by the Tokugawa shogunate, was followed by reforms aimed at building a strong centralized administration. These changes, and in particular the abolition of the samurai monopoly of arms and the establishment of a European-style army, led to rebellions even among those who had helped overthrow the Tokugawa. Opposition to the new order was ruthlessly crushed. Once the country had been unified, the new conscript army's first targets were mineral-rich neighbor Korea and Chinese Manchuria. Japan defeated first China and then Russia to secure them. Its transformation from a closed feudal society into an industrialized world power was complete.

WARS OF THE MEIJI RESTORATION

Satsuma Revolt

DATE January–September 1877

FORCES Imperial: 34,000 plus marines and police; Satsuma: 20–40,000

LOCATION Southern Kyushu, Japan

CASUALTIES Satsuma: only 400 samurai survived

The Satsuma clan played a key role in the Meiji Restoration (see below) but refused to accept plans for a standing army structured along European lines. In early 1877 Saigo Takamori, their leader, angry at the rejection of his proposal for an invasion of Korea, marched on Kumamoto Castle in southern Kyushu. The government responded swiftly, sending a unit to disarm the rebels, then, when they refused to back down, the full army to crush them. The conflict dragged on for six months, until the battle of Shiroyama in September. The mainly conscript Imperial army was well equipped and organized. Saigo's troops, with just a white cloth tied to their arms to identify themselves, fought with their swords. They also had Enfield rifles, but these were no match for modern heavy artillery and they were blasted to pieces. The old samurai order was finished.

WARRIORS FROM KAGOSHIMA
The Satsuma, hard pressed by Imperial forces, recruited a female army, who fought with the naginata, a traditional bladed weapon.

WARS OF THE MEIJI RESTORATION

Boshin War

DATE January 1868–May 1869

FORCES Shogunate: 15,000; Satsuma and Choshu: 5,000

LOCATION Islands of Honshu and Hokkaido, Japan

CASUALTIES No reliable estimates

Sporadic conflict between the ruling Tokugawa shogunate and reformist elements intent on restoring the emperor to power had dragged on for years. By September 1867, armies loyal to the *Bakufu* (the Tokugawa's central administration) were hard pressed by reformist forces. To avoid civil war, the Tosa clan proposed a compromise whereby the shogun Yoshinobu would step down, but retain his privileges in a new parliament responsible to the emperor. Yoshinobu seeing a chance to avert war while keeping de facto control, promptly resigned. Concerned that the Tokugawa would dominate the new parliament, the heads of the rebellious clans, Saigo Takamori of the Satsuma and Kido Kion of Choshu, informed four other clans— the Owari, Echizen, Tosa and Hiroshima—of their intention to seize the palace in

MANCHURIAN MARCH
Japanese troops during the 1894–95 war with China, which left Port Arthur briefly in Japanese hands, before its lease to Russia.

Kyoto. Saigo's troops took the palace on January 3, 1868, and responsibility for the country's government reverted immediately to the Meiji emperor. Yoshinobu attacked Kyoto but, despite outnumbering the Satsuma and Choshu armies and support from French military advisers, his forces were routed in the first battle near Toba and fled to Edo. During the weeks that followed, an ever-growing Imperial army advanced eastward, securing oaths of loyalty from local *daimyo* (barons) as they went. Faced with such opposition,

Yoshinobu surrendered before a shot was fired. The seat of government was moved to Edo (now renamed Tokyo) and the Meiji era began. The Aizu clan still resisted, however. Despite the mismatch between the Imperial army's western-made arsenal and the Aizu's Japanese blades, it took a month of fighting to suppress them, ending with the mass suicide of the Aizu's elite warriors. The final resistance was ended in May 1869 when the self-declared republic of Ezo, set up on Hokkaido by a former *Bakufu* official, was crushed by Meiji forces.

NOGI MARESUKE
The new Japanese army had officers such as Nogi, who fought at Port Arthur.

RUSSO–JAPANESE WAR

Siege of Port Arthur

DATE August 1904–January 1905

FORCES Japanese: 90,000; Russian: 40,000

LOCATION Modern-day Lushun, Liaotung peninsula, Manchuria

CASUALTIES Japanese: 60,000 Russian: 40,000

At the end of the Boxer Rebellion (see p.251) Russia was left in occupation of the Liaotung peninsula, including Port Arthur. In 1903, when Russia reneged on an agreement to withdraw from the area, Japan, fearful of further encroachments and growing in military confidence, decided to attack. In a tactic that would be repeated at Pearl Harbor in 1941, the Russo–Japanese War began with a Japanese torpedo attack on Russia's Pacific Squadron at Port Arthur. Land forces under General Nogi Maresuke encircled Russian positions and a long siege began. The harbor was surrounded by 22 Russian forts protected by lines of trenches, barbed wire, and Maxim guns. Search lights, grenades, and poison gas were used for the first time by the Japanese. Unused to this new style of mechanized warfare, both sides floundered until Nogi finally realized that the key lay in taking the hill overlooking the harbor. Wave upon wave of Japanese were mown down by machine gun fire as they climbed the steep hill, which was eventually taken at a cost of nearly 20,000 lives. A month later, in January 1905, the Russian garrison finally surrendered.

RUSSO–JAPANESE WAR

Mukden

DATE	February 20– March 10, 1905
FORCES	Japanese: 270,000; Russians: 330,000
LOCATION Modern-day Shenyang, southern Manchuria, China	**CASUALTIES** Japanese: 71,000; Russians: 89,000

While the siege of Port Arthur dragged on, Japanese land forces quickly overran Korea and pushed northward into Manchuria. Defeat at Fuhsien and Liaoyang in the summer of 1904 forced the Russians back to Mukden, the capital city of Manchuria, where they were reinforced via the Trans-Siberian Railway. In March the following year, when Japanese reinforcements arrived after the taking of Port Arthur, the decisive battle for Mukden began. Fresh troops of the

MOSIN NAGANT RIFLE
This style of rifle, introduced in 1891, saw extensive service in the Russo–Japanese War. It was still in use in the 1960s.

WINTER WAR
An assault on a bridge during the Battle of Mukden. The freezing conditions in the Manchurian winter claimed many lives.

Japanese Fifth Army crossed the mountains west of the city and attacked the Russian left flank. A few days later the main attack on the center of Russian lines began and the Japanese Fourth Army appeared on the Russian right flank. The fighting lasted for 19 days as huge numbers of Japanese were repelled by Russian machine-gun fire. A distinctive feature in this and other battles in the Russo–Japanese War was the use of forward observers linked by telephone to gunners who would fire on targets beyond their visual range. It was no longer necessary to see the enemy in order to kill him. Unable to resist the flanking armies, the Russian defensive line was curved backward. The Russian commander, General Kuropatkin, anxious not to be totally surrounded, ordered a general retreat to the north. Mukden was evacuated and the retreat broke the stalemate in the land war, which had now effectively been won by the Japanese.

RUSSO–JAPANESE WAR

Tsushima

DATE	May 27–28, 1905
FORCES Japanese: 4 battleships, 27 cruisers; Russian: 11 battleships, over 20 other ships	
LOCATION Tsushima Strait between Korea and Japan	**CASUALTIES** Japanese: 117 dead; Russian: 4,380 dead, 21 ships sunk

Hoping to overwhelm the Japanese navy through sheer numbers, the Russian government despatched its entire Baltic fleet to the Far East in October 1904. The old problem of Manchuria being such a huge distance from European Russia, which had plagued the Russians' war effort throughout, resurfaced again. The coal-fired warships were not designed for long voyages, and the 18,000-mile (144,000km-) journey took seven months, by which time Port Arthur had fallen and the only harbor the Russians still held was Vladivostok. To get there before the coal ran out, the commander of the Russian fleet, Admiral Rozhdestvenski, decided to sail right through the Japanese-controlled Tsushima Strait. With lights dimmed, the fleet pushed deep into the straits unnoticed until the hospital ship *Orel*, lit up as international law demanded, was spotted by a Japanese patrol. Admiral Togo, commanding the Japanese fleet, sailed out to engage the enemy at Okinoshima. Through poor seamanship, Rozhdestvenski failed to form his fleet into a single battle line and when the two forces engaged Togo was easily able to outmaneuver him. The Japanese fleet was faster and better armed and two-thirds of the Russian fleet was sunk. Its navy in ruins and faced with increasing political unrest at home, the Russian government was forced to sue for peace. Russia withdrew from Manchuria and Japan regained control of Korea.

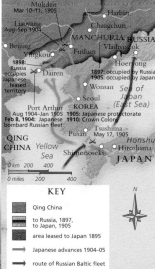

KEY
- Qing China
- to Russia, 1897, to Japan, 1905
- area leased to Japan 1895
- → Japanese advances 1904–05
- → route of Russian Baltic fleet
- ⚔ Japanese victory, with date

NAVAL DISASTER
Here, Russian warships are shown sinking. The Japanese sunk more than 20 Russian ships at Tsushima, leaving the fleet crippled.

NATIONALISM AND MODERNIZATION

FROM 1815 TO 1914 Europe was free of the near constant warfare between major powers that had characterized the preceding centuries. Aside from some sharp but short outbreaks of war between 1848 and 1871, associated with the creation of new nation states in Germany and Italy, armed conflicts were concentrated in marginal areas in or around the Ottoman Empire. But long periods of peace did not lead to the demilitarization of the European powers.

ARMED PEACE

As well as fighting colonial wars, European states armed and trained to fight each other between 1871 and 1914. Except in Britain, which was protected by its navy and therefore able to depend on a small professional army, military service became a standard experience for the European male. As Europe's population grew from around 200 million in 1815 to almost 500 million in 1914, conscription created armed forces of unprecedented size. Improved railroads allowed these large armies to be moved swiftly to a battlefield, while modernized state bureaucracies organized their equipment and supply. By the late 19th century, most European countries were gripped by a militant flag-waving patriotism encouraged by popular newspapers—the first mass media. Armed services were a focus for national pride. Military maneuvers became prominent annual events attended by monarchs and political leaders.

IMPERIAL PRAISE
Austrian emperor Franz Joseph congratulates a recently decorated soldier in Austria-Hungary's mass conscript army.

KEY

small German states
areas in revolt against Louis-Napoleon in 1851
German Confederation
revolts and uprisings, with date
frontiers 1815

EUROPE 1815–52

Following the Napoleonic wars the Congress of Vienna redrew the political map of Europe. The result was three decades of reactionary rule, during which nationalist and republican movements challenged the status quo.

1780–1831

KARL VON CLAUSEWITZ

As a Prussian army officer, Karl von Clausewitz was present at many of the major battles of the Napoleonic wars, including Jena and Waterloo. From 1818 he became superintendent of the Berlin War College, a position that enabled him to develop his historical and theoretical views on warfare. Published posthumously as *On War*, the crucial thrust of his writings was that war ideally constituted "the continuation of politics by other means"— a practical instrument for achieving political goals, which should be limited in its means and its ends. Yet, in his dense and subtle arguments, he also recognized the irrational violence of war and the large measure of chaos and chance involved in armed conflict.

THEORIST OF WAR
Clausewitz only once commanded troops in combat, during the twin battles of Jena and Auerstadt in 1806.

MODERNIZATION

The Prussians set the pace for military modernization with the development of a highly professional general staff responsible for the planning and execution of large-scale warfare. All European armies were forced to follow their example. Far from being reactionary, most European military leaders sought new technologies that would give them the edge in battle. The development of airships and winged aircraft in the early 20th century, for example, was to a large extent driven by the armed forces' interest in their military potential. Great arms factories such as Schneider in France and Krupp in Germany mass-produced ever more powerful artillery pieces and ever more efficient rifles and machine guns. High explosive shells and smokeless propellants took over from solid shot and gunpowder. Naval forces were transformed from wooden sailing ships with cannons to steam-driven ironclads with guns mounted in rotating turrets.

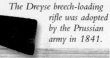

EARLY ZEPPELIN
An early version of the Zeppelin airship is tested. The military implication of such machines was immediately appreciated.

PRUSSIAN RIFLE
The Dreyse breech-loading rifle was adopted by the Prussian army in 1841.

1820–1910
FLORENCE NIGHTINGALE

British nursing reformer Florence Nightingale won fame as the "Lady with the Lamp" who improved the conditions of wounded soldiers in hospitals at Scutari during the Crimean War. She campaigned relentlessly for the reform of army sanitary arrangements, taking a special interest in the British army in India. Her influence stretched far beyond Britain and she was associated with the International Red Cross after its foundation in 1864. Thanks to her achievements, combat deaths in the 20th century for the first time exceeded deaths from disease.

UNLIMITED ENDS

The European wars of the 1848–71 period were in some ways deceptive. Prussia's swift victories over Austria in 1866 and France in 1870–71 appeared to show that modern armies could be effective instruments for fighting limited wars for limited political ends, in line with contemporary thinking. But the battle of Solferino and the battles of the Crimean War showed another side of the coin—how improved firearms and artillery were already making infantry or cavalry attacks on defensive positions increasingly costly, and how the expanding scale of battles could make decisive maneuvers hard to accomplish and effective command almost impossible to exercise. Rather, the policies of Europe's major powers after 1871 implied a belief in sheer numbers (hence the stress on larger and larger conscript armies) and the industrial might to back them up.

ARMS FACTORIES
The Krupp armament factories at Essen, Germany, pioneered the manufacture of steel artillery.

SLIDE TO WAR

Maintaining peace and limiting the destructiveness of war were subjects much discussed in Europe before 1914—the time of the Hague peace conferences and the first Nobel Peace Prize, but European states were thoroughly geared up for conflict. The Franco-Prussian War of 1870–71 was the pivotal point of the period. The creation of a dominant German state via the calculated use of Prussian military power left France desperate for revenge and desperately aware of weakness. Once France was allied with Russia, and Germany with Austria, the scene was set for a general conflict that many European leaders came to view as inevitable.

PEACE DELEGATES
Delegates from 26 countries meet for a peace conference in the Hague in 1899. They discussed issues such as banning the use of poison gas and aerial bombardment.

1750–1914

ITALIAN UNIFICATION

IN THE EARLY 19TH CENTURY Italy was a collection of small states whose rulers included the king of Piedmont and Sardinia in the northwest and the Austrian emperor in Lombardy and Venetia. Through a series of wars and uprisings between 1848 and 1870, Italy was united under the king of Piedmont.

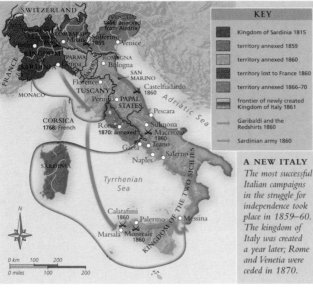

KEY

- Kingdom of Sardinia 1815
- territory annexed 1859
- territory annexed 1860
- territory lost to France 1860
- territory annexed 1866–70
- frontier of newly created Kingdom of Italy 1861
- Garibaldi and the Redshirts 1860
- Sardinian army 1860

A NEW ITALY
The most successful Italian campaigns in the struggle for independence took place in 1859–60. The kingdom of Italy was created a year later; Rome and Venetia were ceded in 1870.

WARS OF ITALIAN INDEPENDENCE

First Custoza

DATE
July 24–25, 1848

FORCES
Austrians: 33,000;
Piedmontese: 22,000

LOCATION
Venetia, northern Italy

CASUALTIES
No reliable estimates

In March 1848 Milan staged an uprising against Austrian occupation and King Carlo Alberto of Piedmont declared war on Austria. Venice also declared its independence of Austria. The Austrian marshal Josef Radetzky withdrew his forces from Milan but took up a defensive position based on the four forts known as the Quadrilateral: Verona, Mantua, Peschiera, and Legnano. The Piedmontese succeeded in taking Peschiera after a siege, but Radetzky, meanwhile, received substantial reinforcements. In July Alberto led an army across the Mincio River and set out to occupy the hill town of Custoza. Radetzky responded with a crushingly superior concentration of forces; in a two-day battle he inflicted a painful defeat on the Piedmontese, the Austrians taking Custoza at bayonet point. Radetzky went on to reoccupy Milan and drove the Piedmontese out of Lombardy. When war was resumed in March 1849 after an armistice, Radetzky again defeated Piedmont at Novara, causing Carlo Alberto to abdicate in favor of his son Vittorio Emanuele. Venice also fell to the Austrians after a siege in August 1849, restoring Austrian authority throughout its Italian territories. Radetzky's generalship so enthused the Austrians that Johann Strauss I wrote a famous march in his honor.

BATTLE SCENE
This impression of the first battle of Custoza depicts a Piedmontese field-cannon battery in operation.

WARS OF ITALIAN INDEPENDENCE

Magenta

DATE June 4, 1859

FORCES French and Piedmontese: 59,000; Austrians: 58,000

LOCATION
Lombardy, northern Italy

CASUALTIES French and Piedmontese: 4,600 killed, wounded, or missing; Austrians: 58,000

FRENCH ENTRY
French troops enter Magenta's market square as the smoke of battle still lingers in the air.

French emperor Napoleon III made a secret treaty with King Vittorio Emanuele II of Piedmont to support him in a war against Austria. In April 1859 the Austrians stumbled into a confrontation with Piedmont that gave France a pretext for military intervention. The efficiency of the French railroad allowed Napoleon to move 130,000 men and a similar number of horses to the war zone, the first mass movement of armed forces by rail in history. Napoleon commanded his army in person, despite a complete lack of military experience. He did no worse, however, than the Austrian commander, Count Franz von Gyulai.

> "The battle of Magenta will count among the most glorious victories of the French army."
>
> *General MacMahon*, reporting to Napoleon III, June 5, 1859

The two sides met in an unplanned encounter at the village of Magenta. Limited French forces attacked from the west across a canal while larger French forces under General MacMahon approached from the north. However, MacMahon's progress was slow and confused, leaving French troops on the canal bridges to hold off far superior Austrian forces through most of the day. The élan of the French soldiers overcame the chaos of command and late in the day MacMahon's men fought their way into Magenta, clearing the Austrians out in house-to-house fighting. The French victory was followed by the capture of Milan.

WARS OF ITALIAN INDEPENDENCE

Siege of Rome

DATE
February 9–July 3, 1849

FORCES
Roman Republic: 20,000; French: 8,000

LOCATION
Rome, central Italy

CASUALTIES
No reliable estimates

In February 1849 Italian radicals declared a Roman Republic, deposing Pope Pius IX as ruler of the city. The king of Naples and French president Louis Napoleon—the future emperor Napoleon III—sent troops to reinstate the pope. The Republic installed a ruling triumvirate, including the famous Italian nationalist Giuseppe Mazzini, to organize the defense of the city. On April 27 they were joined by Giuseppe Garibaldi's legion, a force of irregulars armed with muskets, lances, and daggers. Garibaldi's imposing presence inspired the defenders, who prepared to defend Rome against the French army under General Nicolas Oudinot. On April 29 an initial French infantry assault was repulsed; the forces of the king of Naples were equally driven off. After a month's passive siege, the French resumed the battle for the city on June 3. A final assault broke through the defenses on the night of June 29–30. Garibaldi led 4,000 volunteers out of the city before the French formally entered on July 3.

WARS OF ITALIAN INDEPENDENCE

Solferino

DATE June 24, 1859

FORCES French and Piedmontese: 160,000; Austrians: 160,000

LOCATION Northern Italy

CASUALTIES French and Piedmontese: 17,300, of which 2,500 killed; Austrians: 22,000, of which 3,000 killed

After their defeat at Magenta, Austrian forces retreated eastward, destroying bridges to slow the French and Piedmontese pursuit. Emperor Franz Joseph took over formal command of the army from Gyulai. Early on the morning of June 24 French troops unexpectedly encountered Austrians around the village of Solferino; Napoleon III had believed the enemy was on the other side of the Mincio River. A confused but bloody conflict ensued, spread over a wide area. French foreign legionaries and Zouaves played a prominent part in fighting that lacked any clear overall plan or control. In the village of Solferino itself, Austrians took up position behind a thick cemetery wall from which they were dislodged only after repeated and

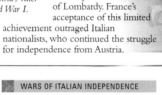

FRANZ JOSEPH
Emperor Franz Joseph, youthful at Solferino, was still Austria's ruler during World War I.

ZOUAVES IN ACTION
French Zouaves advance with bayonets fixed at Solferino. Immediately recognizable by their exotic uniform, Zouaves were an elite light infantry in the French army.

costly assaults. The rifle muskets with which both sides were equipped—firing Minié bullets—showed their deadly effectiveness. The French deployed around 400 rifled cannons that proved far more destructive than the Austrian smoothbore artillery. After nine hours of savage combat (many defenseless wounded were allegedly shot or bayonetted where they lay), Franz Joseph ordered a retreat across the Mincio, which was accomplished with competence.

Happening upon the battle scene, Swiss businessman Henri Dunant was horrified by the spectacle of the wounded lying untended. This provided him with the impulse for founding the International Red Cross. Napoleon, in part because he was sickened by the slaughter, made peace with Franz Joseph the following month, allowing Piedmont to take possession of most of Lombardy. France's acceptance of this limited achievement outraged Italian nationalists, who continued the struggle for independence from Austria.

1807–1882

GIUSEPPE GARIBALDI

The son of a sailor, Guiseppe Garibaldi fled Piedmont after participating in an unsuccessful insurrection at Genoa in 1834. The next 14 years of his life were spent in South America, where he gained plentiful experience of guerrilla warfare. In 1848 he returned to take part in the Italian nationalist revolution. His role in the defense of the Roman Republic in 1849 and, above all, in the invasion of Sicily in 1860 is legendary. He last fought as head of an Italian legion supporting the French Republic in the Franco–Prussian War of 1870–71.

WARS OF ITALIAN INDEPENDENCE

Garibaldi's Redshirts

DATE May 11, 1860–February 13, 1861

FORCES Garibaldi: 5,000; Neapolitans: 25,000

LOCATION Sicily and southern Italy

CASUALTIES No reliable estimates

Sicily and southern Italy were ruled by the Bourbon king Francis II from Naples. In May 1860 Garibaldi sailed from Genoa with around 1,000 followers—the "Redshirts"—and landed at Marsala in Sicily. He marched inland, expanding his forces with local volunteers, and defeated a Neapolitan force at Calatafimi before occupying Palermo. Support from the British navy allowed Garibaldi to cross back to the mainland in August. Naples fell almost without a fight and Garibaldi defeated the Neapolitans again at Volturno on October 26. The Redshirts then joined Piedmontese forces advancing south to besiege Francis II's remaining troops in Gaeta, which surrendered in February 1861. The next month a united kingdom of Italy was established under Vittorio Emanuele II, but still excluding Rome and Venice.

STREET BATTLE
Garibaldi leads his red-shirted followers into the city of Palermo on May 27, 1860, overpowering the Bourbon garrison.

WARS OF ITALIAN INDEPENDENCE

Second Custoza

DATE June 24, 1866

FORCES Italians: 125,000; Austrians: 75,000

LOCATION Venetia, northern Italy

CASUALTIES Italians: 8,000 killed, wounded, or missing; Austrians: 5,600 killed, wounded, or missing

The Italians seized the opportunity presented by the Prusso–Austrian War to declare war on Austria in 1866, with the intention of annexing Venetia. The Italian army was a composite force that included a contingent of Garibaldi's troops. Commanded by King Vittorio Emanuele and his general Alfonso La Marmora, the Italians crossed the Mincio to invade Venetia. Austrian troops under Archduke Albert marched west from Verona to the north of the Italians, attempting to wheel behind them and cut them off from the rear. This maneuver failed and a confused battle resulted. The Austrians' rifled artillery outperformed the Italian smoothbore guns, and an improvised charge by Austrian lancers sustained heavy losses but unnerved the Italians. The Austrians were victorious, but neither this nor an Austrian naval victory at Lissa made any difference, since defeat by Prussia obliged the Austrians to cede Venetia in any case.

RISE OF THE GERMAN EMPIRE

BETWEEN 1864 AND 1871, Prussia's chief minister Otto von Bismarck led his country into three wars that resulted in the unification of Germany under the Prussian king. First came a brief, one-sided conflict with Denmark in which Prussia took over the duchies of Schleswig and Holstein; then, in alliance with Italy, the Seven Weeks War with Austria in 1866 that gave Prussia dominance over the smaller German states; and finally a war with France that concluded with the provinces of Alsace and Lorraine integrated into a new German Empire. The main instrument of Prussian victory was an army led by a professional general staff, skilled in mobilization via railroad networks and committed to decisive offensive warfare.

SEVEN WEEKS WAR

Sadowa

DATE July 3, 1866	
FORCES Austrians and allies: 240,000; Prussians: 245,000	
LOCATION Between Königgrätz and Sadowa, Bohemia	**CASUALTIES** Austrians and allies: 38,000 killed or wounded; Prussians: 9,500 killed or wounded

When Austria declared war on Prussia in June 1866, Prussian chief of staff Helmuth von Moltke set in motion a bold offensive. Making maximum use of railroads, the Prussians rapidly advanced over 200,000 men to the border. On the principle of "march divided, fight united," Moltke split his forces into three field armies—the Army of the Elbe and the First and Second Armies. The Austrians, commanded by Ludwig Benedek, dawdled indecisively while the Prussians thrust southward. Armed with breech-loading rifles and fighting in small units, the Prussians inflicted heavy losses on Austrian infantry attacking in dense columns. The three Prussian armies converged upon the Austrians positioned on high ground near the fortress of Königgrätz. Moltke's plan was for his Elbe and First Armies to restrain the Austrians while his Second Army delivered a crushing blow to the right flank. The day of the battle brought driving rain and near disaster for the Prussians. Through a breakdown in communications, the Second Army did not receive the order to attack. The Elbe and First Armies attacked at dawn but were greatly outnumbered. By 11 a.m. their attack had stalled and they were driven back. The Prussians were saved by Benedek's inertia in failing to press home a counterattack and by the superiority of their rifles and artillery. In the early afternoon the Second Army at last received the order to move. Its onslaught from the flank forced Benedek to withdraw. The Austrian emperor Franz Joseph sought a ceasefire three weeks later.

FAST-FIRING RIFLES
Prussian troops, firing their Dreyse needle guns, mow down Austrian infantry in the Svib Forest on the Prussian left.

> "This policy cannot succeed through speeches and songs; it can only be carried out through blood and iron."
>
> *Chancellor Otto von Bismarck*, 1886

FRANCO–PRUSSIAN WAR

Metz

DATE August 16–18, 1870	
FORCES Prussians and allies: 188,000; French: 113,000	
LOCATION West of Metz, eastern France	**CASUALTIES** Prussians and allies: 21,000 killed or wounded; French: 13,000 killed, wounded

After Bismarck manipulated French emperor Napoleon III into a declaration of war against Prussia in July 1870, the Prussians and their German allies mobilized rapidly, concentrating 300,000 men in three armies on the French border by the end of the month. The French forces, assembled in confusion to meet this threat, were armed with the Chassepot rifle, with an effective range of 5,000ft (1,500m) to the German Dreyse rifle's 2,000ft (600m), and the Mitrailleuse, an early machine gun. However, Prussian breech-loading artillery was far superior to French muzzle-loaders. In early encounters the Prussians suffered substantial casualties but forced the French to retreat through outflanking moves. Bazaine, in command of the French left wing in Lorraine, was a courageous officer out of his depth. In mid-August his forces west of Metz withdrew toward Verdun to avoid being encircled. As they headed westward, they ran into a corps of the Prussian Second Army at Mars-la-Tour. Taken by surprise and greatly outnumbered, the Prussians risked annihilation if the French pressed an attack. A desperate cavalry charge under von Bredow disrupted French artillery and deterred the French from any bold initiatives until the main Prussian forces caught up with the battle. The Prussians cut off the Verdun road and Bazaine ordered his men to withdraw eastward toward Metz, taking up a strong defensive position from Gravelotte in the south to St. Privat in the north. On August 18 the Prussians attacked in force, suffering appalling losses advancing over open ground into French infantry fire. But Bazaine failed to organize a counterattack as the Prussians faltered. Eventually, with Saxon troops taking St. Privat and threatening to outflank the French right, Bazaine withdrew into Metz. The French had won a defensive battle on balance of casualties but suffered a decisive strategic defeat. Besieged inside Metz, Bazaine's forces were in effect removed from the war and capitulated in October 1870.

SPIKED HELMET
Prussia adopted the "Pickelhaube" helmet in 1842. The spike was purely decorative. This headgear was worn until World War I.

DEATH RIDE
Prussian cavalry under von Bredow charge the French guns at Mars-la-Tour on August 16, 1870. Half the force of 800 failed to return.

FRANCO–PRUSSIAN WAR

Sedan

DATE
September 1–2, 1870

FORCES Prussians:
200,000; French: 120,000

CASUALTIES Prussians:
9,000 casualties;
French: 200,000
killed, wounded,
or taken prisoner

LOCATION
Sedan, on the
Meuse River

The French Army of Châlons under Patrice MacMahon, with Emperor Napoleon III in attendance, set out to relieve Bazaine in Metz. However, they were driven into a loop of the Meuse River at Sedan and there encircled by Moltke. On September 1 Prussian guns positioned on hills overlooking Sedan mercilessly battered the French from beyond the range of any artillery response. The wounded MacMahon was replaced first by Auguste Ducrot, then by Emmanuel de Wimpffen, but neither could coordinate attempted breakouts. French cavalry distinguished themselves by their bravery in charging the Prussian lines near the village of Floing, but these were futile gestures in the face of concentrated infantry firepower. An observer commented of the slaughter of one body of horsemen that "so thorough a destruction by a single volley" had never

DEFENDING THE FLAG
A French engraving celebrates the heroism of the country's soldiers in defeat. They were badly let down by their senior officers.

> "Who can describe the consternation written on every face…the siege of the newspaper kiosks, the triple line of readers gathering around every gas lamp?… Then there is the menacing roar of the crowd, in which stupefaction has begun to give way to anger. Next there are great crowds moving along the boulevards and shouting, 'Down with the Empire!'"

WITNESS TO WAR

EDMOND DE GONCOURT

Famous diarist Edmond de Goncourt describes the reaction of the Parisian people as news of the defeat at Sedan filters through. The capitulation at Sedan was followed on September 4 by the overthrow of Napoleon III's Second Empire and the proclamation of a republic in Paris.

been witnessed. With his forces suffering heavily under the relentless artillery bombardment, Napoleon III decided on surrender to end the

slaughter. The following day the emperor met Bismarck to agree on terms and was then taken off into captivity, along with the entire army.

SWORD BAYONET

CHASSEPOT
The French Chassepot bolt-action rifle was superior to the Prussian Dreyse.

CHASSEPOT RIFLE

FRANCO–PRUSSIAN WAR

Siege of Paris

DATE September 19,
1870–January 28, 1871

FORCES
French: 420,000;
Prussians and
allies: 700,000

LOCATION
Paris

CASUALTIES
French: 4,000 killed,
24,000 wounded

After their victory at Sedan, the Prussians headed for Paris. A defense of the capital was prepared under the leadership of General Louis Trochu.

Although Trochu's forces were poor, the fortifications around Paris were formidable. In early October firebrand Léon Gambetta left Paris by balloon to organize the Armies of National Defense in the provinces. The Prussians were obliged to mount campaigns against these forces, while their lines of communication came under attack from guerrillas (*francs-tireurs*), provoking reprisals against the civilian population. Trochu mounted a series of sorties from the Paris defenses that were all repulsed. On January 5 the Prussians began bombarding Paris with heavy siege guns, but this, if anything, stiffened the morale of the population.

Famine was taking hold, however, and a last major breakout attempt on January 18 failed with heavy losses. The provincial armies were also being routed after a few spirited successes. An armistice was agreed to on January 28. In the ensuing peace agreement the newly founded German Empire, proclaimed at Versailles, took Alsace and most of Lorraine from France and extorted massive reparations payments from the defeated country.

SIEGE GUNS
The bombardment of Paris by Krupp guns played little part in deciding the siege, although it destroyed forts around the city.

1815–1898

OTTO VON BISMARCK

Known as the "Iron Chancellor," Bismarck was a diplomat before being appointed chief minister by King Wilhelm I in 1862. His skillful diplomatic maneuvers and ruthlessly calculating use of military power achieved the unification of Germany under Prussian leadership. As German Chancellor from 1871 to 1890 he maintained peace and ensured German security by playing off other powers against one another. After his dismissal by Emperor Wilhelm II, Germany slipped down the slope to World War I.

1750–1914

THE CRIMEAN WAR AND RUSSIA IN ASIA

BY THE 19TH CENTURY RUSSIAN EXPANSION was coming into conflict with an increasingly weak Ottoman Empire and, in Siberia, with the frontiers of a series of Muslim powers ill-equipped to oppose Russian military might. Where outside powers viewed the prospect of further enlargement of the czar's domains with alarm, as in the case of Ottoman Turkey, Russia's ambitions could be opposed. The Crimean War, which resulted from this, stymied Russian ambitions to seize the remains of Turkish territories in the Balkans. In the Caucasus and central Asia, however, despite some residual British interest in keeping the Russian frontier from touching that of British India, local Muslim powers fought long, hard, and ultimately in vain.

THE CRIMEAN WAR

Alma

DATE
September 20, 1854

FORCES Allies: 26,000 British, 37,000 French, 7,000 Turks; Russians: 35,000

LOCATION
Alma River, Crimea, Ukraine

CASUALTIES British: 2,000; French: 1,000; Russians: 6,000

In 1853 a quarrel between Russia and Ottoman Turkey over the czar's right to protect the Orthodox church in Turkish territory flared up into war. Russia occupied two Turkish provinces and defeated a Turkish fleet at Sinope. In March 1854 Britain and France stepped in to prevent a total Ottoman collapse. Allied forces under Lord Raglan and Marshal St. Arnaud landed 30 miles (50km) north of Sebastopol, and encountered the Russians well

ALMA ASSAULT
In the background can be seen the smoke from Russian guns on Telegraph Hill.

dug in on the Alma River. The British faced the main Russian positions, and although they were soon across the river, they suffered heavy casualties and had to give ground. Defective leadership and inferior muskets, however, forced the Russians to retreat.

THE CRIMEAN WAR

Inkerman

DATE
November 5, 1854

FORCES
Allies: 8,500 British; 7,000 French; Russians: 35,000

LOCATION Near Inkerman, northeast Crimea, Ukraine

CASUALTIES British: 2,357; French: 1,700; Russian: 11,800

After Alma, the Allies pressed on inland, occupying a strategic ridge commanding the approaches to Sebastopol, which the Russians had left undefended. Wave upon wave of Russian assaults, supported by artillery, failed to dislodge the Allies. In the fierce fighting, British casualties reached more than one in four. Exhausted, they were on the brink of retreat, and saved only by a timely intervention by the French under General Bosquet.

"…with a cheer that was many a noble fellow's death-cry, they flew into the smoke of the batteries, gaps in our ranks, but ere they were lost from view the plain was strewed with their bodies…"

WITNESS TO WAR

WILLIAM HOWARD RUSSELL

Russell was sent in 1854 by *The Times* to cover the Crimean War, so becoming the first ever war correspondent. This is his account of the Charge of the Light Brigade.

THE CRIMEAN WAR

Balaclava

DATE
October 25, 1854

FORCES
Allies: 15,000; Russians: 25,000

LOCATION West coast of Crimea, south of Sebastopol

CASUALTIES
British: Light Brigade 247 out of 673

In October Russian forces advanced on the Allied base at Balaclava. Three incidents marked this otherwise minor engagement: the defense of the Highlanders ("The Thin Red Line") against a determined Russian charge; the successful charge of the British Heavy Brigade against great odds; and the charge of the British Light Brigade under Lord Cardigan, which arose from a series of misunderstandings and resulted in huge casualties from the Russian artillery as the brigade charged uphill. The battle was indecisive. The British force returned to Sebastopol; the Russians retained their guns and their positions.

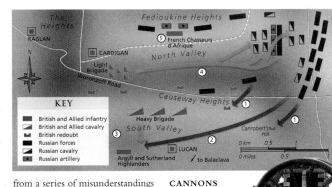

KEY

▬	British and Allied infantry
◣	British and Allied cavalry
▬	British redoubt
▬	Russian forces
◣	Russian cavalry
▲	Russian artillery

① Russians capture Canrobert's Hill and other redoubts

② Russian cavalry attack Argyll and Sutherland Highlanders

③ Charge of the Heavy Brigade drives off Russian cavalry

④ Charge of the Light Brigade against Russian artillery; driven off with heavy losses

⑤ French Chasseurs attack Fedioukine Heights in support of Light Brigade Charge

CANNONS
Field artillery, like this muzzle-loading cannon, played a key role in both sieges and field battles in the Crimea.

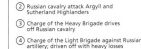

Worm for extracting unfired charge from gun barrel

Elevating wheel for changing angle of fire

FIELD GUN

FATEFUL CHARGE
The Light Brigade charges as Russian artillery scythes through its lines. The guns on the heights in the foreground were silenced by French chasseurs.

THE CRIMEAN WAR

Sebastopol

DATE October 17, 1854–September 9, 1855

FORCES
Allies: 40,000 (including 15,000 Sardinians); Russians: 40,000

LOCATION
West coast of Crimea, Ukraine

CASUALTIES
No reliable estimates

The final phase of the Crimean War centered around the year-long siege of Sebastopol. Menshikov, the Russian commander, strove, with limited effect, to relieve it. Many of the city's defenders were sailors, and the "genius" of the defense was the military engineer Colonel Todleben (see box). After surviving a winter for which they were ill-prepared, the Allies embarked on naval raids that opened the Sea of Asov in east Crimea. A successful attack on outworks in June was followed by a check to the British—now commanded by General Simpson—at the Great Redan. But, after a last, unsuccessful, effort by the Russian land army to relieve

CRIMEA MEDAL
This British medal has a Sebastopol bar for the Brigade of Rifles.

Sebastopol and a second, expensive, British assault of the Redan, the French, commanded by Marshal Pélissier, overwhelmed the vital strongpoint of Malakof and a Russian surrender became inevitable.

DIGGING IN
British Guardsmen are seen here working on the trenches outside the besieged city of Sebastopol.

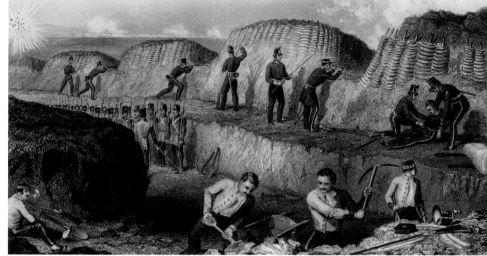

1818–1884

COLONEL FRANZ TODLEBEN

Franz Todleben was a Russian of German descent who learned his trade in the school of engineers in St. Petersburg before entering the army in 1836. He served in the Caucasus with forces fighting Shamyl's guerrillas before being sent to assist Menshikov in the Crimea. He was responsible for maintaining and reconstructing fortifications at Sebastopol, well protected to seaward but vulnerable on the landward side. His reinforcement of the defense works greatly prolonged the city's resistance. Only a colonel in 1853, he became the leading spirit of the defense, and by the end of his career he commanded the whole Russian army.

1750–1914

THE CAUCAUSUS WAR

Shamyl's Caucasus Uprising

DATE
1817–59

FORCES
Russians: varied
Muslim guerrillas: Varied

LOCATION
Northern Caucasus

CASUALTIES
No reliable estimates

During the Crimean War Russia was also engaged in a morale-sapping guerrilla war beyond the Caucasus mountains against Muslim (primarily Chechen) rebels. Earlier in the century Russia had won suzerainty over the Daghestan from Persia, and the Russian grip on the Caucasus was further strengthened by Turkey's retreat from the Black Sea in 1829. A Muslim resistance movement against Russia arose, led by Ghazi Mollah, who was succeeded on his death in 1817 by his disciple, Imam Shamyl. Shamyl was born in southern Daghestan, joined a

RESISTANCE LEADER
Imam Shamyl inspired resistance to Russian rule long after he was captured in 1859. Chechen nationalists still invoked his example in the 21st century.

learned Sufi (mystic) order and made the *hajj* (pilgrimage to Mecca) in 1828, where he met the Algerian nationalist Abd el-Qadir (see p.240), from whom he probably learned much about guerrilla warfare. Using these tactics against the Russians, he also managed to unite the notoriously fractious Caucasian peoples against Russia and won many victories. The Russians resorted to employing an enormous army, allegedly 500,000 men strong, which crushed the resistance and captured Shamyl. He was imprisoned in August 1859, exiled to Kaluga near Moscow and later, having met the czar, was allowed to retire to Mecca and Medina.

RUSSIA IN CENTRAL ASIA

Conquest of Bokhara

DATE
May 20, 1868

FORCES
Russians: Unknown;
Bokharans: Unknown

LOCATION Uzbekistan, 100 miles (150km) west of Samarkand

CASUALTIES
No reliable estimates

The nomads of central Asia, who had produced great conquerors in the distant past, were little match for the disciplined regular armies of the 19th century. Raids by Muslim guerrillas encouraged local Russian governors to take the initiative in subduing the central Asian khanates of Khiva and Bokhara. Envoys from Russia and Britain to Bokhara were treated with arrogance and contempt, and in 1842 two British officers were imprisoned and killed. In the early 1860s the Bokharans managed to fend off Russian advances, but in May 1866 they were defeated. The Russians then established a governor-general of Turkestan, on the Jaxartes (Syr-Darya) River. The war resumed in 1868, when the emir was forced to accept vassal status. Khiva was formally annexed by the Soviet Union in the 1920s.

RUSSIA IN CENTRAL ASIA

Conquest of Khiva Khanate

DATE
1873

FORCES
Russians: 10,000;
Khivans: Unknown

LOCATION Uzbekistan, 25 miles (37km) west of Amu-Darya River

CASUALTIES
No reliable estimates

A revolt against Russian exploitation, or, from another point of view, the frequent raids of fanatical Muslims on Russian garrisons, provoked a series of expeditions against the khanates of Bokhara, Khiva, and Kokand. In 1839 a large Russian expedition led by General Prevosky against Khiva, which lay south of the Aral Sea, had ended, like previous attempts, in disaster. But in 1847 the Russians built a fort at the mouth of the Syr-Darya River and occupied some Khivan territory. Khiva's fate was sealed after the Russian capture in 1865 of Tashkent, the commercial center of the region. A large-scale expedition under General Kaufmann, starting from three separate points, took over the khanate almost without a fight in 1873. The rulers were expelled and Khiva became a protectorate of Russia.

OTTOMAN DECLINE AND THE BALKANS

FROM AROUND 1700 THE DECLINE OF THE Ottoman Empire became increasingly apparent. The Sultan was no longer able to recruit good soldiers, rampant inflation undermined the economy and fueled social unrest, and, perhaps most critically, technological progress lagged behind Europe. Napoleon conquered Ottoman Egypt (1798), and Russia took Moldavia and Wallachia in the Russo–Turkish War of 1828–29. Mahmud II (1808–39) attempted army reform and massacred the corrupt Janissaries, who had formed the elite of the Turkish army, but he lost Greece (1829) and Serbia (1839). By the late 19th century the "Eastern Question"—what would happen to the Ottoman Empire as it collapsed—dominated European diplomacy.

RUSSO–TURKISH WARS

Izmail

DATE
December 22, 1790

FORCES
Russians: unknown;
Turks: 35,000

LOCATION On Danube River, 110 miles (70km) southwest of Odessa

CASUALTIES
Russians: unknown;
Turks: 26,000

Izmail, a Turkish fortress that guarded the Danube and the route to Constantinople, changed hands several times during the Russo–Turkish Wars of the late 18th century. In 1790, after a siege, it was finally taken by assault and the garrison, and many Turkish civilians, were slaughtered. The

RUSSIAN GENERAL
Mikhail Kutuzov fought with distinction at Izmail and would later force Napoleon's retreat from Moscow in 1812.

A FORTRESS FALLS
Russian troops approach Izmail by boat as the town burns. The Turkish garrison fought to the bitter end.

victorious commander was the military genius Alexander Suvorov, the greatest of all Russian generals. Throughout his long career, he never lost a battle, though unhappy relations with Czar Paul I held his career back for several years. Suvorov's innovative offensive operations included long rapid marches followed by sudden, fierce attacks. Adored by his men, he shared their ordeals, but insisted on detailed training with complex drill and top physical stamina. He insisted that fewer casualties were suffered in an all-out attack than during a protracted siege, maintaining that "The bullet is a fool; the bayonet is a fine fellow."

THE GREEK WAR OF INDEPENDENCE

Missolonghi

DATE May 7, 1825–April 22, 1826

FORCES
Turks: 4,000 (and 5,000 Egyptians);
Greeks: 5,000

LOCATION North coast of Gulf of Patras, Greece

CASUALTIES Estimates unreliable, but Greek losses very high

The expectations created by revolutions in America and France, the success of an Albanian uprising in 1807, and growing awareness of their history and culture, strongly encouraged by the Greek Orthodox Church, inspired the Greeks to begin a struggle for independence from Ottoman Turkey in 1821. The nationalists soon gained control of the Peloponnese, declared a Greek republic and, despite an outbreak of civil war in 1822, fended off Turkish counterattacks. In 1825 an Egyptian army led by Ibrahim Pasha intervened at the sultan's request. The Turks, under Reshid Pasha, were already

POET'S OATH
The English poet Lord Byron takes an oath on the tomb of Botzaris, a Greek nationalist leader. Byron fought on the Greek side but died of fever at Missolonghi in 1824.

> "If we are not taken off with the sword, we are like to march off with an ague in this mud basket... better [to die] martially than marsh-ally..."
>
> *Lord Byron*, letter to Charles Franklin from Missolonghi, **FEBRUARY 5, 1824**

besieging the Greek stronghold of Missolonghi. Ibrahim joined Reshid later that year, and when the Greeks lost command of the sea after a naval mutiny, it was no longer possible to keep Missolonghi supplied. Conditions in the town began to deteriorate rapidly. Outlying forts and defenses

ISLAND MASSACRE
In 1822 the inhabitants of Chios joined the anti-Turkish uprising. In retaliation up to 20,000 were killed.

were gradually captured and, with hunger and disease taking hold, the garrison staked everything on a last, desperate sortie in April 1826. It was a forlorn effort, rendered entirely hopeless when a misunderstanding over orders caused chaos, and the Turks rushed into the town. Some defenders reached the forests on Mount Zygos, where most were later killed. The struggle of the Greeks aroused widespread sympathy throughout Europe, inspiring volunteers, including the poet Byron.

THE GREEK WAR OF INDEPENDENCE

Navarino

DATE	October 20, 1827
FORCES	Turks: 3 battleships, 17 frigates; British: 7 battleships, 10 frigates
LOCATION Off southwest Peloponnese, Greece	**CASUALTIES** British: 660; Turks: up to 10,000

By a treaty of 1827, Britain, France, and Russia agreed to demand an immediate armistice in the Greek War of Independence. The British commander in the Mediterranean, Admiral Codrington, with his French opposite number, put the proposition to the Greeks, who accepted. Ibrahim Pasha, with the Turco–Egyptian fleet in the harbor of Navarino (Pylos), rejected it but

THE SEA ABLAZE
Turkish warships burning at Navarino. Losses at the battle crippled the Turkish fleet and left their land forces isolated.

agreed verbally not to attack without further orders from the Turkish court. Codrington later heard that Ibrahim Pasha's ships were preparing to leave the harbor; Ibrahim apparently considered his promise applied only at sea, and did not prevent him from burning Greek villages on land. When the Turks rejected an Allied ultimatum, Codrington drew up his forces outside Navarino Bay in an impressive show of strength. The Turco–Egyptian fleet formed a horseshoe formation, but Codrington sent his ships in two lines to anchor alongside the enemy. His orders were to intimidate, not fight, but when the captain of a British frigate was fired upon, fighting became general. The three Allies cooperated remarkably well and one of the most one-sided naval battles in history ended with the destruction of three-quarters of Ibrahim Pasha's fleet (three battleships, 17 frigates, 42 corvettes, plus auxiliaries) without losing a single Allied ship. The battle, the last major engagement between wooden warships, effectively assured Greek independence.

OTTOMAN RIFLE
This ornate piece, inlaid with mother of pearl, would have been more suitable for ceremonies than for action.

> "The Turks were clumsy sailors; they felt ill at ease… but above all, they felt a dread of Greek fire-ships, which made them imagine every vessel that approached them to be one. "
>
> *Samuel Gridley Howe*, 1828

EGYPTIAN–OTTOMAN WAR

Konya

DATE	December 21, 1832
FORCES	Turks: unknown Egyptians: unknown
LOCATION 120 miles (200km) south of Ankara, Turkey	**CASUALTIES** No reliable estimates

Muhammad Ali was probably born in Albania, in about 1769. He accompanied Ottoman forces to Egypt in 1798 to face the French invaders and there gained high repute as commander of the Albanian troops, and in the chaos following the French withdrawal he was sufficiently popular in Cairo to be acclaimed ruler in 1805. The weakness of the Turkish government meant that the khedive, the governor of Egypt, was in effect independent. Muhammad Ali claimed to be merely the sultan's representative, but he disposed of the previous rulers, the Mamelukes, and extended his authority into Arabia, capturing Mecca and Medina, and took over the Sudan. He also supported the sultan against the Greek nationalists. Muhammad Ali reformed the Egyptian army along European lines. He set up military and naval schools, sending promising students to Europe, and boosted industry. He showed his ability as a general in the field when he marched his army through Syria into Anatolia in 1832 and easily defeated Reshid's Turkish forces at the battle of Konya. The war resumed in 1839, but Muhammad Ali once again defeated the sultan. Afraid of a total Ottoman collapse, the British forced him to leave Syria in 1841, but he was confirmed as the independent ruler of Egypt.

RUSSO–TURKISH WAR

Plevna

DATE	July–December 1877
FORCES	Turks: 400,000; Russians and allies: 100,000
LOCATION Pleven, 75 miles (120km) SW of Bucharest, Romania	**CASUALTIES** Turks: 7,000; Russians: 30,000

1877 saw the 12th Russo–Turkish war in 200 years. The Turkish general Osman Pasha was on his way to assist his forces besieged by the Russians at Nicopol, but on hearing that they had already surrendered (on July 17), he proceeded to the town of Plevna, which had a small Turkish garrison but no fortifications. The move went undetected by Russian spies, and Osman began building defenses and gun emplacements (he had up-to-date Krupp guns) and

A KING WATCHES
Alexander, king of Romania, commander of the Russian forces, watches the final action at Plevna which forced Osman Pasha's retreat.

BACK FROM THE WAR
A Russian soldier returns from the Russo-Turkish war, both his uniform and expression careworn.

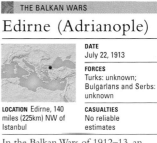

carrying out detailed mapping of the area. General Schuldner's Russians were ordered to occupy Plevna, but arrived too late. A long siege ensued, involving enormous Russian and allied forces—over 100,000—which, badly led, launched numerous unsuccessful and costly assaults. As Russian numbers swelled still further, their weight of numbers, together with the arrival of General Todleben, hero of Sebastopol (see p.261), eventually told, and Osman surrendered on December 10. His holding of the town for five months had wrecked the Russian war strategy.

THE BALKAN WARS

Edirne (Adrianople)

DATE	July 22, 1913
FORCES	Turks: unknown; Bulgarians and Serbs: unknown
LOCATION Edirne, 140 miles (225km) NW of Istanbul	**CASUALTIES** No reliable estimates

In the Balkan Wars of 1912–13, an alliance of Serbia, Montenegro, Greece, and Romania conquered large portions of remaining Ottoman territories in Europe, including Thrace, and then fought each other over the spoils. In the First Balkan War, Bulgaria and Serbia took Edirne from the Turks after a siege that included possibly the world's first aerial bombardment. The great powers, nervous about the Balkan conflict, tried to end the fighting, but, following a revolution in Turkey in January 1913, war was renewed, with Turkey allied with Serbia and Romania against Bulgaria. Turkey retook Edirne and held it at the war's end.

PALACE REVOLUTION
Enver Pasha heads the 1913 revolution that brought the Young Turk movement to power. He led Turkey in the Second Balkan War.

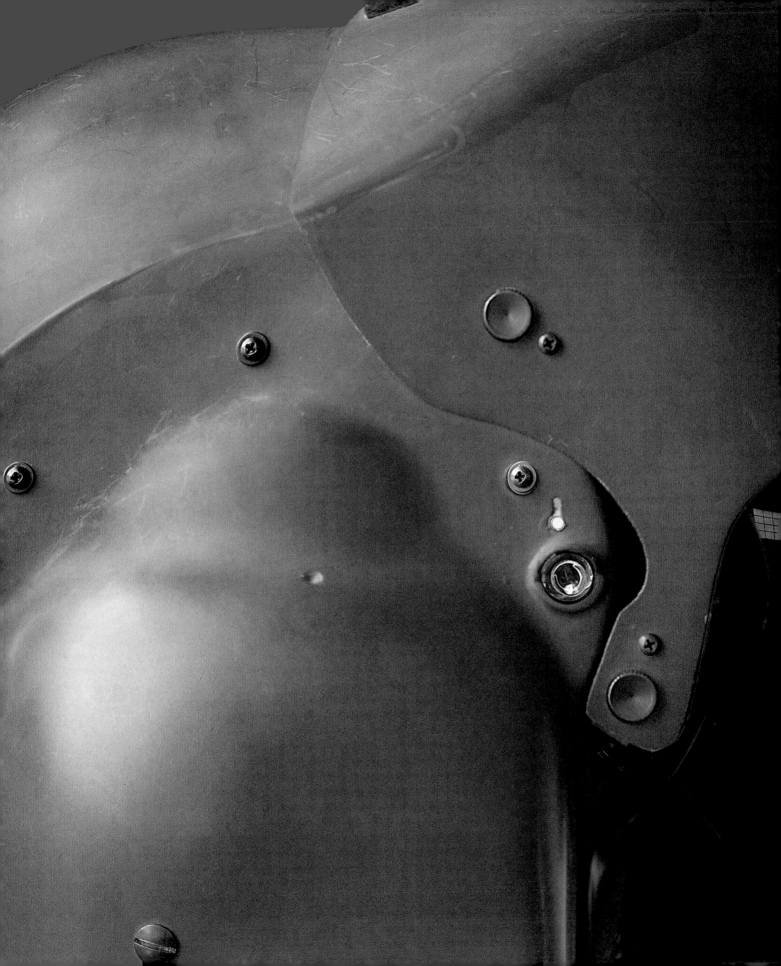

ERA OF
WORLD WARS
1914–PRESENT

GLOBAL WARFARE

THE OUTBREAK OF WAR BETWEEN THE major European powers in 1914 initiated a struggle for world domination that lasted until the late 1980s. Vast resources were devoted to weapons, both in terms of technological development and mass production, creating a destructive potential on a terrifying new scale. The very destructiveness of modern warfare deterred major powers from fighting all-out war with one another after 1945, but smaller-scale conflicts proliferated.

The two mighty global conflicts that dominated the history of the 20th century, World War I (1914–18) and World War II (1939–45), were in many ways linked. In Europe, both could be seen as a single struggle by Britain, France, and Russia to resist German domination, a struggle that could only be won with the additional involvement of the United States. But World War II also developed a Pacific and Asian dimension in the war waged by the United States, Britain, and China against Japan. Whereas World War I at least started as a straightforward conflict between states, by the time of World War II a three-sided ideological battle between extreme nationalist regimes, liberal democracies, and communists had complicated the struggles between the great powers. The scale of the world wars was monumental—more than 70 million people lost their lives in the two conflicts. It was the age of "total war," with the entire

LOOMING STORM
Adolf Hitler at a Nazi rally at Nuremberg, Germany, in 1933.

resources of modern states mobilized in pursuit of victory. And if the whole of a nation's economy and civilian population was devoted to the war effort, it followed logically that factories and civilians were legitimate targets for military action. In World War II the number of civilian deaths far exceeded that of military personnel.

WORLD WAR TECHNOLOGY

The development of military technology in the 1914–45 period was mostly an offshoot of general scientific and technological progress. Many of the weapons that shaped the character of the world wars were in place before 1914, including rapid-fire rifles, machine-guns, artillery firing high explosive shells, and submarines and mines at sea. The advent of aircraft—which, like motor vehicles and the radio, was not specifically intended for military purposes— was probably the single most radical innovation during the world wars. If air power failed to achieve the independent war-winning potential its most enthusiastic advocates envisaged, it nonetheless had a

1914 Outbreak of World War I (p.268)	**1926** Wall Street Crash causes global slump	**1939** Nazi–Soviet Pact sparks World War II	**1941** Japan attacks Pearl Harbor; US enters World War II (p.322)	**1948** Communist takeover of Czechoslovakia	**1950** Outbreak of Korean War (to 1953) (p.334)	**1956** Suez crisis in Egypt

1925 Civil war in China

1936–1939 Spanish Civil War (p.294)

1945 German surrender ends war in Europe

1954 End of French colonial rule in Indochina

1910   **1930**   **1945**   **1950**

1917 Russian Revolution

1925 Stalin comes to power

1940 Nazi conquest of western Europe

1941 Nazi invasion of USSR

1945 Atomic bombs dropped on Nagasaki and Hiroshima (p.329)

1947 India and Pakistan gain independence

1948 State of Israel founded

1955 Warsaw Pact established

1958 Start of China's "Great Leap Forward" agricultural and industrial reforms

1922 Soviet Union established

1933 Hitler becomes German chancellor

1950 China invades Tibet

BRITISH RECRUITMENT, WORLD WAR I   **MARK IV WORLD WAR I TANK ENGINE**   **GERMAN TROOPS, CRETE, 1941**

dramatic effect both on land and sea battles, as well as in the strategic bombing of enemy populations and industrial centers.

HOT AND COLD WARS

The period after 1945 was shaped by two factors: the introduction of nuclear weapons—the power of which was demonstrated in the destruction of the Japanese cities of Hiroshima and Nagasaki in August 1945—and the confrontation between the United States and the Soviet Union as the Americans dedicated themselves to stopping the global spread of communism. By the 1950s both "superpowers" had nuclear weapons and were engaged in a race to build more powerful warheads and more effective delivery systems. The destructive power of each side's nuclear armory was soon so great that, under sane leadership, they had to agree on avoiding full-scale war. But this Cold War stand-off left plenty of scope for superpower involvement in "hot wars" at a regional level, from Korea in the 1950s to Vietnam in the 1960s and Afghanistan in the 1980s. In principle, much of the new technology made warfare more impersonal and distant—from the dropping of bombs on an unseen target to the pressing of a button that launched a missile against a city thousands of miles away—but most of the fighting in the Afghan mountains or the Vietnamese jungle remained as much a face-to-face infantry battle as ever.

NEW WORLD ORDER

The disintegration of the Soviet Union in 1991 left the United States as the undisputed world superpower. With no major enemy to counterbalance its power, the United States and its allies have, rightly or wrongly, been tempted to intervene in regional or civil conflicts in order to prevent massacre, punish aggression, or effect regime change. These enterprises have been hampered by the increasing intolerance of the public in western countries for casualties on their own side, which has led to a growing reliance on aircraft with precision-guided munitions and remote-controlled drones as a way of projecting power. Highly developed arms industries have deluged the world with mass-produced automatic weapons, fueling a chronic state of permanent warfare in some areas. Since 1945 one of the worst regions for ongoing conflict has been Africa, where, as in Europe in the Middle Ages, it has often been hard to distinguish war from violence. In the 21st century the western response to Islamic terrorism has presented the possibility of permanent war on a global scale, in which major powers are unable to locate an enemy against whom to deploy their high-tech weaponry. The potential for a nuclear Third World War, at least for the moment, has vanished. But, predictably, there is still no prospect of peace on earth.

READY TO STRIKE
A UK-built Rapier surface-to-air missile launcher and tracker from the 1970s. Although now obsolete, this system represented cutting-edge Cold War-era technology.

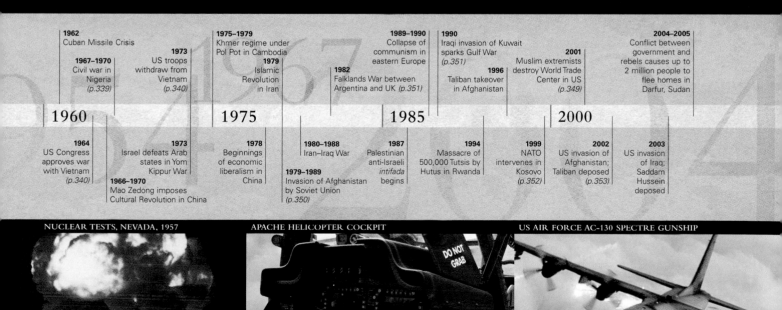

NUCLEAR TESTS, NEVADA, 1957 · APACHE HELICOPTER COCKPIT · US AIR FORCE AC-130 SPECTRE GUNSHIP

WORLD WAR I

ON JULY 28, 1914, Austria–Hungary declared war on Serbia after the assassination of Archduke Franz Ferdinand by a Serb extremist. Within a week the major powers of Europe were at war; as Russia mobilized in support of Serbia, Austria–Hungary's ally Germany mobilized against Russia and its ally France, and Britain entered the conflict in support of France and Belgium. By the time the war had ended, four years later, it had cost an estimated 15 million lives.

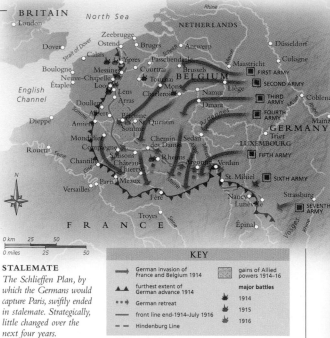

MASS WARFARE

The causes of World War I have been endlessly debated, but it perhaps suffices to say that if states are divided into hostile alliance systems and engaged in an arms race, as the European powers were, then war is highly likely. The scale of the conflict was vast from the outset—in the first week Germany alone mobilized 3.5 million men. The soldiers were swiftly moved to frontier zones by train and thrown into the attack. The unprecedented firepower of artillery, machine guns, and rapid-fire rifles brought to bear upon these mass armies produced awesome casualties even before stalemate set in at the end of 1914. The long haul that followed allowed modern industrialized nations to demonstrate the enormous killing power they could generate through the mass-manufacture of artillery shells and other munitions. The war soon spread, and the Ottoman Empire joined Germany, and Italy joined Britain and France. But it was the entry of the United States into the war in April 1917, provoked by German submarine warfare, that gave the conflict pretensions of being a "world war."

STALEMATE
The Schlieffen Plan, by which the Germans would capture Paris, swiftly ended in stalemate. Strategically, little changed over the next four years.

KEY

→	German invasion of France and Belgium 1914	▨	gains of Allied powers 1914–16
▲▲	furthest extent of German advance 1914		**major battles**
▶▶▶	German retreat	✹	1914
——	front line end-1914–July 1916	✹	1915
– –	Hindenburg Line	✹	1916

PROPAGANDA
Britain's Field Marshal Kitchener appeals for volunteers to join the British army in a famous poster. New techniques of advertising, developed to promote consumer goods, were applied to selling the war.

ASSASSINATION VICTIMS
Archduke Franz Ferdinand, heir to the throne of Austria–Hungary, and his wife Sophie were shot dead by Bosnian Serb Gavrilo Princip on June 28, 1914, precipitating World War I.

MACHINE GUNNERS
British troops resting in shallow trenches. Their Vickers machine guns could fire 450 rounds per minute.

TECHNOLOGY

Technologically, the war was a mix of old and new. Even if cavalry failed to find an effective role where trench warfare prevailed, horses were still crucial for hauling supplies and artillery. Away from railroad lines, armies advanced as fast as a man could march. Tanks began to appear in the Allied forces on a significant scale toward the end of the war. Other new land weapons, such as poison gas and flamethrowers, made war more gruesome but were of limited effect. Aircraft took over the reconnaissance role from cavalry and provided aerial spotters to direct artillery fire. Hundreds of fighters battled for air superiority over the Western Front and German airships dropped bombs on London and Paris. By 1918 aircraft were increasingly used in support of troops, while submarines and mines proved their worth in naval warfare, upstaging even the much-touted Dreadnought battleships.

DREADNOUGHT AND ZEPPELIN
Airships were among the latest military technology. Naval reconnaissance was one of the functions of German Zeppelins.

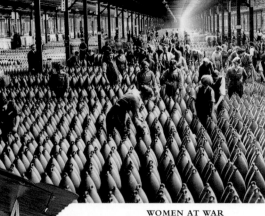

WOMEN AT WAR
Women were drafted into dangerous jobs such as shell manufacturing to fill labor shortages while men were at the front.

Thick, semi-cantilever wing

Fabric-covered plywood decking

Nonretractable undercarriage

GERMAN FIGHTER
The Fokker D.VII was a late-war single-seat fighter. Its top speed was 117mph (187kph).

GAS MASK
This German mask has a cylindrical air filter as well as goggles and a hood.

TRENCH WARFARE

Generals on the Western Front have been much criticized for launching offensives that achieved little gain at the expense of huge casualties. The combination of barbed wire, machine guns, and rapid-fire rifles gave defense the upper hand. The use of artillery bombardment on a massive scale to prepare the way for infantry attacks proved largely ineffectual once troops were dug into deep trenches, although improvements in tactics, such as the use of creeping barrages, did help. Communications, mostly by telephone land line, were thoroughly inadequate for the proper command and control of such large armies. Both sides found it difficult to exploit any breakthroughs that they achieved. However, tactics evolved that permitted a return to more fluid warfare in 1918.

THE WAR ENDS
After a final German offensive and Allied counteroffensive in 1918, hostilities ended with still no Allied troops in Germany territory.

KEY

→ Kaiserschlacht (Kaiser's battle) 1918

▲▲ German offensive March–July 1918

→ Allied counteroffensives 1918

▬ front line at Armistice November 11, 1918

major battles
⚔ 1917
⚔ 1918

THE COST OF WAR

The strain on morale, both at the front and among civilians, became a crucial factor in a long war with very high casualties. Those states that could not command the loyalty of their citizens eventually fell apart under the pressure of total war. The Russian Empire was first to collapse in the two revolutions of 1917. Austria–Hungary disintegrated into its various national components in the last stages of the war. In Germany, now reduced to near-starvation by a British naval blockade and clearly facing defeat in the field by the fall of 1918, Kaiser Wilhelm II was forced to abdicate, replaced by a republic founded amid political chaos. The Ottoman Empire was the last to go, falling shortly after the war's end. The carnage on the battlefields of the Great War was unprecedented, combat deaths alone totaling between 8.5 and 10 million. Around 2 million German soldiers, 1.8 million Russian, 1.4 million French, 1 million Austro–Hungarian, 900,000 British Empire, and 50,000 Americans died in the fighting. The outcome of the war was not peace and stability, but more conflict.

ARMISTICE DAY
American soldiers and French civilians celebrate victory over Germany on November 11, 1918.

Map labels: BRITAIN, London, North Sea, NETHERLANDS, Rhine, Zeebrugge, Düsseldorf, Dover, Ostend, Bruges, Antwerp, Strait of Dover, Calais, Dunkirk, Ypres, Passchendaele, Cologne, Boulogne, Lys, Messines, Brussels, Maastricht, Aachen, Étaples, Loos, Lens, Tournai, BELGIUM, Arras, Mons, Maubeuge, Namur, Liège, GERMANY, Dieppe, Somme, Albert, Péronne, St. Quentin, Dinant, Coblenz, Cambrai, Amiens, Cantigny, Noyon, Chemin des Dames, Ardennes, Sedan, Mainz, Mondidier, Compiègne, Aisne, Soissons, Reims, Argonne, Verdun, LUXEMBOURG, Rouen, Seine, Oise, Château-Thierry, St. Mihiel, Trier, Moselle, Chantilly, Marne, Châlons-sur-Marne, English Channel, Versailles, Paris, Belleau Wood, Fère, Nancy, Luneville, Strasbourg, Troyes, Seine, Épinal, Meuse, Moselle, Vosges, Rhine, FRANCE

0 km 25 50 / 0 miles 25 50

1914

GERMANY HAD LONG PLANNED ITS STRATEGY for a war on two fronts against Russia and France. Assuming that the Russians would be slow to mobilize, the Germans intended to win a lightning victory over France and then transfer their forces to the Eastern Front. The Schlieffen Plan envisaged fighting a holding action on the Franco–German border while the main German forces advanced into France through neutral Belgium. Victory over France was to take six weeks, after which Germany would transfer its forces to the Eastern Front. Instead, the invasion of Belgium brought Britain into the war and French and British forces pushed the Germans back from the Marne, while on the Eastern Front a smaller German army was unexpectedly victorious.

THE WESTERN FRONT

German invasion of Belgium

DATE
August 4–25, 1914

FORCES
Belgians: 117,000
Germans: 750,000

LOCATION
Belgium, northwest Europe

CASUALTIES
Belgians: 30,000
Germans: 2,000

On August 4 an advanced force of six German brigades crossed the Belgian border and attacked Liège. The city itself was quickly taken, but the fortresses around it held out for long enough to threaten the Germans' tight timetable. Bombarded by heavy howitzers, including a couple of huge 16½in (420mm) siege guns, the forts were subdued by August 16. The main German invasion began the next day, 48 hours behind schedule. Von Bülow's Second and Third Armies advanced down the Meuse River, taking Namur, while the First Army, commanded by General Alexander von Kluck, occupied Brussels on August 20. The king and his government retreated to Antwerp, however, where elements of the Belgian army held out until October. The stiffness of Belgian resistance outraged the Germans, who adopted a preplanned policy of *schrechlichkeit*— the cowing of the population through terror. Groups of civilian hostages were executed whenever the Germans judged that Belgians had been guilty of sabotage. At Dinant 612 civilians were rounded up and shot in the town square. Louvain, a famous Belgian city of culture, was looted and burned in medieval fashion. These actions outraged world opinion and hardly needed to be exaggerated by Allied propagandists.

HOWITZER SHELL
A 16½-inch high-explosive shell was too much for Belgian steel-clad fortifications.

BIG BERTHA
The 16½in (420mm) Mörser howitzer, the original "Big Bertha" used at Liège, is readied for action.

THE WESTERN FRONT

Battle of the Frontiers

DATE
August 7–25, 1914

FORCES
French: 1 million
Germans: 725,000

LOCATION
Eastern France from Ardennes to Lorraine

CASUALTIES
French: 200,000
Germans: also heavy

France's plan for the war required an all-out offensive across its eastern border to regain the lost provinces of Alsace and Lorraine. French generals believed the attacking élan of their troops offered the best prospect of victory. At first the Germans fell back—it was part of their plan to allow the French to advance, the better to trap them by encirclement. Then the French infantry and cavalry sustained massive casualties from German machine-gun and artillery fire. A French captain, Charles de Gaulle, wrote, "It had become clear that not all the courage in the world could withstand this fire." With the French decimated, German commander Crown Prince Rupprecht could not resist going on to the offensive, which was also costly, as the French held a line in front of Nancy and Verdun.

RETREAT
Exhausted British soldiers wake to another day's marching during the retreat from Mons.

Barrel much shorter than traditional field gun

BRITISH 4½IN HOWITZER
This light British howitzer replaced the field gun as the primary weapon of trench warfare. Firing heavier shells at a higher trajectory, it provided vital infantry support.

THE WESTERN FRONT

Mons and Le Cateau

DATE
August 23–26, 1914

FORCES
British: 150,000
Germans: 320,000

LOCATION
Western Belgium and northeast France

CASUALTIES
British: 10,000
Germans: 8,000

In line with prewar planning for cooperation with France, the British Expeditionary Force (BEF) was sent across the English Channel to take up position on the right of the French line. Advancing into Belgium, the BEF found itself directly in the line of march of von Kluck's First Army. The two forces met in front of Mons, where the British fought a brief holding action that showed the effectiveness of their rapid rifle fire. Retreating, the BEF's II Corps, under Smith-Dorrien, fought a more substantial day-long rear-guard action at Le Cateau. At the expense of heavy casualties, this allowed the British retreat to continue relatively unmolested. Marching 18–25 miles (30–40km) a day in hot weather, they continued south with the French on their left, arriving east of Paris at the start of September.

THE EASTERN FRONT

Tannenberg

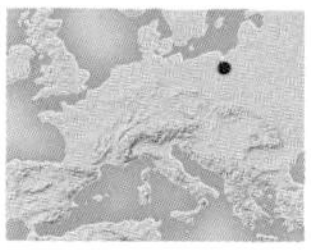

DATE
August 22–29, 1914

FORCES
Russians: 150,000
Germans: 210,000

LOCATION
East Prussia,
northeast Europe

CASUALTIES
Russians: 140,000
Germans: 20,000

The Russian army mobilized far more quickly and efficiently than its enemies had believed possible. However, its forces were split between taking on the Germans and the

PAPAKHA

The winter hat had an oval cockade in Romanov colors.

COAT

BEBOUT

RUSSIAN UNIFORM

Khaki was adopted by the Russians as the color for their uniforms as early as 1907. The knife was carried by a gunner, to be used at close quarters, instead of a bayonet.

Austro–Hungarians. The First and Second Russian armies invaded East Prussia, where, in accordance with the Schlieffen Plan, the Germans stood on the defensive. Failing to stop the First Army at Gumbinnen on August 20 and threatened with encirclement by the Second Army to the south, German Eighth Army commander Prittwitz proposed abandoning East Prussia. He was instantly dismissed and replaced by Hindenburg, with Ludendorff transferred from Belgium as his chief of staff. The Germans were fully informed of Russian movements, both through aerial reconnaissance and through listening to Russian radio transmissions. Exploiting the excellent railroad network of East Prussia, almost the entire German Eighth Army was transferred southward to face the Russian Second Army, leaving only a screening force in front of the

First Army. Second Army commander General Alexander Samsonov, advancing to encircle the German forces that he believed to be far to the north, marched straight into a trap. Even when he was attacked on both flanks on August 27, he continued to press forward, hoping to break through the Germans' center. The consequence was the complete encirclement of his forces, which were soon in total disarray, shattered by German artillery. Fewer than 10 percent escaped the cordon around them. Samsonov shot himself.

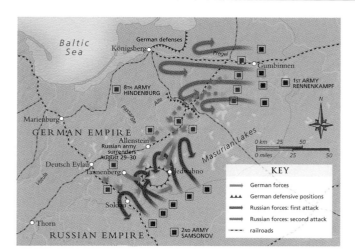

1847–1934

PAUL VON HINDENBURG

Hindenburg was called from retirement in 1914 to command the German Eighth Army. His victory at Tannenberg, in partnership with chief of staff Erich von Ludendorff, made him a national hero. Hindenburg was placed in command of the German armed forces in 1916, but Ludendorff exercised real control. German president from 1925 to 1934, Hindenburg legitimized Hitler's rise to power in the 1930s.

RUSSIAN CAPTIVES
Estimates of Russian prisoners taken at Tannenberg range from 95,000 to 125,000. Between 300 and 500 Russian guns were also captured.

THE WESTERN FRONT

First Marne

DATE	September 6–9, 1914
FORCES	French: 1 million; British: 125,000; Germans: 1,275,000
LOCATION East of Paris, northeast France	**CASUALTIES** Up to 100,000

By early September the German armies that had force-marched for a month through Belgium and France were exhausted and their lines of command and supply were overextended. Von Kluck's First Army, scheduled to circle west of Paris, changed direction to pass east of the city. When General Joseph Gallieni, in command of the Paris garrison, received confirmation of this through aerial reconnaissance, he asked French commander-in-chief Joffre to authorize an attack on von Kluck's exposed flank. Joffre was already vigorously preparing his forces for a stand against the

COMBAT DEATH
By the end of 1914 over half a million soldiers had been killed on the Western Front.

Germans south of the Marne. On September 6 the French Sixth Army carried out the flank attack, catching von Kluck by surprise and forcing him to turn to face the onslaught. This opened a gap between his army and the rest of the German forces. British commander Sir John French was prodded reluctantly to advance into this gap, along with more enthusiastic French armies. The fighting was evenly balanced, the French Sixth Army at one point receiving reinforcements from Paris ferried in taxis. But German chief of staff Helmut von Moltke, out of touch with the fighting and shocked by the level of casualties, had lost the will to direct the battle. On September 9 one of his staff officers ordered a general retreat.

> "A soldier who can no longer advance must guard the territory already held, no matter what the cost. He must be killed where he stands rather than draw back."
>
> *Joseph Joffre*, on the eve of the battle of the Marne, 1914

UNDER FIRE
Seen here are British soldiers from the First Middlesex regiment under shell fire as they reach the Marne River, France, September 8, 1914.

THE WESTERN FRONT

First Aisne

DATE	September 13–18, 1914
FORCES	Numbers unknown
CASUALTIES	Numbers unknown
LOCATION Northeast of Paris, France	

Falling back from the Marne, the German right wing dug in along the north bank of the Aisne River, where the Chemin des Dames ridge provided a natural defensive position. Pursuing French and British forces crossed the river under fire, but attempts to take the ridge by frontal assault were repulsed by a German counterattack. It was a brutal demonstration of the costly ineffectiveness of frontal attacks on entrenched troops with artillery support, a lesson being learned all along the front. The land between the Aisne and the English Channel, however, was still open country. During the fall Allied and German armies made a series of attempts to outflank one another in this area, drawing ever closer to the coast in the "Race to the Sea."

THE WESTERN FRONT

First Ypres

DATE	October 19– November 22, 1914
FORCES	Numbers unknown
CASUALTIES	Germans: 135,000 British: 55,000 French: 20,000
LOCATION Flanders, northeast France and Belgium	

The Race to the Sea ended in carnage at a salient in front of the town of Ypres, which was held by the BEF with French support. The Germans launched a series of attacks that repeatedly threatened a breakthrough against the British, but the rapid rifle fire of experienced British soldiers inflicted heavy losses on German troops, many of whom were volunteers with only eight weeks' training. The death of 25,000 student volunteers earned the battle its German name, *Kindermord* ("Massacre of the Innocents"). The British also suffered appalling casualties that effectively wiped out the prewar professional army. As winter set in, the opposing armies dug in; three years later, they were still there.

TRENCH COMBAT

In the early days of the trenches, percussion grenades were often equipped with streamers, a parachute, or a propeller to ensure that they would fall headfirst and so detonate on hitting the ground. Medieval-seeming clubs, often homemade, were found useful for night raids and patrols.

BRITISH NAIL CLUB

GERMAN METAL ROD

FRENCH P2 GRENADE

BRITISH MK III PERCUSSION GRENADE

ITALIAN TRENCH CLUB

THE WESTERN FRONT, 1915

IN 1915 THE COMBATANT COUNTRIES began to marshal their resources for a long war. While waiting for industries to gear up for the mass-manufacture of munitions, both sides ran short of artillery shells. Britain and France drew on the manpower reserve of their empires to supplement their armies at the front. Neither side was committed to passive defense or a war of attrition. The Allies in particular were eager to retake the areas of France and Belgium that were under German occupation. But the line of trenches that stretched from the English Channel to the Swiss border left no room for flanking maneuvers, while frontal attacks repeatedly failed against trenches fronted by barbed wire and defended by machine guns.

THE WESTERN FRONT

Second Ypres

DATE
April 22–May 25, 1915

FORCES
Allies: unknown;
Germans: unknown

LOCATION
Flanders, northeast
France, and Belgium

CASUALTIES
Allies: 69,000
Germans: 38,000

The only major German offensive of the year, carried out by the Fourth Army against the Ypres salient, was intended to take advantage of Germany's new weapon, chlorine gas. After a heavy artillery bombardment, on the afternoon of April 22 the gas was released from almost 6,000 canisters and drifted toward the Allied line on an east wind. With no protection, the French colonial troops holding the sector stumbled to the rear in a choking panic. German infantry advanced through the empty trenches but did not have sufficient reserves to exploit the breakthrough effectively. The sector next to the gap in the line was held by troops of the Canadian Expeditionary Force, which had begun fighting on the Western Front in February. By the time they were attacked with chlorine gas, on April 24, they had improvised protection with water- or urine-soaked cloths around their mouths. The battle developed into a costly series of attacks and counterattacks in which the Canadians played a distinguished role. The Allies eventually withdrew to a line closer to Ypres.

REINFORCEMENTS
A truck mounted on railroad tracks carries German soldiers to the front at Ypres.

CHEMICAL WARFARE

From April 1915 poison gas—including chlorine, phosgene, cyanide, and mustard gas—was used extensively by both sides in the war. Although much feared and hated—especially mustard gas, which caused temporary blindness, blistered skin, and ruined lungs—gas was responsible for fewer than 5 percent of war casualties, killing around 91,000 soldiers.

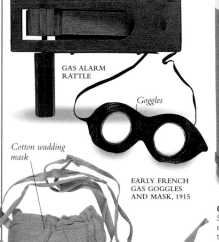

GAS ALARM RATTLE

Goggles

Cotton wadding mask

EARLY FRENCH GAS GOGGLES AND MASK, 1915

GERMAN GAS SHELLS

GAS SHELLS
Shells were a much more effective way of delivering gas to enemy lines than depending on the wind. Liquid gas in the shells evaporated on impact.

THE WESTERN FRONT

Artois–Loos

DATE
September 25–
November 4, 1915

FORCES
Numbers unknown

LOCATION
Artois, 85 miles (135
km) north of Paris

CASUALTIES
British: 50,000
Germans: 25,000

French commander Joffre planned a grand offensive against the vast salient of German-occupied French territory south of Flanders. While half a million of his men attacked in Champagne, on the southern side of the salient, his Tenth Army would strike on the northern side at Vimy. British commander Sir John French reluctantly agreed to support the Vimy operation by attacking in the adjoining sector around Loos. The British infantry advanced behind a cloud of chlorine gas, but its effect was partly negated when gas drifted back to the British lines. Nonetheless, the British and French made considerable gains on the first day. As so often happened, however, reserves were not moved up quickly enough to exploit the advantage. When British reserves did arrive, on the second day, thousands were mown down as they marched into German machine-gun fire. It was another case of small gains for heavy losses, and it cost French his job; he was replaced by Sir Douglas Haig.

GAS ATTACK
British troops advance behind a cloud of chlorine gas, released with smoke to make its direction visible.

Barrel rifled to increase range and velocity

Recoil chambers

GERMAN 76MM MINENWERFER
The German Minenwerfer (bomb-thrower) came in three sizes, this 76mm gun being the smallest.

Elevation gauge

Fired by pull lanyard

Detachable wheels for transportation

"In Flanders field the poppies blow…"

John McCrae, In Flanders Fields, 1915

IN THE TRENCHES

If the Somme was the Via Dolorosa of the British army, Passchendaele was very nearly its Calvary. Wishful thinking led Haig, the British commander-in-chief, to believe that the German army was finally at breaking point and so he ordered an offensive that he thought would smash its will to fight. By now the idealism of 1914 had passed away, along with hundreds of thousands of soldiers on both sides. Inured to suffering though they might be, the troops who fought at Passchendaele would be inducted into a whole new theater of horror.

"Any dent in the ground you'd stick your head down as far as you could ram it. There might be a shell-hole, there might not, but you had to lay flat on the ground when these creeping barrages came, and they were terrible things. You don't think you're coming out of it. There's the blast of them, you know, and you can hear the steel, awful sound, piece of steel as it goes by you. It would cut you in half, a piece of that shell. You can't imagine it—every night, every night, every night."

Private W. G. Bell, 9th Battalion Army Cyclist Corps, 1917

The offensive began in July 1917. Half-crazed by the sound of shelling, the scarcely trained, bewildered soldiers on both sides were often reduced to dehumanized husks, barely able to comprehend their surroundings, let alone act effectively as fighting troops. Advancing over the top, following in the wake of the steel rain of their own creeping barrage, the infantry faced a many-headed death, by shell splinters, exploding mines, machine-gun fire, the slice of cold steel, or the lung-choking agony of gas. The first few days of fighting won control of a tiny salient beyond Messines Ridge, a sliver of land that served only as a more effective killing field for the German defenders.

"Darkness alternates with light as bright as day. The earth trembles and shakes like a jelly…and those men who are still in the front line hear nothing but the drum-fire, the groaning of wounded comrades, the screaming of fallen horses, the wild beating of their own hearts, hour after hour, night after night. Even during the short respite granted them, their exhausted brains are haunted in the weird stillness by recollections of unlimited suffering. They have no way of escape, nothing is left them but ghastly memories and resigned anticipation…. The battle-field is really nothing but one vast cemetery."

Gerhard Gurtler, a German soldier and former theology student from Breslau in a letter four days before his death, AUGUST 14, 1917

OVER THE TOP
Canadian troops advance into action from their trench. The chances of reaching the German lines alive were slim.

Along the Menin Road, the British columns marched to their doom. The deadly storm of the preliminary bombardment snapped the spine of German resistance, but it also reduced the canal-crossed terrain to a pock-marked, churned-up slurry of mud. With unseasonal rains added to this quagmire, the Allied assault became hopelessly enmired. Nobody could pass to the front except over duck-boards and the troops thus channeled became all the more easy targets for German shells and snipers. Those who strayed from the path met an awful end, literally drowning in the mud, their lungs clogged with filth, and little or nothing could be done to save them.

WAITING IN THE TRENCHES

Private R. Le Brun, 4th Canadian Division, 1917

66 It was one of our infantrymen and he was sitting on the ground, propped up on his elbow with his tunic open. I nearly vomited. His insides were spilling out of his stomach and he was holding himself and trying to push all this awful stuff back in. When he saw me he said, 'Finish it for me, mate. Put a bullet in me. Go on. I want you to. Finish it!' He had no gun himself. When I did nothing, he started to swear. 99

Three blood-soaked months later, the original objective of Passchendaele village was almost in the Allies' hands. On October 26 a new push was made, spearheaded by the Canadian divisions. In just one day they suffered 12,000 casualties, for a gain that could measured at an inch for each man fallen. Haig's great gamble had barely dented the German line and nearly another year would pass and a string of "final offensives" be launched before the agony of the two armies would end. Only the rows of white crosses, the swaying blood-red fields of poppies, and a host of diaries, letters, and poems bear witness to those who fell.

66 **If you could hear, at every jolt, the blood Come gargling from the froth-corrupted lungs, Obscene as cancer, bitter as the cud.** 99

Wilfred Owen,
Dulce et Decorum est, 1918

1916–1917

IN 1916 THE VAST BATTLES OF Verdun and the Somme killed soldiers in their hundreds of thousands, while generals struggled vainly to find a tactical approach that would allow them to achieve and exploit a breakthrough. By mid-1917 the Germans stood on the defensive on the Western Front, the French were ruled by caution, and the British army continued to grow and attempt ambitious offensives. Meanwhile, as Germany suffered under naval blockade by the British fleet, the German high command took the momentous decision to resort to unlimited U-boat warfare in February 1917. This brought the United States into the war the following April, though it was a year before the Americans had an impact on the battlefield.

THE WESTERN FRONT

Verdun

DATE
February 21–
December 18, 1916

FORCES
Germans: 1,000,000
French: 200,000

LOCATION
120 miles (195km) east
of Paris

CASUALTIES
Germans: 355,000
French: 400,000

General Erich von Falkenhayn, German chief of general staff in succession to Moltke, planned an attack on the French fortified city of Verdun in order, he later wrote, "to bleed the French army white." Von Falkenhayn intended Verdun to be a killing ground on which French infantry would be slaughtered by his artillery. After an initial bombardment in which a million shells were fired in 21 hours, the Germans advanced rapidly through two lines of trenches and took Fort Douaumont, one of a number of forts protecting Verdun. Joffre put Pétain in command and ordered him to hold Verdun at all costs. All troops and supplies into Verdun had to travel along a single road (soon named the Voie Sacrée, or "Sacred Way") under German artillery fire. Above the battlefield, squadrons of fighter aircraft fought for command of the air—crucial, since aircraft acted as spotters for artillery. On the ground, the garrison of Fort Vaux put up a heroic resistance until overrun on June 7. After a last supreme effort in July, the Germans fell back on the defensive. The French retook Fort Douaumont in October and by December the front was more or less back where it started. By then Falkenhayn had been fired.

DOUAUMONT
A doorway and bunker at Fort Douaumont, one of the most heavily armed forts at Verdun.

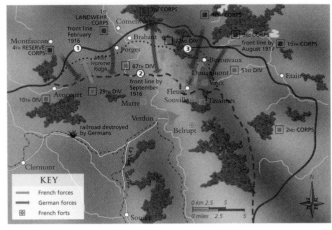

CARNAGE AT VERDUN
Around half a million men died at Verdun in 1916. The Germans proved incapable of inflicting massive casualties on the French without suffering similar losses themselves.

1856–1951

GENERAL PÉTAIN

Henri-Philippe Pétain's role at Verdun made him a national hero. Appointed commander-in-chief of the French army in the spring of 1917, he succeeded in queling mutinies with a judicious mixture of concessions and punishments. He was a cautious and methodical commander who believed "artillery now conquers a position and infantry occupies it." Head of the collaborationist Vichy regime after France's defeat in 1940, he was sentenced to death at the end of World War II. He was later reprieved and died in prison.

ERA OF WORLD WARS

THE NORTH SEA

Jutland

DATE May 31, 1916

FORCES (British and Germans in total) ships: 274; seamen: 70,000

LOCATION North Sea, 75 miles (120km) off the Danish coast

CASUALTIES British: 14 ships sunk, 6,784 men killed; Germans: 11 ships, 3,039 men

Despite the prewar excitement over competition in battleship-building, Jutland was the only major encounter between the British Grand Fleet and the German High Sea Fleet in the war. Battle-cruiser squadrons from both sides, commanded respectively by Admiral Sir David Beatty and Admiral Franz von Hipper, set out into the North Sea followed by their main fleets, commanded by Admiral Sir John Jellico and Admiral Reinhard Scheer.

When the battle cruisers made contact, Hipper drew the British southward toward the High Sea Fleet. Having taken a battering, Beatty reversed the maneuver, drawing the Germans north to meet the more powerful Grand Fleet, heading at full steam toward the action. Twice the two main fleets engaged one another, but the Germans managed to slip away to safety. Cheated in its expectations of a new Trafalgar, much of the British public was outraged by Jellico's caution at Jutland. But, even if the balance of losses favored the Germans, the battle in effect confirmed Britain's naval superiority.

U-BOATS
Following Jutland, the Germans turned to unrestricted U-boat warfare.

THE ROYAL NAVY
HMS Lion, *HMS* Princess Royal, *and the* Queen Mary *at Jutland, shortly before the* Queen Mary *sank.*

COSTLY FAILURE
French troops advance on a broad front along the Aisne River.

THE WESTERN FRONT

Nivelle Offensive

DATE April 16–May 9, 1917

FORCES French: 1.2 million; Germans: unknown

LOCATION Between Rheims and Soissons, eastern France

CASUALTIES French: 187,000; Germans: 167,000

General Robert Nivelle replaced Joffre as French commander-in-chief in December 1916. He claimed to be able to "win the war in 48 hours" by concentrating his forces in a single massed attack and applying new tactics. After a "lightning" bombardment of enemy lines, his infantry would advance on a wide front behind a rolling barrage, supported by tanks. Nivelle's plan suffered its first setback when the Germans unexpectedly withdrew to the strong Hindenburg Line defenses. The offensive was then repeatedly postponed because of bad weather. By the time the attack went ahead on April 16, the Germans were fully prepared. The French tanks were picked off by artillery fire and the rolling barrage was too far ahead of the infantry, which was consequently cut down by machine guns and shells.

WORLD WAR I RIFLES

European armies entered World War I armed with bolt-action rifles firing spring-loaded clips of multiple rounds inserted into the magazine. In general there was little incentive to attempt radical innovation during the war. Instead, efforts were concentrated on mass production.

Rifles were typically accurate up to 3,000ft (900m) and skilled infantryman might be able to fire 15 rounds a minute. The French 8mm Lebel was less accurate than the British Enfield 0.303 or the German 7.92mm "Gewehr." and began to be replaced by the Berthier from 1916.

BRITISH LEE ENFIELD .303 RIFLE

Wire cutters

Bolt

Foresight

FRENCH 8MM LEBEL (1893 MODEL)

Magazine holding eight bullets

Ammunition clip

GERMAN 7.92MM MAUSER "GEWEHR" (1898 MODEL)

Rear sight

Bayonet fitting

ARTILLERY BARRAGE
British soldiers fire an 8-in howitzer during the battle of the Somme. The British had too few heavy artillery pieces and too many of their shells failed to explode.

The Somme

DATE July 1– November 18, 1916	
FORCES Allies: 750,000 on first day	
LOCATION Between Albert and Péronne, eastern France	**CASUALTIES** British: 420,000; French: 200,000; Germans: 500,000

In 1915 French commander-in-chief General Joffre planned a major offensive for the following year. It was to be a joint Anglo–French operation at the junction between the two allies' forces at the Somme. The German offensive at Verdun in February 1916 changed the strategic situation. Now Joffre urged the British to go ahead with the Somme offensive to take the pressure off Verdun; French participation was sharply reduced. General Douglas Haig, commander of British forces in France since December 1915, planned the destruction of German defenses by preparatory bombardment. The infantry would then advance behind a rolling bombardment and occupy enemy lines almost unopposed. Tactical instructions for the battle stated, "The assaulting troops must push forward at a steady pace in successive lines...." The preparatory bombardment started on June 24; the British fired over a million shells along a 18½-mile (30km) front, while a score of mines were exploded under German strongpoints. Yet none of this seriously affected the well-built German trenches. As tens of thousands of heavily laden British soldiers plodded across no man's land on the morning of July 1, the rolling barrage lifted ahead of them and Germans emerged from their bunkers to man their machine guns. The barbed wire in front of the German trenches had not been destroyed. The infantry, many of them New Army volunteers, were mown down in swathes. In one day the British army suffered 57,470 casualties, 21,392 of them killed or missing. One of Haig's staff, praising the valor of the men,

1852–1931

JOSEPH JOFFRE

An officer of engineers, Joseph Joffre became chief of the French general staff in 1911. He was committed to the principle of "offensive spirit" and adopted the disastrous plan for all-out attack with which the French army started the war. The failure of costly offensives in 1915–16, culminating at the Somme, lost him political support and led to his replacement by Nivelle in December 1916. He was promoted to marshal but reduced to a figurehead for the rest of the war.

commented that the assault "only failed of success because dead men can advance no farther." On the southern wing of the offensive, the French did better. Over following days and months gains were made. The battle certainly achieved its objective of drawing German artillery and troops away from Verdun. It provided the British army with an effective, if bloody, education in warfare. It also exacted a heavy toll from the German army, whose own attacks met the same fate as those of the Allies. But the Somme had not been intended as part of a war of attrition; it was supposed to achieve a decisive military advantage. Yet the last action of the Somme campaign, on November 13, was the capture of Beaumont Hamel, which had been one of Haig's first-day objectives.

KEY

— British front line July 1
— French front line July 1
— front lines end July
--- front lines Sept 1
-·-·- front lines Oct 1
--- British front line Nov 18
--- French front line Nov 18

THE WESTERN FRONT

Vimy Ridge

DATE April 9, 1917

FORCES
British, Canadians, and Germans: unknown

LOCATION
7½ miles (12km) northeast of Arras

CASUALTIES
Canadian: 3,598 killed; Germans: 10,000 captured

The British launched an attack in front of Arras in April 1917 as their contribution to the Nivelle Offensive.

AIR DEFENSE
World War I saw the first use of antiaircraft guns. They began as specially mounted machine-guns.

The first day of the British operation was a notable success, especially for the Canadian Corps, commanded by General Sir Julian Byng. The Canadians' target was the formidable German defensive system on Vimy Ridge. A five-day artillery bombardment heralded the coming offensive, but the defenders were taken by surprise when Canadian troops emerged from tunnels that had been dug to bring them closer to the German line. Advancing through snow, they were almost on top of the defenders before the Germans responded. Many were captured in their bunkers. Although the initial success was not exploited, the gain of the ridge was an important victory.

THE WESTERN FRONT

Messines

DATE June 7–14, 1917

FORCES British and empire: 9 divisions (plus 3 in reserve); Germans: 5 divisions (plus 4 in reserve)

LOCATION
9 miles (15km) southeast of Ypres

CASUALTIES
Germans: 25,000; Allies: 17,000

The British Second Army, commanded by General Sir Herbert Plumer, carried out a successful attack on the German salient at Messines Ridge through effective use of mining. Starting in January 1917, more than 26,000ft (8,000m) of tunnels were dug under the German lines. German engineers dug countermines and succeeded in destroying one of the British tunnels, but 19 others were ready and packed with explosives on the morning of June 7. Their simultaneous explosion at 3:10 a.m. was clearly heard in London. Some 10,000 German soldiers were killed and Allied infantry were able to advance and obtain all the key objectives by the afternoon. The Germans launched a series of counterattacks over the following days, but these were repulsed with heavy losses. By June 14 the whole Messines salient was in Allied hands.

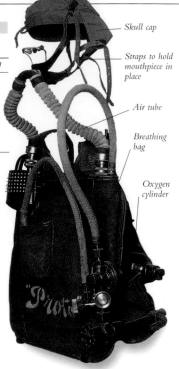

- *Skull cap*
- *Straps to hold mouthpiece in place*
- *Air tube*
- *Breathing bag*
- *Oxygen cylinder*

BREATHING APPARATUS
Working underground demanded special breathing equipment. The bags on this British gear contained compressed oxygen, which was released through air tubes.

THE WESTERN FRONT

Passchendaele

DATE
July 31–November 10 1917

FORCES
Allies: unknown; Germans: unknown

LOCATION
Ypres salient, Flanders

CASUALTIES
Allies: 250,000 (70,000 killed); Germans: similar

The Third Battle of Ypres, popularly known as Passchendaele, was a British-led Allied offensive planned by General Haig, who had long believed in the potential for a decisive breakthrough in Flanders. Haig gained grudging authorization for the operation from sceptical British prime minister David Lloyd George, partly through arguing that it might lead to the seizure of German submarine bases at Blankenberghe and Ostende on the Flanders coast. The success at Messines was taken by Haig as confirmation of his view that the German army was near to breaking point. After a preparatory bombardment lasting 15 days and delivering four million shells, the offensive began along an 11-mile (18km) front at dawn on

> **"Men with serious wounds…crawled for safety into new shell holes, and now the water was rising about them and, powerless to move, they were slowly drowning."**
>
> *Edwin Vaughan,*
> 8th Warwickshire Regiment

July 31, with the British Fifth Army under General Sir Hubert Gough flanked by supporting British and French formations. Commanded by Crown Prince Rupprecht, the Germans had prepared a defense in depth, with a relatively lightly held front line backed by powerful counterattack divisions. After small initial gains, the Allied forces found themselves bogged down in low-lying terrain that had been rendered virtually impassable by a combination of artillery bombardment and heavy rain. In September and early October, with General Sir Herbert Plumer now in command, the British achieved a series of limited but real successes with "bite and hold" tactics—infantry making small-scale advances and never outrunning their artillery support. By October 4 they had taken Polygon Wood and Broodseinde. Instead of taking this chance to declare a victory and stop, however, Haig continued the offensive against Passchendaele Ridge, telling his officer, "The enemy is faltering…a good decisive blow might lead to decisive results." This was not apparent to his troops, mostly Anzac and Canadian, who carried out the final stages of the offensive, floundering in mud as weather

worsened and facing fresh German reserves liberally supplied with mustard gas. The Canadians finally captured the remains of Passchendaele village on November 6, after which a halt was called. The cost of the battle was a subject of controversy at the time and has remained so ever since. Clearly, if Allied forces suffered heavy casualties and were demoralized by fighting in such conditions, the same was true for the Germans. However, the distinguished British military historian John Keegan has written, "The point of Passchendaele…defies explanation."

DESTRUCTION AT YPRES
Allied troops in the ruins of the city of Ypres, devastated many times over by shell fire. St. Martin's Church and the Cloth Hall can be seen in the background.

THE ITALIAN FRONT

Caporetto

DATE October 27–
November 12, 1917

FORCES Italians: 41
divisions; Austrians: 29
divisions; Germans: 7
divisions

LOCATION
Isonzo River,
Italian Alps

CASUALTIES Italians:
40,000; Germans and
Austrians: 20,000

Italy entered the war against Austria–Hungary in 1915. After a series of engagements along the Alpine frontier, in August 1917 the Italians at last achieved a breakthrough. Seriously weakened by massive losses in their

MOUNTAIN ARTILLERY
Alpine mountains were difficult terrain for fighting. The Austro–German victory at Caporetto shifted the war down to the plains.

Eastern Front war against Russia, the Austro–Hungarians appealed to Germany for military support. Seven divisions from Hutier's Eighth Army at Riga were transferred to the Italian Front, combining with Austrian divisions to form a new army under German General Otto von Below. Italian commander General Luigi Cadorna was aware of this move and put his numerically superior forces on the defensive, however, von Below achieved local superiority at the point of attack,

forcing a general Italian retreat. The Italian forces were probably saved from a complete rout by the Austro–German forces' lack of cavalry or motorized vehicles. A line was stabilized along the Piave River, where British and French troops arrived to join the Italians.

HUTIER TACTICS

Pioneered by German commander Oskar von Hutier, these tactics involved infiltrating small units of elite stormtroopers between enemy strongpoints after a brief "hurricane" artillery barrage. Heavily armed with mortars, flamethrowers, and machine guns, the stormtroopers sought maximum penetration in depth, leaving ordinary infantry to mop up enemy troops behind them. Used at Caporetto, Hutier tactics later helped the Germans re-create mobile warfare on the Western Front in the fighting of spring 1918.

THE WESTERN FRONT

Cambrai

DATE
November 20–
December 7, 1917

FORCES British: 8
divisions with 476
tanks; German: 20
divisions

LOCATION
Southeast of Arras,
northeast France

CASUALTIES British:
45,000; German: 50,000

Cambrai was the first battle in which tanks were used effectively on a large scale. British Tank Corps chief of staff Colonel John Fuller was allowed to mastermind an attack led by tanks with infantry following. There was no preparatory bombardment to alert the German defenders. Instead, a thousand guns opened up as the tanks lumbered toward the German lines in early dawn light. Operating in pairs armed respectively with six-pounder guns and machine-guns, the armored vehicles rolled through the barbed wire, opening the way for the infantry. Many Germans surrendered. Although 179 tanks were lost, along much of the front they reached their objectives, in places advancing 5 miles (8km). Church bells were rung in Britain to celebrate a great victory, but the success was not followed up. Using their new Hutier infiltration tactics, the Germans counterattacked so effectively that ultimately the honors were even.

1861–1928

DOUGLAS HAIG

One of the most controversial figures in British military history, Sir Douglas Haig became commander-in-chief of the British army in December 1915. His unshakeable self-confidence was based on religious belief: "I know quite well that I am…a tool in the hands of the Divine Power." His persistence in costly offensives in 1916-17 was at times stubbornly unimaginative, but his grasp of the open warfare of 1918 made him the architect of victory.

SHELLED LANDSCAPE
Australian troops pass along duckboards at Passchendaele. There were many instances of heavily laden troops slipping off such boards and drowning in mud.

OTTOMANS IN WORLD WAR I

IN 1913 THE OTTOMAN EMPIRE came under the control of Turkish nationalist generals led by Enver Pasha, who took the empire into the war as an ally of Germany in October 1914. The defense of the Dardanelles in 1915 stirred national pride, but other campaigns in the Caucasus, Mesopotamia, and Palestine overstretched the empire's resources. Mounting Turkish nationalism created problems in the multinational empire, especially with the Armenians and Arabs. Defeat in 1918 was followed by the disintegration of the empire.

DARDANELLES

Gallipoli

DATE February 19, 1915–January 9, 1916

FORCES Allies: 480,000 Turks: unknown

CASUALTIES British and imperial: 205,000; French and French colonial: 47,000; Turks: 300,000

LOCATION Dardanelles Straits, Turkey

The Gallipoli campaign started as an Allied naval operation aimed at breaking through the Dardanelles Straits into the Sea of Marmara and capturing Constantinople, knocking Turkey out of the war and opening the sea route to Russia's southern ports on the Black Sea. Begun on February 19, 1915, the naval operation was largely inspired by British First Lord of the Admiralty Winston Churchill. It proved a predictable failure. British and French battleships could not progress until Turkish mines had been cleared, but clearing the mines was impossible under the threat of Turkish shore batteries. A last attempt to force the straits with 16 battleships on March 18 was abandoned with four vessels either sunk or beached and two severely damaged. A fallback plan to land troops on the Gallipoli peninsula and seize the Turkish forts dominating the straits was by then already in hand. British General Sir Ian Hamilton was put in charge of a landing force of 75,000 men that included the Anzac Corps from Australia and New Zealand, the British 29th Division, and a French colonial division. The landings on April 25 were almost a success. British troops arriving at one beach were shot up by Turkish machine guns, but most of the forces got safely ashore. Subsequent confusions and hesitation, however, ended up with the Allies

GALLIPOLI STAR

A medal was awarded to Turkish Gallipoli veterans. The battle excited Turkish national pride after decades of Ottoman decline.

AUSSIE GRIT

An Australian soldier carries a wounded colleague. Of the 322,000 Australians who served in the war, 280,000 were casualties.

restricted to shallow beachheads as a result of Turkish counterattacks. Under the overall command of German general Liman von Sanders, the Turkish defenders performed with skill and determination, Mustafa Kemal Pasha playing a prominent and inspiring role. Suffering from heat and dysentery, the Allied troops held onto their toehold into midsummer while reinforcements were organized. In early August a new offensive was launched. On August 6–7, Anzac, British, and Gurkha forces staged an assault on the Sari Bair mountains, while fresh British troops landed farther north at Suvla Bay. The mountain assault narrowly failed to take the peak of Chunuk Bair and was thrown back

by a counterattack led by Kemal. The forces at Suvla Bay failed to act quickly enough, allowing the Turks to create a defensive line that successfully resisted the British on August 21. By the fall, the only question was how to extract the Allied forces. Troops were filtered out over a period of a month without the Turks realizing what was happening and with hardly a single casualty.

ANZAC COVE

Anzac troops at Gaba Tepe, where they landed on April 25, 1915. They made little headway over the mountainous terrain.

KEY

- Ottoman Empire 1914
- British Empire 1914
- Russian Empire 1914
- area of Arab revolt (1916–18)
- Russian/Turkish front 1917
- Turkish lines at surrender, 1918
- Turkish forces
- Allied forces
- Allied forces under Col. T.E. Lawrence
- French forces
- Russian forces

0 km 400 800
0 miles 400 800

1881–1938

MUSTAFA KEMAL (ATATÜRK)

Known as Atatürk ("Father of the People"), Mustafa Kemal Pasha was the founder of modern Turkey. His inspiring role at Gallipoli made him a national hero, and he went on to fight in Palestine and the Caucasus. After the defeat of the Ottoman Empire, he set up a revolutionary government in May 1919. He led the fight against the partitioning of Turkey, won a war against Greece in 1921–23, and founded the Turkish republic in 1924.

MESOPOTAMIA

Siege of Kut

DATE December 7, 1915–April 30, 1916

FORCES Anglo-Indian: 12,000 in Kut, 30,000 relief; Turks: 30,000

LOCATION Between modern-day Baghdad and Basra

CASUALTIES Anglo-Indian: all in Kut killed or imprisoned; Turks: 10,000

When the Ottoman Empire entered the war, an expeditionary force of the British Indian army was sent to invade southern Mesopotamia (Iraq), then under Ottoman rule. After occupying Basra the expedition's commander sent a divisional strength force under General Sir Charles Townshend north to capture the town of Kut al-Amara

in September 1915. Townshend was then ordered to continue north to take Baghdad. His force came within 20 miles (32km) of the city before it encountered substantial Turkish resistance. Feeling his lines of communication were overstretched, Townshend withdrew to Kut, and by December he was encircled by the Turks. After failing to take Kut by assault, the Turks dug a trench system strong enough to keep Townshend's men in and keep a relief force out. Between January and April 1916 the British made four attempts to break through the Turkish lines with troops sent north from Basra, but on each occasion they were repulsed. Ravaged by hunger and disease, the forces inside Kut surrendered on April 30. More than a third of those marched off to captivity died in Turkish labor camps.

PALESTINE

Megiddo

DATE September 19–26, 1918

FORCES British and Commonwealth: 69,000; Turks and Germans: 32,000

LOCATION Palestine

CASUALTIES British and Commonwealth: 853; Turks: unknown

In early fall the British commander General Allenby launched a major offensive against the Turks north of Jerusalem. Surprise enabled his forces to break through trenches held by General Liman von Sanders' Turkish and German troops on Palestine's coastal plain. Fleeing Turkish forces surrendered in their thousands.

THE MIDDLE EAST

The Arab Revolt

DATE June 5, 1916–October 1918

FORCES Numbers fluctuated

LOCATION Arabia, Palestine, and Syria

CASUALTIES No reliable estimates

The increasingly nationalistic Ottoman government in Constantinople alienated many of the empire's Arab subjects. Britain encouraged Sherif Hussein ibn Ali of Mecca to declare an Arab revolt against Ottoman rule in June 1916. Support for the revolt wavered until December 1916, when Hussein's son Feisal, aided by British adviser Colonel T. E. Lawrence and a British warship, successfully defended the port of Yenbo from a Turkish attack. In July 1917 Feisal captured Aqaba, which became the base for

1888–1935

LAWRENCE OF ARABIA

T. E. Lawrence was an archeologist before World War I transformed him into an intelligence officer. He was instrumental in obtaining British backing for Feisal ibn Hussein and fought with Feisal in the campaign from the defense of Yenbo in 1916 to the entry into Damascus in 1918. He subsequently became convinced that the Arabs had been betrayed in the postwar peace settlement. He wrote several accounts of his experiences, the most famous being *The Seven Pillars of Wisdom*.

operations north into Palestine. The Arab guerrillas operated in support of British regular forces commanded by General Sir Edmund Allenby, which broke through the Turkish Beersheba–Gaza line into Palestine in the fall of 1917 and occupied Jerusalem the following December. The Arab guerrillas carried out raids on Turkish

road and rail communications and tied down large numbers of Turkish troops. In 1918 they carried out combined operations with British regular forces, using armored cars as well as camels and horses. British and Arab cavalry occupied Damascus on October 1, 1918. Some isolated Turkish strongholds were still resisting Arab forces in 1919. Many Arabs felt betrayed by postwar arrangements in the Middle East, which saw Syria and Palestine come under French and British rule respectively (mandated by the League of Nations), rather than under Arab control.

DESERT WARRIORS
Arab guerrillas amassing in Palestine during the Arab revolt.

Bullet-proof shield

Yellow paint provided camouflage in the desert

Relatively light, the gun could be towed by horses or tractor

On average, gun crews fired six to 10 rounds per minute

Hydraulic recoil mechanism

DESERT ARTILLERY
This British 10-pounder mountain gun, primarily used in India, saw extensive use in Mesopotamia and Palestine.

THE EASTERN FRONT

THE FIGHTING ON THE EASTERN FRONT never developed into the static stalemate seen in the west. Yet, although the Germans repeatedly defeated the Russians, who were hampered by problems with supply, organization, and command, victories proved impossible to exploit to any decisive effect. The Germans easily defeated Serbia and Romania, but Russian troops continued to fight well into spring 1917. Meanwhile, Germany's ally Austria–Hungary was becoming a liability, theatening to break apart into its national components under the pressure of war. The political disintegration of the Russian Empire eventually undermined the Russian soldiers' will to fight, allowing the Germans to impose a punitive peace at Brest-Litovsk in March 1918.

EASTERN FRONT

Gorlice-Tornow

DATE May 2–June 22, 1915

FORCES German: 120,000; Austro-Hungarian: 120,000; Russian: 56,000

LOCATION Galicia, modern-day Poland

CASUALTIES German, Austro-Hungarian: 90,000; Russian: heavy

The weakness of the Austro-Hungarians led Germany to transfer substantial forces to the Galician Front in spring 1915. Under the command of Field Marshal August von Mackensen, the newly formed German Eleventh Army launched a major offensive in the Gorlice-Tarnow sector. A four-hour preliminary bombardment along a 30-mile (50km) front had a devastating effect on poorly equipped Russian troops packed into shallow forward trenches. They broke and fell back 15 miles (25km) in the first two days and continued to fall back thereafter, despite the arrival of reinforcements and attempted counteroffensives. In seven weeks the Russians were driven out of Galicia, Lvov falling on June 22.

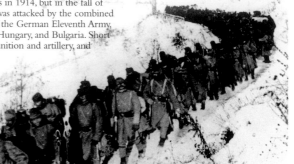

SCHWARZLOSE
The Schwarzlose 8mm machine gun was a standard weapon of the Austro-Hungarian army. It had a flash eliminator on its barrel.

EASTERN FRONT

Serbia

DATE October 6–November 23, 1915

FORCES German, Austrian, Bulgarian: 300,000; Serbian: 200,000

LOCATION Serbia

CASUALTIES Serbian: 50,000

Serbia rebuffed three Austro-Hungarian offensives in 1914, but in the fall of 1915 it was attacked by the combined forces of the German Eleventh Army, Austria-Hungary, and Bulgaria. Short of ammunition and artillery, and weakened by typhus, the Serbs retreated south. French troops entered southern Serbia in November, but by then the Serbs were cut off in Kosovo. In appalling winter weather, hundreds of thousands of Serbian soldiers and civilians retreated across the mountains to the Albanian coast, many dying of hunger, cold, and disease.

WINTER OPERATIONS
Austro-Hungarian troops advance along a Serbian mountain road. Snowfall brought military operations to an end in November.

EASTERN FRONT

Brusilov Offensive

DATE June 4–September 20, 1916

FORCES Russian: 573,000; Austro-Hungarian: 448,000

LOCATION From the Pripet Marshes south to Czernowitz

CASUALTIES Both sides: 500,000–1 million killed, wounded or imprisoned

In the summer of 1916 General Alexei Brusilov, commander of the Russian Southwest Front, advocated new offensive tactics. Instead of attacking on a narrow front after a prolonged preparatory bombardment that ensured the enemy would know the attack was coming and have reserves in position to counter any breakthrough, he wanted a coordinated offensive along a broad front, each army attacking with only brief artillery preparation. The Russian high command reluctantly authorized him to proceed on June 4. Brusilov's four armies faced Austro-Hungarian troops comfortably dug in to deep trenches. Attacking at points along a 350-mile (550km) front, the Russians achieved total surprise. The initial bombardment was unusually accurate and many of the Austrians were still cowering in their deep shelters when taken prisoner. By the end of June the Russians had advanced 60 miles (100km) in Galicia, while also making significant gains farther north. The Austro-Hungarian Seventh Army was virtually destroyed. Throughout the summer, however, the Russians suffered from lengthening supply lines and the loss of surprise. By August German reinforcements were arriving in quantity from the Western Front; the German high command also took effective control of the Austro-Hungarian army. The offensive came to halt having ultimately made small gains at high cost. The scale of the losses put immense strain on the morale of the Russian and Austro-Hungarian empires.

> "I received hundreds of telegrams... All wanted to let me know that the great heart of the country was beating in sympathy with the well-loved soldiers of my victorious armies."
>
> *General Alexei Brusilov, on the support for the offensive, 1916*

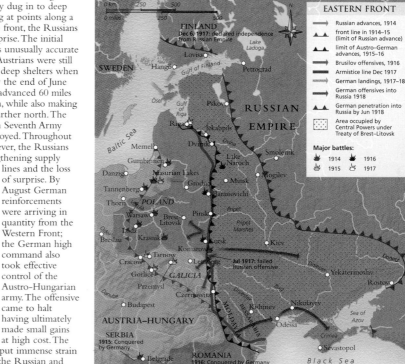

EASTERN FRONT

- Russian advances, 1914
- front line in 1914–15 (limit of Russian advance)
- limit of Austro-German advances, 1915–16
- Brusilov offensives, 1916
- Armistice line Dec 1917
- German landings, 1917–18
- German offensives into Russia 1918
- German penetration into Russia by Jun 1918
- Area occupied by Central Powers under Treaty of Brest–Litovsk

Major battles:
- 1914
- 1915
- 1916
- 1917

FINLAND
Dec 6, 1917: declared independence from Russian Empire

SWEDEN

RUSSIAN EMPIRE

Jul 1917: failed Russian offensive

AUSTRIA–HUNGARY

SERBIA
1915: Conquered by Germany

ROMANIA
1916: Conquered by Germany

Black Sea

EASTERN FRONT

Kerenski Offensive

DATE
July 1–August 3, 1917

FORCES
Numbers unknown

CASUALTIES
Russian: several hundred thousand killed, wounded, or taken prisoner

LOCATION
Galicia, modern-day Poland

In March 1917 Tsar Nicholas II abdicated in the face of mass demonstrations in Petrograd. A provisional government took power, committed to continuing the war as a patriotic defense of the nation. In May a moderate socialist, Alexander Kerenski, became minister of war. He appointed General Brusilov as commander-in-chief, with the task of mounting a major summer offensive.

BEFORE THE FALL
Russian soldiers kneel before Czar Nicholas II. The czar's decision to assume command of the armed forces meant that he was held personally responsible for military reverses.

Kerenski believed that a successful offensive would restore the morale of the army and align patriotic sentiment behind the provisional government. He seriously underrated the decline in discipline in the armed forces, where soldiers' councils (*soviets*) challenged the authority of officers and peasant soldiers were eager to get home to seize land from large estates. Launched on July 1 after a two-day preliminary barrage the offensive at first made progress, especially against the Austrians in the south, but quickly ran out of steam as German reserves came into play. When the Germans mounted a counteroffensive in the second half of July, the Russian armies disintegrated.

> "Even if we are not fully confident of success, we should go on the offensive.... The faster we throw our troops into action, the sooner their passion for politics will cool."
>
> *Russian General Mikhail Alexeev,* before the offensive, MARCH 30, 1917

EASTERN FRONT

The Bolshevik Revolution

DATE
November 1917–March 1918

FORCES
Bolshevik, Czarist: no reliable estimate of numbers

LOCATION
Russia

CASUALTIES
No reliable estimate

After the abdication of Czar Nicholas II in March 1917, even the most extreme revolutionaries at first accepted the need to continue the war to protect the revolution against "German militarism." In April,

however, Bolshevik leader Vladimir Ilyich Lenin returned from exile (with German help) and committed his party to a policy of immediate peace. After the failure of the Kerenski Offensive (see above), Russia had no effective army with which to defend itself. At the start of September, German forces captured the port of Riga and advanced along the Baltic, posing a direct threat to Petrograd. General Lavr Kornilov, who had

ENEMY AT THE GATE
This 1917 Russian poster calls the workers of Petrograd to join the revolution and fight the czar's army.

replaced Brusilov as commander-in-chief, intended to restore discipline in the army and abolish the soldiers' soviets as a prelude to resuming the defense of the country, but his bid to take control of Petrograd in mid-September failed. Lenin's Red Guards—armed workers and politicized soldiers and sailors— were more successful. On November 7–8 they seized control of the capital and Lenin assumed power at the head of a revolutionary government. He immediately declared Russia at peace, in the context of a general appeal to soldiers in all countries to rise up against their capitalist rulers and end the war. More practically, the Bolshevik government asked Germany for an armistice, which was agreed to on December 16. Peace negotiations followed at the German military headquarters of Brest-Litovsk. The Germans were eager to

take maximum advantage of Russia's weakness. When the Bolsheviks stalled, following Leon Trotsky's line of "neither war nor peace," Germany launched a largely unopposed offensive in mid-February 1918 that carried them hundreds of miles farther east. On March 3 the Bolsheviks bit the bullet and signed a peace treaty that lost Russia around 30 percent of its prewar population.

1870–1924

VLADIMIR LENIN

When World War I started, Russian revolutionary politician Vladimir Lenin was in exile in Switzerland, where he denounced the war as an "imperialist" venture. After the fall of the czar, he accepted a German offer of transport to Russia. His single-minded devotion to world revolution led him to accept the peace of Brest-Litovsk in March 1918, but also to wage ruthless war against his enemies in the Russian Civil War and the Russo-Polish War.

ARMED PARADE
Armed workers parade in Petrograd on May Day 1917. The Russian capital's name had been patriotically changed from the too Germanic St. Petersburg early in the war.

1918

THE LAST YEAR OF THE WAR brought titanic battles on the Western Front as the stalemate of the trenches finally broke. The Germans' gamble on unlimited submarine warfare had brought the United States into the war, but they believed victory was still possible before American troops arrived in force. Large-scale German offensives begun in March 1918 achieved substantial gains but no knock-out punch, and from July the Allies counterattacked. Facing military defeat and political collapse, Germany was forced to accept armistice terms in November.

ERA OF WORLD WARS

Spring Offensives

DATE
March 21–June 3, 1918

FORCES
German: 74 divisions,
British: 30 divisions

LOCATION Western
Front from Flanders to
the Marne River

CASUALTIES
Allied: 500,000;
German: 400,000

Ludendorff planned "to deliver an annihilating blow to the British before American aid can become effective." The Kaiserschlacht, or Michael Offensive, began at 4:40 a.m. of March 21, 1918, when some 6,600 guns—many firing gas shells—and 3,500 trench mortars opened up a hurricane of fire on British trenches at the Somme. Stunned by the intensity of the bombardment, the British troops were in poor shape to resist German infantry infiltrating their positions in thick mist and attacking from the flanks and rear. Although some British units fought to the last man, many surrendered or retreated in confusion. The Germans took 21,000 prisoners on the first day. By March 27 they had advanced 40 miles (65km) through an 50-mile-(80km-) wide gap punched in the Allied line. But the offensive then ran out of momentum. Hungry German troops stopped to plunder food stores, while French forces joined in to

INFANTRY ADVANCE
Germans troops advance during the Kaiserschlacht offensive. Many carried grenades, flamethrowers, and machine guns.

stiffen British resistance. On April 9 Ludendorff launched a new offensive in Flanders. Attacking a sector held by a Portuguese corps and exhausted British units transferred from the Somme for a rest, the Germans advanced 3 miles (5km) on the first day. In response to the emergency, Marshal Ferdinand Foch was appointed Allied Supreme Commander to coordinate defensive operations. Once again the offensive ran out of steam and by April 29 both sides had fought to a standstill. A further offensive on the Aisne in late May brought the Germans within 55 miles (90km) of Paris. The combined effect of these offensives was to exhaust and demoralize the German army, using up irreplaceable manpower, and without achieving any decisive objective.

"Every position must be held to the last man... With our backs to the wall...each of us must fight on to the end."

General Haig, order of the day, APRIL 11, 1918

STORMTROOPERS
Elite stormtroopers spearheaded the Kaiserschlacht offensive, pressing deep into enemy lines.

Belleau Wood

DATE
June 6–26

FORCES
Numbers Unknown

LOCATION Between the
Aisne and the Marne
river, east of Paris

CASUALTIES
American: 9,777,
German: numbers
killed unknown, 1,600
taken prisoner

By May 1918 half a million American soldiers had arrived in France. On June 6 the US 2nd Division was given the task of recapturing Belleau Wood. The 4th Marine Brigade attacked across an open field swept by German machine-gun fire, taking heavy casualties. The Marines and 3rd Infantry Brigade succeeded in taking the wood, but it was reclaimed by the Germans, who were not definitively evicted until June 26. The battle showed the fighting qualities of American troops, but also their inexperience, which was to cost them dearly.

1860–1948

JOHN PERSHING

A veteran of wars in the Philippines and Mexico, General John Pershing was selected to lead the American Expeditionary Force and persuaded US politicians of the need for an army numbering millions. Once in Europe, he mostly kept American troops unified under his command, leading them through a costly learning process in the final offensives. He believed the armistice was a mistake and that the Germans should have been totally defeated.

PARIS SHELL DAMAGE
The spring offensives brought German guns within 55 miles (90km) of Paris, which was hit by over 300 shells.

Second Marne

DATE
July 15–August 3, 1918

FORCES
Numbers unknown

LOCATION
Marne River, east of
Paris

CASUALTIES
French: 95,000;
British: 13,000;
American: 12,000;
Germans: 168,000

Just as it did four years earlier, the tide of the war in 1918 turned at the Marne River. On July 15 the Germans launched the last of the series of offensives that they had begun on March 21, striking on a front from the Marne to Rheims.

However, Allied commander Foch was already preparing his own attack farther west. The German offensive at first went well, troops establishing bridgeheads across the Marne, but it was already stalled when the Allied counteroffensive opened at dawn on July 18. Commanded by the aggressive French general Charles Mangin, it was primarily a French operation, although American divisions played a prominent role. With over 500 tanks and more than 1,000 aircraft committed, the Allies fought their way forward, progressing 6 miles (10km) in the first two days. The Germans were forced to stage a general withdrawal over two weeks, falling back behind the Aisne to the positions they had held before the spring offensives.

FINAL OFFENSIVES

Final Allied Offensives

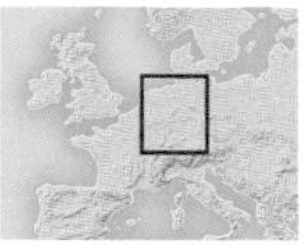

DATE
August 8–
November 11, 1918

FORCES
Allied / German: no
reliable estimate of
numbers

LOCATION
Eastern France

CASUALTIES
No reliable estimate

At dawn on August 8, 1918, British, Canadian, and Australian infantry advanced behind over 400 tanks against German positions in front of Amiens. They were supported by 800 aircraft carrying out ground-attack missions and dropping ammunition to advancing troops. By the afternoon the Allies had achieved a breakthrough, progressing about 7 miles (12km) on what Ludendorff called the "black day of the German army." Although the Amiens offensive quickly ground to a halt, it was a sign of things to come. The strength of the German army was failing while, with the arrival of the Americans, Allied numbers were

GUN CREW
American infantry press forward among shell-shattered trees. Two men are operating a 37mm machine-gun.

increasing. The British naval blockade was inflicting immense hardship on German civilians and causing supply problems for the army. German aircraft was hopelessly outnumbered and German tanks were few and cumbersome. The effectiveness of US forces was demonstrated on September 12, when the First American Army attacked the St. Mihiel salient, taking more than 13,000 prisoners in a day. In the last week of September, when Allied forces broke through the formidable Hindenburg Line defenses, Ludendorff told his superiors that it was necessary to seek an armistice. Many German troops were demoralized and unready to fight to the death—340,000 Germans surrendered in the last four months of

the war—but stiff fighting continued through weeks of political and diplomatic maneuvering. On October 30 sailors of the German High Seas Fleet mutinied at Kiel, sparking uprisings in many German cities. On November 9 Germany became a republic and an armistice was agreed to two days later, taking effect at 11 a.m. on November 11.

CANAL CROSSING
British troops are addressed by their brigadier after crossing the St. Quentin Canal, a part of the Hindenburg Line, in late September 1918.

1865–1937

ERICH LUDENDORFF

Victories at Liège and Tannenberg made the previously obscure staff officer Ludendorff a German national hero. He masterminded the German war effort from August 1916, creating a centrally controlled war economy and ruthlessly pursuing total victory. After the war he promoted the myth that the German army had been "stabbed in the back" by socialists and Jews, and became a leading figure in the early Nazi movement.

MARK IV TANK

TANKS WERE FIRST USED BY THE BRITISH DURING THE SOMME OFFENSIVE ON SEPTEMBER 15, 1916. EARLY MODELS WERE SLOW AND UNRELIABLE BUT SHOWED THE VEHICLE'S OVERWHELMING POTENTIAL.

In 1915 the British began designing a secret new vehicle, using the American Holt caterpillar tractor as the basis for its chassis. The Mark IV, introduced in 1917, incorporated thicker armor plating than the Mark I, unveiled the year before. Like all the early models, the Mark IV was a heavy tank in which mobility was sacrificed to armor. It was employed to lead infantry across no man's land, smashing a path through barbed wire and trenches.

STRENGTHS AND WEAKNESSES

Although they defied machine guns, heavy tanks were still vulnerable to artillery fire. When operated over muddy ground pitted with shell holes, they constantly bogged or broke down. At the battle of Cambrai in 1917 about 324 British heavy tanks, authorized to carry out a mass attack on firm ground, demonstrated what the vehicle could achieve if properly used. Lighter, quicker tanks such as the British Whippet and the French Renault FT-17—which introduced the rotating gun turret—proved their worth in the more open warfare of the war's later stages.

Vision slit for driver · Machine gun · Access hatch · Metal crawler tracks · Sponson with six-pounder gun · Tank name · ME9828 · DEVIL · Track tensioner

HELL ON TRACKS
Over 1,000 Mark IV tanks were built, more than any other model of its day. The tank went from concept to successful design over the course of World War I.

SPECIFICATION	
Origin Britain	**Speed** Up to 4mph (6.4kph)
Date of Launch 1917	**Horsepower** 105
Crew Six	**Weight** 28 tons

DITCHED TANK
Mark IVs frequently failed to cope with the mud, trenches, and enormous shell craters of the Western Front battlefields.

INSIDE THE MARK IV *The tank's crew had to operate in a hot, fume-filled interior with poor visibility and no communication with the outside, unless infantry tapped messages on the armor.*

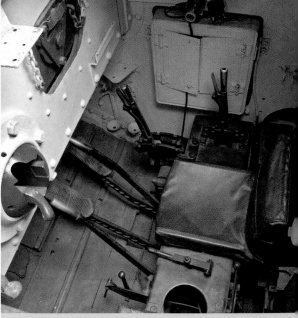

DRIVER'S SEAT *An officer and a driver sat side by side at the front of the Mark IV. The driver had to bring the tank to a halt to turn it, which made it an easy target.*

LEVER *This secured the escape hatch—on the roof of the tank—from the inside.*

GUN *Two crew manned each of the tank's quick-firing six-pounders.*

TRACK PLATE *The tank moved on two loops of metal links running around rollers. On uneven ground this was far superior to wheels.*

STEEL PLATE *Mark III and IV tanks had thicker armor than earlier models to withstand German armor-piercing bullets. Even so, the impact of bullets on the outside sent splinters flying on the tank's inside, so the crew had to wear protective clothing.*

SHELLS *These rounds were shelved by the sponson for easy access. Some are spent.*

ENGINE *Mark IV tanks ran on 105hp Daimler engines. The engine was exposed so that crew could keep it lubricated, but the downside was the noise and the smoke, as well as the need to dodge moving engine parts. The sheer weight of early tanks meant that the engines often overheated and wore out quickly.*

VISION PORTS *Enemy troops quickly learned to train their fire on tanks' vision ports, so crews began to wear face masks.*

ME 9828

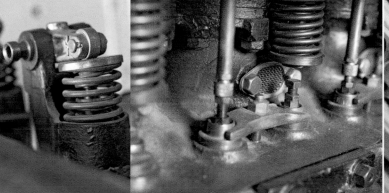

BETWEEN THE WARS

IN 1918 THE PIOUS HOPE was expressed that World War I would prove to have been a war to end wars. An international organization, the League of Nations, was set up in the war's immediate aftermath to preserve peace and promote disarmament. This impulse was maintained through the following decade: in August 1928, 15 countries, including Britain, Germany, France, the United States, and Japan, signed the Kellogg–Briand Pact, solemnly outlawing war. Yet within less than five years of that agreement, Germany had a Nazi government dedicated to rearmament and aggressive expansionism, and Japan had already embarked on the first of the military adventures that would lead to World War II.

ERA OF WORLD WARS

SOVIET STATUE
Vera Muhkina's worker and farmer statue was made for the Soviet pavilion at the Paris Exhibition of 1937. Soviet communism seemed an inspiring example to millions worldwide.

AFTER WORLD WAR I

Germany never shook off the bitterness of defeat or accepted the financial sacrifices it was forced to make by the terms of the peace treaty. When reparation payments fell behind in 1923, Franco–Belgian forces occupied the industrial Ruhr; Germany's economy, already heavily in debt, hyperinflated. Meanwhile the

establishment of the first communist government in the Soviet Union created an ideological division that complicated power relations between the states. Although much of public opinion had shifted against the glorification of warfare—as shown by a surge of antiwar literature in the late 1920s—some ex-servicemen came out of World War I with a devotion to militarism and nationalism, exemplified by the fascists, who took power in Italy in 1922, and the German Nazi Party, which attempted a coup in 1923.

CRAZY MONEY
At the peak of the hyperinflation in Germany in 1923, a note for nine billion marks would not have bought a cup of coffee.

AGAINST WAR
Erich Remarque's 1929 novel All Quiet on the Western Front *was one of the books that established the image of World War I as a "futile slaughter."*

CIVIL AND COLONIAL WARS

Between 1918 and 1923 the major armed conflicts were essentially a settlement of leftover issues from World War I. In Russia a complex and immensely destructive civil war left the Bolsheviks in control of most of the fomer Russian Empire, while a short, sharp war with Poland established Russia's western border. Turkish nationalists defied a carve-up of Anatolia decreed by a peace treaty imposed on the old Ottoman Empire and fought a successful war with Greece to establish the nation of Turkey. Colonial powers devoted some of the air power developed in World War I to "imperial policing" operations—the Italians against rebels in Libya, the French and Spanish against Abd el-Krim in Morocco, and the British against Kurds and Shi'ites in Iraq. The use of

aerial bombardment—sometimes with poison gas—to intimidate tribal peoples was regarded as an economic way of upholding authority.

ITALIAN INVADERS
Italian troops with local people during the invasion of Ethiopia in 1935. European democracies failed to react to Italy's aggression.

SLIDE TO WAR

NAZI LEADER
Adolf Hitler displays the Iron Cross he won in World War I on his Nazi uniform. His early experience of war shaped his brutal world view of life as the survival of the strongest.

The 1930s was a decade of widening warfare, culminating in World War II. The collapse of German democracy under the impact of economic depression allowed Adolf Hitler's Nazi Party to come to power in 1933. Hitler's mission was to reverse the verdict of World War I. He greatly enhanced German power by joining Austria and the Sudetenland area of Czechoslovakia to the Reich. In Japan, militarists gained control of the government and followed an expansionist policy in Asia, seizing Manchuria in 1931 and embarking on a full-scale invasion of China in 1937. Italy's conquest of Ethiopia—a League of Nations member state—in 1935–36 produced such a timid response that "collective security" was dead. When civil war broke out in Spain in 1936, Italian fascists and German Nazis fought for the Nationalist side, while the Soviet Union backed the Republican government.

STAR OF DAVID
Hitler blamed the Jews for Germany's defeat in World War I. From 1939 Jews in German-occupied Europe were forced to wear this yellow star.

JAPAN AT WAR
Japanese troops near Nanjing celebrate their invasion of China in 1937. The start of the Sino-Japanese conflict is sometimes regarded as the true beginning of World War II.

1883–1945

BENITO MUSSOLINI

Blustering Italian dictator Mussolini came to power in 1922 after threatening to march on Rome with his black-shirted, paramilitary, fascist combat squads. The hostility of Britain and France to his invasion of Ethiopia in 1935–36 led him to form an alliance with Hitler. Italian troops participated in the Spanish Civil War, but Mussolini hesitated to enter World War II until June 1940. Driven from power when the Allies invaded Italy in 1943, he was seized by the Germans and set up as a puppet ruler in northern Italy. Italian partisans killed him at the end of the war.

1914–PRESENT

AIR WARFARE

The warfare of the 1930s differed from that of World War I primarily in the increased role of air power. The heavy casualties caused by the Japanese bombing of Nanking in China and the German air force's destruction of Guernica in Spain suggested that a war between the major powers might begin with the immediate laying of waste of cities from the air. As rearmament got under way in the second half of the 1930s, the key focus was on aircraft. Only the Germans devised tactics for using aircraft in conjunction with tanks and other ground forces.

FIGHTER PLANE
The German Messerschmitt Bf109 was one of the high-performance monoplanes introduced in the 1930s.

BACK TO WAR
British munition workers stack up artillery shells in November 1939, as Europe is once more plunged into a major war.

RUSSIA AND CHINA AT WAR

THE AREA OF THE GREAT EURASIAN LANDMASS stretching from the Baltic to the Pacific was the site of upheaval and wars in the early half of the 20th century. In the former Russian Empire, the Soviet Union was founded after extensive warfare defeated enemies of the revolution and established new borders. In China, a Kuomintang (Nationalist) government struggled to establish its rule nationwide, resisted by warlords and communists. Exploiting China's weakness, the Japanese encroached on northern China in a series of military operations between 1931 and 1933, occupying Manchuria and forcing the Chinese to withdraw all troops north of Beijing. But their full-scale invasion of China in 1937 failed to achieve a swift victory, despite the capture of major cities.

RUSSIAN CIVIL WAR

Russian Civil War

DATE May 1918–November 1920

FORCES Bolsheviks: 800,000 (October 1920); Whites: c.300,000 (end 1918); foreign forces: 180,000 (end 1918)

LOCATION Former Russian Empire

CASUALTIES Total casualties: 10 million

In mid-1918 the Russian Bolshevik government was threatened by a variety of forces: Czech former prisoners of war, who took control of the trans-Siberian railroad; forces from Britain, France, the United States, and Japan, which occupied areas around key ports; nationalist groups in Ukraine and other ethnically distinct areas; and the "White" armies led by czarist officers—most prominently General Anton Denikin and Admiral Alexander Kolchak—who wished to suppress the revolution. Bolshevik leader Leon Trotsky built up the Red Army from scratch. Like the White armies, it was commanded by former czarist officers, the most effective of whom was Mikhail Tukhachevsky. Trotsky exercised control from an armored train that traveled between the various fronts. Cavalry came into its own in a war of raids fought by relatively small formations spread over vast areas. Great barbarity was shown by both sides as they terrorized the peasantry to extract conscripts and

grain. The White forces were poorly led, crippled by internal divisions, and could not rally popular support. Kolchak was captured by the Bolsheviks and executed in February 1920. Most of Denikin's forces were

evacuated from Black Sea ports the following month. White general Peter Wrangel attempted a final offensive from the Crimea in June to coincide with Russia's war with Poland, but he too was forced to flee in November.

RED CAVALRY
A detachment of the Bolshevik First Cavalry Army advances across Russia. Led by Semyen Budenny, the Red cavalry played a major role both in the Russian Civil War and the Polish–Bolshevik War.

POLISH–BOLSHEVIK WAR

Warsaw

DATE May 7–October 12, 1920

FORCES Russians: 200,000; Poles: 200,000

LOCATION Outside Warsaw

CASUALTIES Russians: c.80,000 killed or wounded, 60,000 taken prisoner; Poles: 50,000 killed or wounded

In May 1920, with the support of Ukrainian nationalists led by Simon Petlyura, Polish forces under Jozef Pilsudski invaded Ukraine and seized Kiev. It was Pilsudski's aim to push the borders of newly independent Poland as far as possible to the east. The Russian Red Army counterattacked in force, retaking Kiev on June 12. The Bolsheviks continued with the offensive, hoping to win Poland for the revolution. Military advisors,

headed by the French general Maxime Weygand, were dispatched to Warsaw by the western European powers, who feared that a Bolshevik capture of Poland would lead to further Russian incursions into Germany. By August 13 the Red Army's Western Army Group under Tukhachevsky was enveloping Warsaw to the north and south while the Southwest Army Group was engaged in front of Lvov. On August 16 Pilsudski personally commanded a surprise counteroffensive of around 20,000 troops into a weak spot identified by Polish intelligence between the Bolshevik armies. A simultaneous blow against the northern flank of Tukhachevsky's forces threatened to trap his army in a pincer movement. The Russians were forced into a disorganized withdrawal eastward over the Niemen River into Belorussia and Ukraine, where further fighting saw the Polish

army victorious. Under heavy pressure from the western European powers, an armistice was agreed on October 12. Both the Bolsheviks and the powers of western Europe considered Poland to be on the verge of defeat before the Battle of Warsaw, also

known as the Miracle at the Vistula; the unexpected Polish victory crippled the Bolshevik forces. The Treaty of Riga, signed on March 18, 1921, gave a securely independent Poland western Ukraine and Belorussia, which they held for the next 18 years.

1867–1935

MARSHAL JOZEF PILSUDSKI

Before World War I, Pilsudski took part in Polish agitation for freedom from Russian rule. During the war he led the Polish Legion, which fought with the Austro–Hungarian army against Russia. As ruler of Poland from 1918 he launched the war with the Bolsheviks that left Poland in control of western Ukraine and Belorussia. After retiring in 1923, he returned to rule with dictatorial powers in 1926.

CHINESE "BANDIT SUPPRESSION"

The Long March

DATE	October 16, 1934–October 20, 1935
FORCES	80,000 in initial Communist outbreak from Jiangxi
LOCATION 6,200 miles (10,000km) from Ruijin to Wuqizhen	**CASUALTIES** Unknown, but 9,000 arrived at Wuqizhen

Until 1927 the Chinese Communist Party supported the Kuomintang under Jiang Jieshi (Chiang Kai-Shek) in unifying China under a nationalist government. The Kuomintang then turned on the communists, however, massacring many and forcing the survivors to flee the major cities. In the early 1930s Jiang Jieshi launched a series of campaigns to destroy their remaining bases. Communist-controlled Jiangxi was encircled by government troops and placed under blockade. Communist leaders, including Mao Zedong, decided to stage a breakout to the southwest. Short of supplies—

GUERRILLA LEADER
Mao Zedong emerged as the leader of the communists during the Long March. He advocated a peasant revolutionary war.

only one in three troops spearheading the march had rifles—the communists nonetheless broke out of encirclement and headed west then north in search of a safe base. Intermittent small-scale fighting was a constant drain on manpower, but hardship and disease caused most losses as the march crossed high mountains and trackless swamps.

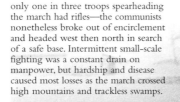

JAPAN INVADES CHINA

Japanese Invasion of China

DATE July 1937–January 1938
FORCES Chinese: 2,150,000; Japanese/Manchurian: 450,000
LOCATION China	**CASUALTIES** Total at Shanghai: c.200,000; Chinese at Rape of Nanking: c.250,000

On July 7, 1937, a clash between Japanese and Chinese troops at Beijing's Marco Polo bridge precipitated a full-scale war in which the Kuomintang and the communist Chinese fought as allies against the Japanese. The heaviest fighting occurred at Shanghai, where Japanese troops carried out amphibious landings with strong naval and air support from August 13. By September 12 Japanese forces were inside the city, but fierce Chinese resistance continued from street to street. In early November Chinese forces carried out a fighting withdrawal. With Shanghai in their hands, the Japanese advanced on Nanking, where Chinese soldiers failed to put up substantial resistance, despite outnumbering their enemy. The Japanese subjected the city to aerial bombardment and then unleashed six weeks of brutality and massacre upon civilians and prisoners of war alike. Between 200,000 and 300,000 people were killed, many after rape or torture.

SWARMING THE WALL
A regiment of Japanese infantry marches onto a section of the Great Wall of China near Beijing in November 1937.

THE NOMONHAN INCIDENT

Nomonhan

DATE May 28–September 16, 1939
FORCES Soviet and Mongolian: 65,000; Japanese: 28,000
LOCATION Border between Manchuria and Outer Mongolia	**CASUALTIES** Soviet: 24,000; Japanese: 18,000

Japan pushed troops from Manchuria into a region disputed with the Soviets across the Khalkin-Gol River. Soviet general Georgi Zhukov was sent to repel the intrusion with a well-equipped force dominant in numbers. On August 20 he launched an attack near the small village of Nomonhan with armored brigades and mechanized infantry. Remnants of the Japanese forces retreated into Manchuria, after which a ceasefire was agreed to. The victory freed the Soviets from the threat of fighting on two fronts when Germany invaded in 1941.

SOVIET ARMOR
The Red Army prepares for battle. With the outbreak of World War II in western Europe, Nomonhan attracted little world attention.

SPANISH CIVIL WAR

IN JULY 1936 ARMY OFFICERS tried to overthrow Spain's left-wing Popular Front government, but the attempted coup was successfully resisted by workers' militias. The resulting civil war lasted for three years and cost at least 600,000 lives. Around 40,000 volunteers fought in the International Brigades for the government, or Loyalist, side, which also received arms and aircraft from the Soviet Union. Over 60,000 troops from fascist Italy and the German Condor Legion fought for the rebels, or Nationalists, led by General Francisco Franco. Britain and France maintained a strict neutrality that contributed to Franco's victory.

Land held by Nationalist forces
Jul 1936
Oct 1937
Jul 1938
Feb 1939

Land held by Loyalist forces
Feb 1939
— temporary independence, with dates

ATTRITION
As the Nationalists won more territory in the north, the conflict became a war of attrition.

SPANISH CIVIL WAR
Advance from Africa

DATE
August–September 1936

FORCES
Army of Africa: 34,000

CASUALTIES
No reliable estimates

LOCATION
Spanish Morocco, Badajoz, Toledo

The Spanish army's rebellion launched on July 18, 1936, at first looked like it would fail. Its most experienced forces were the Foreign Legionnaires and Moroccans in Spanish Morocco. Since the navy was loyal to the government, these troops could not cross to Spain.

The head of the African forces, General Franco, requested assistance from fascist Italy and Nazi Germany. The arrival of German Junkers Ju-52 transport aircraft at the end of July allowed Franco to fly 15,000 troops across to Seville in 10 days, the first airlift in history. With air cover provided by Italian Savoia-Marchetti bombers, other troops were ferried by boat across the straits. The Army of Africa marched north to Badajoz and west to Toledo, massacring thousands of militiamen and suspected Loyalist sympathizers along the way. At Toledo on September 28 it relieved the Nationalist garrison in the Alcazar fortress, which had been under siege for 10 weeks. The next target was Madrid.

MESSERSCHMITT BF 109
Messerschmitt Bf 109 fighter planes saw their first combat with the German Condor Legion in the Spanish Civil War.

SPANISH CIVIL WAR
Defense of Madrid

DATE
November 6–23, 1936

FORCES
Nationalists: c.50,000;
Loyalists: unknown

CASUALTIES
No reliable estimates

LOCATION
Madrid, Spain

In October 1936 Madrid was under threat from the Army of Africa in the south and General Emilio Mola's forces in the north. The first arrival of Soviet military supplies was followed on November 8 by the first detail of the International Brigades. By then, Nationalist troops were already in the suburbs and the government had fled to Valencia, leaving General José Miaja in command. Madrid came under artillery and aerial bombardment, but remarkably its defenses held. The 11th International Brigade, a variety of makeshift militias—including anarchist, communist, and women's brigades—loyal army units, and a small quantity of Soviet tanks and aircraft fought the Army of Africa to a standstill. Madrid stayed besieged for the rest of the war.

IMPROVISED DEFENSES
Spanish Loyalists establish a machine-gun post behind a barricade of rice sacks, ready to resist the Nationalist penetration of Madrid.

SPANISH CIVIL WAR
Guadalajara

DATE
March 8–16, 1937

FORCES Loyalists: 20,000; Nationalists: 45,000

CASUALTIES
Loyalists: 7,000; Italians and Nationalists: 5,000

LOCATION Guadalajara, 40 miles (65km) NE of Madrid, Spain

In February 1937 the International Brigade held Franco's Nationalists in desperate fighting in the Jarama valley, east of Madrid. Italian general Mario Roatta decided to attack toward Guadalajara, intending to join up with Franco's forces. The initial advance on March 8, spearheaded by over 100 light tanks supported by artillery, broke through the thinly held Loyalist line, but the Italians were hampered by snow and sleet, for which they were ill prepared. Franco remained passive, allowing the Loyalists to transfer forces from the Jarama front. These included the Garibaldi Battalion, largely composed of antifascist Italians, who found themselves fighting an Italian civil war on Spanish soil. On March 12 the Loyalists mounted a counterattack, deploying Soviet T-26 tanks that outgunned the Italian armor. Loyalist aircraft carried out ground-attack missions to devastating effect, and the Italians were driven back in disarray. A small defensive victory, Guadalajara gave a boost to Loyalist morale and dented the prestige of fascist Italy.

WAR POSTER
A Loyalist poster calls for unity in pursuit of victory—a vain hope given the political divisions within the Republican camp.

"A battle is in progress not merely to defend a people from a savage aggressor, but to destroy something that…will eventually crush the people of all democratic countries."

Bill Paynter, British International Brigade member, MAY 1937

Guernica

DATE
April 26, 1937

FORCES
Germans: 43 aircraft;
Basque: none

CASUALTIES
Germans: none;
Basque civilians: c.300

LOCATION
Basque country,
northern Spain

The Basque area of northern Spain supported the Republic because it offered them regional self-government. In spring 1937 General Mola launched a campaign against the Basque country, threatening to raze it to the ground "if submission was not immediate." The Basques put up a brave fight, but in late April they were falling back toward Guernica, a market town of symbolic importance as the "cradle of Basque culture." The German Condor Legion under Wolfram von Richthofen was conducting air attacks in support of the Nationalist offensive—officially attacking military targets, but expressly "without regard for the civilian population." On the afternoon of April 26 the Condor Legion struck at Guernica. They might

have been delivering a blow against Basque morale, or they might have been seeking to destroy a bridge to block the withdrawal of Basque forces. Either way, the effect was devastation. The Heinkel He-51s went in first, followed by Junkers transports roughly adapted for bombing missions. In wave after wave of "shuttle" attacks, dropping a mix of incendiaries and 550lb (250kg) bombs, they destroyed two-thirds of Guernica's buildings. Basque spokesman Father Alberto Onaindaia, who arrived at Guernica at the same time as the aircraft, described seeing He-51 fighters

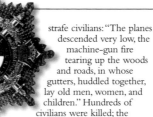

strafe civilians: "The planes descended very low, the machine-gun fire tearing up the woods and roads, in whose gutters, huddled together, lay old men, women, and children." Hundreds of civilians were killed; the bridge said to be the primary target of the raid was not hit. Reports from foreign journalists who witnessed the aftermath ensured that Guernica would become synonymous with the ruthless bombing of a civilian population.

PICASSO'S GUERNICA
Picasso's painting for the Paris Exhibition of 1937 helped fix Guernica as a symbol of the inhumanity of aerial bombardment.

Teruel

DATE December 15,
1937–February 20, 1938

FORCES Unknown

CASUALTIES Loyalists:
60,000 killed, wounded,
or taken prisoner;
Nationalists: 50,000
killed, wounded, or
taken prisoner

LOCATION
Aragon,
eastern Spain

By the winter of 1937 the Nationalists had overrun the Basque country and were preparing a decisive offensive against Madrid. To forestall this attack, General Vicente Rojo launched an offensive against the Nationalist-held city of Teruel. The attack achieved complete surprise, trapping a Nationalist garrison inside Teruel. Franco responded as the Loyalists had hoped by transferring forces to the Aragon front. The fighting took place on bleak, rocky terrain during one of the coldest winters on record. Many soldiers on both sides froze to death. On January 8, after house-to-house fighting, Teruel fell to the Loyalists, but they were themselves threatened with encirclement as the major Nationalist forces began to arrive. Amid recriminations between rival political factions, the Loyalists achieved a fighting withdrawal under aerial and artillery bombardment, once more bested by the Nationalists' growing materiel and numerical superiority.

Ebro

DATE July 24–
November 16, 1938

FORCES Loyalists: 80,000
in original offensive

CASUALTIES
Loyalists: 70,000
killed or wounded;
Nationalists: 36,500
killed or wounded

LOCATION
Southern Catalonia,
Spain

In summer 1938, facing almost certain defeat, the Loyalists launched a major offensive across the Ebro River, hoping that, if they demonstrated their ability to fight, the western democracies might yet come to their aid. Under General Juan Modesto, troops crossed the river by boat on the night of July 23–24, the rest of the force crossing on pontoon bridges the following day. By August 1 they had advanced 25 miles (40km), but the Nationalists held a strong position at Gandesa. Both sides suffered heavy casualties in frontal assaults on entrenched positions. Nationalist artillery and air strikes by German Ju-87 Stuka dive-bombers wore down the Popular Army, the remnants of which were driven back to their start point by mid-November. A Nationalist victory in the war was now a formality, completed by April 1, 1939.

VICTORIOUS NATIONALISTS
Spanish Nationalist troops enter Barcelona in January 1939 in Italian-made minitanks. The city's Loyalist defenders fled to France.

HITLER'S WAR

WORLD WAR II CONSISTED OF two more or less distinct conflicts, one fought in Europe and North Africa, the other in the Pacific and Asia. Between them they are thought to have caused the deaths of over 50 million people. The European war was a conflict of Hitler's own making, planned and, to a great extent, executed by him.

NAZI TRIUMPHS

The war in Europe began on September 1, 1939, when Germany invaded Poland, so provoking a declaration of war by Britain and France. A pact with the Soviet Union, signed just days earlier, allowed Hitler to concentrate on the Western Front after Poland's defeat. Germany was not superior to the Allies in numbers of tanks, but it had developed *Blitzkrieg* tactics, combining air power and armored divisions to achieve rapid victory in mobile warfare. In a series of lightning campaigns between 1939 and 1941, Hitler extended German control over most of Europe, with only Britain remaining undefeated. When Germany invaded the Soviet Union in June 1941, the war took on an unprecedented scale and savagery. The following December, after the Japanese attack on Pearl Harbor, Hitler declared war on the United States, which was already heavily involved in support of Britain.

KEY

Greater German Reich, 1942	Axis satellites
Finland and area occupied by Finland	Allied territories
areas occupied by Germany	neutral states
Italy and areas occupied by Italy	Vichy France and its territories

THE GREATER GERMAN REICH
By 1942 the Greater German Reich covered much of central Europe. The invasion of the Soviet Union sowed the seeds of Hitler's ultimate defeat.

SS INSIGNIA
The SS was a Nazi elite formation that performed well in battle but was responsible for many atrocities. In particular, SS personnel played a key role in the administration of death camps where millions of Jews and others were murdered.

1889–1945

ADOLF HITLER

Austrian by birth, Adolf Hitler served in the Germany army in World War I and was decorated for bravery. After Germany's defeat in 1918, he entered right-wing nationalist circles and, in 1923, as head of the Nazi Party, led a failed coup in Munich. The Great Depression turned the Nazis into Germany's largest single political party. After becoming chancellor in 1933 with the support of German conservatives, Hitler instituted a personal dictatorship. His goals were to make Germany dominant in Europe, destroy the Jews, and reduce the Slavs to servitude. Although early in the war he supported *Blitzkrieg* tactics, his personal control over the German war effort was disastrous. He survived an assassination attempt in 1944 but committed suicide the next year amid the ruins of Berlin.

THE TIDE TURNS

After December 1941 Germany's hopes of victory rested on crushing the Soviet armies and reducing Britain to submission by a submarine blockade, which would leave the United States confronted by a "fortress Europe" impossible to assault. But from the end of 1942, the tide of battle on the Eastern Front turned with the German defeat at Stalingrad, while in 1943 the U-boat menace was tamed. Victorious in North Africa, Allied troops landed in southern Europe in 1943, taking Germany's main ally, Italy, out of the war. Hitler was thrown back on his belief in secret weapons that might swing the war around, but although Germany developed the first operational jet aircraft and cruise and ballistic missiles—the V1 and V2—these were created too late to have a decisive effect on the war's outcome.

GERMAN SOLDIER
Despite technological advances, much of the war was fought by soldiers such as this German infantryman, with rifles, machine guns, and other weapons little different from those of World War I.

GERMAN JET
The world's first operational jet fighter, the Messerschmitt Me 262, was used in the defense of Germany from July 1944.

Jumo 004 turbojet engine

NAZI LEADERS
Top German Nazi leaders and senior officers visit the West Wall (also known as the Siegfried Line), which was built to defend Germany's western border. Those present include Hitler himself (far right) and SS chief Heinrich Himmler (center, with glasses).

ALLIED VICTORY

Gradually, the United States and the Soviet Union brought their manpower and industrial potential to bear—a remarkable achievement for the Soviets, who had lost most of their industrial regions to German occupation. The Allies produced weapons that were sometimes less sophisticated than their German equivalents, but sturdy and manufactured in vast numbers. The German airforce—the Luftwaffe—was worn down by the British and American strategic bombing offensive that reduced German cities to ruins. By the time of the D-Day landings in June 1944 it could no longer provide effective air support, while Allied airforces had developed an impressive ground-attack capability. None of the major combatants broke under the strain of war; despite a revolt by German generals, the German people fought for Hitler to the last. The alliance led by US president Franklin D. Roosevelt, British prime minister Winston Churchill, and Soviet dictator Josef Stalin also held firm in pursuit of "unconditional surrender." The war ended in 1945 with the Western Allies and the Soviet Union occupying Germany.

1879–1953

JOSEF STALIN

Born in Georgia, Stalin was one of the leaders of the 1917 Bolshevik Revolution. Throughout the 1920s he extended his power inside the Soviet Communist Party, building up a personal dictatorship. In the 1930s he purged potential rivals, including much of the Red Army officer corps. His pact with Hitler in 1939 paved the way for World War II. After the German invasion of 1941, which Stalin refused to see coming, he rallied the people with appeals to Russian patriotism. His conduct of the war was resolute but hugely wasteful of soldiers' lives.

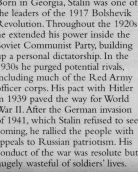

RED VICTORY
Soviet soldiers advance through the center of Berlin in May 1945. By this time, street fighting and aerial bombardment had reduced much of the city to rubble.

1914–PRESENT

BLITZKRIEG

THERE WAS A STARK CONTRAST in attitudes between the two sides at the outset of World War II in Europe. Britain and France had not wanted war and had little enthusiasm for offensive action. In the 1930s the French had spent a large proportion of their military budget on the Maginot Line, a series of fortifications on the border with Germany intended for a static,

defensive war. Nazi Germany, on the other hand, was imbued with a spirit of ruthless aggression. German *Blitzkrieg* tactics were based on speed and decisiveness, hitting the enemy hard at his weakest points and exploiting breakthroughs with maximum mobility. Tanks and aircraft were the key weapons that would enable Germany to win this "lightning" war.

THE POLISH CAMPAIGN

Defeat of Poland

DATE September 1–October 5, 1939	
FORCES Germans: 1.25 million; Poles: 800,000	
LOCATION Poland	**CASUALTIES** Germans: 14,000 killed, 30,000 wounded; Poles: 66,000 killed, 200,00 wounded

At dawn on September 1, 1939, German forces invaded Poland without a declaration of war. Poland was exposed to attack in the north from East Prussia and to the south from Slovakia—a German puppet state—as well as along its long western border. Underequipped and thinly spread, Polish forces were sliced apart by German armored spearheads supported by bomber aircraft. The

POLISH CAVALRY
In 1939 the Polish army had 40 cavalry regiments, none of which was able to make any impact on the fighting. The Germans still relied heavily on horses for transportation.

Polish airforce was quickly wiped out, most of its aircraft destroyed while still on the ground. On September 3 Britain and France declared war in response to the invasion but remained passive, doing nothing to relieve pressure on Poland. Polish forces withdrew to the Vistula River, concentrating around Warsaw. By September 15, the Polish capital was surrounded; two days

later, at German invitation, the Soviet army occupied eastern Poland. On September 27, after 10 days of aerial bombardment, Warsaw surrendered, although pockets of resistance held out until October 5. Tens of thousands of Poles escaped to continue the war as armed forces in exile.

1888–1954

HEINZ GUDERIAN

A staff officer in 1918, Guderian became an expert in armored warfare and in the mid-1930s persuaded his superiors in the German army—the Wehrmacht— to let him form the first *panzer* (tank) divisions. He developed and applied the theory of *Blitzkrieg* and led tank forces in the invasion of Poland and the battle of France. Dismissed in December 1941, when the invasion of Russia ran into difficulties, he was recalled in 1943, becoming Hitler's chief of staff in 1944.

THE WINTER WAR

The Winter War

DATE November 30, 1939–March 12, 1940	
FORCES Finns: 175,000; Soviets: 1 million	
LOCATION Finnish-Soviet border	**CASUALTIES** Finns: 25,000 killed; Soviets: 127,000 killed

In November 1939 Stalin demanded that Finland cede part of the Karelian Isthmus to the Soviet Union. When the Finns refused, the Soviets launched a hasty attack, expecting the operation to be a formality. But led by veteran Marshal Carl Mannerheim, the Finnish army held its fortified line north of Leningrad, inflicting heavy casualties. Soviet columns soon became bogged down in snow and freezing conditions and were cut apart by Finnish ski troops, who enjoyed unhampered mobility.

SKI TROOPS
Finnish troops operating on skis in white winter camouflage ran rings around Soviet units, most of which had no winter equipment. Thousands of Soviet soldiers died of cold.

In February the Soviets delivered a properly prepared attack against the Mannerheim Line in overwhelming force. The Finns sued for peace the following month and the Soviets took what they had originally asked for.

Foresight | *Cheek rest*

ANTITANK RIFLE
The Finnish Lahti L39 rifle was nicknamed the "Elephant Gun" for its huge recoil. It weighed 105lb (48kg) unloaded.

Plywood skis for balance

THE NORWEGIAN CAMPAIGN

The Norwegian Campaign

DATE April 8–June 9, 1940	
FORCES Germans: 10,000; Allies: 24,000 (Norwegians: 12,000)	
LOCATION Norway	**CASUALTIES** Germans: 5,500; Allies: 7,300 (Norwegians: 1,800)

Neutral Scandinavia was a vital source of iron ore for Germany. Britain and France made plans to invade Norway, but Germany acted more decisively. On April 8 British ships laying mines in Norwegian waters ran into German convoys carrying troops to Norwegian ports. The next day the Germans occupied Denmark unopposed and paratroopers seized Oslo. Allied landings to counter the German invasion began on April 14 but failed to take German-held Trondheim; Allied troops there were evacuated by May 3. At Narvik the Royal Navy inflicted heavy losses on German ships, but it took until May 27 to drive the Germans from the port. Military disaster in France led to the withdrawal of all Allied troops from Norway.

THE BATTLE OF FRANCE

The Battle of France

DATE
May 10–June 25, 1940

FORCES Germans:
3.3 million men, 2,600
tanks; Allies: 2.8 million
men, 3,600 tanks

LOCATION
France, Netherlands,
and Belgium

CASUALTIES Germans:
111,000; French:
290,000; British: 68,000

On May 10, 1940, the Germans
launched a long-awaited offensive
in the west. Making bold use of air
attack and paratroopers, they crushed
the neutral Netherlands in four days

VICHY BADGE
*Pétain's Vichy-based
government replaced
many traditional
symbols with new
ones such as this
double-headed ax.*

GERMAN BOMBER
*The two-seater Junkers Ju 87 Stuka dive-
bomber was used as "aerial artillery" in
support of tanks, making a major contribution
to German victories in Poland and France.*

and sent the Belgians reeling. Much
of the French army and the British
Expeditionary Force advanced into
Belgium to confront what they
assumed to be the main German
advance. However, after much debate,
Hitler and his generals adopted Erich
von Manstein's plan for a powerful
armored thrust farther south, through
the supposedly impassable forests
of the Ardennes. Three columns of
German tanks and motorized infantry
emerged from the Ardennes and
crossed the Meuse River on May 13.
With Stuka dive-bombers giving
aerial support, they broke
clean through the French
line and wheeled north
toward the Channel coast,
threatening to cut off Allied
armies in Belgium. Fighting
off counterattacks by de
Gaulle's 4th Armored

VICTORY MARCH
*Victorious German troops march
through the center of Paris on
June 14, 1940, after taking the
city without a fight. Paris
remained under German
occupation for
more than four years, until
August 25, 1944.*

Division at Laon and
British tanks at Arras,
the Germans reached
the English Channel on May
22. With most other Channel
ports lost, the Allied armies fell back
on Dunkirk. This refuge might also
have fallen but for Hitler's decision to
halt the armored advance for two
days, allowing the Allies to organize a
defensive perimeter. A desperate
operation was improvised by Allied
naval forces, supplemented by small
civilian craft, to evacuate troops under
constant air attack. By the time
Dunkirk fell on June 4, some 338,000
soldiers had been taken off, two-thirds
of them British. While the remaining
French forces put up strong resistance
to the Italians, who Mussolini led
into the war on June 10, their
armies disintegrated whenever
confronted by the Germans,
as morale collapsed. The fall
of Paris on June 14 was
followed on June 21
by a capitulation
signed in the same
railroad carriage

used for the signing of the November
1918 armistice. Two-thirds of
France was placed under German
occupation, the rest coming under the
collaborationist government of Marshal
Philippe Pétain, ruling from Vichy.

FIELD CAP

SS PANZER JACKET

SS ENGRAVED BELT

SS PANZER UNIFORM
*There were 10 German panzer divisions in
the army that defeated France in 1940. SS
units fought as part of 1st Panzer Division
at Dunkirk and SS Panzer divisions were
seen as an elite formation later in the war.
Panzer divisions transformed the
effectiveness of tanks, allowing commanders
such as Guderian and Rommel to exploit
their potential for maneuverability.*

RESISTANCE STAMP
*This false stamp was used by the French
Resistance. It is recognizable by a changed
design around the eye, showing the recipient
that they could trust the letter's contents.*

The Battle of Britain and the Blitz

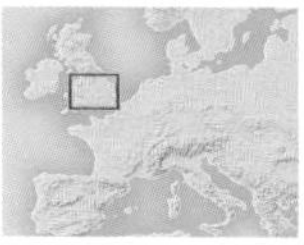

DATE Battle of Britain: Jul–Oct 1940; Blitz: Sep 1940–May 1941

FORCES Luftwaffe: 1,464 fighters, 1,380 bombers; RAF: 900 fighters

LOCATION Southern and central Britain

CASUALTIES B. of Britain: Luftwaffe: 1,887 aircraft; RAF: 1,023 aircraft; Blitz: 43,000 British civilians

Laminated-wood propellor blade

Clearview laminated cockpit

SUPERMARINE SPITFIRE
The all-metal Spitfire was the only RAF fighter that could take on and beat the Messerschmitt Bf 109. This Mark V model was personalized by a Canadian pilot.

Squadron markings

Liquid-cooled, V-12, Rolls-Royce engine

Elliptical section wing housing machine guns

Light metal alloy fuselage

Stabilizing wheel

After defeating France, Hitler hoped that the British would sue for peace, but, under the leadership of Winston Churchill, Britain instead adopted a posture of defiance. Hitler then ordered preparations for a cross–Channel invasion and instructed the Luftwaffe "to overcome the British air force with all means at its disposal." The British Fighter Command was well prepared to meet a German air offensive. A chain of radar stations was in place to pass warning of approaching enemy aircraft to operations rooms, where the progress of the air battle could be monitored. Pilots at fighter bases were in constant readiness for takeoff. After preliminary clashes over the English Channel in July 1940, Luftwaffe operations began in earnest in mid-August. Whenever weather permitted, fleets of bombers

with fighter escorts were sent across in daylight from airfields in France. In clashes over southern England, RAF Spitfires took on the German escorts, while Hurricane fighters attacked the German bombers. Fighter Command chief Hugh Dowding had a clear objective: to keep his fighter force in operation. The British aircraft industry could make up for aircraft losses, but trained pilots were in short supply; the RAF fighter squadrons depended on a mix of nationalities, including British, Canadians, New Zealanders, Australians, South Africans, Czechs, Poles, and other Europeans. Most dangerous to the British were German attacks on fighter airfields, but these were rarely pursued with sufficient concentration. In general,

the Germans had the edge in air combat but lacked clear objectives. On September 7 the main focus was arbitrarily shifted from bombing airfields to mass raids on London. By late October, all thought of an invasion had been abandoned. Air operations then focused on night bombing raids. The Germans wreaked devastation on London and other

British cities, but they failed to develop a viable heavy bomber, limiting the impact of attacks, which never exceeded 500 tons of bombs dropped a night. The "Blitz" showed no signs of breaking the British will to resist. The raids passed their peak by the end of May 1941, as aircraft were withdrawn for the invasion of Russia.

> "Let us therefore brace ourselves to our duties and so bear ourselves that, if the British Empire and the Commonwealth last for a thousand years, men will still say: 'this was their finest hour.'"
>
> *Winston Churchill,* JUNE 18, 1940

LONDON'S BURNING
St. Paul's Cathedral stands surrounded by smoke and fire after an air raid on London in December 1940 during the Blitz. As well as 40,000 killed, 50,000 civilians were injured in the bombings.

1914–PRESENT

1874–1965

WINSTON CHURCHILL

British war leader Winston Churchill was a soldier before he was a politician, seeing action against the Mahdi at Omdurman in 1898. His role in promoting the Gallipoli operation when First Lord of the Admiralty in World War I earned him a reputation as an impulsive adventurer lacking in judgment. During the 1930s, as a maverick Conservative MP, he led opposition to the policy of appeasement of Hitler and pressed for rapid rearmament. In 1939 he returned to control of the Admiralty and, despite bearing much of the responsibility for the debacle in Norway in 1940 (see p.298), became prime minister at the head of a coalition government just as the German invasion of France began. His defiant speeches helped to rally the British people behind a policy of "no surrender" through the most difficult days of the war. In July 1945 he was evicted from office by British voters just months after victory in Europe.

WAR IN THE MEDITERRANEAN

ITALY'S ENTRY INTO THE WAR in June 1940 turned the Mediterranean into a theater of conflict. Defeats for the Italians—by the British in North Africa and the Greeks in Albania—drew German forces into the region. In the end, Germany paid heavily for its commitment to the desert war in North Africa, but when the Allies invaded Italy it failed utterly to prove itself the "soft underbelly" of Europe that Churchill had hoped. When Italy surrendered to the Allies in 1943, the Germans continued a vigorous resistance on the Italian peninsula.

THE BATTLE FOR CRETE
Crete

DATE
May 20–June 1, 1941

FORCES Allies: 42,500; Axis: 22,000 men, 600 Ju-52 transports, 80 gliders

LOCATION
Crete, eastern Mediterranean

CASUALTIES Allies: 2,000 killed, 12,000 prisoner; Axis: 4,000 killed

In April 1941 German forces overran Yugoslavia and Greece. Allied troops—mostly from Australia and New Zealand—were evacuated to Crete. German general Kurt Student devised an airborne operation to seize the island, but the Allies knew, from Enigma codebreakers (see p.305), every detail of his plans. As the Seventh Airborne Division dropped on May 20, the Germans suffered more than 50 percent casualties. But Allied forces were poorly equipped, with no air cover. They mistakenly let the Germans take control of an airstrip at Maleme, allowing elite mountain troops with heavy equipment to land. The Royal Navy evacuated about half the Allied force via the port of Sphakia.

BEFORE THE DROP
German paratroopers fly toward Crete. The death rate suffered in the jump, and by German glider troops, was so high that Hitler banned further large-scale airborne operations for the rest of the war.

THE NORTH AFRICAN CAMPAIGN
Gazala

DATE
May 26–June 21, 1942

FORCES
Axis: 110,000 men, 560 tanks; Allies: 125,000 men, 850 tanks

LOCATION
Western Desert, Libya

CASUALTIES
Axis: 60,000; Allies: 88,000

German general Erwin Rommel's Afrika Korps and their Italian allies engaged in a struggle for control of North Africa that swayed back and forth across the Western Desert. In the spring of 1942 the British were holding a defensive line stretching south from Gazala, near Tobruk. Rommel decided to lead his tanks around the southern end of the line and drive up to the coast, cutting the British Eighth Army off from the rear. At first this bold maneuver went badly, newly delivered Grant tanks taking a heavy toll of Rommel's armor. The German tanks were trapped on the eastern side of the British line, with British minefields behind them and tanks in front of them. But a screen of German 88mm antitank guns prevented British armor from coming in for the kill. With consummate skill, Rommel broke the stranglehold and turned the tables, driving the British back into Egypt. The Germans advanced to the key port of Tobruk and took it in a day, capturing 33,000 prisoners.

THE NORTH AFRICAN CAMPAIGN
El Alamein

DATE October 23–November 4, 1942

FORCES Axis: 104,000 men, 489 tanks; Allies: 195,000 men, 1,029 tanks

LOCATION 60 miles (100km) west of Alexandria, Egypt

CASUALTIES Axis: 25,000 and 30,000 prisoner; Allies: 14,400

By July 1942 Rommel's Panzerarmee Afrika had driven the British Eighth Army deep inside Egypt and was threatening the naval base at Alexandria and the Suez Canal. The advance was halted at a defensive line stretching from El Alamein south to the impassable Qattara Depression. Despite holding this line, General Claude Auchinleck was dismissed as Eighth Army commander and replaced by General Bernard Montgomery. The new commander set about building up his forces for a major offensive. Composed of British, Australian, New Zealand, Indian, South African, and Free French formations, the Eighth Army faced a formidable enemy position consisting of extensive minefields defended by infantry and antitank guns, with panzer divisions held in the rear. The German forces had serious supply problems, however, and Rommel himself was ill.

Montgomery planned a frontal offensive closer in spirit to World War I than to Blitzkrieg. An artillery barrage would prepare the way for infantry to advance through the minefields, clearing a path along which tanks would follow. Montgomery intended it to be "a killing match" rather than the "tip-and-run" mobile warfare at which Rommel excelled. Resisting pressure from Churchill for haste, Montgomery set the offensive for the night of October 23. At 9:40 p.m. some 600 guns opened up in the largest preparatory bombardment since 1918, switching to a creeping barrage as infantry advanced into the minefields with bayonets fixed. Sappers worked to clear antitank mines and mark taped corridors for the armor to follow. The fighting was bloody, confused, and inconclusive. As the offensive became bogged down, Montgomery struggled to persuade his tank commanders to advance through uncleared minefields. On October 27, with Rommel back, the Germans launched an

GEORGE CROSS
This is Britain's highest medal for bravery not under enemy fire. Two seamen got it after El Alamein for recovering vital codes from a U-boat.

DESERT SURRENDER
Gripping images such as this surrender of a German tank crew were achieved by reenacting El Alamein battle scenes shortly after the event for the cameras—an effective contribution to Allied propaganda.

1891–1944

ERWIN ROMMEL

Rommel first commanded tanks in May 1940 during the invasion of France. He took to the role with such flair that he was chosen to lead the Afrika Korps the following year. His desert victories made him a legend—Churchill praised him as "a daring and skillful opponent." In command of Normandy at the time of D-Day, he was badly wounded when an RAF fighter strafed his car. In October 1944, he committed suicide to avoid trial in connection with the plot to assassinate Hitler.

Invasion of Sicily

DATE
July 10–August 17, 1943

FORCES
Allies: 180,000;
Axis: 260,000

LOCATION
Sicily, Italy

CASUALTIES
Allies: 16,000;
Axis: 160,000
(including prisoners)

After the surrender of the remaining Axis forces in North Africa in May 1943, the Allies set their sights on crossing to Sicily, from where they intended to launch an invasion of the Italian mainland. Around 3,000 ships were assembled for the operation, codenamed *Husky*. General George

AMPHIBIOUS LANDINGS
The landings in Sicily revealed the Allies' skill at seaborne operations, which would be crucial to the invasion of Normandy.

Patton's US Seventh Army was to take the west of the island, while Montgomery's British Eighth Army took the east. The weather was bad on invasion day, with high winds and rough seas. Airborne landings went badly, and many troops in gliders drowned. Amphibious landings generally went well, however. The island's defenses were well managed by Field Marshal Albert Kesselring, who escaped with 100,000 Axis troops from Messina to mainland Italy. Allied commanders were distracted by an unseemly race to reach Messina first—a contest won by Patton.

Monte Cassino

DATE January 17–
May 18, 1944

FORCES
Allies: 670,000;
Axis: 360,000

LOCATION
75 miles (120km) south
of Rome, Italy

CASUALTIES
Allies: 105,000;
Axis: 80,000

The Allied invasion of mainland Italy in September 1943 was followed by a grim fight northward up the Italian peninsula, contested by the Germans at every point (Italy itself having surrendered). The strongest German defensive position was the fortified Gustav Line, which at its western end ran along a ridge on which stood the historic monastery of Monte Cassino. Despite Allied landings at Anzio, behind the Gustav Line, in January 1944, the defense continued to hold. On February 15, 1944, the monastery was destroyed in a raid by Allied bombers. Despite this, New Zealand troops failed in an assault on the ridge over the following days. It was eventually taken the following May in a costly assault by Polish troops under General Anders.

RUINED MONASTERY
The remains of the monastery of Monte Cassino after the war had moved on in May 1944. The decision to bomb the monastery has remained a controversial one.

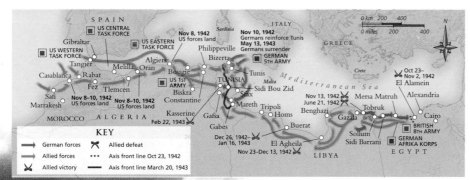

KEY

→ German forces	✕ Allied defeat
→ Allied forces	···· Axis front line Oct 23, 1942
✕ Allied victory	— Axis front line March 20, 1943

armored counteroffensive. It was a costly failure, halted by British artillery and air support. Montgomery launched a fresh offensive on the night of November 1–2, when New Zealand troops succeeded in clearing a corridor for the tanks. A brutal series of engagements followed as British armored divisions drove forward into artillery fire and counterattacks by German panzers. Realizing that the British were "gradually battering us out of our position by sheer brute force," on November 4, Rommel ordered a full retreat. Through bad judgment and bad luck the Eighth Army bungled the pursuit, letting most of Rommel's forces escape. But, combined with the Allied landings in French North Africa that followed, El Alamein effectively sealed the fate of Germany's North African adventure.

BERNARD LAW MONTGOMERY

Montgomery was put in charge of the Eighth Army in August 1942 after Gott, the first choice, died in a plane crash. He skillfully restored morale, while his insistence on heavy reinforcements before taking the offensive thoroughly paid off. Commanding Allied land forces in the Normandy invasion, he showed the same taste for a methodical application of force. However, his relations with American generals, including Eisenhower, were poor, and his belief that the war could be won with a Ruhr offensive led to a disastrously risky airborne operation at Arnhem in fall 1944.

WAR AT SEA

COMMAND OF THE SEAS WAS ESSENTIAL to the Allied war effort in the European theater. Without it the Atlantic supply line to Britain would have been cut and crucial operations—from the evacuation of Dunkirk to the Normandy invasion—could not have taken place. Despite some spectacular operations by German surface vessels, Allied naval dominance was contested more effectively by mines and submarines. This came close to throttling the Allied war effort, just as had been the case in World War I. Where they had sufficient range, the Luftwaffe's land-based aircraft constituted the most intractable menace to the British Royal Navy, the carrier aircraft of which achieved some spectacular offensive successes, but were unable to provide effective fleet air defense.

WAR AT SEA
River Plate

DATE
December 13, 1939

FORCES Axis: Pocket battleship *Graf Spee*; Allies: 1 heavy cruiser, 2 light cruisers

LOCATION Off mouth of Rio de la Plata, between Uruguay and Argentina

CASUALTIES Axis: *Graf Spee* scuttled; Allies: 1 ship disabled, 2 badly damaged

In the first months of the war the German pocket battleship *Graf Spee*, under Captain Hans Langsdorff, roamed the South Atlantic, preying upon Allied merchant shipping. The surface raider was tracked down by a Royal Navy cruiser squadron led by Commodore Henry Harwood. The heavy cruiser *Exeter* and the light cruisers *Ajax* and *Achilles* had no armament to match the *Graf Spee's* 11-in guns, but nonetheless carried the fight to the Germans. After 80 minutes of fighting, the *Exeter* was a burning wreck, while both *Ajax* and *Achilles* had sustained severe damage. But the *Graf Spee* had also been hit and Langsdorff sought refuge in Montevideo harbor in neutral Uruguay. Four days later, wrongly convinced that he was trapped by superior British forces, he steamed to the mouth of the harbor and sank the *Graf Spee* with explosives.

SCUTTLED SHIP
The Graf Spee *is scuttled at the entrance to Montevideo harbor on December 17. Its commander, Captain Langsdorff, committed suicide three days later.*

WAR AT SEA
Sinking of the Bismarck

DATE
May 18–28, 1941

FORCES Axis: 1 heavy cruiser, 1 battleship; Allies: 2 aircraft carriers, 55 other ships

LOCATION
North Sea and North Atlantic

CASUALTIES Axis: 2,100 dead on *Bismarck*; Allies: 1,500 dead

In May 1941 the German battleship *Bismarck*, then the world's most powerful warship, slipped out of Gdynia, Poland, accompanied by the heavy cruiser *Prinz Eugen*. Its mission was to destroy Allied merchant shipping. The German ships were sighted in a Norwegian fjord by a British reconnaissance aircraft and were tracked to an area between Iceland and Greenland. There they were intercepted by the battleship *Prince of Wales* and the battle cruiser *Hood*. The *Bismarck's* accurate 15-in guns proved devastatingly effective. One shell penetrated the *Hood's* deck and blew it up—there were only three survivors. The *Prince of Wales* was also severely damaged. *Bismarck* separated from *Prinz Eugen* to head for a port in occupied France. The Royal Navy assembled all available forces to give chase. *Bismarck* was twice attacked by Swordfish biplanes. The second attack, delivered from *Ark Royal* on May 26, scored a hit that wrecked the

BISMARCK SURVIVORS
Some of the 110 survivors from the sinking of the Bismarck *are taken on board British cruiser* Dorsetshire.

Bismarck's steering mechanism. No longer able to escape its pursuers, trapped under fire from battleships *Rodney* and *King George V*, the blazing *Bismarck* was finally sunk by two torpedos from the cruiser *Dorsetshire*.

WAR AT SEA
Taranto

DATE
November 11, 1940

FORCES British: 21 aircraft; Italians: 6 battleships, 9 cruisers, 8 destroyers

LOCATION
Southern Italy

CASUALTIES British: 2 aircraft; Italians: 2 battleships, 1 cruiser

The British raid on Taranto was the first exclusively air–sea battle in history. The aircraft carrier *Illustrious* launched 21 Fairey Swordfish biplanes in a night attack on the Italian fleet in harbor. The first wave of 12 aircraft reached Taranto at around 11 p.m., and a follow-up wave attacked from the northwest an hour later. Although flares dropped by the aircraft to illuminate their targets also helped Italian gunners, only two of the slow-flying Swordfish were shot down. Torpedos released at low altitude struck three Italian battleships, while a cruiser was damaged by bombs. The raid was carefully studied by the Japanese before Pearl Harbor.

Battle of the Atlantic

DATE Peak period: August 1940–May 1943	
FORCES August 1940: 27 German U-boats; 1943: over 400 U-boats	
LOCATION North Atlantic	**CASUALTIES** Allies: 3,500 merchant ships, 175 warships; Germans: 783 submarines

The battle of the Atlantic was an attempt on a vast scale by Germany to blockade Britain, crippling its war effort. The battle began in earnest in the summer of 1940, after the fall of France. The German U-boat forces, commanded by Admiral Karl Dönitz, were then able to operate from bases on France's Atlantic coast. The British responded with a convoy system, with groups of merchant ships escorted by naval warships. Using sonar to detect submarines and depth charges to sink them, escort vessels succeeded in limiting losses of merchant shipping. After the United States entered the war in December 1941, Allied losses rose steeply. Operating just off the US coast, U-boats sank over 150,000 tons of shipping in one month. They could now refuel at sea, giving them almost limitless range. They were also growing in numbers, since Dönitz had won Hitler's backing for the submarine war. The U-boats reached the peak of effectiveness in March 1943, sinking 260,000 tons of Allied shipping. Then, with startling rapidity, the tide turned. In April and May U-boat losses were so heavy that they were withdrawn from the North Atlantic. The causes of this reversal included ocean patrols by Allied long-range B-24 Liberator and Sunderland aircraft, the use of escort carriers to provide convoys with their own air cover, and improved radar to spot submarines on the surface. But most importantly, decoded radio traffic allowed groups of frigates to attack U-boats where groups ("wolf packs") were forming. Thereafter, losses to U-boats were at a level that did not seriously threaten the Allied war effort.

ENIGMA MACHINE
The prime means of communication in World War II was the radio, so codes were vital to stop an enemy from listening in. With the aid of captured German Enigma encoding machines, the Allies deciphered enough German naval messages to make a vital difference to the submarine battles in the Atlantic.

GERMAN U-BOAT TACTICS

Around September 1940 German U-boats began to hunt in packs of 15 or 20 for maximum effect against convoys. The submarines would spread out across the sea lanes in the mid-Atlantic. When one of them located a convoy, it maintained contact while radioing headquarters with the news. Headquarters broadcast a homing signal which guided other U-boats on to their prey. Once assembled, they would track the convoy by day and attack at night, often penetrating the escort screen on the surface to savage the merchant shipping. If detected, they dived and took evasive action.

CRAMPED CONDITIONS
U-boats had a crew of around 50, who would be at sea for weeks at a time. Consequently, conditions on board could be horribly cramped.

SUBMARINE ATTACK
A German torpedo strikes a British merchant ship in 1941. Merchant seamen had one of the most unenviable jobs in the war, unable even to fight back against their attackers.

> "Stand by for the depth-charge attack! They are falling right alongside now. A roar and a crash in the control room enough to crack our eardrums."
>
> *Heinz Schaeffer, U-977—66 Days Underwater*

INVASION OF THE SOVIET UNION

THE CONFLICT INITIATED BY HITLER'S invasion of the Soviet Union in June 1941 was both a racial war waged by Germany upon Slavic peoples viewed by Nazi ideology as inferiors and a fight to the death between Europe's two most powerful dictatorships. Warfare took on an unsurpassed savagery. Hitler ordered the German army to conduct a "war of annihilation" against communists and Jews. The Soviet response was pitiless in its determination and ruthless expenditure of soldiers' lives. Hitler planned a short war—the last *blitzkrieg*—but the Soviets refused to give in when seemingly beaten. In the long haul they organized war production better than the Germans and found commanders who counterattacked with flair and won a string of victories.

GERMAN INVASION OF SOVIET UNION

Barbarossa

DATE June 22–September 1941	
FORCES Axis: 4 million men, 3,600 tanks; Soviets: 2.3 million men, 10,000 tanks	
LOCATION Western Soviet Union (modern Ukraine, Belarus, Russia)	**CASUALTIES** Axis: 400,000; Soviets: 1 million (plus 3 million taken prisoner)

The German invasion of the Soviet Union (Operation *Barbarossa*) was one of the largest military operations in history. Only a fifth of the immense force that Hitler assembled consisted of armored or motorized formations; there were 3,600 tanks assigned to the invasion but 700,000 horses. The invasion force was divided into three: Army Group North, striking toward Leningrad; Army Group Center, advancing on Smolensk and Moscow; and Army Group South, heading for Kiev, in the Ukraine. Soviet dictator Joseph Stalin had clear warnings of the invasion from intelligence sources but chose to ignore them. Soviet forces were badly deployed in forward positions, strung out along the length of the border. The German onslaught began early on the morning of June 22 with a massive artillery bombardment and air attacks on Soviet airfields. German panzer groups and motorized infantry swiftly enveloped Soviet forces in forward positions, trapping hundreds of thousands in pockets from which

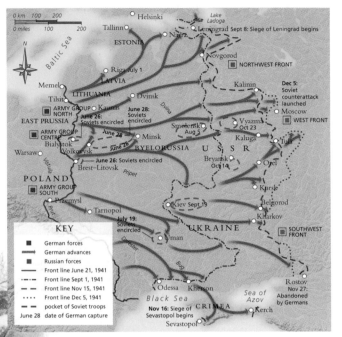

KEY

- German forces
- German advances
- Russian forces
- Front line June 21, 1941
- Front line Sept 1, 1941
- Front line Nov 15, 1941
- Front line Dec 5, 1941
- pocket of Soviet troops
- June 28 date of German capture

HITLER'S ALLIES
Romanian troops fight on the Eastern Front. Around 300,000 Romanians took part in Operation Barbarossa, alongside 250,000 Italians, and other allies of Germany.

there was no escape. These pincer movements continued as the Germans drove deep into Soviet territory, with around 300,000 Soviet troops captured in the Smolensk pocket in mid-July and over 600,000 at Kiev in September. Yet, despite these vast military disasters, Soviet resistance remained fierce. Hitler had envisaged total victory in three months; Barbarossa was falling far behind its timetable.

GERMAN INVASION OF SOVIET UNION

Moscow

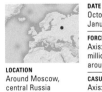

DATE October 2, 1941–January 7, 1942	
FORCES Axis: around 1.5 million; Soviets: around 1.5 million	
LOCATION Around Moscow, central Russia	**CASUALTIES** Axis: 250,000; Soviets: 700,000

In early October 1941 the Germans launched a belated drive to capture Moscow. It seemed for a time that the capital might be abandoned, but the Soviet leadership recovered its nerve and stiffened resistance. The German offensive ground forward, with much of October spent overcoming Soviet forces in the Vyazma–Bryansk pocket.

As fall rains turned dirt roads to mud, the German army literally bogged down. The onset of winter in mid-November froze the mud and the German advance regained momentum, but by then General Georgi Zhukov had organized a defensive line in front of Moscow. Advance German units reached the outskirts of the city on November 30, but their forces were in bad shape, having no winter clothing or equipment. Meanwhile, Zhukov prepared a counteroffensive. Attacking north and south of Moscow on December 5, fresh Soviet reserves struck the exhausted Germans, while airborne troops and partisans carried the fight behind the German lines. By early January the Germans had been driven back halfway to Smolensk.

WINTER WARFARE
In December 1941 alone around 133,000 German soldiers suffered from frostbite. They had not been given winter equipment because the Soviets were supposed to have been defeated by October.

Siege of Leningrad

DATE September 8, 1941–January 27, 1944

FORCES Axis: unknown; Soviets: 200,000 plus 3 million civilians

LOCATION Leningrad (now St. Petersburg), western Russia

CASUALTIES Axis: unknown; Soviets: around 800,000 dead

Leningrad was Germany's Army Group North's prime objective in Operation *Barbarossa*. As the Germans advanced from the south, the city was also threatened by the Finns, who occupied the Karelian peninsula. Leningraders

SIEGE CITY
Soviet armored vehicles patrol a Leningrad street. Street signs warned pedestrians which side to walk on to avoid German shellfire.

worked feverishly to construct lines of antitank defenses and Zhukov was sent to the city in August to galvanize resistance. Nonetheless, Leningrad would probably have fallen but for Hitler's preference for subjecting the city to a slow death by blockade. The city was surrounded by mid-September, under constant artillery fire and air attack, with inadequate reserves of food and fuel. In late November Lake Ladoga, to the east of Leningrad, froze over. An "Ice Road" was improvised over the frozen lake and through forests and swamps to bring at least minimal supplies into the city. Despite these heroic efforts, hundreds of thousands died of starvation and cold in the first winter of the siege. Supplies improved through 1942, using boats across the lake in the summer, and in January

1943 a combined offensive by Soviet troops inside and outside Leningrad opened up a land corridor to enable supply by road and rail. German forces remained in place on the southern edge of the city for another year before they were driven off in the general westward advance of Soviet forces.

TANKBUSTER
This Soviet 76mm antitank gun had a range of 14,200 yards (13,000m).

Shield to protect crew

Double baffle muzzle break

Kursk

DATE July 5–15, 1943

FORCES Axis: 900,000 men, 2,700 tanks; Soviets: 1.3 million men, 3,500 tanks

LOCATION Around Kursk, Ukraine

CASUALTIES Axis: 210,000; Soviet: 178,000

By the summer of 1943 rapid Soviet advances in the wake of Stalingrad (see p.308), followed by German counterattacks, had left a large Soviet salient bulging into German-held territory around Kursk. The Germans massed around two-thirds of their entire armored forces and aircraft on the Eastern Front for a pincer attack, intending to destroy all the Soviet

WAR WINNERS
Soviet T-34 tanks come under fire at Kursk. Heavily armed, reliable, and easy to manufacture, the T-34 made a vital contribution to winning the war.

forces in the salient. The attack on the northern sector would be made by Walther Model's Ninth Army while Erich von Manstein commanded the assault from the south. Soviet leaders were fully informed of the offensive by the Lucy spy ring in Switzerland. Zukhov prepared a defense in depth, with minefields, trenches, and antitank guns, backed up by massed tank formations. Intelligence from German prisoners told the Soviets the timing of the attack, so they opened the battle early on July 5 with a bombardment of the assembling German forces. The Soviet air force also launched a preemptive strike against Luftwaffe airfields, triggering air battles involving thousands of aircraft. Advancing into the Soviet defenses, the German army in the northern pincer stalled in the face of fire from antitank guns and

tankbusting aircraft. After a week, this arm of the offensive petered out. In the south, Hoth's Fourth Panzer Army did better, hammering a way through to Prokhorovka, 20 miles (30km) inside the Soviet defenses. Soviet reserves, the Fifth Guards Tank Army, were rushed forward. The two forces clashed on July 12. Around 800 Soviet T-34s streamed forward, seeking to close with the heavier German Tiger and Panther tanks and Ferdinand self-propelled guns, which were trying to pick off the Soviet tanks at long range. By the end of the day the Soviets had lost around 300 tanks, the Germans less than 100, but the Soviets could better afford the losses. Hitler called off the offensive and by July 15 the Soviets were pressing forward toward Kharkov, leaving behind the battlefield littered with burned-out tanks and charred bodies.

SOVIET MEDAL
The Order of the Red Star was instituted in 1930 for valor in defense of the Homeland. The image in its center shows a soldier with fixed bayonet.

GERMAN INVASION OF SOVIET UNION

Stalingrad

DATE September 1942–February 2, 1943

FORCES Axis: 500,000 (290,000 inside Stalingrad); Soviets: more than 1 million

LOCATION Stalingrad (now Volgograd) on Volga River, Russia

CASUALTIES Axis: 500,000; Soviets: 750,000

In late June 1942 German Army Group South launched an offensive in the Caucasus to capture the vital Baku oil fields and so cripple the Soviet war machine. At Hitler's insistence the offensive also struck at Stalingrad, a major industrial center on the Volga. While Army Group A advanced into the Caucasus, Army Group B, comprising Friedrich Paulus's Sixth Army and Hermann Hoth's Fourth Panzer Army, headed for Stalingrad.

The city's defense was entrusted to 62nd Army under General Vasili Chuikov, a young officer with no experience of wartime command. From September 13 the Germans attacked the Stalingrad perimeter with great ferocity, driving the Soviets back to an irregular strip along the west bank of the Volga. Soviet troops clung on, fighting for every building. Supplies and reinforcements were ferried across the Volga each night under German artillery fire. Half-destroyed apartment blocks and factory buildings—the Dzerzhinsky Tractor Works, the Red

TAKING AIM
A German soldier lines up a target in Stalingrad. Snipers on both sides took a particularly heavy toll on officers, necessitating a steady stream of replacements.

October Factory— were defended like fortresses. When the Germans got inside, fighting continued room by room and floor by floor. Hitler declared publicly that the Germans would never leave the city; Stalin ordered Stalingrad to be held at any price. A second push in October took the Germans to within 220yds (200m) of the Volga; in November they reached the riverbank. But still the Soviets

fought on in pockets of resistance, the two armies, in Chuikov's phrase, "gripping each other in a deadly clutch." Meanwhile, Zhukov viewed the massive German effort to take Stalingrad as an opportunity to encircle them. On November 19, he launched Operation *Uranus*, attacking in strength from north and south of Stalingrad, smashing through Italian, Romanian, and Hungarian troops on the German flanks. The Soviet pincers met on November 23, snapping shut a trap behind Paulus's Sixth Army. Instead of allowing the German forces inside Stalingrad to attempt a breakout, Hitler decided to keep them supplied by an airlift, a task that proved utterly beyond the Luftwaffe's capacity. Receiving no more than 10 percent of the supplies they needed, the Germans inside Stalingrad began slowly to starve. Fending off an attack by a German relief force, Zhukov's forces ground forward through

SHATTERED CITY
Soviet soldiers advance through the ruins of Stalingrad to reinforce "Pavlov's House," a building held by Sergeant Jakob Pavlov of Forty-Second Guards Regiment with a handful of men.

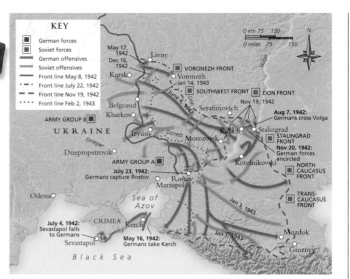

SNIPER RIFLE

Soviet sharpshooters used a 7.62mm Mosin-Nagant infantry rifle with a telescopic sight. Top sniper Vasili Zaitsev was credited with killing 149 Germans at Stalingrad.

Telescopic sight

December, tightening the noose around the city as freezing winter weather set in. No help came from Army Group A, which was forced by Soviet pressure to extricate itself from the Caucasus and withdraw some 160 miles (250km) to the west. Tortured by frostbite and malnutrition, through January 1943 the Germans were driven back into the center of Stalingrad, fighting on despite a desperate shortage of ammunition. On January 30 Hitler promoted Paulus to field marshal. That day, the German headquarters in Stalingrad was overrun and Paulus surrendered. All resistance ceased on February 2.

> "We have fought for 15 days for a single house....
> Already by the third day 54 German corpses are strewn in
> the cellars, on the landings and the staircases."
>
> *An officer of 24th Panzer Division, October 1942*

1914–PRESENT

BOMBER OFFENSIVE

THE BRITISH AND AMERICAN BOMBER OFFENSIVE in Europe was, according to Allied chiefs of staff, intended to achieve the "destruction and dislocation of the German military, industrial, and economic system, and the undermining of the morale of the German people." In daylight raids from 1942 to 1945 the USAAF's Eighth Air Force lost 26,000 killed; RAF Bomber Command's night bombing cost 56,000 lives—half of all aircrew who took part. But the Germans were forced to devote massive resources to home defense, including a third of their artillery and the cream of the Luftwaffe. German armed forces were deprived of essential supplies, especially fuel. And hundreds of thousands of German civilians died in their ruined cities.

BOMBER OFFENSIVE

Hamburg

DATE
July 24–August 3 1943

FORCES British: 791 bombers; American: 127 bombers

LOCATION
Hamburg, northern Germany

CASUALTIES
German: 50,000 civilians killed; Allied: 108 bombers lost

Britain's RAF adopted nighttime bombing because their aircraft could not survive over Germany in daylight. Incapable of hitting a target with any accuracy, they launched mass attacks with fleets of heavy bombers against cities, hoping the sheer scale of destruction would deliver a decisive blow. By contrast, the USAAF was committed to precision raids on industrial and military targets. The attacks on the port city of Hamburg in the summer of 1943 were a combined effort by the RAF at night and American B-17s by day. The Germans had developed a sophisticated system of defense against night bombing; radar operators on the ground tracked the bombers and guided night fighters on to their targets. Antiaircraft fire was also directed by radar. Over Hamburg the RAF deployed a new countermeasure known as "window." Bombers scattered strips of aluminum foil, which confused German radar, leaving the night fighters and flak guns blind. On the night of July 27–28, 735 British bombers dropped 2,326 tons of explosives and incendiaries in just over an hour.

Aided by the weather conditions, this intensive bombardment generated a firestorm that swept through the city, killing an estimated 46,000 people.

> "In spite of all that happened at Hamburg, bombing proved a comparatively humane method. For one thing, it saved the youth of this country and of our allies from being mown down by the military as it was in the war of 1914–1918."

WITNESS TO WAR

AIR MARSHAL SIR ARTHUR HARRIS

Head of RAF Bomber Command from 1942 to the end of the war in Europe, Harris was an unwavering advocate of the bombing of enemy cities. He believed that his bombers could have won the war outright if they had been given the resources with which to conduct raids on a large enough scale.

DAYLIGHT RAIDERS
USAAF B-17 Flying Fortresses drop bombs over Germany. The Americans were tasked with precision bombing, but poor visibility affected accuracy.

BOMBER OFFENSIVE

Dambusters

DATE May 16–17, 1943

FORCES British: 19 Lancaster bombers, 133 aircrew

LOCATION
Ruhr, northern Germany

CASUALTIES British: 8 bombers lost, 53 aircrew killed, 3 taken prisoner; German: 1,200 drowned

British scientist Dr. Barnes Wallis devised a way of breaching dams in the Ruhr, Germany's industrial heartland. He created a "bouncing bomb" that would skip across the water, hopping over an antitorpedo barrier, and sink straight down after hitting the dam, detonating underwater against the concrete wall. Lancaster bombers were adapted to carry the special bombs under their fuselage. The RAF created an elite force, 617 Squadron, specifically for the mission. They had to release the bombs at a precise altitude and distance from the dams while flying through dense antiaircraft

BREACHED DAM
The Möhne dam shows a gaping cavity after the Lancaster bombing raid. An official German report described the aftermath as "a dark picture of destruction."

fire. Led by wing commander Guy Gibson, they attacked by night and breached the Möhne and Eder dams and damaged two others.

BOMBER OFFENSIVE

Schweinfurt

DATE
August 17, 1943

FORCES American: 376 bombers; German: 250 fighters

LOCATION
Bavaria, southern Germany

CASUALTIES American: 167 bombers, 482 aircrew; German: 27 aircraft

Dedicated to attacking German war industries, the USAAF decided to bomb a ball-bearing factory at Schweinfurt and an aircraft factory at Regensburg. These two missions were combined in the hope of overstretching German air defenses. The targets were deep inside Germany, far beyond the range of US escort fighters. The Regensburg force, equipped with extra fuel tanks, was to fly on to North Africa after the bombing; the Schweinfurt bombers had to make it back to their bases in eastern England. As soon as the glistening fleets of B-17s crossed into Germany, Messerschmitt 109s and Focke-Wulf 190s swarmed to attack them. The bombers took heavy punishment before reaching their targets and then were expected to fly a steady course through flak to achieve an accurate drop. Not surprisingly, many went far astray, even bombing open countryside. The Schweinfurt target, masked by a smokescreen, was virtually undamaged. By the time survivors limped in to land in North Africa or East Anglia, over a quarter of the original bomber force had been lost.

BLACKOUT
A German poster tells citizens that "the enemy sees your light" as bombers swoop overhead.

Berlin and Big Week

DATE
November 18, 1943–
March 25, 1944

FORCES
Berlin: 900 RAF
bombers; Big Week:
1,000 USAAF bombers

LOCATION
Germany

CASUALTIES
No reliable estimates

In the winter of 1943–44 the RAF launched 16 mass night raids on Berlin, accompanied by diversionary raids on other cities, driven by the belief that destruction of the capital would force a German surrender. General Carl Spaatz refused to devote the USAAF's bombers to the Berlin offensive, instead preparing attacks on specific sectors of the German war economy, culminating in the mass daylight raids of Big Week. Both air forces were hampered by bad weather, but otherwise the Americans were the more successful. The accuracy of British raids had improved through using De Havilland Mosquitos as "pathfinder" aircraft, but the Americans now had fighter escorts; the Mustangs not only enabled the bombers to do their job, but also shot down large numbers of German day fighters.

> "We can wreck Berlin from end to end if the USAAF will come in on it. It will cost us between 400 and 500 aircraft. It will cost Germany the war."
>
> *Sir Arthur Harris*, in a letter to Churchill, **November 1943**

MUSTANG FIGHTER
The North American P-51 Mustang was a high-performance long-range fighter that for the first time gave Allied bombers effective escort to targets deep inside Germany.

Ploesti

DATE
April–August 1944

FORCES
Raids by over 1,000
USAAF bombers

LOCATION
Ploesti, Romania

CASUALTIES
Total losses: 305
USAAF bombers and
3,000 air crew

In summer 1944 Allied air forces made a concerted attempt to destroy German oil supplies. The most important target was the Ploesti oil field, Germany's largest single source of oil. Over a five-month period the US Fifteenth Army Air Force's B-24 Liberators carried out 24 raids on Ploesti, flying out of bases in Italy. The oil fields were heavily defended and bomber losses were high, but large areas of Ploesti blazed through the summer, and by mid-August oil production had ceased.

Dresden

DATE
February 13–14, 1945

FORCES RAF: 796
Lancasters and 9
Mosquitos; USAAF:
311 B-17s

LOCATION Dresden,
Saxony, southeast
Germany

CASUALTIES 30,000–
60,000 civilians;
9 Lancaster bombers

By early 1945 the loss of fighter aircraft in air combat and shortages of fuel had eroded Germany's ability to defend its airspace. Much artillery had been diverted from antiaircraft duties to the defense of Germany's borders. At the end of January 1945 the Allies decided to attack communications centers in eastern Germany, where the German army was retreating in the face of advancing Soviet forces. Dresden was on a list of cities where, a British memo stated, "a severe blitz will not only cause confusion in the evacuation from the East but will also hamper the movement of [German] troops from the West." In February 1945 Dresden was an overcrowded city, its prewar population of 650,000 swollen to over a million by an influx of refugees, German soldiers, Allied prisoners of war, and foreign slave laborers. It had previously been the target of only two relatively small raids by the USAAF. On the night of February 13–14, the RAF attacked in two waves, 244 aircraft bombing at low level at around 10:15 p.m. and the main force of 529 aircraft following up at 1:30 a.m. The mix of incendiaries and high explosives created a vast firestorm, as it had at Hamburg, gutting much of the city and burning or asphyxiating every individual in its path. The USAAF followed up with a daylight raid on the 14th, but by then they were bombing ruins.

RUINED CITY
The decision to bomb Dresden was widely criticized on the grounds that it was not a military target and that the war was in any case already virtually won.

NORDEN BOMBSIGHT
The USAAF's sophisticated Norden bombsight allowed an experienced bombardier to achieve accurate bombing as long as visibility was good and enemy flak was not too furious.

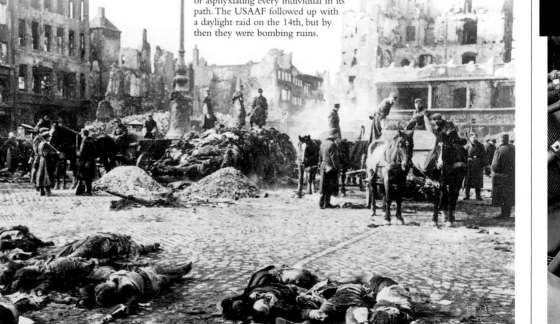

BOEING B-17 FLYING FORTRESS

A SLEEK FOUR-ENGINED BOMBER, THE BOEING B-17 WAS THE PRINCIPAL AIRCRAFT USED BY THE USAAF IN ITS WORLD WAR II BOMBING CAMPAIGN IN EUROPE.

The B-17 was a complex war machine that required 10 men to operate; a pilot, co-pilot, navigator, radio operator, bombardier, flight engineer, and four gunners. It was bristling with guns (hence the "Flying Fortress" soubriquet), capable of flying at high altitude, and had a maximum speed of nearly 300mph (500kmh).

BOMB RUN
The risk of being hit by a bomb from another B-17 above was one of the hazards of combat.

These features were expected to make it capable of carrying out daytime missions without fighter escort. The B-17s flew in a tight pattern calculated to make their guns give mutually supporting fire against enemy fighters while avoiding shooting one another. Nonetheless, in practice the bombers suffered heavy losses to German fighters whenever their missions were unescorted. Flak also took its toll. The Norden bombsight, with which B-17s were equipped, took over control of the aircraft in the final stage of the bomb run, giving a good chance of an accurate drop in good visibility, but allowing no evasion of enemy fire. Flying in a B-17 at high altitude was not a comfortable experience. The aircraft was not pressurized and it was freezing cold. The rear gun turret could only be reached on all-fours, but the most uncomfortable position was that of the ball-turret gunner, sitting in his bubble underneath the fuselage with his knees drawn almost up to his chest. Yet the B-17 was a popular aircraft with its crews, who respected it as a sturdy, reliable machine that could take a lot of punishment and still get safely home. In addition to its bombload, it was equipped with 13 Browning machine guns.

Rudder

12448

Tail gun turret

PROPELLORS *Measuring 11ft 6in (3.5m) in diameter, the propellors enabled the plane to fly at 30,000ft (9,000m). They were attached to four 1,200hp radial engines.*

TURBO ENGINES *A turbo supercharger system allowed the engines to run at full power between 20,000 and 30,000ft (6,000 and 9,000m).*

BOMBS *The B-17 could transport a bombload of up to 6,000lb (2,724kg) for a distance of approximately 2,000 miles (3,200km). Each bomb was marked with two yellow stripes at both ends; this indicated that it contained TNT.*

SPECIFICATION

Origin United States	**Wingspan** 103ft 9in (31.6m)
Top Speed 302mph (486kph)	**Length** 74ft 4in (22.7m)
Date of Launch 1941	**Weight** 36,135lb (16,391kg)

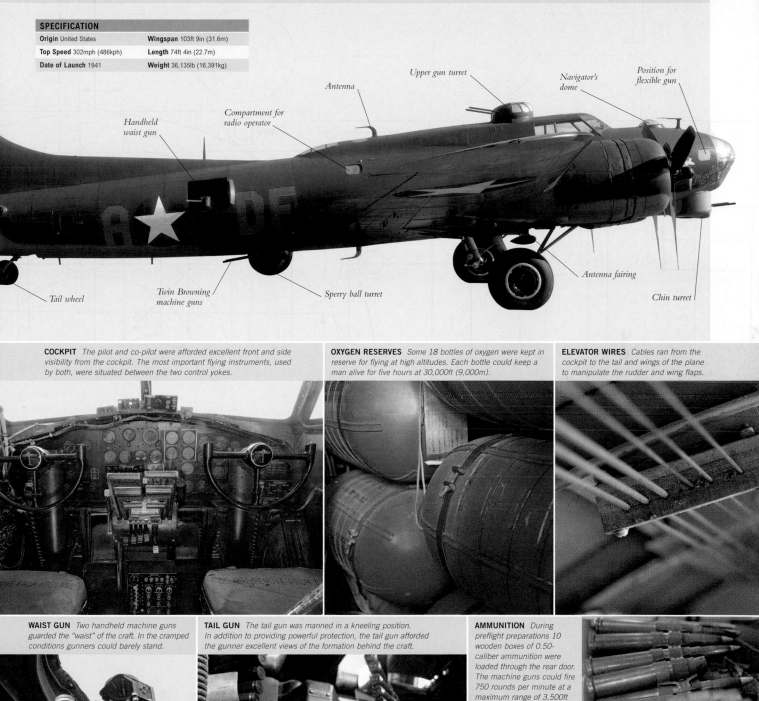

Antenna

Compartment for radio operator

Upper gun turret

Navigator's dome

Position for flexible gun

Handheld waist gun

Antenna fairing

Tail wheel

Twin Browning machine guns

Sperry ball turret

Chin turret

COCKPIT *The pilot and co-pilot were afforded excellent front and side visibility from the cockpit. The most important flying instruments, used by both, were situated between the two control yokes.*

OXYGEN RESERVES *Some 18 bottles of oxygen were kept in reserve for flying at high altitudes. Each bottle could keep a man alive for five hours at 30,000ft (9,000m).*

ELEVATOR WIRES *Cables ran from the cockpit to the tail and wings of the plane to manipulate the rudder and wing flaps.*

WAIST GUN *Two handheld machine guns guarded the "waist" of the craft. In the cramped conditions gunners could barely stand.*

TAIL GUN *The tail gun was manned in a kneeling position. In addition to providing powerful protection, the tail gun afforded the gunner excellent views of the formation behind the craft.*

AMMUNITION *During preflight preparations 10 wooden boxes of 0.50-caliber ammunition were loaded through the rear door. The machine guns could fire 750 rounds per minute at a maximum range of 3,500ft (1,060m). Each magazine contained 365 rounds.*

OPERATION OVERLORD

D-Day

DATE June 6, 1944

FORCES Invasion force: 154,000 men, 6,500 ships, 13,000 aircraft; German: unknown

LOCATION Coast of Normandy, northern France

CASUALTIES Allies: 4,500 killed (2,500 American); German: unknown

The Allies planned the invasion of northern Europe, Operation Overlord, for May 1944. They selected five beaches in Normandy as the landing point while mounting an elaborate deception operation to make the Germans believe the blow would fall farther east on the Pas de Calais. Eisenhower was appointed Allied supreme commander, with Montgomery as commander of land forces. Montgomery's insistence on increasing the number of troops and landing craft devoted to the operation forced a postponement to June 5. Everything was ready for that date except the weather; a gale blew up and the invasion had to be halted. Faced with an uncertain weather forecast for the following day, Eisenhower made the brave decison to go ahead regardless. The vast armada of landing craft set off across the Channel in the middle of the night while American and British airborne troops ahead of them carried out parachute and glider landings, with mixed success, inland from the invasion beaches. The German defenses on the Normandy coast were only partially complete and manned mostly by second-rate troops. The defenders were

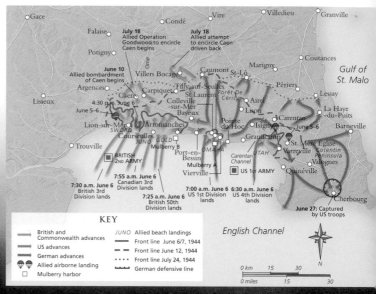

KEY

	British and Commonwealth advances	**JUNO**	Allied beach landings
	US advances		Front line June 6/7, 1944
	German advances		Front line June 12, 1944
	Allied airborne landing		Front line July 24, 1944
	Mulberry harbor		German defensive line

> ## "The beach was strewn with wreckage, a blazing tank, bundles of blankets and kit, bodies and bits of bodies. One bloke near me was blown in half by a shell…"
>
> *British Gunner Charles Wilson*, Gold Beach, June 6, 1944

taken totally by surprise when Allied warships opened fire on the coastal fortifications. Although troops of 12 nationalities took part, the invasion force was primarily American, British, and Canadian. The bad weather had caused a higher tide than usual, creating unexpected problems getting ashore—

OPERATION OVERLORD

The Allied invasion of France was the largest shore-to-shore invasion in history; eight divisions were suppported by 6,500 ships and 12,000 aircraft. Artificial "Mulberry" harbors were floated across the Channel.

many heavily laden soldiers sank without trace exiting their landing craft in too-deep water. Nonetheless, the American landing at Utah beach and the British and Canadian landings on Sword, Juno, and Gold went more or less to plan. The American landing at Omaha beach did not. Most of the Americans' tanks and artillery sank without reaching shore. Lightly equipped infantry were pinned on the beach under fire from concrete bunkers on the cliffs above. By the end of a long day the Americans had fought their way off the beach, but at heavy cost.

1890–1969

DWIGHT D. EISENHOWER

In 1942 Eisenhower was appointed commander of US forces in Europe over the heads of hundreds of more senior officers. He acquitted himself well during the Allied invasions of North Africa, Sicily, and mainland Italy in 1942–43, justifying his selection as supreme commander for the Normandy invasion. He showed fine diplomatic skills, although his decision to advance into Germany on a broad front was hotly contested by Montgomery. Eisenhower never shirked responsibility for decisions he made, however, and deservedly received much of the credit for Germany's defeat. After the war he was NATO's first commander-in-chief and president of the United States from 1953 to 1961.

GERMANY DEFEATED IN THE WEST

THE FAILURE OF AN ATTEMPT to assassinate Hitler in the wake of the D-Day landings ensured that the war would have to be fought to a finish. Once the Allies had broken out of Normandy they rapidly liberated most of France and Belgium, and hopes were high for victory before Christmas. But Allied supply lines were stretched to the limit and German resistance once more stiffened. There were delays in bringing Antwerp into use as a supply port and Montgomery's attempted breakthrough at Arnhem failed. Hitler's winter counterattack in the Ardennes gave the Allies a nasty shock, but the balance of forces meant the Germans had no realistic chance of avoiding defeat in 1945. On the Western Front, at least, the end of the war was near.

ALLIED INVASION OF FRANCE

Normandy

DATE June 6– July 25, 1944

FORCES Allied: 2 million; German: 1 million

CASUALTIES Allied: 40,000 killed, 170,000 wounded; German: 240,000 killed or wounded

LOCATION Normandy, northern France

The D-Day landings were followed by a tough battle to break out of the Normandy beachhead. The British and Canadians were stuck short of Caen while the Americans struggled up the Cotentin peninsula toward Cherbourg. The balance of the battle shifted inexorably in favor of the Allies because they were more capable of reinforcing their position.

TAKING COVER
The fighting in Normandy was a hard slog in which small gains were dearly bought. The woody terrain favored the defense.

Mulberry floating harbors handled a continuous flow of men and supplies from England. The Germans, by contrast, had great difficulty bringing up troops and armor along a bomb-damaged transport network under constant Allied air attack. After a failed attempt to outflank Caen to the west in the last week of June, Montgomery threw forward three armored divisions west of the city in Operation Goodwood on July 18 while Caen was flattened by heavy bombers. Goodwood was costly and failed to produce a breakout, but it did pin substantial German forces, helping the Americans break through toward Avranches in the last week of July.

ALLIED INVASION OF FRANCE

Falaise

DATE July 25– August 20, 1944

FORCES German: 250,000; Allied: unknown

CASUALTIES German: 100,000 killed or wounded; Allied: 40,000 killed or wounded

LOCATION Southern Normandy

On July 25 US Twelfth Army Group launched an offensive west of St.-Lô that turned into the long-awaited breakout from Normandy. Patton's US Third Army debouched into open country and turned east, intending to link up with British and Canadians advancing from Caen and trap German forces in a pocket south of Falaise. Instead of allowing a withdrawal to the Seine, Hitler ordered a counteroffensive on August 7. This only carried more tanks deeper into encirclement. Over the following days attacks by Allied aircraft pulverized German panzers and trucks. Though 100,000 German troops escaped, their losses were shattering.

OPERATION MARKET GARDEN

Arnhem

DATE September 17–26, 1944

FORCES Allied: 30,000 airborne troops

CASUALTIES British: 6,800; American: 4,000; Polish: 400; German: 3,300

LOCATION Southeastern Netherlands

Montgomery was convinced that a concentrated thrust into the Ruhr, under his command, would win the war. Denied the full resources he wanted by Eisenhower, who was committed to a "broad front" approach, "Monty" devised Operation Market Garden. Airborne forces were to seize a series of bridges in the German-occupied Netherlands, opening the way for British XXX Corps to push rapidly into northern Germany. On September 17 three airborne divisions were dropped by parachute and glider. US 101st captured canal crossings at Eindhoven, but US 82nd initially failed to take the bridge at Nijmegen, which was only taken after fierce fighting the next day. British 1st Airborne, dropped outside Arnhem, could not take the vital final bridge over the Rhine and were counterattacked by SS panzer divisions. Around 2,700 paratroops were withdrawn from Arnhem across the Rhine on the night of September 25–26. The rest of the survivors surrendered. It had been, in the famous phrase, "a bridge too far."

30-round magazine

BREN GUN
This British light machine-gun weighed just 22lb (10kg), giving it potential for use by airborne forces.

BRITISH PARATROOPERS
Soldiers of 1st British Airborne advance with Sten guns through Oosterbeek, a suburb of Arnhem. More than 7,000 troops were killed or taken prisoner.

ARDENNES COUNTEROFFENSIVE

Bulge

DATE December 16, 1944–January 15, 1945

FORCES American: 80,000; German: 200,000

CASUALTIES Allied: 80,000 (including prisoners); German: 70,000–100,000 (including prisoners)

LOCATION Ardennes, southern Belgium

In winter 1944 Hitler gambled on a counteroffensive in a last desperate attempt to turn the war around. It was intended as a repetition of the great German success of 1940, with tanks emerging unexpectedly from the Ardennes, punching holes in a weak sector of the Allied line. Launched on December 16, the offensive achieved complete surprise. Bad weather prevented the Allies from using their airpower, but troops of US 1st Army fought courageously to slow German progress. Sepp Dietrich's SS panzer divisions soon ran out of steam, but farther south Erich von Manteuffel's Fifth Panzer Army swept around Bastogne toward the Meuse. On December 22 the weather cleared and Allied aircraft hammered German forces that were already running out of fuel. Patton's Third Army reached Bastogne on December 26, where heavy fighting continued into the new year. The failed offensive cost both sides dearly, but the Allies could afford the losses, while the Germans could not.

GERMANS SURRENDER
US troops guard German prisoners at Malmedy, Belgium, in December 1944. Malmedy was the site of a German massacre of Allied prisoners earlier in the month.

ALLIED INVASION OF GERMANY

Rhineland

DATE February 8–March 28, 1945

FORCES Allied: 1.25 million; German: 150,000

CASUALTIES German: 60,000, plus 250,000 prisoners; Allied: 22,000

LOCATION Western Germany

In the spring of 1945 the Allies had to fight their way through to the Rhine and then across the river itself into the heart of Germany. In the north, British, Canadian, and American troops under Montgomery had a hard fight forward in atrocious February weather. The Germans released the water from the Schwammenauel dam, blocking all progress at the southern end of this sector for two weeks.

RHINE CROSSING
A tank of US 2nd Armored Cavalry crosses a pontoon bridge over the Rhine at Darmstadt. The 1,050ft (320m) bridge was built in 5 hours and 55 minutes.

Farther south, forces under US command were eager to show they could do better than Montgomery. Patton sent the armored spearheads of his US Third Army to batter a way through the Eiffel region and reach the Rhine on March 7. On the same day part of US Ninth Armored Division found an intact bridge over the Rhine at Remagen, which they boldly seized before it could be blown up. This bridgehead was only

> "Thousands of white parachutes dropped through an inferno of flak, while Dakotas crashed in flames..."
>
> *US Pilot Pierre Clostermann,* airborne assault on the Rhine, March 24, 1945

grudgingly exploited, as Montgomery methodically prepared a massive Rhine crossing farther north at Wesel. Patton upstaged Montgomery with a daring amphibious crossing, without air or artillery support, on March 22. Montgomery's sledgehammer blow was delivered the following day. With a series of bridgeheads established on the east bank, by the end of March the German position was indefensible.

1885–1945

GEORGE S. PATTON

Charismatic and headstrong, General Patton embodied the aggressive spirit of mobile tank warfare. He was relieved of command after striking a shell-shocked soldier when leading the US Seventh Army in Sicily in 1943 but reemerged as commander of the US Third Army in the breakout from Normandy. Always at odds with Montgomery, he went his own way in the last stages of the war, ending up deep inside Czechoslovakia. In 1945 he was killed in a car accident in Germany.

1914–PRESENT

GERMANY DEFEATED IN THE EAST

IN THE FINAL STAGES OF THE WAR Soviet forces, well supplied by their ever-expanding war industries and by deliveries from the United States, were getting stronger all the time. From June 1944 the Germans had to divide their resources between the Eastern and Western Fronts, as well as fighting in Italy and defending their cities against air attack. Despite mutual suspicions, no major fissure opened up between the Western Allies and the Soviet Union that the Germans might have exploited. After years on different sides, when Soviet and American troops met on the Elbe River in central Germany on April 25, 1945, it was as friends. Fearful of Soviet vengeance, the Germans fought for Hitler to the end.

EASTERN FRONT

Operation Bagration

DATE
June 23–July 28, 1944

FORCES Soviet: 1.7 million men, 2,700 tanks; German: 800,000 men, 450 tanks

LOCATION
Belorussia

CASUALTIES
Soviet: 178,000;
German: 350,000

By the summer of 1944 Germany and its allies had suffered around five million casualties in three years of fighting on the Eastern Front. The Red Army now prepared to drive German forces off Soviet soil. Three army groups, or "fronts," were to attack north and south of the Pripet Marshes, aiming to catch the German Army Group Center in their pincers. They would then clear the Germans out of Belorussia and advance into Poland. The offensive struck simultaneously on six axes along a 620-mile- (1,000km-) front, crushing understrength German formations. Using maximum speed and aggression the Soviet armies repeatedly cut off and annihilated Germans committed to static defense by orders from Hitler for "no retreat." In the rear, around 250,000 Soviet partisans mopped up German remnants and cut supply lines. The Third Belorussian Front from the north and the First Belorussian Front from the south met at the city of Minsk on July 3, trapping a large part of German 4th and 9th armies to the east. Pressing on through the rest of July, the First Belorussian Front reached the Vistula River at the end of the month. Germany had suffered a catastrophic defeat.

STALIN ORGANS
Katyusha multiple rocket launchers, known as "Stalin Organs," could deliver a salvo of 4 tons of explosives. The Germans feared them more than conventional artillery.

EASTERN FRONT

Warsaw Uprising

DATE August 1–2, October 1944

FORCES Polish Home Army: 20,000–40,000; German garrison in Warsaw: 10,000

LOCATION
Warsaw, Poland

CASUALTIES Polish Home Army: 50,000; civilians: 220,000

On August 1, 1944, with the Soviet First Belorussian Front approaching Warsaw, the Polish Home Army mounted an armed uprising against the German occupation forces. Led by General Tadeusz

POLISH CROSS
This cross was awarded to servicemen who displayed exemplary courage in battle.

Bor-Komorowski, Polish fighters soon took control of more than half the city. For reasons that remain controversial, the Soviet army halted its advance on August 2. Undoubtedly, Soviet forces needed to regroup after headlong progress, but it was also true that Stalin intended to install his own communist-dominated Polish government and had no love for the anti-Soviet Home Army. The pause allowed the Germans

RESISTANCE FIGHTERS
Members of the Polish Home Army defend an improvised position. The resistance fighters were only lightly equipped but of indomitable spirit.

to concentrate on suppressing the uprising, which they did with consummate brutality and ruthlessness. On October 2 the last remnants of the Home Army surrendered.

EASTERN FRONT

Budapest

DATE December 26, 1944–February 14, 1945

FORCES
Numbers unknown

CASUALTIES Soviet: 80,000 killed, 240,000 wounded; German and Hungarian: 40,000 killed, 62,000 wounded

LOCATION
Budapest, Hungary

Between August and October 1944, Soviet forces swept through Romania and Bulgaria. A thrust north from Belgrade forced a passage over the Danube in late November and Budapest was put under siege at Christmas. Hitler ordered the city held at any cost and transferred panzer divisions south from Poland in a failed attempt to break the siege. Troops within the city tried a breakout on February 11 but were slaughtered in the attempt. After some of the most vicious fighting of the war, Budapest fell to the Soviets on February 14.

ERA OF WORLD WARS

EASTERN FRONT

Berlin

DATE
April 16–May 2, 1945

FORCES Soviet: 2 million; German: 750,000

LOCATION
Berlin, Germany

CASUALTIES Soviet: 305,000 killed or wounded; German unknown

In late March 1945 Eisenhower informed Stalin that he did not intend to race for Berlin. The Soviets could have the honor of taking the Nazi capital—and the casualties. Instead, Stalin set up his own race for Berlin between the First Ukrainain Front under Marshal Ivan Konev and the First Belorussian Front under Zhukov. Zhukov's offensive, led by Chuikov's Eighth Guards Army, opened on April 16 with a fiasco at Seelow Heights, where Soviet forces became stuck in a traffic jam under German fire. Konev made smoother progress and both fronts were in the Berlin suburbs by April 21. After a moment when rivalry got out of hand and Zhukov's troops fought Konev's, Stalin determined that Zhukov take the center and the credit. The remaining German forces fought tenaciously, taking a toll on Soviet armor with their antitank *panzerfaust*. Artillery shells rained down on the center of the city, where Hitler prepared for defeat in his bunker under the Reich Chancellery. On April 30 a Rifle Corps Division of Eighth Guards Army broke into the Reichstag building, fighting up through the floors to raise the Red Flag on the roof. Hitler committed suicide on the same day. On May 2, after futile prevarications, the German commander in Berlin surrendered.

1896–1974

GEORGI ZHUKOV

Of lowly origins, Marshal Zhukov rose to be an officer through the Russian Revolution. He became known as a tank specialist in the 1930s and masterminded the victory over the Japanese at Nomonhan in 1939. Appointed chief of staff in January 1941 and deputy commissar for defense in August 1942, he was associated with every major Soviet battle from the defense of Moscow through Stalingrad and Kursk to Bagration and the battle for Berlin. His most valuable quality was his readiness to stand up to Stalin, ensuring military expertise had a proper voice in decision-making.

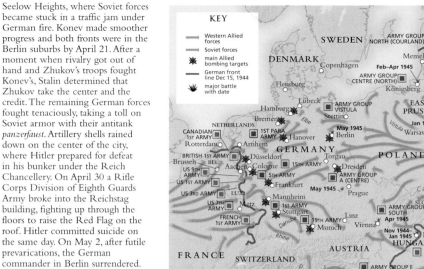

KEY

⎯ Western Allied forces
⎯ Soviet forces
✹ main Allied bombing targets
⎯ German front line Dec 15, 1944
✹ major battle with date

HOLED EAGLE
A bronze eagle, symbol of the Nazi Reich, shows bullet holes received during the street fighting in Berlin.

SHOWING THE FLAG
Yevgeny Khaldei's famous image of a Soviet soldier raising the Red Flag on the Reichstag was shot from an aircraft, a daylight re-creation of an event that happened on the night of April 30.

1914–PRESENT

THE PACIFIC WAR

THE ORIGINS OF THE PACIFIC WAR lay in Japan's expansionist policies in Asia. US opposition to the Japanese invasion of China, and to the installation of Japanese troops in French Indochina, led in 1941 to an American-led embargo on oil sales to Japan. This presented the Japanese with a stark choice between abandoning imperial ambitions or fighting a war they could hardly hope to win.

JAPAN'S GAMBLE

Japan's war goals were to conquer China and overthrow the rule of European colonial powers in Southeast Asia, creating a "Greater Asian Co-Prosperity Sphere" under Japanese leadership. The Europeans, either at war with or already conquered by Nazi Germany, were singularly ill-equipped to defend their colonies. Taking on the United States, however, was considered unrealistic by many Japanese leaders. Admiral Isoruku Yamamoto, commander of the Japanese combined fleet, said "I shall run wild for the first six months or a year, but I have utterly no confidence for the second or third year." But army leader General Tojo Hideki, Japanese prime minister from October 1941, argued that swift initial victories would put Japan in a position of power that the United States would have to learn to live with: "America will be outraged at first, but then she will come to understand."

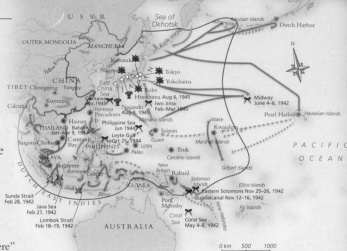

PACIFIC THEATER
At the height of the war, Japan's front line was over 21,000 miles (35,000km) in extent.

KEY

——	Japanese offensives 1941–42
——	Japanese perimeter June 1942
····	Allied offensives 1943
- - -	Allied offensives 1944
——	Allied offensives 1945
⚔	Japanese victory
✕	Japanese defeat
◉	Japanese bases from 1942
◉	Allied bases 1942
✹	major Allied bombing target
♟	atom bomb targets

NAVAL FLAG
This Rising Sun flag was used by the Japanese navy, a force modeled to a large extent on the British Royal Navy.

BATTLESHIP *YAMASHIRO*
Japanese admirals were committed to the importance of battleships, in practice largely irrelevant to a naval war fought by aircraft carriers.

EMBITTERED CONFLICT

The Japanese achieved the early successes they needed in 1941–42 through the quality of their naval aviation and of their infantry, which was especially good at operating in jungle conditions. But after the shock of Pearl Harbor, there was no way the United States would ever come to an accommodation with imperial Japan, even though President Franklin D. Roosevelt placed the defeat of Germany first on the United States' list of priorities. Japanese mistreatment of prisoners of war was a factor that further embittered a struggle characterized by mutual racial contempt. The Japanese were notoriously reluctant to surrender, but American soldiers rarely gave them a chance to do so. Despite its importance in the origins of the war, China turned out not to be a decisive theater, even though millions died there in the fight against Japanese occupation. Instead, the war was primarily decided in the Pacific, in duels between aircraft carriers and brutal battles from island to island.

UNITED we are strong

UNITED we will win

MIGHTY ALLIES
This poster lauds the alliance between Britain, the US, China, and the USSR. The Soviets joined the war against Japan a week before it ended.

SUICIDE BOMBERS
USS Bunker Hill *was struck by Japanese kamikaze aircraft in May 1945. The ship suffered over 600 casualties.*

ATOM BOMBER
The B-29 Enola Gay *returning to Tinian Island after dropping an atom bomb on the Japanese city of Hiroshima.*

NUCLEAR WARFARE

In the late 1930s scientists made governments aware of the immense destructive potential of atomic fission. Whereas Germany and Japan made little progress with nuclear weapons programs, the US invested $2 billion in the top-secret Manhattan Project, which eventually employed around 120,000 people nationwide. Dropped on the Japanese cities of Hiroshima and Nagasaki in August 1945, atom bombs were a triumph of American technological prowess, opening a new, dangerous era in warfare.

DEFEATING JAPAN

The overwhelming success of the United States in war production gave the Japanese no chance in the long term. In 1944 American factories produced nearly 100,000 aircraft and over 16 million tons of shipping, easily enough to cope with the demands of war in the Pacific and Europe at the same time. The products of this extraordinary feat of economic organization were put at the service of the ever-improving American armed forces. By 1944 both American aircraft and their pilots were so superior that only the adoption of "kamikaze" suicide tactics could allow the Japanese to inflict any serious damage on their enemy. Pitting the spirit of samurai self-sacrifice against overwhelming odds was an admission of failure. Yet, even facing total destruction, many Japanese military leaders still resisted surrender in August 1945.

SURRENDER
Japanese general Yoshijiro Umezo signs surrender documents on board USS Missouri *in Tokyo Bay, September 2, 1945.*

JAPAN'S HIGH TIDE

IN 1941 JAPAN'S WAR PLAN WAS to invade Southeast Asia and some Pacific islands while simultaneously attacking the US Pacific fleet in its base at Pearl Harbor in Hawaii. This attack, the Japanese reasoned, would stun the Americans and give Japan time to consolidate its conquests and establish a defensive perimeter from the Aleutian Islands, off the coast of Alaska, to Burma (now Myanmar). It was a risky plan that, to a remarkable degree, succeeded in its initial goals. Through cracking Japanese codes, the Allies knew of the enemy's general intentions but were sent reeling by the speed and shock of the Japanese onslaught. Japan, its admiral Chuichi Nagumo declared, had "woken a sleeping giant and filled her with a terrible resolve."

THE JAPANESE OFFENSIVE

Pearl Harbor

DATE December 7, 1941

FORCES Japanese: 353 planes; Americans: 90 ships, 300 planes

CASUALTIES Japanese: 130 pilots, 29 planes; Americans: 2,403 soldiers and civilians, 18 ships, 186 planes

LOCATION
Pearl Harbor, Oahu Island, Hawaii

On November 26, 1941, a fleet of 31 ships, including six aircraft carriers, sailed from Japan under the command of Admiral Chuichi Nagumo. US intelligence, monitoring Japanese war preparations, missed the fleet, which maintained strict radio silence. At dawn on December 7 the first wave of Japanese aircraft took off from the carriers 250 miles (400km) north of Hawaii. Despite the threat of war with Japan, peacetime Sunday routines were being observed at the US base, which was completely unprepared for the Nakajima torpedo bombers that skimmed in at low altitude and the Aichi dive-bombers that plunged from above. These planes were followed by horizontal bombers flying steadily through antiaircraft fire to blast already blazing ships, and Zero fighters that strafed American aircraft on their airfields. The story on the ground was one of individual courage amid collective chaos. Despite the immense damage caused, the Pearl Harbor attack was a partial failure, because US fleet carriers were out of port and therefore survived.

BLAZING WARSHIPS
A rescue launch looks for survivors from US warships in Pearl Harbor. Japan had meticulously prepared for the attack, developing special armor-piercing bombs.

MITSUBISHI A6M ZERO FIGHTER

EII-142

DEADLY FIGHTERS
Japanese Zero fighters escorted the bombers to Pearl Harbor. Fast—up to 350mph (560kph)—and highly maneuverable, they could outperform any US aircraft of the time.

"I was asked to go into the water and get sailors out that had been blown off the ships. Some were unconscious, some were dead.... I brought out I don't know how many."

John Garcia, US serviceman, Pearl Harbor, 1941

THE JAPANESE OFFENSIVE

Hong Kong

DATE December 8–25, 1941

FORCES Japanese: 40,000; British and Commonwealth: 15,000

LOCATION Hong Kong, southern China

CASUALTIES Japanese: 3,000; British and Commonwealth: 15,000 killed or captured

Reviewing its military commitments in 1940, Britain concluded that the colony of Hong Kong was indefensible, since Japanese forces held the Chinese mainland north and south of the city. But it was too prestigious a possession to be abandoned, and its garrison was actually reinforced with two Canadian battalions in October 1941. On December 8 Japanese troops crossed the border from China. Operating with artillery and air support, they drove the British back to Hong Kong Island. The first Japanese attempts to cross the straits were repulsed, but on the night of December 18–19, they established a bridgehead. Thrusting across the island, they split the defending forces in two. One half surrendered on Christmas Eve, the other on Christmas Day.

POPULAR PISTOL
Many Japanese officers possessed Nambu 8mm pistols. This one has an enlarged trigger, which could be fired while wearing gloves.

TAKING POSSESSION
Japanese troops ride into Hong Kong after the surrender of the British garrison. They occupied the city until the end of the war.

THE JAPANESE OFFENSIVE

Singapore

DATE December 8, 1941–February 15, 1942

FORCES Japanese: 55,000; British and Commonwealth: 140,000

LOCATION Malaysia and Singapore, Southeast Asia

CASUALTIES Japanese: 3,500; British and Commonwealth: 9,000 killed, 130,000 captured

On December 8, 1941, Japanese forces landed in Thailand and the Malay peninsula. Two days later the British warships the *Prince of Wales* and the *Repulse* set out from Singapore to impede the landings, but both were attacked by Japanese aircraft and sank with the loss of over 800 lives. Meanwhile, Japanese troops advanced down both sides of the peninsula. Although outnumbered by British and Commonwealth troops, their speed of movement and superiority in the air created an impression of overwhelming force. The British commander General Arthur Percival prepared a last-ditch defense of Singapore, blowing up the causeway linking it to the mainland. On February 9, however, the Japanese succeeded in landing on the island. Believing that he faced far superior forces, Percival surrendered on February 15. The British prime minister Winston Churchill called it "the worst disaster…in British military history."

BRITISH SURRENDER
Japanese troops march British soldiers out of Singapore. Many British men would die of mistreatment, malnutrition, and disease.

THE JAPANESE OFFENSIVE

The Philippines

DATE December 8, 1941–May 6, 1942

FORCES Japanese: 55,000; Americans and Filipinos: 130,000

LOCATION Philippines, Southeast Asia

CASUALTIES Japanese: 12,000; Americans and Filipinos: 100,000 captured

The Philippines were defended by American and Filipino forces under General Douglas MacArthur. He had around 200 aircraft that were expected to play a key role in the defense, but on the first day of the war an attack by Japanese bombers and fighters from Formosa (now Taiwan) destroyed most of this air force on the ground at Clark Field, on Luzon island. With the Japanese in control of the air, American naval forces withdrew and the surviving B-17 bombers were evacuated. Japanese troops under General Masaharu Homma began a series of landings that the Americans were powerless to stop. MacArthur concentrated his forces around the capital, Manila, and in late December carried out a skillful fighting withdrawal to a defensive line on the Bataan peninsula. Some 83,000 American and Filipino troops took up positions on each side of jungle-clad Mount Natib, terrain that was considered impassible. But the Japanese infiltrated the jungle around the defenders' flanks, forcing a further withdrawal to a reserve position in late January. Along with 25,000 civilian refugees, MacArthur's forces were now crowded in a limited space, short of rations, harassed by air and artillery bombardment, and fighting off amphibious landings behind their lines. US president Roosevelt made it clear they could expect no relief. On March 12 MacArthur was pulled out, leaving with the promise "I shall return." Racked by malnutrition and tropical diseases, the troops on Bataan surrendered on April 8. About 25,000 of them died while being herded to a prison camp by their Japanese captors—the infamous "Bataan Death March."

1880–1964

GENERAL MACARTHUR

Defeat in the Philippines was a low point in General Douglas MacArthur's distinguished career. As Supreme Allied Commander in the southwest Pacific from February 1942 he masterminded the "island-hopping" strategy, advancing to Japan island by island and bypassing Japanese strongholds. This strategy took him back to the Philippines in October 1944. After the Allied victory, Douglas acted as head of the forces in Japan.

RIVER CROSSING
Japanese soldiers cross a river in the Philippines after the US defeat. The mix of horses and tanks—Type 89 medium models—was typical.

HONORING JAPAN
This medal was the 7th in eight grades of the Order of the Rising Sun, awarded to Japanese civilians or soldiers.

BOMB DAMAGE
A Japanese Mogami-class cruiser lists heavily after being struck by US dive-bombers. The battle of Midway shifted the balance of naval air power in the Pacific in favor of the United States.

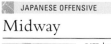

Midway

DATE June 4, 1942

FORCES Japanese: 20 ships, 275 planes; US: 26 ships, 321 planes

CASUALTIES Japanese: 2,500 men, 5 ships; US: 307 men, 2 ships

LOCATION Midway Island, Pacific Ocean

In spring 1942 Japan's Admiral Yamamoto, who felt that his naval aircraft and pilots were superior to those of the US, sought to advance Japan's defensive perimeter in the Pacific and draw the US Pacific Fleet into battle. Yamamoto planned joint attacks on the Aleutian islands in the northern Pacific and on the US base at Midway Island, to which he sent four aircraft carriers and 16 other warships. US intelligence, having had great success with codebreaking, provided the Pacific Fleet commander Admiral Chester Nimitz with details of the Japanese plan. Nimitz chose to ignore the attack in the Aleutians and focus

his forces on Midway. He had three carriers at his disposal—the *Enterprise*, the *Hornet*, and the *Yorktown*—and sent two battle groups to Midway. The morning of June 4 began with a heavy raid by Japanese naval aircraft against airfields on Midway. They were preparing a second raid when they came under attack from American naval aircraft. Devastator torpedo bombers from the *Hornet* found the Japanese carriers first, but all 15 were shot down by Zero fighters. A wave of torpedo bombers from the *Yorktown* was similarly savaged, although US Wildcat fighters did their best to keep the Zeros occupied. Concentrating on the low-flying torpedo bombers, however, the Japanese fighters missed the arrival of Douglas Dauntless dive-bombers from the *Yorktown* and the *Enterprise*, which plunged down on the Japanese carriers. Within five minutes three of the Japanese carriers were burning hulks. The fourth carrier delivered a counterstrike against the *Yorktown* before being destroyed in turn by dive-bombers from the *Enterprise*. It was an overwhelming US victory.

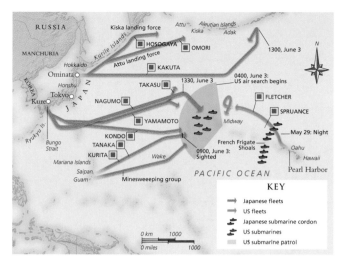

> "I saw this glint in the sun and it just looked like a beautiful, silver waterfall, these dive-bombers coming down. I'd never seen such superb dive-bombing."

US pilot Jimmy Thatch, recalling the battle of Midway, 1942

FIGHT BACK

IN 1942 THE JAPANESE NAVY continued its offensive in the Pacific instead of standing on the defensive as initially planned. This policy led to the heavy losses at Midway that marked a turning point in the Pacific War. From then on, the Americans advanced from island to island toward Japan, achieving overwhelming naval superiority in large-scale carrier battles and exploiting the expertise of US Marines in amphibious warfare. "Island-hopping" eventually brought Japan within range of American bombers that devastated its cities. The belated entry of the Soviet Union into the war against Japan, coinciding with nuclear bombings, brought Japan to surrender in August 1945 without the need for a costly invasion of the Japanese mainland.

Coral Sea

DATE	May 4–8, 1942
FORCES	US: 2 carriers, 21 other warships; Japanese: 3 carriers, 13 other warships
LOCATION South of the Solomon islands, Pacific Ocean	CASUALTIES US: 1 carrier, 74 aircraft; Japanese: 1 carrier, 80 aircraft

In April 1942 American intelligence informed Admiral Nimitz of a Japanese plan to seize Tulagi island in the Solomons and Port Moresby in New Guinea. A US naval force under Admiral Frank Fletcher, including fleet carriers *Yorktown* and *Lexington*, was sent to contest the landings, which were supported by a Japanese naval force under Admiral Takeo Takagi, with fleet carriers *Zuikaku* and *Shokaku* and light carrier *Shoho*. Skirmishes between naval aircraft and warships began on May 4, but the main forces at first failed to locate one another. On May 7 American aircraft sank *Shoho*, causing the Japanese to cancel the Port Moresby landing. On May 8 a long-range duel was fought between the fleet carriers. American Dauntless dive-bombers scored three hits on the *Shokaku*, which barely stayed afloat, while *Lexington* was struck by two air-launched torpedos and a bomb exploded on *Yorktown*'s flight deck. *Yorktown* remained operational, but *Lexington* could not be saved. Fires on board caused two massive explosions that sank the ship before the end of the day. It was the first time a naval battle had been fought beyond visual range.

CARRIER LEADER
An American carrier task group led by USS Essex *heads into action in the Philippine Sea in 1944.*

PRAYER FLAG
All Japanese servicemen carried prayer flags, which took the form of the flag of Japan, with them into battle. On the background friends and relatives wrote prayers and blessings.

Scale showing degrees relative to equator

Adjustable eyepiece

NAVAL SEXTANT
This sextant was used by Japanese naval officers in the Pacific to calculate latitude. It operated on the same principles as the navigational devices of the age of sail.

Guadalcanal

DATE August 7, 1942– February 7, 1943
FORCES US: 19,000 rising to 50,000; Japanese: 3,000 rising to 25,000
LOCATION Solomon islands, Pacific Ocean	CASUALTIES US: 6,100; Japanese: 25,000

After the victory at Midway (p.325), American commanders in the Pacific were eager to take the offensive. They targeted the island of Guadalcanal when it was discovered that the Japanese were building an airstrip there—later known as Henderson Field. On August 7, 1942, after an air and naval bombardment, US Marines went ashore unopposed, taking the lightly defended airstrip the following day. But at sea the battle went badly at first for the Americans. On the night of August 8–9 a Japanese naval force sank four US cruisers off Savo island, forcing a withdrawal of American warships that left the Marines cut off from supplies and with no naval support or air cover. The arrival of Marine aircraft at the airstrip only marginally improved their position. But the Japanese failed to exploit the opportunity to land troops in sufficient numbers before the US Navy returned in strength. A prolonged battle followed on land and sea. Japanese warships sailed down the "Slot" to Guadalcanal each night to land reinforcements and shell Henderson Field—a maneuver the Americans called the "Tokyo Express." US Marines fought desperate battles against suicidally courageous Japanese infantry, holding a perimeter around the airstrip in unhealthy, difficult jungle conditions. Crucially, the Americans now had much the better of a series of naval battles in which both sides suffered substantial losses. From mid-November they were able to reinforce and supply the forces on Guadalcanal. At the start of February 1943 Japan successfully evacuated most of its surviving troops, taking off 13,000 men for the loss of only one destroyer.

MORTAR SQUAD
US Marines bombard Japanese positions on Guadalcanal. The American ability to resupply their troops with ammunition was critical to their ultimate success.

Burma

DATE January 1942–August 1945

FORCES British and Commonwealth: 30,000; Japanese: 30,000

LOCATION Burma

CASUALTIES (initial invasion) British: 13,000; Japanese: 4,000

The Japanese invaded British-ruled Burma in January 1942, chiefly to cut the supply line to Chinese Nationalist forces in Kunming. Despite an intervention by Chinese forces organized by US General Stilwell, General Slim's British, Indian, and African troops could not prevent the Japanese from occupying the country. The terrain was ideal for Japanese infantry to show their prowess at jungle warfare, although Brigadier Orde Wingate's Chindits and General Frank Merrill's Marauders would later show that the British and Americans were also capable of fighting in the jungle. In January 1944 the Japanese renewed their advance, crossing the border into India, but were repulsed at Imphal and Kohima, where British-led forces showed a fresh resolve. The

WINGATE'S CHINDITS

British General Wingate set up the Chindits as a long-range penetration force operating behind Japanese lines. They were sometimes air-dropped into jungle clearings.

following December Slim launched a major offensive. As his Fourteenth Army advanced southward, the Japanese set out to hold Mandalay at all costs, but were defeated there in March 1945. The following May the Burmese capital, Rangoon, fell to combined sea and airborne landings.

Philippine Sea

DATE June 15–20, 1944

FORCES US: 20,000 Marines, 15 carriers; Japanese: 32,000 men, 9 carriers

LOCATION Marianas islands, Pacific Ocean

CASUALTIES US: 16,500 men, 129 aircraft; Japanese: 31,000 dead

In June 1944 the United States invaded the Marianas, aiming to put the Japanese mainland in range of American bombers. In support of the landings, the US Navy sent an imposing fleet including 15 aircraft carriers and 12 battleships under the command of Admiral Raymond Spruance. After a four-day bombardment, US Marines went ashore at Saipan on June 15. Some 20,000 landed on the first day, but they were pinned down close to the beaches as Japanese troops launched fierce counterattacks from strong defensive positions. At sea, too, the Japanese fighting spirit remained undaunted. The Japanese navy steamed into the Philippine Sea, intent on destroying naval forces by combined attacks from carrier-borne and island-based aircraft—although almost all of the latter had already been wiped out by American naval aircraft. Spruance took up position west of Tinian, where his fleet came under air attack on the morning of June 19. Detected by radar, the waves of aircraft from Japanese carriers were met by hundreds of US Navy fighter aircraft directed on to them by combat controllers aboard ships. Most of the Japanese planes that survived were either shot down by antiaircraft fire from US warships or destroyed as they tried to land on island airstrips. The Japanese lost some 300 aircraft in a single day, in what became known as the "Marianas Turkey Shoot." Two Japanese aircraft carriers were also sunk by American submarines. The following afternoon, determined to complete the victory, carrier task-force commander Admiral Marc Mitscher sent over 200 aircraft

CRUISER AT BAY

A Japanese heavy cruiser under attack in Manila Bay from US carrier-based bombers. Despite its frantic evasive maneuvers, it was sunk.

VOUGHT F4U CORSAIR

The Corsair, introduced into carrier service in 1944, gave US naval pilots a fighter that could trounce the Japanese Zero. Its top speed was 440mph (710kph).

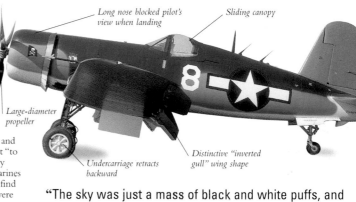

Long nose blocked pilot's view when landing

Sliding canopy

Large-diameter propeller

Undercarriage retracts backward

Distinctive "inverted gull" wing shape

to attack the Japanese fleet at extreme range. They sank a fleet carrier and damaged other warships for little loss, but on the nighttime return trip many aircraft ran out of fuel and ditched. Mitscher ordered the fleet "to turn on the lights"—an extremely dangerous ploy with enemy submarines around—so that the pilots could find their way home. Eighty aircraft were lost, although most of the crews were saved. Meanwhile, on Saipan a tough battle continued into July, ending with mass suicides by Japanese soldiers and civilians.

> "The sky was just a mass of black and white puffs, and in the midst of it planes already hit, burning and crashing into the water below."
>
> *Lieutenant Don Lewis*, US navy bomber pilot's account of an attack, June 20, 1944

PACIFIC WAR

Leyte Gulf

DATE
October 23–26, 1944

FORCES Allies: 35 carriers, 177 other ships; Japanese: 4 carriers, 62 other ships

LOCATION Around the Philippines

CASUALTIES Allies: 3 carriers, 4 other ships; Japanese: 4 carriers, 21 other ships

The decision by the US to invade the Philippines in October 1944 owed much to the personal agenda of General MacArthur, who in 1942 had famously promised to "return." He chose Leyte, one of the smaller islands, as the site for the first landings. The Japanese navy decided to contest the invasion, despite a lack of naval aircraft after their defeat at the Philippine Sea. They devised a complex plan in which a decoy force would draw away US carriers, thus enabling Japanese

battleships and cruisers to engage the rest of the Allied fleet. Aircraft flying from airfields in the Philippines would provide air cover. However, Japanese resources were inadequate to carry out this ambitious plan effectively. Two cruisers from Admiral Kurita's Centre Force, moving north from Brunei, were sunk by a US submarine on October 23, and the next day the massive battleship *Musashi* was destroyed by US naval aircraft in the Sibuyan Sea. The Japanese decoy force drew away much of Admiral William Halsey's Third US Fleet, but on October 25, Admiral Thomas Kinkaid's Seventh US Fleet shattered a force of Japanese warships in the Surigao Strait. The remaining battleships and cruisers of Japanese Center Force slipped through to engage the escort carriers and destroyers protecting the landing beaches. The Allies lost two of their carriers and three destroyers, but two of Kurita's cruisers were also sunk and he withdrew to save his remaining battleships.

ON THE BEACH
Some of the 130,000 US troops landed on Leyte Island take up position on a beach. The conquest of the island took two months.

PACIFIC WAR

Iwo Jima

DATE February 19–March 24, 1945

FORCES
Americans: 70,000;
Japanese: 22,000

LOCATION Pacific Ocean, 625 miles (1,000km) se of Tokyo

CASUALTIES
Americans: 28,700;
Japanese: 1,000 prisoner, 20,000 dead

The tiny volcanic island of Iwo Jima was targeted by the United States as a stepping-stone to the invasion of Japan, and a potential base for escort fighters. Guessing the intentions of the US, Japan reinforced the island's defenses in the winter of 1944–45. General Kuribayashi Tadamichi made Iwo Jima into a

fortress of pillboxes, bunkers, tunnels, trenches, and fortified caves, densely defended by an array of artillery. Rejecting suicidal charges, Tadamichi instructed his men to fight from cover and hold out as long as humanly possible. Aware of the strength of Iwo Jima's defenses, American military leaders planned to use poison-gas shells fired from warships to flush out the Japanese, but President Roosevelt flatly refused to authorize this. Still, the conventional bombardment of the island in the weeks prior to the landings was prolonged and heavy. It had little effect. The first wave of Marines approached the beaches at 8:30 a.m. on February 19, the lead landing craft strafing the beaches with rocket and cannon fire while supporting air and naval forces battered Japanese positions. But when amphibious vehicles

came ashore, they quickly bogged down in the steep volcanic sand. The Marines were pinned on increasingly crowded beaches, exposed to fire from artillery on the heights of Mount Suribachi and machine guns in pillboxes just inshore. Sheltering in shallow foxholes amid the wreckage of burning vehicles, the Marines suffered almost 2,500 casualties on the first day—but 30,000 of them got ashore. By the morning of February 23, they had fought their way to the top of Mount Suribachi, where they twice planted a flag, the second time for the camera. It was not until late March that resistance in the tunnels and caves was finally subdued. Only 1,000 Japanese surrendered, mostly those too badly wounded to kill themselves.

GLORY FLAG
US Marines raise the Stars and Stripes on Mount Suribachi, Iwo Jima, to create a potent symbol of US triumph.

PACIFIC WAR

Okinawa

DATE April 1–July 2, 1945	
FORCES Japanese: 130,000; Americans: 250,000, Allied fleet: 1,300 ships	
LOCATION Okinawa and Ryukyu Islands	**CASUALTIES** Americans: 38,400 (land forces); Japanese: 120,000 dead

After Iwo Jima, the seizure of the rugged island of Okinawa was the logical next step toward an invasion of Japan. The island's commander, General Ushijima Mitsuru, created similar fortifications to those on Iwo Jima in mountainous terrain in the south of the island. He intended to hold out for as long as possible while Japanese aircraft based in Formosa and southern Japan battered the Allied fleet. The landings on April 1, 1945, by the US Tenth Army, a force of army and marines under General Simon Bolivar Buckner, were unopposed. American soldiers swiftly occupied the island's center and took a relatively short time to overcome resistance in the north. But Ushijima's forces in the southern mountains slowed American progress to a crawl. Meanwhile, on April 6 the Japanese began mass air attacks on the Allied fleet off Okinawa. Raids by up to 700 aircraft in a day overwhelmed the fleet air defenses. Many Japanese pilots were committed to *kamikaze* missions, using their aircraft as flying bombs to crash onto the decks of US warships. American losses were heavy, with destroyers on radar picket duty between the fleet and the air bases suffering very heavily. But the attacks cost the lives of around 1,900 Japanese pilots. On land, American soldiers fought a savage struggle to clear bunkers, caves, and tunnels. Using flamethrowers or grenades to clean out strongpoints, they often killed everyone inside, including civilians. General Buckner was among those who died in a bloodbath that lasted into July. General Ujishima and other senior Japanese commanders committed ritual suicide before resistance ceased.

KEEPING WATCH
Sailors on the battleship West Virginia *watch for Japanese aircraft off the coast of Okinawa. The ship was damaged in a* kamikaze *attack that killed four men.*

KAMIKAZE PILOTS

The first Japanese "special attack units" were organized during the battle of Leyte Gulf in October 1944. Almost certain to be killed in unequal air battles, elite pilots crashed their aircraft on enemy warships so they would at least not die in vain. Later, suicide tactics became a way of using expendable young pilots to some effect— Japan was too short of fuel to give recruits proper flight training before sending them into action. The few surviving experienced fliers provided a fighter escort.

DEATH CLOUD
The mushroom cloud rises over Nagasaki. The lowest estimates of the immediate death tolls from the atom bombs are 140,000 at Hiroshima and 80,000 at Nagasaki.

PACIFIC WAR

Bombing of Japan

DATE June 1944–August 1945	
FORCES American: up to 500 bombers per raid	
LOCATION Japan	**CASUALTIES** American: up to 512 aircraft lost; Japanese: 500,000 dead

In June 1944 the introduction of B-29 bombers, with twice the range of B-17s, brought Japan within range of US air bases in China. At first raids did not go well, with substantial losses to mechanical failure. From late November 1944 B-29s began flying from bases in the Marianas, but still their high-altitude daylight raids were relatively ineffectual. In March 1945, under General Curtis LeMay, new tactics were adopted. B-29s were sent in at low altitude by night, carrying a maximum load of incendiary bombs. Since most areas of Japanese cities consisted of close-packed wooden buildings, fire-bombing was frighteningly effective. On March 9–10 a raid by 279 B-29s caused a firestorm that destroyed a quarter of Tokyo and killed around 80,000 people. As city after city was subjected to such attacks, the population fled to the countryside and industrial production plummeted. On August 6 and 9, B-29s from Tinian island dropped atom bombs on Hiroshima and Nagasaki, destroying the cities and incurring massive loss of life. Japan surrendered on August 15.

FAT MAN
The bomb dropped on Nagasaki was nicknamed "Fat Man." The destruction it wrought on the city was slightly mitigated by the hills that blocked blast and radiation.

> **"We call upon the government of Japan to proclaim now the unconditional surrender of all Japanese armed forces.... The alternative for Japan is prompt and utter destruction."**
>
> *Potsdam Declaration issued by Allied leaders,* July 26, 1945

CONFLICTS SINCE 1945

SINCE THE END OF WORLD WAR II there has been no return to full-scale conflict between major powers, but nor has there been a single day without a war going on somewhere around the globe. Weapons systems of great destructive power and technological sophistication have been developed, a whole category of which—nuclear weapons—has not been used since 1945.

THE COLD WAR

From the late 1940s to the late 1980s, the two superpowers—the United States and the Soviet Union (the USSR)—continuously prepared for a Third World War that never happened. From the 1950s they engaged in a nuclear arms race that led within a decade to the era of "mutually assured destruction" (MAD), a strategic deadlock in which nuclear war was prevented by the certainty that both sides would suffer an unacceptable level of damage if one broke out. While this balance of fear prevented a world war, an American-led struggle against the spread of communism was instead fought out in a series of local wars. Whereas in the first half of the 20th century "total war" had seemed to develop almost naturally, with combatants using as much destructive power as they could muster, the Korean War of 1950–53 in contrast set the pattern for "limited war": limited in scope, with US soldiers fighting Chinese troops in Korea but no American attacks on China itself, and limited in weaponry, since the United States did not use the atom bombs it possessed. Many of the wars fought in the nuclear age—for example, in Vietnam—were, even so, massively destructive, partly because the limits on the conduct of war made it difficult to achieve a swift, decisive result.

COLD WAR ALLIANCES
As confrontation mounted, the USSR and US sought security in alliance networks. The danger of nuclear conflict led to a spread of wars in areas where they did not face each other directly.

KEY			
US, allies, and satellite states		**USSR and allies**	
▦	US and original NATO 1949	▦	USSR
▦	later NATO	▦	Warsaw Pact 1955
▦	NATO dependencies 1960	▦	Communist satellite states
▦	other nations allied to the Western Bloc by treaty	▦	China
■	major US and NATO overseas bases	■	major Soviet overseas base
		⚓	Cold War flashpoint
		⚓	major US fleet

SPUTNIK
A Soviet poster celebrates its space program, which was closely linked to its development of military missiles.

THE COLD WAR
Until the 1990s, annual May Day parades in Moscow were a regular occasion for the Soviet Union to show off its military hardware.

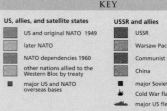

MISSILE SILO
An intercontinental ballistic missile (ICBM) in its hardened silo. ICBMs formed the core of America's nuclear armory from the 1960s.

NUCLEAR TESTING
US troops witness an atomic test at close range in the Nevada Desert. Almost 100 such tests were carried out in Nevada in 1951–62.

WEAPONS DEVELOPMENT

The development of nuclear weapons dominated military budgets in the Cold War era. Until the 20th century it had been impossible to kill someone you could not see. Once ballistic missiles, developed from the German V-2 rocket of World War II, were combined with nuclear warheads, everywhere on the planet was vulnerable to a nuclear strike at the touch of a button on a different continent. The evolution of conventional weapons was less dramatic. Although jet aircraft had replaced propeller-driven planes, and missiles were used alongside guns, the battles between Israel and its Arab neighbors in the 1960s and 1970s were not fundamentally different from those of World War II. The radical areas of development came in computerized command and control, "smart" guidance systems, and electronic countermeasures. By the 1980s it was superiority on the electronic battlefield, rather than the possession of greater numbers of tanks, aircraft, or missiles, that won wars.

GUERRILLA WARFARE

Guerrilla tactics proved a consistently effective counter to the technological superiority of major powers. Evolved from the theory and practice of Mao Zedong's communist forces in China in the 1930s and 1940s and of anti-Nazi partisans in Europe in World War II, guerrilla struggle was, until the 1970s, principally a form of revolutionary warfare practiced by those fighting colonialism and imperialism. Guerrillas sought to avoid battle except on their own terms, denying their enemy targets for his superior firepower while inflicting a steady stream of losses through hit-and-run attacks. Counterinsurgency techniques varied between trying to beat the guerrillas at their own game and seeking high-tech solutions, from exploiting the rapid mobility of helicopters to the area-bombing of jungles and mountains by B-52s.

VIETNAM WAR
US soldiers enter a Vietnamese village in May 1967. Much of th US war in Vietnam was fought by infantry operating on foot, with little technological advantage over the guerrilla enemy.

NUCLEAR CARRIER
USS Enterprise *was the world's first nuclear-powered carrier when commissioned in 1961. Carriers have become a crucial Instrument of power projection, bringing air power swiftly to bear in war zones.*

THE NEW WORLD ORDER

The end of the Cold War in the late 1980s removed the immediate threat of a nuclear holocaust, but a "new world order" proved elusive. The new era was characterized by wars of intervention by the United States and its allies, no longer held in check by the fear of a Soviet response. There were also wars of state disintegration in the former Soviet Bloc and Yugoslavia. In some parts of the world—the Congo, for example, and the Sudan—a state of chronic warfare existed. The declaration of a "war on terror" by the United States in the wake of the 9/11 terrorist attacks in 2001 seemed to blur the distinction between war and peace. The world was saturated with automatic weapons, often in the hands of irregular "troops" who were no more than children. As the specter of major war between great powers receded, the prospect of endless small wars seemed increasingly probable.

1914-PRESENT

THE CHINESE CIVIL WAR

THE CHINESE CIVIL WAR OF 1945–49 was the culmination of a lengthy struggle for control of the country that had started in 1911, when the Manchu dynasty of emperors was overthrown and China was declared a republic. As the country descended into chaos during the 1920s, two main political groups fought for power: the Nationalist Kuomintang led by Jiang Jieshi (Chiang Kai-Shek) and the Chinese Communist Party and its People's Liberation Army, led by Mao Zedong. The necessity of suppressing the Japanese invasion of China after 1937 brought the two factions together in an uneasy alliance for the duration of World War II, but Japan's defeat by the Allies in August 1945 soon re-opened the domestic conflict.

THE CHINESE CIVIL WAR

Opening Campaign

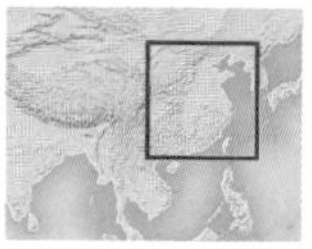

DATE
August 1945–
January 10, 1946

FORCES
Communists: 100,000;
Nationalists: 110,000

LOCATION
Eastern China
and Manchuria

CASUALTIES
Communists: c.45,000;
Nationalists: unknown

Japan's defeat left a power vacuum in many parts of China, as the Japanese had previously controlled most of the east coast, the populous river valleys of the interior, and the northern province of Manchuria. As Nationalist forces retook the coastal cities, the Communists occupied Manchuria, supplied with enough arms for 600,000 soldiers. These weapons were taken from the Japanese by the Soviet army, which had invaded the province at the very end of the war. After peace talks broke down in October 1945, a Nationalist army moved into the province and forced the Communists northward. Their defeat was avoided only after US-led talks resulted in a ceasefire on January 10, 1946.

THE CHINESE CIVIL WAR

Manchuria

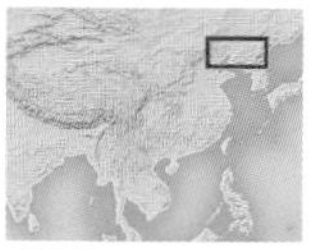

DATE
April 14, 1946–
November 1948

FORCES
Communists:
c.1 million;
Nationalists:
c.1 million

LOCATION
Manchuria,
north-east China

CASUALTIES Unknown

The halt in fighting in Manchuria gave both sides time to regroup. Five million Nationalist forces were soon

deployed in a line across northern China, cutting Manchuria off from the rest of the country and attacking Communist bases to the west and south. By the end of 1946 the Nationalists had captured 165 Communist-held towns, taking

---

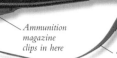

Hand-operated breechbolt

Ammunition magazine clips in here

Shoulder strap

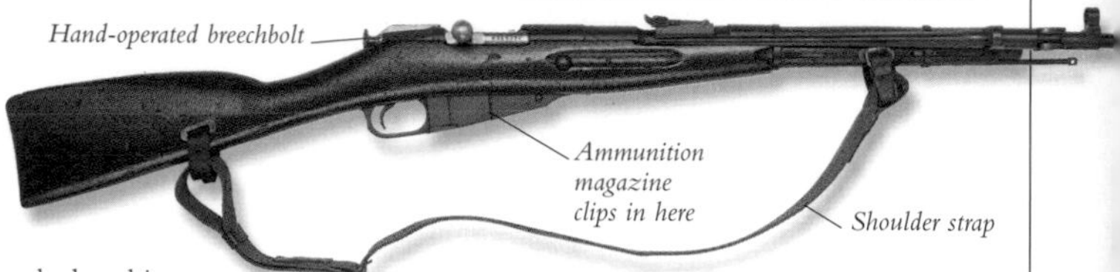

CARBINE RIFLE
The Soviet-made and supplied Mosin-Nagant Model 1944 carbine was the standard rifle of the Communist troops.

their capital, Yan'an, in March 1947. But while the Nationalists won the major offensives, the Communists won the small-scale clashes, killing or capturing 400,000 Nationalist troops during 1947 and acquiring some much-needed heavy artillery in the process. In December 1947 the Communists sent the 600,000-strong Fourth Field Army under Lin Piao on the offensive in Manchuria. Isolating the Nationalist armies from each other, they completed the conquest of the province in November 1948.

SHENYANG
The Communist Fourth Army took the strategic city of Shenyang on November 1, 1948, a major defeat for Nationalist forces.

THE CHINESE CIVIL WAR

Xuzhou

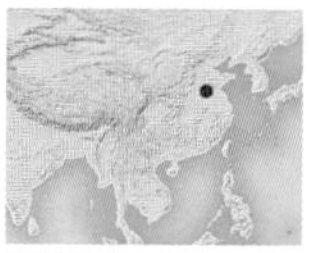

DATE
September 1948–
January 10, 1949

FORCES
Communists: 500,000;
Nationalists: 500,000

LOCATION
Shandong province,
eastern China

CASUALTIES
Communists: unknown
Nationalists: 200,000

The decisive battle in the campaign for eastern China—and the biggest formal battle of the civil war—took place in the winter of 1948–49. In September the Communists' Third Field Army under Ch'en Yi pushed east from Shaanxi province into Shandong, the province south of Beijing. The Nationalist Seventh Army led by General Du Yuming was overwhelmed and its troops driven south toward the Huai He River. Du Yuming halted at the key railroad junction of Xuzhou,

1893–1976

MAO ZEDONG

Mao Zedong was born in Shaoshan, Hunan, the son of a peasant farmer. He was educated locally and left Hunan in 1918 to work in the National University library in Beijing. There he discovered Marxism and in 1921 became a founder member of the Chinese Communist Party. Mao's main contribution to the Communists' strategy was his belief in the need for grassroots political action to build up support among the rural peasantry. This enabled the Communists to wage a lengthy rural guerrilla campaign before they had experience and equipment to field a large, regular army in late 1947.

where he fielded more than 500,000 men. His position was immediately broken when four divisions in the center of his line defected to the Communists. This was consistent with the Nationalist failure to command and support its troops, 800,000 of whom deserted to the Communists during the

CAPTURED
Communist soldiers captured at Xuzhou are shown here with their weapons. This group was unlucky, as by this stage of the war, most prisoners were Nationalists.

civil war. Two arduous battles against the exposed wings of the Nationalist army took place during November and December as the Communists cut the Nationalists' communications, encircled their troops, and bombarded them into submission, eventually taking Xuzhou on January 10. Faced with large amounts of equipment falling into Communist hands, Jiang Jieshi ordered his air force, which had had total air superiority during the battle, to bomb his own formations, killing many of his own troops.

Seizure of Tianjin and Beijing

DATE
January 15 and 22, 1949

FORCES
Communists:
c.500,000;
Nationalists: unknown

LOCATION
Northeast China

CASUALTIES
No reliable estimates

As a result of their victory at Xuzhou, the Communists had broken the stalemate with the Nationalists. From then on, their momentum was irresistible. Their firepower was now immense, their troops were far more mobile than those of the Nationalists—

ON PARADE
Banners bearing photographs of Mao Zedong and slogans were carried in parades to create enthusiasm for the Communist authorities.

whose number they now exceeded—and most importantly their motivation and political commitment was total. The Nationalists were increasingly weak, divided, and overstretched. The Communists now controlled all northern and eastern China with the exception of the isolated cities of Tianjin and Beijing. Lin Piao's Fourth Field Army captured Taijan on January 15 and then took Beijing unopposed seven days later. Marching with sound trucks blaring continuous revolutionary refrains, the Communist troops entered the city "in high spirits. As they marched up the streets, the crowds lining the sidewalks… burst into applause," as one western observer recorded in his diary. Here and elsewhere, civilians tired of years of Japanese occupation and civil war welcomed the Communists as the one force that could end the fighting and unite the country. After the capture of Beijing, the Communists could now strike south toward Shanghai and the Nationalist capital at Nanjing.

> ## "Welcome to the People's Army on its arrival in Beijing! Congratulations to the people of Beijing on their liberation!"
>
> Communist slogans broadcast by troops entering Beijing, **January 22, 1949**

Yangtze Incident

DATE
April 20, 1949

FORCES
British: unknown;
Chinese: unknown

CASUALTIES
British: 117 killed
or wounded

LOCATION 139 miles
(224km) up the
Yangtze River, China

One of the oddest incidents of the civil war occurred on the Yangtze River. On April 20, 1949, Communist guns fired on the frigate HMS *Amethyst* as it sailed upriver from Shanghai with supplies for the British community in Nanjing; 17 soldiers were killed and another 30 wounded. Three other British naval vessels attempted but failed to rescue the ship, resulting in 70 further casualties. HMS *Amethyst* remained off an island in the river for more than 14 weeks, its crew suffering extreme hardship in the hot summer weather, until the night of July 30–31 when Lieutenant-Commander J. S. Kerans broke free and sailed the 139 miles (224km) down to the sea at a speed of more than 22 knots to avoid the gunfire from five lines of forts along the river. It is not clear why the Communists attacked and detained the ship, other than a suspicion that it might be carrying arms for the Nationalists, but the incident served notice on the international community that the Communists would aggressively assert Chinese sovereignty over the entire nation, including what had previously been recognized as an international waterway.

Conquest of the South

DATE
April 1949–April 1950

FORCES
Communists:
unknown;
Nationalists:
unknown

LOCATION
Southern China

CASUALTIES
No reliable estimates

Following their successes in the north and east, Communist troops moved south in April. Nanjing, the Nationalist

capital, fell without a fight on April 24 and Shanghai in May. The Nationalists held a supreme council on July 16, at which they decided to evacuate to the island of Taiwan, taking the national gold reserves and art collection with them. As the Communist army prepared to enter Guangzhou, the last remaining major Nationalist city in the south, Mao Zedong stood on top of the Gate of Heavenly Peace in Beijing on October 1, 1949, to announce the formation of the People's Republic of China. Facing defeat and capture, Jiang Jieshi fled on December 10 to Taiwan, giving up control by April 1950 of all but this and some small islands to the Communist victors.

VICTORY
Revolutionary propaganda posters from 1949 showed jubilant crowds cheering Mao Zedong, the new Communist leader of the People's Republic of China.

SHANGHAI
The Nationalist troops in Shanghai, seen here parading along the Bund waterfront on November 12, 1948, imposed martial law on the city as they prepared to defend it from Communist attack. In the end, the Communists easily took the city the following May.

THE KOREAN WAR

AFTER 1945 KOREA WAS DIVIDED between a Soviet-backed North and an American-backed South. A North Korean invasion of the South in summer 1950 brought a US-led UN intervention in which 15 other countries took part, while Chinese troops entered the war after UN forces invaded the North. By the end of the war in 1953, over 39,000 US and other UN forces, around a million Chinese, and 3–4 million Koreans had died.

KEY

- area controlled by North Korean forces Sep 15, 1950
- front line Sep 15, 1950
- US offensives Sep 15–Oct 24, 1950
- Chinese offensives Oct 1950
- front line Nov 24, 1950
- front line Jan 25, 1951
- ceasefire line Jul 27, 1953
- US navy

THE KOREAN WAR
North Korea's invasion of the South in June 1950 was seen as a test of US global credibility. The front lines in the war moved sharply across the peninsula but, after three years of bitter conflict, stabilized more or less where they had begun.

THE KOREAN WAR

Inchon

DATE September 15–27, 1950

FORCES North Korean: 20,000; UN/South Korean: 40,000

LOCATION Inchon and Seoul, Korea

CASUALTIES North Korean: 14,000; UN/South Korean: 671 killed, 2,758 wounded

MacArthur devised an amphibious landing at Inchon, 200 miles (320km) north of the Pusan perimeter, to capture Seoul and cut the enemy's communications. This operation, entrusted to X Corps under General Edward Almond, was hazardous, for the approach to Inchon lay along a barely navigable seaway dotted with uncharted rocks and reefs. After preliminary air and naval bombardment, US Marines began the assault at 6:15 a.m. on September 15, securing the port defenses and part of the town by midnight. Casualties in the landings were light, but the same was not true of the subsequent capture of Seoul, where North Korean troops fought to the death, although outnumbered and outgunned. On September 26 UN and South Korean forces driving north from the Pusan perimeter met up with X Corps. North Korean forces had been captured, melted into the hills, or retreated into the North.

INVASION TIDE
UN forces pour into Inchon after the US landing. The huge rise and fall of the tide at Inchon was a major hazard for the operation.

THE KOREAN WAR

The Pusan Perimeter

DATE August 1–September 15, 1950

FORCES (End August): North Korean: 98,000; UN/South Korean: 180,000

LOCATION Southeast of Korean peninsula

CASUALTIES US: 3,600 killed

On June 25, 1950, North Korean forces invaded South Korea, capturing the capital, Seoul. The US secured a resolution in the UN Security Council authorizing intervention to counter the aggression, which it was able to do since the Soviet Union was boycotting the Council. General Douglas MacArthur was appointed commander of UN forces in Korea. The first US troops were rushed into South Korea on July 1, but they were thrown into headlong retreat by the North Koreans, who included veterans of the Chinese Civil War. At the start of August, under General Walton Walker, American and South Korean troops succeeded in stabilizing a defensive perimeter around the port of Pusan. Walker's forces were too limited to man the whole perimeter, but intelligence gave him warning of the location of North Korean attacks and allowed him to concentrate men at crucial points. North Korean ruler Kim Il-Sung ordered General Kim Chaik to take Pusan by September 1 at all costs, but UN forces received constant reinforcements, including the first British troops at the end of August.

Meanwhile, extended North Korean supply lines were pulverized from the air and by naval bombardment. By early September MacArthur was confident that Pusan was safe and he could take the offensive.

NORTH KOREAN SOLDIER
A North Korean People's Army soldier handles Soviet-supplied munitions. The North Koreans fought with World War II-vintage Soviet equipment, including T-34 tanks.

MORTAR CREW
US troops (left) fire a heavy mortar against North Korean positions. The perimeter they held at Pusan was just 80 miles (130km) from north to south.

The Invasion of the North

DATE
October 9–
December 24, 1950

FORCES Chinese/North
Korean: 300,000–
400,000; UN: 250,000

LOCATION
North Korea

CASUALTIES Chinese:
40,000 killed; US 11,700
(718 killed)

By October 1950 North Korean forces had been cleared out of South Korea. Instead of standing on the defensive, MacArthur requested permission to press on into the North. Although worried about provoking a Chinese intervention, US president Harry Truman gave authorization, stipulating that troops should not advance to the Yalu River, the border with China. The US Eighth Army headed up the west coast, taking the northern capital, Pyongyang, on October 12 and continuing northward almost unopposed, while X Corps was shifted to the east coast of North Korea, landing at Wonsan. The movement of X Corps proved a tortuous operation, and it was not established ashore until October 26. By then, the first reports were coming in of clashes with Chinese soldiers who had infiltrated northern Korea. After some hesitation, MacArthur decided not to take the Chinese threat seriously and, on November 24, ordered a final drive to the Yalu River, which he believed would end the war. Within two days of beginning this advance, the Eighth Army came under attack from Chinese infantry, hundreds of

JET COMBAT
The F-86 Saber was America's latest jet fighter at the time of the Korean War. Sabers fought air battles with Soviet MiGs over the Yalu River, the first aerial combats between jet aircraft.

Air intake for turbojet engine

35-degree swept wing

Underwing fuel tank

thousands of whom were concealed in the mountains. On November 28 the Eighth Army was ordered to withdraw, but the Chinese had taken up position on the road behind them. UN troops had to fight their way southward through ambushes and roadblocks, suffering heavy losses of men and equipment. In the east, US Marines had advanced through the mountains to the Chosin reservoir. Coming under attack from Chinese

ICY WEATHER
A US machine-gun squad lies exhausted after combat against communist forces. Korea's winter was harsh and troops on both sides suffered from frostbite and exposure.

SOVIET MIG-15
The Soviet Union supplied MiG-15 jet fighters and pilots to back the Chinese in North Korea. According to US estimates, 792 MiGs were shot down in the war.

and North Korean forces, they fought their way back along a narrow road to the coast at Hungnam, suffering as much from the cold as from enemy action. Marine General Oliver Smith put a brave face on it, telling the press his men were not retreating but "just attacking in a new direction." But the UN forces had suffered a serious reverse. X Corps had to be evacuated by sea to Pusan, while the Eighth Army retreated into South Korea.

Ridgway's Meatgrinder

DATE January 25–
April 21, 1951

FORCES (Spring 1951)
Chinese: 542,000;
North Korean:
197,000;
UN: 270,000

LOCATION
Korea, to the north and
south of Seoul

CASUALTIES
No reliable estimates

In January 1951 a renewed communist offensive drove UN forces back south of Seoul. The US considered evacuating its forces from Korea, or using atom bombs to halt the Chinese. However, General Matthew Ridgway, field commander after the death of Walton Walker, stopped the rout. He set up a UN line from coast to coast and began an advance up the peninsula, using air and artillery bombardment to destroy the enemy without infantry assaults. The Chinese responded to Ridgway's "meatgrinder" with costly "human wave" attacks, attempting to swamp the firepower with sheer numbers. In three months of slaughter

VETERANS MEMORIAL
For years Korea was "the forgotten war." The Korean War Veterans Memorial in Washington, D.C., was not created until 1995.

Ridgway pushed the front line back to the border between North and South. In April he was promoted to UN commander, after MacArthur's dismissal for advocating attacks on China. In summer 1951 the war settled down to a stalemate, lasting through two years of peace talks.

NIGHT FIRE
A US 155mm howitzer fires at night. This was the kind of weapon Ridgway used to grind down the Chinese infantry.

NUCLEAR SUBMARINE

NAUTILUS WAS THE WORLD'S FIRST NUCLEAR-POWERED SUBMARINE. ITS ADVENT DURING THE EARLY PART OF THE COLD WAR MARKED A REVOLUTIONARY NEW STEP IN NAVAL WARFARE.

SPECIFICATION

Origin United States	**Date of launch** 1954	**Crew** 116
Tonnage 4,092 tons	**Length** 219ft (67m)	**Max speed** 23 knots
Max depth 700ft (213m)	**Armament** 6 x 21in (53cm) torpedo tubes	

The brainchild of a US Navy team headed by Hyman G. Rickover, *Nautilus* came into service in 1954. Its nuclear power plant meant that it could operate for long periods without refueling or surfacing. In January 1955 *Nautilus* demonstrated its strengths by making a record-breaking underwater voyage of 1,381 miles (2,222km) in 90 hours. In 1958, after several failed attempts, it became the first submarine to travel under the ice cap to the North Pole. *Nautilus* was, however, a transitional technology. It was not outstandingly fast under water and it was armed with conventional torpedoes. Aside from its power plant, its major novelties were having no gun on deck and having a bunk for each crew member, instead of the shift system for use of bunks found on earlier submarines. By 1959 it was already being superseded by submarines that, through improved hull design and the use of new materials, could travel faster under water and at far greater depths than before. Whereas *Nautilus* had been designed for the same role as earlier submarines (to attack surface shipping), its immediate successors were primarily built as part of US strategic nuclear forces. Armed with Polaris missiles, their function was to make nuclear deterrence a reality, providing a platform for nuclear missiles that was both mobile and hard to track and attack. In conventional warfare, nuclear-powered submarines found other new roles, including missile attacks on surface vessels and hunting down enemy submarines. *Nautilus* was retired in 1980 and is preserved in Connecticut.

LAUNCH
Draped with flags and bunting for its maiden launch in January 1954, Nautilus *plunges into the Thames River at Groton, Connecticut.*

TORPEDO *Torpedoes were the main armament of the Nautilus. This one was a spare and could be loaded just after another one had been fired.*

EXTERIOR *The exterior of the Nautilus included a flattened area on the upper part of the hull that formed an area on which the crew members could stand.*

COUNTERMEASURES *This electronic equipment was used to foil attempts to track the ship.*

HYDROPLANE CONTROLS *Located on the port side of the submarine and operated by three men facing toward the bow, these are the main controls for steering and diving. The gauges show depth, trim, and course.*

WATERTIGHT *Doors such as this, which could be locked tight against water pressure, were closed in times of action or emergency.*

CONTROL ROOM *This periscope stands at the nerve center of the ship.*

WATER LEVELS *These dials indicated the amount of water in the submarine's ballast tanks.*

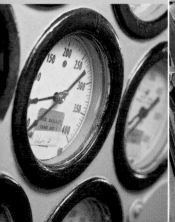

ALARMS *These color-coded alarms were sounded when the submarine was about to dive or when there was a danger of collision with another undersea object, warning the crew to shut the watertight doors.*

POST-COLONIAL WARS

THE ECONOMIC WEAKNESS OF MANY NATIONS after World War II, and international pressure for colonial self-determination, led to the gradual breakup of the European empires after 1945. Most colonies achieved independence through increasing self-government and negotiation, but both Portugal and, to a lesser extent, France tried to retain their empires, resulting in costly liberation wars in, among other places, Indochina, Algeria, and Angola. Rapid decolonization of Angola by Portugal and the Congo by Belgium left both new countries ill-equipped to cope with independence, resulting in lengthy civil wars, while ill-conceived colonial boundaries caused numerous problems after independence, notably in Nigeria and the Indian subcontinent.

ERA OF WORLD WARS

VIETNAMESE INDEPENDENCE

Dien Bien Phu

DATE
March 13–May 7, 1954

FORCES
French: 16,000;
Vietminh: 80,000

LOCATION
100 miles (160km)
west of Hanoi

CASUALTIES French:
8,500 killed, 10,000
taken prisoner;
Vietminh: 23,000

The fight for Vietnamese independence from French rule that began in 1946 reached its climax in the siege of Dien Bien Phu. In an attempt to break the stalemate in the war, the French commander-in-chief Henri Navarre decided to entice the Vietminh guerrillas to a battle in which French firepower could decimate their largely peasant army. In this goal, he underestimated the skill and resourcefulness of the Vietminh commander, General Giap. French airborne troops seized Dien Bien Phu, a strategic village deep in Vietminh territory, but were in turn besieged by the Vietminh, who fortified the surrounding hills with heavy artillery to stop the French from flying in supplies. After eight weeks of heavy bombardment, the French garrison surrendered, only 3,300 of its troops surviving the siege and subsequent imprisonment. The defeat led, within two months, to an armistice that ended French colonial rule in Vietnam, and the rest of Indochina, and seriously weakened the prestige of France.

1912–

GENERAL VO NGUYEN GIAP

Giap joined the Communist Party in 1933 but fled to China when the French colonial government banned the party in 1939. There he became an aide to Ho Chi Minh, the Vietnamese Communist leader, and from 1942–45 helped him organize Vietminh resistance to Japanese occupation. In 1946 Giap took command of the Vietminh, leading them to victory against the French and then, from 1965, the Americans, his use of guerrilla tactics enabling him to defeat two technologically superior forces.

CELEBRATING VICTORY
Fifty years on, Vietnamese soldiers march to celebrate the victory over the French at Dien Bien Phu, one of the key moments in the fight for independence.

CONGO CRISIS

Congo Crisis

DATE June 30, 1960–
November 25, 1965

FORCES Congolese
and mercenaries:
unknown; UN
peacekeepers: 19,828

LOCATION Mainly in the
southern Congo
province of Katanga

CASUALTIES
Congolese: unknown;
UN peacekeepers: 250

The Belgian government's rushed decision to grant independence to the Congo created a series of crises. Within days of independence, the province of Katanga declared its independence and sought help from mercenaries, forcing the UN to send in troops to keep the peace. UN forces regained control in January 1963, only for the north and east of the country to break away in 1964. Peace was eventually restored in 1965 by a coup led by General Mobutu, whose corrupt government remained in power until 1997.

MERCENARY FORCE
Rebel Katanga employed these Belgian mercenaries, many of whom had previously been employed by the colonial government.

ALGERIAN INDEPENDENCE

Algiers

DATE September 30,
1956–September 1957

FORCES French army:
40,000; FLN: 36,000

LOCATION
Algiers, capital
of Algeria

CASUALTIES French
army: 83,000; FLN:
153,000; civilians:
80,000 (all minimum
figures, 1954–62)

The failure of the French government to grant Algerians independence led nationalists to form the guerrilla Front Libération de Nationale (FLN) in 1954. At first the FLN's 800 fighters were heavily outnumbered by the 20,000-strong French army and concentrated on isolated terrorist attacks in rural areas. These met with a violent response from the French, but helped the FLN to increase its strength and unite the Algerian Arabs and Berbers behind it. In 1956 the FLN switched its campaign to Algiers, hoping that its many streets and alleys afforded better protection than open countryside. On September 30 the FLN planted bombs at three sites, including the offices of Air France. The FLN then launched a campaign that saw more than 8,000 bombings and shootings a month, including the assassination of the mayor of Algiers in broad daylight in December and a general strike in 1957. As the violence escalated, General Massu,

"INDICT MASSU!"
General Jacques Massu's use of torture and kidnap made him a war criminal in the eyes of freedom fighters.

ce général de l'armée française est un
CRIMINEL DE GUERRE
il fait l'apologie de la torture
so___uf, dehors, le protège
INCULPEZ MASSU!

"France without Algeria would be no France."

Pierre Mendès-France,
Prime Minister of France, 1954

commander of the French Tenth Parachute Division, acquired police powers in early 1957. These he used with savage effect, torturing FLN suspects to acquire information and kidnapping and killing others to intimidate the population. By September Massu had shattered the FLN in Algiers. Despite this success, French army plots against their own government and international pressure forced the French to grant Algerian independence in July 1962.

BIAFRA WAR

Biafra War

DATE May 30, 1967–
January 15, 1970

FORCES
Nigerians: 250,000;
Biafrans: 150,000

LOCATION
Southeast Nigeria

CASUALTIES
Nigerians: 100,000;
Biafrans: 100,000;
civilians: 1 million

HUMANITARIAN CRISIS
The main casualties of the Biafran war were civilians, caught up in the fighting and killed by malnutrition and disease.

The Ibo of southeast Nigeria had dominated the central government and military since independence in 1960 but felt threatened when proposals to strengthen the government in 1966 led to anti-Ibo massacres in the north. After efforts to reach a settlement failed, Colonel Odumegwu Ojukwu, Ibo governor of the southeast region, declared its independence as the Republic of Biafra. The French and Rhodesians supported the rebels, the Soviet Union the Nigerians. Fear of genocide kept the Biafrans fighting until superior Soviet weaponry, a naval blockade, and starvation led to Biafra's unconditional surrender in 1970.

ANGOLAN INDEPENDENCE

Angola

DATE
November 10, 1975–
February 17, 1976

FORCES
MPLA: 40,000;
UNITA: 30,000;
FNLA: 20,000;
Cubans: 20,000

LOCATION
West-central Africa

CASUALTIES Unknown

Alone among the European nations, Portugal had fought hard to retain control over its African empire and granted its five colonies independence only after a military coup in Portugal in April 1974. Since 1961 the Portuguese had been fought in Angola by three independence movements: the left-wing Popular Movement for the Liberation of Angola (MPLA), the Angola National Liberation Front (FNLA), and the National Union for the Total Independence of Angola (UNITA). On national independence in November 1975, the MPLA seized control, backed by Cuban forces armed with Soviet tanks, and attacked the other two groups. MPLA troops soon defeated the FNLA and secured control over most of the country by February 1976, receiving widespread international recognition as the legitimate government. However, Cuban involvement in the war prompted the US and South Africa to step up their support for UNITA, resulting in a vicious conflict that continued until the assassination of the UNITA leader, Jonas Savimbi, and a ceasefire in April 2002, which lasts precariously to this day.

INDO–PAKISTAN WAR

Indo–Pakistan War

DATE
December 3–16, 1971

FORCES Bangladeshis:
100,000; Pakistanis:
80,000 (in Bengal)

LOCATION West
and East Pakistan;
India; Kashmir

CASUALTIES
Indians: 7,000;
Pakistanis: unknown,
93,000 taken prisoner

The partition of British India in 1947 created new Muslim-majority West Pakistan and East Pakistan, two disconnected areas separated by 1,094 miles (1,760km) of Hindu India. Relations between India and Pakistan flared into violence in 1947–48 and again in 1965. The third war erupted after a political crisis in Pakistan's eastern province of Bengal. Although the Bengalis were Muslims, they had nothing in common with Pakistanis in the west. Their political and economic grievances came to a head in December 1970, when Sheikh Mujibur Rahman's Awami League, which sought Bengali autonomy, won a massive election victory. The Pakistani military overturned the result and arrested Rahman, whose party called a general strike and on March 26, 1971, declared Bengal independent as Bangladesh. In the violence that followed, more than 6 million Bengalis fled for safety to India, some pursued across the border by the Pakistani army. As India prepared to defend itself, the Pakistanis launched a preemptive air strike against the Indian air force on December 3. The Indians responded by invading Bengal. Tank battles also broke along the shared western border as both sides sought to readjust the border in their own favor. Pakistan's resistance soon collapsed, as it could not maintain communication lines between the two halves of the country across a hostile India. The East Pakistan army unconditionally surrendered to the Indians after 13 days' fighting. Bangladesh was now independent.

FRONT LINE COMBAT
Pakistani troops aim a bazooka at Indian lines as Indian troops threaten their lines in East Pakistan, now Bangladesh.

TANK WARFARE
One of the biggest battles of the brief Indo–Pakistan war was a massive tank engagement in southern Kashmir on December 6, 1971.

THE VIETNAM WAR

IN THE 1960s THE UNITED STATES became committed to defending the government of South Vietnam against communist-led guerrillas and allies in the North Vietnamese regular army. By 1969 over half a million US military personnel had been despatched to Vietnam. The war proved too costly for the American public to stomach and a US withdrawal in early 1973 was followed two years later by victory for North Vietnam. The conflict cost the lives of 58,336 Americans and over a million Vietnamese.

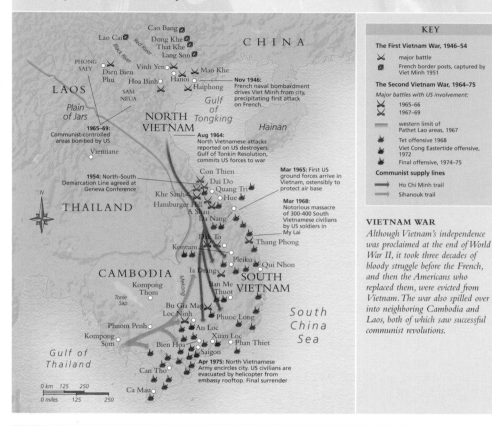

KEY

The First Vietnam War, 1946–54

✗ major battle

✗ French border posts, captured by Viet Minh 1951

The Second Vietnam War, 1964–75

Major battles with US involvement:

✗ 1965–66

✗ 1967–69

— western limit of Pathet Lao areas, 1967

☘ Tet offensive 1968

☘ Viet Cong Eastertide offensive, 1972

☘ Final offensive, 1974–75

Communist supply lines

→ Ho Chi Minh trail

→ Sihanouk trail

Nov 1946: French naval bombardment drives Viet Minh from city, precipitating first attack on French

Aug 1964: North Vietnamese attacks reported on US destroyers. Gulf of Tonkin Resolution, commits US forces to war

1965–69: Communist-controlled areas bombed by US

1954: North–South Demarcation Line agreed at Geneva Conference

Mar 1965: First US ground forces arrive in Vietnam, ostensibly to protect air base

Mar 1968: Notorious massacre of 300–400 South Vietnamese civilians by US soldiers in My Lai

Apr 1975: North Vietnamese Army encircles city. US civilians are evacuated by helicopter from embassy rooftop. Final surrender

VIETNAM WAR

Although Vietnam's independence was proclaimed at the end of World War II, it took three decades of bloody struggle before the French, and then the Americans who replaced them, were evicted from Vietnam. The war also spilled over into neighboring Cambodia and Laos, both of which saw successful communist revolutions.

THE VIETNAM WAR

Cedar Falls

DATE
January 8–26, 1967

FORCES
US and Vietcong: no reliable estimates

LOCATION
37 miles (60km) northwest of Saigon

CASUALTIES US: 409; South Vietnamese: 19; Viet Cong: 750 killed, 280 prisoners

Operation Cedar Falls was designed to clear communist forces out of their long-established base area in the "Iron Triangle" outside Saigon. A blocking force was put in place as an "anvil," while helicopter and ground assaults provided a "hammer" against which to crush the enemy. The operation started spectacularly on January 8 with a fleet of 60 helicopters flying in troops to seize the village of Ben Suc. Over the following weeks US troops searched the encircled zone, destroying tunnel complexes used by the guerrillas. But relatively few enemy were engaged, most slipping away through the US cordon. The 19-day operation ended with the destruction of Ben Suc and the forced evacuation of its population.

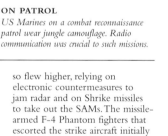

ON PATROL

US Marines on a combat reconnaissance patrol wear jungle camouflage. Radio communication was crucial to such missions.

THE VIETNAM WAR

Rolling Thunder

DATE March 2, 1965–October 31, 1968

FORCES US: 306,380 sorties, 643,000 tons of bombs dropped

LOCATION
North Vietnam

CASUALTIES US: 938 aircraft, 1,084 crew; North Vietnam: 118 aircraft, 52,000 killed

After a number of earlier "retaliatory raids," the United States initiated a systematic air campaign against North Vietnam in March 1965. Operation Rolling Thunder lasted for over three years. US Navy and Marine aircraft launched raids from carriers in the Gulf of Tonkin and from Marine airbases in South Vietnam; the US Air Force operated out of bases in Thailand; and B-52s of US Strategic Air Command flew in from Okinawa and Guam. US airmen encountered formidable air defenses. North Vietnam had Soviet-supplied SA-2 surface-to-air missiles (SAMs) and antiaircraft guns, plus

B-52 STRATOFORTRESS

The Boeing B-52 was designed as a strategic nuclear bomber, but was effective in Vietnam as a high-altitude conventional bomber.

MiG-17 and MiG-21 fighters. Areas along the Chinese border and around major cities were off limits, and MiG fighters operated from safe bases in these sanctuaries. The Americans soon learned that low-level raids incurred heavy losses from antiaircraft guns, and

so flew higher, relying on electronic countermeasures to jam radar and on Shrike missiles to take out the SAMs. The missile-armed F-4 Phantom fighters that escorted the strike aircraft initially had no guns and were flown by pilots trained for interceptor missions rather than dogfights. The strike aircraft had difficulty hitting precision targets because they were armed with conventional free-fall bombs or with Bullpup missiles that had to be guided onto a target with a joystick—no easy task under combat conditions. The political goal of the air offensive was to persuade the North Vietnamese to stop promoting the war in the South by punishing them. In this, it patently failed.

GROUND FIRE

North Vietnamese antiaircraft battery guns such as these were very effective against low-flying attack aircraft.

THE VIETNAM WAR

Tet Offensive

DATE January 31–
March 2, 1968

FORCES Viet Cong/North
Vietnamese: 84,000;
US: 500,000; South
Vietnamese: 350,000

LOCATION
South Vietnam

CASUALTIES Viet Cong/
North Vietnamese:
45,000; US: 9,000; South
Vietnamese: 11,000

In early 1968 General Vo Nguyen Giap, defense minister of North Vietnam, launched an offensive intended to win the war. Simultaneous attacks on towns and cities throughout South Vietnam by Viet Cong guerrillas and North Vietnamese Army (NVA) troops were to promote a popular uprising and undermine the American position in South Vietnam militarily and politically. As a prelude to the main offensive, on January 21 the NVA laid siege to the American Marine base at Khe Sanh, near the demilitarized zone that separated North and South Vietnam, threatening the Americans with a repeat of Dien Bien Phu (see p.338).

BAZOOKA
The Viet Cong used bazookas during the Tet Offensive, although the US no longer employed them in the Vietnam War.

The main offensive followed on January 31, timed to coincide with the Tet holiday, when many South Vietnamese soldiers would be on leave. Communist forces seized key positions in over 100 towns or cities, including the capital, Saigon, and the former imperial capital, Hue. In Saigon a Viet Cong platoon shot its way into the US embassy compound, although they were killed before they could enter the building itself. Within a few days most urban areas had been reclaimed by American and South Vietnamese forces— the latter fighting with impressive commitment and determination. Scattered fighting continued in Saigon until early March, but it was Hue that saw the heaviest and most prolonged combat. The imperial citadel was captured by NVA troops on January 31 and then held against a South Vietnamese counterattack. In February US Marines became engaged in a house-to-house battle to retake the city, supported by naval gunfire. By the time Hue was retaken on March 2, half of the city's buildings had been damaged or destroyed and the US had suffered 1,500 casualties. The siege of Khe Sanh lasted until April 8, also

AIR CAVALRY
US 1st Cavalry Division troops leap from their Bell UH-1 helicopter during a reconnaissance mission.

ending in defeat for the NVA. Altogether, the offensive was a military disaster for the communist forces. The Viet Cong guerrillas had emerged from hiding into open battle, and as a result had been slaughtered. There was no popular uprising in their support and the South Vietnamese troops held firm. But politically

the offensive—taking place in a US presidential election year—dealt a mortal blow to the US intervention, convincing the American public and politicians that the war could not be won. On March 31 President Johnson opened peace negotiations with North Vietnam.

PURPLE HEART
The Purple Heart is a decoration given to wounded US servicemen. Around 200,000 were awarded during the Vietnam War.

THE VIETNAM WAR

Eastertide Offensive

DATE March 30–
July 11, 1972

FORCES
North Vietnam:
200,000; South
Vietnam: 500,000

LOCATION
South Vietnam

CASUALTIES North
Vietnam: 100,000;
South Vietnam: 50,000

By 1972 US ground forces had ceased combat operations and were pulling out of Vietnam. The South Vietnamese Army had taken over the fighting, although still with American air and naval support. Abandoning guerrilla tactics for open warfare, on March 30 the North Vietnamese Army (NVA) launched a full-scale invasion of South Vietnam with Soviet T-54 tanks and 130mm artillery. The offensive was launched on three axes: from the north toward Quang Tri and Hue, through the Central Highlands to Kontum, and in the south toward An Loc. President Richard Nixon responded by resuming bombing of North Vietnam. In Operation Linebacker,

KOREAN SUPPORT
A South Korean soldier kneels beside a Vietnamese woman. Some 4,400 Koreans died fighting on the US side in Vietnam.

the Americans used new smart bombs to devastate the NVA supply system. American aircraft, including B-52s, also inflicted heavy losses on the forces invading the South. For the first

month the NVA made good progress. An Loc and Kontum were put under siege and, on May 1, Quang Tri fell to NVA tanks. South Vietnamese soldiers and civilians fled south, but a defensive line was stabilized in front of Hue. From late May the tide turned. On July 11 the siege of An Loc was lifted,

although Quang Tri was not retaken until September. The invasion failed, but it left North Vietnamese troops inside South Vietnam's borders, where they stayed after a peace deal with the US in January 1973. It was these troops that brought about the fall of Saigon to North Vietnam in 1975.

AH-64 ATTACK HELICOPTER

THE AH-64 ATTACK HELICOPTER, DESIGNED FOR AN ANTITANK ROLE, USES MANY OF THE SOPHISTICATED OFFENSIVE AND DEFENSIVE TECHNOLOGIES THAT DOMINATE THE MODERN BATTLEFIELD.

The first American attack helicopter, the AH-1 Cobra, was introduced by the US Army during the Vietnam War to give fire support to assault helicopters landing troops in hostile territory. By the time the AH-64 Apache entered service in 1984, attack helicopters had found a new role as tank-busters. Developed by McDonnell Douglas (now Boeing), the AH-64 performed effectively in Operation Desert Storm in 1991 and has since been used in the US invasion of Afghanistan in 2001 and the US and British invasion of Iraq in 2003. The version shown here is an AH-64D Longbow.

ATTACK AND DEFENSE

The AH-64 is a twin-engined helicopter with a crew of two. The co-pilot/gunner sits in front with the pilot above and behind. Firepower includes a chain gun and 70mm rockets, but the primary armament consists of up to 16 Hellfire antiarmor missiles. Using the helicopter's sophisticated target-acquisition and fire-control systems, the crew has only to select targets and fire; the missiles will lock onto the targets and do the rest. This "fire and forget" capacity means the

helicopter can take evasive action as soon as it has fired. It was once feared that the slow-moving helicopter would be too vulnerable in battle, but the AH-64D benefits from a variety of defensive systems— for example, suppressing infrared radiation so the helicopter is not located by heat-seeking missiles, and giving warning of incoming missiles so that countermeasures can be deployed. Using thermal imaging, the Apache can operate in all weathers and at night, hugging the terrain to avoid detection by enemy radar.

Fully articulated main rotor blade

Infrared scanner turret

Automatic defense system sensors

STUB WINGS
Rockets and missiles are mounted under the helicopter's wings.

CHAIN GUN AND FEED MECHANISM *The 30mm chain gun can fire up to 1,200 rounds of ammunition at 625 rounds per minute.*

HIDAS *This Longbow uses the Helicopter Integrated Defensive Aids System (HIDAS) to sense threats automatically and perform the necessary countermeasures.*

WIRECUTTER
Shearing blades are placed at strategic points on the helicopter's airframe to cut through any wires—such as power or telephone cables—that threaten to bring the craft down.

FLARE CONTAINER *Flares mounted in this container, which is attached near the tail of the helicopter, can be fired by the craft's automatic defense systems.*

MAIN ROTOR DRIVE *The fully articulated main rotor blades are attached to the hub by stacks of laminated steel straps. They can easily be folded or removed for transportation by air or ship.*

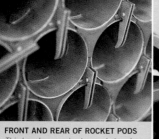

FRONT AND REAR OF ROCKET PODS
This Longbow carries two rocket pods, each capable of launching 19 rockets.

MISSILE *The Apache can carry up to 16 air-to-surface Hellfire missiles on four 4-rail launchers.*

TAIL ROTOR
The two blade units of the small tail rotor are crossed at a 55-degree angle to reduce noise.

AH-64D LONGBOW
This AH64-D Longbow attack helicopter was built by the American military for the British army.

Mast-mounted radar dome

Armor-protected turbo engine

Tail rotor drive

SPECIFICATION			
Origin United States		**Date** 2004	
Fuselage length 60ft (15.5m)		**Main rotor diameter** 48ft (14.6m)	
Overall height 16ft 3in (4.95m)		**Cruise speed** 140 knots	

Chain gun and ammunition feed

Nonretractable landing gear

Rocket and missile launchers

Flare container

Lockable tail wheel

DO NOT GRAB

PILOT'S CONTROLS Although the co-pilot is in charge of firing the helicopter's weapons, the pilot is able to override these controls and fire the weapons himself.

SAFTEY BELT
The impressive array of safety features built into the seats and structure of the Apache mean that crew members have a 95 percent chance of surviving ground impacts when descending at a rate of 42ft (12.8m) per second.

CANOPY JETTISON The armored canopy covering the pilot and co-pilot can be jettisoned in an emergency.

PILOT'S MONOCLE The monocle provides thermal imaging for night vision.

JETTISON PIN STOWAGE

CANOPY JETTISON   TURN 90° PUSH

PILOT'S COCKPIT All of the helicopter's systems are displayed on two screens situated in both the pilot's and co-pilot's cockpits. The crew can manage these systems using the buttons located around the outside of each screen.

ISRAEL'S WARS

THE DECISION TO CREATE THE independent Jewish state of
Israel out of the former British mandate of Palestine in 1948
led to five major wars in the region and a long-running
intifada ("uprising") by Palestinians fighting for their own
homeland. The continuing animosity between the Jews and
the Arabs has destabilized the region for more than half
a century and shows little sign of abating in the near future.

ISRAEL AT WAR

*On four occasions
since it gained
independence,
Israel has invaded
and occupied
neighboring
territory, although
it now holds only
the West Bank, the
Gaza Strip, and
the Golan Heights.*

KEY

- Israel in 1949
- occupied by Israel after 1967 war
- occupied by Israel after 1973 war
- occupied by Israel after 1967 war reoccupied by Egypt after 1973 war
- demilitarized zone held by UN after Israel–Syria agreement, 1974, and 2nd Sinai agreement, 1975
- → route of Israel's invasion of Lebanon 1982
- Palestinian refugee camps 1982
- ++++ disputed border

ERA OF WORLD WARS

ISRAELI INDEPENDENCE

Israeli Independence

DATE May 15, 1948–July 20, 1949

FORCES Arabs: 22,500–25,500; Israelis: c.30,000

LOCATION Former British mandate in Palestine

CASUALTIES Arabs: 8,000–15,000; Israelis: 4,000; Palestinian refugees: 700,000

On the day the last British troops left
Palestine, May 14, 1948, Israel declared
its independence. The next day, armies
from Egypt, Transjordan (Jordan), Syria,
Lebanon, and Iraq attacked. Although
outnumbered, the Israeli forces were
better trained and armed. The Israelis
also had a unified command and
shorter supply lines, unlike the
overextended Arabs. Above all, the
Israelis were fighting for their survival,
while their opponents had no common
strategy. The initial Arab attacks had
taken place by June and thereafter were
slowly reversed, the Israelis eventually
occupying the entire British mandate
aside from the West Bank and the Gaza
Strip. Ceasefires eventually brought
the conflict to a close in July 1949.

SINAI CAMPAIGN

Sinai Campaign

DATE October 29–November 7, 1956

FORCES Israelis vs. Egyptians; Anglo–French forces, UN peacekeepers

LOCATION Sinai peninsula between Israel and Egypt

CASUALTIES No reliable estimates

Tension between Egypt and Israel
escalated from 1955 after a series of
terrorist raids against Israel were
launched from the Gaza Strip. The
new president of Egypt, Gamal Abdel
Nasser, closed the Gulf of Aqaba and
sealed Eilat, Israel's only port on the
Red Sea. In July 1956 he nationalized
the Suez Canal Company; its shares
were owned mainly by the British
government and French investors.
Fearful of an Arab attack, Israel struck
first and invaded Sinai. It had first
secretly agreed on its strategy with

PORT SAID

*A small boy stands
bewildered in the
ruins of Port Said
in November 1956
as a British tank
crews look on.*

the British and
French, who
then issued an
ultimatum for a
halt to military
action. When
both sides refused,
British and French planes attacked
Egyptian bases and airborne troops
landed at Port Said on October 31 in
order to seize the canal. Pressure from
the UN and US forced a ceasefire on
November 7 and the withdrawal of
the Anglo–French forces. Israeli troops
evacuated Sinai in March 1957, having
lifted the blockade of Eilat and reduced
the threat of attacks from Gaza. UN
peacekeepers were then stationed to
keep Israel and Egypt apart.

SIX–DAY WAR

Six-Day War

DATE June 5–10, 1967

FORCES Israelis: 264,000; Egyptians, Jordanians, Iraqis, Syrians: 410,000

LOCATION West Bank, Golan Heights, and the Sinai peninsula

CASUALTIES No reliable estimates; Palestinian refugees: 300,000

Egyptian pressure led to the withdrawal
in May 1967 of UN peacekeepers
installed after the Sinai campaign,
followed swiftly by a renewed
Egyptian naval blockade of Eilat
and a massing of Egyptian, Jordanian,
Iraqi, and Syrian troops along Israel's
borders. Once again, Israel took the
initiative. Its air force launched a
devastating series of raids against the
Egyptian air force, destroying four-fifths
of it on the ground and giving Israel
total air superiority. Similar action was
taken against Jordan and Syria. Israeli
troops then invaded Sinai and reached
the Suez Canal on June 8. At the same
time, Israeli tanks and paratroopers
entered Jordanian-held East Jerusalem
and occupied the entire West Bank of
the Jordan River. Israel also retaliated
against 20 years of Syrian shelling by
occupying the Golan Heights and
advancing 30 miles (48km) into Syria.
By the time fighting stopped on June
10, Israel had doubled its territory,
reduced the length of its borders, and
removed its cities from the range of
enemy guns. However, it now had
600,000 extra Palestinians under its
control, and the likelihood of more
retaliatory action in the future.

CLOSE-QUARTERS COMBAT

*An Israeli soldier in a trench prepares to
throw a hand grenade against Syrian lines
on the disputed territory of the Golan
Heights during the Six-Day War.*

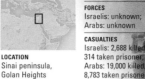

PHANTOM
At the time of the Yom Kippur War the Israeli air force possessed the Phantom, the MiG, and the Mirage.

SA-6

Egypt's surface-to-air missiles (SAMs) posed a considerable threat to Israeli planes during the Yom Kippur War. SA-6 missile launchers supplied by the Soviet Union shot down over 100 Israeli aircraft in the early days of the war, largely because Israeli pilots were not aware that their radar made them visible to the enemy. Once their radar warning receivers were reprogrammed, the threat from the missiles was reduced considerably.

WARHEAD
The warhead itself weighs 123lb (56kg)

MOTOR
The missile is propelled by a solid fuel rocket motor

SPECIFICATION

Origin Soviet Union		**Date** 1973
Weight 1,320lb (600kg)		**Top speed** Mach 2.8
Max altitude 39,370ft (12,000m)		

▨ YOM KIPPUR WAR

Yom Kippur War

DATE October 6–24, 1973

FORCES
Israelis: unknown;
Arabs: unknown

CASUALTIES
Israelis: 2,688 killed,
314 taken prisoner;
Arabs: 19,000 killed,
8,783 taken prisoner

LOCATION
Sinai peninsula,
Golan Heights

Despite its military success in the Six-Day War, Israel did not win a political victory, since none of the defeated Arab states were prepared to make peace in return for their territory. Egypt, in particular, felt humiliated by Israeli military superiority and its loss of the Sinai peninsula, and waged a three-year campaign of bombardments and raids across the Suez Canal, known as the War of Attrition, which ended only in August 1970. Under its new leader, Anwar Sadat, in alliance with Syria, Egypt planned a surprise attack on Israel for October 6, 1973, the Day of Atonement, or Yom Kippur, one of the holiest days of the Jewish calendar. The Israelis were caught unawares as Egyptian forces crossed the Suez Canal and headed into Sinai, supported by surface-to-air missile batteries and portable antitank missiles that respectively reduced Israeli air effectiveness and immobilized its tanks. Prime Minister Meir of Israel sought aid from the Americans, who were slow to respond until the Soviet Union began to resupply the Egyptians and Syrians. President Nixon then set up an emergency supply line of arms to Israel. Despite their initial success, the Egyptians outreached their defensive cover and had ground to a halt by October 9. The Israelis then turned the tables on October 16. A helicopter assault disabled the Egyptian air defenses, allowing General Ariel Sharon of Israel to break through between two Egyptian armies and cross the canal on to the West Bank, there encircling the Third Egyptian Army. In the

ISRAELI COUNTERATTACK
On October 16, 1973 Israeli tanks rush to engage the Egyptian armies in Sinai — ten days after the outbreak of the war.

north, the Syrians attacked the Golan Heights, but despite their numerical weakness, Israeli defenders managed to knock out almost 900 Syrian tanks and advanced to within 25 miles (40km) of Damascus, the Syrian capital. A ceasefire established by the UN ended the conflict on October 24.

▨ INVASION OF LEBANON

Invasion of Lebanon

DATE June 6, 1982–
June 10, 1985

FORCES Israelis and
Christian Phalangists
vs. PLO, Syrians, and
Muslim Lebanese

LOCATION
Southern Lebanon

CASUALTIES Israelis:
675; Arab troops and
civilians: 17,825

After the creation of Israel in 1948, more than 110,000 Palestinian refugees fled north to Lebanon. The Palestinian Liberation Organization (PLO) moved its headquarters to Lebanon in 1970 and by the 1980s represented a militant community of more than 300,000 refugees. The Palestinian presence so destabilized Lebanon that in 1975 it erupted in civil war. As Christian and Muslim communities fought for power, a Syrian force intervened in 1976 to support the Muslims. The PLO had been using Lebanon as a base from which to launch rocket attacks on northern Israel since 1968; Israel therefore invaded in 1982 to create a buffer zone between itself and the Palestinians, as well as to counteract growing Syrian influence in the country. Israeli tanks advanced toward the

YASSER ARAFAT
Yasser Arafat was chairman of the PLO from 1969 until his death in 2004. Israeli intervention forced him out of Lebanon in 1983.

capital and besieged strongholds in West Beirut. Although many Palestinians were evacuated in late August to friendly countries, Christian militias allied to the Israelis attacked two Palestinian refugee camps at Sabra and Chatila in West Beirut on September 18, killing 800 people. International outrage at this massacre and huge protests in Israel led to an Israeli withdrawal from West Beirut by the end of the month. After lengthy diplomacy, Israel withdrew most of its troops from Lebanon in June 1985, leaving a residual force and an Israeli-supported militia in a small buffer zone. Israel finally withdrew from this zone in 2000.

AFTERMATH OF AN EXPLOSION
West Beirut suffered constant bombardment from land, sea, and air during the 10-week siege of 1982, which caused great loss of life.

MODERN WEAPONS

THE INTRODUCTION OF the German Sturm-Gewehr assault rifle in 1944 pointed the way to a new era in which bolt-action magazine rifles, still common at the end of World War II, were replaced by lighter automatic or semiautomatic rifles. Weapons such as shoulder-launched surface-to-air missiles and rocket-propelled grenades (RPGs) have enabled infantry to take on helicopters and tanks. Manufactured in massive quantities, modern small arms have amply equipped guerrillas and terrorists as well as regular armies across the world.

GUERRILLA WEAPON
Angolan UNITA guerrillas, opposed to the country's government, train to use AK-47 Kalashnikov assault rifles. More than 40 million AK-series rifles are thought to have been manufactured.

Foresight

Integral folding bipod

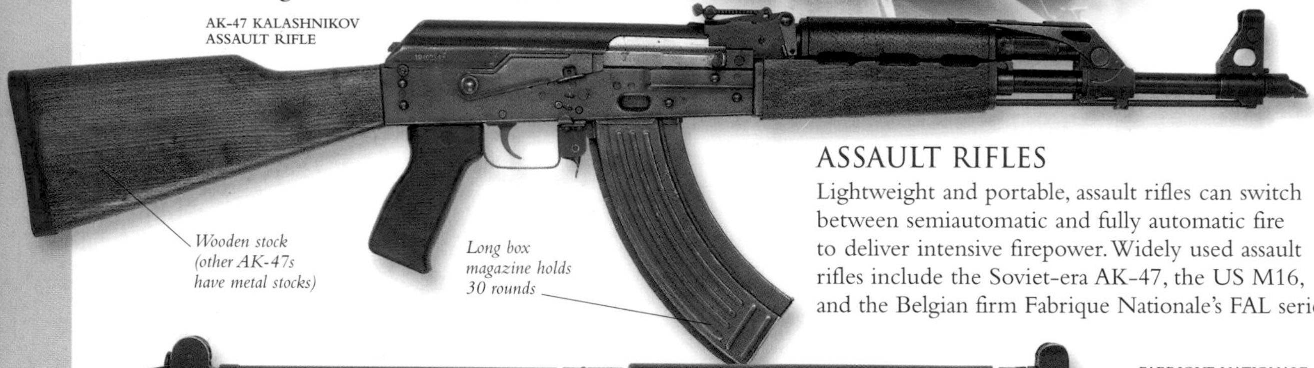

AK-47 KALASHNIKOV ASSAULT RIFLE

Wooden stock (other AK-47s have metal stocks)

Long box magazine holds 30 rounds

ASSAULT RIFLES

Lightweight and portable, assault rifles can switch between semiautomatic and fully automatic fire to deliver intensive firepower. Widely used assault rifles include the Soviet-era AK-47, the US M16, and the Belgian firm Fabrique Nationale's FAL series.

FABRIQUE NATIONALE FAL PARA ASSAULT RIFLE

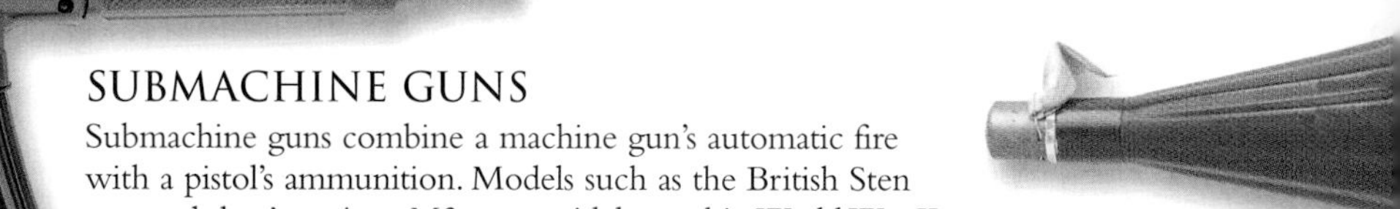

Folding skeleton butt

Warhead

IRAQI ROCKET LAUNCHER
The Al-Nasirah RPG is the Iraqi version of the Soviet RPG7. This weapon is cheap to purchase, easy to use, and can take out an armored vehicle.

HECKLER & KOCH MP5 SUBMACHINE GUN

Locking pin for stock assembly

Safety catch / firing selector

SUBMACHINE GUNS

Submachine guns combine a machine gun's automatic fire with a pistol's ammunition. Models such as the British Sten gun and the American M3 were widely used in World War II. The Sten was replaced by the Sterling in the 1950s, but the US Army largely abandoned submachine guns. Models such as the German MP5 continue to equip special forces, for whom its small size is a distinct advantage.

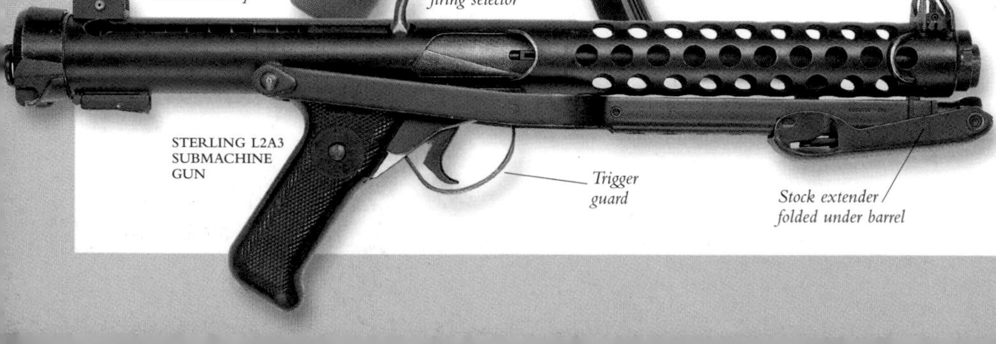

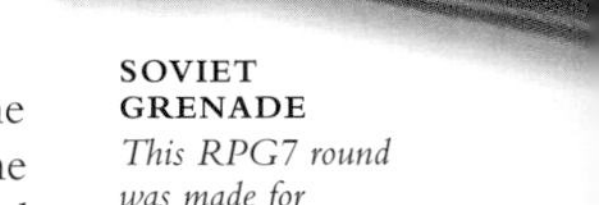

SOVIET GRENADE
This RPG7 round was made for use by Soviet paratroopers. Its "shaped charge" warhead can punch a hole in a tank.

STERLING L2A3 SUBMACHINE GUN

Trigger guard

Stock extender folded under barrel

GENERAL-PURPOSE MACHINE GUN,
BRITISH ARMY ISSUE

Cartridge

*Gun is not normally
handheld, so bipod aids firing*

M60 MACHINE GUN

MACHINE GUN BULLET CLIP

ALL-PURPOSE
*Most armies carry a General-Purpose
Machine Gun, or GPMG, which
can be used with a bipod or tripod, or
mounted on vehicles and helicopters.*

Pistol grip

HEAVY MACHINE GUNS

Despite the high rate of fire of assault rifles, armies still
need heavier belt-fed machine guns—distinguished by
their larger caliber ammunition, longer range, and higher
volume of fire. The belt feed means these weapons require
two men to operate them, and their weight necessitates
that they be disassembled and carried by several soldiers.

STANDARD ISSUE
*The M60 machine gun was
the standard US Army squad
machine gun during the Vietnam
War. Although in service for over 30
years, it was never a popular weapon.*

RIFLE GRENADE
*This US M16 assault rifle is
equipped with an M203 grenade
launcher. Such launchers are
of limited range but can be
effective antipersonnel weapons.*

Carrying handle

Plastic stock

*Barrel of grenade
launcher*

M16 A1 ASSAULT RIFLE

AL-NASIRIYAH ROCKET LAUNCHER

*Rocket exhaust
vent*

MASKED FIGHTERS
*Iraqi insurgents brandish RPGs in front
of a burning US vehicle. The man on the
left carries more grenades for reloading.*

SOVIET PG-7 ROCKET-
PROPELLED GRENADE

*Collapsible
stabilizing fin*

GRENADE LAUNCHERS

Rifle grenades are fired from ordinary rifles or from
shotgun-style grenade launchers. The most famous grenade
launcher is the Soviet-developed RPG7, which has
become a familiar feature of guerrilla warfare and terrorist
activity. Its warhead, which propels a jet of molten metal
onto the target, can penetrate almost any tank armor.

GUERRILLAS AND TERRORISTS

EVENTS SUCH AS THE CHINESE CIVIL WAR, the Vietnam War, and Castro's victory in Cuba established the practice of guerrilla warfare as a revolutionary activity peculiar to communist or anticolonialist groups, although in the 1980s US-backed Contras in Nicaragua and *mujahideen* in Afghanistan showed it was a strategy that could serve any political cause. Terrorism could be an adjunct to guerrilla activity—for example, through assassination or sabotage—but beginning in the 1960s terrorism developed into a form of warfare in its own right. Terrorist groups ranged from those pursuing local causes and limited ends to those envisaging nothing less than the downfall of international capitalism, from a Marxist or Islamicist viewpoint.

CASTRO AND CUBA

Castro and Cuba

DATE
November 25, 1956–
January 1, 1959

FORCES
Guerrillas: 300;
Cuban armed forces:
30,000 (May 1958)

LOCATION
Cuba

CASUALTIES
No reliable estimates

Fidel Castro was arrested for his part in an uprising against Cuban dictator Fulgencio Batista in 1953. Released from jail two years later, Castro went to Mexico, where he gathered a band of armed followers. In December 1956 he landed in Cuba with 81 men, but this flimsy force was swiftly dispersed by the Cuban army. Castro took refuge in the Sierra Maestra mountains with a few survivors, including the unit's doctor, Ernesto "Che" Guevara. Reinforced by anti-Batista elements from Cuban cities, they embarked on hit-and-run attacks against army outposts. In the summer of 1958 Batista launched a large-scale military operation to clear the guerrillas out of the sierra, but his poorly led forces were repeatedly outfought and retreated in disarray. Batista had by now lost the support of the United States and was facing strikes, mutinies, and sabotage in urban areas. Castro's men began to occupy towns without encountering serious resistance. Batista fled the country on January 1, 1959, and Castro assumed power.

REBEL BAND
Fidel Castro in June 1957 with members of his guerrilla band, including "Che" Guevara (seated, second from left).

> "How close we could look into a bright future should two, three, or many Vietnams flourish throughout the world with their share of deaths and their immense tragedies, their everyday heroism and their repeated blows against imperialism."

WITNESS TO WAR
ERNESTO "CHE" GUEVARA

In his message to the Tricontinental Conference in January 1966, the rebel leader Guevara painted a vision of guerrilla wars springing up around the world that would overwhelm the capacity of the "American imperialists" to respond.

BAY OF PIGS

Bay of Pigs

DATE April 17–19, 1961

FORCES Cuban exiles:
1,300 men; Castro's
forces: unknown

LOCATION
La Playa Girón,
south coast of Cuba

CASUALTIES
Cuban exiles: 120 killed,
1,180 taken prisoner;
Castro's forces: 3,000

The United States quickly decided that Castro had to be overthrown. The CIA organized a brigade of Cuban exiles and trained them to fly B-26 bombers. Preparations were far advanced when John F. Kennedy, who was eager to avoid direct US involvement, became US president. Initial B-26 strikes intended to take out the Cuban air force were scaled down and failed. The invasion force then went ashore at the Bay of Pigs without air cover. US naval and air forces did not intervene as the Cuban exiles, pummeled from the air, were overwhelmed by Castro's numerically superior troops.

EXILE MEMORIAL
A monument erected by Cuban exiles in Miami, Florida, commemorates those who died in the Bay of Pigs invasion.

BOLIVIA

Bolivia

DATE
November 3, 1966–
October 9, 1967

FORCES Guevara's
guerrillas: 50;
Bolivian Rangers: 600

LOCATION
Bolivia

CASUALTIES
All guerrillas killed,
captured, or dispersed

In November 1966 Argentine-born Ernesto "Che" Guevara, one of Fidel Castro's closest associates, entered Bolivia in disguise and set up a guerrilla camp with a small band of followers. Including as many Cubans as Bolivians, the group had no support from the local population. In

FALLEN HERO
The Bolivian armed forces proudly display Guevara's body to the world's press after his execution on October 9, 1967.

March 1967 the camp was overrun by government forces; from then on the guerrillas were constantly on the move. They outfought the Bolivian army in small engagements, but were short of food and other essential supplies. Once Bolivian Rangers trained by the US were deployed from late July, Guevara's men suffered serious casualties. On October 8 the surviving guerrillas were surrounded by Rangers. After a two-hour firefight, most were dead or taken prisoner. A wounded Guevara was among those captured; he was shot the following day.

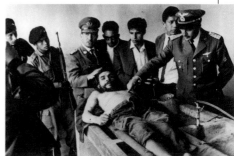

THE RISE OF MODERN WARFARE

BETWEEN 1750 AND 1914 European armies and those of countries founded by European settlement, such as the United States, achieved an unquestionable preeminence in military technology and organization. An ever wider gulf opened up between those forces that adopted western methods and armaments and those that did not—Japan being the only nonwestern country to cross this divide decisively. Mass armies, new firearms, and new forms of transportation and communication allowed western states to extend their rule over much of the planet.

Many wars in the 18th and 19th centuries crossed continents and created modern nations. The Seven Years War (1756–63), which opens this period, has been called the first true "world war," because its European combatants fought in India and North America as well as in Europe itself. Warfare was central to the creation of the United States, from the Revolutionary War (1775–83) against British rule through the wars against Mexico and American Indian peoples to the Civil War (1861–65). In Europe, the great convulsions of the French revolutionary and Napoleonic wars (1792–1815) were followed by a century of more limited but still decisive conflicts, which brought Germany and Italy into being as nation-states. Elsewhere, many wars occurred when western powers imposed their rule on Asian or African peoples, such as the British in India and east Africa and the French in Southeast Asia and west Africa.

MOBILE FIREPOWER
Artillery such as this field cannon played a pivotal role in the Civil War.

UNIFORM DISCIPLINE

By the mid-18th century European countries had uniformed, strictly hierarchical, and professional armies, for which the Prussians under Frederick the Great set the standard. Infantry armed with flintlock muskets and bayonets, and trained to fight in strict lines, squares, or columns, formed the core of the army. Often recruited from the dregs of society, the soldiers were disciplined by draconian punishments, although attempts were also made to inspire them with regimental pride. Cavalry remained the elite arm, executing functions such as screening, reconnaissance, and shock charge, while artillery had become a vital, fully mobile part of armies on the battlefield. Yet the Revolutionary War showed the potential vulnerability of a professional European army in difficult terrain and against an irregular enemy. As they became aware of the limitations of formally disciplined formations, the European powers recruited irregular skirmishing cavalry, often

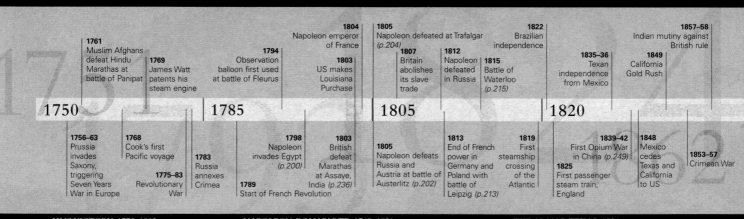

						1804	1805			1822			1857–58
	1761					Napoleon emperor	Napoleon defeated at Trafalgar			Brazilian			Indian mutiny against
	Muslim Afghans				**1794**	of France	(p.204)			independence			British rule
	defeat Hindu	**1769**			Observation			**1807**	**1812**		**1835–36**	**1849**	
	Marathas at	James Watt			balloon first used	**1803**		Britain	Napoleon	**1815**	Texan	California	
	battle of Panipat	patents his			at battle of Fleurus	US makes		abolishes	defeated	Battle of	independence	Gold Rush	
		steam engine				Louisiana		its slave	in Russia	Waterloo	from Mexico		
						Purchase		trade		(p.215)			

1750   1785   1805   1820

1756–63	**1768**		**1798**	**1803**	**1805**	**1813**	**1819**	**1839–42**	**1848**	
Prussia	Cook's first		Napoleon	British	Napoleon defeats	End of French	First	First Opium War	Mexico	
invades	Pacific voyage	**1783**	invades Egypt	defeat	Russia and	power in	steamship	in China (p.249)	cedes	**1853–57**
Saxony,		Russia	(p.200)	Marathas	Austria at battle of	Germany and	crossing	**1825**	Texas and	Crimean War
triggering	**1775–83**	annexes		at Assaye,	Austerlitz (p.202)	Poland with	of the	First passenger	California	
Seven Years	Revolutionary	Crimea	**1789**	India (p.236)		battle of	Atlantic	steam train,	to US	
War in Europe	War		Start of French Revolution			Leipzig (p.213)		England		

HMS VICTORY, 1778–1812   **NAPOLEON BONAPARTE, 1769–1821**   **THE ALAMO, TEXAS, 1836**

WARS SINCE 1980

THE DECADE AFTER 1980 MARKED the final years of the Cold War, with conflicts in Afghanistan, Nicaragua, and elsewhere adding to the tension between the United States and the Soviet Union. This situation changed in 1985, when Mikhail Gorbachev became leader of the Soviet Union and began to reform its monolithic structure. As the Soviet Union weakened its hold on eastern Europe, and itself collapsed entirely in 1991, the Cold War came to an end. In its place, long-buried ethnic conflicts resurfaced in Chechnya and Yugoslavia, while the threat posed by the Iraqi dictator Saddam Hussein led to three major wars in the Middle East. Since 2001 Islamic fundamentalist terrorism has become a main contributor to world instability.

SOVIETS IN AFGHANISTAN

Soviets in Afghanistan

DATE December 25, 1979–February 1989

FORCES Soviets: 175,000; Mujahideen: unknown

CASUALTIES Soviets: 97,000; Afghans: 180,000; civilians: 1.5 million killed, 6 million refugees

LOCATION Afghanistan

The conflict in Afghanistan that lasted almost the entire length of the 1980s had its genesis in July 1973, when the country's monarchy was overthrown and a republic established under Muhammad Daoud. Islamic leaders opposed to his modernizing government fled to neighboring Pakistan, where in 1975 they set up the *mujahideen* ("holy warriors") to overthrow Daoud's regime. The assassination of Daoud in April 1978 by the Revolutionary Council, and his replacement with a communist-led government, prompted the US to support the *mujahideen* the following July. Alarmed by American-armed instability on its southern border, the Soviet Union sent in 85,000 troops to support the Afghan government in December 1979. The Afghan army swiftly disintegrated as soldiers deserted, leaving Soviet troops to fight a *mujahideen* familiar with the mountainous terrain and largely supported by the local population. As a result, the Soviets could hold only the major towns, while their attempts to subdue the countryside through aerial bombardment and siege tactics sent millions of refugees fleeing to Pakistan and other neighboring countries. By 1985 guerrilla warfare was being conducted in every province, convincing the new Soviet government of Mikhail Gorbachev to cut its losses and leave. A phased withdrawal of Soviet troops began in May 1988 and was finally completed the following February. Within three years the *mujahideen* took control and an Islamic republic was set up, but civil war between rival groups broke out in December 1992, allowing the extremist Taliban regime to seize power in September 1996.

STINGER POWER
American-supplied Stinger surface-to-air missiles proved effective in downing Soviet helicopter gunships and transport planes.

IRAN–CONTRA AFFAIR

Contras in Nicaragua

DATE January 1984–February 25, 1990

FORCES Contras: 15,000; Nicaraguans: unknown

CASUALTIES No reliable estimates

LOCATION Nicaragua

ON PATROL
A group of guerrilla Contra rebels patrols a river in Nicaragua.

The Sandinista Liberation Front overthrew dictator Anastasio Somoza of Nicaragua in 1979. Alarmed by the arrival of a left-wing Central American government, the US under Ronald Reagan armed the opposing National Democratic Front—the "Contras." Although the Sandinistas' Daniel Ortega won the presidential election in November 1984, the US continued to support the Contras, even after Congress cut off their funding. A secret US plan to sell arms to Iran and pass the revenues on to the Contras caused a scandal in November 1986, but US support continued until the Sandinistas were defeated in elections in 1990.

IRAN–IRAQ WAR

Iran–Iraq War

DATE September 22, 1980–August 8, 1988

FORCES Iraqis: unknown; Iranians: unknown

CASUALTIES Iraqis: unknown; Iranians: 1.5 million (100,000 Iranians and Kurds killed by poison gas)

LOCATION Iran–Iraq border

In July 1979 Saddam Hussein seized power as president of Iraq. Kurds, Shi'as, and others opposed his Sunni regime, while neighboring Iran was still in turmoil after the revolution that had just overthrown the shah. Iraq viewed this event with concern, as it feared revolution might spread across the border. Saddam, therefore, took the opportunity to unify his own country by attacking Iran, using as a pretext a dispute about the ownership of the strategic Shatt al-Arab waterway between the two countries. Saddam attacked in September 1980, expecting an easy victory against a disorganized enemy, but the Iranians resisted fiercely, the war settling into a stalemate with huge loss of life on both sides. An uneasy peace ended the war in 1988.

TROUBLE ON THE HORIZON
Iraqi soldiers at Khorramshahr in southwest Iran watch as smoke rises in the distance in 1981 during the Iran–Iraq War.

FALKLANDS WAR

Falklands War

DATE March 19–June 14, 1982

FORCES British: 28,000; Argentines: unknown

CASUALTIES British: 982 killed or wounded; Argentines: 13,113 killed, wounded, or taken prisoner

LOCATION Falkland islands, South Atlantic

Argentina had long claimed the remote British colony of the Falkland Islands in the southern Atlantic Ocean as its own. In 1982 Argentina took advantage of the British willingness to negotiate the islands' future (and a consequent reduction of British naval strength in the region) to invade. On March 19, 1982, a group of Argentine civilians posing as scrap-metal dealers landed on the dependency of South Georgia and claimed it for Argentina. As Britain prepared to evict them, Argentine troops invaded the Falklands. Britain then sent a recovery task force to the islands, retaking South Georgia on April 25 and then attacking Argentine positions on the Falklands. Argentina had the better of the naval campaign, using air-launched Exocet missiles to sink a total of six British ships, although the British generally got the better in the skies. On May 21 British troops landed on East Falkland and took the capital, Port Stanley, on June 14, liberating the islands.

SEA HARRIERS
The superior maneuverability and firepower of the British Sea Harriers proved no match for the Argentine planes, 26 of which were brought down during the conflict.

ASHORE
With little military presence in the area, the British task force had to be sent 8,000 miles (13,000km) down the Atlantic to the Falklands.

GULF WAR

Gulf War

DATE August 2, 1990–March 3, 1991

FORCES International coalition: 680,000; Iraqis: unknown

CASUALTIES Coalition troops: 1,378; Iraqis: 22,000; civilians: 2,300

LOCATION Kuwait and Iraq

The ending of the Iran–Iraq war in 1988 left Iraq impoverished. One of its biggest creditors was neighboring Kuwait, where high oil production was keeping the price of Iraqi oil exports depressed, making it difficult for Iraq to repay its debts. In August 1990 Saddam Hussein invaded and easily occupied Kuwait, which Iraq had long claimed as its 19th province, seizing its massive oil industry. With one-fifth of the world's oil reserves in the hands of a ruthless dictator, the international community feared what Iraq might do next. The UN imposed sanctions on Iraq to force it to withdraw from Kuwait, while the US put together a coalition of 29 nations, including Saudi Arabia and the Gulf States, to oppose Iraq. After a six-week air attack, the coalition attacked Iraqi forces on the ground on February 24, 1991. After four days of fighting, the coalition liberated Kuwait, the war formally ending on March 3. High-tech weaponry—notably "smart" cruise missiles capable of hitting targets with almost pinpoint accuracy and American F-117 "stealth" bombers able to evade radar detection—helped the coalition to achieve a swift victory, while Iraq's largely conscript army was no match for the well-equipped and well-trained coalition forces. The war also marked the use of environmental warfare, as Iraq set fire to three-quarters of Kuwait's oil wells, causing massive ecological damage throughout the Gulf region.

SMOKE SCREEN
American troops watch as Kuwaiti oil fields burn in the distance, the fires creating massive smoke screens as black as night.

1934–

NORMAN SCHWARZKOPF

General Norman Schwarzkopf served two combat tours in Vietnam, later rising through the ranks to become commander-in-chief of US Central Command and commander of operations of Desert Storm, the campaign to liberate Kuwait. "Stormin' Norman" Schwarzkopf was an inspirational leader, and under his command allied forces speedily retook Kuwait while sustaining only minimal casualties. He retired from military service in 1992 as a four-star general.

WAR IN CHECHNYA

Chechnya

DATE December 11, 1994–August 29, 1996; September 23, 1999–

FORCES Chechens and Russians: unknown

LOCATION Chechnya, southern Russia

CASUALTIES Chechens: 200,000 killed, 400,000 refugees; Russians: 10,000 killed

The breakup of the Soviet Union in 1991 brought previously suppressed nationalist tensions to the surface in the new Russian Federation. In November 1991 the province of Chechnya in the northern Caucasus declared its independence, a move ignored by the Russians, who tried to negotiate a settlement. When fighting broke out in the capital, Grozny, between pro- and anti-independence campaigners, Russian troops invaded Chechnya in December 1994. After considerable loss of life and the death of the Chechen leader, both sides agreed to end the conflict in August 1996; Russia withdrew its troops but both sides postponed agreement on the future status of Chechnya. In 1999 a series of bombs exploded in Russian cities. The Russians blamed the separatists, although many thought the Russian security services, aiming to ensure the election of Vladimir Putin as Russian president, were responsible. Russian forces reinvaded the province in September 1999; the conflict continues to this day with considerable loss of life.

RUSSIAN FIREPOWER
A Russian Grad missile launching system fires at rebel positions on the outskirts of the war-torn Chechen capital, Grozny.

WAR IN FORMER YUGOSLAVIA

Yugoslavia

DATE March 2, 1992–November 21, 1995

FORCES Yugoslavians: unknown; NATO-led peacekeepers: 60,000

LOCATION Bosnia

CASUALTIES Bosnians: 100,000 killed, 1.3m refugees; Serbs and Croats: 50,000

In 1980, after the death of Yugoslavia's communist leader, Yosip Broz Tito, the country's constituent republics began to break away from each other. Tensions rose after the election to the Serbian leadership in 1987 of Slobodan Milosevic, who campaigned for a Greater Serbia that would unite all Serbs in Yugoslavia. In June 1991, fearing total Serbian domination of Yugoslavia, Slovenia and Croatia declared their independence, quickly followed by Macedonia. The Serb-dominated Yugoslav army fought brief wars against both Slovenia and Croatia before peace was restored in January 1992. Multiethnic Bosnia feared that it would then be divided between Croatia and Serbia and declared its independence in March. A three-way conflict broke out, with the Bosnian Muslims—the biggest single

WAR CRIMES
Bosnian Muslims bury the 8,000 Muslims massacred by Serb forces in the so-called "UN safe haven" of Srebrenica on July 11, 1995.

> "Belligerents target civilians in order to expel or eradicate segments of the population, or for the purpose of hastening military surrender."
>
> *UN secretary-general Kofi Annan*, on the origins of ethnic cleansing, 1999

MACHINE GUN
This M72 light machine gun was used in the Bosnian conflict.

ethnic group—defending themselves against both Croat and Serb forces. By summer 1993 the Serbs were in control of 70 percent of the country, killing or expelling all non-Serbs through a new policy of "ethnic cleansing." The UN imposed sanctions against Serbia and set up six Muslim "safe havens." These, however, were poorly defended, allowing the Serbs to overrun them in 1995, killing 8,000 Muslims in Srebrenica. After NATO stepped in to enforce a peace settlement by bombing Serb positions, a deal was reached in November 1995 between Serbia, Croatia, and Bosnia, setting up two separate states within Bosnia—a Serb republic and a Muslim–Croat federation.

WAR IN FORMER YUGOSLAVIA

Kosovo

DATE March 1, 1998–June 10, 1999

FORCES Serbs and Croats: unknown; NATO forces: unknown

LOCATION Kosovo province, southern Serbia

CASUALTIES 940,000 refugees

In March 1989 Serbian leader Slobodan Milosevic removed the autonomy of the province of Kosovo, largely inhabited by Albanians, and suppressed any dissent. The Albanians formed the Kosovo Liberation Front (KLA), confronting Serb troops for the first time in January 1998. In March Serbia sent in thousands of troops to flush out the militants, attacking villages and massacring inhabitants. Peace talks in Paris proposed full autonomy with the possibility of independence after three or five years. When Serbia refused to accept this, NATO intervened and bombed Serbia in an 11-week campaign. The Serbs responded with a renewed policy of ethnic cleansing, forcing 640,000 Kosovans to flee their homes. In June 1999 Milosevic eventually capitulated; Serb troops left the province to be replaced by NATO peacekeepers. The future of the province remains to be decided.

TO THE HILLS
During the Kosovan war thousands of Kosovo Albanians fled for safety into the highlands of Albania and Macedonia.

Afghanistan

DATE October 7–December 6, 2001

FORCES Afghans: unknown; coalition forces: unknown

CASUALTIES Coalition forces: 219; Afghan troops: unknown; Afghan civilians: 1,300

LOCATION Afghanistan

Following the al–Qaeda terrorist attacks on New York and Washington on September 11, 2001, the US government accused Afghanistan's Taliban government of sheltering al-Qaeda and its leader, Osama bin Laden. After the Taliban refused to surrender bin Laden to the US, American and British forces invaded Afghanistan. Other countries provided troops and equipment. Pakistan, Uzbekistan, and Tajikistan provided air bases from which US aircraft launched bombing missions, while special services ground troops worked with the Afghan Northern Alliance, which had been fighting the Taliban

FIRE POWER
Anti-Taliban Pashtun soldiers, loyal to the postwar interim governor of Kandahar, patrol the city on December 16, 2001.

since 1996. The Taliban quickly collapsed in the north, leading to defections in the south and successes for anti-Taliban militias. The capital, Kabul, fell on November 18 and the city of Kandahar—the Taliban power base—on December 6. Despite this success, neither bin Laden nor the Taliban leadership were captured, while resistance still continues in the mountains in the center of the country and along the frontier with Pakistan.

SPY IN THE SKY
The US military made use of its unmanned Predator spy planes for surveillance and reconnaissance in the war against the Taliban.

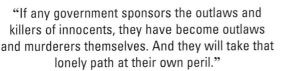

> "If any government sponsors the outlaws and killers of innocents, they have become outlaws and murderers themselves. And they will take that lonely path at their own peril."
>
> *US President George W. Bush* in his address to the nation, October 7, 2001

Invasion of Iraq

DATE March 20–April 14, 2003

FORCES Coalition forces: 345,000; Iraqis: 350,000

CASUALTIES Coalition forces: 13,543 killed or wounded; Iraqi troops: c.21,000 killed or wounded

LOCATION Iraq

As part of the US-led "war on terror" launched after the al-Qaeda attacks of September 11, 2001, US president George W. Bush stepped up international pressure against Saddam Hussein of Iraq, accusing him of supporting international terrorism and developing chemical, biological, and nuclear weapons of mass destruction (WMDs). UN weapons inspectors arrived in the country in November 2002, backed by a UN mandate warning the Iraqi government of severe consequences if it failed to cooperate. The chief inspector, Hans Blix, reported to the UN on March 7, 2003, that Iraq was complying with the search but that he needed more time to complete his inspection. The US and Britain refused to accept this and began a bombing campaign against Iraq on March 20, to force it to comply with UN resolutions. The US-led coalition then invaded Iraq in a high-tech "shock and awe" campaign, capturing the capital, Baghdad, on April 9 and Tikrit, Hussein's hometown and the last major target, on April 14. A US-led provisional government then took power until free elections for a new parliament and government could be held in January 2005. Saddam Hussein was captured on December 13, 2003, and awaits trial for war crimes. Subsequent weapons inspections have revealed that there were no WMDs in Iraq. The prime reason for the invasion was the removal of the Iraqi dictator. The invasion sparked international protests against the US and Britain in particular, and also began a major insurrection inside Iraq against the coalition occupation, which cost many more US and British lives than the invasion itself.

TOPPLING SADDAM
Across Iraq, statues of the dictator Saddam Hussein were toppled from their pedestals and his image eradicated from public buildings and billboards.

SHOCK AND AWE
Laser-guided missiles, smart bombs, and other high-tech weaponry set Baghdad and other Iraqi cities alight during the allied invasion of Iraq in March 2003.

INDEX

Illustrations are shown in *italic* except where there are battle entries for the subject on the same page.

ACKNOWLEDGMENTS

Dorling Kindersley would like to thank Peter Smithurst, Philip Abbott, and Rod Joyce at the Royal Armouries, Leeds; Eleanor Holmes at The Imperial War Museum; Natalie Finnigan at Duxford; Les Smith, Mark Sheriff, and Matthew Buck at Firepower, the Royal Artillery Museum; Major Tim David of the MOD; Staff Sargent Carl Bird at RAF Dishforth.

Key: a = above, b = below, c = center,
l = left, r = right, t = top, f = far, s = sidebar

akg-images: 13acl, 15cl, 15bc, 17cr, 19tr, 19acr, 21cr, 30c, 37bl, 38bl, 39tc, 41tc, 48br, 48bcl, 55br, 57c, 66tr, 67cr, 79b, 80bl, 86b, 86t, 87tl, 87tr, 88bl, 92b, 94tr, 96b, 108bl, 108br, 109cfl, 110c, 110bl, 114bl, 118br, 119tr, 119cr, 119bl, 134, 143bl, 143br, 144ac, 150bl, 151cfl, 158bl, 163b, 165b, 184bl, 186br, 186ac, 191br, 198br, 202b, 258tr, 258b, 258cbr, 263c, 285bl, 290ac, 292tr, 297cb, 305b, 311b, 321br, 326c. **Alamy Images:** 19tl, 39b, 49ac, 68b, 72t, 111cfr, 121bl, 147br, 170t, 182br, 199acr, 201tr, 219br, 222b, 227cl, 243tr. **Archivi Alinari:** 25tr. **Altitude:** 158br. **Ancient Art & Architecture Collection:** 34acl, 51bl, 51bl, 51acl, 62tr, 64tr, 64c, 67b, 72bl, 73tr, 81t, 92cl, 92c, 94b, 95c, 96c, 103t, 132bl. **Associated press:** 333b. **Artothek:**152t. **Aviation Picture Library:** 335cr. **Bibliothèque Nationale de France, Paris:** 85. **Bildarchiv Preußischer Kulturbesitz, Berlin:** 77tr. **www.bridgeman.co.uk:** 11bc, 33tl, 35tr, 36cr, 47ac, 57ttr, 60tl, 60bc, 60br, 64b, 69br, 72br, 78b, 79tl, 80t, 82tr, 91tr, 91cl, 95b, 97b, 98t, 100c, 101bl, 107cra, 120br, 133br, 136br, 137tr, 138c, 143tl, 150br, 151br, 153b, 155cra, 155cbr, 158crb, 158cfl, 159tr, 159b, 160bl, 160t, 160t, 161tr, 161cla, 163tc, 173cb, 173crb, 174cfl, 179bl, 187tr, 196br and bl p197, 199bcr, 201b, 208cl, 222tc, 234cl, 237bl, 262tr; /MARCEL ANDRE Baschet © ADAGP, Paris and DACS, London, 2005 235c. **British Library, London:** 75tr. © **The British Museum:** 28tr, 37tc. **Corbis:** 4b, 6bc, 7tl, 7bc, 10bl, 11br, 16bl, 16br, 18br, 19br, 23acl, 25b, 27c, 27c, 32cr, 34Across 34-5, 39bcr, 40tc, 41bl, 42bl, 45b, 47br, 48tr, 48acr, 50bl, 52r, 53bcl, 54bl, 55tr, 56cl, 56br, 60bl, 63tr, 66, 71cr, 73b, 74br, 75br, 76c, 76tr, 79tr, 87cr, 89b, 89r, 90tl, 90bl, 97r, 99b, 100b, 100t, 102c, 113tr, 115cl, 116bl, 122br, 123b, 127bl, 129b, 134bl, 137ca, 140bl, 141tc, 141b, 142br, 148bl, 154cb, 158cra, 163tr, 167b, 168b, 171br, 172b, 175cra, 178tr, 178br, 178tcr, 179cal, 185bl, 187br, 190cl, 190b, 191cl, 193tc, 193b, 198t, 204b, 210acl,

211tr, 215b, 216bcr, 217br, 217bcr, 217t, 218br, 218t, 220acr, 221tr, 222cr, 24b/p225 b, 224bcr, 225tl, 225acr, 225bcfl, 226tr, 226cl, 227bl, 227br, 230tr, 230bl, 231tr, 231bl, 232tr, 233tb, 235t, 238acl, 240bl, 242tr, 242br, 248tr, 248bcr, 249br, 250tc, 251bl, 251bcr, 254br, 255bl, 257tl, 259br, 261acr, 267bl, 267br, 268tl, 269br, 271cr, 272acl, 273acl, 274tr, 275b, 276acl, 278br, 279tc, 279br, 282b, 283tr, 285br, 286cr, 287tr, 288b, 290tr, 290bl, 290br, 291tl, 291tr, 291bc, 293tr, 293bl, 297tl, 297tr, 297br, 298cra, 302bl, 302t, 303tl, 303br, 312tl, 314tr, 3 14b, 316t, 317cr, 319cl, 320tr, 320c, 321tl, 321bl, 321b, 321cbl, 322tr, 324, 327br, 328c, 328br, 329tr, 329cb, 329bl, 330cl, 330bl, 330b, 331tl, 331cl, 331tl, 332bl, 333tl, 334cr, 334bl, 335tl, 335cb, 335bcl, 336cl, 337t, 338cl, 338b, 339cr, 339al, 339b, 340cr, 341tr, 341b, 342tl, 344tr, 344br, 344ar, 345acl, 345bl, 345cbr, 347b, 348tl, 348bl, 348br, 349tl, 349tr, 349bl, 349br, 350bl, 350br, 351br, 352cl, 352t, 353c, 353c, 353, 353bl. **Defence Picture Library:** 7bl, 351bl. **DK Images:** Dave King (c) Dorling Kindersley, Courtesy of Warwick Castle, Warwick 211bfr; / 61tl, 62CR; //Courtesy of the Wallace Collection London 139cr; /Alistair Duncan 78tl, 82b, 87b; /American Museum of Natural History 170tr, 170tr, 170cr, 170cr; /Andy Crawford 90cr, 197c; /Andy Crawford/Imperial War Museum 319cr; /Ashmolean museum bl/ British Museum 8, 10br, 14tr, 14cr, 14bc, 14br, 14rfbc, 17tc, 18acl, 19bl, 20bl, 25rfbc, 42br, 52bl, 52bl, 54cl, 55tc, 55bl, 67br, 90br, 114br; /Capitoline museums, Rome 50tr; /Collection of Jean-Pierre Verney 271cal, 272br, 273ac, 273acr, 277bc, 277b, 284tl; /Collection of the University Museum of Newcastle 11bl; /Conacultinah-mex 164bl; /Confederate Memorial Hall 224cl, 230cfr; /Courtesy Michael Butler Collection 296cl; /Courtesy of the National Museum, Delhi 128br; /Courtesy of 95th Rifles and Re-enactments, Living Heritage 146bl; /Courtesy of Churchill College Archive, Cambridge University 94tl; /Courtesy of David Edge 205ac, 205t, 208cr; /Courtesy of H. Keith Melks Collection 299br; /Courtesy of the Board of the Trustees of the Royal Armouries 109vtr; /Courtesy of the Board of Trustees of the Armouries 104tr, 104clb, 104car, 105tr, 105bcr, 105cfr, 115bc, 142bl, 152cr, 176car, 184br, 184bfr, 186c, 188ac, 188t, 189bc, 189b, 196tr, 200c, 208b, 210bc, 210acr, 210b, 211bl, 211br, 211bfl, 213c, 214c, 241tr, 244bcr, 245br, 245bfr, 253c, 259cr, 346bl, 346ac, 346tbc, 346x, 347tl; /Courtesy of the Ministry of Defence

Pattern Room Nottingham 347c; /Courtesy of the Ministry of Defence Pattern Room, Nottingham 298cb, 347b; /Courtesy of the National Army Museum, London 202t; /Courtesy of the National Museum, New Delhi 136bl; /Courtesy of the Order of the Black Prince 107bl, 119br; /Courtesy of the Pitt Rivers Museum Oxford 104c, 105tr; /Courtesy of the Pitt Rivers Museum, University of Oxford 138tr, 138bc, 139tl, 139br; /Courtesy of the Powell-Cotton Museum, Kent 140cr; /Courtesy of The Royal Green Jackets Museum, Winchester 209c, 244bl; /Courtesy of the University Museum of Newcastle 34cl; /Courtesy of the University of Newcastle 35flac; /Courtesy of the Wallace Collection London 122cr; /Courtesy of Warwick Castle 154ct; /Courtesy of Warwick Castle, Warwick 188c; /Courtesy of the Wallace Collection London 138cr, 138bvl, 139tr; /Courtesy the Wallace Collection, London 138b; /Courtesy Warwick Castle, Warwick 145bcr, 146bc; /Courtesy of Robin Wigginton, Arbour Antiques Ltd, Stratford upon Avon 189tr, 189cr; /Coutesy of Robin Wigington, Arbour Antiques Ltd, Stratford upon Avon 109ca; /Danish National Museum 63cr, 70bl, 70tr, 70tcr; /Dave King 144br; /Dave King, Confederate Memorial Hall, New Orleans 183bl; /Dave King, courtesy of Gettysburg National Military Park 198bl; /Dave King/Confederate Memorial Hall, New Orleans 228tr; /Dave Kingle 219bl; /English Heritage 42ac; /Ermine Street Guard 38br, 43c, 43bl, 43bcl, 43bfl, 43flac, 43flac, 43flbc; /Firepower 156, 180, 191cr, 238bl, 238br, 238bcfr, 238bfl, 238br, 273br, 307tr; /Gary Ombler 182bl, 182br, 206bl, 206br, 206cbl, 207bc, 207br, 207bcfl, 207cbfr, 207cbr, 207cbr, 207t, 300dl; /Geoff Dann 61br, 63b, 115cr, 215c; /Geoff Dann / Dorling Kindersley / Scottish United Services Museum, Edinburgh Castle (c) National Museums of Scotland 161cbr; /Geoff Dunn, courtesy of the Royal Green Jackets 240br; /Geoff Dunn/National Museums of Scotland 260bcr; /Gettysburg National Military Park 230ac, 231tc; /Imperial War Museum 299ca; /Imperial War Museum 163c, 288tr, 289tl, 289tr, 289br, 289br, 289acfr, 289acr, 289bcfl, 289bcfr, 289bcl, 289bcr, 302cb, 305cfl; /Imperial War Museum, London 311cr; /IWM 266bl, 270tl, 270cl, 273acr, 273frac, 278tr, 291ac, 311tc, 311br, 323tl; /Joe Cornish 23tr, 118bl; /John Heseltine 47bl; /John Spaull, courtesy of Civil War Museum, Bardstown, Kentucky 182t; /Judith Miller/Cooper Owen 43bc; /Judith Miller/Wallis and Wallis 196cl, 235bl; /Kate Clow 78c; /Kim Sayer 81b; /Lynton Garceiner, Courtesy of the Natural History Museum 216t; /Max Alexander 46bl,

75bl, 88cr; /Museum of London 32tr, 32cl, 32bc, 32acl, 32acr, 32b, 32btc, 33c, 33bcl, 70tcr, 71tl; /Museum of Mankind 219tr; /National Maritime Museum 69tr, 69ar, 99tr; /Nick Sayer 88tr; /Nigel Hicks 20tl; /Paul Kenwood 115cfl; /Peter Chadwick/Museum of Artillery 246tr; /Pitt Rivers Museum Oxford 101c, 102t; /Rob Reichenfeld 112br; /Robin Wigginton, Arbour Antiques Ltd, Stratford upon Avon 148tl; /Royal Armouries 173tr, 173tr, 173tr, 173tr, 173ac, 178tc; /Scottish United Services Museum, Edinburgh © National Museums of Scotland 323cr; /Scottish United Services Museum, Edinburgh Castle, © National Museums of Scotland 1c; /Simon James 47tr; /The Wallace Collection 112c; /The Wallace Collection 188bc, 189bcl; /Tony Souter 123 cr; /Trustees of the National Museums of Scotland 153cla, 237br; /US Army Military Institute 223acr; /US Military Institute 226br; /Wallace Collection 58, 106c, 119bc, 119bcr, 121br, 130, 131, 143cra, 143cal, 143cr, 145br, 146cb, 147c, 150tr, 150cbl, 151cal, 160car, 212acr, 263tl, 269br; /Wallis & Wallis 210cr; /Warwick Castle 81c, 112cb; ? 123ca, 123cfl, 126bcl; Andrew Chernack 341cr; Andy Crawford/Imperial War Museum 318bl; Museum of Artillery, The Rotunda, Woolwich, London 190cr; Collection of Jean-Pierre Verney 271cafl, 272bfr; Conacultinah-mex 165tr, 166bc; Courtesy of Robin Wigginton, Arbour Antiques Ltd, Stratford upon Avon 109cr; Courtesy of the Board of Trustees of the Armouries 332tr, 346abc, 347tc, 347t, 352cr; Courtesy of the Bradbury Science Museum, Los Alamos 329bcr; Courtesy of the Old Flying Machine Company 327cr; Courtesy RAF Wittering, Cambridgeshire 351t; Gary Ombler 342cr, 342bl, 342bc, 342acl, 342acr, 342bcl, 342bcr, 343bl, 343bc, 343br, 343acr, 343bc, 343bcr; 343t; Geoff Dan 60tr; Imperial War Museum 309tl, 326tr; Joe Cornish 211tl; Martin Plomer 326cl; Museum of London 70tc; Royal Artillery Museum, Woolwich 99tl; Scottish United Services Museum, Edinburgh Castle. Copyright National Museums of Scotland 155bcl; US Army Military History Institute 225cb. **The Art Archive:** 0, 2, 6tc, 6tr, 6br, 7tc, 7tr, 10bc, 11tr, 12c, 12b, 13tr, 13bl, 13tr, 15tr, 16flac, 17bl, 18tr, 21b, 24bc, 26bl, 26frbc, 27bl, 28bl, 29dps, 30tr, 31bl, 34c, 35cr, 36cl, 36bl, 40t, 43bl, 43car, 45flac, 46Main picture, 49b, 52c, 53br, 62cr, 62bc, 65b, 65t, 67tl,70br, 71b, 73cl, 74bl, 80b, 93b, 93tr, 98br, 101bl, 102b, 103cl, 105car, 107br, 109br, 110tr, 110br, 112tr, 113b, 114c, 118c, 121tl, 126br, 126c, 127bc, 128tl, 128bl, 129tl, 129tr, 132c, 133tr, 133bl, 140br, 142cl, 143clb, 144cra, 145cbl, 145t, 146cra, 147bl, 147t, 148acl, 148bb, 149bl, 149t, 153cbr, 154bl,

154t, 155btc, 156tr, 161b, 162cra, 165tcr, 166tc, 166bl, 166br, 167tr, 167tcl, 168t, 170br, 175cal, 182bc, 183tr, 183br, 184tr, 185c, 191tr, 192ac, 194tc, 194bl, 195tr, 195b, 196bc, 196acr, 197tl, 197cfr, 199tr, 200ac, 201tl, 204tr, 205acl, 205b, 208tr, 212c, 212b, 213b, 213t, 214bl, 215tr, 216bcl, 219c, 220tr, 220, 221bl, 221br, 223b, 225cr, 225cbn, 231br, 234bl, 235bl, 236bcl, 238tr, 240tr, 241tl, 241br, 241bcr, 243tl, 243b, 244tr, 245tr, 245acl, 246br, 247tl, 247cr, 247b, 248b, 249tr, 249c, 250tr, 250b, 251tr, 251br, 252tr, 252c, 252bl, 253tr, 253b, 254bl, 255tr, 255cl, 255cr, 255ac, 256tr, 256bl, 257tr, 257bl, 257bc, 259tl, 259bl, 260tc, 260b, 261acl, 262bc, 262br, 263tr, 266br, 266br, 269tl, 269tr, 270tr, 270cb, 271b, 272tr, 273bl, 276bl, 277tc, 277tr, 278tl, 279bl, 281tr, 282tr, 283bl, 284tr, 285c, 286tcc, 287b, 292bl, 292br, 294br, 300, 302cra, 317tr, 317br, 322b, 333cr; /© Succession Picasso/DACS, 2005 295ac. **Mary Evans Picture Library:** 21tr, 23bl, 111t, 114tr, 130cl, 131tr, 131tr, 152br, 171tl, 199bl, 209bl, 209t, 214t, 236t, 263bc. **Werner Forman Archive:** 6bl, 33r, 54ac, 55acl, 98bc, 104ca, 140c, 172cfl, 173rd, 175b. **GreatBuildings.com:** Ronald Soong 22b. **Getty Images:** 22tr, 116tl, 228b/p229 b, 236br, 237tr, 244bc, 245bl, 280, 295cb, 296cb, 338cr, 338ac, 340bcl, 346t, 350t, 351cr, 353bcr. **John Hamill:** 177b. **Robert Harding Picture Library:** 175bl. © **Michael Holford:** 96. **Robert Hunt Library:** 277cl, 279tr, 294tr, 294bl, 298, 304cb, 304, 306cla, 306b, 307dl, 308bl, 311bl, 317b, 318cb, 319b, 323tr, 323cl, 323bl, 323 br, 326br, 327c. **The Kobal Collection:** 290cl. **Korean War Academy:** 176bl. **Lonely Planet Images:** 176b. **The Military and Historical Image Bank:** 185br, 193cr, 195acl, 217bl, 234cr, 261tcc, 282acl, 286c, 295tc. © **National Maritime Museum, London:** 149br, 200bl, 206tr. **National Portrait Gallery, London:** 187br. **The National Trust:** 70tl. **Peter Newark's Military Pictures:** 170bl, 190tr, 194br, 218bl, 223bcr, 228cl. **National Museums & Art Galleries On Merseyside:** © National Maritime Museum 69c. **Novosti (London):** 7bl, 92tr, 120bl, 121tr, 126cl, 162b, 163cb, 261bl, 262d, 285tr, 292tl, 307db, 308b. **Ann & Bury Peerless:** 136b, 137cfl, 137cr. **Photolibrary Wales:** 111b. **popperfoto.com:** 302bl, 305tr, 340cb. **Rex Features:** 266br, 324br, 332br, 345tl, 352b. **Royalty Free Images:** Corbis 192bl. **Science & Society Picture Library:** 31c. **Stadt Pohlheim:** 50bl. **Texas Historical Commission:** 216b. **Thomas Mallon McCorgray:** 57bc. **Tokugawa Reimeikai:** 17r. **Topfoto.co.uk:** 34cfl. **TRH Pictures:** 209cl, 283bc, 286bl, 287tc, 298cal, 299tc, 301tr, 303cl, 318c, 332c. **Ullstein Bild:** 276br.